W. B. YEATS'S ROBARTES-AHERNE WRITINGS

Modernist Archives Series

From letters, journals, and notebooks to unpublished or out of print works, unfamiliar but important writings in translation and forgotten articles, Bloomsbury's *Modernist Archives* series makes available to researchers at all levels historical archival material that can reconfigure received views of Modernist literature and culture.

Annotated throughout and supported by extensive contextual essays by leading scholars, the *Modernist Archives* series is an essential resource for anyone with a serious interest in 20th Century Literature and Culture.

Titles in series
David Jones on Religion, Politics, and Culture, edited by Thomas Berenato, Anne Price-Owen and Kathleen Henderson Staudt

Ezra Pound and Globe Magazine: The Complete Correspondence, edited by Michael T. Davis and Cameron McWhirter

Forthcoming titles
The Correspondence of Ezra Pound and the Frobenius Institute, 1930–1959, edited by Ronald Bush and Erik Tonning

David Jones's The Grail Mass and Other Works, edited by Thomas Goldpaugh and Jamie Callison

Edith Ayrton Zangwill's The Call, edited by Stephanie Brown

Ezra Pound's and Olga Rudge's The Blue Spill, edited by Mark Byron and Sophia Barnes

Global Modernists on Modernism, edited by Alys Moody and Stephen J. Ross

Man Into Woman, edited by Pamela L. Caughie and Sabine Meyer

W. B. YEATS'S ROBARTES-AHERNE WRITINGS

FEATURING THE MAKING OF HIS "STORIES OF MICHAEL ROBARTES AND HIS FRIENDS"

Edited by Wayne K. Chapman

BLOOMSBURY ACADEMIC
LONDON • NEW YORK • OXFORD • NEW DELHI • SYDNEY

BLOOMSBURY ACADEMIC
Bloomsbury Publishing Plc
50 Bedford Square, London, WC1B 3DP, UK
1385 Broadway, New York, NY 10018, USA
29 Earlsfort Terrace, Dublin 2, Ireland

BLOOMSBURY, BLOOMSBURY ACADEMIC and the Diana logo are trademarks of Bloomsbury Publishing Plc

First published in Great Britain 2018
This paperback edition published in 2021

Cover design: Daniel Benneworth-Gray
Cover image © Edward Steichen/Condé Nast/Getty Images

A catalogue record for this book is available from the British Library.

A catalog record for this book is available from the Library of Congress.

ISBN: HB: 978-1-4725-9513-3
PB: 978-1-3502-1074-5
ePDF: 978-1-4725-9515-7
eBook: 978-1-4725-9514-0

Series: Modernist Archives

CONTENTS

LIST OF ILLUSTRATIONS

(excluding facsimiles on pages 52–63, 188–271, 322–39, and 352–59)

EDITORIAL PREFACE TO MODERNIST ARCHIVES

Archival excavation and thick contextualization are becoming increasingly central to scholarship on literary modernism. In recent years, the increased accessibility and dissemination of previously unpublished or little-known documents and texts has led to paradigm-shifting scholarly interventions on a range of canonical authors (Beckett, Eliot, Joyce, Pound and Woolf, among others), neglected topics (the occult, "primitivism," fascism, eugenics, book history, the writing process), and critical methodologies (genetic criticism, intertextuality and historical contexts). This trend will surely only increase as large-scale digitization of archival materials gathers pace and existing copyright restrictions gradually lapse. *Modernist Archives* is a book series that aims to channel, extend and interrogate these shifts by publishing hitherto unavailable or neglected primary materials for a wider readership. Each volume also provides supporting, contextualizing work by scholars, alongside a critical apparatus of notes and references.

The impetus for *Modernist Archives* emerges from the editors' well-established series, *Historicizing Modernism*. While *Historicizing Modernism*'s focus is analytical, *Modernist Archives* will make accessible edited and annotated versions of little-known sources and avant-texts. The monographs and edited collections in *Historicizing Modernism* have revealed the extent to which contemporary scholars are increasingly turning toward archival and/or unpublished material in order to reconfigure understandings of modernism, in its broader historical rootedness as well as in its compositional methodologies. The present series extends this empirical and genetic focus.

Understanding and defining such primary sources as a broad category extending to letters, diaries, notes, drafts and marginalia, the *Modernist Archives* series produces volumes that not only unearth significant unpublished material and provide original scholarship on this material, but which also develop cutting-edge editorial presentation techniques that preserve as much information as possible in an economical and accessible way. Also of note is the potential for the series to explore collections pertaining to the relations between literary modernism and other media (radio, television), or important cultural moments. The series thus aims to be an enabling force within modernist scholarship.

It is becoming ever more difficult to read this extraordinary period of literary experimentation in isolation from contextualizing archival material, sometimes dubbed the "gray canon" of modernist writing. The difficulty, we suggest, is something like a loss of innocence: once obviously relevant materials are actually accessible, they cannot be ignored. They may challenge received ideas about the limits or definition of modernism; they may upend theoretical frameworks, or encourage fresh theoretical reflection; they may require new methodologies, or revise the very notion of "authorship"; likewise, they may require types of knowledge that we never knew we needed—*but there they are.*

However, while we are champions of historical, archival research, *Modernist Archives* in no way seeks to influence the results or approaches that scholars in this area will utilize in the exciting times ahead. By commissioning a wide range of innovative and challenging editions, this series aims to once more "make strange" and "make new" our fundamental ideas about modernism.

Matthew Feldman
Erik Tonning

ACKNOWLEDGMENTS

The editor and publisher gratefully acknowledge the following permissions granted to reproduce the copyright material in this book: United Agents LLP, on behalf of Caitriona Yeats and the Yeats Estate, for permission to quote the unpublished materials by W. B. Yeats; the Council of Trustees of the National Library of Ireland for approving the reproduction of manuscripts by W. B. Yeats in their possession; Oxford University Press for permission to quote from *The Collected Letters of W. B. Yeats* (copyright 1985, including all subsequent InteLex CD-ROM and online editions); Simon and Schuster, Inc. (Scribner) for permission to reprint poetry and prose by W. B. Yeats (save for correspondence) in copyright in the United States, including (1) *The Collected Works of W. B. Yeats*, vol. 1: *The Poems, Revised* by W. B. Yeats, edited by Richard J. Finneran, copyright 1928 by The Macmillan Company, renewed 1956 by Georgie Yeats (all rights reserved), and (2) *A Vision: The Revised 1937 Edition*, vol. 14, by W. B. Yeats, edited by Margaret Mills Harper and Catherine E. Paul, copyright 1937 by W. B. Yeats, copyright renewed 1965 by Bertha Georgie Yeats and Anne Butler Yeats; as well as Ed Victor Ltd. for approval to quote extracts from *World Within World* by Stephen Spender (copyright 1951), reprinted by kind permission of the Estate of Stephen Spender. For permission to reprint the editor's own work, thanks are due to James S. Rogers, Editor, *New Hibernia Review* 17.1 (for a shorter version of the last chapter), and to John Morgenstern, Executive Editor, Clemson University Press (for text adapted on pages 34–45).

With advice, encouragement, and assistance received from the following persons, this book benefitted in various ways: Lauren Arrington, Charis Chapman, Lauren Crisp, Matthew Feldman, Matthew Gibson, Warwick Gould, Meg Harper, James Harte, Jessica Heim, Clara Herberg, Merv Honeywood, Aaron M. Lisec, Neil Mann, Gerry Ó Luing, Catherine Paul, Jim Rogers, Linda Shaughnessy, and Erik Tonning. For a one-semester sabbatical to typeset most of the extracts and transcriptions found in this book, and for financial support of fieldwork as well as a research assistant, the editor is grateful to Clemson University, to the Department of English, and to the Center for Electronic and Digital

Publishing then under his direction. Special thanks are due to Michael Cronin and the staff of Boston College-Ireland for services and temporary office space in Dublin. Neil Mann was particularly helpful in assisting with the proofreading of this book, in the late stage of its production, and by contributing valuable suggestions to the transcriptions of Part Four and elsewhere.

Every effort has been made to trace copyright holders and to obtain their permission for the use of copyright material. The publisher apologizes for any errors or omissions in the above list and would be grateful if notified of any corrections that should be incorporated in future reprints or editions of this book.

EDITORIAL PRINCIPLES

Aside from correspondence, the unpublished manuscripts quoted or reproduced in this book are all part of the W. B. Yeats Collection at the National Library of Ireland. A small part of these are housed separately among the Occult Papers of W. B. Yeats (Accession No. 5554).

Transcriptions shall preserve the idiosyncrasies of Yeats's spelling, punctuation, and manner of revising as much as possible. The whole word is given when that seems intended, even though letters are missing or elided with a stroke, as often with the "-ing" ending. When a precise spelling is unclear, a standard spelling may be substituted. A word will be left incomplete if Yeats seems to have abandoned it that way. Overwritings are formalized within enlarged curly braces { }. Illegible words are represented thus: [?]. A conjectural reading thus: [?word]. And a partly conjectural reading thus: every[?thing]. When Yeats uses drawn lines and arrows in revising, these features are replicated graphically to help the reader relate the editor's transcriptions to their originals. Yeats's underlinings and "stet." notations are retained, as are his caret symbols. Where he has inserted extra lines, or parts of lines, the line spacing is increased to allow room to accommodate this interlineation. Blots, bleeds, and physical damage are noted only when the text is affected.

The following conventions represent the physical features of Yeats's texts: roman type indicates the use of black ink; *italic type* indicates pencil; and **boldface type** indicates typescript or print. Transcriptions that make these distinctions will also employ notes and collations in an apparatus. In such cases, the word "*lacking*" indicates that some material is missing; "*del*" is an abbreviation for "deleted," "*rev from*" for "revised from," and "*rev to*" for "revised to." The editor has been able to match photographs of holograph materials and facing transcriptions for most of the evidence submitted. The exceptions are transcriptions that have been incorporated into the editor's commentary, including selections from the early Robartes-Aherne dialogues as well as the entire "Appendix by Michael Robartes." This abandoned composition in the handwriting of Mrs. Yeats is streamed for economy, with her scribal additions indicated within angle brackets < > and those of the editor entered in square brackets [ ]. In streamed transcriptions, the editor may indicate vertical space omitted by introducing [...] in the appropriate position in the text. Strikeouts are everywhere indicated with a line through the deleted word, parts of words, parts of lines, and whole lines. Cancellation of two or more consecutive lines is represented by a vertical bracket in the left margin. Frequently there are earlier cancellations within such blocks, and these are represented with horizontal lines. Generally, editorial queries and glosses on the revision of textual matter are noted parenthetically.

ABBREVIATIONS

Frequently cited works by W. B. Yeats and others are given standard abbreviations. Most of those selected for use in this book became standardized in *Yeats Annual.* Bibliographic details may also occur in commentary and notes when relevant to context, and with the abbreviation explained in first instance. Of Yeats's works frequently cited, generally these will be Macmillan's standard editions and the *Variorum Editions* of the poems and plays. Because Scribner has so far issued as many as six versions of Yeats's collected poems edited by Richard J. Finneran, three of them with different paginations, the "*Varorium Poems*" (*VP*) is reliably cited in preference to *The Collected Works of W. B. Yeats, Volume I: The Poems* in its second edition (1997), which is sometimes also cited. In this way confusion is avoided or minimized. See the editors' headnote in *YVEC* (xvi) for a detailed explanation. Similarly, citations for books owned and sometimes annotated by Yeats or his wife are sometimes given as listed both in Wayne K. Chapman's *The W. B. and George Yeats Library: A Short Title Catalog* (*WBGYL*), based on the library as it was received by the National Library of Ireland, and in the older, less complete compilation of Edward O'Shea (*YL*).

AS	Automatic Script
Au	*Autobiographies* (London: Macmillan, 1955).
AVA	*A Vision: An Explanation of Life Founded upon the Writings of Giraldus and upon certain Doctrines attributed to Kusta Ben Luka* (London: T. Werner Laurie, 1925).
AVB	*A Vision* (1937; revised, London: Macmillan, 1962).
BL Add.	Additional Manuscript, The British Library, London (followed by number).
CL Intelex	*The Collected Letters of W. B. Yeats*, gen. ed. John Kelly, Oxford University Press (Intelex Electronic Edition) 2002; letters cited by accession number.
CVA	*A Critical Edition of Yeats's A Vision (1925)*, ed. George Mills Harper and Walter Kelly Hood (London: Macmillan, 1978).
CW	*The Collected Works of W. B. Yeats* (followed by vol. number)

CW1	*Volume I: The Poems (Second Edition)*, ed. Richard J. Finneran (1989; New York: Scribner, 1997).
CW2	*Volume II: The Plays*, ed. David R. Clark & Rosalind E. Clark (New York & London: Palgrave, 2001; New York: Scribner, 2001).
CW13	*Volume XIII: A Vision (1925)*, ed. Catherine E. Paul & Margaret Mills Harper (New York: Scribner, 2008).
CW14	*Volume XIV: A Vision (1937)*, ed. Margaret Mills Harper & Catherine Paul (New York: Scribner, 2015).
E&I	*Essays and Introductions* (London and New York: Macmillan, 1961).
Ex	*Explorations*, selected by Mrs. W. B. Yeats (London: Macmillan, 1962; New York: Macmillan, 1963).
FFTIP	*Fairy and Folk Tales of the Irish Peasantry*, edited and selected by W. B. Yeats (London: Walter Scott, 1888).
L	*The Letters of W. B. Yeats*, ed. Allan Wade (London: Rupert Hart-Davis, 1954; New York: Macmillan, 1955).
LDW	*Letters on Poetry from W. B. Yeats to Dorothy Wellesley*, 1940 (London: Oxford University Press, 1964).
Life	Roy F. Foster, *W. B. Yeats: A Life*, 2 vols.
Life1	*Volume 1: The Apprentice Mage* (Oxford: Oxford University Press, 1997).
Life2	*Volume 2: The Arch-Poet* (Oxford: Oxford University Press, 2003).
LTWBY	*Letters to W. B. Yeats*, ed. Richard J. Finneran, George Mills Harper and William M. Murphy with Alan B. Himber, 2 vols. (London: Macmillan; New York: Columbia University Press, 1977).
Mem	*Memoirs: Autobiography—First Draft Journal*, transcribed and ed. Denis Donoghue (London: Macmillan, 1972; New York: Macmillan, 1973)
Myth	*Mythologies* (London and New York: Macmillan, 1959).
M2005	*Mythologies*, ed. Warwick Gould & Deirdre Toomey (London: Macmillan, 2005).
MYV1, 2	George Mills Harper, *The Making of Yeats's "A Vision": A Study of the Automatic Script*, 2 vols. (London: Macmillan; Carbondale and Edwardsville, IL: Southern Illinois University Press, 1987).
NLI	Manuscripts in the National Library of Ireland (followed by number).
OBMV	*The Oxford Book of Modern Verse 1895–1935*, chosen by W. B. Yeats (Oxford: Clarendon Press, 1936).
PASL	*Per Amica Silentia Lunae* (London: Macmillan, 1918).
SMR	*Stories of Michael Robartes and his Friends: An Extract from a Record Made by his Pupils: and a play in prose* [*The Resurrection*] (Dundrum: Cuala Press, 1931; *facsimile*: Shannon: Irish University Press, 1970).

VP	*The Variorum Edition of the Poems of W. B. Yeats*, ed. Peter Allt and Russell K. Alspach (New York: The Macmillan Company, 1957). Cited from the corrected third printing of 1966.
VPl	*The Variorum Edition of the Plays of W. B. Yeats*, ed. Russell K. Alspach assisted by Catherine C. Alspach (London and New York: Macmillan, 1966). Cited from the corrected second printing of 1966.
VSR	*The Secret Rose, Stories by W. B. Yeats: A Variorum Edition*, ed. Phillip L. Marcus, Warwick Gould and Michael J. Sidnell (1981; second edition, London: Macmillan, 1992).
Wade	Allan Wade, *A Bibliography of the Writings of W. B. Yeats*, 3rd ed., rev. Russell K. Alspach (London: Rupert Hart-Davis, 1968). Item nos. and/or page nos. preceded by "p."
WBGYL	*The W. B. and George Yeats Library: A Short-Title Catalog*, Wayne K. Chapman (Clemson, SC: Clemson University Digital Press, 2006; online: http://blogs.clemson.edu/press/2006/04/15/the-w-b-and-george-yeats-library-a-short-title-catalog-by-wayne-chapman/.
WSC	*The Wild Swans at Coole* (London: Macmillan, 1919).
WWB1, 2, 3	*The Works of William Blake Poetic, Symbolic, and Critical, edited with lithographs of the illustrated "Prophetic Books," and a memoir and interpretation*, Edwin John Ellis and William Butler Yeats, 3 vols. (London: Bernard Quaritch, 1893).
YA	*Yeats Annual* (London: Macmillan, 1982–2000; Palgrave, 2001–2007; Open Book Publishers, 2013–), cited by issue number.
YAACTS	*Yeats: An Annual of Critical and Textual Studies* (publishers vary, 1983), cited by issue number.
YL	*A Descriptive Catalog of W. B. Yeats's Library*, Edward O'Shea, (New York and London: Garland Publishing, 1985). Item numbers and/or page numbers preceded by "p."
YO	*Yeats and the Occult*, ed. George Mills Harper (Toronto: Macmillan of Canada; Niagara Falls, NY: Maclean-Hunter Press, 1975).
YPM	Wayne K. Chapman, *Yeats's Poetry in the Making: "Sing Whatever Is Well Made"* (London: Palgrave Macmillan, 2010).
YVEC	*W. B. Yeats's "A Vision": Explications and Contexts*, ed. Neil Mann, Matthew Gibson, and Claire Nally (Clemson, SC: Clemson University Press, 2012).
YVP	*Yeats's Vision Papers*, George Mills Harper (General Editor) assisted by Mary Jane Harper.
YVP1	*Volume 1: The Automatic Script: 5 November 1917–18 June 1918*, ed. Steve L. Adams, Barbara J. Frieling and Sandra L. Sprayberry (London & Iowa City: Macmillan & University of Iowa Press, 1992).

YVP2 *Volume 2: The Automatic Script: 25 June 1918–29 March 1920*, ed. Steve L. Adams, Barbara J. Frieling and Sandra L. Sprayberry (London & Iowa City: Macmillan & University of Iowa Press, 1992).

YVP3 *Volume 3: Sleep and Dream Notebooks, Vision Notebooks 1 and 2*, Card File, ed. Robert Anthony Martinich and Margaret Mills Harper (London & Iowa City: Macmillan & University of Iowa Press, 1992).

YVP4 *Volume 4: "The Discoveries of Michael Robartes," Version B ("The Great Wheel" and "The Twenty-Eight Embodiments")*, ed. George Mills Harper and Margaret Mills Harper, with Richard W. Stoops, Jr. (London: Palgrave, 2001).

INTRODUCTION

A few years ago, the prospect of reconstructing the genesis of Yeats's final, completed work of prose fiction presented itself, as it were, in three portents—a single manuscript notebook, a later holograph addition dissevered in fragments, and a packet bearing corrected proofs for *Stories of Michael Robartes and His Friends: An Extract from a Record Made by His Pupils: and a Play in Prose* (Cuala Press, 1931; abbreviated *SMR*)—each a part of the W. B. Yeats Collection at the National Library of Ireland. Since then, construction toward that objective came to pass with the addition of numerous related materials, the number of which is suggested by the list of "Manuscript Materials Cited" at the end of this book. One begins, necessarily, with the origin of characters in the *Secret Rose* triptych of the late-1890s, followed by a selection of unpublished dialogues of 1917–1920 because those works embody the narrative frame, or bones, of Yeats's creative enterprise from the first year of his marriage. By adhering to the sequence of composition through the 1930s, then, the book was able to become the first genetically conceived, chronologically arranged edition of all Yeats's Robartes-Aherne writings. As the reader chooses, these writings may be considered as autonomous constituents of the whole or viewed in terms of Yeats's on-going pre-occupation with two very extraordinary characters.

This volume's archival excavations focus on the processes of writing and publishing, literary adaptation and innovation, philosophical discovery by occultation, and interrogation of self-textualizing doubles who often blur distinctions between author and character, actuality and art. Yeats's preface to *Michael Robartes and the Dancer* (Cuala, 1921) made a promise that he could not keep. Because no account had been given "of Robartes himself" (were we to imagine him to be a real person), Yeats said that he, aided by Aherne, would see publication of "the great mass of [Robartes's] letters and table talk" almost before the ink were able to dry on that little "hand-printed" chapbook ([v–vi]; see page 115 below). *A Vision* (1925) made good with a handsome payment, following assorted notes on the lyrics "An Image from a Past Life" and "The Second Coming" and on his "plays for dancers." But the debt was still owed when he conceded in *A Packet for Ezra Pound* (Cuala, 1929) that his invention of "an unnatural story of an Arabian traveller…I must amend and find a place for some day because I was fool enough to write half a dozen poems that were unintelligible without it" (25). Subsequently, he added a footnote to *A Packet for Ezra Pound* (SPEC COL/ PR5906.A553 1929, Emory University), the setting copy for *A Vision* (1937), wherein he cited "Stories of Michael Robartes" as the "amended version" he had meant.

I have included the first two drafts (untitled) of what became the dialogue "The Discoveries of Michael Robartes," otherwise presented by George Mills Harper and Margaret Mills Harper in Volume 4 of *Yeats's Vision Papers* (London: Palgrave, 2001), only because the drafts are unavailable there either in image or transcription. Thus, the exercise books are presented here without quoting at length the dialogues in *YVP4*, including the extracts of "Version B." Similarly, the silently edited versions of "Appendix by Michael Robartes" and "Michael Robartes Foretells," published in 1975 by Walter Kelly Hood, have been replaced and given context by *literatim* transcriptions, critical apparatus, and commentary, as is usual for an edition of creative work. Other normative features include the use of procedures established for transcriptions and photo-facsimiles in the distinguished Cornell Yeats series, except that presentation of manuscripts in relation to commentary, at times resembling blocks of unpublished documents interspersed with chapters, most resembles the organization employed by David R. Clark and James B. McGuire in *W. B. Yeats: The Writing of "Sophocles' King Oedipus"* (Philadelphia: American Philosophical Society, 1989). That precedent seems especially well-suited for textual-genetic methodology and chronological sequencing in a multilayered source history, though the five-part structure of the present volume, spanning forty years of Yeats's writing in a single vein, also follows M. J. Sidnell and W. K. Chapman in *The Countess Cathleen: Manuscript Materials* (Cornell, 1999), which traces Yeats's writing and rewriting of the play during a comparable period of time. Elsewhere, in "Mr. Yeats, Michael Robartes and Their Circle" (*YO* 225–54), Michael Sidnell proved an inspiration to an economical and accessible presentation of the entire "set" of Robartes-Aherne writings, which seemed possible by his example. Of course, nothing was to surpass the inspiration of Yeats's published stories, poems, prefaces, notes, and supposed "extracts" from the "Robartes MSS" themselves, including the unpublished dialogues and other writings, both early and late.

The organization here is organic, involving the division of content into sections by time and alternating between published and unpublished texts. The book's five parts are as follows:

"Part One: 1896–1897, *The Secret Rose* Triptych" begins with "A Note on the Texts" although anticipated by commentary in this introduction. Here the objective is to present the celebrated precursor texts that inspired the later dialogues, poems, notes, extracts, and "Stories" in response to philosophical substance, style, and above all Yeats's creation of two vividly portrayed characters as well as a conflicted, flawed narrator. Part One is, then, an exhibition of the early tales of

Michael Robartes, Owen Aherne, and the unnamed but Yeats-like narrator. The 1908 version of "Rosa Alchemica," "The Tables of the Law," and "The Adoration of the Magi" serves as the base text of a simplified critical edition of the three stories, with variants of one or more lines provided from both the original and the later (1925 and 1932) versions just to illustrate shifts in style and perspective to and from Yeats's important attempt to make a canonical body of his writings, inclusive of the three stories as first published together at the Shakespeare Head Press, in volume 7 of *The Collected Works in Verse and Prose of William Butler Yeats*.

"Part Two: 1917–1920, Unpublished Dialogues and Extracts" examines the reintroduction of Robartes and Aherne as characters after a lapse of twenty years. The burden of this part of the book, with its somewhat disparate body of dispersed fictions, is to articulate a myth Yeats began in stages to disguise his wife's role in the genesis of the philosophical core of *A Vision* (1925). He engaged these characters in the construction of a fictitious narrative frame and generated a substantial amount of unpublished work about the same time they began resurfacing in his poetry. The texts explored here are (1) the unfinished dialogue between Yeats and Aherne called "Anglo Ireland: a conversation," (2) the first two drafts of the Robartes-Aherne dialogues eventually called "The Discoveries of Michael Robartes," and (3) the rejected manuscript in Mrs. Yeats's hand, "Appendix by Michael Robartes," an early effort to develop the Wheel, or "Diagram," of the fictional magus Giraldus. Also considered is the complexly related process by which the verse-dialogue "The Phases of the Moon," kindred to "Ego Dominus Tuus," came into being, as well as the verse-monologue "The Double Vision of Michael Robartes."

"Part Three: 1919–1925, Published Poems, Notes and Extracts" presents selections from *The Wild Swans at Coole* (1919), *Michael Robartes and the Dancer* (1920), *The Cat and the Moon and Certain Poems* (1924), and *A Vision* (1925), including prefaces and notes for *Later Poems* (1922), *Four Plays for Dancers* (1921), and both the longer and shorter interjections made by Owen Aherne (signed "O.A." or "O. Aherne"). These were derived from the narrative frame—that is, with characters revived to deflect attention from the reality of WBY's discoveries actually accomplished by communicating with various "spirit guides" mediated by his wife. The assembled lyrics of Part Three include "Ego Dominus Tuus," "The Phases of the Moon," "The Double Vision of Michael Robartes," "Michael Robartes and the Dancer," "An Image from a Past Life," "The Second Coming," "The Gift of Harun-Al-Rashid," "The Lover Speaks," and "The Heart Replies" (the latter two eventually coalesced to form "Owen Aherne and His Dancers," I and II). The plays Yeats discussed by resorting to this gambit are *The Only Jealousy of Emer*, *The Dreaming of the Bones*, and *Calvary*.

"Part Four: 1929–1931, The Making of 'Stories of Michael Robartes and His Friends'" features facsimiles and a *literatim* transcription of the single tale that Yeats eventually composed from recycled fictional elements of the 1920s. Published in

1931 before it occurred to him that the work might one day serve as a preliminary movement for a revised edition of *A Vision*, "Stories of Michael Robartes and His Friends: An Extract from a Record Made by His Pupils" first counterpointed and accompanied Yeats's play *The Resurrection*, about the dispensation of the Christian era at the end of the Hellenic one. Thus, a comparative analysis of themes and motifs receives a good deal of the editor's attention. As commentary is followed by a major exposition of 83 pages, both the epigraph "Huddon, Duddon and Daniel O'Leary" (from holograph) and a diplomatic rendering of the 1931 Cuala Press printing of "Stories" are presented with illustrations by artist Edmund Dulac, figures of the Unicorn, the Wheel, and Giraldus introduced at the same points established in that edition.

"Part Five: 1932–1937, Afterword: Unpublished and Published Additions Prepared for *A Vision* B" concludes this study by presenting two fairly late augmentations to the "Stories of Michael Robartes" after its release in 1932. Once Yeats decided to append "Stories" to *A Vision* revised, beside the latter's designated introduction, in *A Packet for Ezra Pound*, he next had to address the problem of integrating essentially extraneous material. Did he not already consider the 1931 "Stories of Michael Robartes" to be a complete work of fiction before joining it to the dissimilar treatise? Sometime in 1932–1933, he wrote and even corrected an epilogue for *A Vision* as if it were to extend the 1931 "Stories." Called "Michael Robartes Foretells," the epilogue was soon abandoned, and by 1934 Robartes's prophecies seem to have been little more to Yeats than divertissements for entertaining high-brow Bloomsbury literati, especially Virginia Woolf and the young Stephen Spender. Likewise, this section of the study closes with the late, somewhat lurid addition to the tale, referred to here as "Denise's Story," written in July 1936 to entertain (and possibly to shock) Lady Gerald Wellesley. The addition was not introduced until Yeats corrected page proofs of *A Vision* in 1937. Both the rejected "Michael Robartes Foretells" and the accepted addition appear in photo-reproductions following commentary on their making.

MICHAEL ROBARTES

As a literary persona and protagonist, Michael Robartes made his debut in the April 1896 issue of *The Savoy*, where he is presented by a comparatively sallow, unnamed narrator (the sympathetic eye-witness to a tragedy), as one whose "passion for universal ideas" blindly leads to "martyrdom" at the hands of an ignorant mob during a religious revival: "A few years ago," the story begins,

> an extraordinary religious frenzy took hold upon the peasantry of a remote Connemara headland; and a number of eccentric men and women, who had turned an old custom-house into a kind of college, were surprised at prayer…by a mob of fishermen, stone masons, and

> small farmers, and beaten to death with stones, which were heaped up close at hand to be ready for the next breach in the wave-battered pier. Vague rumours of pagan ceremonies and mysterious idolatries had for some time drifted among the cabins; and the indignation of the ignorant had been further inflamed by a priest, unfrocked for drunkenness, who had preached at the road-side of the secret coming of the Antichrist. (See page 16, below; *VSR* 126)

On Maud Gonne's authority, the first of three biographical models proposed for Robartes is an ubiquitous figure in Dublin magical circles, a Captain Roberts, possibly John Dobrée Anderson Roberts (ret. 1890), the leading dark magician in "The Sorcerers," whose art had passed down "from his father, and [whose] one word which he had repeated several times was Arabic" (*Myth* 40; see *M2005* 26, 235–36, and 367–68). As a romantic figure with a physical resemblance to Michael Robartes—"whose wild red hair, fierce eyes, sensitive, tremulous lips and rough clothes, made him look...something between a debauchee, a saint, and a peasant" (*Myth* 271)—Samuel Liddell MacGregor Mathers is an obvious possibility, too, for having invited Yeats, in 1887, "to join an Order of Christian kabalists, 'the Hermetic Students,'" and for instructing Yeats in *scrying*, "a form of meditation that has perhaps been the intellectual chief influence on my life up to perhaps my fortieth year" (*Mem* 26–27). Then an equally obvious candidate is George Russell because of Yeats's dedication "TO | A. E." in the 1925 *Secret Rose* triptych, to acknowledge him as fellow mystic, poet, and life-long friend, scarcely to mention the dedicatory letter of 1897, which reads in part: "My Dear A.E.—I dedicate this book to you because, whether you think it well or ill written, you will sympathize with the sorrows and the ecstasies of its personages, perhaps even more than I do myself" (*VSR* 233). Moreover, verdicts by Russell in *The Irish Statesman* on *A Vision* (1925) and on *A Packet for Ezra Pound* (1929), with high praise for *Stories of Michael Robartes* (1931) in letters, were most valued.

Another obvious point, though one that tends to be overlooked in our scholarship, is the role that Michael Robartes played as a projection of Yeats in the love poetry written in 1895–1896 and published in *The Saturday Review* and *The Savoy* at the time of his affair with Olivia Shakespear and then rearranged, among poems written for Maud Gonne of slightly earlier date, under revised titles in *The Wind Among the Reeds* (1899). This proto-Modern exemplum of Symbolism introduced the first of a host of short dramatic monologues that became one of Yeats's signatures. Three of the eight Olivia Shakespear poems assume the identity of Robartes as the speaker, chronologically in the first, fourth, and sixth ones written. They are, respectively, "Michael Robartes asks Forgiveness because of his Many Moods," "Michael Robartes bids his Beloved be at Peace," and "Michael Robartes remembers Forgotten Beauty." To be sure, Yeats's failed progress in his love affair with this woman and his temporary contentment complicates one's view of the poetic sequence made to dramatize conflicts produced in his personal life. He could not have seen when he first produced these poems as biographical artifacts and then, in three years, began to edit them together as a collection, given the range of speakers attributed to be "principles of the mind" rather than "actual personages" (*VP* 803), that one's conception of the whole might eventually simplify. For the 1906 *Poetical Works,* Yeats revised the titles again (namely *VP* poems 44, 52, 53, 54, 55, 56, 57, 58, 59, 62, 63, 64, 65, 66, 69, 71, 72, 73, 74, 75, and 76), suppressing various imaginary personae of *The Wind Among the Reeds* in favor of a single voice. Thus, collectively and at once, Aedh, Mongan, Michael Robartes, and Red Hanrahan gave way to more transparent, co-referential identities: that of "He," "The Poet," "The Lover." Michael Robartes's poems became "The Lover asks Forgiveness because of his Many Moods," "He bids his Beloved be at Peace," and "He remembers Forgotten Beauty" when the three "personages" or "principles of the mind" in Yeats's 1899 endnote coalesced without making an issue of the hermetic background of the poems and their speakers. Providently (for our purposes), he had allowed that "only students of the magical tradition will understand me when I say that 'Michael Robartes' is fire reflected in water" whereas "Hanrahan is fire blown by the wind" and "Aedh…is fire burning by itself"; however, for uncommon and common readers alike, he made a familiar distinction between Robartes and the other personae, adducing that

> Hanrahan is the simplicity of an imagination too changeable to gather permanent possessions, or the adoration of the shepherds; and Michael Robartes is the pride of the imagination brooding upon the greatness of its possessions, or the adoration of the Magi; while Aedh is the myrrh and frankincense that the imagination offers continually before all that it loves. (*VP* 803)

Although the assignment of speakers was not the metaphysical science that it sounds, the speaker in "Michael Robartes asks Forgiveness because of his Many Moods" (or "The Twilight of Forgiveness" in *The Saturday Review* of 2 November 1895) certainly sounds like a learned wizard, if not entirely expert as an instructor in the art of love-making, with the invocation of fifteen ceremonious lines (6–20) on the occult sources of his many moods in inverted commas:

> If this importunate heart trouble your peace
> With words lighter than air,
> Or hopes that in mere hoping flicker and cease;
> Crumple the rose in your hair;
> And cover your lips with odorous twilight and say,
> 'O Hearts of wind-blown flame!
> 'O Winds, elder than changing of night and day,

'That murmuring and longing came,
'From marble cities loud with tabors of old
'In dove-gray faery lands;
'From battle banners fold upon purple fold,
'Queens wrought with glimmering hands;
'That saw young Niamh hover with love-lorn face
'Above the wandering tide;
'And lingered in the hidden desolate place,
'Where the last Phoenix died
'And wrapped the flames above his holy head;
'And still murmur and long:
'O Piteous Hearts, changing till change be dead
'In a tumultuous song:'
And cover the pale blossoms of your breast
With your dim heavy hair,
And trouble with a sigh for all things longing for rest
The odorous twilight there.

The poem's Pre-Raphaelite ardor for the beloved, muted eroticism, and vague twilight imagery ("dim heavy hair" etc.) are characteristic of the early Yeats and A.E. The line "O Hearts of wind-blown flame" seems to denote a Red Hanrahan trait, but the last four lines foreshadow the next two poems assigned to Michael Robartes as a speaker, suggesting consistency of purpose, as John Harwood notes in *Olivia Shakespear and W. B. Yeats: After Long Silence* (London: Macmillan Press, 1989), 71.

"Michael Robartes bids his Beloved be at Peace" had been entitled "The Shadowy Horses," the first lyric in *The Savoy* (of January 1896) to appear beneath the banner "Two Love Poems," its companion being "The Travail of Passion." In *The Wind Among the Reeds*, Yeats attached a long note to associate the Shadowy Horses of the poem with "horse-shaped…Formorian divinities" and the horses of the sea-god Mannannan, as well as the sea with "the drifting indefinite bitterness of life" and "many Irish voyages to the islands of enchantment" from mythology, with directions provided from "the magical tradition" (*VP* 808). As a consequence, Robartes became an explorer of the distant points of the compass:

I hear the Shadowy Horses, their long manes a-shake,
Their hoofs heavy with tumult, their eyes glimmering white;
The North unfolds above them clinging, creeping night,
The East her hidden joy before the morning break,
The West weeps in pale dew and sighs passing away,
The South is pouring down roses of crimson fire:
O vanity of Sleep, Hope, Dream, endless Desire,
The Horses of Disaster plunge in the heavy clay:

Beloved, let your eyes half close, and your heart beat
Over my heart, and your hair fall over my breast,
Drowning love's lonely hour in deep twilight of rest,
And hiding their tossing manes and their tumultuous feet.

The eroticism has become more explicit with the positioning of the lovers in bed together and with the so-called "hair-tent" configuration noted by Harwood to distinguish Olivia Shakespear from Maud Gonne in these poems. Psycho-sexual conflict is dramatized in a way that caught the attention of the young James Joyce, who imitated the best features of the poem in *Chamber Music* XXXVI (1907) and then gave over the result for reprinting in Ezra Pound's famous anthology *Des Imagistes* (1914). Understandably, Yeats took Joyce's effort to be a compliment: "There is a poem on the last page of his *Chamber Music* which will, I believe, live. It is a technical and emotional masterpiece" (*L* 598–99).

"Michael Robartes remembers Forgotten Beauty," initially published in *The Savoy* (July 1896) as "O'Sullivan Rua to Mary Lavell" and thus associated with Red Hanrahan and his beloved in the popular "Stories of Red Hanrahan" cycle within *The Secret Rose* (1897), also caught the eye of the self-critical Joyce, who shows that his younger, Yeatsian self, Stephen Dedalus, had enough of the poem by heart to quarrel with its terms. Here is the Yeats:

When my arms wrap you round I press
My heart upon the loveliness
That has long faded from the world;
The jewelled crowns that kings have hurled
In shadowy pools, when armies fled;
The love-tales wove with silken thread
By dreaming ladies upon cloth
That has made fat the murderous moth;
The roses that of old time were
Woven by ladies in their hair,
The dew-cold lilies ladies bore
Through many a sacred corridor
Where such gray clouds of incense rose
That only the gods' eyes did not close:
For that pale breast and lingering hand
Come from a more dream-heavy land,
A more dream-heavy hour than this;
And when you sigh from kiss to kiss
I hear white Beauty sighing, too,
For hours when all must fade like dew
But flame on flame, deep under deep,

Throne over throne, where in half sleep
Their swords upon their iron knees
Brood her high lonely mysteries.

Joyce's response, from Stephen's second diary entry of 6 April [1902] in *A Portrait of the Artist as a Young Man* (New York: Viking, 1970), 251:

> Michael Robartes remembers forgotten beauty and, when his arms wrap her round, he presses in his arms the loveliness which has long faded from the world. Not this. Not at all. I desire to press in my arms the loveliness which has not yet come into the world.

Significantly, as Sidnell notices (see *YO* 242), "Just before Robartes was resurrected [in *WSC*], Yeats saw this reflection of his early work in Joyce's self-image (as Yeats firmly characterized Dedalus [in *L* 599])." The poem itself, hinting at the disaster of "endless Desire" brought by the Shadowy Horses and of the death of love in "Aedh laments [The Lover mourns for] the Loss of Love" (*VP* 152), is oddly elegiac at a moment when love seems cloyed, foreshadowing Robartes's very personal confession, in 1931, that once fulfilment is realized, "it ends" though "desire does not end" (*SMR* 9, *AVB* 40; but see pages 172–73 below). The somnolent tone, incantatory rhythms involving repetition of "rose" and "flame on flame," and images of "clouds of incense" and twilight gods whose eyes do not close mimic the atmosphere of the supposed hallucinatory sequence in "Rosa Alchemica," the climactic riot of the senses before the story's celebrated catastrophe:

> The dance wound in and out, tracing upon the floor the shapes of petals that copied the petals in the rose overhead....After a little I had grown weary, and stood under a pillar watching the coming and going of flame-like figures; until gradually I sank into a half-dream, from which I was awakened by seeing the petals of the great rose...falling slowly through the incense-heavy air, and, as they fell, shaping into the likeness of living beings of an extraordinary beauty. Still faint and cloud-like, they began to dance, and as they danced took a more and more definite shape, [including Eros veiled]... for Eros alone of divinities is altogether a spirit, and hides in passions not of his essence if he will commune with a mortal heart. So that if a man love nobly he knows Love through infinite pity, unspeakable trust, unending sympathy; and if ignobly through vehement jealousy, sudden hatred, and unappeasable desire; but unveiled Love he never knows. (*Myth* 288–89)

The narrator, whose hesitation permits these observations, is encouraged by Robartes to get back into the dance: "Into the dance! There is none that can be spared out of the dance; into the dance! Into the dance! That the gods may make them bodies out of the substance of our hearts" (289). Succumbing to the "magnetic power" (271) of his instructor, the unwilling initiate finds himself "dancing with an immortal august woman" who terrifies him when he realizes that "her eyelids had never quivered" and he surmises that she is "more or less than human…drinking up my soul as an ox drinks up a wayside pool" (290). The dance fails for him; the initiation fails; and he falls into a swoon because he is not like Robartes, only a former fellow student from Paris who has written an academic monograph on alchemy entitled *Rosa Alchemica*, "somewhat in the manner of Sir Thomas Browne" (267). To the narrrator, the former self of Robartes had already died: "This is not Michael Robartes at all; Michael Robartes is dead; dead for ten, for twenty years perhaps" (279). Hence it is easy for the narrator to believe, as the common thread joining the three stories of the triptych, that at daybreak Robartes has been finished off by crazed revivalists who destroy his make-shift college by stoning him and his followers. Indeed, Yeats's revisions allow for that deduction, too, with greater degrees of ambiguity inversely related to some stylistic shifting, in 1908 and 1925, toward a plainer, more muscular prose. Adding emphasis by recurrence, the same narrator refers to Robartes's "terrible destiny" (and that of "his brotherhood") in "The Tables of the Law" (303), and then confirms "the death of Michael Robartes" in "The Adoration of the Magi" by saying that the oldest of the itinerant wise men had heard it from a disembodied voice that "came out of the air over the waters" (310).

Incredibly, after twenty years, when Robartes is reintroduced into Yeats's writing, he is no less a Pre-Raphaelite and idealist than he had ever been on the subjects of love and beauty; and, unlike the timid narrator of "Rosa Alchemica," he is not one to hold back. He travels light, as we notice in "The Phases of the Moon," and, like the poet in "Adam's Curse," is something of an antiquarian, an admirer of old books and their precedents. We see this in "Michael Robartes and the Dancer" when their authority fails to gain advantage in a quarrel with his dancer—"I have principles to prove me right. / It follows from this Latin text…" (*VP* 386, ll. 42–43)—accepting the part of an avuncular, slightly foolish prophet to avouch the principles of the *Speculum Angelorum et Hominum* by Giraldus but to leave it to Yeats to explain their "diagrams and pictures in the traditional knowledge of a certain obscure Arab tribe" (853). Like the poet a connoisseur of visual art, Robartes meets his old friend Owen Aherne (coincidentally, on the very same day that Macmillan publishes *Per Amica Silentia Lunae*) on 18 January 1918, in front of a painting called *The Adoration of the Magi* (NLI 36,263/7, Exercise Book 1, folios 6^v and 7^r; see page 72 below). He had only recently returned to the English-speaking world, to London, from a twenty-year sojourn in the desert, among the tents and camels of the Judwalis. He has taken quarter in the Borough of St Pancras, it seems, a short walk from Yeats's lodgings in Bloomsbury. Hence they gossip about him, compare accounts of his misdeeds as a storyteller, and, being of the generation of Pater and Verlaine, critique modern times in their view of the past.

The "phantasmagoria" of which Yeats wrote in the unpublished dialogues and in his *Collected Poems* (*VP* 821) before extending its use to "A General Introduction for my Work" (*E&I* 509), and which Sidnell defines as cognate with "elaborate fiction" and "imaginative construction" (*YO* 226), begins with this reunion. "The word [*phantasmagoria*] insists on the unity and the equal status in reality of a great variety of thought, images, and experience of very various origin"; so the reunion of Robartes and Aherne becomes the first accretion in "an aggregate of fragments, a constructed ruin affirming the unrealizable unity" (226). The epitome and end of the *phantasmagoria*, in this sense, will be the "compound narrative" (252) of "Stories of Michael Robartes and His Friends." But the resurrection of Robartes in the poetry of 1918–1921 highlights most the distinction between the personalities of Yeats and Robartes. As to which of the two is the "creative force," Sidnell argues that "at times Mr. Yeats is no more than Robartes' scribe, at others his opponent; Robartes is not merely a character *in* a story but a character *with* a story in search of an author" (231). We are, of course, reminded of the influence of Walter Pater (*Imaginary Portraits*), Walter Savage Landor (*Imaginary Conversations*), and Luigi Pirandello (*Six Characters in Search of an Author*). Yeats so delighted in confuting his identity with Robartes in 1919 that the character, referred to as "a certain friend" in "A People's Theatre: A Letter to Lady Gregory," was credited with writing two of Yeats's poems:

> Are we approaching a supreme moment of self-consciousness, the two halves of the soul separate and face to face? A certain friend of mine has written upon this subject a couple of intricate poems called *The Phases of the Moon* and *The Double Vision* respectively, which are my continual study, and I must refer the reader to these poems for the necessary mathematical calculations. (*Ex* 259)

Warwick Gould contributes to the idea of the Robartes "set" by relating the series to the structural principle of the *Arabian Nights*, which is to gain time with the propagation of a substantial body of frame tales in the form of poems, the fictionalized notes attached to them and three plays, and short integrative pieces laid at several key points in *A Vision* (1925). For Gould, "Stories of Michael Robartes" constitutes a second set to "hold ground" for *A Vision* (1937, revised). This thesis is introduced in an important essay, "'A Lesson for the Circumspect': W. B. Yeats's Two Versions of *A Vision* and the *Arabian Nights*," in which the role of progenitor passes from Princess Scheherazade (George Yeats) to Robartes as source of the tales, usually told second-hand by Yeats or Aherne. (See *The* Arabian Nights *in English Literature*, ed. Peter L. Caracciolo [London: Macmillan Press, 1988], 244–80.) Noting Yeats's memorable encounter with *Arabian Nights* in childhood (see *WBGYL* 689 [*YL* 676]), Gould's case is made on the adult versions that Yeats would have known: the translations of John Payne (1882–84), Richard Burton (1885–88), and Powys Mathers (1923; see *WBGYL* 258 [*YL* 251]). This procedure circumvents the weaknesses of Suheil Bushrui's overly broad discussion in "Yeats's Arabic Interests" (see *In Excited Reverie*, ed. A. Norman Jeffares and K. G. W. Cross [London: Macmillan, 1965], 280–314), which tends to make undemonstrated claims or blanket statements almost impossible to verify in the vastness of English- and Arabic-language texts with which Bushrui is presumably familiar as a practicing Baha'i, citing Yeats but often withholding alleged Arabic instances. Like Sidnell, Gould is particularly keen on two Kusta ben Luka tales of Yeats's devising, "The Gift of Harun Al-Rashid" (as tribute to "love voice and all") and the "wisdom" frame tale "The Dance of the Four Royal Persons" (ostensibly by Owen Aherne on the authority of the "Robartes MSS" but with doubts about "authenticity"). Both tales establish the structural frame on which stands the 1925 version of *A Vision*, Books I and II, entitled "What the Caliph Partly Learned" and "What the Caliph Refused to Learn" (see texts, notes, and commentary in Part Three, pages 133–40, below, and the section called "Inventions and Extracts for *A Vision*...[1925]," pages 142–64). These "pastiches" in *AVA* are exquisitely rendered counterfeits the writing of which delighted Yeats as he applied himself to the long labor of writing and rewriting the treatise he likened to "stylistic arrangements of experience comparable to the cubes in the drawing of Wyndham Lewis and to the ovoids in the sculpture of Brancusi" (*AVB* 25); in "Desert Geometry or The Gift of Harun Al-Raschid," these are the "signs and shapes" of a young woman's wisdom, "All those abstractions that you fancied were / From the great Treatise of Parmenides; / All, all those gyres and cubes and midnight things / Are but a new expression of her body" (*AVA* 126; *VP* 469, lines 181–85).

Without the direct knowledge of a Bushrui, much of what Yeats wrote, sired by inspiration and excitement, will seem purely invented. Initially, Robartes's big discovery in the dialogues went without father until the blank spaces left for names could be filled there in consultation with more knowledgeable friends such as Edward Denison Ross, director of the School of Oriental Languages at London University. Even the mysteriously mimetic dance of Luka's bride and of the Royal Persons has its origin in the dance of Robartes's initiates in "Rosa Alchemica," rather than in some account of sand-divination (not cited) in Charles M. Doughty's *Travels in Arabia Deserta* (1888), according to Bushrui (306). Not even Giraldus and the Latin title of the *Speculum Angelorum et Hominum* had been decided at first pass, by Christmas 1917, as an occult holy book with obvious affinity to the *Kabbala Denudata* (1677) of Christian Knorr von Rosenroth, selectively translated by MacGregor Mathers as *The Kabbalah Unveiled* (London: George Redway, 1887; *WBGYL* 1305 and 1305a [*YL* 1292 and 1292a]). By January 1918, if not before, Yeats had the English he wanted for the title of Giraldus's Arabic source, *The Way of Souls between the Moons and the Suns*, reminiscent of W. T. Horton's *The Way of the Soul, a Legend in Line and Verse* (1910) and of Cecil French's *Between Sun and Moon: Poems and Woodcuts* (published in 1922 but dedicated to Yeats in November 1917 "In token of what he has given to the world").

Attribution of the historical Kusta ben Luka, as a plausible author of antecedent wisdom for Giraldus in the *Speculum*, was certainly suggested by Denison, with possible collusion by Iseult Gonne, at that time supervised by Denison as a student and employee, thanks to Yeats (see pages 77–80, below). The non-alliterating Arabic title would not have fit in an allotted space in a slightly later draft, suggesting one reason why "TARĪQUAT UN-NUFŪS BAYN AL-QUMÚR WA'L-SHUMUS" (*YVP4* 17, n. 24, and 70, n. 30) was later abandoned. On the other hand, the name "Judwali," for the Arab tribe that accepted Robartes as a member and medical doctor, became a permanent element in Yeats's fable. For, as Mrs. Yeats confided to Bushrui, Yeats "wanted a 'fable' for his philosophical treatise and…'he went to Denison Ross for a fable'" (296). Gould introduces the term "*cante-fable*" to be more precise (276, n. 20). "There is no tribe," Bushrui ventures, "nor has there ever been one" by the name of Judwali; "'Judwal' (correctly 'jadwal') in Arabic means a stream or canal or a mathematical table or diagram; hence Yeats's reference to the Judwalis as 'diagrammatists'" (295). Mrs. Yeats thought that her husband had made Ross to feel that his brains were being picked, but she also said that, "although the 'Judwalis' might not have existed, the 'sand diagrams' were part of the Order to which Yeats belonged" (297). Equally helpful, Bushrui suggests that the Sābians of Mesopotamia (present-day Iraq) are the nearest fit for Robartes's adopted tribe—a suggestion to connect Luka, Bedouin culture, and Caliph Harun Al-Rashid save for errors in Yeats's dating (297–302) or in the exercise of poor judgment, as Aherne prefers.

Sources known to Yeats in popular culture are also implied. One of these is a two-act play, Lord Dunsany's *The Tents of the Arabs*, an inversion of the pastoral tradition in which Arcadia is displaced by the desert as the home of untravailed wisdom, opposed to the corrupting influence of beautiful, populated cities. Produced at the Abbey Theatre on 24 May 1920, the play was published in *Plays of Gods and Men* (1917) and part of Yeats's library in the 1920s (*YA* 4 [1986]: 282), where it joined company with several of Dunsany's Pegana tales by the time George Russell applauded Yeats by observing, in 1932, a stylistic kinship between the latter and *Stories of Michael Robartes and His Friends*. (See pages 312 and 320, n. 2, below.) Popular attention commanded by the great Victorian translations of *Arabian Nights* might profit a master of short fiction, as Robert Louis Stevenson had shown in a series of *New Arabian Nights* built on clusters of stories mostly set in contemporary London, told by "my Arabian author," and presented in the nested structure of the tales of Sheherazade. Yeats owned the Scribner edition of 1913 (*YA* 4: 288). Gould points out that Yeats's sentiment favored a Balzacian adaptation, a "Western Thousand and One Nights" (264–65), which would tend to make "Stories of Michael Robartes" as *smart* today as the magic realism of Juan Rulfo's *Pedro Páramo* and Salman Rushdie's mixture of magic and mythology in *Two Years Eight Months and Twenty-Eight Nights: a Novel.* In March 1934, Yeats wrote prematurely to one of his learned advisers, Frank Pearce Sturm, announcing completion of his "new version" of *A Vision* and anticipating criticism that he had failed to transform Robartes into a Buddhist. In truth, he had scarcely tried, but the reason he gave is apt to this discussion:

> I required a man whose thought was not too far removed from European tradition, to comment on it. The Buddhist is[,] like the Vedantist[,] interested in the individual, whereas I had to deal with natural individuality, the individuality of civilizations. My world is Balzac's world. (*CL InteLex* 6017)

By the end of this introduction, I will offer a defense of Yeats's premise that within "Stories of Michael Robartes" one finds some of his best writing. For now, however, the objective is to complete the snapshot of a protagonist who is an unrepentant, somewhat wounded mystic, also a charming, ridiculous, self-effacing tragicomedian. We know that Edmund Dulac's woodcut "Portrait of Giraldus" was intended to resemble Yeats, turbaned and behind a beard. It seems likely that in acknowledging Robartes's covert activities as a British expatriate involved in an Arab uprising against Ottoman rule, there was a motive to associate him with attested bravery in the person of "young Colonel Lawrence," whom he fought beside to balance pleasure and danger "lest [his old] bones might soften" (*SMR* 10, *AVB* 41). Bushrui says that Mrs. Yeats told him that the two books that influenced Yeats the most were "Doughty's *Arabia Deserta* and T. E. Lawrence's *The Seven Pillars of Wisdom*" (294). Lawrence and his exploits were the stuff of a living legend from 1919 onward, sensationalized by the international media; hence his own account of it was much in demand after publication of the first edition in 1926. Although Yeats's personal copy was not entirely cut (*WBGYL* 1104 [*YL* 1094], he expressed "great pleasure" in nominating Lawrence (a.k.a. Thomas Edward Shaw) to the Irish Academy of Letters and in commending the author, on 26 September 1932, when writing to recognize Lawrence's acceptance of the nomination, because "you are among my chief of men, being one of the few charming and gallant figures of our time, & as considerable in intellect as in gallantry & charm" (*CL InteLex* 5743).

In "good light," Robartes is seen to be "lank, muscular, clean-shaven, with an alert, ironical eye" (*SMR* 6); he is "that inspired man" (18) whose uncanny visions arise before him always as he awaits his morning tea. The theme "Concerning love," written out on the last page of Yeats's manuscript notebook as a practice run for the confessional climax of Robartes's life's story, is rewritten in the guise of Kantian logic. Making account of himself at the request of his precociously sexual pupil, Denise de Lisle Adam, Robartes is no longer of the same mind as he had been when he directed a school for Christian Cabalists on the pier in "Rosa Alchemica":

> Love contains all Kant's antinomies but it is the first that poisons our lives. Thesis, there is no beginning; antithesis, there is a beginning; or,

> as I prefer[,] thesis, there is no end…[for] desire does not end. Life is no series of emanations from divine reason such as the cabalists imagine, but an irrational bitterness,…no waterfall but a whirlpool, a gyre. (9)

By the same token, "the terror that is to come" (19) is a prophecy informed by experience but also derived from Kant's third antinomy:

> Thesis: freedom; antithesis: necessity.…Every action of man declares the soul's ultimate, particular freedom, and the soul's disappearance in God; declares that reality is a congeries of beings and a single being; nor is this antinomy an appearance imposed upon us by the form of thought but life itself which turns, now here, now there, a whirling and a bitterness. (21)

Ergo: "Love war because of its horror, that belief may be changed, civilization renewed. We desire belief and lack it.…Belief is renewed continually in the ordeal of death" (22). (Cf. *AVB* 40 and 52–53; see *YPM* 3–5 and pages 173–74, below.)

Gallantry suffers when it becomes *recklessness*, a term Yeats equated with *sprezzatura*, or riding without a bit in "In Memory of Major Robert Gregory." Not one to hold back, Robartes goes too far until he is reined in by his more orthodox companion and chronicler, Owen Aherne: "You are not sane when you talk like that" (22). Nevertheless, the two old men, accompanied by ecstatic-eyed Mary Bell and the as-yet-unhatched third egg of Leda, plunge absurdly ahead into another adventure in the sands of Arabia, presumably their last, considering the passing of time noted in the unfinished epilogue "Michael Robartes Foretells" (see pages 316–17 and 322–23, below).

OWEN AHERNE

As a Yeatsian mask in these tales, the second most important is a conflicted character who serves both Yeats and Robartes as a foil. Given similar interests as students in Paris during their university days, Aherne and Robartes follow separate paths until chance reunites them in winter 1917–1918, after twenty years and the latter's disappearance at the end of "Rosa Alchemica." Owen Aherne is the protagonist of "The Tables of the Law" (1896), and, like Robartes, his background is sketchy although scholarship has extended to him a kind of genealogy, or Herne family history in Ireland and in Yeats's fiction of the 1890s until about 1903—that is, in the stories "The Rose of Shadow" and "The Cradles of Gold" (where the name is spelled "Herne" and "Hearne," respectively, meaning "heron") and in the abandoned novel *The Speckled Bird*, in which Yeats presents his "most personal mask," to whom he gave the name Michael Hearne; as Warwick Gould states (in "'Lionel Johnson Comes First to Mind," *YO* 275):

> In "philosophic" terms, the Herne characters throughout Yeats are birds of the margin. Michael Hearne, who would sound familiar to readers of *Reveries over Childhood and Youth*, is the "Speckled Bird" of the title, and as his epiphany by the shore on the west coast of Ireland shows, he takes his name, oddly enough, not from the unspeckled heron, but from Jeremiah's owl.

Jeremiah 12.19: "Mine heritage is unto me as a speckled bird, the birds round about are against her; come ye, assemble all the beasts of the field, come to devour." Taken into context separately, both symbols are meaningful. Michael Hearne, Owen Aherne (whose name is anagrammatic for "Hearne"), and the narrator of *The Secret Rose* triptych are "three of a kind," according to Gould, who argues convincingly that Yeats modeled "the psychological type" of Owen Aherne on the life-models of close friends Lionel Johnson and John O'Leary (277). In outline, the argument is compressed in a long note in *M2005* 399–400.

Like Aherne, Johnson and O'Leary were divided characters; while both were Catholic, the latter most resembled Aherne by age, physical appearance, commitment to act with "passion for abstract right" yet with "detachment from his own enthusiasm," giving "his whole life a curious and solitary distinction" (*E&I* 510). Like Aherne, the old Fenian, with whom Yeats lived for a time and famously quarreled on the subject of magic, "had the nature, which is half monk, half soldier of fortune, and must needs turn action into dreaming, and dreaming into action; and for such there is no order, no finality, no contentment in this world" (*Myth* 294). Perhaps more monkish than O'Leary though dreaming of action in the self-defining poem "Mystic and Cavalier," Lionel Johnson seems clearly the model for Owen Aherne in connection with Joachimist theology and possibly bringing to Yeats's attention two eighteenth-century members of the Herne family: the Irish revolutionary Captain John Aherne and Dr. Maurice Aherne, "priest, librarian at the Bibliotheque Mazarine in Paris, and Professor of Dogmatic Divinity in Maynooth" (*M2005* 399; see *YO* 277–83). One might add that Yeats's *reintroduction* of Owen Aherne at Ballylee in an unpublished dialogue of 1917, "Anglo Ireland: a conversation," only to quarrel with Yeats on sectarian ground, recalls strong clerical reaction against *The Countess Cathleen* in 1899, when the play premiered in company with *The Heather Field* by Edward Martyn of Tillyra Castle, a Roman Catholic sensitive to objections voiced by the Church for alleged heresy by Yeats and for sacrilegious treatment of revered symbols by players in the role of the evil merchants (see pages 37–42, below).

It is odd that Yeats's memory lapsed in his 1919 Preface to *The Wild Swans at Coole*, referring there to Owen as "John Aherne," a name that he fancied reading in a list of "men prosecuted for making a disturbance at the first production of 'The Play Boy' which may account for his animosity to myself" in "The Phases of the Moon." Unconsciously, Yeats may have been thinking of old Captain John Aherne if he were not making a joke. Nevertheless, Owen's brother John was born in that instance, reappearing in a note in *Later Poems* (1922–31) to acknowledge a supposed real person, "or some near relation to the man that was" the original Owen Aherne (*VP* 821). In the same note, Yeats said such poems would remain obscure until his "philosophy of life...has found some detailed exposition in prose," which by then had only just moved beyond the unpublished Robartes-Aherne dialogues to the extracts of "Version B," and to the actual drafting of *A Vision* (1925). The inscription, which refers to Robartes's "friend John Aherne" as the person through whom Yeats obtained "fragments, partly extracts from letters...to John Aherne, & partly records of conversation" (*YVP4* 141), either mistakes John for Owen or introduces John in Yeats's narrative as Owen's brother and correspondent as in "Stories of Michael Robartes," where he speaks for Owen after the latter's departure with Robartes and Mary Bell. In the inscription of 1920, Yeats writes that Robartes had returned to Mesopotamia in the spring of 1919; and this news is followed by four folios of dialogue largely copying the content of Robartes's account of himself in "The Discoveries of Michael Robartes" (typescript, holograph, and untitled manuscript), anticipating Owen Aherne's account in the "Introduction" to *AVA*, the direct antecedent of Yeats's reversion to Robartes speaking in first-person in *SMR*. Moreover, Owen Aherne and Michael Robartes tramp around Ireland together in "1922 and 1923," according to brother John (in *SMR* 23), extended to "1919, 1922, and 1923" in *AVB* 53, a contradiction in itself if Robartes were actually in Arabia. But contradiction is specially emphatic when Owen's testimony in *AVA* vouches for Robartes's return to Mesopotamia following the armistice, after which, "from that day to this [May 1925,] I have heard neither of him nor from him" (xxii). Yeats's amendment of the note in *Later Poems* for *The Collected Poems* (1933–50) says that only one of the friends, Michael Robartes, "has but lately returned *from* Mesopotamia" (*VP* 821; emphasis added), contradicting both *SMR* and *AVB*, as well as the rejected epilogue "Michael Robartes Foretells," where, conspicuously, Robartes's absence has become the burden of his disciples. Chronology, therefore, is relative. Like truth, time in the Robartes tales is elastic and extremely subjective, no matter who is entrusted with narrating them.

While Robartes's cosmic analogy of an "egg that turns inside-out perpetually without breaking its shell" is the sort of thing "that always sets Owen off" (*SMR* 1, *AVB* 33), Aherne himself is a case history of susceptibility and fanatical devotion to received wisdom passed down from mysterious old books, in his case the twelfth-century philosophy of Joachim of Flora in a thirteenth-century compendium called the *Liber inducens in Evangelium aeternum*. Aherne recovers and, later, spurns the book. His desire to learn the significance of his discovery by applying its lost doctrine to himself, as in a crucible, reflects, too, the narrator's divided sympathy in "The Tables of the Law." The present is 1896 in the triptych, a vaguely stated number of years after the narrator had made the acquaintance of Robartes and Aherne as a student in Paris, when they had "belonged to a little group which devoted itself to speculations about alchemy and mysticism" (*Myth* 294). After that, c. 1886, Robartes and his "brotherhood" in Ireland meet their "terrible destiny" in "Rosa Alchemica" and Aherne meets the narrator in part I of "The Tables of the Law." In part II, it is 1896, and the narrator trails Aherne from bookstalls along the river side of Dublin's quays to his old house for their last meeting, soon after which, in "The Adoration of the Magi," the narrator is visited "late into the night" by "three very old men" with an incredible tale about the birth of the future, an avatar born to an Irish prostitute in Paris as if in fulfillment of a vision by Robartes and the gospel of the Eternal Evangel, from the lost *Expositio in Apocalypsin*, "that the Kingdom of the Father was past, the Kingdom of the Son passing, the Kingdom of the Spirit yet to come" in "complete triumph of the Spirit…over the dead letter" (296). In sympathy, the chronology of the combined narrative seems to fluctuate in a wave pattern (see 267, 302–03, and 308). Just as Robartes and Aherne eventually serve each other as mirror and complement in the frame stories and poems within and outside *A Vision* (1925, 1937), so the narrator in "The Tables of the Law" projects something of himself in the nature of his subject:

> More orthodox in most of his beliefs than Michael Robartes, [Aherne] had surpassed [Robartes] in a fanciful hatred of all life, and his hatred had found expression in the curious paradox—half borrowed from some fanatical monk, half invented by himself—that the beautiful arts were sent into the world to overthrow nations, and finally life herself, by sowing everywhere unlimited desires, like torches thrown into a burning city. (294)

The narrator is not Yeats but of the older generation of Robartes and Aherne. In late 1917, when Yeats was "getting old—over fifty," Robartes remarks that "that seems young only to you & me"; and a short while later in the manuscript Yeats is criticized for "misrepresenting" them "under the influence of Paul Verlaine and Walter Pater, both writers who belonged by right of birth to our older generation" (see pages 74 and 82, below). The protagonists and the narrator are roughly twenty years Yeats's senior, and well into their fifties in November 1902, when Yeats, at 37, met James Joyce for the first time. About a year later, the 22-year-old Joyce expressed great admiration for *The Tables of the Law. / The Adoration of the Magi* (London: privately printed, 1897), which he purchased from a bookstall along the River Liffey, convincing Yeats that reprinting them had merit worth acknowledging in a short preface destined for the Elkin Mathews edition of 1904: "I do not think I should have reprinted them had I not met a young man the other day who liked them very much and nothing else at all that I have written" (*VSR* 234 and 265). The back flyleaf in Lily Yeats's presentation copy is inscribed "James Joyce in 1904" (in *WBGYL* 2460 [*YL* 2428]), and a letter from Arthur Symons's to Mathews, recommending Joyce for the Vigo Cabinet series, attests that Yeats meant Joyce: "Oddly enough it is to him that Yeats refers in the prefatory note to 'Tables of the Law in that very series!'" (MS Princeton, 9 October 1906). In *Stephen Hero*, fragmentary forerunner of *A Portrait of the Artist as a Young Man*, Stephen Dedalus lectures to his friend Lynch from having recently acquired an interest in Franciscan literature, thanks to Yeats:

> He had found on one of the carts of books near the river an unpublished book containing two stories by W. B. Yeats. One of these stories was called *The Tables of the Law* and in it was mentioned the fabulous preface which Joachim, abbot of Flora, is said to have prefixed to his Eternal Gospel. This discovery, coming so aptly upon his own researches, induced him to follow his Franciscan studies with vigour…[to] deliver himself boldly of the whole story of *The Tables of the Law*, every word of which he remembered.…The atmosphere of these stories was heavy with incense and omens and the figures of the monk-errants, Ahern and Michael Robartes strode through it with great strides.…Civilisation may be said indeed to be the creation of its outlaws.…These inhabit a church apart; they lift their thuribles wearily before their deserted altars; they live beyond the region of mortality, having chosen to fulfil the law of their being. (James Joyce, *Stephen Hero* [New York: New Directions, 1963], 176–78)

Stephen's depiction by his third-person narrator betrays the Romantic nature of his particular enthusiasm, one too recently acquired for him to appreciate the horrible consequence of Owen Aherne's discovering "the law of [his] being" so that he "could only express or fail to express [that] being…[when] God has made a simple and an arbitrary law that we may sin and repent!" (*Myth* 305). Aherne's misery ("I am not among those for whom Christ died" [305]), echoed in Robartes's cry that "Jesus does not understand my despair" (*SMR* 9–10, *AVB* 41), is consequent to his whole-hearted devotion to the Order of the Alchemical Rose. His happiness sinks into a state of "dejection and listlessness" because, paradoxically, the gospel of Joachim allows him to see "the whole": "and how can I come again to believe that a part is the whole? I have lost my soul because I have looked out of the eyes of the angels" (*Myth* 306).

But neither the "half-initiated" narrator of Yeats's story nor young Stephen Dedalus see Aherne's dilemma the way he sees it—or even in the same way. On the one hand, the former is terror-stricken and recoils into a reflexive attitude of orthodox prayer and rejection: the Order was "not of this earth," but a legion "seeking over this earth for whatever souls it could gather within its glittering net" (307). On the other hand, Stephen is mainly struck by the beautiful expression Yeats's narrator imparts to this terror:

> Stephen was fondest of repeating to himself this beautiful passage from *The Tables of the Law*: ["]Why do you fly from our torches which were made out of the wood of the trees under which Christ wept in the gardens of Gethsemane? Why do you fly from our torches which were made of sweet wood after it had vanished from the world and come to us who made it of old tunes with our breath.["] (*Stephen Hero* 178)

Out of respect for Yeats as an artist, and perhaps for Joachimist doctrine (threads of historical theory that will lead to the Viconian cycle of *Finnegans Wake*), Joyce withheld this material when he expanded the scene in the fifth chapter of *A Portrait*, where Stephen seriously articulates his theory of beauty, derived from a synthesis of Aristotle and Aquinas undercut by the fatuous remarks of Lynch. In the *Stephen Hero* draft, however, the narrator only slightly misrepresents the 1897 text that Joyce had before him or copied from memory. A pastoral world made "of old tunes with our breath" hardly comes to the same thing as the epochal "old *times*" made "with our breath" in Yeats's text (emphasis added; see *VSR* 164; also pages 25–26, below, lines 352–56), which finds its complement in an old prayer to fend off spiritual assailants that the narrator recites at the end of "The Adoration of the Magi," continuing his retreat to withdrawal completely from the quest known to great artists. Some of these are listed in the provenance of the *Liber inducens in Evangelium aeternum* (*Myth* 297). Joyce's slip was perhaps Freudian, or possibly a mis-transcription by an editor. Who is to say?

Unlike Robartes, Aherne is not really the presiding persona of a single lyric poem, but more of an "actual personage" rather than a "principle of the mind." He speaks in "The Phases of the Moon," mainly to prompt Robartes's recitation and to continue the antipathy to Yeats that had started as an amusement to the poet in the philosophical dialogues of 1917–20. Yeats sings; Robartes sings; but Aherne does not, in spite of strong feelings.

Then, remarkably, Yeats combined in *The Tower* (1928) two personal poems that he had written on 24 and 27 October 1917, within days of taking a much-younger bride, reissuing these poems under one title, "Owen Aherne and his Dancers." Originally entitled "The Lover Speaks" and "The Heart Replies," the poems (as "I" and "II") reassigned the zone of identity of their first-person speaker to Aherne though doing little to disguise the fact that the central question his heart tries to answer points to Yeats, who did not use a disguise when printing the two parts separately in *The Dial* (June 1924) and in *The Cat and the Moon* (July 1924). In the latter, it bore company with "The Gift of Harun Al-Rashid" and its Robartesian note relating matter from "a letter of Owen Ahern's" that Yeats says he plans to publish in *A Vision*. The courtship triangle to which the resolved 1928 poem alludes features a man who has crossed the threshold of fifty: "How could she mate with fifty years that was so wildly bred? / Let the cage bird and the cage bird mate and the wild bird mate in the wild. // …I did not find in any cage the woman at my side" (*VP* 450, II, lines 15–16 and 19). "Owen Aherne and his Dancers," with all its reticence about the principle of desire and its worry over running from love "unsought / Upon the northern upland" (later "…Norman upland" in lines 1–2 of part I), a reference to Iseult Gonne in Normandy, seems a fitting title for the poem leading up to the series "A Man Young and Old." By then, Yeats was 63, but Aherne would have been at least an octogenarian!

By the 1920s, Aherne had essentially become Robartes's historian and curator of the "Robartes MSS," including a mass of extracts from conversations and letters, all fictitious. On the day these two old men are reunited, Yeats's *Per Amica Silentia Lunae* had just been published, to Aherne's disapproval. Far from concurring, however, Robartes is "shocked" and "puzzled" to discern real authority, the voice of "dogmatic certainty" on the subject of the Antithetical self that Yeats's essays should not have possessed because Robartes alone, except for the Judwalis, "held that doctrine in the form in which [Yeats] cast it" (see page 74, below). Aherne supposes that Yeats has only presented "speculations as certainties" with a motive to recruit followers for a California cult. Following another such remark (that the doctrine of the Antithetical self was the "one original thing" in Yeats's two essays), Robartes admits that, "[s]ince I have seen this book of his[,] I have not been able to rest: I have longed to talk to somebody, & I do not know a soul but you" (see pages 75–76, below, in the unpublished writings). Besides registering alarm, Yeats has also impressed Robartes, who begins to teach Aherne the mysteries he has acquired, explaining first, in his rooms, the meaning of the woodcuts in the *Speculum* of Giraldus, and then venturing to Ireland with Aherne as traveling companion, secretary, and disciple. Eventually they stop at Thoor Ballylee, "where Mr Yeats had settled for the summer, and words were spoken… slightly resembling those in 'The Phases of the Moon,'" and quarrel but come to an understanding in London, where Aherne had produced "eighty or ninety pages of exposition" (*AVA* xxi). To reconcile Robartes's teachings with the system Aherne had cast too much in the character of Christianity, the project is handed over to Yeats ("a man," according to Aherne, "who has thought more of the love of woman than of the love of God," to which Robartes rebuts: "I want a lyric poet, and if he cares for nothing but expression, so much the better, my geometry will take care of the truth" [xxi]). As Aherne describes the arrangement, an appointment had been set up with Yeats at Woburn Buildings, where Robartes

> talked of his travels and his discovery, and as during the night I had thought the matter over and thought myself well out of a troublesome and thankless work, I helped his exposition. He had brought the Giraldus diagrams, and they seemed to interest Mr Yeats at first sight as much as they had Robartes himself. Mr Yeats consented to write the exposition on the condition that I wrote the introduction and any notes I pleased,

> and would have persuaded me to accept a portion of the profits but this I refused as later on I may publish my own commentary. (xxii)

Thus Yeats becomes the "editor" of the Robartes Papers and Aherne the "author" of the "Introduction" to *AVA*, "The Dance of the Four Royal Persons," and the four interjected notes in Book IV, "The Gates of Pluto," usually with a dig at Yeats and, sometimes, a dram of sarcasm aimed at Robartes, whose departure in "declining years" translates into "silence that has closed round him [and] made it natural to write, as I know he wished that I should, as if his conversation and his foibles were already a part of history" (xxii–xxiii). Indeed, the main frame of Robartes's life-story, from near martyrdom in "Rosa Alchemica" to his return to desert oblivion after the armistice, is recycled from successive tellings in the Robartes-Aherne dialogues, allowing for the elasticity of memory as already mentioned.

Unlike Robartes, Owen Aherne changes. He is not the same as we left him in "The Tables of the Law." By 1931 and 1937, with Robartes's return to London, Aherne is fading, becoming a menial, "stout and sedentary, bearded and dull of eye" (*SMR* 6, *AVB* 37). His animating principle is defined succinctly by John Duddon: "Aherne is a pious Catholic, thinks it Pagan or something of the kind and hates it, but he has to do what Robartes tells him, always had to from childhood up" (*SMR* 4, *AVB* 35). Aherne takes the pratfalls incumbent to missions determined by Robartes in a vision. He pulls a shoeless Daniel O'Leary into his car to rescue him from rampaging musicians; takes a crack on the head, in place of Duddon's patron and mate, Peter Huddon, and is taken to a chemist's shop, muttering; sets and clears table for the others; meets and fetches adulterers Bond and Bell from an old fool's funeral in Ireland; but protests the insanity of Robartes's rhetoric when taken too far in praise of war. On cue, Aherne unlocks a cabinet and fetches "a bit of goatskin" and "an old battered book" (*SMR* 7, *AVB* 37), having heard the coming story, as it seems, many times before. Barbara L. Croft, in *Stylistic Arrangements: A Study of William Butler Yeats* (Lewisburg, PA: Bucknell University Press), accounts for the change in Aherne as a need Yeats saw in the protocol of the writing from 1919 onward:

> Though never identical because of Aherne's preoccupation with Christianity, Aherne and Robartes were originally much more alike. Even as late as "The Phases of the Moon"…both Robartes and Aherne seem to be initiates in the system of *A Vision*, and it is Aherne who begs Robartes to sing the changes of the moon. Aherne has no primary scruples there. It was only as the material was reworked over the years that Yeats saw the need to polarize the two characters, allowing Aherne to assume some of the qualities of the narrator of the early stories: "Rosa Alchemica," "The Tables of the Law," and "The Adoration of the Magi." (102)

In the epistolary conclusion of "Stories," only John Aherne is left to represent the attitudes of his brother and to speculate about literary prospects for the diary Owen kept during Ireland's civil war. Though now ancient himself, John is allowed to wonder: "Should I live, and my brother consent, I may publish some part of it..." (*SMR* 23, *AVB* 53).

PUPILS AND FRIENDS

Moreover, part of the record left to develop in the literary afterlife of Robartes and Aherne has been kept by "Robartes' pupils in London and contains his diagrams and their explanations," as well as "Duddon's long narrative" (ibid.), the latter of which may also exist, excerpted, in "Stories of Michael Robartes and His Friends." The first page of Yeats's manuscript indicates that "Stories" was to consist of a letter "~~from Daniel O'Leary to John Ahern edited by WB Yeats~~" before the piece became, in a few lines, "an extract from a manuscript book" (see page 175, below). Yeats confused himself (throughout part I) about which of two pupils, O'Leary or Duddon, was supposed to have written the extract. On folio 1^{r}, we learn that the log was "compiled" in "May 1924" though the date of John Aherne's letter, on folio 25^{r}, is given as "Feb 1930." These dates are coordinate with *AVA* and *SMR* but problematic for *AVB*, the publication of which Yeats must have understood would actually require more years of revising prior to Macmillan production. So flexibility on dating to preserve a seemingly contemporary setting was achieved by leaving those dates out of the Cuala and Macmillan editions. Also, in 1930, he introduced into Aherne's letter a footnote on the early version of *A Vision*: "I published an inaccurate, obscure, incomplete book, called 'A Vision.' It lies beside me now, corrected, clarified and completed after five years' work and thought" (*SMR* 24; see pages 260–61 and 264–65, below). The note was cut when a setting copy of *SMR* for *AVB* was prepared for Macmillan in December 1934. The rejected epilogue for *AVB*, "Michael Robartes Foretells," would have added another seven years to the arithmetic and extended the record of the pupils, not to mention the projected life-expectancies of Robartes, the Aherne brothers, and Yeats himself.

As Gould says, "the Robartes 'set' kept growing" ("A Lesson for the Circumspect" 251), and the procedure for writing a book of extracts by four Robartes pupils, like the chain-sequence of tales in *SMR*, might take its cue from *Arabian Nights*, as discussed earlier. Had Yeats lived a few years longer, he might have imagined what explanations the students had copied into the record, what extracts, what diagrams. After all, John Aherne remained in touch with some of them. John Duddon, for example, was responsible for supplying him with the photograph of a woodcut from the *Speculum*: "Plato symbolized by the word 'memory' a relation to the timeless, but Duddon is more literal and discovers a resemblance between your face and that of Giraldus" (*SMR* 24, *AVB* 54). To put it another way, a postscript to John Aherne's letter (on 27^v of the holograph) reads: "I enclose some photographs Duddon took of Wood Cuts in Speculum. He says that Gyraldus…is a portrait so like you…that he may [have] been one of your incarnations. I cannot myself see the resemblance." Referring to "photographs" (plural) and "Wood Cuts" acknowledges artwork already published a first time in *AVA* ("The Great Wheel" and "Portrait of Giraldus" by Edmund Dulac), a fact that informs the observation Yeats made to his sister Elizabeth, on 1 February 1932, when he cited improvements in the typesetting of text (with exceptions) and praised the figures for being nicely integrated with the materiality of the text: "The illustrations look exceedingly well[,] better I think than in the Vision. They suit the type & paper" (*CL InteLex* 5580). Otherwise imperfect, the book (including *The Resurrection*) was published in March at the Cuala Press.

Over the years, the scholarly reception of "Stories" has been somewhat checkered. In her early study, Virginia Moore wrote approvingly of the work as appended fiction in *AVB* but disparagingly of the Robartes fables in *AVA*:

> The embarrassing Robartes material has undergone a metamorphosis. It is subsumed under the section "Stories of Michael Robartes and His Friends," but not without new interweavings of fantasy that introduce four new characters, "normal" and not to be fooled: Peter Huddon, John Duddon, Daniel O'Leary, and Denise de L'Isle Adam. Very cannily Yeats is providing ballast for his balloon. In the story, Robartes has still found his *Speculum Angelorum et Hominorum* (now corrected to *Hominum*), but in Vienna, not Cracow; the book is bound not in calf, but in pigskin; and his joining of the Judwali tribes in Arabia is now preceded by an old Arab explaining that his two whorls have the same meaning as Robartes' single wheel—and so forth. Back in London after wisdom garnering, Robartes is teaching Duddon, Huddon, O'Leary, and Denise, when in walk John Bond and Mary Bell with a strange story. (*The Unicorn: William Butler Yeats' Search for Reality* [London: Macmillan, 1954], 362–63)

Completing her paragraph with a summary of plot, Moore thereafter renders a verdict: "Fantasy, all; yet not without certain symbolic meanings and overtones—too many to explore here—consonant with Yeats' chief purpose" (364). *A Vision* revised was a better book, accordingly, and Moore extended as metaphors Robartes's elastic Cosmic egg and Leda's "lost egg":

> The body-proper of the book, as compared to the 1925 edition, shows an enormously increased clarity and cogency. Not only have Yeats' philosophical studies alerted and disciplined his mind. The intervening twelve years have meant doctrinal integration. Whereas formerly he walked gingerly among eggshell ideas, now he moves boldly and without breakage. (364)

In less than ten years, Helen Vendler opened Chapter 1 of her influential book *Yeats's VISION and the Later Plays* (Oxford: Oxford University Press, 1963), with some carefully chosen, dismissive *bons mots*:

> The tales which preface *A Vision*—the "Stories of Michael Robartes and His Friends"—now have a faded antiquarian savor in their remoteness, their rather perverse and precious humor, and their artificial tone. They serve as a fictional frame for the system, linking it to that elusive compilation of Giraldus, the *Speculum Angelorum et Hominum*, which it so mysteriously resembles. Yeats must have enjoyed the elaborateness of his stage scenery, and the tales hint at the spirit in which the book is to be taken. (7)

Critical approval, here, obviously involves taste in addition to an ordinary appraisal of a work of fiction based on the exigencies of character, story, and style. But something else is afoot in more extreme forms of censure to be found when sensibility reviles the use of fiction in the service of philosophy. That line was crossed in "Stories of Michael Robartes," according to Richard Finneran in his paper *The Prose Fiction of W. B. Yeats: The Search for "Those Simple Forms"* (Dublin: Dolmen Press, 1973), because the "material strikes me as so limited in purpose and so intimately connected with the philosophical system as to be distinct from the prose fiction proper" (37). Hence there is nothing more to say about it, denying, as well, Yeats's return to prose fiction in the "Introduction by Owen Aherne" to *A Vision* (1925). Another extreme example of censure by reason of association may be found in the absolute rejection of "Stories" from the body of work selected by G. J. Watson to represent Yeats's *Short Fiction*, published in London by the Penguin Group in 1995. Watson suggests that Yeats's title is misguided, for it is "only one 'story' in the material that forms the prolegomena for *A Vision*"; and he asserts that it "is hardly a story from any point of view but, rather, a crudely obvious vehicle in which Yeats takes the opportunity to expound his philosophical ideas" (x). In light of the principle of "phantasmagoria" that Yeats generalized to all of his writings, especially as the principle applies to the Robartes tales, it is hard to swallow Watson's opinion that "Stories," in particular, lacks "the very thinnest of fictional veneers" (x).

Unlike Watson, William H. O'Donnell is less categorical and more conflicted, including a whole, last chapter to "Stories of Michael Robartes" in his survey of fiction, *A Guide to the Prose Fiction of W. B. Yeats* (Ann Arbor: UMI Research Press, 1983), but being of two minds about the story in its own right and taken as the capstone of the three magical tales of 1896 and 1897, especially "Rosa Alchemica." His views are informed by a faulty assumption that "Stories" was primarily intended to join the "Introduction to the Great Wheel" (1928) so-called in *A Packet for Ezra Pound* of 1929. Thus "[t]he primary function of 'Stories of Michael Robartes,' together with the farcical details in the 'Introduction to the Great Wheel' [or "Introduction to 'A Vision'" in *AVB*] is to offset the high seriousness of the main text" (145). I partly agree with this statement but must save a small yet important point of textual-genetic hair-splitting for the end of the introduction at hand, after completing this review of criticism. Perhaps a matter of taste or regard for "high seriousness" over "humorous" or "farcical" details contributed to O'Donnell's impression that "comedy is more important than doctrines" in "Stories," motivating his frown upon the use of "comedy to remind" people that Yeats was "aware of the occult world's frequent excesses" and upon his "distancing with comedy" in both *AVA* and *AVB*, amounting to much of the Robartes "set" (notable exceptions being notes and poems, unpublished writings, and the *Secret Rose* triptych *sans* "The Adoration of the Magi," the latter deemed "little more than a simple fable illustrating occult doctrine" [128]). For O'Donnell, the negatives in *SMR* are preponderate: "comic ridicule" undermines "serious doctrine" "nearly everywhere"; Robartes and Aherne are "ridiculous disciples" yet fantasy enhances "the Robartes myth behind which Yeats hides" defensively against unsympathetic readers; the "love-war-art schema fails clumsily"; the exemplary qualities of old Mr. Bell are taken to "hilarious extremes"; and Yeats's abandoned affection for *Axël*'s "romantic asceticism" is regretted when he pairs off silly Denise de Lisle Adam with respectable Mary Bell, artist's promiscuous model and adulterous Helen-like bearer of Leda's egg, respectively. Still, the story is better than the "humorless and unsuccessful adaption" that Yeats composed and abandoned as an epilogue for *AVB*, "Michael Robartes Foretells." Given O'Donnell's view of the "brazen hilarity" of "Stories of Michael Robartes," "very little merit" is a disappointing final assessment of it when a pile of adjectives suggests otherwise: "hilarious," "fantastic," "playful," "elaborately comic," "bizarrely comic," "intentionally bizarre," and "amused delight." Despite biographical inferences about Maud Gonne and her fondness for caged song-birds, the indigenous nature of the Irish cuckoo, and the Yeatses' interest in the nest-building of pet canaries, O'Donnell wisely registers a cautionary note about the danger of pushing too hard for parallels between the doctrines of *A Vision* and the tales of Robartes's pupils and friends: "we must remain cautious of overemphasizing doctrinal allusions in these ludicrous tales" (146). After all, we must recognize that Yeats was not writing autobiography. As he told Pound in 1918, "I intend these tales & dialogues to be simply works of art. I will use certain philosophical ideas to give subjective hardness as Dante used Aquinas.... Subjective hardness is what we [are] all trying to get in different ways" (*CL InteLex* 3447).

So it is interesting that in Hazard Adams's *The Book of Yeats's Vision: Romantic Modernism and Antithetical Tradition* (Ann Arbor: University of Michigan Press, 1995) almost everything is a matter of art; even the apparent seriousness of the philosophy, or "system," is a fiction to which "Stories" became attached in 1937, though Adams never fully considers the implication of delayed marriage in the parallel making of these materials. His important early work *Blake and Yeats: The Contrary Vision* (1955, 1968) provided necessary background but not the thesis of the later study, which may be seen in the context of more recent theory-driven literary studies. Nor were speculations so much a part of the early inquiry. The later book complements, as a sequel, *The Book of Yeats's Poems* (1990), and follows insights developed in *Philosophy of the Literary Symbolic* (1983). R. P. Blackmur and Northrop Frye are his acknowledged exemplars in *The Book of Yeats's Vision*, with its short chapter on "Stories" in the final state of *A Vision*, where Yeats "is himself absorbed into the fiction that he has already said he has made" (40):

> "Stories" sits in *A Vision* as an example of a major characteristic of antitheticality. That is the employment of a "both-and" in opposition to an "either-or" logic. In an antithetical work an author can be a character in his own fiction, in this particular case, doubly fictive. (41)

According to this conception, Aherne is "typically primary in attitude" whereas Robartes is antithetical, "not particularly concerned about…inaccuracies, even the report of his death" (41 and 42). As parodies of primary and antithetical types, Aherne and Robartes are central to a "narrative [that] is full of parody and verges on farce" (44), and that parody, according to Adams, "is mainly of Yeats's own most serious ideas and even of himself" (44). Not surprisingly, the most informative section of the chapter deals with Robartes's anti-Kantian application of Kant's first and third antinomies of pure reason, the first applied, as we have seen, in the professed tension between *love* and *desire*, and the second involving *the soul's freedom* versus *the laws of nature*, "a whirling and a bitterness"; in relation to these, Aherne presents us with the historical principle as "progressive toward synthesis" whereas Robartes's view is "spiral" and represents "the antithetical historical impulse" (55–57). On the other hand, in connection with the system of *A Vision*, parodies involving Robartes's pupils and friends sometimes strain credibility. For instance, to draw a parallel between the quaternary of pupils and the four Faculties presented in *A Vision*, a case is not convincingly made for the correlation Duddon (Will), O'Leary (Creative Mind), Denise (Mask), Huddon (Body of Fate). Adams presents the parody as such (among others) after stating that he is only "tempted" to do so and conceding that it bears resemblance by way of "vague comic correspondence," that it is not a "systematic" one, and that "one should not expect system in something that is clearly a parody of it" (46). Elderly Mr. Bell is seen as Yeatsian self-parody, missing O'Donnell's good sense not to push too hard for parallels in *A Vision*, but also to reckon that old Bell is one of Yeats's favorite comic butts, and therefore "a caricature of the Irish country gentry" (141). But for Adams, "Stories" parodies the "technical aspects" of *A Vision*, its antithesis, and so "opposes any possible tendency on our part to take [the book of Yeats's vision] too solemnly and literally" (57).

If there is a tendency in our scholarship to stretch a bit too far to find in Yeats's lesser characters confirmation of the principles of the system, it seems also true that actual persons figuring in Yeats's life-story often become, like Yeats himself, part of the game of speculation. In Croft, for example, more than we need to know is offered on Maud Gonne and Olivia Shakespear for Mary Bell as a "Madonna figure for the new age" (122), around whom is built a shaky trinity of old Bell (a Joseph figure who serves God) as the ostensible father of her son, a bastard Christ, and John Bond, "the parallel to the Holy Ghost who, like a cuckoo, leaves his offspring to hatch" in the old man's nest (123). Mr. Bell is also prefigured in Sir William Gregory, just as Olivia Shakespear, Lady Gregory, and Mrs. Yeats "merge" in Mary and as John Bond, John Duddon, Mr. Bell, and Daniel O'Leary coalesce into a portrait of Yeats, "each representing a certain period in his life" (124). On firmer ground, because Yeats puts sign-posts in the narrative, Huddon = War, Duddon = Art, Denise = Love, and "theater-reforming" O'Leary seems most to represent Yeats's viewpoint as a dramatist (118–19). The last connections are also made by Adams.

For reading "Stories" through the prism of *A Vision B*, the most useful, recent study is probably Elizabeth Müller's "The Mask of Derision in Yeats's Prologue to *A Vision* (1937)," published in 2013 in *Yeats Annual* 19 and built on the work of Adams, Steven Helmling, and Eugene Korkowski, which she handily summarizes as follows:

> For Adams, the self-derisiveness in the Prologue indicates that the system itself is not to be taken seriously: it is a no-system and the book must be treated as a piece of antithetical uncertainty, a fine construction and a fictional challenge which Yeats wrote in a fit of light-hearted *sprezzatura*. For Helmling, the Prologue bears witness to Yeats's role as *eirôn*, "the wise man who enlightens others by playing the fool with them": eventually, self-derisiveness backfires and the reader feels compelled to endorse the *eirôn*'s position, in this case, Yeats's "indictment of materialist, bourgeois, 'modern culture.'" These various readings, thought-provoking as they might be, seem incomplete, for more is at stake here than mere criticism....Korkowski seems nearer the mark when he asserts that the sheer medley of fact and fiction, the many loopholes and disavowals in both real and fictitious accounts are merely part of the technique of the *satura* which consists in making "bitter and difficult learning" palatable. As Korkowski makes clear, the improbable medley aims at more than parody and satire.... (128)

The "Prologue," as Müller defines it, consists of a "true account" and a "fictional account." The true one consists of the three parts of *A Packet for Ezra Pound*: "Rapallo" (omitting part VI from the 1929 edition, including Yeats's "Meditations upon Death," I and II); "Introduction to 'A Vision'" (formerly known as "Introduction to the Great Wheel"); and "To Ezra Pound" (a dedication veiled as a letter to dispatch "the introduction of a book which will, when finished, proclaim a new divinity" [*AVB* 27]). Yeats's fictional account is his "Stories of Michael

Robartes and His Friends," also in its 1937 state. What interests us here is that account, wherein Müller's "main development" is about "the kind of coherence I detect under the guise of nonsense" (128). The first, or "true," account introduces biography and history as fair game to be treated in the Prologue's second part "under the guise of nonsense," since "biography seems inextricably bound up with history" (132). Hence the structural key to "Stories" is that principle, somewhat misaligned with the numbered sections within *AVB* (and the mis-numbered sections of *SMR*), but punctuated by two significant intrusions by Robartes into the sequence of stories told by his pupils and friends, followed by the coda of John Aherne's letter to Yeats (the obverse of Yeats's letter to Pound in the true account). The first stories, about art and told by O'Leary and Duddon, "culminate in Robartes's recounting his personal story of unrequited love"; and these are followed by love stories, told by Denise and Bond, which in turn impel Robartes "to announce the new historical dispensation" (132).

It might be noted here, however, that in the biography and history of the text both Denise's scene-stealing side-show performance and Robartes's ironic response—to say that her story "will be a full and admirable introduction" for the one John Bond has to tell (*AVB* 42)—were entirely absent in *SMR* and not introduced until almost the last minute into the 1937 page proofs. His deadpan comment on her shocking revelation that a sexual *ménage* maintains her chemistry with and hold on to the male rivals Huddon and Duddon also acknowledges Robartes's recognition that she has just demeaned the painful account he has made of himself, the ballet dancer, and "the ignorant girl of the people" with whom he "cohabited" when he found remnants of the *Speculum* only because the girl had thrown him out of bed and had not yet set fire to the rest of the book (*SMR* 7–8, *AVB* 38 and 40; see pages 176–80 and 204–21, below). After Denise had begged Robartes to tell his story, she is prevented from reciprocating in the 1931 version because of the entrance of John Bond and Mary Bell, ushered in by Aherne. As a self-standing work of art, "Stories" did not then have to deal with this episode because it did not exist, until circumstances quite apart from *A Vision* inspired Yeats to write it into Duddon's extract, in part III. (See pages 291–94 and 340–59, below.)

Yet aside from that complication—a disruptive one with regard to a symmetrical "coherence" to be made of the text because the love-story of guests John Bond and Mary Bell had really no counterpart in 1931—Müller seems on the right track. Both true and fictional accounts in the 1937 Prologue involve "carefully interw[oven] threads which run...in a complex criss-cross pattern" (133); and "[w]hat seems at first a reverberating medley of masks and costumes in the Prologue finally resolves itself into distinct antinomies, as the trios turn into twos" (132). In this, the editor takes satisfaction from seeing confirmed certain inferences he has made in the textual-genetic study of Yeats's poetry in relation to literary history. To fit himself into a long critical tradition, Yeats found it useful, for example, to juxtapose Shakespeare and Jonson, or Jonson and Donne:

> A few of his pairings, or *dyads*—any two recurrently linked sources of content and/or form in an adaptive complex—played conspicuous roles in the formation of his poetic theory and in his gradual mastery of the poetic craft. Perhaps conveniently located in the same zone of the memory (and for good reasons), such pairings developed by association in the manuscripts and eventually surfaced in the published work, often in modified form. (Wayne K. Chapman, *Yeats and English Renaissance Literature* [London: Macmillan Press, 1991], 69)

Just so, Müller thinks that Yeats, like Plato in the *Theaetetus*, develops his philosophy from opposites in the Prologue "under the aegis of the Dyad" (142). For my part, the Primary-Antithetical *dyad* reflects the habit of mind exercised in both editions of *A Vision*, particularly in "The Twenty-Eight Embodiments" (or "… Incarnations"), and is a very useful concept to account for real people and characters in Yeats's work. Take, for example, the symbolic doubles Sphinx and Buddha in "The Double Vision of Michael Robartes," as well as Huddon and Duddon in "Stories," juxtaposed cones that wax and wane on a pivoting "dancer"; or the female doubles of ballet dancer and "girl of the people" in "Stories," as well as Iseult Gonne and Mrs. Yeats in "Owen Aherne and his Dancers," juxtaposed cones pivoting on Robartes and Aherne (or Yeats, initially, in the latter case). To this habit of the mind, we owe the duo Robartes and Aherne, themselves, as well as the unnamed narrator of the *Secret Rose* triptych—and before that the title character of the short novel *John Sherman* (1891) and his *alter ego* the Reverend William Howard, with the pseudonymous author "Ganconagh" playing along in "Ganconagh's Apology" until Yeats signed himself in the preface that accompanied the novel in the seventh volume of the 1908 *Collected Works*, joined with the triptych narratives and the fairy story "Dhoya."

From the view of a text and its making, it makes no sense to focus too narrowly, reductively, or dependently on *A Vision* to appreciate a work that has had an independent life, at least one conceived at first to share covers with another text for part of its life. After all, "Stories of Michael Robartes and His Friends" was written to accompany *The Resurrection* when Yeats rewrote the play and incorporated fresh material into a relatively small body of older fiction to make a new story to complement. Extraordinarily, the unhatched egg of Leda transferred from the old edition of the play to become a new device to enhance the story. An effort to address this blind spot has been made in this study (see pages 166–74, below), but a sustained colloquy on the two works is certainly welcome. Conversely, an additional study or two might consider the reason why Yeats did not let *A Vision* stand alone with the "Introduction" he had written in the form of *A Packet for*

Ezra Pound (1929). We know that, on 14 December 1930, he sent to his agent, Hansard Watt, a proposal to include with the revised treatise several works in prose to make "a seventh volume" for Macmillan's "ordinary collected edition" of his work (*CL InteLex* 5419). For this, he wanted a book "about the same size as 'Essays'" to conclude with *A Vision* but preceded by "1. The two little volumes of 'Diaries' published at Cuala [*Estrangement*, 1926; and *The Death of Synge*, 1928]. / 2. A collection of philosophic stories about to be published at Cuala [i.e., *SMR*]. / [and thereafter] 3. 'A Packet for Ezra Pound' published at Cuala two years ago." The fourth tier of the proposed volume, *A Vision*, was no longer "the crude book published by Laurie," and "[t]he philosophic stories, which were written this summer and are amongst the best things I have written, expound its fundamental ideas." *A Packet for Ezra Pound* was to serve as the "Introduction" to *A Vision*, and the two sections from the "Diaries" that Yeats believed "probably my best critical writings" were sufficiently related to the treatise "not to seem out of harmony." He was most keen on getting such a volume into the proposed Edition de Luxe and offered suggestions on a way forward in spite of complications. But one point was emphatic. He said: "***I don't want to publish 'A Vision' by itself for various reasons***" (bold italics added). Shall we ever know what these "various reasons" were? Or know why the "Diaries" selections were excluded from the plan, as good as they were? Or how those selections might have influenced our reading of *A Vision* and *vice versa*? Moreover, how did "Stories" happen to change positions with the "Introduction" so that outside matter might be regarded as falling within the circumference of *A Vision* and, indeed, to be interpreted as a preliminary element or partial Prologue? On this last point, I concur with George Mills Harper, dean of Yeats studies on the subject of *A Vision*, when he says: "outside of Yeats's carefully written introduction [provided in *A Packet*, revised] I consider much of the remaining cover material as extraneous" (*YAACTS* 6: 293; see page 166, below). So far, the critical implications of this judgment remain largely unexplored in the scholarship, which would include, recently, Margaret Mills Harper's "'The clock has run down and must be wound up again': *A Vision* in Time," in *Yeats and Afterwords*, ed. Marjorie Elizabeth Howes and Joseph Valente (Notre Dame, IN: University of Notre Dame Press, 2014), 189–212.

W. B. Yeats's Robartes-Aherne Writings is a tool that should enable scholars to pursue answers to these questions. I am not wise enough to offer an opinion on whether *A Vision* is true or not. Partisans on both sides of the question, believers and non-believers alike, may puzzle out an answer for themselves as the topic is beyond the scope of this book. The role of *fiction* in relation to the philosophy of *A Vision*, I think it is fair to say, resembles the apposition of cake and bread, to expropriate an analogy that I quote properly in the last chapter. I tend to agree with Yeats and Russell that the brisk new style one witnesses in the evolution of the Robartes pieces, transacted over a forty-year period, is laudable, perfectly suited to the nature of the writing, which is the stuff of fables and tall tales. I like to think that, whatever fate awaits Robartes (antithetical-but-not-final man), Aherne, and their pupils and friends, our lot is to imagine and to make sense of their unruly lives (endowed by Yeats as characters of fiction) as we understand the laws of modern literature. These characters are part of Yeats's creative history, and thus part of an extraordinary story in its own right. Margaret Harper tells me that Yeats desired to *live the system* in the same way these characters do, outlandishly, in the "double-coned truth" he lived out. I believe she's right. Paradoxically, they all belong to the truth that dies into art. In other words, I must be satisfied merely to rest my agnostic case without verdict on the "truth" of the system itself, because *that* question is not relevant, *ipso facto*, to this book's purpose to reconstruct the genesis of the Robartes-Aherne writings by inducing the published and unpublished materials to tell their own story. I suppose wisdom and skepticism in the world of fable may not be altogether opposed to one another. On the one hand, objectivity is hard. On the other, as Yeats explained to Pound about modern art and literature: "Subjective hardness is what we [are] all trying to get in different ways.…All the rest is haycocks in the flood."

Part One: 1896–1897 (1908)

The Secret Rose Triptych—

Early Tales of Michael Robartes and Owen Aherne

(from *The Collected Works*, 1908)

"Rosa Alchemica" (1896), "The Tables of the Law" (1896), and "The Adoration of the Magi" (1897): A Note on the Texts

Two of these stories, "Rosa Alchemica" and "The Tables of the Law," first appeared in *The Savoy* (London), issues of April and November 1896, respectively. The third story, "The Adoration of the Magi," joined the second in a private printing entitled *The Tables of the Law. | The Adoration of the Magi* (London, 1897; cited as "1897T; *Wade* 24), thereafter reprinted together in *The Tables of the Law and The Adoration of the Magi* (London: Elkin Mathews, 1904 and 1905; *Wade* 25) and in *The Tables of the Law; & The Adoration of the Magi* (Stratford-upon-Avon: Shakespeare Head Press, 1914; *Wade* 26). "Rosa Alchemica" appeared without their company in *The Secret Rose* (London: Lawrence & Bullen, 1897; *Wade* 21), in the American (Dodd, Mead) edition of 1897 (*Wade* 22), in the Dublin (Maunsel) edition of 1905 (*Wade* 23), and in *Stories of Red Hanrahan: The Secret Rose: Rosa Alchemica* (London and Stratford-upon-Avon: A. H. Bullen, 1913; *Wade* 104), including its American complement (New York: Macmillan, 1914; *Wade* 105). The three stories first appeared together in *The Collected Works in Verse and Prose*, volume 7 (Stratford-upon-Avon: Shakespeare Head Press, 1908; *Wade* 81), which provides the base text for the readings that follow.

The chief aim here is to provide reading texts of the stories as they appeared in that momentous edition, with simple glosses to exceptional passages from the earliest and latest states of their writing and rewriting. To that end, a list of "Substantial Variants" from earlier printings is presented after each text is completed (with the variant source designated accordingly: either "***The Savoy***" or "**1897T**," for the first printing). Likewise, substantial revisions made from the 1908 base text are noted for later variants (designated "**1925, 1932**" in the corresponding list). These later amendments occurred when the stories were first set off as a group, dedicated in the year of *A Vision* "to | A. E." (George Russell, one of the live models for Michael Robartes), and reprinted in the English and American Macmillan editions of *Early Poems and Stories* (1925; *Wade* 147 and 148), copy text for the corrected page proofs of 1931–1932 (NLI 30,030), selected by editors Warwick Gould, Phillip L. Marcus, and Michael Sidnell to serve as base text in *The Secret Rose Stories by W. B. Yeats: A Variorum Edition*, 2nd ed., revised & enlarged (London: Macmillan, 1992). For our purposes, "Substantial" shall be defined as involving one or more full lines of text, usually more. The intricacies of punctuation, syntax, minor usage, spelling, typography, and the like are left to the *Variorum Edition*, to which the reader is nevertheless encouraged to refer such stylistic matters. Also recommended is the magnificent tome: W. B. Yeats, *Mythologies*, ed. Warwick Gould and Deirdre Toomey (London: Palgrave Macmillan, 2005; *M2005*), especially its encyclopedic commentary, "Explanatory and Textual Notes," and several appendices.

ROSA ALCHEMICA

O blessed and happy he, who knowing the mysteries of the gods, sanctifies his life, and purifies his soul, celebrating orgies in the mountains with holy purifications.—*Euripides*

I

It is now more than ten years since I met, for the last time, Michael Robartes, and for the first time and the last time his friends and fellow students; and witnessed his and their tragic end, and endured those strange experiences, which have changed me so that my writings have grown less popular and less intelligible, and driven me almost to the verge of taking the habit of St. Dominic. I had just published *Rosa Alchemica*, a little work on the Alchemists, somewhat in the manner of Sir Thomas Browne, and had received many letters from believers in the arcane sciences, upbraiding what they called my timidity, for they could not believe so evident sympathy but the sympathy of the artist, which is half pity, for everything which has moved men's hearts in any age. I had discovered, early in my researches, that their doctrine was no merely chemical phantasy, but a philosophy they applied to the world, to the elements and to man himself; and that they sought to fashion gold out of common metals merely as part of an universal transmutation of all things into some divine and imperishable substance; and this enabled me to make my little book a fanciful reverie over the transmutation of life into art, and a cry of measureless desire for a world made wholly of essences.

I was sitting dreaming of what I had written, in my house in one of the old parts of Dublin; a house my ancestors had made almost famous through their part in the politics of the city and their friendships with the famous men of their generations; and was feeling unwonted happiness at having at last accomplished a long-cherished design, and made my rooms an expression of this favourite doctrine. The portraits, of more historical than artistic interest, had gone; and tapestry, full of the blue and bronze of peacocks, fell over the doors, and shut out all history and activity untouched with beauty and peace; and now when I looked at my Crevelli and pondered on the rose in the hand of the virgin, wherein the form was so delicate and precise that it seemed more like a thought than a flower, or at the grey dawn and rapturous faces of my Francesca, I knew all a Christian's ecstasy without his slavery to rule and custom; when I pondered over the antique bronze gods and goddesses, which I had mortgaged my house to buy, I had all a pagan's delight in various beauty and without his terror at sleepless destiny and his labour with many sacrifices; and I had only to go to my bookshelf, where every book was bound in leather, stamped with intricate ornament, and of a carefully chosen colour: Shakespeare in the orange of the glory of the world, Dante in the dull red of his anger, Milton in the blue grey of his formal calm; and I could experience what I would of human passions without their bitterness and without satiety. I had gathered about me all gods because I believed in none, and experienced every pleasure because I gave myself to none, but held myself apart, individual, indissoluble, a mirror of polished steel: I looked in the triumph of this imagination at the birds of Hera, glowing in the firelight as though they were wrought of jewels; and to my mind, for which symbolism was a necessity, they seemed the doorkeepers of my world, shutting out all that was not of as affluent a beauty as their own; and for a moment I thought as I had thought in so many other moments, that it was possible to rob life of every bitterness except the bitterness of death; and then a thought which had followed this thought, time after time, filled me with a passionate sorrow. All those forms: that Madonna with her brooding purity, those rapturous faces singing in the morning light, those bronze divinities with their passionless dignity, those wild shapes rushing from despair to despair, belonged to a divine world wherein I had no part; and every experience, however profound, every perception, however exquisite, would bring me the bitter dream of a limitless energy I could never know, and even in my most perfect moment I would be two selves, the one watching with heavy eyes the other's moment of content. I had heaped about me the gold born in the crucibles of others; but the supreme dream of the alchemist, the transmutation of the weary heart into a weariless spirit, was as far from me as, I doubted not, it had been from him also. I turned to my last purchase, a set of alchemical apparatus which, the dealer in the Rue le Peletier had assured me, once belonged to Raymond Lully, and as I joined the *alembic* to the *athanor* and laid the *lavacrum maris* at their side, I understood the alchemical doctrine, that all beings, divided from the great deep where spirits wander, one and yet a multitude, are weary; and sympathized, in the pride of my connoisseurship, with the consuming thirst for destruction which made the alchemist veil under his symbols of lions and dragons, of eagles and ravens, of dew and nitre, a search for an essence which would dissolve all mortal things. I repeated to myself the ninth key of Basilius Valentinus, in which he compares the fire of the last day to the fire of the alchemist, and the world to the alchemist's furnace, and would have us know that all must be dissolved before the divine substance, material gold or immaterial ecstasy, awake. I had dissolved indeed the mortal world and lived amid immortal essences, but had obtained no miraculous ecstasy. As I thought of these things, I drew aside the curtains and looked out into the darkness, and it seemed to my troubled fancy that all those little points of light filling the sky were the furnaces of innumerable divine alchemists, who labour continually, turning lead into gold, weariness into ecstasy, bodies into souls, the darkness into God; and at their perfect labour my mortality grew heavy, and I cried out, as so many dreamers and men of letters in our age have cried, for the birth of that elaborate spiritual beauty which could alone uplift souls weighted with so many dreams.

II

My reverie was broken by a loud knocking at the door, and I wondered the more at this because I had no visitors, and had bid my servants do all things silently, lest they broke the dream of my inner life. Feeling a little curious, I resolved to go to the door myself, and, taking one of the silver candlesticks from the mantelpiece, began to descend the stairs. The servants appeared to be out, for though the sound poured through every corner and crevice of the house there was no stir in the lower rooms. I remembered that because my needs were so few, my part in life so little, they had begun to come and go as they would, often leaving me alone for hours. The emptiness and silence of a world from which I had driven everything but dreams suddenly overwhelmed me, and I shuddered as I drew the bolt. I found before me Michael Robartes, whom I had not seen for years, and whose wild red hair, fierce eyes, sensitive, tremulous lips and rough clothes made him look now, just as they used to do fifteen years before, something between a debauchee, a saint, and a peasant. He had recently come to Ireland, he said, and wished to see me on a matter of importance; indeed, the only matter of importance for him and for me. His voice brought up before me our student years in Paris, and remembering the magnetic power he had once possessed over me, a little fear mingled with much annoyance at this irrelevant intrusion, as I led the way up the wide staircase, where Swift had passed joking and railing, and Curran telling stories and quoting Greek, in simpler days, before men's minds, subtilized and complicated by the romantic movement in art and literature, began to tremble on the verge of some unimagined revelation. I felt that my hand shook, and saw that the light of the candle wavered and quivered more than it need have upon the Mænads on the old French panels, making them look like the first beings slowly shaping in the formless and void darkness. When the door had closed, and the peacock curtain, glimmering like many-coloured flame, fell between us and the world, I felt, in a way I could not understand, that some singular and unexpected thing was about to happen. I went over to the mantlepiece, and finding that a little chainless bronze censer, set, upon the outside, with pieces of painted china by Orazio Fontana, which I had filled with antique amulets, had fallen upon its side and poured out its contents, I began to gather the amulets into the bowl, partly to collect my thoughts and partly with that habitual reverence which seemed to me the due of things so long connected with secret hopes and fears. 'I see,' said Michael Robartes, 'that you are still fond of incense, and I can show you an incense more precious than any you have ever seen,' and as he spoke he took the censer out of my hand and put the amulets in a little heap between the *athanor* and the *alembic*. I sat down, and he sat down at the side of the fire, and sat there for awhile looking into the fire, and holding the censer in his hand. 'I have come to ask you something,' he said, 'and the incense will fill the room, and our thoughts, with its sweet odour while we are talking. I got it from an old man in Syria, who said it was made from flowers, of one kind with the flowers that laid their heavy purple petals upon the hands and upon the hair and upon the feet of Christ in the Garden of Gethsemane, and folded Him in their heavy breath, until He cried against the cross and his destiny.' He shook some dust into the censer out of a small silk bag, and set the censer upon the floor and lit the dust which sent up a blue stream of smoke, that spread out over the ceiling, and flowed downwards again until it was like Milton's banyan tree. It filled me, as incense often does, with a faint sleepiness, so that I started when he said, 'I have come to ask you that question which I asked you in Paris, and which you left Paris rather than answer.'

He had turned his eyes towards me, and I saw them glitter in the fire-light, and through the incense, as I replied: 'You mean, will I become an initiate of your Order of the Alchemical Rose? I would not consent in Paris, when I was full of unsatisfied desire, and now that I have at last fashioned my life according to my desire, am I likely to consent?'

'You have changed greatly since then,' he answered. 'I have read your books, and now I see you among all these images, and I understand you better than you do yourself, for I have been with many and many dreamers at the same cross-ways. You have shut away the world and gathered gods about you, and if you do not throw yourself at their feet, you will be always full of lassitude, and of wavering purpose, for a man must forget he is miserable in the bustle and noise of the multitude in this world and in time; or seek a mystical union with the multitude who govern this world and time.' And then he murmured something I could not hear, and as though to someone I could not see.

For a moment the room appeared to darken, as it used to do when he was about to perform some singular experiment, and in the darkness the peacocks upon the doors seemed to glow with a more intense colour. I cast off the illusion, which was, I believe, merely caused by memory, and by the twilight of incense, for I would not acknowledge that he could overcome my now mature intellect; and I said: 'Even if I grant that I need a spiritual belief and some form of worship, why should I go to Eleusis and not to Calvary?' He leaned forward and began speaking with a slightly rhythmical intonation, and as he spoke I had to struggle again with the shadow, as of some older night than the night of the sun, which began to dim the light of the candles and to blot out the little gleams upon the corner of picture-frames and on the bronze divinities, and to turn the blue of the incense to a heavy purple; while it left the peacocks to glimmer and glow as though each separate colour were a living spirit. I had fallen into a profound dream-like reverie in which I heard him speaking as at a distance. 'And yet there is no one who communes with only one god,' he was saying, 'and the more a man lives in imagination and in a refined understanding, the more gods does he meet with and talk with, and the more does he come under the power of Roland, who sounded in the Valley of Roncesvalles the last trumpet of the body's will and pleasure; and of Hamlet, who saw them perishing away, and sighed; and of Faust, who looked for them up and down the world and could not find them; and under the power of all those countless divinities who have taken upon themselves spiritual bodies in the minds of the modern poets and romance writers, and under the power of the old divinities, who since the Renaissance have won everything of their ancient worship except the sacrifice of birds and fishes, the fragrance of garlands and the smoke of incense. The many think humanity made these divinities, and that it can unmake them again; but we who have seen them pass in rattling harness, and in soft robes, and heard them speak with articulate voices while we lay in deathlike trance, know that they are always making and unmaking humanity, which is indeed but the trembling of their lips.'

He had stood up and begun to walk to and fro, and had become in my waking dream a shuttle weaving an immense purple web whose folds had begun to fill the room. The room seemed to have become inexplicably silent, as though all but the web and the weaving were at an end in the world. 'They have come to us; they have come to us,' the voice began again; 'all that have ever been in your reverie, all that you have met with in books. There is Lear, his head still wet with the thunder-storm, and he laughs because you thought yourself an existence who are but a shadow, and him a shadow who is an eternal god; and there is Beatrice, with her lips half parted in a smile, as though all the stars were about to pass away in a sigh of love; and there is the mother of the God of humility who cast so great a spell over men that they have tried to unpeople their hearts that he might reign alone, but she holds in her hand the rose whose every petal is a god; and there, O swiftly she comes! is Aphrodite under a twilight falling from the wings of numberless sparrows, and about her feet are the grey and white doves.' In the midst of my dream I saw him hold out his left arm and pass his right hand over it as though he stroked the wings of doves. I made a violent effort which seemed almost to tear me in two, and said with forced determination: 'You would sweep me away into an indefinite world which fills me with terror; and yet a man is a great man just in so far as he can make his mind reflect everything with indifferent precision like a mirror.' I seemed to be perfectly master of myself, and went on, but more rapidly: 'I command you to leave me at once, for your ideas and phantasies are but the illusions that creep like maggots into civilizations when they begin to decline, and into minds when they begin to decay.' I had grown suddenly angry, and seizing the *alembic* from the table, was about to rise and strike him with it, when the peacocks on the door behind him appeared to grow immense; and the *alembic* fell from my fingers and I was drowned in a tide of green and blue and bronze feathers, and as I struggled hopelessly I heard a distant voice saying: 'Our master Avicenna has written that all life proceeds out of corruption.' The glittering feathers had now covered me completely, and I knew that I had struggled for hundreds of years, and was conquered at last. I was sinking into the depth when the green and blue and bronze that seemed to fill the world became a sea of flame and swept me away, and as I was swirled along I heard a voice over my head cry, 'The mirror is broken in two pieces,' and another voice answer, 'The mirror is broken in four pieces,' and a more distant voice cry with an exultant cry, 'The mirror is broken into numberless pieces'; and then a multitude of pale hands were reaching towards me, and strange gentle faces bending above me, and half wailing and half caressing voices uttering words that were forgotten the moment they were spoken. I was being lifted out of the tide of flame, and felt my memories, my hopes, my thoughts, my will, everything I held to be myself, melting away; then I seemed to rise through numberless companies of beings who were, I understood, in some way more certain than thought, each wrapped in his eternal moment, in the perfect lifting of an arm, in a little circlet of rhythmical words, in dreaming with dim eyes and half-closed eyelids. And then I passed beyond these forms, which were so beautiful they had almost ceased to be, and, having endured strange moods, melancholy, as it seemed, with the weight of many worlds, I passed into that Death which is Beauty herself, and into that Loneliness which all the multitudes desire without ceasing. All things that had ever lived seemed to come and dwell in my heart, and I in theirs; and I had never again known mortality or tears, had I not suddenly fallen from the certainty of vision into the uncertainty of dream, and become a drop of molten gold falling with immense rapidity, through a night elaborate with stars, and all about me a melancholy exultant wailing. I fell and fell and fell, and then the wailing was but the wailing of the wind in the chimney, and I awoke to find myself leaning upon the table and supporting my head with my hands. I saw the *alembic* swaying from side to side in the distant corner it had rolled to, and Michael Robartes watching me and waiting. 'I will go wherever you will,' I said, 'and do whatever you bid me, for I have been with eternal things.' 'I knew,' he replied, 'you must need answer as you have answered, when I heard the storm begin. You must come to a great distance, for we were commanded to build our temple between the pure multitude by the waves and the impure multitude of men.'

III

I did not speak as we drove through the deserted streets, for my mind was curiously empty of familiar thoughts and experiences; it seemed to have been plucked out of the definite world and cast naked upon a shoreless sea. There were moments when the vision appeared on the point of returning, and I would half-remember, with an ecstasy of joy or sorrow, crimes and heroisms, fortunes and misfortunes; or begin to contemplate, with a sudden leaping heart, hopes and terrors, desires and ambitions, alien to my orderly and careful life; and then I would awake shuddering at the thought that some great imponderable being had swept through my mind. It was indeed days before this feeling passed perfectly away, and even now, when I have sought refuge in the only definite faith, I feel a great tolerance for those people with incoherent personalities, who gather in the chapels and meeting-places of certain obscure sects, because I also have felt fixed habits and principles dissolving before a power, which was *hysterica passio* or sheer madness, if you will, but was so powerful in its melancholy exultation that I tremble lest it wake again and drive me from my new-found peace.

When we came in the grey light to the great half-empty terminus, it seemed to me I was so changed that I was no more, as man is, a moment shuddering at eternity, but eternity weeping and laughing over a moment; and when we had started and Michael Robartes had fallen asleep, as he soon did, his sleeping face, in which there was no sign of all that had so shaken me and that now kept me wakeful, was to my excited mind more like a mask than a face. The fancy possessed me that the man behind it had dissolved away like salt in water, and that it laughed and sighed, appealed and denounced at the bidding of beings greater or less than man. 'This is not Michael Robartes at all: Michael Robartes is dead; dead for ten, for twenty years perhaps,' I kept repeating to myself. I fell at last into a feverish sleep, waking up from time to time when we rushed past some little town, its slated roofs shining with wet, or still lake gleaming in the cold morning light. I had been too preoccupied to ask where we were going, or to notice what tickets Michael Robartes had taken, but I knew now from the direction of the sun that we were going westward; and presently I knew also, by the way in which the trees had grown into the semblance of tattered beggars flying with bent heads towards the east, that we were approaching the western coast. Then immediately I saw the sea between the low hills upon the left, its dull grey broken into white patches and lines.

When we left the train we had still, I found, some way to go, and set out, buttoning our coats about us, for the wind was bitter and violent. Michael Robartes was silent, seeming anxious to leave me to my thoughts; and as we walked between the sea and the rocky side of a great promontory, I realized with a new perfection what a shock had been given to all my habits of thought and of feelings, if indeed some mysterious change had not taken place in the substance of my mind, for the grey waves, plumed with scudding foam, had grown part of a teeming, fantastic inner life; and when Michael Robartes pointed to a square ancient-looking house, with a much smaller and newer building under its lee, set out on the very end of a dilapidated and almost deserted pier, and said it was the Temple of the Alchemical Rose, I was possessed with the phantasy that the sea, which kept covering it with showers of white foam, was claiming it as part of some indefinite and passionate life, which had begun to war upon our orderly and careful days, and was about to plunge the world into a night as obscure as that which followed the downfall of the classical world. One part of my mind mocked this phantastic terror, but the other, the part that still lay half plunged in vision, listened to the clash of unknown armies, and shuddered at unimaginable fanaticisms, that hung in those grey leaping waves.

We had gone but a few paces along the pier when we came upon an old man, who was evidently a watchman, for he sat in an overset barrel, close to a place where masons had been lately working upon a break in the pier, and had in front of him a fire such as one sees slung under tinkers' carts. I saw that he was also a voteen, as the peasants say, for there was a rosary hanging from a nail on the rim of the barrel, and as I saw I shuddered, and I did not know why I shuddered. We had passed him a few yards when I heard him cry in Gaelic, 'Idolaters, idolaters, go down to Hell with your witches and your devils; go down to Hell that the herrings may come again into the bay'; and for some moments I could hear him half screaming and half muttering behind us. 'Are you not afraid,' I said, 'that these wild fishing people may do some desperate thing against you?'

'I and mine,' he answered, 'are long past human hurt or help, being incorporate with immortal spirits, and when we die it shall be the consummation of the supreme work. A time will come for these people also, and they will sacrifice a mullet to Artemis, or some other fish to some new divinity, unless indeed their own divinities, the Dagda, with his overflowing cauldron, Lug, with his spear dipped in poppy-juice lest it rush forth hot for battle, Aengus, with the three birds on his shoulder, Bodb and his red swineherd, and all the heroic children of Dana, set up once more their temples of grey stone. Their reign has never ceased, but only waned in power a little, for the Sidhe still pass in every wind, and dance and play at hurley, and fight their sudden battles in every hollow and on every hill; but they cannot build their temples again till there have been martyrdoms and victories, and perhaps even that long-foretold battle in the Valley of the Black Pig.'

Keeping close to the wall that went about the pier on the seaward side, to escape the driving foam and the wind, which threatened every moment to lift us off our feet, we made our way in silence to the door of the square building. Michael Robartes opened it with a key, on which I saw the rust of many salt winds, and led me along a bare passage and up an uncarpeted stair to a little room surrounded with bookshelves. A meal would be brought, but only of fruit, for I must submit to a tempered fast before the ceremony, he explained, and with it a book on the doctrine and method of the Order, over which I was to spend what remained of the winter daylight. He then left me, promising to return an hour before the ceremony. I began searching among the bookshelves, and found one of the most exhaustive alchemical libraries I have ever seen. There were the works of Morienus, who hid his immortal body under a shirt of hair-cloth; of Avicenna, who was a drunkard and yet controlled numberless legions of spirits; of Alfarabi, who put so many spirits into his lute that he could make men laugh, or weep, or fall in deadly trance as he would; of Lully, who transformed himself into the likeness of a red cock; of Flamel, who with his wife Parnella achieved the elixir many hundreds of years ago, and is fabled to still live in Arabia among the Dervishes; and of many of less fame. There were very few mystics but alchemical mystics, and because, I had little doubt, of the devotion to one god of the greater number and of the limited sense of beauty, which Robartes would hold an inevitable consequence; but I did notice a complete set of facsimiles of the prophetical writings of William Blake, and probably because of the multitudes that thronged his illumination and were 'like the gay fishes on the wave when the moon sucks up the dew.' I noted also many poets and prose writers of every age, but only those who were a little weary of life, as indeed the greatest have been everywhere, and who cast their imagination to us, as a something they needed no longer now that they were going up in their fiery chariots.

Presently I heard a tap at the door, and a woman came in and laid a little fruit upon the table. I judged that she had once been handsome, but her cheeks were hollowed by what I would have held, had I seen her anywhere else, an excitement of the flesh and a thirst for pleasure, instead of which it doubtless was an excitement of the imagination and a thirst for beauty. I asked her some question concerning the ceremony, but getting no answer except a shake of the head, saw that I must await initiation in silence. When I had eaten, she came again, and having laid a curiously wrought bronze box on the table, lighted the candles, and took away the plates and the remnants. So soon as I was alone, I turned to the box, and found that the peacocks of Hera spread out their tails over the sides and lid, against a background, on which were wrought great stars, as though to affirm that the heavens were a part of their glory. In the box was a book bound in vellum, and having upon the vellum and in very delicate colours, and in gold, the alchemical rose with many spears thrusting against it, but in vain, as was shown by the shattered points of those nearest to the petals. The book was written upon vellum, and in beautiful clear letters, interspersed with symbolical pictures and illuminations, after the manner of the *Splendor Solis*.

The first chapter described how six students, of Celtic descent, gave themselves separately to the study of alchemy, and solved, one the mystery of the Pelican, another the mystery of the green Dragon, another the mystery of the Eagle, another that of Salt and Mercury. What seemed a succession of accidents, but was, the book declared, the contrivance of preternatural powers, brought them together in the garden of an inn in the South of France, and while they talked together the thought came to them that alchemy was the gradual distillation of the contents of the soul, until they were ready to put off the mortal and put on the immortal. An owl passed, rustling among the vine-leaves overhead, and then an old woman came, leaning upon a stick, and, sitting close to them, took up the thought where they had dropped it. Having expounded the whole principle of spiritual alchemy, and bid them found the Order of the Alchemical Rose, she passed from among them, and when they would have followed was nowhere to be seen. They formed themselves into an Order, holding their goods and making their researches in common, and, as they became perfect in the alchemical doctrine, apparitions came and went among them, and taught them more and more marvellous mysteries. The book then went on to expound so much of these as the neophyte was permitted to know, dealing at the outset and at considerable length with the independent reality of our thoughts, which was, it declared, the doctrine from which all true doctrines rose. If you imagine, it said, the semblance of a living being, it is at once possessed by a wandering soul, and goes hither and hither working good or evil, until the moment of its death has come; and gave many examples, received, it said, from many gods. Eros had taught them how to fashion forms in which a divine soul could dwell, and whisper what they would into sleeping minds; and Ate, forms from which demonic beings could pour madness, or unquiet dreams, into sleeping blood; and Hermes, that if you powerfully imagined a hound at your bedside it would keep watch there until you woke, and drive away all but the mightiest demons, but that if your imagination was weakly, the hound would be weakly also, and the demons prevail, and the hound soon die; and Aphrodite, that if you made, by a strong imagining, a dove crowned with silver and bad it flutter over your head, its soft cooing would make sweet dreams of immortal love gather and brood over mortal sleep; and all divinities alike had revealed with many warnings and lamentations that all minds are continually giving birth to such beings, and sending them forth to work health or disease, joy or madness. If you would give forms to the evil powers, it went on, you were to make them ugly, thrusting out a lip, with the thirsts of life, or breaking the proportions of a body with the burdens of life; but the divine powers would only appear in beautiful shapes, which are but, as it were, shapes trembling out of existence, folding up into a timeless ecstasy, drifting with half-shut eyes, into a sleepy stillness. The bodiless souls who descended into these forms were what men call the moods; and worked all great changes in the world; for just as the magician or the artist could call them when he would, so they could call out of the mind of the magician or the artist, or if they were demons, out of the mind of the mad or the ignoble, what shape they would, and through its voice and its gestures pour themselves out upon the world. In this way all great events were accomplished; a mood, a divinity, or a demon, first descending like a faint sigh into men's minds and then changing their thoughts and their actions until hair that was yellow had grown black, or hair that was black had grown yellow, and empires moved their border, as though they were but drifts of leaves. The rest of the book contained symbols of form, and sound, and colour, and their attribution to divinities and demons, so that the initiate might fashion a shape for any divinity or any demon, and be as powerful as Avicenna among those who live under the roots of tears and of laughter.

IV

A couple of hours after sunset Michael Robartes returned and told me that I would have to learn the steps of an exceedingly antique dance, because before my initiation could be perfected I had to join three times in a magical dance, for rhythm was the wheel of Eternity, on which alone the transient and accidental could be broken, and the spirit set free. I found that the steps, which were simple enough, resembled certain antique Greek dances, and having been a good dancer in my youth and the master of many curious Gaelic steps, I soon had them in my memory. He then robed me and himself in a costume which suggested by its shape both Greece and Egypt, but by its crimson colour a more passionate life than theirs; and having put into my hands a little chainless censer of bronze, wrought into the likeness of a rose, by some modern craftsman, he told me to open a small door opposite to the door by which I had entered. I put my hand to the handle, but the moment I did so the fumes of the incense, helped perhaps by his mysterious glamour, made me fall again into a dream, in which I seemed to be a mask, lying on the counter of a little Eastern shop. Many persons, with eyes so bright and still that I knew them for more than human, came in and tried me on their faces, but at last flung me into a corner with a little laughter; but all this passed in a moment, for when I awoke my hand was still upon the handle. I opened the door, and found myself in a marvellous passage, along whose sides were many divinities wrought in a mosaic, not less beautiful than the mosaic in the Baptistery at Ravenna, but of a less severe beauty; the predominant colour of each divinity, which was surely a symbolic colour, being repeated in the lamps that hung from the ceiling, a curiously-scented lamp before every divinity. I passed on, marvelling exceedingly how these enthusiasts could have created all this beauty in so remote a place, and half persuaded to believe in a material alchemy, by the sight of so much hidden wealth; the censer filling the air, as I passed, with smoke of ever-changing colour.

I stopped before a door, on whose bronze panels were wrought great waves in whose shadow were faint suggestions of terrible faces. Those beyond it seemed to have heard our steps, for a voice cried: 'Is the work of the Incorruptible Fire at an end?' and immediately Michael Robartes answered: 'The perfect gold has come from the *athanor*.' The door swung open, and we were in a great circular room, and among men and women who were dancing slowly in crimson robes. Upon the ceiling was an immense rose wrought in mosaic; and about the walls, also in mosaic, was a battle of gods and angels, the gods glimmering like rubies and sapphires, and the angels of the one greyness, because, as Michael Robartes whispered, they had renounced their divinity, and turned from the unfolding of their separate hearts, out of love for a God of humility and sorrow. Pillars supported the roof and made a kind of circular cloister, each pillar being a column of confused shapes, divinities, it seemed, of the wind, who rose as in a whirling dance of more than human vehemence, and playing upon pipes and cymbals; and from among these shapes were thrust out hands, and in these hands were censers. I was bid place my censer also in a hand and take my place and dance, and as I turned from the pillars towards the dancers, I saw that the floor was of a green stone, and that a pale Christ on a pale cross was wrought in the midst. I asked Robartes the meaning of this, and was told that they desired 'To trouble His unity with their multitudinous feet.' The dance wound in and out, tracing upon the floor the shapes of petals that copied the petals in the rose overhead, and to the sound of hidden instruments which were perhaps of an antique pattern, for I have never heard the like; and every moment the dance was more passionate, until all the winds of the world seemed to have awakened under our feet. After a little I had grown weary, and stood under a pillar watching the coming and going of those flame-like figures; until gradually I sank into a half-dream, from which I was awakened by seeing the petals of the great rose, which had no longer the look of mosaic, falling slowly through the incense-heavy air, and, as they fell, shaping into the likeness of living beings of an extraordinary beauty. Still faint and cloud-like, they began to dance, and as they danced took a more and more definite shape, so that I was able to distinguish beautiful Grecian faces and august Egyptian faces, and now and again to name a divinity by the staff in his hand or by a bird fluttering over his head; and soon every mortal foot danced by the white foot of an immortal; and in the troubled eyes that looked into untroubled shadowy eyes, I saw the brightness of uttermost desire as though they had found at length, after unreckonable wandering, the lost love of their youth. Sometimes, but only for a moment, I saw a faint solitary figure with a veiled face, and carrying a faint torch, flit among the dancers, but like a dream within a dream, like a shadow of a shadow, and I knew by an understanding born from a deeper fountain than thought, that it was Eros himself, and that his face was veiled because no man or woman from the beginning of the world has ever known what love is, or looked into his eyes, for Eros alone of divinities is altogether a spirit, and hides in passions not of his essence if he would commune with a mortal heart. So that if a man love nobly he knows love through infinite pity, unspeakable trust, unending sympathy; and if ignobly through vehement jealousy, sudden hatred, and unappeasable desire; but unveiled love he never knows. While I thought these things, a voice cried to me from the crimson figures: 'Into the dance! there is none that can be spared out of the dance; into the dance! into the dance! that the gods may make them bodies out of the substance of our hearts'; and before I could answer, a mysterious wave of passion, that seemed like the soul of the dance moving within our souls, took hold of me, and I was swept, neither consenting nor refusing, into the midst. I was dancing with an immortal august woman, who had black lilies in her hair, and her dreamy gesture seemed laden with a wisdom more profound than the darkness that is between star and star, and with a love like the love that breathed upon the waters; and as we danced on and on, the incense drifted over us and round us, covering us away as in the heart of the world, and ages seemed to pass, and tempests to awake and perish in the folds of our robes and in her heavy hair.

Suddenly I remembered that her eyelids had never quivered, and that her lilies had not dropped a black petal, or shaken from their places, and understood with a great horror that I danced with one who was more or less than human, and who was drinking up my soul as an ox drinks up a wayside pool; and I fell, and darkness passed over me.

V

I awoke suddenly as though something had awakened me, and saw that I was lying on a roughly painted floor, and that on the ceiling, which was at no great distance, was a roughly painted rose, and about me on the walls half-finished paintings. The pillars and the censers had gone; and near me a score of sleepers lay wrapped in disordered robes, their upturned faces looking to my imagination like hollow masks; and a chill dawn was shining down upon them from a long window I had not noticed before; and outside the sea roared. I saw Michael Robartes lying at a little distance and beside him an overset bowl of wrought bronze which looked as though it had once held incense. As I sat thus, I heard a sudden tumult of angry men and women's voices mix with the roaring of the sea; and leaping to my feet, I went quickly to Michael Robartes, and tried to shake him out of his sleep. I then seized him by the shoulder and tried to lift him, but he fell backwards, and sighed faintly; and the voices became louder and angrier; and there was a sound of heavy blows upon the door, which opened on to the pier. Suddenly I heard a sound of rending wood, and I knew it had begun to give, and I ran to the door of the room. I pushed it open and came out upon a passage whose bare boards clattered under my feet, and found in the passage another door which led into an empty kitchen; and as I passed through the door I heard two crashes in quick succession, and knew by the sudden noise of feet and the shouts that the door which opened on to the pier had fallen inwards. I ran from the kitchen and out into a small yard, and from this down some steps which descended the seaward and sloping side of the pier, and from the steps clambered along the water's edge, with the angry voices ringing in my ears. This part of the pier had been but lately refaced with blocks of granite, so that it was almost clear of seaweed; but when I came to the old part, I found it so slippery with green weed that I had to climb up on to the roadway. I looked towards the Temple of the Alchemical Rose, where the fishermen and the women were still shouting, but somewhat more faintly, and saw that there was no one about the door or upon the pier; but as I looked, a little crowd hurried out of the door and began gathering large stones from where they were heaped up in readiness for the next time a storm shattered the pier, when they would be laid under blocks of granite. While I stood watching the crowd, an old man, who was, I think, the voteen, pointed to me, and screamed out something, and the crowd whitened, for all the faces had turned towards me. I ran, and it was well for me that pullers of the oar are poorer men with their feet than with their arms and their bodies; and yet while I ran I scarcely heard the following feet or the angry voices, for many voices of exultation and lamentation, which were forgotten as a dream is forgotten the moment they were heard, seemed to be ringing in the air over my head.

There are moments even now when I seemed to hear those voices of exultation and lamentation, and when the indefinite world, which has but half lost its mastery over my heart and my intellect, seems about to claim a perfect mastery; but I carry the rosary about my neck, and when I hear, or seem to hear them, I press it to my heart and say: 'He whose name is Legion is at our doors deceiving our intellects with subtlety and flattering our hearts with beauty, and we have no trust but in Thee': and then the war that rages within me at other times is still, and I am at peace.

Substantial Variants

Epigraph from *The Bacchanals* of Greek tragedian Euripides (c. 480–406 BC); see *M2005* 366.

1–6 A few years ago an extraordinary religious frenzy took hold upon the peasantry of a remote Connemara headland; and a number of eccentric men and women, who had turned an old custom-house into a kind of college, were surprised at prayer, as it was then believed, by a mob of fishermen, stone masons, and small farmers, and beaten to death with stones, which were heaped up close at hand to be ready for the next breach in the wave-battered pier. Vague rumours of pagan ceremonies and mysterious idolatries had for some time drifted among the cabins; and the indignation of the ignorant had been further inflamed by a priest, unfrocked for drunkenness, who had preached at the road-side of the secret coming of the Antichrist. I first heard of these unfortunates, on whom passion for universal ideas, which distinguishes the Celtic and Latin races, was to bring so dreadful a martyrdom, but a few weeks before the end; and the change in my opinions which has made my writings so much less popular and intelligible, and driven me to the verge of taking the habit of St. Dominic, was brought about by the strange experiences I endured in their presence.¶ I… *The Savoy*

118–34 connected with secret hopes and terrors. When I turned I saw Robartes standing in the middle of the room and looking straight before him as though he saw some one or something I could not, and whispering to himself. He heard me move, and coming toward the fire, sat down and began gazing at the flame. I turned my chair towards him and sat down also and waited for him to speak. He watched the rising and falling of the flame for a moment and began. ¶ I have… *The Savoy*

169–73 power of Lear, and Hamlet, and Lancelot, and Faust, and Beatrice, and Quixote, divinities who took upon… *The Savoy*

200 determination: 'Your philosophy is charming as a phantasy, but, carried to the point of belief, it is a supreme delusion, and, enforced by mesmeric glamour, a supreme crime. You… *The Savoy*

263–67 peace. ¶ We were not long in the train before Michael Robartes was asleep, and, to my excited mind, his face… *The Savoy*

301–16 waves. ¶ Some half a mile to sea, and plunging its bowsprit under at every moment, and lifting it again dripping with foam, was a brown-sailed fishing yawl. ¶ 'A time… *The Savoy*

346–47 were few mediæval or modern mystics other than the alchemical; and… *The Savoy*

375 students, of whom all but one, who was of Cornish descent, were Western Irish, Western Scottish, or French, gave… *The Savoy*

426 yellow, or cities crumbled away and new cities arisen in their places, and… *The Savoy*

428 leaves. I remembered, as I read, that mood which Edgar Poe found in a wine-cup, and how it passed into France and took possession of Baudelaire, and from Baudelaire passed to England

and the Pre-Raphaelites, and then again returned to France, and still wanders the world, enlarging its power as it goes, awaiting the time when it shall be, perhaps, alone, or, with other moods, master over a great new religion, and an awakener of the fanatical wars that hovered in the gray surges, and forget the wine-cup where it was born. The… *The Savoy*

537–73 incense. ¶ I had no thought but to get away, and to forget all. The door of the room opened with a push, and hurrying along the passage, where the bare boards clattered under my feet, I found the front door by the light of a single oil lamp, that hung from the ceiling, mingling its yellow flame with the morning light. I hurried along the pier, between brown nets and old spars, the spray driving in my face; but had not gone far before I met a group of stonemasons going to their morning work. They went a few yards past me and then one of them, an old man with iron-gray hair, turned and cried: 'Idolater, idolater, go back to your dhoules, go down to hell with your she dhoules!' I scarcely heard them, for other voices were in my ears. Voices uttering reproaches that were forgotten the moment they were spoken, as a dream is forgotten on waking. ¶ From that day I have never failed to carry the rosary about my neck, and whenever the indefinite world, which has but half lost its empire over my heart and my intellect, though my conscience and my soul are free, is about to claim a new mastery, I press the cross to my heart… *The Savoy*

THE TABLES OF THE LAW

I

'Will you permit me, Aherne,' I said, 'to ask you a question, which I have wanted to ask you for years, and have not asked because we have grown nearly strangers? Why did you refuse the berretta, and almost at the last moment? When you and I lived together, you cared neither for wine, women, nor money, and had thoughts for nothing but theology and mysticism.' I had watched through dinner for a moment to put my question, and ventured now, because he had thrown off a little of the reserve and indifference which, ever since his last return from Italy, had taken the place of our once close friendship. He had just questioned me, too, about certain private and almost sacred things, and my frankness had earned, I thought, a like frankness from him.

When I began to speak he was lifting to his lips a glass of that old wine which he could choose so well and valued so little; and while I spoke, he set it slowly and meditatively upon the table and held it there, its deep red light dyeing his long delicate fingers. The impression of his face and form, as they were then, is still vivid with me, and is inseparable from another and fanciful impression: the impression of a man holding a flame in his naked hand. He was to me, at that moment, the supreme type of our race, which, when it has risen above, or is sunken below, the formalisms of half-education and the rationalisms of conventional affirmation and denial, turns away, unless my hopes for the world and for the Church have made me blind, from practicable desires and intuitions towards desires so unbounded that no human vessel can contain them, intuitions so immaterial that their sudden and far-off fire leaves heavy darkness about hand and foot. He had the nature, which is half monk, half soldier of fortune, and must needs turn action into dreaming, and dreaming into action; and for such there is no order, no finality, no contentment in this world. When he and I had been students in Paris, we had belonged to a little group which devoted itself to speculations about alchemy and mysticism. More orthodox in most of his beliefs than Michael Robartes, he had surpassed him in a fanciful hatred of all life, and this hatred had found expression in the curious paradox—half borrowed from some fanatical monk, half invented by himself—that the beautiful arts were sent into the world to overthrow nations, and finally life herself, by sowing everywhere unlimited desires, like torches thrown into a burning city. This idea was not at the time, I believe, more than a paradox, a plume of the pride of youth; and it was only after his return to Ireland that he endured the fermentation of belief which is coming upon our people with the reawakening of their imaginative life.

Presently he stood up, saying: 'Come, and I will show you, for you at any rate will understand,' and taking candles from the table, he lit the way into the long paved passage that led to his private chapel. We passed between the portraits of the Jesuits and priests—some of no little fame—his family had given to the Church; and engravings and photographs of pictures that had especially moved him; and the few paintings his small fortune, eked out by an almost penurious abstinence from the things most men desire, had enabled him to buy in his travels. The pictures that I knew best, for they had hung there longest, whether reproductions or originals, were of the Sienese School, which he had studied for a long time, claiming that it alone of the schools of the world pictured not the world but what is revealed to saints in their dreams and visions. The Sienese alone among Italians, he would say, could not or would not represent the pride of life, the pleasure in swift movement or sustaining strength, or voluptuous flesh. They were so little interested in these things that there often seemed to be no human body at all under the robe of the saint, but they could represent by a bowed head, or uplifted face, man's reverence before Eternity as no others could, and they were at their happiest when mankind had dwindled to a little group silhouetted upon a golden abyss, as if they saw the world, habitually from far off. When I had praised some school that had dipped deeper into life, he would profess to discover a more intense emotion than life knew in those dark outlines. 'Put, even Francesca, who felt the supernatural as deeply,' he would say, 'beside the work of Siena, and one finds a faint impurity in his awe, a touch of ghostly terror, where love and humbleness had best been all.' He had often told me of his hope that by filling his mind with those holy pictures he would help himself to attain at last to vision and ecstasy, and of his disappointment at never getting more than dreams of a curious and broken beauty. But of late he had added pictures of a different kind, French symbolistic pictures which he had bought for a few pounds from little-known painters, English and French pictures of the School of the English Pre-Raphaelites; and now he stood for a moment and said, 'I have changed my taste. I am fascinated a little against my will by these faces, where I find the pallor of souls trembling between the excitement of the flesh and the excitement of the spirit, and by landscapes that are created by heightening the obscurity and disorder of nature. These landscapes do not stir the imagination to the energies of sanctity but as to orgaic dancing and prophetic frenzy.' I saw with some resentment new images where the old ones had often made that long gray, dim, empty, echoing passage become to my eyes a vestibule of Eternity.

Almost every detail of the chapel, which we entered by a narrow Gothic door, whose threshold had been worn smooth by the secret worshippers of the penal times, was vivid in my memory; for it was in this chapel that I had first, and when but a boy, been moved by the mediævalism which is now, I think, the governing influence in my life. The only thing that seemed new was a square bronze box which stood upon the altar before the six unlighted candles and the ebony crucifix, and was like those made in ancient times of more precious substances to hold the sacred books. Aherne made me sit down on an oak bench, and having bowed very low before the crucifix, took the bronze box from the altar, and sat down beside me with the box upon his knees

'You will perhaps have forgotten,' he said, 'most of what you have read about Joachim of Flora, for he is little more than a name to even the well read. He was an abbot in Cortale in the twelfth century, and is best known for his prophecy, in a book called *Expositio in Apocalypsin*, that the Kingdom of the Father was passed, the Kingdom of the Son passing, the Kingdom of the Spirit yet to come. The Kingdom of the Spirit was to be a complete triumph of the Spirit, the *spiritualis intelligentia* he called it, over the dead letter. He had many followers among the more extreme Franciscans, and these were accused of possessing a secret book of his called the *Liber Inducens in Evangelium Æternum*. Again and again groups of visionaries were accused of possessing this terrible book, in which the freedom of the Renaissance lay hidden, until at last Pope Alexander IV. had it found and cast into the flames. I have the greatest treasure the world contains. I have a copy of that book; and see what great artists have made the robes in which it is wrapped. The greater portion of the book is illuminated in the Byzantine style, which so few care for to-day, but which moves me because these tall, emaciated angels and saints seem to have less relation to the world about us than to an abstract pattern of flowing lines, that suggest an imagination absorbed in the contemplation of Eternity. Even if you do not care for so formal an art, you cannot help seeing that work where there is so much gold, and of that purple colour which has gold dissolved in it, was valued at a great price in its day. But it was only at the Renaissance the labour was spent upon it which has made it the priceless thing it is. The wooden boards of the cover show by the astrological allegories painted upon them, as by the style of painting itself, some craftsman of the school of Francesco Cossi of Ferrara, but the gold clasps and hinges are known to be the work of Benvenuto Cellini, who made likewise the bronze box and covered it with gods and demons, whose eyes are closed, to signify an absorption in the inner light.'

I took the book in my hands and began turning over the gilded, many-coloured pages, holding it close to the candle to discover the texture of the paper.

'Where did you get this amazing book?' I said. 'If genuine, and I cannot judge by this light, you have discovered one of the most precious things in the world.'

'It is certainly genuine,' he replied. 'When the original was destroyed, one copy alone remained, and was in the hands of a lute-player of Florence, and from him it passed to his son, and so from generation to generation until it came to the lute-player who was father to Benvenuto Cellini, and from Benvenuto Cellini to that Cardinal of Ferrara who released him from prison, and from him to a natural son, so from generation to generation, the story of its wandering passing on with it, until it came into the possession of the family of Aretino, and to Giulio Aretino, an artist and worker in metals, and student of the kabalistic heresies of Pico della Mirandola.

He spent many nights with me at Rome, discussing philosophy; and at last I won his confidence so perfectly that he showed me this, his greatest treasure; and, finding how much I valued it, and feeling that he himself was growing old and beyond the help of its teaching, he sold it to me for no great sum, considering its preciousness.'

'What is the doctrine?' I said. 'Some mediaeval straw-splitting about the nature of the Trinity, which is only useful to-day to show how many things are unimportant to us, which once shook the world?'

'I could never make you understand,' he said, with a sigh, 'that nothing is unimportant in belief, but even you will admit that this book goes to the heart. Do you see the tables on which the commandments were written in Latin?' I looked to the end of the room, opposite to the altar, and saw that the two marble tablets were gone, and that two large empty tablets of ivory, like large copies of the little tablets we set over our desks, had taken their place. 'It has swept the commandments of the Father away,' he went on, 'and displaced the commandments of the Son by the commandments of the Holy Spirit. The first book is called *Fractura Tabularum*. In the first chapter it mentions the names of the great artists who made them graven things and the likeness of many things, and adored them and served them; and the second the names of the great wits who took the name of the Lord their God in vain; and that long third chapter, set with the emblems of sanctified faces, and having wings upon its borders, is the praise of breakers of the seventh day and wasters of the six days, who yet lived comely and pleasant days. Those two chapters tell of men and women who railed upon their parents, remembering that their god was older than the god of their parents; and that which has the sword of Michael for an emblem commends the kings that wrought secret murder and so won for their people a peace that was *amore somnoque gravata et vestibus versicoloribus*, heavy with love and sleep and many-coloured raiment; and that with the pale star at the closing has the lives of the noble youths who loved the wives of others and were transformed into memories, which have transformed many poorer hearts into sweet flames; and that with the winged head is the history of the robbers who lived upon the sea or in the desert, lives which it compares to the twittering of the string of a bow, *nervi stridentis instar*; and those two last, that are fire and gold, are devoted to the satirists who bore false witness against their neighbours and yet illustrated eternal wrath, and to those that have coveted more than other men the house of God, and all things that are His, which no man has seen and handled, except in madness and in dreams.

'The second book is called *Lex Secreta*, and describes the true inspiration of action, the only Eternal Evangel; and ends with a vision, which he saw among the mountains of La Sila, of his disciples sitting throned in the blue deep of the air, and laughing aloud, with a laughter that was like the rustling of the wings of Time: *Cœlis in cæruleis ridentes sedebant discipuli mei super thronos: talis erat risus, qualis temporis pennati susurrus.*'

'I know little of Joachim of Flora,' I said, 'except that Dante set him in Paradise among the great doctors. If he held a heresy so singular, I cannot understand how no rumours of it came to the ears of Dante; and Dante made no peace with the enemies of the Church.'

'Joachim of Flora acknowledged openly the authority of the Church, and even asked that all his published writings, and those to be published by his desire after his death, should be submitted to the censorship of the Pope. He considered that those whose work was to live and not to reveal were children and that the Pope was their Father; but he taught in secret that certain others, and in always increasing numbers, were elected, not to live, but to reveal that hidden substance of God which is colour and music and softness and sweet odour; and that these have no father but the Holy Spirit. Just as poets and painters and musicians labour at their works, building them with lawless and lawful things alike, so long as they embody the beauty that is beyond the grave, these children of the Holy Spirit labour at their moments with eyes upon the shining substance on which Time has heaped the refuse of creation; for the world only exists to be a tale in the ears of coming generations; and terror and content, birth and death, love and hatred, and the fruit of the Tree, are but instruments for that supreme art which is to win us from life and gather us into eternity like doves into their dove-cots.

'I shall go away in a little while and travel into many lands, that I may know all accidents and destinies, and when I return, will write my secret law upon those ivory tablets, just as poets and romance writers have written the principles of their art in prefaces; and when I know what principle of life, discoverable at first by imagination and instinct, I am to express, I will gather my pupils that they may discover their law in the study of my law, as poets and painters discover their own art of expression by the study of some Master. I know nothing certain as yet but this—I am to become completely alive, that is, completely passionate, for beauty is only another name for perfect passion. I shall create a world where the whole lives of men shall be articulated and simplified as if seventy years were but one moment, or as they were the leaping of a fish or the opening of a flower.'

He was pacing up and down, and I listened to the fervour of his words and watched the excitement of his gestures with not a little concern. I had been accustomed to welcome the most singular speculations, and had always found them as harmless as the Persian cat who half closes her meditative eyes and stretches out her long claws before my fire. But now I would battle in the interests of orthodoxy, even of the commonplace: and yet could find nothing better to say than: 'It is not necessary to judge everyone by the law, for we have also Christ's commandment of love.'

He turned and said, looking at me with shining eyes: 'Jonathan Swift made a soul for the gentlemen of this city by hating his neighbour as himself.'

'At any rate, you cannot deny that to teach so dangerous a doctrine is to accept a terrible responsibility.'

'Leonardo da Vinci,' he replied, 'has this noble sentence: "The hope and desire of returning home to one's former state is like the moth's desire for the light; and the man who with constant longing awaits each new month and new year, deeming that the things he longs for are never too late in coming, does not perceive that he is longing for his own destruction." How, then, can the pathway which will lead us into the heart of God be other than dangerous? why should you, who are no materialist, cherish the continuity and order of the world as those do who have only the world? You do not value the writers who will express nothing unless their reason understands how it will make what is called the right more easy; why, then, will you deny a like freedom to the supreme art, the art which is the foundation of all arts? Yes, I shall send out of this chapel saints, lovers, rebels and prophets: souls who will surround themselves with peace, as with a nest made with grass; and others over whom I shall weep. The dust shall fall for many years over this little box; and then I shall open it; and the tumults, which are, perhaps, the flames of the last day, shall come from under the lid.'

I did not reason with him that night, because his excitement was great and I feared to make him angry; and when I called at his house a few days later, he was gone and his house was locked up and empty. I have deeply regretted my failure both to combat his heresy and to test the genuineness of his strange book. Since my conversion I have indeed done penance for an error which I was only able to measure after some years.

II

I was walking along one of the Dublin quays, on the side nearest the river, about ten years after our conversation, stopping from time to time to turn over the books upon an old bookstall, and think, curiously enough, of the terrible destiny of Michael Robartes, and his brotherhood; when I saw a tall and bent man walking slowly along the other side of the quay. I recognized, with a start, in a lifeless mask with dim eyes, the once resolute and delicate face of Owen Aherne. I crossed the quay quickly, but had not gone many yards before he turned away, as though he had seen me, and hurried down a side street; I followed, but only to lose him among the intricate streets on the north side of the river. During the next few weeks I inquired of everybody who had once known him, but he had made himself known to nobody; and I knocked, without a result, at the door of his old house; and had nearly persuaded myself that I was mistaken, when I saw him again in a narrow street behind the Four Courts, and followed him to the door of his house.

I laid my hand on his arm; he turned quite without surprise; and indeed it is possible that to him, whose inner life had soaked up the outer life, a parting of years was a parting from forenoon to afternoon. He stood holding the door half open, as though he would keep me from entering; and would perhaps have parted from me without further words had I not said: 'Owen Aherne, you trusted me once, will you not trust me again, and tell me what has come of the ideas we discussed in this house ten years ago?—but perhaps you have already forgotten them.'

'You have a right to hear,' he said, 'for since I have told you the ideas, I should tell you the extreme danger they contain, or rather the boundless wickedness they contain; but when you have heard this we must part, and part for ever, because I am lost, and must be hidden!'

I followed him through the paved passage, and saw that its corners were choked, and the pictures gray, with dust and cobwebs; and that the dust and cobwebs which covered the ruby and sapphire of the saints on the window had made it very dim. He pointed to where the ivory tablets glimmered faintly in the dimness, and I saw that they were covered with small writing, and went up to them and began to read the writing. It was in Latin, and was an elaborate casuistry, illustrated with many examples, but whether from his own life or from the lives of others I do not know. I had read but a few sentences when I imagined that a faint perfume had begun to fill the room, and turning round asked Owen Aherne if he were lighting the incense.

'No,' he replied, and pointed where the thurible lay rusty and empty on one of the benches; as he spoke the faint perfume seemed to vanish, and I was persuaded I had imagined it.

'Has the philosophy of the *Liber Inducens in Evangelium Æternum* made you very unhappy?' I said.

'At first I was full of happiness,' he replid, 'for I felt a divine ecstasy, an immortal fire in every passion, in every hope, in every desire, in every dream; and I saw, in the shadows under leaves, in the hollow waters, in the eyes of men and women, its image, as in a mirror; and it was as though I was about to touch the Heart of God. Then all changed and I was full of misery, and I said to myself that I was caught in the glittering folds of an enormous serpent, and was falling with him through a fathomless abyss, and that henceforth the glittering folds were my world; and in my misery it was revealed to me that man can only come to that Heart through the sense of separation from it which we call sin, and I understood that I could not sin, because I had discovered the law of my being, and could only express or fail to express my being, and I understood that God has made a simple and arbitrary law that we may sin and repent!'

He had sat down on one of the wooden benches and now became silent, his bowed head and hanging arms and listless body having more of dejection than any image I have met with in life or in any art. I went and stood leaning against the altar, and watched him, not knowing what I should say; and I noticed his black closely-buttoned coat, his short hair, and shaven head, which preserved a memory of his priestly ambition, and understood Catholicism had seized him in the midst of the vertigo he called philosophy; and I noticed his lightless eyes and his earth-coloured complexion, and understood how she had failed to do more than hold him on the margin: and I was full of an anguish of pity.

'It may be,' he went on, 'that the angels whose hearts are shadows of the Divine Heart, and whose bodies are made of the Divine Intellect, may come to where their longing is always by a thirst for the divine ecstasy, the immortal fire, that is in the passion, in hope, in desire, in dreams; but we whose hearts perish every moment, and whose bodies melt away like a sigh, must bow and obey!'

I went nearer to him and said: 'Prayer and repentance will make you like other men.'

'No, no,' he said, 'I am not among those for whom Christ died, and this is why I must be hidden. I have a leprosy that even eternity cannot cure. I have seen the whole, and how can I come again to believe that a part is the whole? I have lost my soul because I have looked out of the eyes of the angels.'

Suddenly I saw, or imagined that I saw, the room darken, and faint figures robed in purple, and lifting faint torches with arms that gleamed like silver, bending, above Owen Aherne; and I saw or imagined that I saw, drops, as of burning gum, fall from the torches, and a heavy purple smoke, as of incense, come pouring from the flames and sweeping about us. Owen Aherne, more happy than I who have been half initiated into the Order of the Alchemical Rose, and protected perhaps by his great piety, had sunk again into dejection and listlessness, and saw none of these things; but my knees shook under me, for the purple-robed figures were less faint every moment, and now I could hear the hissing of the gum in the torches. They did not appear to see me, for their eyes were upon Owen Aherne; now and again I could hear them sigh as though with sorrow for his sorrow, and presently I heard words which I could not understand except that they were words of sorrow, and sweet as though immortal was talking to immortal. Then one of them waved her torch, and all the torches waved, and for a moment it was as though some great bird made of flames had fluttered its plumage, and a voice cried as from far up in the air: 'He has charged even his angels with folly, and they also bow and obey; but let your heart mingle with our hearts, which are wrought of divine ecstasy, and your body with our bodies, which are wrought of divine intellect.' And at that cry I understood that the Order of the Alchemical Rose was not of this earth, and that it was still seeking over this earth for whatever souls it could gather within its glittering net; and when all the faces turned towards me, and I saw the mild eyes and the unshaken eyelids, I was full of terror, and thought that they were about to fling their torches upon me, so that all I held dear, all that bound me to spiritual and social order, would be burnt up, and my soul left naked and shivering among the winds that blow from beyond this world and from beyond the stars; and then a faint voice cried, 'Why do you fly from our torches that were made out of the trees under which Christ wept in the Garden of Gethsemane? Why do you fly from our torches that were made of sweet wood, after it had perished from the world and come to us who made it of old times with our breath?'

It was not until the door of the house had closed behind my flight, and the noise of the street was breaking on my ears, that I came back to myself and to a little of my courage; and I have never dared to pass the house of Owen Aherne from that day, even though I believe him to have been driven into some distant country by the spirits whose name is legion, and whose throne is in the indefinite abyss, and whom he obeys and cannot see.

Substantial Variants

4 moment? I never expected you, of all men, to become 'a spoilt priest.' When… *The Savoy*

27–29 world. At the Jesuit school in Paris he had made one of the little group, which used to gather in corners of the playing field, or in remote class rooms, to hear the speculative essays which we wrote and read in secret. More… *The Savoy*

46–76 *rev. to* The photographs and engravings were from the masterpieces of many schools; but in all the beauty, whether it was a beauty of religion, of love, or of some fantastical vision of mountain and wood, was the beauty achieved by temperaments which seek always an absolute emotion, and which have their most continual, though not most perfect expression in the legends and vigils and music of the Celtic peoples. The certitude of a fierce or gracious fervour in the enraptured faces of the angels of Francesca, and the august faces of the sibyls of Michael Angelo; and the incertitude, as of souls trembling between the excitement of the spirit and the excitement of the flesh, in wavering faces from frescoes in the churches of Siena, and in the faces like thin flames, imagined by the modern symbolists and Pre-Raphaelites, had… 1925, 1932

83–85 box; like those made in ancient times of more precious substances to hold the sacred books; which stood before the six unlighted candles and the ebony crucifix upon the altar. Aherne… *The Savoy*

102–17 *rev. to* wrapped. This bronze box was made by Benvenuto Cellini, who covered it with gods and demons, whose eyes are closed to signify an absorption in the inner light.' He lifted the lid and took out a book bound in leather, covered with filigree work of tarnished silver. 'And this cover was bound by one of the binders that bound for Canevari; while Giulio Clovio, an artist of the later Renaissance, whose work is soft and gentle, took out the beginning page of every chapter of the old copy, and set in its place a page surmounted by an elaborate letter and a miniature of some one of the great whose example was cited in the chapter; and wherever the writing left a little space elsewhere, he put some delicate emblem or intricate pattern.' ¶ I… 1925, 1932

168–71 *rev. to* men wealth and woman, and have thereby and therefore mastered and magnified great empires. ¶ 'The… 1925, 1932

200–10 *rev. to* and will gather pupils about me that they may discover their law in the study of my law, and the Kingdom of the Holy Spirit be more widely and firmly established.' ¶ He… 1925, 1932

249–55 the destinies of the little group of fellow students who had shared so many speculations at the school in Paris, and particularly of the terrible destiny of Michael Robartes and his disciples, when I saw a tall, bent man walking slowly in front of me. He stopped presently at a little shop, in the window of which were blue and white statues of the Virgin and gilded statues of St. Patrick and his crozier. His face was now half turned towards me, and I recognized in the lifeless mask with dim eyes what had been the resolute, delicate face of Owen Aherne. I walked towards him, but had not gone many yards before he turned away, as though he had seen me, and went hastily down a side street. ¶ During... *The Savoy*

269–73 he answered; 'for having told you the ideas, it is necessary that I tell you the terrible danger they contain; but when you have heard, we part for good and all: I must be hidden away, for I am lost.' ¶ I... *The Savoy*

274 were shrouded with cobwebs and gray with dust; and, when he opened the door of the chapel, I saw that... *The Savoy*

276 He sat down wearily, not seeming to notice whether I was standing or sitting, and pointed... *The Savoy*

280–362 know. Before I had done more than read a sentence here and there, I turned from them, for Aherne had begun to speak in a low monotonous voice. ¶ 'I am outside the salvation of Him who died for sinners, because I have lost the power of committing a sin. I found the secret law of my life, and, finding it, no longer desired to transgress, because it was my own law. Whatever my intellect and my soul commanded, I did, and sin passed from me, and I ceased to be among those for whom Christ died.' And at the name of Christ he crossed himself with that involuntary gesture which marks those who have crossed themselves from childhood. 'At first I tried to sin by breaking my law, although without desire; but the sin without desire is shadowy, like the sins of some phantom one has not visited even in dreams. You who are not lost, who may still speak to men and women, tell them that it is necessary to make an arbitrary law that one may be among those for whom Christ has died.' ¶ I went over and stood beside him and said: ¶ 'Prayer and penance will make you like other men.' ¶ 'Not,' he replied, 'unless they can take from me my knowledge of the secret law.' ¶ I used some argument, which has passed out of my memory, but his strong intellect, which seemed all the stronger and more active from contrast with the weary monotony of his voice, tore my argument in pieces. I had gone on to heap argument on argument, had he not risen and led me from the chapel, repeating, 'We part for good and all; for I must be hidden away.' ¶ I followed, intending to come to him again the next day; but as I stood in the door of the house a sudden hope came into my mind, and I said: ¶ 'Will you lend me the *Liber Inducens in Evangelium Æternum* for a few days, that I may have it examined by an expert?' ¶ 'I have burned the book and flung the box into the sea.' ¶ When I came the next day with a Jesuit Father from the College of St. Francis Xavier, the house was locked up and apparently empty once more. *The Savoy* [text ends here].

294–96 *rev. to* misery; and in... 1925, 1932

311–15 *rev. to* angels who have hearts of the Divine Ecstasy, and bodies of the Divine Intellect, need nothing but a thirst for the immortal element, in hope... 1925, 1932

355–57 *rev. to* world? ¶ It... 1925, 1932

The Adoration of the Magi

I was sitting reading late into the night a little after my last meeting with Aherne, when I heard a light knocking on my front door. I found upon the doorstep three very old men with stout sticks in their hands, who said they had been told I should be up and about, and that they were to tell me important things. I brought them into my study, and when the peacock curtains had closed behind us, I set their chairs for them close to the fire, for I saw that the frost was on their great-coats of frieze and upon the long beards that flowed almost to their waists. They took off their great-coats, and leaned over the fire warming their hands, and I saw that their clothes had much of the country of our time, but a little also, as it seemed to me, of the town life of a more courtly time. When they had warmed themselves—and they warmed themselves, I thought, less because of the cold of the night than because of a pleasure in warmth for the sake of warmth—they turned towards me, so that the light of the lamp fell full upon their weather-beaten faces, and told the story I am about to tell. Now one talked and now another, and they often interrupted one another, with a desire, like that of countrymen, when they tell a story, to leave no detail untold. When they had finished they made me take notes of whatever conversation they had quoted, so that I might have the exact words, and got up to go. When I asked them where they were going, and what they were doing, and by what names I should call them, they would tell me nothing, except that they had been commanded to travel over Ireland continually, and upon foot and at night, that they might live close to the stones and the trees and at the hours when the immortals are awake.

I have let some years go by before writing out this story, for I am always in dread of the illusions which come of that inquietude of the veil of the Temple, which M. Mallarmé considers a characteristic of our times; and only write it now because I have grown to believe that there is no dangerous idea which does not become less dangerous when written out in sincere and careful English.

The three old men were three brothers, who had lived in one of the western islands from their early manhood, and had cared all their lives for nothing except those classical writers and old Gaelic writers who expounded an heroic and simple life; night after night in winter, Gaelic story-tellers would chant old poems to them over the poteen; and night after night in summer, when the Gaelic story-tellers were at work in the fields or away at the fishing, they would read to one another Virgil and Homer, for they would not enjoy in solitude, but as the ancients enjoyed. At last a man, who told them he was Michael Robartes, came to them in a fishing-boat, like St. Brandan drawn by some vision and called by some voice; and spoke of the coming again of the gods and the ancient things; and their hearts, which had never endured the body and pressure of our time, but only of distant times, found nothing unlikely in anything he told them, but accepted all simply and were happy. Years passed, and one day, when the oldest of the old men, who travelled in his youth and thought sometimes of other lands, looked out on the grey waters, on which the people see the dim outline of the Islands of the Young—the Happy Islands where the Gaelic heroes live the lives of Homer's Phæacians—a voice came out of the air over the waters and told him of the death of Michael Robartes. They were still mourning when the next oldest of the old men fell asleep while reading out the Fifth Eclogue of Virgil, and a strange voice spoke through him, and bid them set out for Paris, where a woman lay dying, who would reveal to them the secret names of the gods, which can be perfectly spoken only when the mind is steeped in certain colours and certain sounds and certain odours; but at whose perfect speaking the immortals cease to be cries and shadows, and walk and talk with one like men and women.

They left their island, at first much troubled at all they saw in the world, and came to Paris, and there the youngest met a person in a dream, who told him they were to wander about at hazard until those who had been guiding their footsteps had brought them to a street and a house, whose likeness was shown him in the dream. They wandered hither and thither for many days, but one morning they came into some narrow and shabby streets, on the south of the Seine, where women with pale faces and untidy hair looked at them out of the windows; and just as they were about to turn back because Wisdom could not have alighted in so foolish a neighborhood, they came to the street and the house of the dream. The oldest of the old men, who still remembered some of the modern languages he had known in his youth, went up to the door and knocked, but when he had knocked, the next in age to him said it was not a good house, and could not be the house they were looking for, and urged him to ask for some one that they knew was not there and go away. The door was opened by an old over-dressed woman, who said, 'O, you are her three kinsmen from Ireland. She has been expecting you all day.' The old men looked at one another and followed her upstairs, passing doors from which pale and untidy women thrust out their heads, and into a room where a beautiful woman lay asleep in a bed, with another woman sitting by her.

The old woman said: 'Yes, they have come at last; now she will be able to die in peace,' and went out.

'We have been deceived by devils,' said one of the old men, 'for the immortals would not speak through a woman like this.'

'Yes,' said another, 'we have been deceived by devils, and we must go away quickly.'

'Yes,' said the third, 'we have been deceived by devils, but let us kneel down for a little, for we are by the deathbed of one that has been beautiful.' They knelt down, and the woman who sat by the bed, and seemed to be overcome with fear and awe, lowered her head. They watched for a little the face upon the pillow and wondered at its look, as of unquenchable desire, and at the porcelain-like refinement of the vessel in which so malevolent a flame had burned.

Suddenly the second oldest of them crowed like a cock, and until the room seemed to shake with the crowing. The woman in the bed still slept on in her death-like sleep, but the woman who sat by her head crossed herself and grew pale, and the youngest of the old men cried out: 'A devil has gone into him, and we must begone or it will go into us also.' Before they could rise from their knees, a resonant chanting voice came from the lips that had crowed and said: 'I am not a devil, but I am Hermes the Shepherd of the Dead, and I run upon the errands of the gods, and you have heard my sign, that has been my sign from the old days. Bow down before her from whose lips the secret names of the immortals, and of the things near their hearts, are about to come, that the immortals may come again into the world. Bow down, and understand that when they are about to overthrow the things that are to-day and bring the things that were yesterday, they have no one to help them, but one whom the things that are to-day have cast out. Bow down and very low, for they have chosen for their priestess this woman in whose heart all follies have gathered, and in whose body all desires have awaked; this woman who has been driven out of Time and has lain upon the bosom of Eternity. After you have bowed down the old things shall be again, and another Argo shall carry heroes over sea, and another Achilles beleaguer another Troy.'

The voice ended with a sigh, and immediately the old man awoke out of sleep, and said: 'Has a voice spoken through me, as it did when I fell asleep over my Virgil, or have I only been asleep?'

The oldest of them said: 'A voice has spoken through you. Where has your soul been while the voice was speaking through you?'

'I do not know where my soul has been, but I dreamed I was under the roof of a manger, and I looked down and I saw an ox and an ass; and I saw a red cock perching on the hayrack; and a woman hugging a child; and three old men, in armour studded with rubies, kneeling with their heads bowed very low in front of the woman and the child. While I was looking the cock crowed and a man with wings on his heels swept up through the air, and as he passed me, cried out: "Foolish old men, you had once all the wisdom of the stars." I do not understand my dream or what it would have us do, but you who have heard the voice out of the wisdom of my sleep know what we have to do.'

Then the oldest of the old men told him they were to take the parchments they had brought with them out of their pockets and spread them on the ground. When they had spread them on the ground, they took out of their pockets their pens, made of three feathers, which had fallen from the wing of the old eagle that is believed to have talked of wisdom with St. Patrick.

'He meant, I think,' said the youngest as he put their ink-bottles by the side of the rolls of parchment, 'that when people are good the world likes them and takes possession of them, and so eternity comes through people who are not good or who have been forgotten. Perhaps Christianity was good and the world liked it, so now it is going away and the immortals are beginning to awake.'

'What you say has no wisdom,' said the oldest, 'because if there are many immortals, there cannot be only one immortal.'

Then the woman in the bed sat up and looked about her with wild eyes; and the oldest of the old men said: 'Lady, we have come to write down the secret names,' and at his words a look of great joy came into her face. Presently she began to speak slowly, and yet eagerly, as though she knew she had but a little while to live, and in the Gaelic of their own country; and she spoke to them many secret powerful names, and of the colours, and odours, and weapons, and instruments of music and instruments of handicraft belonging to the owners of those names; but most about the Sidhe of Ireland and of their love for the Cauldron, and the Whetstone, and the Sword, and the Spear. Then she tossed feebly for a while and moaned, and when she spoke again it was in so faint a murmur that the woman who sat by the bed leaned down to listen, and while she was listening the spirit went out of the body.

Then the oldest of the men said in French to the woman who was still bending over the bed: 'There must have been yet one name which she had not given us, for she murmured a name while the spirit was going out of the body,' and the woman said, 'She was but murmuring over the name of a symbolist painter she was fond of. He used to go to something he called the Black Mass, and it was he who taught her to see visions and to hear voices. She met him for the first time a few months ago, and we have had no peace from that day because of her talk about visions and about voices. Why! it was only last night that I dreamed I saw a man with a red beard and red hair, and dressed in red, standing by my bedside. He held a rose in one hand, and tore it in pieces with the other hand, and the petals drifted about the room, and became beautiful people who began to dance slowly. When I woke up I was all in a heat with terror.'

This is all the old men told me, and when I think of their speech and of their silence, of their coming and of their going, I am almost persuaded that had I gone out of the house after they had gone out of it, I should have found no footsteps on the snow. They may, for all I or any man can say, have been themselves immortals: immortal demons, come to put an untrue story into my mind for some purpose I do not understand. Whatever they were, I have turned into a pathway which will lead me from them and from the Order of the Alchemical Rose. I no longer live an elaborate and haughty life, but seek to lose myself among the prayers and the sorrows and the multitude. I pray best in poor chapels, where the frieze coats brush by me as I kneel, and when I pray against the demons I repeat a prayer which was made I know not how many centuries ago to help some poor Gaelic man or woman who had suffered with a suffering like mine.

Seacht b-páidreacha fó seacht
Chuir Muire faoi n-a Mac,
Chuir Brighid faoi n-a brat,
Chuir Dia faoi n-a neart,
Eidir sinn 'san Sluagh Sidhe,
Eidir sinn 'san Sluagh Gaoith.

Seven paters seven times,
Send Mary by her Son,
Send Bridget by her mantle,
Send God by His strength,
Between us and the faery host,
Between us and the demons of the air.

Substantial Variants

52–57 *rev. to* a dying woman would give them secret names and thereby so transform the world that another Leda would open her knees to the swan, another Achilles beleaguer Troy. ¶ They... 1925, 1932

99–103 *rev. to* sign. The woman who lies there has given birth, and that which she bore has the likeness of a unicorn and is most unlike man of all living things, being cold, hard and virginal. It seemed to be born dancing; and was gone from the room wellnigh upon the instant, for it is of the nature of the unicorn to understand the shortness of life. She does not know it has gone, for she fell into a stupor while it danced, but bend down your ears that you may learn the names that it must obey.' Neither of the other two old men spoke, but doubtless looked at the speaker with perplexity, for the voice began again: 'When the Immortals would overthrow... 1925, 1932

109–12 *rev. to* Eternity. ¶ The voice... 1925, 1932

142–43 down the names of the immortals,' and... 1897T

145–50 and, in English, with the accent of their own country; and she told them the secret names of the immortals of many lands, and of the colours, and odours, and weapons, and instruments of music and instruments of handicraft they held dearest; but most about the immortals of Ireland and of their love for the cauldron, and the whetstone, and the sword, and the spear, and the hills of the Shee, and the horns of the moon, and the Grey Wind, and the Yellow Wind, and the Black Wind, and the Red Wind. Then she tossed feebly a while... 1897T

154–66 *rev. to* one Immortal.' ¶ 'Yet it seems,' said the youngest, 'that the names we are to take down are the names of one, so it must be that he can take many forms.' ¶ Then the woman on the bed moved as in a dream, and held out her arms as though to clasp the being that had left her, and murmured names of endearment, and yet strange names, 'Harsh sweetness', 'Dear bitterness', 'O solitude', 'O terror', and after lay still for awhile. Then her voice changed, and she, no longer afraid and happy but seeming like any dying woman murmured a name so faintly that the woman who sat by the bed bent down and put her ear close to her mouth. ¶ The oldest of the old men said in French, 'There... 1925, 1932

Part Two: 1917–1920

Unpublished Dialogues and Extracts—

The Resurrection of Robartes and Aherne

Imaginary Conversations, "The Phases of the Moon," and the Robartes Monologue in *The Wild Swans at Coole*

The Robartes-Aherne dialogue "The Phases of the Moon" was first published on March 11, 1919, in the Macmillan trade edition of *The Wild Swans at Coole* (London and New York; *Wade* 124), which substantially augmented the 1917 Cuala Press collection of 29 lyrics, *The Wild Swans at Coole, Other Verses and a Play in Verse* (*Wade* 118), with 15 additional poems, as a rule published simultaneously in English and American magazines in 1917 and 1918, besides those privately printed by Clement Shorter in *Nine Poems* (October 1918).[1] "The Phases of the Moon" became a companion to the dialogue "Ego Dominus Tuus" with the verse-dedication "A Prayer on going into my House" intervening, making no question that the three poems together dramatized the poet (as *Ille*, seeking the image of his anti-self; as Sinbad, "myself for portions of the year"; and as "*the man within*," ridiculed in third-person by a fictional Owen Aherne, resurrected from a short story of 1896, "The Tables of the Law"). Together, the three poems introduced to the body of Yeats's poetry a new setting, that of Thoor Ballylee, near Coole Park and Gort, a village in Co. Galway. Aherne's companion in the poem is Michael Robartes, also a fictional character. Yeats wrote, feigning that they were actual men, that both Aherne

> and Robartes, to whose namesake I had attributed a turbulent life or death, have quarrelled with me. They take their place in a phantasmagoria in which I endeavour to explain my philosophy of life and death.... To some extent I wrote these poems as a text for exposition.[2]

In "Ego Dominus Tuus," Yeats had already brought Robartes back to life from an apparently fatal stoning at the end of the story "Rosa Alchemica" (1896), and Robartes's death had even been announced in another story, "The Adoration of the Magi" (1897). Dated in manuscript "Dec 5. 1915" (NLI 30,358, 67^{r}), "Ego Dominus Tuus" was originally published in America in *Poetry* (Chicago) and in the UK in *The New Statesman*, respectively, in October 1917 and 17 November 1917 issues, some twenty years after publication of the stories. *Ille*'s fellow, *Hic*, observes that, "Under your old wind-beaten tower, where still | A lamp burns on beside the open book | That Michael Robartes left, you walk in the moon, | … still trace, | Enthralled by the unconquerable delusion, | Magical shapes" (*VP* 367: 2–7). Aside from an elliptical allusion to "a Bedouin's horse-hair roof" in line 29, no other sign of Robartes, returned from Mesopotamia, occurs in the poem—nor anywhere else in the body of the philosophical treatise *Per Amica Silentia Lunae*, to which the poem was attached as a prolusion. Eventually, "The Phases of the Moon" served the first Book of *A Vision* ("What the Caliph Partly Learned" in

1925 and "The Great Wheel" in 1937) in the same way. Thus placing the two poems in apposition to one another in *The Wild Swans at Coole* is doubly significant as is, by later association, the relationship between *Per Amica Silentia Lunae* and *A Vision*. However, it is also possible to identify a specific genetic link between these texts based on the evidence of an unpublished dialogue entitled "Anglo Ireland. | a conversation" (NLI 30,103).

The word "conversation" is a clue to a common source in Yeats's reading. Walter Savage Landor and, specifically, his *Imaginary Conversations* were commended for demonstrating "calm nobility when the pen was in his hand," despite "the daily violence of his passion when he laid it down" (*Myth* 328). "A poet, when he is growing old, will ask himself if he cannot keep his mask and his vision without new bitterness, new disappointment" (342). As the poet of "Lines Written in Dejection," an eight-poem sequence of 1916 within *The Wild Swans at Coole* collection, Yeats himself had reached the crisis of middle age; consequently, he posed for all poets a question that was really self-referential:

> Could he if he would, knowing how frail his vigour from youth up, copy Landor who lived loving and hating, ridiculous and unconquered, into extreme old age, all lost but the favour of his Muses?
>
> The mother of the muses we are taught
> Is memory; she has left me; they remain
> And shake my shoulder urging me to sing. (342)[3]

In *A Vision*, Landor is numbered with the "*Antithetical* men" (*Mask* at Phase Three *AVA* 19, 42; *AVB* 84, 109) but enlisted among the "*Daimonic*" men of Yeats's own Phase Seventeen, with Dante and Shelley: "Landor has been examined in *Per Amica Silentia Lunae*. The most violent of men, he uses his intellect to disengage a visionary image of perfect sanity…seen always in the most serene and classic art imaginable" (*AVA* 78–79 and *AVB* 144–45). George Harper and Walter Hood have noted that Landor's name frequently occurs in the Automatic Script.[4] Yeats's lyric poem "To a Young Beauty," written in 1918, famously celebrates not only Yeats's affection for the beautiful Iseult Gonne, but also, I believe, much-annotated imaginary conversations between Landor as a character and various literary figures though John Donne was not one of them.[5] The evidence that we have from Yeats's reading notes in the six-volume *Imaginary Conversations* he owned (edited by Charles G. Crump [London: Dent, 1909]) is of sufficient quantity to warrant the account of an appendix to this commentary.[6] After proposing to Iseult Gonne and marrying on the rebound the young Georgina Hyde-Lees, in October 1917, Yeats exulted in a Landorian "calm nobility" with pen in hand, a profound satisfaction that had followed temporary disappointment:

I know what wages beauty gives,
How hard a life her servant lives,
Yet praise the winters gone:
There is not a fool can call me friend,
And I may dine at journey's end
With Landor and with Donne. (*VP* 336, ll. 13–18)

Yeats's praise of "winters gone" might well recall months spent writing at Stone Cottage, Sussex, with Ezra Pound in the winters of 1914–1916.[7] The following excerpts suggest as much and provide context for Yeats's reading and preparation for his adaptation of Landor in "Anglo Ireland. | a conversation," the dress-rehearsal for "The Phases of the Moon" in late 1917:

1. WBY to John Quinn, 19 Dec. [1915], from Woburn Buildings: "Ezra is to read Landor to me in the evenings. Last year I made him read Sagas & Doughty's Arabian travels & he was very bored till I allowed him to raise his spirits with Sordello" (*CL InteLex* 2831).[8]
2. WBY to Aleck Shepeler, [26 December 1915], from Stone Cottage: "…I am writing a letter to Leo Africanus, my 'daimon' & reading Landor" (*CL InteLex* 2838).[9]
3. WBY to Lady Gregory, [7 January 1916], from Stone Cottage: "… Ezra is reading out Walter Savage Landor in the evenings. It has great occasional beauty but much repetition of a few dominant thoughts" (*CL InteLex* 2844).
4. WBY to John Quinn, 29 November 1917, Stone Cottage: "…I am writing a new play, a fourth Cuchulain Play in the manner of the Noh, and a dialogue in the manner of Landor. My wife is an old friend of Dorothy Pound's so it is likely we shall see much of Ezra, at least if he can bear the country for a while, or we the town" (*CL InteLex* 3367).

For reasons that I have argued elsewhere,[10] the writing of "The Phases of the Moon" must have occurred before two of the philosophical Robartes-Aherne prose dialogues were written, called "The Discoveries of Michael Robartes" and eventually edited, selectively, by George M. Harper and Margaret M. Harper. "Yeats decided some time in 1918 to compose a book based on the revelations of the AS,…order[ing] the material in a series of conversations between Ahearne and Robartes," say the Harpers (*YVP4* 11). Catherine Paul and Margaret Harper, in their critical edition of *AVA*, date the writing of the Robartes-Aherne manuscripts from November 1917 to "the latter months of 1919," citing as key Yeats's letter to Quinn of 29 November 1917. In my reconstruction of the composition sequence of Yeats's Noh adaptations, including an unfinished fifth play (a "summary of 1918"), Yeats's plan, on 14 January 1918, to collect "my four or five Noh plays" (*L* 644) is also significant and dovetails with the conclusion of a years-long series of negotiations with the Gregorys and the Congested Districts Board for the purchase of Ballylee Castle, as well as with delayed plans for a honeymoon fishing-tour and layover at Coole demesne to supervise renovation of the Yeatses's new home in Ireland.[11] Due to George Yeats's influenza, the couple remained in rented quarters in Oxford until after Easter 1918. Though starting the dialogue "Anglo Ireland. | a conversation" months before that, the scene was indeed imagined and constructed from memory.

See NLI 30,103, folio 1, where (in part) the dialogue begins between the author and Owen Aherne as follows:

> WB Yeats.
> I stood here just now waiting for you, watching
> the gre[y] tower ~~in~~ through the ash trees, & a crow
> flying suddenly brought up again all the emotion
> all the emotion with which I first saw this
> building nearly thirty years ago. I do not know
> what it is in the flight of a crow accross grey
> stone that suggests something wild & ancient.
> . . .
> Owen Aherne.
> at Tullyhan was a
> I was staying ~~there when I heard~~ — that ~~is May~~
> year ago now — when I heard that ~~you wanted this house~~. (ll. 1–7, 13–14)

All six folios of this manuscript measure approximately 7-by-5 inches and are of lined notebook paper (20 light blue lines horizontally) with two holes punched on the left-hand side for use in a ring-binder, from which the six leaves have been removed. From this beginning to the end of the last folio, the dialogue has been written straight through, on rectos only, and characteristically in black ink. Even revisions were made with the same instrument, perhaps at a single sitting on the 29th of November 1917.

To give directions on renovations, Yeats had visited Ballylee on October 5th and wrote the next day to Miss Hyde-Lees, who would not become Mrs. W. B. Yeats for another two weeks, to report "mudd & litter ever[y]where" but assuring her that "[i]t looks so different in spring with the island full of daffodils." Deciding to delay her introduction to Ballylee, he directed her to "go straight to Stone Cottage & then when I have roofed & cleared the castle you can come & see it," equating the howling of the wind in the chimney with his longing to see her and equating himself with "Sinbad [of *Arabian Nights*] thrown upon the rocks & weary."[12] The swirling of the crows in the manuscript, like the flight of the falcon in "The Second Coming" and the "sudden thunder of the mounting swan" in "Coole Park and Ballylee, 1931," simulates a common enough sight but one noted as an omen in conjunction with the tower because of history and the emotion that Yeats attached to his own first impression of it, when his coveting of the property began, between 1897 and 1899, during his initial summers at Coole and Tillyra, the ancestral home of Edward Martyn. Tullaghan and its strange well, located south of Sligo, is the setting for Yeats's Cuchulain play *At the Hawk's Well*. Traveling about the Yeats Country, Aherne learned of the poet's acquisition.

See NLI 30,103, folio 2, which continues Aherne's speech from folio 1:

> You wanted this house. ~~Edward Martyn~~
> ...I longed to ask you
> why for it seemed an uncomfortable sort of place...
> WB Yeats.
> When I first saw, rising above its cottages, a
> ~~ford~~ between an ~~old ford~~ ford with ancient stepping
> stones & a bridge almost as ancient, no
> separate wall or garden but the trail ~~cut~~ carts
> passing under walls it seemed that ~~Lancelot~~
> ~~the knight of Arthur~~ I was in the Mort D'Arthur....
> Owen Aherne
> ~~You would set up~~ a symbol of unity of being
> of a people whose classes are distinct but not
> separate from [one] another. ~~That~~ The Tower rising out of
> a lowly life — its expression & its master (folio 2, ll. 1, 3–4, 6–11, 15–18)

On 4 January 1917, Yeats used a generous offer by Edward Martyn to bargain with the CDB for reduction of the price of Ballylee. Martyn, a Catholic who took the side of the clergy during the so-called "*Countess Cathleen* Row" of 1899, and Aherne, devout Catholic turned to dereliction in "The Tables of the Law," are of one party, like *Hic* versus *Ille* (or Willy). Aherne assumes the role of Landorean dialectician. The argument at this point is more reminiscent of later poems such as "The Tower" (II) "Meditations in Time of Civil War" (I-II), and "Blood and the Moon" (I-II) as Yeats listens to Aherne make the case for renovations at Ballylee as the fashioning of a personal symbol both *new* and *more* than merely Victorian nostalgia for "unity of being" in the old feudal order. In this imaginary conversation between himself and a creature of his invention, Yeats tries to define the tower as his personal symbol with Irish national and probably universal implications that he was simultaneously beginning to explore in the Robartes-Aherne dialogues.

Thus, Aherne continues, on NLI 30,103, folio 3:

> It suggests to me some thing new, some thing more
> intimate than a Morte D'Arth[ur]...
> he[re] lived perhaps
> the old medieval gaelic life & ~~in the house~~
> of some Catholic gentle man, who ~~in the sevent[eenth]~~
> ...had to carry his sword perhaps...to spain or France
> & died...fighting for some alien cause...
>
> WB Yeats
> If you come a little this way, I will show you
> where Mary Hynes used to live — the cottage is
> gone now some [?birch] bushes mark the place.
> ~~You remember rafterys song.~~ She
> was one of the tenants of the owner of this Tower
> & came to it often with butter & eggs & the like
> You remember the song. (ll. 1–2, 6–9, 14–20)

At this point, suppressing the local legend of Mary Hynes as Helen of Ballylee and the blind poet Anthony Raftery as Homer,[13] Yeats introduces a locution familiar to us from the final version of "The Phases of the Moon," namely the recitation of song at the inducement of Aherne. Only it is Yeats the character who begins singing to himself, rather than Robartes to Aherne, until Yeats the poet decides that it is still too early in the work for singing, and the impulse is arrested, postponed until folio 6.

See NLI 30,103, folio 4, begun with an unprecedented reference to Yeats singing:

> Owen Aherne.
> ~~I know you think I am getting back on~~ the old subject
> ~~& losing my way about~~
> What are you murmering
> WB Yeats
> ~~Milton~~ Ill Penseroso.
> quote (folio 4, ll. 1–5)

The prompt to insert "quote" (l. 5) from Milton's "Il Penseroso" (l. 4) could be to any passage, but it can hardly be doubted, because of the iconographic alignment of the scene with Samuel Palmer's famous illustration *The Lonely Tower* in *The Shorter Poems of John Milton* (London: Seeley, 1889) and to the reference to "the spirit of Plato" to which its caption[14] directs us:

> Or let my Lamp at midnight hour,
> Be seen in some high lonely Tow'r,
> Where I may oft outwatch the *Bear*,
> With thrice great *Hermes*, or unsphere
> The spirit of *Plato* to unfold
> What Worlds, or what vast Regions hold
> The immortal mind that hath forsook
> Her mansion in this fleshly nook:
> And of those *Dæmons* that are found
> In fire, air, flood, or underground,
> Whose power hath a true consent
> With Planet, or with Element. ("Il Penseroso," ll. 85–96)[15]

This passage produces the only reference to Plato in Milton's poem. Aherne makes a brusque comment on Yeats's manner of delivery "murmuring" as to suggest a gaggle of "wild geese," cleverly capitalized at one point to call too-obvious attention to the flight of the Irish Jacobite army, in 1691, at the end of the Williamite War in Ireland, and to the partisan political divide between Catholics such as Sarsfield and Aherne and Protestants such as Yeats and the author of "Il Penseroso." To Yeats's prompt to quote lines from Milton's poem in the dialogue, Aherne retorts (also in a cancelled passage) that Yeats's murmuring suggests a gaggle of wild geese and "to you some Platonist. You protestants have your quotations but I do not see much Platonics about you" (folio 4, ll. 6–8). If Aherne is not too subtle, but even gruff, in censuring Yeats's singing and his Protestantism—as one unfit to choose the tower as an "emblem" (ll. 15–16) in spite of all his poems about Ireland—he asks pardon: "Forgive me" (l. 12). Yet Aherne's disapproval runs deep, it seems, extending to Platonists generally and to Yeats in particular ("I do not see much Platonics about you"). If the suggestion is that Yeats might be a fraud, the accuser bears Landor's prejudice against Plato.[16] (See note 6 and Landor, *Imaginary Conversations*, vol. 1, "Diogenes and Plato," where, for instance, Diogenes criticizes Plato for being "learned and scholastic" [p. 100 and *passim*].)

Thereafter, the character named "WB Yeats" can only seem to defend himself by making superficial counter-assertions based on his rights by deed, the assurance of his solicitor, and the material evidence of the property (pieces of stone and thatch, clods of "earth from the garden"). He claims that he is literally entitled to sing because he bought all these. But the poet, in reality, is not satisfied with the argument; so for the better part of folio 5 the defense is withdrawn in a series of violent strokes (see facsimile and facing transcription below). In effect, the poet backs up to the bottom of folio 4 (to Aherne's "Forgive me") to pursue a more conciliatory tack in the dialogue, allowing differences to remain between the speakers. In order to claim the tower to be his own "fit emblem," Yeats recognizes that he "must sing wisdom" (folio 5, l. 12). This recognition constitutes an important tactical moment transferred to two later stages of work. Defending his right and intention to sing as a poet of Ireland, Yeats also speaks with vehemence and somewhat redirects his devotion: "I have so sung & shall so sing…that young men will remember <my> ~~me & my~~ tower <& me>. I <sang love> long enough ~~sung enough of love songs, & so~~ now I must sing wisdom" (ll. 9–12). Differences compound. Aherne asserts, "This tower suggests fights" though Yeats points out to him that the wall by the river bears stones that had once been part of Ballylee's chapel (ll. 13–16, all cancelled). Then, as space runs out on folio 5, at line 17, Aherne's sectarian critique of "You protestants" becomes even more pointed as, in NLI 30,103, folio 6,

> …the emblem ~~of the Protestant rule~~
> would be
> ~~[of] Ireland, is always~~ some house with a high domain wall
> ~~& I am ready to admit~~ Though I am ready to admit
> that…those eighteenth century land owners
> were good gardeners
> & behind that wall I am ready to admit an
> excellent garden ~~made in 1~~ first dug in 1750 &
> in 1760 let us say. But these ancient stones — (ll. 2–8)

whereupon "Anglo Ireland. | a conversation" breaks off unexpectedly:

> but what are you murmering
> WB Yeats
> lines from El Penseroso.
> I am thinking of George Burkeley (ll. 9–11)

Wisdom is not a chapel, and Aherne concedes the point. But neither is it an eighteenth-century Big House "with a high domain wall." He makes jest with barely disguised irony, allowing that decay brought on by "landowners"[17] in the great age of Protestant Anglo-Ireland provided "an excellent garden." The years cited signify a range of dates intersected by the lives of Yeats's four favourite writers of that time except Swift, who died in 1745. Precisely why those lines from "Il Penseroso" (first intended for folio 4) should elicit from Aherne's opponent the name "George Burkeley," misspelled as a conflation of Burke and Berkeley, remains an unsolved mystery of the dialogue because the singing of the poet's persona interrupts Aherne's argument, which seems to be antithetical to that of Milton's Platonist. Yet it is impossible to say with certainty because the dialogue abruptly ends.

A good start but a false one, in many ways, in relation to "The Phases of the Moon" as we know it. In embryonic state, including unexpected departures in later drafts, the poem promised "simple" wisdom which could not have fully anticipated, as a prolusion, the philosophical toil of *A Vision* for the next two decades. In fact, Yeats's conception of the poem changed radically in the course of its writing, although the scene was always pastoral and bound to the atmosphere, if not the location, of Thoor Ballylee. Among the manuscripts of "The Phases of the Moon" on file at the National Library of Ireland, in NLI 13,587 (21), are two sheets (three pages) of holograph material as well as one folio (two pages) from the Occult Papers of W. B. Yeats (NLI Collection List No. 60) to disclose a very different mode of exposition from what we have seen in the Yeats-Aherne dialogue and different, still, from the one later devised for the poem with Robartes and Aherne as speakers. The first speech of the fragment renders imagery parallel to that applied to Fand and the Sidhe in *The Only Jealousy of Emer*, seductresses who "drop their hair upon" men, "Lap them in cloudy hair or kiss their lips" (*VPl* 549, ll. 214a and 214), to steal men's souls. We find Cuchulain conversing with an immortal, Aengus, who may not leave him until death, one who begins to chant, when asked "What is that you reckon on your fingers" the familiar opener, "Twenty & eight the phases of the moon | The full & the moons dark and all the crescents [etc.]" (cf. *VP* 373, ll. 31ff.), continuing for 21 lines in that vein until he reaches a long hiatus of three manuscript pages. Aengus's disappearance at the end of the next fragment has precedent in the tale "The Only Jealousy of Emer" in Lady Gregory's *Cuchulain of Muirthemne*. Except for the hiatus, we have 5 pages constituting the introductory and concluding parts of the work's frame. Essentially narrative in conception, the surviving fragments of this version of "The Phases of the Moon" present a visionary speaker, Aengus (identified by name at one point) who is disguised much as he had been in Yeats's narrative poem "Baile and Aillinn" (1903): a "crude ragged man" here, as elsewhere "an old man" with "ragged long grass-coloured hair," "that old gaunt crafty one" (*VP* 190, ll. 25–26 and 193, l. 100). Impossible to know how the dialogic between Aengus and the author's surrogate Cuchulain developed in full, what remains of the draft reflects Yeats's attempt to bring animation to his first poem about "the system."[18]

Among the revelations that the manuscripts have in store for us, besides the Landorian imaginary conversation between Yeats and Aherne as a prototype, is that the poem's relations at stage two were Yeats's own early poems "The Harp of Aengus" (*VP* 219, l. 2: "young Aengus in his tower of glass") and "Under the Moon" (*VP* 209, l. 8: "Land-of-the-tower, where Aengus has thrown the gates apart"). Although the second stage of composition ended where the poem begins in the poem's third and final stage, Yeats "system," as delivered in lines 31–123 of "The Phases of the Moon," seems to have been in place. The mystical Robartes had only to take possession of it from Aengus. Conjecturally, this surgical procedure may have begun by lifting the numbered pages (the extant frame) of the Aengus-Cuchulain version from early draft material intended for the play *The Only Jealousy of Emer* in NLI 8774 (14), with which Yeats struggled and chose to set aside in preference to *The Dreaming of the Bones*. Paper types are a match and the lacunae are roughly correspondent. Transposing speakers from Aengus to Robartes, reverting to Aherne from his dialogue with Yeats, and dispatching the latter to his high tower as Milton's Platonist, at close distance but beyond detecting Aherne's dismissal of Ballylee's "stark | Austerity, a place set out for wisdom | That [Yeats] will never find" (*VP* 377, ll. 126–28)—all of this will have occurred by or before June 1918, because of renewed work on the "Cuchulain Play," with completion of the poem, finally, with the return of proofs for *The Wild Swans at Coole* (1919) on 4 October 1918.

In revising the poem at stage three, the narrative preface of lines 1–7 began to take shape around the "rocks & briars," an "uneven road," and "that late scarce risen dwindling crescent" of the moon, in keeping with the actual scene of Yeats's new property but with a symbolic shift to the iconography of Samuel Palmer's illustration, "The Lonely Tower," from "a crow across grey stone that suggests something wild & ancient" and "the circling overhead of hundreds of crows before they settle in the tree tops for the night" (NLI 30,103, folio 1, ll. 6–7 and 9–11). The well-known picture in *The Shorter Poems of John Milton* bore beneath it less than four complete lines of "Il Penseroso" (ll. 85–88), ones that represented for Yeats a passage he thought, at two points, the character Yeats might quote in the imaginary conversation, in effect serving the composition of "The Phases of the Moon" as an exploratory first draft in prose. Palmer's illustration was also accompanied by an explanatory note to direct the reader's attention to the constellation of stars hanging over the tower in the engraving as in Milton's poem, instead of crows; and the caption drew attention to two shepherds, seated in the foreground, who "speak together of the mysterious light above them." In the latter, the "spirit of Plato" presides, in contrast to Aherne's expression of doubt, in the first draft, that there was much "Platonics" to be seen in Yeats. Always prone to oppose his author and *alter ego* (Yeats), the fictitious Aherne eventually contributes to *A Vision* (1925) its "Introduction," where he discloses that

> On a walking tour in Connaught we [he and Robartes] passed Thoor Ballylee where Mr Yeats had settled for the summer, and words were spoken between us slightly resembling those in "The Phases of the Moon," and I noticed that as his [Robartes's] friendship with me grew closer, his animosity against Mr Yeats revived. (*AVA* pp. xx-xxi)

The depiction is a convenient way to suggest a parallel between the poem and the rustic elegy "Shepherd and Goatherd," written in March 1918 and similarly advancing, by means of the Goatherd's song, the tenets of occult philosophy, in that case the doctrine of "Dreaming Back." As travelling men, the duo Robartes and Aherne in "The Phases of the Moon" bear semblance to Eros and Anteros, mythical opposites who journey about creation trying to find one another and complete oneself, until each, according to Milton, succeeds, "kindles and repairs the almost faded ammunition of his Deity by the reflection of a coequal and *homogeneal* fire. Thus mine author sung it to me."[19] The "crux" of "The Phases of the Moon," as I have said elsewhere at length (see notes 14 and 18), is therefore *both* Miltonic and Platonic, as affirmed in Yeats's slightly clipped attribution of authority left in Aherne's request that Robartes should "Sing…the changes of the moon once more; | True song, though speech: 'mine author sung it me'" (*VP* 373, ll. 29–30). The reference to Plato in Milton's tract on divorce is both a rhetorical obligation and a tribute. However, out of context in Yeats, it is an obscurity, an element of mystery, a part of the Yeatsian "phantasmagoria."

Faithful to his "First Principle," Yeats was determined not to write "directly" of his own personal experience "as to someone at the breakfast table" (*E&I* 509). Dialogues, as Yeats read in *Plato and Platonism* (the likely reason that Pater appears in the poem), move intelligence up the ladder of the dialectical process. In the second draft, Aengus observes that man "longs | To come into possession of himself" (NLI 13,587 [21], 13^{v}). The dialogue's *processus*, according to Pater, is one with this objective since it involves "that dynamic, or essential, dialogue of the mind with itself."[20] So Pater helped define a literary genre for Yeats, it would appear, if Milton suggested a philosophical basis for its development: "the essence of that method, of 'dialectic' in all its forms, as its very name denotes, is dialogue, the habit of seeking truth by means of question and answer, primarily with one's self."[21] Tactically, as a framing architecture, Aherne's "Introduction" and his piece "The Dance of the Four Royal Persons" were also components of the phantasmagoria, positioned on opposite sides of "The Phases of the Moon" in the preliminary pages and opening section of *A Vision* (1925), with parenthetical intrusions elsewhere signed "O.A." The necessity to invent a tactical device with which to introduce one or more set-pieces of verse interspersed with conversation was important, at first occurring as interruptions by the murmuring of speaker-Yeats, prompting Aherne to ask what Yeats is singing (NLI 30,103, folios 4 and 6); secondly by Cuchulain's query to Aengus on what he is reckoning on his fingers (NLI 13,587 [21], 13^{r}); and finally Aherne's request to hear Robartes's recitation of the phases as "Mine Author sung it me" (NLI 13,587 [21], 2^{v}). Robartes is given the spotlight in the poem, and the source material for *A Vision,* according to Aherne's assertion, is said to be the "Robartes MSS" (*AVA* 10). But Aherne, we recall, bears an antithetical relation to the persona that Yeats has fashioned for himself, very like one's impression of Landor when reading and then imitating the *Imaginary Conversations*. In precisely that enterprise, Yeats becomes "part of his own phantasmagoria," and we therefore "adore him because nature has grown intelligible," part of our own collective "creative power" (*E&I* 509).

❧

Apart from "The Phases of the Moon," the only other poem first collected in *The Wild Swans of Coole* (1919) and put to later use in *A Vision A* and *A Vision B* is "The Double Vision of Michael Robartes,"[22] though other lyrics of 1918 are kindred. For instance, "The Saint and the Hunchback" foreshadows Yeats's depiction of Phases 26 and 27 on the Wheel of Incarnation, and "A Prayer on Going into My House," "Two Songs of a Fool," and "Another Song of a Fool" all celebrate the empathy of husband (W. B. Yeats, dreamer, fool, scholar) and wife (George Yeats, dream-mate, speckled cat, butterfly) as succeeded by such delightful contemporary poems about their mystical exploits as "Solomon and the Witch," "An Image from a Past Life," and the Complementary Dream lyric "Towards Break of Day" from *Michael Robartes and the Dancer*. In his study of the making of *The Wild Swans at Coole* poems, Stephen Parrish argues that, "[b]y pairing 'The Phases of the Moon' with 'The Double Vision of Michael Robartes' at the close [of the poetry collection in 1919], Yeats clearly intended to signal his turn away from the prevailing mode of the 1917 [Cuala Press] volume and his work from his marriage onward."[23] Yeats's pairing of the poems was also attempted through the agency of Ezra Pound, on 15 July 1918, for consideration by the editors of *The Little Review*, with notice given to the particular stage reached in the writing of Yeats's Robartes-Aherne dialogues in prose:

> My dear Ezra: I send you "The Phases of the Moon" which should go with "The Double Vision" if you want to use that? …I am now at the 30th page of my prose dialogue expounding the symbol & there will be 3 dialogues of some 40 pages each, full of my sort of violence & passion.… (*CL InteLex* 3461)

Neither poem subsequently appeared in *The Little Review*, nor anywhere else before publication of *The Wild Swans at Coole* in March 1919.

However, unlike "The Phases of the Moon," which uses verse to introduce figuratively the philosophical matter to follow it in plain prose in *A Vision*, "The Double Vision of Michael Robartes" is quoted there on various occasions, briefly, and always embedded in texts that serve as glosses to help explain the meaning of its unusual imagery, particularly that of juxtaposed Sphinx and Buddha reconciled by the girl dancing between them, "outdanc[ing] thought," a state of "Mind moved yet seem[ing] to stop | As 'twere a spinning-top" (*VP* 384 ll. 43–4; *CW1* 173), completing for the reader a geometrical figure summoned to the mind's eye as in the poet's vision. The explanation given for this in *A Vision A*:

> In the *Beatitude* and in the states that immediately follow, the man is subject to his *Daimon* only, and there is no alternation of sleeping and waking. In the *Beatitude* communication with the living is through that state of soul, where an extreme activity is indistinguishable from an equal passivity. (*CW13* 196; *AVA* 238)

This occurs in part X of Book IV, "The Gates of Pluto," unique to *A Vision A* and its investment in the fictitious Robartes's supposed Arabian authority, Kusta ben Luka, on the Dreaming Back and on spiritual cycles approaching and following the discarnate Phase 15. In Book III of *A Vision A*, in part of the final movement of "Dove or Swan" withheld from *A Vision B*, lines 9–12 are quoted to characterize "the last gyre," with which "must come a desire to be ruled or rather, seeing that desire is all but dead, as adoration of force spiritual or physical, and society as mechanical force [is] complete at last" (*AVA* 213). With these earlier glosses gone by 1937, a new Book II called "The Completed Symbol" reproduced three full stanzas of the poem to illustrate the conjunction of opposites as "heraldic supporters guarding the mystery of the fifteenth phase" (with the caveat that Christ should have been substituted for Buddha, according to the instructors):

> Although I saw it all in the mind's eye
> There can be nothing solider till I die; I saw by the moon's light
> Now at its fifteenth night.
>
> One [the Sphinx] lashed her tail; her eyes lit by the moon
> Gazed upon all things known, all things unknown,
> In triumph of intellect
> With motionless head erect.
>
> The other's [the Buddha's] moonlit eyeballs never moved,
> Being fixed on all things loved, all things unloved,
> Yet little peace he had,
> For those that love are sad. (*VP* 383 ll. 25–36; *CW1* 173)

An earlier gloss to the same passage occurs in the typescript of the dialogue "The Discoveries of Michael Robartes," where Robartes explains to Aherne that "[t]he images at fifteen do not [a]ffect the automatic portions of the mind at all[;] for[,] being each one separate and complete[,] they cannot start any sequence of thought and image[;] the mind in their presence is stationary in a Buddha[-] or Sphinx[-] like trance of wonder" (*YVP4* 41 and 58 n.139). "All thought becomes an image" at that stage in "The Phases of the Moon" (*VP* 374 l. 58; *CW1* 166), and Yeats felt that the latter helped clear up the "too obscure" symbolism of "The Double Vision of Michael Robartes" (letter to Ezra Pound, cit. *YVP4* 4) and so gave priority to the former in *The Wild Swans at Coole* and both editions of *A Vision*.

The metaphor of the dancer as representative of the mind in trance-like, passive state could only be suggested, of course, by the example of the actual George Yeats in the creation of the automatic script (AS). But the AS itself proved to be a fertile source for the origin of poetry, as the emergence of "The Double Vision of Michael Robartes" shows, from the session of 7 January 1919 (*YVP2* 162–63 and *MYV2* 198–202). The contemporary plays were sometimes complexly related to the events of these sessions and grew occasionally from a number of sessions and therefore part of the making of *A Vision*. Out of the analogy between the beatific mind/soul negotiating the counterpointed "evil and good" of Sphinx and Buddha, or Christ, grew in 1918–19 a line of inquiry on the Evil Genius. To take up first the last of Yeats's original four "plays for dancers," *Calvary* began as a "Judas play" and wound up as a "Christ play" with thematic and constructive parallels born out of Yeats's second Noh play, *The Dreaming of the Bones*.[24] A "reconstructive interpretation" of *Calvary* from the evidence of the AS has been made by Janis Haswell.[25] Perhaps the choral speeches in the manuscript (NLI 30,361) and those of the First Musician in the second draft are all that remains of a Sinn Feiner (as in *The Dreaming of the Bones*) conversing "with Judas in the streets of Dublin" (*L* 645) from first conception. In manuscript, in the opening "Song of folding & unfolding [of the cloth]," "The savior of men dreams his bitter dream | Sees those that mocked him," dreaming himself back through the psychic trauma of the last moments of his life, repeatedly enduring the mockery of those whom he has saved. Thus he carries an invisible cross in an "Asiatic street," not a Dublin roadway, the gist of the plot borne by the arguments of the ungrateful Lazarus and the arch-betrayer, Judas. The "Song for the folding and unfolding of the cloth" in the published version of 1921 displaces Christ with a symbolic bird, following the precedents of hawk, sea-bird, and birds crying in loneliness, wheeling overhead in the plays that accompanied *Calvary* in *Four Plays for Dancers* (Macmillan, 1921; *Wade* 129):

> Motionless under the moon-beam,
> Up to his feathers in the stream,
> Although fish leap, the white heron
> Shivers in a dumbfounded dream. (*VPl* 780, ll. 1–4; *CW2* 329)

Christ "stands amid a mocking crowd" and the First Musician sings:

Oh, but the mockers' cry
Makes my heart afraid,
As though a flute of bone
Taken from a heron's thigh,
A heron crazed by the moon,
Were cleverly, softly played. (*VPl* 781–82, ll. 31–6; *CW2* 330)

The pronouncement of mockery and ensuing demonstration of it by the chorus and by the Roman Soldiers at the play's end recall Yeats's vituperative treatment of the subject in the poem "Nineteen Hundred and Nineteen":

Mock mockers after that
That would not lift a hand maybe
To help good, wise or great
To bar that foul storm out, for we
Traffic in mockery. (*VP* 432, ll. 108–112; *CW1* 213)

And in that poem, the insipient modern age is brought on with the Platonic Year, "Whirl[ing] out new right and wrong," reminiscent of that pivotal girl in "The Double Vision of Michael Robartes," near the middle of the poem, with the remembered effect of "Loie Fuller's Chinese dancers enwound | A shining web, a floating ribbon of cloth" seemingly changed into a "dragon of air," "hurr[ying] them off on its own furious path" (ll. 49–51 and 53).

The dancer in "The Double Vision of Michael Robartes" may indeed "represent the swirl of creation," as Matthew DeForrest has suggested,[26] anticipating the conclusion of "Dove or Swan" and "All Souls' Night: An Epilogue" in *A Vision*. In Yeats's first monologue in twenty years to identify its speaker as Michael Robartes (that is, since *The Wind Among the Reeds*), "The Double Vision" not only anticipates the title-poem of his next collection, *Michael Robartes and the Dancer*, but also, to be fair to Robartes's alter ego, "Owen Aherne and his Dancers" in *The Tower*. The iconography of "The Double Vision" differs from that of the waxing and waning male and female gyres juxtaposed in *A Vision A* by analogy to Blake's "The Mental Traveller."[27] Rather, the whirling dancer, mediating between two countervailing cosmic polarities, anticipates the tensions between male doubles in the burlesque triangles of *Stories of Michael Robartes and His Friends* (1931), wherein even Michael Robartes in his quest for wisdom of the ages "falls violently in love with a ballet-dancer who had not an idea in her head" but whose rejection of him leads to his accidental discovery of the book of Giraldus when thrown from the bed of "an ignorant girl of the people" (*SMR* 7). These matters will be addressed in later sections of the present study. Suffice it to say here that once Yeats had reintroduced Aherne and Robartes to the public in "The Phases of the

Moon" and "The Double Vision of Michael Robartes," and but briefly in "Ego Dominus Tuus," an excuse for their absence of a generation was improvised in a note first introduced in *Later Poems* (1922). Quoted in part at the outset of this commentary, the note is given in full on page 114, below, functioning in its own way as a pivot to the next section.

Notes

1. See *YPM* 92–95. The "Play in Verse" in the title is *At the Hawk's Well*, the first of several "plays for dancers" that Yeats wrote in the manner of the Japanese theater of the Noh.
2. In *Later Poems* (1922), Yeats notes that Robartes had "lately returned from Mesopotamia, where he has partly found and partly thought out much philosophy" (*VP* 821).
3. O'Donnell attributes sources for the first reference to Landor (above) as being, on the one hand, the dialogue "Machiavelli and Michel-Angelo" in *Imaginary Conversations*, IV, p. 192 (see note 6 below for my account of Yeats's readings in Landor), but also a letter to John Forster's *Walter Savage Landor: A Biography* (London: Chapman and Hall, 1869), II, p. 12. The quotation from Landor's poem "Memory" (ll. 1–3) is found in volume II, p. 273, of Landor's *Poems, Dialogues in Verse, and Epigrams* in Yeats's library (also cited in note 6 below). W. B. Yeats, *Later Essays*, ed. William H. O'Donnell, pp. 294, n. 19 and 299, n. 58.
4. *A Critical Edition of Yeats's* A Vision *(1925)*, Notes, p. 15, n. 42.
5. R. H. Super, in "Dining with Landor," *YAACTS* 5 (1987), speculates that "Donne is of the party, no doubt, both because of the obvious care with which his poems are wrought and because he too [like Landor] was scarcely known in his day" (143).
6. A comprehensive account of Yeats's reading notes in Landor's *Imaginary Conversations* and elsewhere is available in Wayne K. Chapman, "'Something Intended, Complete': Major Work on Yeats Past, Present, and Yet to Come," in *Yeats, Philosophy and the Occult*, ed. Matthew Gibson and Neil Mann (Clemson, SC: Clemson University Press, 2016), "Appendix—Annotations in the Writings of Walter Savage Landor in Yeats's Library." In volumes 1–2, Landor drew attention to his wit and epigrammatic *bons mots*, aspects of his style of writing especially noted in the check marks and strokes Yeats made, and later made by his wife, in the margins and endpapers of vol. 3, in "Dialogues of Literary Men," regarding successive speeches of Landor as a character in "The Abbé Delille and Walter Landor" dialogue (e.g., "In poetry there is a greater difference between the good and the excellent than there is between the bad and the good" [p. 270]); or in vol. 4, pp. 234–99, in "Southey and Landor," for checks and strokes *passim*; or in vol. 5, starting at "Dialogues of Famous Women" and emphasizing "Marchese Pallavicini and Walter Landor"; or in vol. 6 and "Florentine, English Visitor, and Landor." Although receiving less notice than *Imaginary Conversations*, even Crump's editions of *The Longer Prose Works* (1911) in 2 vols. and *Poems, Dialogues in Verse, and Epigrams* (1909) in 2 vols. show Yeats actively engaged with Landor's fictitious exploits.
7. A. Norman Jeffares, *A New Commentary on* The Poems of W. B. Yeats (Stanford, CA: Stanford University Press, 1984), 143.
8. On "Sagas & Doughty's Arabian travels"—see William Morris and Eiríkr Magnússon (trans.), *The Saga Library* (London: Bernard Quaritch, 1891–1905), 6 vols. (*WBGYL* 1407; *YL* 1395); and Charles M. Doughty, *Wanderings in Arabia: Being an Abridgement of* Travels in Arabia Deserta, ed. Edward Garnett (London: Duckworth, 1908), 2 vols. (*WBGYL* 551; *YL* 539). Later, Yeats acquired an unabridged version of 1923 (*WBGYL* 550; *YL* 538). The reference to "Sordello," as a source among Yeats's books, is possibly to volume 3 of *The Poetical Works of Robert Browning*: entitled *Paracelsus, Christmas-Eve and Easter-Day, Sordello* (London: Chapman and

Hall, 1865), with original drawings and notes by John Butler Yeats (*WBGYL* 305; *YL* 297). Cf. Ezra Pound's *Canto* II. On 29 January [1915], Yeats wrote to Lady Gregory: "At night Ezra reads out Doughty's 'Arabia Deserta' & Some Icelandic Saga" (*CL InteLex* 2592). On 5 March [1915], he wrote to her in more specifics: "I did much work & read nearly the whole of Wordsworth & had read out Doughty's 'Arabia Deserta,' 2 vols 'Grettir the Strong' 'Burnt Nigal' & some small sagas, & Brownings 'Sordello'" (*CL InteLex* 2611).

9. On "I am writing a letter to Leo Africanus"—see W. B. Yeats, "The Manuscript of 'Leo Africanus,'" ed. Steve L. Adams and George Mills Harper, in *YA* 1 (1982): 3–47; rpt. in *YA* 19 (2013): 289–335; see also James Longenbach, *Stone Cottage: Pound, Yeats, and Modernism* (Oxford: Oxford University Press, 1988), 187–89 and 193–94, on WBY's reading Landor in preparation for his communication with Leo.
10. *YPM* 130 and 320 (notes 10 and 11).
11. *YPM* 103–110 and 314–16 (notes 14–26).
12. W. B. Yeats and George Yeats, *The Letters*, ed. Ann Saddlemyer (Oxford: Oxford University Press, 2011), 10–12. Another letter that Yeats sent his wife later (on August 18 [or 19?] [1918]) similarly worries about bad weather and an avian phenomenon prior to her joining him: "This afternoon I go to Ballylee unless the rain, which threatens, comes in earnest. Three aero-planes have just passed over flying low & causing much fright among the crows. That is all my news" (23).
13. Yeats's *Celtic Twilight* piece "Dust Hath Closed Helen's Eye" (first published in *The Dome* in October 1899) was his earliest literary account of Hynes and Raftery at Ballylee, including Lady Gregory's translation of the bard's song; see *Mythologies*, ed. Warwick Gould and Deirdre Toomey, 14–19 and 224–31. For the impact of the Hynes-Raftery story on what was to have been Yeats's most ambitions Noh play, see *YPM* 97–127.
14. See text, Palmer plate, and notes in Wayne K. Chapman, *Yeats and English Renaissance Literature* (London: Macmillan Press, 1991), 188–96, 260–62, and Pl. 9; also *YA* 8 (1991): 59–77 & illus. (plate 4); and *YPM* 136–42 and 321–323.
15. John Milton, *Complete Poems and Major Prose*, ed. Merritt Y. Hughes (Indianapolis: Odyssey, 1957), 74.
16. Harper and Hood comment that, in draft materials correspondent with Yeats's treatment of Phase 18, on p. 81 of *A Vision A* (1925), Yeats added in parenthesis: "note—Landor hated Plato" (*CVA* Notes, p. 23, 8n).
17. Perhaps Aherne roughly pinpoints in the mid-eighteenth century the decline of country estates as had been portrayed in Maria Edgeworth's *Castle Rackrent; an Hibernian Tale taken from facts and from the Manners of the Irish Squires before the year 1782* (1832). Yeats praised Edgeworth, whose novel he gave prominence of place in his *Representative Irish Tales* (1891; rpt. Gerrards Cross, UK: Colin Smythe, 1979), observing that, "[w]hen writing of people of her own class she saw everything about them as it really was. She constantly satirized their recklessness, their love for all things English, their oppression of and contempt for their own country" (28).
18. I began documenting this discovery in my doctoral dissertation in 1988, which became *Yeats and English Renaissance Literature* in 1991, the same year I published a sustained focus on the making of "The Phases of the Moon" in *Yeats Annual* (see note 61, above). In three years, Stephen Parrish published *The Wild Swans at Coole: Manuscript Materials* (Ithaca, NY: Cornell University Press, 1994), with its high-fidelity images and diplomatic transcriptions, which permitted various improvements, in 2010, in *YPM*, including the addition of the single folio filed away among materials related to *A Vision*, making a contiguous unit at the conclusion of the Aengus-Cuchulain dialogue.
19. John Milton, *The Doctrine and Discipline of Divorce* (1644), I.vi. The Richard Garnett edition of the *Prose of Milton* (London: Walter Scott, 1894) is the probable source of Yeats's quotation.

20. Walter Pater, *Plato and Platonism* (London: Macmillan, 1893; *WBGYL* 1549 [*YL* 1538]), 166–67.
21. Pater, *Plato and Platonism*, 161.
22. The final movement of this commentary, on "The Double Vision of Michael Robartes," follows closely the case made for the poem in my chapter "'Metaphors for Poetry': Concerning the Poems of *A Vision* and Certain Plays for Dancers," in *YVEC*, especially 225–28.
23. Stephen Parrish, "Introduction" to W. B. Yeats, *The Wild Swans at Coole: Manuscript Materials*, ed. Stephen Parrish (Ithaca, NY: Cornell University Press, 1994), xxxv.
24. See W. B. Yeats, *"The Dreaming of the Bones" and "Calvary": Manuscript Materials*, ed Wayne K. Chapman (Ithaca, NY: Cornell University Press, 2003), especially xxxv-xlii, for a detailed account. This source will recur in the treatment of Yeats's notes to three of his Noh adaptions in *Four Plays for Dancers* (1921).
25. Janis Haswell, "Resurrecting *Calvary*: A Reconstructive Interpretation of W. B. Yeats's Play and Its Making," in *YA* 15 (2002): 159–89.
26. Matthew DeForrest, W. B. Yeats's *A Vision*: "Dove or Swan," in *YVEC* 153.
27. See Chapman, "Metaphors for Poetry," 237–39, as well as *YPM* 154–85 (the latter for a sustained treatment of "Blake, Swedenborg, and *A Vision*: A Case for Recombinate Influence").

[NLI 30,103, folio 1]

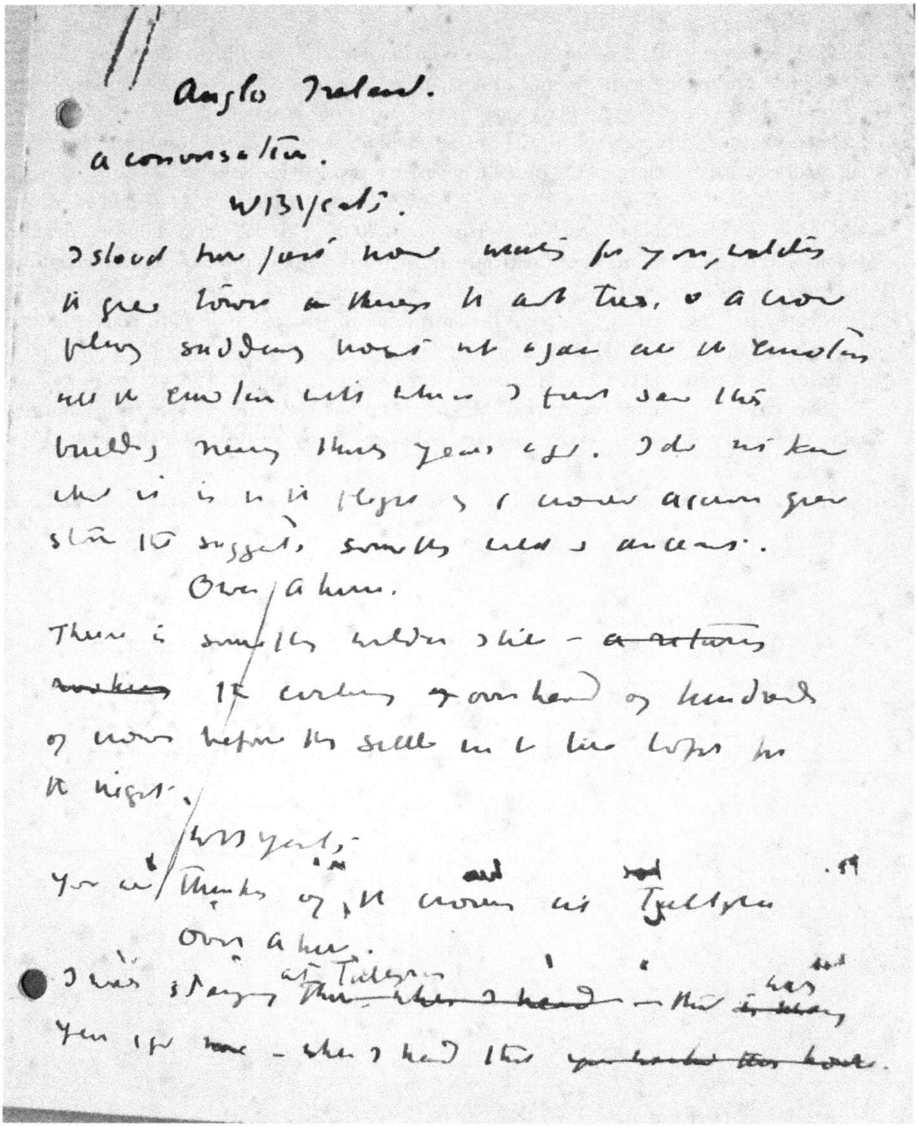
Anglo Ireland.

a conversation.

WBYeats.

[NLI 30,103, folio 1]

Anglo Ireland.

a conversation.

WB Yeats.

I stood here just now waiting for you, watching
the gre[y] tower ~~in~~ through the ash trees, & a crow
flying suddenly brought up again all the emotion
all the emotion with which I first saw this
building nearly thirty years ago. I do not know
what it is in the flight of a crow accross grey
stone that suggests something wild & ancient.

Owen Aherne.

There is something wilder still — ~~a returning~~
~~rookery~~ the circling ~~of~~ over head of hundreds
of crows before they settle in the tree tops for
the night.

WB Yeats

~~[?]~~ [?] [?and] ~~god~~ [?]
You are thinking of the crows at Tullyhan
^

Owen Aherne.

at Tullyhan was a
I was staying ~~there when I heard~~ — that ~~is May~~
year ago now — when I heard that ~~you wanted this house~~.

[NLI 30,103, folio 2]

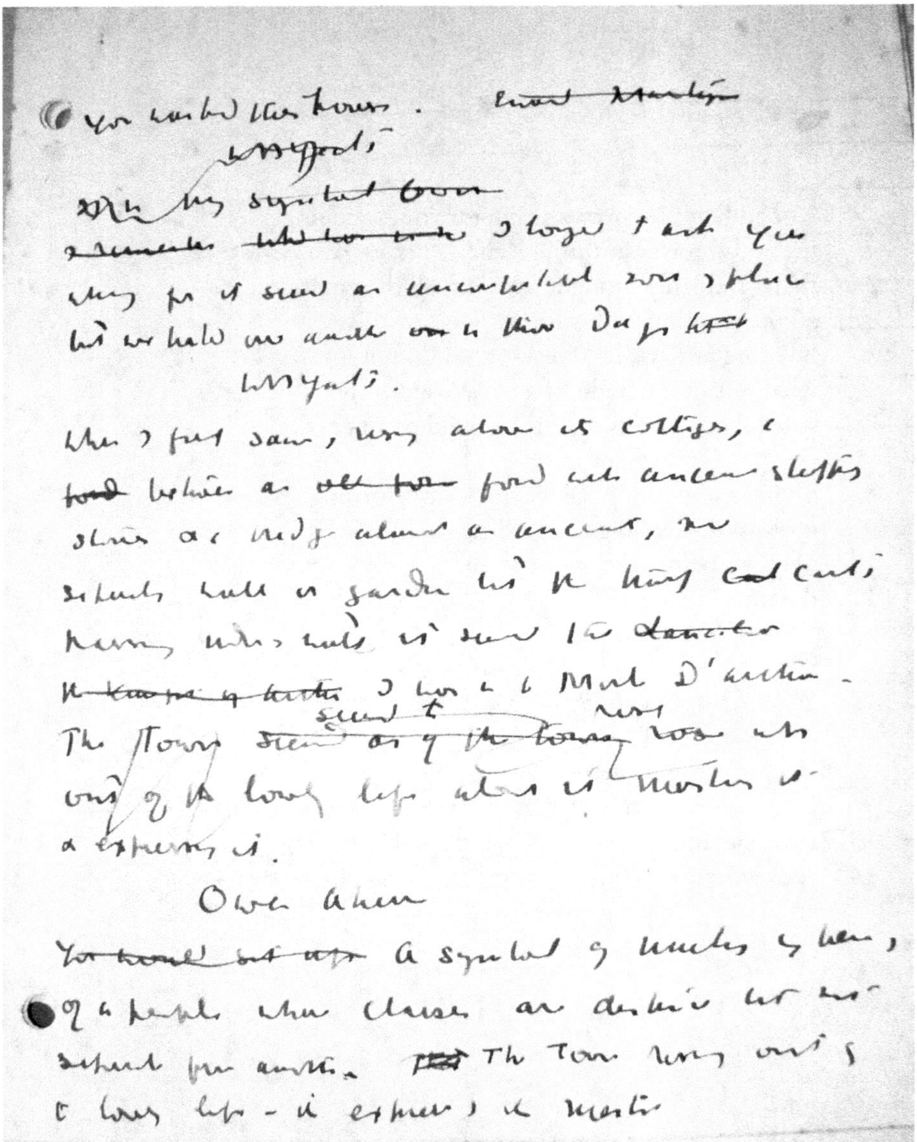

[NLI 30,103, folio 2]

You wanted this house. ~~Edward Martyn~~
~~WB Yeats~~
~~It is my symbol Owen~~
~~I remember who was in the~~ I longed to ask you
why for it seemed an uncomfortable sort of place
but we hated one another ~~on~~ in those days ~~but~~
WB Yeats.
When I first saw, rising above its cottages, a
~~ford~~ between an ~~old ford~~ ford with ancient stepping
stones & a bridge almost as ancient, no
separate wall or garden but the trail ~~cut~~ carts
passing under walls it seemed that ~~Lancelot~~
~~the knight of Arthur~~ I was in the Mort D'Arthur.
seemed to rise
The Tower ~~seemed as if the tower rose~~ up
out of the lowly life about it mastering it
& expressing it.
Owen Aherne
~~You would set up~~ a symbol of unity of being
of a people whose classes are distinct but not
separate from [one] another. ~~That~~ The Tower rising out of
a lowly life — its expression & its master

[NLI 30,103, folio 3]

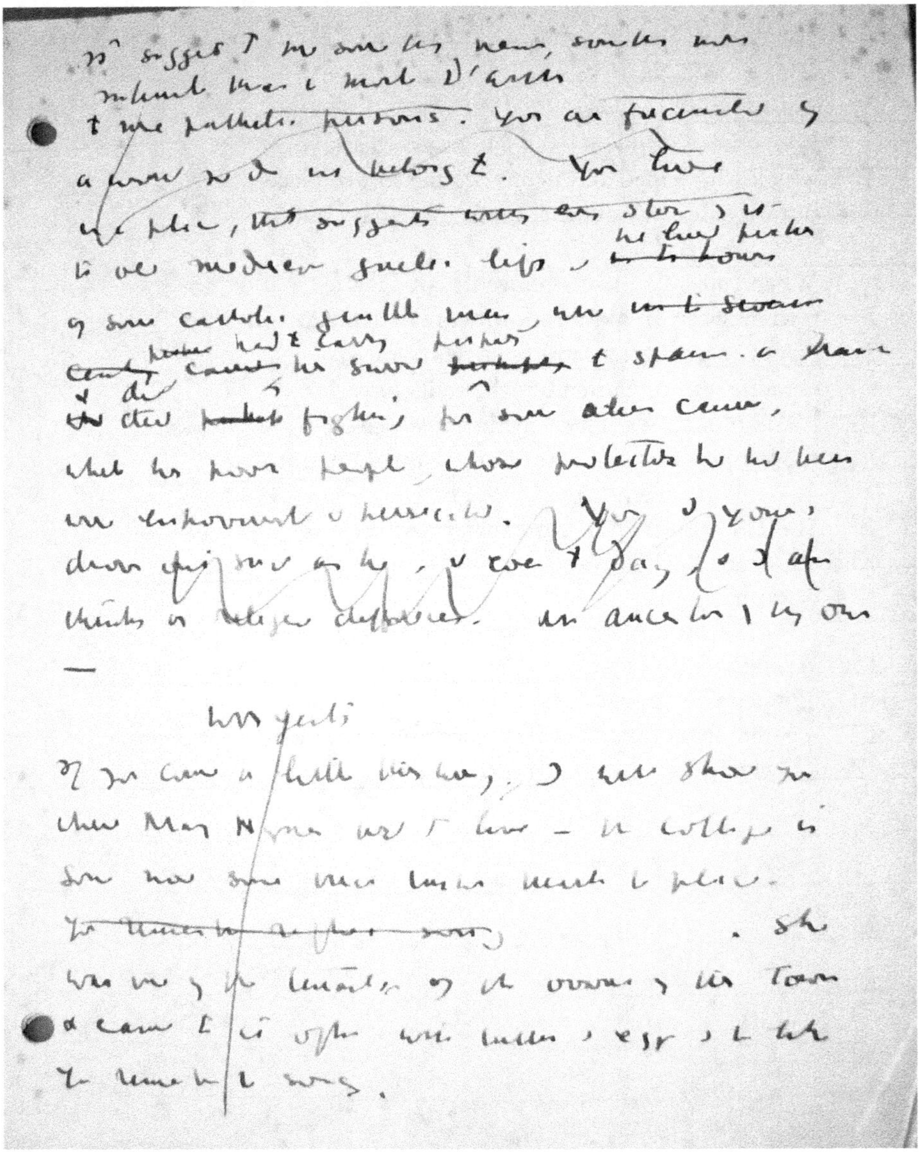

[NLI 30,103, folio 3]

It suggests to me some thing new, some thing more
intimate than a Morte D'Arth[ur]
to me pathetic persons. You are fascinated by
a world you do not belong to. You live
in a place, that suggests with every stone of it
he[re] lived perhaps
the old medieval gaelic life & ~~in the house~~
of some Catholic gentle man, who ~~in the sevent[eenth]~~
~~perhaps~~ had to carry perhaps
~~century carried~~ his sword ~~perhaps~~ to spain or France
& died ^
~~who died perhaps~~ fighting for some alien cause,
which his poor people, whose protector he had been
were empoverished & persecuted. ~~You & yours~~
~~drove out such as he, & even to day, & I am~~
~~thinking o[f] religious differences~~. An ancester of my own
—

WB Yeats
If you come a little this way, I will show you
where Mary Hynes used to live — the cottage is
gone now some [?birch] bushes mark the place.
~~You remember rafterys song.~~ She
was one of the tenants of the owner of this Tower
& came to it often with butter & eggs & the like
You remember the song.

[NLI 30,103, folio 4]

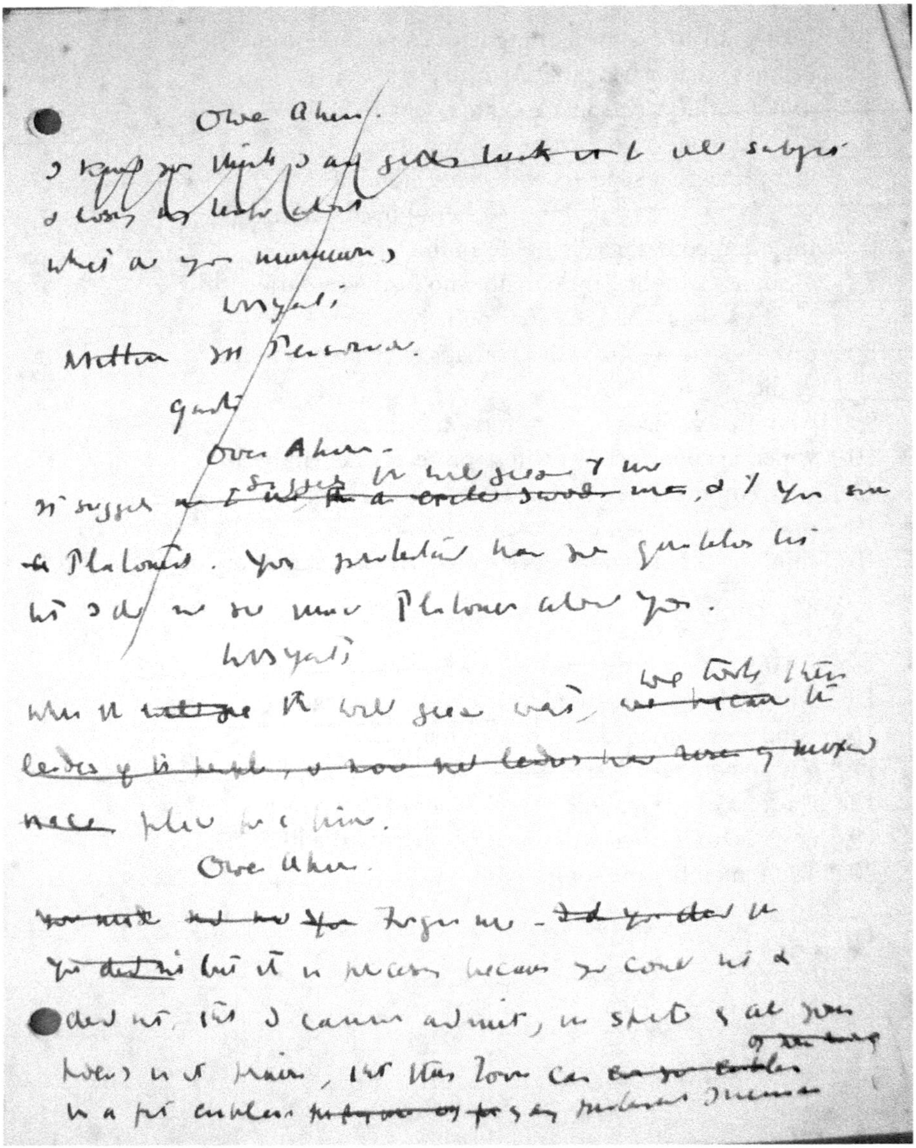

[NLI 30,103, folio 4]

Owen Aherne.
~~I know you think I am getting back on~~ the old subject
~~& losing my way about~~
What are you murmering
WB Yeats
~~Milton~~ Ill Penseroso.
quote
Owen Aherne.
suggests the Wild Geese to me
It suggests ~~[?not] to me~~ ~~the an excited swords man~~, & to you some
~~a~~ Platonist/ You protestants have your quotations but
but I do not see much Platonics about you.
WB Yeats we took their
When the ~~Wild gee~~ the wild geese went, ~~we became~~ the
~~leaders of the people, & now new leaders have risen of~~ mixed
~~race~~ place for a time.
Owen Aherne.
~~You made~~ ~~no no You~~ Forgive me. ~~I do~~ ~~You did~~ the
~~You did not~~ but it is precisely because you could not &
did not, that I cannot admit, in spite of all your
~~of new songs~~
poems in its praise, that this tower can ~~be your emblem~~
be a fit emblem ~~for my self~~ ~~for~~ for any protestant Irishman

[NLI 30,103, folio 5]

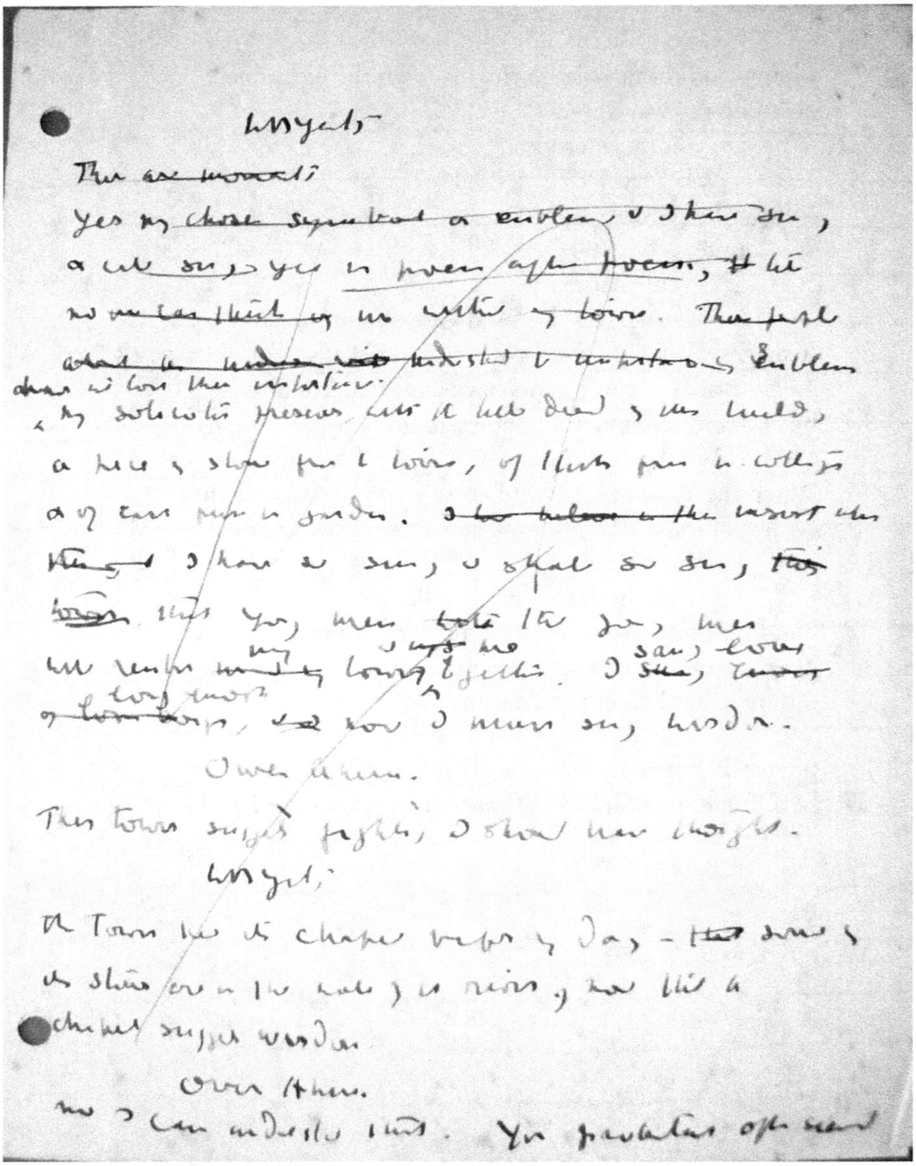
WBYeats

[illegible]

Owen Aherne.

This tower suggests fights, I should have thought.

WBYeats

The Tower [illegible]

Owen Aherne.

Now I can understand that. [illegible]

[NLI 30,103, folio 5]

[WB Yeats]
1 ~~There are moments~~
2 Yes my ~~chosen symbol or emblem, & I have~~ sung
3 & ~~will sing~~ yes ~~in poem after poem,~~ ~~th~~ till
4 ~~no one can think of~~ me without ~~my tower.~~ ~~These people~~
{E
5 about us ~~under will~~ understand the importance of {emblems
[?draw] not lose their importance.
6 ^ my solicitor preserves, with the little deed of this build[ing],
7 a piece of stone from the tower, of thatch from the cottage
8 & of earth from the garden. ~~I have believed in the~~ insist upon
9 ~~the [?]~~, & I have so sung & shall so sing ~~This~~
10 ~~tower~~ that young men ~~with~~ that young men
my & ~~myself~~ me sang love
11 will remember ~~me & my~~ tower ^ together. I ~~sung~~ ~~enough~~
long enough
12 ~~of love songs~~, ~~& so~~ now I must sing wisdom.
Owen Ahern.
13 This tower suggests fights, I should have thought.
WB Yeats
14 The tower had its chapel before my day — ~~that~~ some of
15 its stones are in the wall by the river, not that a
16 chapel suggests wisdom.
Owen Aherne.
17 No I can understand that. You protestants often seem

[NLI 30,103, folio 6]

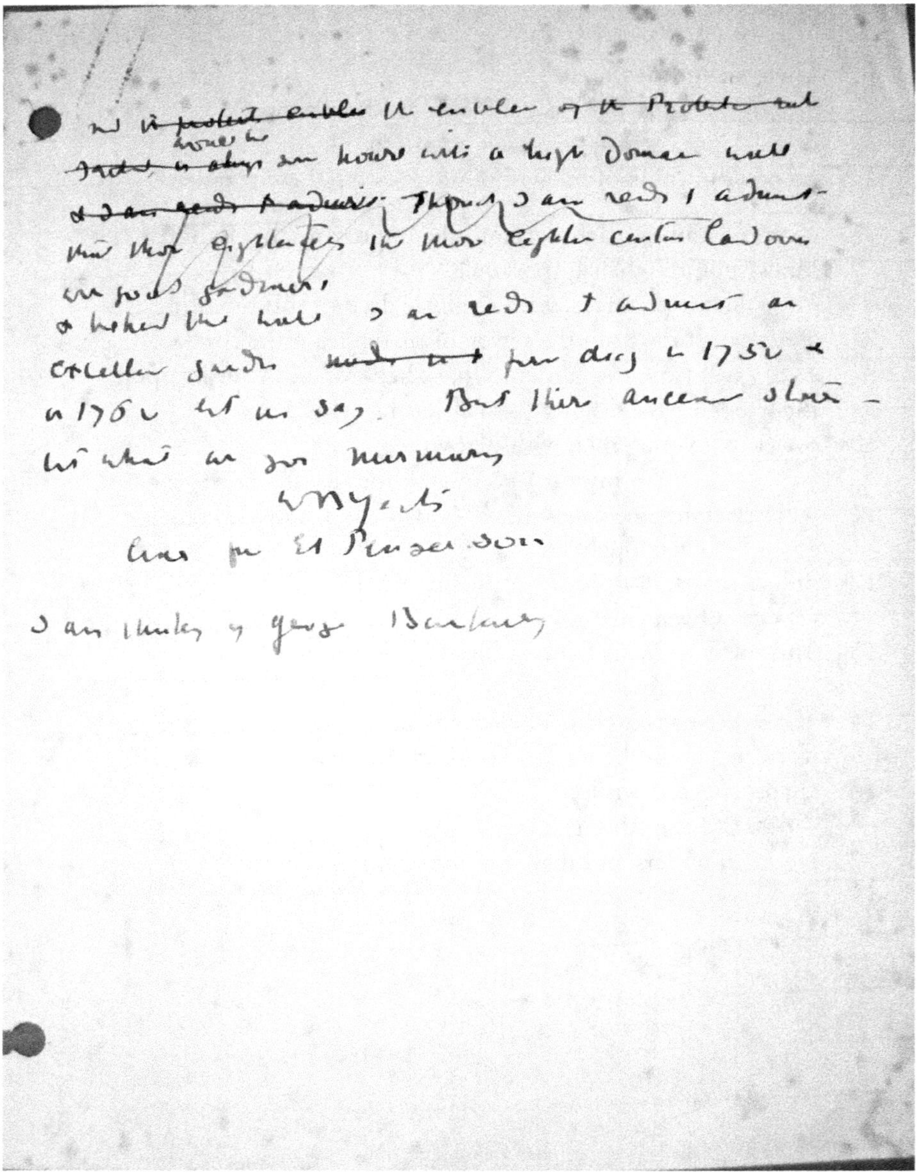
W B Yeats

I am thinking of George Berkeley

[NLI 30,103, folio 6]

1 not ~~to protest emblems~~ the emblem ~~of the Protestant rule~~
would be
2 ~~Ireland, is always~~ some house with a high domain wall
3 ~~& I am ready to admit~~ Though I am ready to admit
4 that those eighteenth that those eighteenth century land owners
5 were good gardeners
6 & behind that wall I am ready to admit an
7 excellent garden ~~made in 1~~ first dug in 1750 &
8 in 1760 let us say. But these ancient stones —
9 but what are you murmering
WB Yeats
10 lines from El Penseroso.
11 I am thinking of George Burkeley

Creating Story in "The Discoveries of Michael Robartes," 1917–1920

Mystification and a degree of bewilderment were fostered when Yeats began to mix his autobiographical and bibliographical facts. Misstatements might always be corrected, but the phantasmagorical elements that were a signature of his early poems and stories also took a surprising turn as sources ostensibly shifted from the Celtic West to the Mystic Middle East. The return of Michael Robartes, as we have seen, followed the reintroduction of Owen Aherne into Yeats's creative writing shortly after his marriage in October 1917. Unexpectedly, a foreshadowing of that return suddenly manifested itself in the "Magical shapes" of an open book that Robartes had left, to be found in "Ego Dominus Tuus," a poem of late 1915. Our last glimpse of Robartes before that incident was in "The Adoration of the Magi" (1897), in which he encountered three old men, the story's symbolic Magi, having come upon them "in a fishing-boat, like St. Brandan drawn by some vision and called by some voice"; similarly, years later, "a voice came out of the air over the waters and told [the eldest of these men] of the death of Michael Robartes" (28–29, ll. 38–49). The coincidence of disembodied voices must have been at least one of the ways George Yeats's initiation of the automatic script, on or about 27 October 1917, would summon to Yeats's mind creatures of his own invention from the past, lying dormant the while but still quick with life apart from their author and recognized as vestiges of imaginative life at the *fin de siècle*.

Not long after Aherne had sprung again from Yeats's pen to engage the poet in an imaginary conversation at Ballylee, both aged, the idea of resurrecting Aherne's alter ego, Michael Robartes, must have dawned on Yeats, who aimed to publish the occult knowledge obtained from interviews with his wife as medium and with various spirit guides. Important to Yeats as a man and, according to George Harper, especially as an artist, was the "conviction that the Communicators had come to excite [Yeats's] imagination at a time when the well of inspiration was drying up" (*MYV1* xii). The book that Yeats envisioned eventually became, after a thorough-going reconceptualization, *A Vision: An Explanation of Life founded upon the Writings of Giraldus and upon Certain Doctrines Attributed to Kusta Ben Luka* (1925; *AVA*) and, finally, *A Vision* (1937; *AVB*), rewritten once again after having dropped the pretense of Arabic authority. "The book," writes Harper, "was in truth an unusual collaboration, for which George [Yeats] received little credit—and she wanted none" (*MYV1* 19). However, prior to the book's first published iteration, Yeats began adapting the findings of this collaboration to the form of a dialogue entitled "The Discoveries of Michael Robartes." Therein, occasionally, Robartes and Aherne refer to Yeats overtly, although the work resembles a Platonic dialogue (with Robartes in the role of Socrates and Aherne as friend and disciple) more than a conversation poem the likes of "Anglo Ireland," where differences of opinion are exposed, debated, and, if not settled after a heated exchange, broken off as irreconcilable. Both "Anglo Ireland" and the much longer, eventually typed "Discoveries of Michael Robartes" were left unfinished. The latter extended to a narrative "Version B," which altogether abandoned dialogue form a few pages beyond a headnote signed "WBY. June 1920" (*YVP4* 141).

Margaret Mills Harper's *Wisdom of Two: The Spiritual and Literary Collaboration of George and W. B. Yeats* (Oxford University Press, 2006) is recommended on the nature and progress of joint research undertaken by the Yeatses, particularly by Mrs. Yeats's until the mid-1920s. Generally, she says, Yeats's verse-dialogues fit into one of two types: "First, there are poems in which speakers agree or form separate statements that the poem joins into a deeper idea, such as 'Adam's Curse'... [and, second, there are][o]thers, like...'Ego Dominus Tuus,' [that] feature characters who differ in opinion but one of whom has all of the poet's sympathy, creating essentially false dialogues reminiscent somehow of vaudeville, one stand-up figure feeding the other all the good lines" (*Wisdom of Two* 234–35). Into the second group falls the long, unfinished prose dialogue of Robartes and Aherne that Yeats undertook in his first attempt to organize the findings of the automatic scripts.

"The Discoveries of Michael Robartes" and "Version B," transcribed and annotated for Palgrave Macmillan by editors George Mills Harper and Margaret Mills Harper, assisted by Richard W. Stoops, Jr. (2001), presents a small mountain of evidence to which *W. B. Yeats's Robartes-Aherne Writings* happily refers and supplements without repeating much from the already published scholarship, including *Yeats's "Vision" Papers*, in general, because the object here is not to study the genesis of *A Vision* per se. Rather, the focus is on two vital *premises* of those manuscript materials—first, that George Yeats's actual role in the creative process was to have been kept secret by an elaborate invention of fictitious agents, and, second, that those agents constituted a story in itself, aside from the philosophical burden they were made to carry. On the face of it, the premises of the story are audacious—that characters taken from Yeats's fiction are *real* people. Not merely characters, Robartes and Aherne may therefore engage each other and prepare to confront their author outside the stories from which they originated, returned home after long separation, much older but still *in character*. Moreover, Robartes has died at least once, the first time in "Rosa Alchemica," and he does not dispute the fact. The *story* of the reunion of Robartes and Aherne begins to address that circumstance, on page 1 of "The Discoveries of Michael Robartes" in typescript (*YVP4* 13), a stage of the writing featured by the Harpers for sake of clarity but not exactly where the dialogue began in first draft.

Precisely when Yeats began writing the piece is not certain; "some time in 1918" (*YVP4* 11), roughly correspondent with the final conversion of "The Phases of the Moon" into a Robartes-Aherne dialogue would be a good guess,[1] some time earlier than the holograph copy of "The Discovery of Michael Robartes" (62–108), the nine-page insert presented as an appendix (108–13), an untitled manuscript (119–34), and of course the typescript (13–44) and "Version B" (141–246)—"some 500 pages," according to the Harpers (1).[2] "Among the astonishing mass of miscellaneous pages…not included" in *YVP4* (but referenced in notes) are two, lined composition booklets that rehearse recursively the accounts that Aherne and Robartes make to each other when they meet unexpectedly at the National Gallery in London. In fact, the opening sequence is rehearsed twice in 19 folios, beginning with the following:

FROM NLI 36,263/7

Exercise Book 1, first draft—folio 1^r

Aherne.
How strange I should meet a man who
~~was~~
so ~~thought your history~~ ~~has been~~ ~~written~~ &
~~your~~ death announced ~~twenty years~~ ago
~~so~~ & whose history was written twenty years
ago, ~~& that we should meet~~, & that we should
be talking on for five minutes as though
I had never believed him dead, & changed all
my religious faith because [of] it.
Robartes
Yes I knew of the [?announcement], for I had read
~~that exagerated~~ Rosa Alchemica when it
came out in the Savoy – a young French poet
had brought a copy to Crackow – but why should I
correct [it]. Mr Yeats was a man of twenty
when we knew him: we were both ~~men of~~ old
men – ~~ten or~~ fifty years old I ~~think~~ should
think, & in the late eighties & early nineties
a man romanticizes everything, even his elders.
Aherne

Exercise Book 1, first draft—folio 2^r

Yet if you do not object to being described as dead.
And I can well understand that after that tragic
riot, & your harrow[ing] escape you wished for some

new manner of life, you might well have corrected the
description of you – half ~~deboche & that's~~ [?]
~~diebachee half~~ peasant &
Robartes. thats
A literary manner of the time – ~~that was when~~ – he
was ~~in love with Irish peasants, & his~~ friends read
Verlaine ~~& [?] the Café de le Paix~~. Even I
a mere ~~[?triviality] became a romantic~~ person[alit]y
& ~~because I knew the Café~~ de le Paix [?dissipated]
yet ~~what more prosaic than~~ my interests, chemical
~~experiments, a little medium perhaps, astronomic~~
ordinary
~~symbolism, & some old conjuring books common~~
~~enough in the east~~. Some very ordinary meeting
where there were girls who danced & a little
incense, with [?] ~~that in her eyes its in hi~~ in her eyes
The mistery of some pagan ceremonies copied from
Walter Pater ~~was perhaps responsible for the whole~~
~~masterpiece~~.

[from folio 1ᵛ]

He turned me into a romantic personality because
Villiers de Lisle Adams was not yet
dead & yet what am I but a very
ordinary civilian.

Following the encounter with Yeats in "Anglo Ireland. | a conversation," Aherne marvels that he should now "meet a man, Robartes, "whose death was announced and whose history was written twenty years ago"[3] by Yeats, and that after five minutes' talk, he should never have believed that announcement, which adversely affected his religious faith. Robartes clearly recalls the literary incident as a young French poet had once given him occasion to read the story "Rosa Alchemica," as it appeared in *The Savoy* (April 1896). We surmise that Robartes had been in Cracow, Poland, at that time because that was the place of publication for the fictitious *Speculum Angelorum et Homenorum* [sic] of Giraldus (see *AVA* frontispiece, later cited as *Speculum Angelorum et Hominum* in *SMR* and *AVB*). Yeats had been "a man of twenty" (c. 1885) when Robartes and Aherne were "both old men" of fifty, which, with the passing of 33 years, would make them eighty-five in 1918 and Yeats fifty-three. Of course, Aherne wants to make an issue of the "tragic riot" at the end of the story, rather than to allow the treatment of Robartes to be dismissed as merely characteristic of "a literary manner of the time," as Robartes does, who finds it incredible that he should be mistaken for a "romantic personality" himself. For it was that younger Yeats who, being "in love with the Irish peasants" and under the spell of Paul Verlaine's poetry, as well as, presumably, the romance of other famous clients of the Café de la Paix, Paris[4] (with which Robartes acknowledges some connection), exaggerated Robartes's numerous "prosaic" interests and transformed "a very ordinary meeting" with dancing girls and incense into "the mystery of some pagan ceremonies copied from" *Marius the Epicurean: His Sensations and Ideas* (1885) by Walter Pater. Under these circumstances, "very ordinary citizen" Robartes became "a romantic personality" because the age of Villiers de l'Isle-Adam, the author of *Axël*, "was not yet dead."[5]

But Aherne will have no excuses for his own part and turns to a personal beef with Yeats, bringing to the dialogue the Catholic perspective he represented in "Anglo Ireland," only this time applied to the habitués of the Olde Cheshire Cheese tavern in London, home of the Rhymers' Club, which Yeats co-founded in 1890 with Ernest Rhys.

Exercise Book 1, first draft—folio 3^{r}

Aherne
I too ~~was a little misrepresented~~ was changed out of
all recognition. I have certainly ~~because I believe~~
I have for many years been a practising Catholic
the
but I am not ~~the~~ narrow voteen he has pictured,
I have a perfectly free mind where freedom matters
~~I have believed myself a man of the modern world~~
history
~~& thus my faith is founded~~ on ~~reason~~ & science

[from folio 2^{v}]

nor have I ceased, of course in a
innocent sense to be a man of the
world.

[folio 3^{r}, continued]

But the late 80's & the early 90's found it could
monks than women
no more tell between ~~saints than sinners~~. You
never knew Dowson, he published his first book two or
three years after your supposed death. He had a way
of de[di]cating his poems to his living friends &
acquaintances & I can remember "Extreme" Unction
for Leonard Smithers, & ~~"Beata Solitudo" for Stan Smithers~~

~~You are right~~ Verlaine ~~was at the bottom of the whole~~
tavern
~~thing~~ with his alternation of chapel & ~~brothel~~
was at the bottom of the whole thing. I wonder if
if you will [like] his
it is why you ~~have seen Yeats~~ new book "Per
Amica Silentia Lunae." It was published to day
Robartes.

Exercise Book 1, first draft—folio 4^r^

I have already seen it for the publish[er] has sent
me a copy & it has puzzled me ~~extremely~~
Aherne
it was not so much puzzle me as shock me: the
writes on | have been weighed & settled
questions he ~~considers have all been settled~~ long ago.
there is not one of them that has not ~~been decided~~ upon
by St Thomas, & ~~it is plain~~ yet it is plain
~~that he~~ Yet he ~~writes [?]~~; or some other great
doctor of the church. It Can he hope to out do
Thomas in learning or in sublity. A man should
learn all these matters, where reason stumbles
to the souls loss, alone ~~[? ?], & say lies~~
progress & ~~say~~ confess he said.
Robartes
I can say that I have been shocked a man
who has sought truth among the camels of

[from folio 3^v^]

I am not shocked at his concerning himself
with such matters, for I have myself

[folio 4^r^ continued]

Arabia "I am not shocked at his writing
I myself
~~on such deep matters,~~ for, I have lived ~~tw~~ 20
years now among the camels & the horse hair
tents ~~for meditation sake, seeking for [&]~~ peace
~~looking for truth~~ ~~that I might se~~ that I sought for the truth
Aherne
You could have found it in a few catec[his]ms

Aherne's complaint is that Yeats, in "The Tables of the Law," makes him out to be a bad Catholic with a penchant for heresy—a "misrepresentation" of character, or libel, as unpleasant as the characterization of Robartes, in "Rosa Alchemica," as "something between a debauchee, a saint, and a peasant" (*Myth* 271). A "man of the world" (in a sense), "not the narrow voteen" depicted by Yeats, Aherne criticizes Yeats's Decadent friends, citing Ernest Dowson as a particular example, who "could no more tell between <monks than women> ~~saints than sinners~~," having dedicated verses to living friends and acquaintances," even to one's publisher.[6] Aherne's mind then springs to Verlaine's notorious obsession for Arthur Rimbaud, shot by the elder poet while lounging in their room at the Hôtel de la Ville de Courtrai, Brussels. Verlaine, "with his alternation of chapel and <tavern> ~~brothel~~, was at the bottom of the whole thing," Aherne alleges. With perhaps enough said of the past, he then changes the subject to Yeats's "new book, *Per Amica Silentia Lunae*," published that very day in both England and America (which would have been 18 January 1918, according to *Wade* 120).

When Robartes claims to be puzzled by the new book, Aherne offers stronger criticism, being "shocked" that Yeats writes on questions "weighed and settled long ago" by St. Thomas Aquinas or "some other great doctor of the Church." But Robartes patiently advances a more temperate line, as "a man who has sought truth among the camels of Arabia"; "I am not shocked at his [Yeats's] concerning himself with such matters, for I have myself…lived 20 years now among the camels and the horse-hair tents." When he might have found truth "in a few catechisms," as Aherne asserts, the reason Yeats's new book puzzles Robartes is its "tone of confidence" disproportionate to the author's small portion of actual "spiritual experience."

Exercise Book 1, first draft—folio 5^{r}

Robartes
But not his tone of confidence. I knew him well once
& I have enquired of his friends & believe that
his spiritual experience has been very slight, a few
broken dreams. & yet especially in a second essay
he writes with an air of authority very telling to
those who have been while still living beyond the
world.
Aherne
He has perhaps noticed, that people are convinced
when one speaks for oneself, as if one has conviction.
He always loved conversation upon such matters
& he may hope that some rich American
~~wh~~ will build for him a kind of great temple

in a California garden, where he may spend
the rest of his life in conversation.
Robartes
If that is his reason one should not speak of those
mockers, for the soul, as I have learned on the
many lives enduring contemplation—and as I believe—
commits every sin. I[n?] 2000 years or 2000 years
ago you & I may have a like ambition

Exercise Book 1, first draft—folio 6r

Aherne
It cannot be gods will that every man should sin.
Robartes
should not
Only [?attitude] of mind matters, & we ~~do not~~
know even if we know his masters his atti[t]udes of
mind—his his way of looking let us say upon
that California garden. I was going to add that
I was more puzzled even than shocked.
You remember his doctrine of the Anti-thetical self.
Aherne
The one original thought in the book.
Robartes
No—its not original, & that is exactly what
puzzles me

Professing to have known Yeats "well once," Robartes has remained interested enough in him to "have enquired of his friends." The essay "Anima Mundi" (*PASL*, part 2) impresses him because of Yeats's "air of authority very telling to those who have been while still living beyond the world." By nuance, this remark might be interpreted as a clever self-compliment—that is, by Yeats about Yeats through this character. But Aherne may be depended upon to undercut Robartes's tepid praise, likening Yeats to a huckster whose false conviction and gift for talk are put to fraudulent purposes, such as persuading a rich patron in America to "build him a kind of great temple in a California garden" (a precursor to the touring evangelist Alexander J. Christ Dowie in Joyce's *Ulysses* or the antihero of Sinclair Lewis's *Elmer Gantry*). Admonishing like a saint ("one should not speak of those mockers, for the soul…commits every sin"), Robartes is rebuffed sharply: "It cannot be God's will that every man should sin." However, it is on Yeats's "attitude of mind" that his book shall be judged, not upon knowing "his masters," but on how he regards "that California garden." Robartes avers that the very derivative nature of the "doctrine of the Antithetical self" in the poem "Ego Dominus Tuus," say, or the essay "Anima Hominis" (*PASL*, part 1), is the source of bewilderment.

With this stated, the first draft of the sequence ends. All preceding rectos and all but two of the versos are cancelled by means of a vertical stroke. At the next opening in the notebook, Aherne and Robartes start over again, or at least roll back their discussion to the point where *PASL* as a topic had been introduced in the first place, to Exercise Book 1, first draft, folio 3^r.

Exercise Book 1, second draft—folio 6^v

~~Aherne~~
~~Robartes~~
Aherne
my favorite
So we meet again & at ~~the same~~ picture
(?)
Titian ^ Adoration of the Magi.
Robartes
~~Th Nat~~ I come to see the and and
which please [?one] because they have that
curious precise articulation of objects seen [in]
sleep, when ~~slee~~ sleep is nearest to vision.
Aherne
I have [been] looking for you. Have you seen

Etc

Exercise Book 1, second draft—folio 7^r

[*The arrow, left, indicates insertion of matter from facing verso, 6^v, above*]

~~A herne~~
Have you read "Per Amica Silentia Lunae," ~~which~~
~~Macmillan & Co have just published for Mr Yeats~~
Robartes
Yes and it has shocked me & puzzled me, shocked
especially in the second of the two essays
by ~~the auth~~ its dogmatic certainty. The authority
tells us exactly ~~how the soul~~ what accomedation
the soul finds after death, & how it is, ~~as it~~
~~were nudged & dandled in [?sight]~~ nourished, as it were,
by its daimon while still living, & it is plain
that he can know nothing of the matter. The truth
is known ~~only to a very few people~~ or perhaps I

should say has been known, for the [?disappearance]
of a ~~very~~ few ~~people~~ persons, who have been able to
see into their life beyond the grave; & Mr Yeats so
far ~~although at the~~ being of the kin of St John of Patmos
broken
has but a few ~~dreams~~ dreams twenty years ago
and may be half forgotten. So at any rate I understand
have
from what you ^ told me.

It was Aherne's turn to speak if the dialogue were simply to continue—or to start over as in folio 1^r—but Yeats hesitated for a moment, perhaps to allow Robartes to declare his favorite painting, *The Adoration of the Magi* by Titian.[7] After all, Yeats has said that, in principle, Robartes represented "the pride of the imagination brooding upon the greatness of its possession, or the adoration of the Magi" (*VP* 802). Aherne is finally given the opening, but the title is queried, possibly due to uncertainty about the work cited. By way of reply, Robartes expresses interest in three figures within the painting, or perhaps three other paintings or painters (with spaces left to fill in their identities later), and he overtly establishes location in the National Gallery, London, though mistaken about Titian's painting, which is in Spain.[8] The "Etc" at the bottom of folio 6^v evidently indicates that banter about other artworks has also been left to fill in later. The exchange on 6^v (left), facing 7^r (right), is inserted by a drawn line and arrow into the latter at the top of the page, where a slightly more detailed discussion of the appearance of authority in *PASL* begins. Notably, Robartes's analysis is less kindly toward Yeats than in the previous draft, likening him to St. John of Patmos, said-author of the apocalyptic Book of Revelation, final chapter of the New Testament. With "but a few broken dreams" to go on, Yeats's revelations are being derided as a come-lately form of false prophecy.

The remainder of Exercise Book 1 (folios 7^v, 8^r, and 9^r) continues in this vein, with reflections built on earlier considerations of Yeats's manner, his questionable motives, and the "doctrine of the Antithetical self" articulated in his *Per Amica Silentia Lunae*, the touchstone of this obviously early manuscript.

Exercise Book 1, second draft—folio 7^v

[*This page is inserted in place of the cancelled speech on the facing page, folio 8^r.*]

Aherne probably
He wants followers ~~I dare say~~ people are attracted by
certainty
Robartes
~~I dare say you [are] right~~ You are right people

do not want the truth so much as to
be rescued from uncertainty. He is ~~probably~~
getting old – over fifty I should say &
though that seems young only to you & me, &
yet I remember that when I ~~began~~ was fifty I
began to feel old. He may feel lonely
at [?] perhaps always writing for those who
never [?share] his desire perhaps in church, or a
meeting house, or perhaps I should say
an Academ[y].

Aherne

I dislike his manner as much as you do
for one should be uncertain about
apart & geographical facts
everything – ~~a few mathematical truths~~
& the like
~~apart which one does not~~, where the spiritual life [is]
concerned which one does not find in the Catecisms.

Exercise Book 1, second draft—folio 8r

Aherne

He wants followers I dare say, & they come hand in
hand by putting ones speculations as certainties,
for men do not so much want truth as to be
rescued from doubt. I ~~[?]~~ dislike his manner
as much as you do though not for the same reason
We can get all the truth there is for a [?penny]
or the Church ~~Catac~~ Catecism, & so one has to
seek beyond it one should stop every free minute in time
to the all how doubtful it all is; but I think
you said that he puz[z]led you.

Robartes.

I cannot make out how he came to the doctrine
of the Antithetical self for I had thought that I
European
a lone ^ & a small wandering sect [of] Arabs among
Asiatics held that doctrine in the form [?] in [?which]
he cast it, & as I have not met him since ~~his~~ my
return to England & have seen no one that has not
heard it from me.

Aherne

Exercise Book 1, second draft—folio 9^{r}

I recall very little more than the ~~prase~~ phrase
—I think it was in the first essay. I read the
book ~~in~~ hastily that I might know how
to thank him for my copy
Robartes
He explains, that every man of genius is the
Or of the circumstance of its life
direct opposite of the primary or [?daily] self ^
as
^ for instance Keats, Synge, Dante Landor
& certain friends of his own~~. &~~ Keats for
~~instance seeks in dreams the~~ denied lately by
circumstance seeks in dreams, & Landor ~~more~~
~~violent a man than any English poet~~ that
most violent of men has the noblest & calmest
style in English. He even contends & finds that
a man of genius, works at what ever task
among those not impossible is hardest to him
for in that way ~~he obtains the greatest possible~~
reaches his direct opposite, & the greatest possibility
degree of his genius: the greater the opposition
the greater the genius.

Interestingly, folio 8^{v}, facing the above at left, bears three views of Thoor Ballylee, an aerial and two side views, all drawn by Yeats and probably inspired by the passage and correlatives in "Ego Dominus Tuus" (e.g., "your old wind-beaten tower," *VP* 367/*Myth* 321, l. 2; with treatments of Dante and Keats, *VP* 367–68/*Myth* 321–22: ll. 17–37 and *VP* 370/*Myth* 323: ll. 51–62) and prose bits in *PASL* on Dante, Synge, Landor, and Keats (*Myth* 326–30, 333, and 342). As a whole, the passage passes as a charming and hilarious exercise in self-deprecation. This conversation continues right on into the second booklet, allowing Aherne only a quick reply to Robartes's closing summation on the topic of genius in Exercise Book 1, folio 9^{r}, before a sustained colloquy by the latter on his life's experiences of the past twenty years. For more than six pages of monologue, we have much of Robartes's story as retold in various places on the way to *SMR* and, finally, *AVB*.

Exercise Book 2 (continuing from Exercise Book 1)—folio 1^{r}

Aherne
Yes I remember thinking it the one original thing in
the essay.

Robartes
But it is not original, & I will show you the
complete doctrine, ~~as~~ if you will come with me to
my rooms. ~~& when you have~~ I will show to you
certain wood cuts in of [*Space left for a book title.*]
a learned doctor of Crackow, & when [*Space left for author name.*]
I have explained them, you['ll] see that he has blundered
on something ~~out~~ ~~altogether~~ beyond his power to invent or
as it seems
^ comprehend. Since I have seen this book of his
I have not been able to rest: I have longed
to talk to somebody, & I do not know a
soul but you. Come ~~as we~~ & if you have no
you how
objection to our walking I will tell ~~you how~~ I
I came upon the old book. After the riot
~~which you & others believed~~ when I was believed to have
been killed I left for the continent, & after

Exercise Book 2—folio 2^r^

the deaths at the under the blows of the rioters of
certain dear friends I had to[o] long no heart for my
old studies. I am now getting [to be] an old man
but all [?through] my youth I have alternated between
periods of ascetic[ci]sm, & periods of pleasure, or
perhaps I should say [?of] excitement, I ~~thik~~ think it
a very natur[al] life. I went to ~~Paris & Rome~~ Paris
to Rome & Vienna
~~to Vienna, & finally to Crackow~~ in pursuit of
a ballet dancer, & there at Vienna we ~~[?] &~~
quarreled. The[n] I tried to forget my troubles
in wine, & in a very few weeks I was tired of
that, & then with some faint stirring of the
old interest I went to Crackow, a ~~great~~
notable for its
~~place~~ of printing as you will remember, and
for the adventures of Dr Dee & E Kelly. There
I took up with a very handsome girl
Of the poor her [= poorer?] classes, ~~who had a~~ ~~& one~~
~~night~~ I took a couple of rooms in a tumble
we were

down old house. One night ~~I was~~ suddenly
thrown out of bed & when I lit the tallow

Exercise Book 2—folio 3r

candle discovered the head of the bed had been
prop[p]ed at ~~one~~ one side by a foot stool, &
an old book bound in calf. In the morning
I found that it was the   of   [*Spaces for title and author.*]
I have spoken of & that it was full of curious
astronomical diagrams ~~&~~ & allegorical
I was deeply interested
emblems cut on wood. ~~We~~ One of the
which
simpler diagrams ^ one [?encountered]
and as all [= always?] in my life
I puzzled over the meaning & origin of beauty in
women. The majority of men although
[?peasants], as all think of it as an ~~origin[al]~~
or accident, which may be united to any kind
of virtue or ~~vi~~ vice, stupidity or talent
as their sayings show "beauty is only
skin deep.["] On the other hand Castiglione
beauty
calls true ~~beauty~~, which one distinguishes from
the mere "promise of physical pleasure
& an easy way to get it,["] as "the sport["]

Exercise Book 2—folio 4r

or monument of the victory of the soul. ~~I then
began to make inquiries~~. However before going
very deeply into the book I tried to find out
something about the author & at last ~~found~~
in the ~~Royal Library a book~~ ~~called~~
______? ________ on the books of the author [*Space for library name.*]
called   had been published [?] in the [*Space for title.*]
year 1599 but of   himself [*Space for author name.*]
I could learn nothing. As no shop or
Library ~~contained~~ I had access to contained
any work of his I assumed that mine was
the only copy of work of his extant.
When I asked my beggar maid where she got [it]

she replied, that she found it, when we
first took possession of the rooms on the
top shelf of a cupboard on the wall. The
previous owner of the room had been
an un[f]rocked priest & he had wandered off
heaven knows where. I had made some
progress with my studies of the Latin text

Exercise Book 2—folio 5^r^

when a quarrel with my beggar maid plunged me in
gloom & wine once more. ~~Then the idea came~~
~~in my head that I would visit the holy lan[d]~~

[inserted from folio 4^v^]

Then I turned soberly against all sensual pleasure
& resolved to

[folio 5^r^, continued]

say my prayers at the holy Sepulchre
And from J~~erusalem~~ I then drifted to
Damascus, I attempt[ed] to get to ~~Messa~~ Mecca
~~half doctor~~ half
~~left in~~ ended up by becoming ~~a sort of~~

[inserted from folio 4^v^]

After ~~coming~~ two or three years
Wandering among arab tribes

[folio 5^r^, continued]

~~a steward to an Arab chief, or rather~~
~~steward, doctor, & [?]~~ thanks [to] a medicine chest
I always carry first doctor, & then general
man of business to an Arab chief. Then one day
old
an Arab, whom I had ~~tread~~ treated medically
~~was turning over~~ opened ~~my~~ *[Blank space left for title.]*
which ~~have~~ I had now thoroughly mastered
& at the sight of the frontispiece cried out
in astonishment. ~~He had he said~~ an
~~Arab book~~ It contained he said
certain doctrines ~~that [?are]~~ peculiar to ~~an old~~ an
arab sect the to which he *[Space left for name of tribe.]*

Exercise Book 2—folio 6[r]

Then one day we were visited by an Arab
of an Arab sect well known at Fez (?) in
to the middle ages. ~~They~~ Among them one
finds the greatest extremes, very holy men
& others exceeding[ly] licentious, or even cruel ~~&~~
~~for the [?sun at back]~~ ~~& all live together~~ & in the same
little wandering ~~tri~~ tribe one will find, ~~the more they~~
the extreme living to tolerable amounts. They lack
moral indignation more than any people I
have met, & one of these an old man
celebrated for his wisdom ~~on seeing that~~
whom I was treating for some complaint cried out
in wonder on seeing the little pages in [a] book
It contained he said certain doctrines of
the & on learning that there were *[Space left for name of tribe.]*
~~diagrams~~ Arab MSS containing these doctrines
~~in that he~~ in his hands I resigned my post
and wandered with him & his people for
years, for my book had now become the
great interest of my life.

In these several pages, at different levels, are two significant developments in Yeats's invention of story. First, Robartes suggests that Aherne accompany him to his lodging to view a book in which woodcuts mirror ideas Yeats has just published in *PASL*, and this ambling away from the scene in the National Gallery constitutes an element of plot. In other words, the characters are now moving spatially while talking—and outdoors, too, on a definite path in the City of London, from Trafalgar Square, in a northerly direction through St. Giles and Bloomsbury to Woburn Place as far as, perhaps, Euston Road on the edge of the Borough of St. Pancras or Regents Park. Secondly, this talk is a *narrative*, almost entirely in one voice, virtually a monologue in which Robartes relates how his own extraordinary travels across Europe to Persia and present-day Saudi Arabia embodied a twenty-year spiritual journey following the catastrophe that Yeats had chronicled in "Rosa Alchemica." The central elements of Robartes's story were first told to Aherne but eventually repeated, in 1931, to Robartes's "pupils" Peter Huddon, John Duddon, Daniel O'Leary, Denise de L'Isle Adam, Mary Bell, and John Bond. A little like the wedding-guest in Coleridge's famous allegorical ballad about expiation and self-discovery, Aherne is apparently transfixed. Talking in this draft passes too swiftly to actually approximate the amount of real time necessary for two, spry, old men to cover the indicated distance. So the process of expanding text in successive stages of writing in the two exercise books will need to be (and was in fact) applied to the much longer manuscript and typescript versions presented in *YVP4*.

Robartes's narrative provides an important hint at dating, thus far, Yeats's progress with the dialogue of Exercise Book 2. At this stage, Yeats had yet to invent the name of Robartes's "learned doctor of Crackow [*sic*]," Giraldus, and the title of the illustrated treatise attributed to him, the *Speculum Angelorum et Hominum*, so he left blank spaces to fill in on folios 1^r, 3^r, 4^r, and 5^r. The fictitious Arabian tribe with which Robartes became associated, the Judwalis in various spellings, had yet to be invented, too, so that blanks were also left in folios 5^r and 6^r. On 16 December 1917, Yeats reported to Lady Gregory that he had broken off work on a "philosophic dialogue" to allow completion of one of his Noh plays, *The Only Jealousy of Emer* (*L* 635). But by 4 January and 10 January 1918, he was able to cite the *Speculum*, Giraldus, and the Judwalis in letters sent, respectively, to Gregory and to Edmund Dulac. For added measure, Yeats wrote Dulac that the *Speculum* of Giraldus compared on profundity and neglect with "the even more profound work of Kusta iben Luka of Bagdad whose honour remains alone in the obscure sect of the Jadwalis" (*CL InteLex* 3384 and 3388). We can conclude from this evidence that, between mid-December and early January, Yeats almost certainly had obtained the assistance of his friend, Sir Edward Denison Ross, who was director of the School for Oriental Languages (London University) and able to provide suggestions for those blanks. Sir Edward's pupil, Iseult Gonne, may have abetted the exercise.[9] Quite naturally, the third, fourth, and fifth fuller drafts of the dialogue would be in position to carry on from there in holograph and typed copy, and they do so in *YVP4* .

The next stage in the plot development of Exercise Book 2, second draft, occurs when Robartes and Aherne come to Yeats's lodging at 18 Woburn Buildings, Euston Road, and consider stopping by to "reproach him."

Exercise Book 2—folio 7^r

[Aherne]
At this moment we are passing Yeats['s] rooms
[?as] this is Woburn Buildings. You can see that
he is in by the light ~~over the w~~ through the
ora[n]ge curtains on the first floor. ~~How strange~~
You & I are
~~that you & I should be~~ quite unknown except
to the few people, who have read his
Rosa Alchemica, & certainly neither of us
would have been chosen ~~to be [?]~~ to be known
in just that way

Robartes
Yes I represented as I remember rightly &
I read the story only once many years ago
Very quixotic & debauched
As ~~half devotee half debauchee~~, & certainly
I think
I have been a very ordinary travellor, & ~~have as~~
~~little sensual~~ have lived a very decent quiet
life
Aherne
He has treated me even worse, for he describes
me as a pious Catholic, who cannot keep

Exercise Book 2—folio 8^r^

himself from curiosity into the most forbidden
subjects. You at any rate know that I have
neither curiosity nor belief out side the
Catecisms, & I can buy that for a penny.

[*Without saying so or indicating as much by means of drawn lines, arrows, and diagonal strokes to signify intent, the whole verso page (7^v^) facing folio 8^r^ would replace the remainder of the latter at this point. Thus, the drawn line that follows is the editor's, not that of Yeats.*]

Robartes
I have a good mind to go in & reproach him.
Aherne
Why should you—he thinks that you are
dead & it is safe[ly] so, & besides he
merely wrote of us in the manner of the
in his
~~early nineties, when he first~~ current ~~then~~
he he & I wrote. Young men [?tend] to
us
~~[?] [?read] themselves~~ He ~~studies you~~ re-created ~~you~~
respectively and
under the influence ^ of Verlaine ~~& in under that~~
of Walter Pater. The two states of emotion
alternated, the first [?honest] passion of the one, the
being
~~delicate uncertainty of the other~~ – ~~was~~ as peppers

on the tongue that made the taste tolerable the
thin claret of the other. It was a proud
~~ger~~ generation & it romanticisd everything

Exercise Book 2—folio 7^{v}

Shall we go in & reproach him
Robartes
I think not, & I think it might pain him
~~& [?]~~ to let him know that he was in error
when he wrote to me as dead. Besides I gather
from what you have told me that one meets
at his rooms writers & painters of the new
generation which has no manner
Aherne
They describe this new manner as ~~sin cety~~ sincerity.
Robartes
Besides why should we reproach him. He misrepresented
us under the influence of Paul Verlaine & of
Walter Pater, both writers who belonged by right
of birth to our older generation. ~~They were thus~~
If they found the cool claret of Pater the more
delightful when they had slightly burned their tongues
than in our generation that supplied the peppar & the
claret. ~~Their style was too elaborate, but contained~~
Aherne
I wish I could show your tolerance. His generation
romanticis[ed] everything even their elders

Exercise Book 2—folio 9^{r}

even its elders. Fortunately the great war
~~has made me~~ has brought back ~~[?]~~ realities of that
~~life, & that romantic generation [?]~~
~~will be soon forgotten. Indeed, & our~~ sobriety.

[inserted from folio 8^{v}.]

I ~~always~~ am always delighted when I think that
The great war has swept away the last
Romanticism
remnants of that unhealthy ~~movement~~; & there
are moments when I prefer even the Café

Ro[y]al & its courtesies. We have now something
novel to think about
~~Robartes~~

[Folio 9^r, continued.]

Robartes

serious
I do not consider the great war ~~serious~~
~~I consider it was a monstrous out~~
~~break of frivolity~~ – ~~The desert~~ sand is
and the desert silence is
serious, ~~& even a mans solitary thought~~
^ but here we are at my door. It is a poor
neighborhood as I warned you but one where
There still
~~[?]~~ I would ~~never have [?] left them~~
had not frivolity ~~rolled its cannon to~~ my
~~very door~~ disturbed – so I am only here because
~~frivolity broke in upon them with their can[non]~~
disturbed the desert sand & the silence
the Turks & the English came ^ with their
frivolous cannon:

[inserted from folio 8^v.]

and yet why should I accuse
the cannon. Only that which [?causes] strange
or withered frivolities. For ~~when I spe~~ at this
moment I am pressing between my fingers some
desert
[?handful] of sand that I carry always in my left
pocket

It seems pretty clear from this that it is too soon for Robartes and Aherne to confront Yeats, except behind his back. To bring these two characters just outside his door to surmise his presence by window-light and to speak of him out of earshot is the same gambit employed in "The Phases of the Moon," only with the scene shifted to Ballylee. For material, here, Yeats has reached back to his first draft in Exercise Book 1, folio 2^r, but with precision and economy. Right away, he plunges into the objections these characters have about the way they were presented in the early stories in *The Savoy* and, reworking his material on the influence of Pater and Verlaine in the first draft, folio 3^r, he lets them voice their complaints covertly. We hear them; but, supposedly, he doesn't. "He re-created us," Aherne says, "under the influence[,] respectively[,] of [Paul] Verlaine and of Walter Pater," the "pepper" and "claret" of "two states of emotion alternated" (8^{r}). The influence caused the author and "his generation" to romanticize. The point was important enough to deserve a recasting on the facing verso (7^{v}) in Exercise Book 2. The Great War of 1914–1918, though, brought back reality and "swept away the last remnants of that unhealthy Romanticism" (8^{v}), and, of that, Robartes is of two minds. On the one hand, there is the desert, sobriety, silence. On the other, juxtaposed, are the courtesies of the Café Royal[10] in the days of Wilde and Beardsley but also, later, the "frivolity of the cannon" and a hint of T. E. Lawrence in the celebrated skirmishes of "the Turks and the English" in the desert sands, a portion of which Robartes keeps in his pocket (9^{r}). At times waxing nostalgic in his ambivalence, he "prefer[s] even the Café Royal and its courtesies" (8^{v}) to war.

But here Robartes and Aherne reach the end of the second draft, not having revealed themselves to Yeats but having arrived, finally, at Robartes's door in a "poor neighborhood" (9^{r}). Judging distance by the number of uncancelled words since folio 7^{r}, Yeats's lodging in Woburn Buildings must be hard by this one. At first, next to Aherne's account of his own splendidly furnished rooms in Pimlico, Westminster, one might expect Robartes's neighborhood to be poor indeed. However, Robartes's "third-rate lodging house" seems to conduce contemplation.

[Folio 9^{r}, continued]

are at
& ~~well here~~ we ~~[?come]~~ my
door—
a third rate lodging house, but here at last
[have] my solitude
I ~~shall escape my friends~~ if any are ~~still living~~
and the contemplation for which ~~I live will not be broken~~.
I live will be a little broken that circumstances admit.

Exercise Book 2—folio 10^{r}

~~Aherne~~.
Wish that I could welcome you under a less
I ~~know you have ample means, & I thought~~ to
pretentious roof
~~find you living under circumstances of~~ greater
~~simplicity.~~ If the founder of our Faith were
to come again, & it were decreed that all had to be
as before I can imagine him searching in vain
for a simple room
among the poor, & ~~among the holy poor~~ for a

room simple enough for the last supper. He would
handful of
be compelled to take a ~~few~~ ^ coppers from ~~peter~~
Peters Bag
~~Peter Boge~~ & change them into gold ~~before~~ he
~~before he came &~~ stood among the pharasees
~~could afford a room simple enough for the last~~
~~supper could find a~~ fitting scenery for the
last supper.
Aherne.
My lodging in Pimblico – with its beauti[ful] furniture,
~~its lo~~ with dropping folds of its red table cloth
and its pictures ~~which heaven~~ ~~I have taken~~ down
~~would be as little suitable or as little~~
~~Robartes~~
could as little pass your test, which I admit
to be admirable.

Positioned on the facing, otherwise clean verso, folio 9^{v}, and of a height equal to the lower third of this page, an inverted spiral, or vortex, has been drawn, the meaning of which is a mystery.

The ascetic simplicity of Robartes's lodging reflects his aesthetics just as the ornamental furnishings of Aherne's comparatively rich house reflects his own. Both are in fact "pretentious." And thus we may recall the picture of dereliction in the Temple of the Alchemical Rose "on the very end of a dilapidated almost deserted pier," as well as in the dust-enshrouded interior of Aherne's house behind Dublin's Four Courts (*Myth* 280 and 304). Robartes's present quarters are not the ampler place he and Aherne will occupy on the (Prince) Albert Road, Regents Park, London, in "The Stories of Michael Robartes and His Friends: An Extract from a Record Made by His Pupils." However, in practice (at this time), Yeats was only working out the source codes for such later work in the drafts of the two exercise books, one labeled "Aherne & Robartes | Dialogue Etc – imperfect."

The next draft is longer, referred to as "Untitled Manuscript" in *YVP4*, a holograph of some thirty pages, the first nine of which are revisions of the second draft of the dialogue presented above—that is, transciptions in *YVP4* 119–24 are correspondent on story whereas pages 124–34 give us Robartes lecturing on the system. Similarly, the fourth draft stage, the first to be called "The Discoveries of Michael Robartes," begins with reworked (and therefore redundant) plot lines, scenes, and characters from the "Untitled Manuscript," the first eleven pages in *YVP4* (62–73, with interpolations) on story followed by thirty-nine pages (74–113) of exposition on the system. The same goes for the typescript: story (13–18) precedes exposition (19–47).

Then something remarkable happened: the process started over again between Robartes and one John Aherne, with dialogue abandoned, in a few pages, in favor of "extracts" from imaginary letters. These extracts presented an alternative method for the exposition of the system, which had grown prolix because of the ongoing discoveries of Yeats and his wife. Still, the new structural basis for "Version B" anticipated *SMR*'s technique of serial story-telling by friends and pupils in extract-form. Yeats wrote in the headnote to "Version B," dated "June 1920":

> In the spring of nineteen nineteen[,] immediately after Michael Robartes['s] return to Mesopotamia[,] I received from his friend John Aherne the following fragments, partly extracts from letters written by Robartes to John Aherne, and partly records of conversations. I offer these to the few friends and disciples of a singular philosophy and visionary. (*YVP4* 141)

This is a major departure from a dialogue structure built on elements of story, because the narrative frame, developed mainly in the year 1918, amounts to such a small share of the whole text—in *YVP4*, a ratio of 4 pages (141–44) to 102 (144–246). It is, however, a transitional step toward the integrative distribution of some of the same story elements in *A Vision* as well as certain poems and notes explanatory introduced in the 1920s.

Still, we have yet to place into our chronology a key part of Yeats's invention, that of "The Great Diagram," or "Great Wheel," itself, which began to emerge in a separate unit, entitled "Appendix by Michael Robartes"[11] and somewhat at a tangent to the "Untitled Manuscript" of *YVP4* (i.e., Draft 3). That unit of work was a necessary rehearsal for the recitation of Robartes in the poem "The Phases of the Moon" (or even of Aengus in the Cuchulain version). As a work of dictation in the hand of George Yeats, the "Appendix" continues to bear witness to the resurrection of Aherne and Robartes as characters and the creation of new ones around Giraldus and his supposed Arab sources. So to that matter, we shall turn next.

Notes

1. See Part Two, above: "Imaginary Conversations, 'The Phases of the Moon,' and the Robartes Monologue in *The Wild Swans at Coole*," as well as notes to "The Phases of the Moon" and "The Double Vision of Michael Robartes." The Harpers are also vague about when Yeats decided Robartes was to become the interpreter of findings. They say only that Yeats queried a spirit guide in an undated "stray MS": "I most wish to know what will help to interpret the script, [so] I would like to ask about symbol after symbol." To this, the Harpers conjecture that either the "Communicator or some other may have suggested that the discoveries of the AS could best be interpreted through Michael Robartes" (*YVP4* 2). The earliest reference to "the imaginary life of Robartes" in the automatic scripts occurred on 6 Dec. 1917 (*YVP1* 149, 519 n. 89).
2. The Harpers completed their study before the dialogues were catalogued and assigned manuscript numbers in the National Library of Ireland, Collection List 60, Occult Papers of W. B.

Yeats (Mss. 34,270–36,285; Accession No. 5554). Not included in *YVP4*, the two notebooks I quote (Popular Exercise Books, one labeled by Yeats "Aherne & Robartes | Dialogue Etc – imperfect") are now part of NLI 36,263/7, a folder also containing "30-odd pages much smaller in size than any other of the MSS" (*YVP4* 12) which are of "special interest" because "important to the growth of the System of *A Vision*" (11).

3. The triptych of related stories in *The Secret Rose* (1897) would generally establish the scene as taking place in late 1917 or early 1918.
4. The Café de la Paix, at the intersection of the Boulevard des Capucines and the Place de l'Opéra, attracted such famous writers of the day as Émile Zola, Gustave Flaubert, Guy du Maupassant, and others.
5. Phillippe-Auguste Villiers de l'Isle-Adam died on 9 Aug. 1889. The play was one of Yeats's sacred books when he went to Paris in 1894, as he acknowledges in his 1924 preface to the H. P. R. Finsberg translation. See Part Five, below, on "Denise's Story."
6. For instance, Leonard Smithers in the case of Dowson's lyric "Extreme Unction"; at this time "Beata Solitudo" and "Stan Smithers" are untraced, perhaps cancelled in manuscript because the names were vaguely recalled.
7. Tiziano Vecellio (c. 1485–1576), better known as Titian, painted *The Adoration of the Magi* (c. 1561), currently located at the Prado Museum in Madrid, Spain.
8. Perhaps Yeats actually had in mind Sandro Botticelli's *The Mystical Nativity*, a favorite at the National Gallery, London, and later cited in *A Vision* (*AVA* 202–3, *AVB* 292 and footnotes). See *YPM* 151–53. The manuscript that the Harpers introduce begins the same way, but then Titian and the title of his painting are crossed out so that one by Carlo Crivelli (c. 1430–1494) may be substituted (*YVP4* 62). The title of the Crivelli, "the story of Griselda," is repeated at the beginning of the typescript (*YVP4* 13).
9. See *YVP4* 49, n. 24, and *CW13* 225, n. 49, and 226, n. 51. See also A. Norman Jeffares, "Iseult Gonne," *YA* 16 (2005): 197–278, especially pp. 235–37, which account for Gonne in the post Yeats had arranged for her in London under Ross's watchful eye. Coincidentally, on 16 Dec. 1917, she visited the Yeatses at Stone Cottage and then joined them again for Christmas at Ashdown Cottage in Forest Row.
10. A famous London restaurant and meeting place at 68 Regents Street, Piccadilly, since 2008 known as the five-star Hotel Café Royal. According to Jeffares, Iseult Gonne inspired Yeats with talk of her Bohemian friends in London, during visits in January 1918, prompting him to write "To a Young Beauty"; and she kept him posted on her meetings with his old friends T. Sturge Moore and Arthur Symons, whose poem "'Deirdre' celebrated a dinner with her in the Café Royal. She helped him with his translation of Baudelaire" (*YA* 16: 237).
11. "Appendix by Michael Robartes," NLI 36,263/7/3, c. Jan.–May 1918.

On Developing The Great Diagram of Giraldus in the "Appendix by Michael Robartes," 1918

On the transmission of texts key to understanding the resurrection of Robartes and Aherne, the following stemma provides an approximate chronology based on evidence and the example of Catherine E. Paul and Margaret Mills Harper in their critical edition of *AVA* (*CW13* xxxiii):

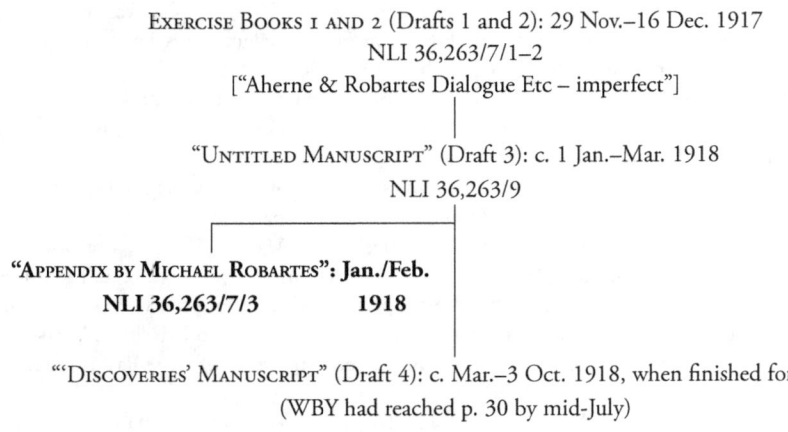

Exercise Books 1 and 2 (Drafts 1 and 2): 29 Nov.–16 Dec. 1917
NLI 36,263/7/1–2
["Aherne & Robartes Dialogue Etc – imperfect"]

"Untitled Manuscript" (Draft 3): c. 1 Jan.–Mar. 1918
NLI 36,263/9

"Appendix by Michael Robartes": Jan./Feb. 1918
NLI 36,263/7/3

"'Discoveries' Manuscript" (Draft 4): c. Mar.–3 Oct. 1918, when finished for typing
(WBY had reached p. 30 by mid-July)
NLI 36,263/4

"'Discoveries' Typescript" (Draft 5): c. 3 Oct. 1918–late 1918
NLI 36,263/3

"Version B": c. late 1918–1920
MS of brief headnote of "June 1920," short Robartes-John Aherne dialogue, and
Extracts ["The Great Wheel" and "The Twenty-Eight Embodiments"]
NLI 30,525 and 36,263/10/1–2

Dating and placing Yeats's dictated monologue "Appendix by Michael Robartes"—presented in the voice of Robartes, with local references to a certain "conversation" with Aherne (in folio 3^r) and to a maligned philosopher by the name of Yeats (in folios 6^r and 9^r)—have been open questions ever since Walter Kelly Hood published his transcription in *Yeats and the Occult*, ed. George Mills Harper (London: Macmillan Press, 1975). Presented as one of two unpublished essays collected and silently emended in Hood's "Michael Robartes: Two Occult Manuscripts" (204–24), the "Appendix" joined company with a second monologue entitled "Michael Robartes Foretells" (which one finds in the Afterword of this study). Hood thought that the two manuscripts were "evidently written for inclusion in *A Vision* (though for two different editions), and both [having] to do with the symbolic figure of Michael Robartes, who is central to the fictional framework of *A Vision*" (204). While partly correct, there are problems with both assertions, the former owing to the fact that it had only just occurred to Yeats, on 12 January 1918 (*CL InteLex* 3389) that his dialogue "The Discoveries of Michael Robartes" might be published as such in the autumn of 1918, when by then he had abandoned the modus of dialogue and even "Version B" cannot quite be said to be an actual manuscript of *AVA*. Likewise, as a discarded story, "Michael Robartes Foretells" was possibly written before Yeats had committed definitely to include *Stories of Michael Robartes and His Friends* (1931), as well as *A Packet for Ezra Pound* (1929) and a third Cuala booklet, into *AVB*, fearing that *A Vision* might not stand alone: "I do not want to publish 'A Vision' by itself for various reasons" (Yeats to H. Watt, 14 Dec. 1930, *CL InteLex* 5419).

The first two drafts of the Robartes-Aherne dialogue occurred before Giraldus and the *Speculum* were given their names, as we've seen, before he broke off, on 16 December 1917, to obtain relief from insomnia and to concentrate on writing the early version of *The Only Jealousy of Emer* (Yeats to Lady Gregory, *CL InteLex* 3375). But instead of returning to the "philosophical dialogue" *after* completing the play, he seems to have continued with the dialogue to some extent—for instance, with respect to research and consultations with Sir Edward Denison Ross (on translating plausible Arabic names) and with Mrs. Yeats as medium and secretary. She took dictation from him for the "Appendix" and drew the eleven fully and partially eclipsed figures of sun and moon (on folio 2^v) that anticipate the range of 28 crescents from "No Moon | Full Sun" at Phase 1 to "No Sun | Full Moon" at Phase 15 incorporated into the third-draft version of the dialogue ("Untitled Manuscript," *YVP4* 125). See figure below (on next page).

As for directions from the spirit guides when work on the dialogue resumed after the holidays, the Yeatses were advised, in the automatic script of 1 January 1918, that matter on "the second circle" would need to "go into another dialogue" (*YVP1* 183, *YVP4* 3). In the "Appendix," Robartes speaks of three concentric circles that "represent the circle of the Heavens," the "inmost" being "merely the Horoscope of Gyraldus himself" while the other two are "symbolical" as drawn in the Great Diagram, "the frontispiece of the *Speculum*" (folio 2^r). Folios 3^r-5^r begin the review of supposed comparative diagrams in the Latin book of Giraldus and an unnamed Arabic one, eventually (in Draft 4) "the TARIQAT UN-NUFUS of Kusta ben Luka" (*YVP4* 64). By 4 January 1918, in Oxford, Yeats was obviously busy with the dialogue again, although working on the play, too, reporting to Lady Gregory that the dialogue would now become

> a series of dialogues about a supposed medieval book, the *Speculum Angelorum et Hominum* by Giraldus, and a sect of Arabs called the Judwalis (diagrammatists). Ross has helped me with the Arabic. I live with a strange sense of revelation and never know what the day will bring. (*CL Intelex* 3384)

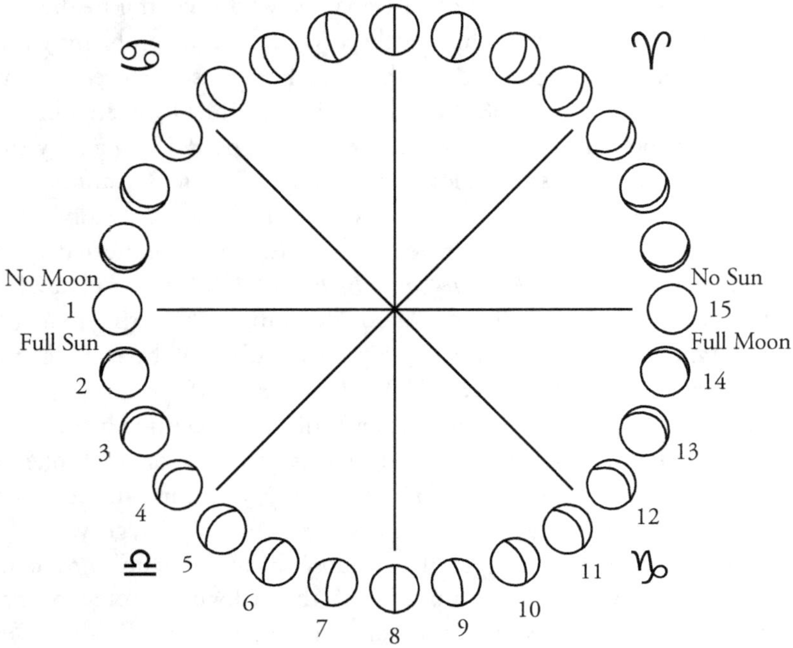

Drawn figure on p. 12 of "Untitled Manuscript" (cf. *YVP4* 125)

Two weeks later, he declared that he had finished his "new Cuchulain play" and was "hesitating on a new one" (*CL InteLex* 3390), though in fact he had only completed the first draft and had but a vague idea for a "Judas play" about Evil Genius (eventually *Calvary*). At the end of folio 5^{r} of the "Appendix," Robartes writes (in the hand of George Yeats): "In the diagram of the Theological Gyraldus the word 'evil' is written at Beauty and the word 'Good' at ugliness." This paradoxical doctrine of the countervailing, inversely polar relationship between beauty and ugliness, good and evil, is entertaining, even humanized by flippant dialogue in "Untitled Manuscript" (Draft 3)—Aherne: "I should think that by your system the further from beauty the greater the desire." Robartes: "In complete ugliness or in complete beauty desire is extinct" (*YVP4* 131). Yet in both the "Appendix" and the dialogue, in this vicinity, several Latinate technical terms are introduced that do not appear elsewhere in Yeats's published writings. More so than in *A Vision*, Hood notices

> a more obvious focus on aesthetic terms in the manuscript than in the book, and the terms gain by emphasis. The bold identification of beauty with what the world considers "evil" links the manuscript to Yeats's earlier work: evil, according to the world, consists in flouting the mores of the bourgeoisie but is, for Yeats, the means by which genius achieves its distinguishing individualism. (207)

In the "Appendix" (folio 6^r^), Robartes says, "The moral struggle is very much as described in Mr. Yeats' 'Anima Hominis' except for a vagueness in a description at second hand and without diagrams" (cf. *Myth* 331–32). "Mr. Yeats is wrong when he describes his famous actress creating a faint Maeterlinckian beauty by reaction from her own dominating primary [state]" (folio 9^r^; cf. *Myth* 326–27; *Per Amica Silentia Lunae* had just been published on 18 January). At the end of Exercise Book 2, as Robartes and Aherne compare the respective simplicity and ornamental furnishings of their lodgings in St. Pancras and Pimlico, just so Yeats makes rapid progress with Draft 3, through familiar territory to Robartes's "less pretentious roof," re-establishing the bond between these old men of another time, one represented by the "pepper" of Paul Verlaine and "cool claret" of Walter Pater (*YVP4* 123–24). Giraldus and the "Speculum Angelorum et Hominis [*sic*]" are named while Kusta ben Luka is left a blank space and his treatise, as in the "Appendix,"is referred to as "The Camels back" (121–22). The circular diagram is introduced and cancelled, illustrating the correspondence between the twenty-eight phases of primary sun and antithetical moon and "the 28 incarnations in different [?phases] of typal man" (125; cf. 126–27). Likewise, in the "Appendix" (folio 3^r^): "These 28 phases represent the 28 incarnations of typal man as I have explained in my conversation with Ahearne [*sic*]." And then we have the coincidence of unusual aesthetic terminology, derived, as Hood speculates, "from the ghostly Instructors or from the Golden Dawn" (107):

> *daemon beneficium*, *Persona Artificans*, and *Mala persona* (the spellings and capitalization are Yeats's own). The origin of the terms is unknown.... In context, the *daemon beneficium* is described by Yeats as a "passion for reality" within a subjective context; why it should be a "beneficent spirit" is not apparent. *Persona Artificans*—the latter is not a legitimate Latin form—is perhaps Yeats's rough translation of some such English phrase as "the shaping mask," suggesting that it artfully creates or shapes personality like the Mask of *A Vision*, and appropriately enough it makes for unity of being. *Mala persona*, evidently to be translated as "evil mask," serves to separate primary from antithetical and vice versa....[T]he *daemon beneficium* is concerned with transcendent reality....*Persona Artificans* suggests the Mask both by translation and from its context....*Mala persona*, though it might be connected by translation with the False Mask of *A Vision*, has least connection with the Faculties. (Hood 207–8)

Two of these terms—"Mala Persona" and "Persona Artificans"—were in use briefly in the automatic script of 24 November 1917 to 11 January 1918 (*YVP1* 111, 129, 131, 160–61, 242). A diagram, consisting of a square enclosed within a circle, was introduced into the Card File to distinguish between ugliness and beauty, "Mala Persona" and "artistic genius" (see *YVP3* 295). In the dialogue of January-March 1918 ("Untitled Manuscript," *YVP4* 126), extracted from parts of two, largely cancelled pages, Robartes describes a similar diagram:

> Mala Persona & Persona Artificans[,] which are written on the cross bars of the solar lunar wheel [of] the European diagram and have been copied by me[,] with certain other names[,] onto the [A]rabic diagram,… [are] from the center or place of balance. Mala Persona[,] which acts in every direction[,] creates the discord between Antithetical & primary & so makes possible the harmonizing action of Persona Artificans with the help of the 28 emblematic wood cuts, which are given by Giraldus.… I can now explain to you artistic genius & its connection with bodily beauty in man & in woman.

This stricken passage is followed by another two pages, half the lines of which are also cancelled, including the following, also cancelled, sentences:

> Mala Persona perpetually increases the clevage between the two halves by creating sin, & Persona Artificans recreates harmonious cooperation. The highest form of subjective genius in man or in woman comes just before or after complete beauty.… I should place the soul of Keats[,] for instance[,] at twelve or 13, [because] the absorption in the antithetic at 14 would be too great. (127)

In Yeats's use of these terms in the "Appendix by Michael Robartes," folios 6^r–9^r, with *Per Amica Silentia Lunae* (1918) very much in the foreground and "Ego Dominus Tuus" somewhat less so, he takes critical aim at himself, as we've seen. This ploy, too, is enacted in the dialogue ("Untitled Manuscript"), nearly three pages further on:

> The impassioned nature of Keats displays more than the others [i.e., Robert Bridges, Lionel Johnson] the mechanics of the phase, & there is no doubt that Yeats is right in saying that he was driven by circumstance & personal defect to seek in the Antithetic what was denied him in the primary: a pure condition of all subjective genius. (*YVP4* 129)

Keats's creative genius "kept Mala Persona so far away that his primary self never closed its objective eye" (129). For once, Yeats's dog Latin was not cancelled in the belief that he might be drafting copy toward publication in the autumn. His aesthetic concerns continued to dominate for another eight pages before he broke off the dialogue, but in a very different way than the mid-sentence exit of the author in the "Appendix"; and yet there is kinship in the observance of "men of remarkable genius who were exceeding[ly] ugly" at the end of this third draft of the dialogue (134–35) and the epitome of ugliness embodied by the Hunchback at the end of the "Appendix" (folios 10ʳ–11ʳ).

In context, then, the evidence points to the creation of an auxiliary device, the "Appendix by Michael Robartes," to explain the esoteric element in the cancelled passages and drawn figure of the wheel, all from Robartes's speeches in the first half of the dialogue as it existed in January 1918. As an appendix, probably it was intended to appear at the end like those appendices inserted later at the end of the "'Discoveries' Manuscript" (*YVP4* 108–13) and the "'Discoveries' Typescript" (44–47). In fact, a sequence of work in loose, unnumbered folios excluded from *YVP4* constitutes a first-draft version of the "'Discoveries' Manuscript" appendix. Somewhat disorderly and incomplete in NLI 36,263/7/4, the unit begins with the heading "Ugliness" (in place of Aherne's name), followed by a disquisition on the poetic beauty of Keats, Rossetti, and others and the placement of Shakespeare in the system of incarnations. Robartes lectures on Rabelais and Phantasmagoria, the skill of Rembrandt, the deformities of the hunchback, and especially the phases after 18, which suggests that some of this material might have been recycled from the missing conclusion of the dialogue at Draft 3. The "Appendix by Michael Robartes" was definitely not conceived as a textual extension of the 1925 edition of *A Vision*, a possibility that Walter Hood raised and that the time-line in the new critical edition recognizes with notable ambiguity (*CW13* xxxii). Moreover, it seems pretty clear that the break in Draft 3 and in the Robartes "Appendix" occurred at the same time, more or less, and perhaps for the same reason. As usual, the automatic script and Yeats's correspondence are highly valued sources.

From 21 December 1917 to 14 January 1918, due to steady work on *The Only Jealousy of Emer*, Yeats was keen to receive instruction from the spirit guides on Cuchulain's place in the emerging system (*YVP1* 164–254 *passim*). From 18 to 25 January, Yeats had a violent case of influenza, but by 7 February, he dictated a letter from Oxford to say, in part, that he and his wife were "very busy" each morning at the Bodleian Library and each evening at work on the system, "growing always more subtle & more profound.... The Cuchulain Play is finished and a Cuchulain poem half done" (Yeats to Edmund Dulac, *CL InteLex* 3405). The next day, he dictated a letter to John Quinn, reporting Robert Gregory's death in Italy, a plan for a fifth Noh play, and affairs relating to his father's welfare in New York (*CL InteLex* 3407). The day after that, he wrote to Iseult Gonne: "I have just finished a new Cuchulain poem full of this new philosophy" (*CL InteLex* 3408). Work on the dialogue and the "Appendix" had swerved into the writing of "The Phases of the Moon" in its Cuchulain-Aengus middle state as a text. (For transcriptions, see Stephen Parrish, ed., *The Wild Swans at Coole: Manuscript Materials* [Ithaca, NY: Cornell University Press, 1994], 346–53; and Chapman, *YPM*

129–35.) That version would have rendered the textual body of the "song" later recited by Robartes. But there were other projects that intervened, including revising *The Only Jealousy*, rewriting *The Dreaming of the Bones*, and consoling Lady Gregory on the loss of her son: "I am trying [to] write something in verse about Robert Gregory but do not know what will come. I am trying a poem in manner like one that Spenser wrote for Sir Phillip Sidney. It may come to nothing" (22 Feb. [1918], *CL InteLex* 3410). The poem was "Shepherd and Goatherd," probably his least successful dialogue in verse. They remained busy in Oxford, hoped to go to Ireland in early March, and planned to spend Easter in Coole. The latter miscarried due to George Yeats's turn with influenza during that pandemic year.

"The Phases of the Moon" was put into final form as a Robartes-Aherne dialogue at Ballylee in the summer of 1918 (*YPM* 237), when the poem completed its evolution from the Yeats-Aherne dialogue "Anglo Ireland: a conversation," of 29 November 1917, and the "new Cuchulain poem" of 9 February 1918. On 27 February, Yeats wrote Dulac to praise the ring Mrs. Yeats had commissioned, noting that it had just been sent to "the makers" and that a poem ("Tom O'Roughly") explained its meaning; but he added: "The Giraldus portrait is a masterpiece & I would like to keep it for a little" (*CL InteLex* 3411). Having commissioned the portrait earlier, presumably with orders for the ring and for "The Great Diagram from the Speculum Angelorum et hominis [*sic*]" interpreted in Robartes's "Appendix," the path was set to continue "The Discoveries of Michael Robartes" as a dialogue. With interruptions, this work advanced another hundred pages by late 1918, when dialogue was abandoned for the "Version B" series of extracts quoted from fictitious letters and conversations—the so-called "Robartes MSS," from which Yeats drew material for prefaces, notes, introductions, and stories for the next two decades.

The following literatim transcription streams for economy the contents of the eleven folios of the "Appendix by Michael Robartes," only vertical slash marks ("|") have been introduced for line breaks in the manuscript and numerous bracketed cues have been used to identify the signs of the zodiac and astrological symbols used by George Yeats in her shorthand. Spellings, capitalizations, and lower case forms are all hers. Strikethroughs appear wherever she cancelled part of the text or was instructed to do so by WBY in the midst of dictation. Folio numbers are indicated within boldface brackets; and, finally, a set of endnotes provide added commentary and highlight some of the details.

APPENDIX BY MICHAEL ROBARTES [NLI 36,263/7/3]

[1r] The Great Diagram from the Speculum Angelorum | et hominis contains the epitome of the philosophy | of human life which has occupied me for | the last twenty years, and which will | occupy me till I die. It cannot however | be fully understood without several | ~~small~~ simpler diagrams, two from the | "Speculum," and two of a somewhat different | nature from the "Camel's Back[.]" The | photograph<s>~~ic~~ ~~reprodu~~ from the diagrams | of the Speculum have been <entitled> ~~numbered~~ | by me <The Great Diagram> and a, b, ~~and c~~ <respectively> <but to> ~~and~~ my own | copies of two diagrams from the "Camel's | back" I have given their Arabic names, | the first "The holy women and the two | Kalendars" because it describes the movements | of two symbolic suns and moons, and <the second> "The | dance of the Eunuch with the favourite wife[.]"[1]

[2r] In the Great Diagram, which is the frontispiece of the | Speculum there are [three] circles one without the | other, and all three represent the circle of | the Heavens. The inmost however is merely the | Horoscope of Giraldus himself placed as we are | taught to place a horoscope for its better understanding[.] | The circle immediately outside that ~~represents~~ | ~~the lunar~~ has to do with certain symbolical | movements of the ☉ [sun] in the present ~~pos~~ position | of the Equinoctial Signs, and from it the whole | past and future of mankind may be judged | and discovered. It is considered both by Gyraldus | and the Arabs who have a similar diagram | to be related to the actual positions of the different | <parts of the> ~~Constellations and of the~~ Zodiac. The outermost | circle which was the first to arouse my | interest is however purely symbolical.[2]

[2v]

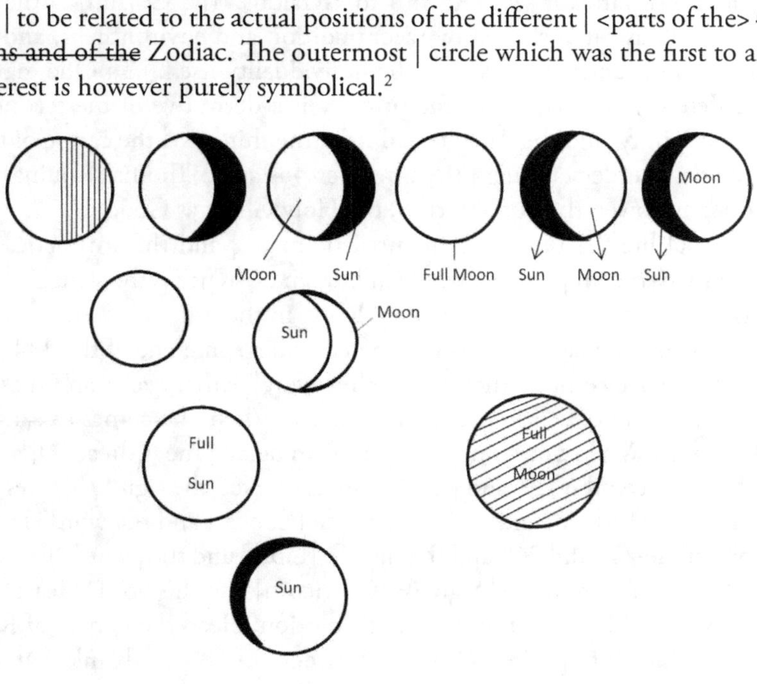

[3r] In the Great Diagram the phases of the ☽ [moon] are set | round it, ~~and drawn more or less naturalistically. The | unilluminated part of the ☽ [moon] being left dark. But in | the Arabic diagram of the same subjects~~ | and it will be noticed that they are not drawn | naturalistically. ~~The~~ [?Notions] ☉ [Sun] and ☽[moon] are combined | into a single symbol, the crescent of the first lunar phase | forming, as it were, upon the face of the ☉ [sun]; and the thin | crescent after the full ☽ [moon] representing not a dark section of | the ☽ [moon] but a symbolical solar crescent. Throughout | 28 steps, or phases ☉ [sun] and ☽ [moon] gain and lose respectively, | the ☽ [moon] gaining until it is full at the 15th phase and | then dwindling till the first phase when the ☉ [sun] is full. | These 28 phases represent the 28 incarnations of | typal man as I have explained in my conversation | with Ahearne.[3] In reality owing ~~to the part that~~ to no soul | ~~is exactly typical~~ being perfect the incarnations are | much more numerous, one has sometimes to go through | the same phase again and again, especially in the earlier | phases. The soul is considered to start at full sun, that | is to say at the dark of the ☽ [moon] and to end the cycle at the | last lunar crescent, after which [paragraph left dangling, incomplete][4]

[4r] When the soul starts its journey at full ☉ [sun] it begins a | symbolical lunar month, and as the ☉ [sun] moves through | a single sign during that month, the certain ~~[?]~~ number | of incarnations are supposed by Gyraldus & the Arab alike | to make up a symbolical year of 336 lives (28 x 12)[.] | This is the symbolical structure so far as it was known | to Gyraldus. The ☉ [sun] is the primary self or the self as | it is shaped by race, tradition and environment, and | the ~~[?]~~ ☽ [moon] is the antithetical self or the individuality itself. | ~~To~~ One may express them differently, and say that | the primary is a derivative of the second person of | (?) the Trinity, and the Antithetical from the third, & | the centre of the circle from the first, understanding | ~~the three persons~~ as St. Thomas Aquinas did, as | the Father as power, the Son as Truth, the Holy Ghost as Good.

In actual life the Primary is naturalistic man, | and the antithetical self the ideal, or ~~image~~ dream | life, the whole of human existence is the struggle | between these two; each to the very least detail | living in the other's loss. Every man who comes into | one's imagination is incarnated under some one of the 28 | **[5r]**phases, but some have come to their phase already in | earlier cycles and these are the stronger or the more | entirely conscious souls. ~~When one comes to examine in | detail the great~~ When one comes to examine in detail | the [G]reat [D]iagram one finds that between the 18th and | 19th phase is marked the sign ♈ [Aries] and the word "Head" is | added, and that the sign ♋ [Cancer] and the word "Loins" are | set between the 25th and 26th and the sign ♎ [Libra] and the | word "Fall" between the 4th & 5th phases, and the | Sign ♑ [Capricorn] and the word "Heart" between the 11th & 12th. | Heart is the climax of Emotion, Head the climax of Reason | ? and Loins which is opposite to Heart is Instinct or | [blank],[5] and the Fall which is opposite Head is the | first departure from Innocence and also the first | awakening of the Ego. The centre of this whole circle, | ~~is~~ where in diagram A Saturn is place[d], is supposed | to be the source of all, and perfect balance. What however | marks this system as different to any known to | me is that the full ☽ [moon] which occurs midway between | Emotion and Reason is described as the state of beauty ~~[?]~~ | while full ⊙ [sun] which occurs midway between loins and | fall is marked state of ugliness.

In the diagram of the Theological Gyraldus the | word "evil" is written at Beauty and the word "Good" | **[6r]** at ugliness. His reason probably was that Beauty binds | the Soul to life where ugliness sets it free, but there | is another reason for the attribution of terms which | occur also in the Arabic text; the antithetical life | struggling always to subdue the primary that full ☽ [moon] or Beauty may be reached, has an entirely individual ideal; | whereas the Primary seeks always to be united to the world | outside itself. The Antithetical life is subjective and | to that degree anarchic, whereas the Primary life | is objective, through the Primary we find our fellows and | our duties toward them. The moral struggle is very | much as described in Mr. Yeats' "Anima Hominis" | except for a vagueness in a description at second hand | and without diagrams.[6] Starting at complete objectivity | the Antithetical develops in a perpetual struggle, | from the first to fifteenth stage it is described | by both old writers as violent, whereas from the 16th | phase to the 28th the Primary is violent. I can only | speak at the moment in general terms and must | even when I have given all the detail possible to me, | <leave> the elucidation of the system very largely to those | who come to make of these diagrams subjects of | meditation.

The Ego from 1 to 15 develops in richness | by seeking the passion for reality, which is even | described by my latin author ~~in the~~ in his italianised | latin as daemon beneficium. **[7r]** The more intense is his passion for reality, the | more does he understand that the objects of his | desire do not exist in the physical world, he is | driven to seek them in the dream world and having | found them there to fashion the primary self into | their expression. This understanding is intensified | by the action of an influence called Mala Persona[,] | which[,] working from within the Antithetical Self and | acting with fullest power at phases 8 and 22 | when Antithetical and Primary are of equal | power[,] withdraws the Antithetical from the | Primary[;] it is the nature of the Primary to | seek <objective> reality and of the Antithetical to seek <subjective> | intensity. Mala persona <before full ☽ [moon]> ~~is~~ therefore <is> ~~[?] [?]~~ tending to | find this intensity by withdrawing from expression. | Left to itself the primary sins, that is to say, | refuses to submit [to] the Antithetical. ~~The intensity | of the [?revolting] contest create[s] the conversion of | being out of which subjective genius is created[.]~~ Persona Artificans as it is called by Gyraldus | acting also from within the antithetical ~~re unites | the shattered halves and thus uniting <makes> [?] genius | possible in the antithetical~~

if the antithetical can | gain the victory re-unites what has been shattered | giving thereby for the first ~~time~~ time the consciousness | of the unity of the being which becomes, where the | contest had been very violent, subjective genius.

[8r] It is no doubt this recognition of sin as the preparation | of genius which has given to the Arab tribe with whom I | have lived their singular tolerance. But it is not only | artistic beauty that is the reward of submission of | primary to antithetical; for this submission which must | always be a service and not a form of in-action, | creates physical beauty. Before however either physical | or Artistic Beauty can come in any great intensity many | lives have to be lived in a state of struggle which in the greater | souls contains every imaginable terror. This struggle centres | about that portion of the ☽ [moon's] path where the word Heart is | written, it is symbolised in the allegorical diagrams of | Gyraldus by such images as the man with his eyes torn | out by an eagle, and by the garroted man, images of | a soul dumb or blinded by a power from within itself. | Every ~~sin~~ effort is towards the personal Ideal[,] every sin | is against it, and men seek solitude and poets describe | mountain and wood.

At the full ☽ [moon] we have complete beauty, physical or | mental, and as the Primary is now entirely lost in the | Antithetical expression of the impossible. In the phase | after the full ☽ [moon], represented in the diagram by a thin solar | crescent, the Primary is re-born, and from this at each | succeeding life the nature is more objective. The process | of development is reversed and the passion for society ~~drives~~ | shows us that we can no longer find within | ourselves the objects of desire. ~~T~~ We cease gradually to | find subjective intensity endurable, and finding no peace | within seek external activity. The passion for reality is | still daemonas beneficium and the effectiveness of our | expression in life corresponds exactly to our sincerity | in seeking an objective form which is in every case the | **[9r]** opposite of the internal state. Mr. Yeats is wrong when he | describes his famous actress creating a faint Maeterlinckian | beauty by reaction from her own dominating primary.[7] | Judging by his description her incarnation is after Beauty, | for the primary is violent and the objectivity enlarging. | Before the full ☽ [moon] the psychology had been as he describes | it[,] but after full ☽ [moon] she is in flight from that faint | delicate beauty once achieved with so much labour. | She has begun to shrink from beauty and pursue | ugliness, she has fallen under the influence of a | new perspective. Before Beauty the Soul sees | utmost energy in the minuteness of harmonious | organization, ~~And after Beauty~~ in a movement inward | or upward, in an always heightening subjectivity. | But now it sees it in the movement of large masses | on a single plane.[8] The whole development from full ☽ [moon] | to full ☉ [sun] is from a desire to rest from subjective | intensity in forms of ~~[?]~~ dwindling emotional energy; in ~~[?]~~ ugliness. Beauty is the complete | expression of the individuality and it is without | desire because it is the goal of desire, and being | complete individuality it is the soul's triumph over the | race.

~~by~~ Complete ugliness is complete objectivity & | is the triumph of the race over the individual.

Every form of ugliness which the soul puts on | represents a passion or an ambition exhausted | **[10r]** and a dismembering of the individual. I find | in the allegorical pictures of Gyraldus that two of | the last phases are represented, the one by the idiot, | the other by a Hunchback. In his commentary he | describes the idiot as that form where the soul can | rest from Spiritual Pride & the Hunchback as its | rest from ambition. In reply to the objection that | the Hunchback is malicious | and that there | should only be good in so much ugliness, as ugliness | frees the soul, he points out that Hunchbacks have | often beautiful eyes or hands, and adds "Even | a little beauty will account for much evil[.]"[9] | These forms are involuntarily assumed but they | may be assumed voluntarily and from that assumption | is sanctity. The soul as it is being set free contemplates | the sorrow and evil of the world and contemplating it not as | before beauty in relation to its own desiring, but in | relation to God who is the Spiritual objectivity. | At phase 26 that is to say between the Hunchback | and the Idiot is the incarnation where the soul frees | itself, though that freedom can only be attained | through a contemplation of ugliness in the mind | **[11r]** prolonged for several ~~life~~ lives and always acting | after the first life of this contemplation, in some | degree upon the body. That freedom once attained | the soul will enforce what ever body, ugly or | beautiful, is suitable for its work. Before this | however it passes symbolically into the axis | the complete balance and the source of energy,[10] [manuscript ends mid-sentence].

Notes

1. References to Arabic titles, possibly derived from *Arabian Nights*, remain untraced. "Camel's back," "The holy women and the two Kalendars," and "The dance of the Eunuch with the favourite wife" do not occur in *AVA* or elsewhere in Yeats's published writings. However, in "Untitled Manuscript" (NLI 36,263/9), "The Camels back" is defined as "an ancient Arab Ms, containing [the] doctrine" of a Bedouin "Arab sect well known at Fez in the time of Leo Africanus" (*YVP4* 122). And various tales involving eunuchs and wives occur in *Arabian Nights*, as well as several Kalendars' tales gathered in Sir Richard Burton's 16-volume, unexpurgated edition of 1885–1888. The parallel, again, between "Appendix by Michael Robartes" and the 3rd-Draft stage of Yeats's "Discoveries" dialogues would appear to be in the characterization of the Arab sect as a range of humanity from "holy men" to "other exceedingly licentious, or even cruel wandering together in tolerable amity" (*YVP4* 122).
2. Walter Kelly Hood (*YO* 210) observes: "The Great Diagram described here is presumably an earlier version of the Great Wheel which appeared in *A Vision* (1925) between pp. xiv and xv, in *Stories of Michael Robartes and His Friends: An Extract from a Record Made by His Pupils: And a Play in Prose by W. B. Yeats* (Dublin: Cuala Press, 1931) between pp. 8 and 9, and in *A Vision* (1937), p. 66. The horoscope of Giraldus does not appear in the Great Wheel. It might be noted that in the last two works Yeats reversed the earlier positions of the astrological signs for Libra and Capricorn." See Chapman, "Metaphors for Poetry," *YVEC* 251, n. 71. I concur

with Hood's association of "Diagram" and "Wheel," considering the drawn figures of a wheel consisting of 28 solar/lunar crescents in the "Untitled Manuscript," p. 13 (cancelled), and the figures drawn on folio 2[v] of the "Appendix."

3. As Hood points out, "The phrasing here is very close to that in Yeats's 1921 notes to *The Only Jealousy of Emer* (*VPl* 566); indeed, this similarity bears on the dating of the 'Appendix.'" I do not believe the evidence here is sufficient in itself to support Hood's claim as the phrasing in Yeats's 1921 note is only part of a long sentence, mostly dissimilar: "The soul through each cycle of its development is held to incarnate through twenty-eight typical incarnations, corresponding to the phases of the moon…" (*VPl* 566). However, it is very much the case that Yeats had taken leave of the Robartes-Aherne dialogues on 16 Dec. 1917 to complete a first draft of *The Only Jealousy* on 14 Jan. 1918, according to his own account in letters to Lady Gregory; see *L* 635 and Steven Winnett, ed., *"The Only Jealousy of Emer" and "Fighting the Waves": Manuscript Sources* (Ithaca, NY: Cornell University Press, 2004), xix.
4. The thought in this sentence is left unfinished, as with the paragraph. Had Yeats not abandoned the "Appendix" early on, without so much as a correction of GY's handwritten MS. for a typist, surely this problem, as well as the blank at 4[r] (see n. 5) and the broken-off ending on 10[r], would have been addressed by Yeats.
5. A question mark stands in the left margin to allow Yeats to fill in the word intended for the blank space.
6. *Per Amica Silentia Lunae* (1918; cf. *Myth* 331–32), hereafter *PASL*.
7. *PASL* (*Myth* 326–27).
8. See *AVA*, p. 129, and *AVB*, p. 70, for Yeats's contrast of primary plane and the antithetical line.
9. Hood notes (*YO* 215), "The Idiot of the 'Appendix' becomes the Fool of Phase 28 in *A Vision* (1925), pp. 115–16. In the following lines, Yeats places an unnamed figure (perhaps the Saint of *A Vision*) at Phase 26, Hunchback at 25, and Idiot at 27; this is at odds with both editions of *A Vision*, in which Hunchback, Saint, and Fool are at Phases 26, 27, and 28, respectively."
10. Abrupt end of "Appendix by Michael Robartes."

Part Three: 1919–1925

Published Poems, Notes, and Extracts—

from *The Wild Swans at Coole* (1919), *Michael Robartes and the Dancer* (1921), *Four Plays for Dancers* (1921), *The Cat and the Moon* (1924), and *A Vision: An Explanation of Life founded upon the Writings of Giraldus and upon certain Doctrines Attributed to Kusta ben Luka* (1925)

Yeats's Preface to *The Wild Swans at Coole* (London: Macmillan, 1919)

This book is, in part, a reprint of *The Wild Swans at Coole*, printed a year ago on my sister's hand-press at Dundrum, Co. Dublin. I have not, however, reprinted a play which may be part of a book of new plays suggested by the dance plays of Japan, and I have added a number of new poems. Michael Robartes and John Aherne, whose names occur in one or other of these, are characters in some stories I wrote years ago, who have once again become part of the phantasmagoria through which I can alone express my convictions about the world. I have the fancy that I read the name John Aherne among those of men prosecuted for making a disturbance at the first production of "The Play Boy," which may account for his animosity to myself.

W.B.Y.

Ballylee, Co. Galway,
September 1918.

Yeats refers to *The Wild Swans at Coole, Other Verses and a Play in Verse* (Dundrum, Co. Dublin: Cuala Press, 1917), which included the play *At the Hawk's Well.* He introduces an element of confusion by assigning Aherne the forename "John," perhaps forgetting that the character's name was "Owen Aherne" in "The Tables of the Law" and that he had recently employed it again in his late-1917 dialogue "Anglo Ireland. | a conversation." Subsequently, one notices that Yeats attempted to correct the error in the note he wrote for this group of poems in *Later Poems* (1922; see p. 114 below). His particular contribution to the "phantasmagoria" here is his "fancy" that John Aherne had been one of the trouble-makers "prosecuted" during the 1907 row at the Abbey Theatre over John Synge's satirical comedy *The Playboy of the Western World.* Such misconduct in the theater is eventually conferred to the character Daniel O'Leary in *Stories of Michael Robartes and His Friends* (1931), where John Aherne is introduced as the brother of Owen. In a letter at the end of the narrative, John observes, in part, that "nobody would have thought the Aherne and Robartes of such fantastic stories real men but for Owen's outcry" (lines 653–55). Aherne's bitterness toward his author, Yeats, is most pronounced in Aherne's last speech and in the italicized direction in the verse-dialogue "The Phases of the Moon."

Michael Robartes makes his first reappearance in Yeats's poetry in the opening stanza of "Ego Dominus Tuus," a dialogue implicitly set on the grounds of the Yeats tower years before he had secured legal title to Ballylee.

EGO DOMINUS TUUS[1]

HIC

On the grey sand beside the shallow stream
Under your old wind-beaten tower, where still
A lamp burns on beside the open book
That Michael Robartes left,[2] you walk in the moon;
And though you have passed the best of life still trace
Enthralled by the unconquerable delusion
Magical shapes.

ILLE

By the help of an image
I call to my own opposite, summon all
That I have handled least, least looked upon.

HIC

And I would find myself and not an image.

ILLE

That is our modern hope and by its light
We have lit upon the gentle, sensitive mind
And lost the old nonchalance of the hand;
Whether we have chosen chisel, pen or brush
We are but critics, or but half create
Timid, entangled, empty and abashed
Lacking the countenance of our friends.

---

[1] Latin for "I am thy master" in Dante Alighieri's *Vita Nuova*. Yeats completed the poem by 5 Oct. 1915, though fair-hand and typed copies entitled "The AntiSelf" are dated "December 1915 (in the Berg and Quinn Collections, respectively, of the New York Public Library). Following printings in *WSC* (1917), *Poetry* (Chicago, Oct. 1917), and *The New Statesman* (17 Nov. 1917), the poem served as the prelude to *Per Amica Silentia Lunae* (1917, pub. 18 Jan. 1918), just as "The Phases of the Moon" later served *AVA* and *AVB*. Also dated "December 1915" there, the poem is made to echo in the opening movement of *PASL*: "At times I remember that place in Dante where he sees in his chamber the 'Lord of Terrible Aspect,' and how…speaking, he said many things among the which I could understand but few, and of these this: ego dominus tuus" (*Myth* 326). Not only was Yeats well-versed in works of Dante, but so was his precocious wife, whose linguistic and philosophic studies from 1910–1912 are featured in 6 of 12 books in their library today, especially *WBGYL* 488 [*YL* 477], *The Vita Nuova of Dante*, ed. Ralph Radcliffe-Whitehead (London: Chiswick Press, 1892), p. 39, which presents the relevant "ego dominus tuus" passage as a set-piece.

[2] First reference to Robartes since 1897. To read in retrospect, because of the poem's proximity to "The Phases of the Moon" in *WSC* (1917, 1919), introduces an ambiguity: Robartes's return to life had not been conceived in 1915. The scene anticipates "Anglo Ireland. | a conversation."

HIC

And yet
The chief imagination of Christendom
Dante Alighieri so utterly found himself
That he has made that hollow face of his
More plain to the mind's eye than any face
But that of Christ.

ILLE

And did he find himself
Or was the hunger that made it hollow
A hunger for the apple on the bough
Most out of reach? and is that spectral image
The man that Lapo and that Guido knew?
I think he fashioned from his opposite
An image that might have been a stony face
Staring upon a bedouin's horse-hair roof[3]
From doored and windowed cliff, or half upturned
Among the coarse grass and the camel dung.
He set his chisel to the hardest stone.
Being mocked by Guido for his lecherous life
Derided and deriding, driven out
To climb that stair and eat that bitter bread,
He found the unpersuadable justice, he found
The most exalted lady loved by a man.

HIC

Yet surely there are men who have made their art
Out of no tragic war, lovers of life,
Impulsive men that look for happiness
And sing when they have found it.

ILLE

No not sing,
For those that love the world serve it in action,
Grow rich, popular and full of influence,
And should they paint or write still it is action:
The struggle of the fly in marmalade.
The rhetorician would deceive his neighbours,
The sentimentalist himself; while art
Is but a vision of reality.

---

[3] An allusion to Robartes's time among the Judwalis? Only if read in retrospect, as in note 2.

What portion in the world can the artist have
Who has awakened from the common dream
But dissipation and despair?

HIC

And yet
No one denies to Keats love of the world;
Remember his deliberate happiness.

ILLE

His art is happy but who knows his mind?
I see a schoolboy when I think of him
With face and nose pressed to a sweet-shop window,
For certainly he sank into his grave
His senses and his heart unsatisfied,
And made—being poor, ailing and ignorant,
Shut out from all the luxury of the world,
The coarse-bred son of a livery stable-keeper—
Luxuriant song.

HIC

Why should you leave the lamp
Burning alone beside an open book.
And trace these characters upon the sands?[4]
A style is found by sedentary toil
And by the imitation of great masters.

ILLE

Because I seek an image not a book.
Those men that in their writings are most wise
Own nothing but their blind, stupefied hearts.
I call to the mysterious one who yet
Shall walk the wet sands by the edge of the stream
And look most like me, being indeed my double,
And prove of all imaginable things
The most unlike, being my anti-self,
And standing by these characters disclose
All that I seek; and whisper it as though
He were afraid the birds, who cry aloud
Their momentary cries before it is dawn,
Would carry it away to blasphemous men.

---

[4] Neither here nor in line 3 is the "open book" Robartes's discovery of work by Giraldus in *AVA*; for "characters upon the sands," cf. "The Gift of Harun Al-Rashid" (156–57), also of later date.

The Phases of the Moon[1]

An old man cocked his ear upon a bridge;
He and his friend, their faces to the South,
Had trod the uneven road. Their boots were soiled,
Their Connemara cloth worn out of shape;
They had kept a steady pace as though their beds,
Despite a dwindling and late risen moon,
Were distant. An old man cocked his ear.

Aherne

What made that sound?

Robartes

A rat or water-hen
Splashed, or an otter slid into the stream.
We are on the bridge; that shadow is the tower,
And the light proves that he is reading still.
He has found, after the manner of his kind,
Mere images; chosen this place to live in
Because, it may be, of the candle light
From the far tower where Milton's platonist
Sat late, or Shelley's visionary prince:
The lonely night that Samuel Palmer engraved,[2]
An image of mysterious wisdom won by toil;
And now he seeks in book or manuscript
What he shall never find.

Aherne

Why should not you
Who know it all ring at his door, and speak
Just truth enough to show that his whole life
Will scarcely find for him a broken crust
Of all those truths that are your daily bread;
And when you have spoken take the roads again?

---

[1] In a copy of *Later Poems*, Mrs. Yeats inscribed beside the poem "Ballylee 1919 Summer" although initial publication occurred in *WSC* (1919) on 11 March. She obviously meant 1918. Anticipated by the Yeats-Aherne dialogue of c. 29 Nov. 1917, "Anglo Ireland. | a conversation" and the onset of the Yeatses' appearance at Coole and Ballylee after Easter 1918, the writing of the Aherne-Robartes version of the poem relates to that of the dialogue in prose "The Discoveries of Michael Robartes" in an early, 1918 stage of composition, where one finds "an almost clean TS of 'The Phases' and two rejected MS pages" (*YVP4* 6). See *YPM* 237, and Stephen Parrish (ed.), *The Wild Swans at Coole: Manuscript Materials* (Ithaca: Cornell University Press, 1994), 314–71.

[2] The allusions of Robartes's first speech are discussed in the preceding commentary (43–44).

Robartes

He wrote of me in that extravagant style
He had learnt from Pater, and to round his tale
Said I was dead; and dead I chose to be.[3]

Aherne

Sing me the changes of the moon once more;
True song, though speech: "mine author sung it me."[4]

ROBARTES

Twenty-and-eight the phases of the moon,[5]
The full and the moon's dark and all the crescents,
Twenty-and-eight, and yet but six-and-twenty
The cradles that a man must needs be rocked in:
For there's no human life at the full or the dark.
From the first crescent to the half, the dream
But summons to adventure and the man
Is always happy like a bird or a beast;
But while the moon is rounding towards the full
He follows whatever whim's most difficult
Among whims not impossible, and though scarred,
As with the cat-o'-nine-tails of the mind,
His body moulded from within his body
Grows comelier. Eleven pass, and then
Athenae takes Achilles by the hair,
Hector is in the dust, Nietzsche is born,
Because the heroes' crescent is the twelfth.
And yet, twice born, twice buried, grow he must,
Before the full moon, helpless as a worm.
The thirteenth moon but sets the soul at war
In its own being, and when that war's begun

---

[3] Critiques of WBY's prose style of the late-1890s recur in his dialogues of 1917–20, precursors to John Aherne's closing complaint in *SMR* and *AVB*, including various takes on the supposed death of Robartes in "Rosa Alchemica" and "The Adoration of the Magi." For example, in *WSC* (1919), Robartes says "dead I chose to be," which acknowledges his absence until now, whereas subsequent tense change to "choose" (as given here) expresses the preference to remain so *as if* dead. Aherne reports in his "Introduction" to *AVA* that Robartes found that misrepresentation to be of service: "but for that rumour I could not have lived in peace in the desert" (154, ll. 39–40).

[4] The tag-quotation, from Milton's *Doctrine and Discipline of Divorce,* refers to Plato. See *YPM* 138–42, and Chapman, "Metaphors for Poetry," *YVEC* 220–25.

[5] On the "twenty-eight 'moon-stations' of the Arabs" and George Yeats's transcription of lines from Chaucer's Franklin's Tale "Touchinge the eighte and twenty mansiouns | That longen to the mone" (Canterbury Tales, F. 1125ff), see *YVEC* 222. From this speech in the poem through his last, Robartes's recitation prefigures "The Great Wheel" and 28 "Embodiments" in *AVA*.

There is no muscle in the arm; and after
Under the frenzy of the fourteenth moon
The soul begins to tremble into stillness,
To die into the labyrinth of itself!

Aherne

Sing out the song; sing to the end, and sing
The strange reward of all that discipline.

Robartes

All thought becomes an image and the soul
Becomes a body: that body and that soul
Too perfect at the full to lie in a cradle,
Too lonely for the traffic of the world:
Body and soul cast out and cast away
Beyond the visible world.

Aherne

All dreams of the soul
End in a beautiful man's or woman's body.

Robartes

Have you not always known it?

Aherne

The song will have it
That those that we have loved got their long fingers
From death, and wounds, or on Sinai's top,
Or from some bloody whip in their own hands.
They ran from cradle to cradle till at last
Their beauty dropped out of the loneliness
Of body and soul.

Robartes

The lovers' heart knows that.

Aherne

It must be that the terror in their eyes
Is memory or foreknowledge of the hour
When all is fed with light and heaven is bare.

Robartes

When the moon's full those creatures of the full
Are met on the waste hills by country men
Who shudder and hurry by: body and soul

Estranged amid the strangeness of themselves,
Caught up in the contemplation, the mind's eye
Fixed upon images that once were thought,
For separate, perfect, and immovable
Images can break the solitude
Of lovely, satisfied, indifferent eyes.

And thereupon with aged, high-pitched voice
Aherne laughed, thinking of the man within,[6]
His sleepless candle and laborious pen.

ROBARTES

And after that the crumbling of the moon.
The soul remembering its loneliness
Shudders in many cradles; all is changed,
It would be the world's servant, and as it serves,
Choosing whatever task's most difficult
Among tasks not impossible, it takes
Upon the body and upon the soul
The coarseness of the drudge.

AHERNE

Before the full
It sought itself and afterwards the world.

ROBARTES

Because you are forgotten, half out of life,
And never wrote a book your thought is clear.
Reformer, merchant, statesman, learned man,
Dutiful husband, honest wife by turn,
Cradle upon cradle, all in flight and all
Deformed because there is no deformity
But saves us from a dream.

AHERNE

And what of those
That the last servile crescent has set free?

ROBARTES

Because all dark, like those that are all light,
They are cast beyond the verge, and in a cloud,
Crying to one another like the bats;
And having no desire they cannot tell
What's good or bad, or what it is to triumph

---

[6] —i.e., the author, Yeats. Aherne's animosity continues from "Anglo Ireland. | a conversation."

At the perfection of one's own obedience;
And yet they speak what's blown into the mind;
Deformed beyond deformity, unformed,
Insipid as the dough before it is baked,
They change their bodies at a word

Aherne

And then?

Robartes

When all the dough has been so kneaded up
That it can take what form cook Nature fancy
The first thin crescent is wheeled round once more.

Aherne

But the escape; the song's not finished yet.

Robartes

Hunchback and saint and fool are the last crescents.
The burning bow that once could shoot an arrow
Out of the up and down, the wagon wheel
Of beauty's cruelty and wisdom's chatter,
Out of that raving tide is drawn betwixt
Deformity of the body and of mind.

Aherne

Were not our beds far off I'd ring the bell,
Stand under the rough roof-timbers of the hall
Beside the castle door, where all is stark
Austerity, a place set out for wisdom
That he will never find; I'd play a part;
He would never know me after all these years[7]
But take me for some drunken country man;
I'd stand and mutter there until he caught
"Hunchback and saint and fool," and that they came
Under the three last crescents of the moon,
And then I'd stagger out. He'd crack his wits.
Day after day, yet never find the meaning.

And then he laughed to think that what seemed hard
Should be so simple—a bat rose from the hazels
And circled round him with its squeaky cry,
The light in the tower window was put out.

---

[7] Aherne's hesitation to turn in at Yeats's door and ring the bell is played out in parallel gambits in "The Discoveries of Michael Robartes" manuscripts and in *AVA*, with settings in Bloomsbury.

The Double Vision of Michael Robartes[1]

I

On the grey rock of Cashel the mind's eye
Has called up the cold spirits that are born
When the old moon is vanishing from the sky
And the new still hides her horn.

Under blank eyes and fingers never still
The particular is pounded till it is man
When had I my own will?
Oh, not since life began.

Constrained, arraigned, baffled, bent and unbent
By these wire-jointed jaws and limbs of wood,
Themselves obedient,
Knowing not evil and good;

Obedient to some hidden magical breath.
They do not even feel, so abstract are they,
So dead beyond our death,
Triumph that we obey.

II

On the grey rock of Cashel I suddenly saw
A Sphinx with a woman breast and lion paw,
A Buddha, hand at rest,
Hand lifted up that blest;

And right between these two a girl at play
That it may be had danced her life away,
For now being dead it seemed
That she of dancing dreamed.[2]

---

[1] In a copy of *Later Poems*, GY inscribed "Glenmalure 1918" beside the poem (see *YPM* 237). The first section in MS is dated "April 1918," and the poem probably remained incomplete when, on 15 July 1918, Yeats confessed to Pound that "'The Double Vision' is too obscure" without "The Phases of the Moon" (*YVP4* 4). However, according to the Harpers (*YVP4* 257, n. 191), the poem (evidently meaning the rest of the poem) grew out of the automatic script of 7 Jan. 1919. Like "The Phases of the Moon," "The Double Vision of Michael Robartes" was an addition to the poems collected in the 1917 Cuala edition of *WSC* when Macmillan's standard edition appeared in March 1919.

[2] The somnambulistic dreaming figure of the girl (without Sphinx and Buddha) seems to emerge from the place of Cormac in GY's automatic writing of 7 Jan. 1919; see *YVP2* 162–64. See also "The Gift of Harun Al-Rashid" ll. 151–58. The metaphor of the dancer as representative of the mind in trance-like, passive state could only be suggested by the example of the actual George Yeats in the creation of the automatic script.

Although I saw it all in the mind's eye
There can be nothing solider till I die;
I saw by the moon's light
Now at its fifteenth night.[3]

One lashed her tail; her eyes lit by the moon
Gazed upon all things known, all things unknown,
In triumph of intellect
With motionless head erect.

That other's moonlit eyeballs never moved,
Being fixed on all things loved, all things unloved,
Yet little peace he had
For those that love are sad.[4]

Oh, little did they care who danced between,
And little she by whom her dance was seen
So that she danced. No thought,
Body perfection brought,

For what but eye and ear silence the mind
With the minute particulars of mankind?
Mind moved yet seemed to stop
As 'twere a spinning-top.

In contemplation had those three so wrought
Upon a moment, and so stretched it out
That they, time overthrown,
Were dead yet flesh and bone.

---

[3] Cf. "The Phases of the Moon," ll. 58–83. The wonder expressed by the narrator, recalls Yeats's definition of Robartes in the early stories and in poems such as "Michael Robartes Remembers Forgotten Beauty" (later "He Remembers Forgotten Beauty"), challenged by Stephen Dedalus in his second diary entry of 6 April [1902] in Joyce's *A Portrait of the Artist as a Young Man*). Yeats asserts that Robartes is "the pride of the imagination brooding upon the greatness of its possession, or the adoration of the Magi," as opposed to Red Hanrahan, who is "the simplicity of an imagination too changeable to gather permanent possessions, or the adoration of the shepherds" (*VP* 802).

[4] This stanza and the two preceding it were reproduced in *AVB* (208) to illustrate the conjunction of opposites as "heraldic supporters guarding the mystery of the fifteenth phase" (with the caveat that Christ should have been substituted for Buddha, according to the instructors). An earlier gloss to the same passage occurs in the typescript of the dialogue "The Discoveries of Michael Robartes," where Robartes explains to Aherne that "[t]he images at fifteen do not affect the automatic portions of the mind at all[;] for[,] being each one separate and complete[,] they cannot start any sequence of thought and image[;] the mind in their presence is stationary in a Buddha[-] or Sphinx[-]like trance of wonder" (*YVP4* 4 and 58, n. 39). "All thought becomes an image" at that stage in "The Phases of the Moon" (*VP* 374, l. 58), and Yeats felt the latter poem helped clear up the obscure symbolism of "The Double Vision of Michael Robartes."

III

I knew that I had seen, had seen at last
That girl[5] my unremembering nights hold fast
Or else my dreams that fly,
If I should rub an eye,

And yet in flying fling into my meat
A crazy juice that makes the pulses beat
As though I had been undone
By Homer's Paragon[6]

Who never gave the burning town a thought;
To such a pitch of folly I am brought,
Being caught between the pull
Of the dark moon and the full,[7]

The commonness of thought and images
That have the frenzy of our western seas.
Thereon I made my moan,
And after kissed a stone,

And after that arranged it in a song
Seeing that I, ignorant for so long,
Had been rewarded thus
In Cormac's ruined house.

---

[5] In *SMR*, Robartes confesses that his passion was an obsession for a particular ballet-dancer that he pursued from Rome to Vienna. One of their many quarrels is the substance of the poem "Michael Robartes and the Dancer."

[6] Helen. In *SMR*, Robartes speaks of the torment of violent love as a passion without end.

[7] On 17 June [1921], Yeats wrote to Frank Pierce Sturm: "The First Part of 'The Double Vision' describes spirits at phase 1 and the last part is spirits at phase 15" (*CL InteLex* 3929).

Yeats's Note from *Later Poems* (London: Macmillan, 1922)

The Phases of the Moon…, *The Double Vision of Michael Robartes…*, *Michael Robartes and the Dancer….*—Years ago I wrote three stories in which occur the names of Michael Robartes and Owen Aherne. I now consider that I used the actual names of two friends, and that one of these friends, Michael Robartes, has but lately returned from Mesopotamia where he has partly found and partly thought out much philosophy. I consider that John Aherne is either the original of Owen Aherne or some near relation of the man that was, and that both he and Robartes, to whose namesake I had attributed a turbulent life and death, have quarreled with me. They take their place in a phantasmagoria in which I endeavor to explain my philosophy of life and death, and till that philosophy has found some detailed exposition in prose certain passages in the poems named above may seem obscure. To some extent I wrote them as a text for exposition. —1922.

On reflection, Yeats corrected his error of mistaking "John" Aherne for Owen. Here Yeats speculates that John (later identified as Owen's brother) "is either the original of Owen Aherne or some near relation of the man," repeating the assertion made in the Preface of *The Wild Swans at Coole* (see p. 102 above) that Owen Aherne and Michael Robartes "take their place in a phantasmagoria in which I endeavour to explain my philosophy of life and death." Eventually, even John Aherne enters the phantasmagoria as a fictitious source in *SMR.*

PREFACE[1]

A few of these poems may be difficult to understand, perhaps more difficult than I know. Goethe has said that the poet needs all philosophy, but that he must keep it out of his work.[2] After the first few poems I came into possession of Michael Robartes' exposition of the *Speculum Angelorum et Hominum* of Geraldus,[3] and in the excitement of arranging and editing could no more keep out philosophy than could Goethe himself at certain periods of his life. I have tried to make understanding easy by a couple of notes, which are at any rate much shorter than those Dante wrote on certain of his odes in the *Convito*,[4] but I may not have succeeded. It is hard for a writer, who has spent much labour upon his style, to remember that thought, which seems to him natural and logical like that style, may be unintelligible to others. The first excitement over, and the thought changed into settled conviction, his interest in simple, that is to say in normal emotion, is always I think increased; he is no longer looking for candlestick and matches but at the objects in the room.

I have given no account of Robartes himself, nor of his discovery of the explanation of Geraldus' diagrams and pictures in the traditional knowledge of a certain obscure Arab tribe,[5] for I hope that my selection from the great mass of his letters and table talk, which I owe to his friend John Aherne,[6] may be published before, or at any rate but soon after this little book, which, like all hand-printed books will take a long time for the setting up and printing off and for the drying of the pages.

W. B. Yeats.

---

[1] From *Michael Robartes and the Dancer* (Churchtown, Dundrum: The Cuala Press, 1921; *Wade* 127); finished "on All Souls Day in the year nineteen hundred and twenty," this collection of 15 lyrics was published in February 1921. Only three of the poems had not appeared elsewhere. Eleven poems, including the three reprinted below, had already appeared, in Nov. 1920, in at least one of the following periodicals: *The Dial*, *The Nation*, and *The New Statesman*. Only "A Prayer for my Daughter" had been published earlier, in Nov. 1919, in *The Irish Statesman*. The collection is often acknowledged as the place where several lyrics on the 1916 Irish rebellion were relocated or first introduced into the Yeats canon after delay, anticipating Yeats's return to public life in 1921 and publication of the Macmillan edition of *Later Poems*. See *YPM* 78–96; cf. Yeats's preface to *The Wild Swans at Coole* (1919) and his note for *Later Poems* (1922), above.

[2] Johann Wolfgang von Goethe (1749–1832), German Romantic poet and dramatist; see *PASL* (*Myth* 344) for a similar thought.

[3] On "Robartes' exposition" of the *Speculum* of Giraldus, see "Creating Story in 'The Discoveries of Michael Robartes,' 1917–1920," above.

[4] Dante Alighieri, *Il Convito* (trans. as *The Banquet*) in the 1887 edition by Elizabeth Price Sayer in Yeats's library (*WBGYL* 477 [*YL* 466]).

[5] The first accounts of the fictitious Arab tribe called the Judwalis by Yeats were made in the manuscript materials for the unpublished dialogue "The Discoveries of Michael Robartes," but the story eventually came out in *AVA*, *SMR*, and *AVB*.

[6] John Aherne, brother of Owen, makes his entrance in *YVP4*, "Version B" first as a speaker, then in extracts from letters. See WBY's preface to *WSC* and note for *Later Poems*, above.

Michael Robartes and the Dancer[1]

He

Opinion is not worth a rush;
In this altar-piece[2] the knight,
Who grips his long spear so to push
That dragon through the fading light,
Loved the lady; and it's plain
The half-dead dragon was her thought,
That every morning rose again
And dug its claws and shrieked and fought.
Could the impossible come to pass
She would have time to turn her eyes,
Her lover thought, upon the glass
And on the instant would grow wise.

She

You mean they argued.

He

Put it so;
But bear in mind your lover's wage
Is what your looking-glass can show,
And that he will turn green with rage
At all that is not pictured there,

She

May I not put myself to college?

He

Go pluck Athena by the hair;
For what mere book can grant a knowledge
With an impassioned gravity
Appropriate to that beating breast,
That vigorous thigh, that dreaming eye?
And may the devil take the rest.

---

[1] Written at "96 Stephens Green, Winter 1918–19," according to Mrs. Yeats (see *YPM* 237), with first appearance in *The Dial*, Nov. 1920. On the poem's connection with the monologue "The Double Vision of Michael Robartes" (final lyric in *WSC* [1919]), see note 5 on that poem, above. If "He" (Robartes) is a mask for Yeats and "She" (the Dancer) "reflects Iseult Gonne, a young dancer encouraged to think, as well as Maud Gonne, an object of desire…identified with shrieking, shrillness, or an 'opinionated mind,'" then "She" "also has affinities with [George Yeats], a young woman not content with a looking-glass and given to replying ambiguously to an older man's questions," writes Margaret Mills Harper (*Wisdom of Two* 236).

[2] As in the several drafts of "The Discoveries of Michael Robartes," the scene is the National Gallery, London. The composite source of "this altar-piece" is addressed in the following note.

She
And must no beautiful woman be
Learned like a man?

He
Paul Veronese[3]
And all his sacred company
Imagined bodies all their days
By the lagoon you love so much,
For proud, soft, ceremonious proof
That all must come to sight and touch;
While Michael Angelo's Sistine roof
His 'Morning' and his 'Night' disclose[4]
How sinew that has been pulled tight,
Or it may be loosened in repose,
Can rule by supernatural right
Yet be but sinew.

She
I have heard said
There is great danger in the body.

He
Did God in portioning wine and bread
Give man His thought or His mere body?

She
My wretched dragon is perplexed.

He
I have principles to prove me right.
It follows from this Latin text[5]

---

[3] Paolo Cagliari (1525–1588), last great Venetian painter better known as Paolo Veronese. The source of the "altar-piece" in line 2, above, has been associated with various paintings entitled *St. George and the Dragon* (e.g., by Tintoretto, Bordone, and others) in the National Gallery, London, and elsewhere. David R. Clark, supported by the manuscript evidence of a name, directs us to a rendition by Giovanni Bellini (1430?–1576) on "one of the predella panels of the Pesaro atlar-piece of which the central panel is the 'Coronation of the Virgin' (Pesaro, Museo Civico)" (*Yeats at Songs and Choruses* [Amherst, MA: University of Massachusetts Press, 1983], 93). Clark also introduced us to the unpublished prose dialogue of 1916 (in *YA* 8 [1991]: 123–43), "The Poet and the Actress," in which George Yeats assisted by making corrections to the typescript. Like "Michael Robartes and the Dancer," it was a dialogue between a beautiful woman and a didactic older man engaged in an aesthetic debate on Yeats's idealized "Theatre of Beauty," a seminal concept for his "plays for dancers."

[4] Michelangelo Buonarroti (1475–1564) finished painting the Sistine Chapel in Rome in 1512; his statues *Morning* and *Night* are in the Medici Chapel, S. Lorenzo, Florence.

[5] Obviously, the fictitious *Speculum Angelorum et Hominum* by Giraldus.

That blest souls are not composite,
And that all beautiful women may
Live in uncomposite blessedness,
And lead us to the like—if they
Will banish every thought, unless
The lineaments that please their view
When the long looking-glass is full,
Even from the foot-sole think it too.

She
They say such different things at school.[6]

---

[6] Margaret Mills Harper asserts that this poem is Yeats's first dialogue "that does not fall neatly into one of two categories," into which either "speakers agree or form separate statements" to combine into "a deeper idea," or they involve one character invested with the poet's sympathy and the other feeding him "all the good lines" like the straight-man in a vaudeville act (*Wisdom of Two* 234–35). Here the characters disagree. The poem advances a view of the Yeatses as being progressive on women's education ("May I not put myself to college?") as "She" undermines Robartes with ironic, one-line cuts.

> The fact that *He* ultimately argues from a "Latin text" while *She* does not theorize but dances…also undermines the male voice's philosophy. The setting in a gallery suggests a quality of artificiality. *He* dramatizes the scene depicted in a painting of Griselda, that quintessential figure of victimized woman, looking for hidden meaning and trying to insert the viewers into the framed scene of the painting, while *She* interrupts his theories. (*Wisdom of Two* 235)

In short, Yeats gives his dancer the last word. It should be noted, too, that Robartes's favorite painting in the National Gallery, after Yeats strikes out Tintoretto's *The Adoration of the Magi* in the manuscript of "The Discoveries of Michael Robartes," is "~~a picture by Crivelli~~…the story of Griselda" (*YVP4* 62).

Harper is right (237) to see Yeats's positioning of the next poem in the collection, "Solomon and the Witch"—a dialogue of 1918 in blank verse, spoken within inverted commas—as pairing with another instance in which the male voice (Landorian Yeats as Solomon) is joined by a younger, female voice (that of George Yeats as "that Arab lady," the Biblical Sheba). Although they fail to achieve a perfect union to annihilate time as lovers, she is not deterred in the achievement of that feat, giving the necessary encouragement that concludes the poem with such gusto: "O, Solomon! let us try again." See *YPM* 21–25. This technique warms the metaphysics of "Chance & Choice," the rubric under which seven folio-pages were puzzled out on that particular theme in an unsorted, early cluster from the extant Aherne-Robartes dialogue (NLI 36,263/7[5]).

AN IMAGE FROM A PAST LIFE[1]

He[2]
Never until this night have I been stirred.
The elaborate star-light has thrown reflections
On the dark stream,
Till all the eddies gleam;
And thereupon there comes that scream
From terrified, invisible beast or bird:
Image of poignant recollection.

She[3]
An image of my heart that is smitten through
Out of all likelihood, or reason,
And when at last,
Youth's bitterness being past,
I had thought that all my days were cast
Amid most lovely places; smitten as though
It had not learned its lesson.

He
Why have you laid your hands upon my eyes?
What can have suddenly alarmed you
Whereon 'twere best
My eyes should never rest?
What is there but the slowly fading west,
The river imaging the flashing skies,
All that to this moment charmed you?

She
A sweetheart from another life floats there[4]
As though she had been forced to linger
From vague distress
Or arrogant loveliness,
Merely to loosen out a tress
Among the starry eddies of her hair
Upon the paleness of a finger.

---

[1] The composition of this poem was dated by Mrs. Yeats as occurring at "Ballylee – Summer 1919"; also "Sept. 1919" (*YPM* 237). Another dialogue dramatizing the wedded life of the Yeatses, the poem first appeared in *The Nation*, 6 Nov. 1920, inspired by Bengali poet Rabindranath Tagore, "In the Dusky Path of a Dream" (see *OBMV* 66: "In the dusky path of a dream I went to seek the love who was mine in a former life"). Yeats's poem follows "Solomon and the Witch."

[2] W. B. Yeats.

[3] George Yeats.

[4] Seemingly Maud Gonne; cf. "The Lover mourns for the Loss of Love" (*VP* 152), which is addressed to Olivia Shakespear. But see note 5, below, on the Over Shadower.

He
But why should you grow suddenly afraid
And start—I at your shoulder—
Imagining
That any night could bring
An image up, or anything
Even to eyes that beauty had driven mad,
But images to make me fonder.

She
Now she has thrown her arms above her head;
Whether she threw them up to flout me,
Or but to find,
Now that no fingers bind,
That her hair streams upon the wind,
I do not know, that know I am afraid
Of the hovering thing night brought me.[5]

Yeats's Note on "An Image from a Past Life"[6]

Robartes writes to Aherne under the date May 12th, 1917. "I found among the Judwalis much biographical detail, probably legendary, about Kusta-ben-Luki.[7] He saw occasionally during sleep a woman's face and later on found in a Persian painting a face resembling, though not identical with the dream-face, which was

---

[5] The "hovering thing" is cognate with the "Over Shadower or Ideal Form" Yeats describes in the final paragraph of his note on the poem, given in the Cuala Press edition of *Michael Robartes and the Dancer* (see below). In the card file kept by the Yeatses to systematize the results of the automatic writing and so-called "Sleep and Dream Notebooks,"an entry labeled "Over shadower" (correspondent with the automatic script of 8 Sept. 1919) gives the following account from Yeats's perspective:

> In all loves is there an over shadower? "Yes & when that is withdrawn there is a lack of sensual desire for a time[.]" "Over shadower is withdrawn when born[.]" "All have the same over shadower until born. Anne [Hyde, mythical ancestor] overshadowed the women I have loved (she is [Mars] [Venus] etc & so suggests [Mars] [Leo] in VII)[.] He who shadows me in Georges eyes not yet born though withdrawn for meditation before birth. Sensual desire returns with complete recovery from last C[ritical].M[oment]. Man always *Victim* for she who over shadows her lovers. *Over shadower* always once made the lover of the over shadowed happy. (*YVP3* 348)

[6] Yeats's note on the poem, written before All Souls' Day (2 Nov.) 1920, the completion date of the collection, returns attention to the fictional frame laid out in his Preface.

[7] References in the note to dated letters sent by Robartes to John Aherne suggest the shift in method *from* dialogue in the unpublished "Discoveries of Michael Robartes" *to* "extracts" from imaginary letters in "Version B," with its dated headnote of "June 1920." The spelling of the Judwali tribe and "Kusta-ben-Luki," later "Kusta ben Luka" (for the historical Qusta ibn Luqa) in *AVA*, are consistent with an early date.

he considered that of a woman loved in another life. Presently he met & loved a beautiful woman whose face also resembled, without being identical, that of his dream. Later on he made a long journey to purchase the painting which was, he said, the better likeness, and found on his return that his mistress had left him in a fit of jealousy." In a dialogue and in letters, Robartes gives a classification and analysis of dreams which explain the survival of this story among the followers of Kusta-ben-Luki. They distinguished between the memory of concrete images and the abstract memory, and affirm that no concrete dream-image is ever from our memory. This is not only true they say of dreams, but of those visions seen between sleeping and waking. This doctrine at first found me incredulous, for I thought it contradicted by my experience and by all I have read, not however a very great amount, in books of psychology and psycho-analysis.[8] Did I not frequently dream of some friend, or relation, or that I was at school? I found, however, when I studied my dreams, as I was directed in a dialogue, that the image seen was never really that of friend, or relation, or my old school, though it might very closely resemble it. A substitution had taken place, often a very strange one, though I forgot this if I did not notice it at once on waking. The name of some friend, or the conceptions "my father" and "at school," are a part of the abstract memory and therefore of the dream life, but the image of my father, or my friend, or my old school, being a part of the personal concrete memory appeared neither in sleep nor in visions between sleep and waking. I found sometimes that my father, or my friend, had been represented in sleep by a stool or a chair, and I concluded that it was the entire absence of my personal concrete memory enabled me to accept such images without surprise. Was it not perhaps this very absence that constituted sleep? Would I perhaps awake if a single concrete image from my memory came before me? Even these images—stool, chair, etc. were never any particular stool, chair, etc. that I had known. Were these images, however, from the buried memory? had they floated up from the subconscious? had I seen them perhaps a long time ago and forgotten having done so? Even if that were so, the exclusion of the conscious memory was a new, perhaps important truth; but Robartes denied their source even in the subconscious. It seems a corroboration that though I often see between sleep and waking elaborate landscape, I have never seen one that seemed a possible representation of any place I have ever lived near from childhood up. Robartes traces these substitute images to different sources. Those that come in sleep are (1) from the state immediately preceding our birth; (2) from the *Spiritus Mundi*[9]—that is to say, from a general store-house of images which have ceased to be a property of any personality or spirit. Those that come between sleeping and waking are, he says, re-shaped by what he calls the "automatic faculty" which can create pattern, balance, etc. from the impressions made upon the senses, not of ourselves, but of others bound to us by certain emotional links through perhaps

---

[8] Yeats is stating the truth about Robartes's knowledge of "psychology and psycho-analysis," for his own acquaintance with those subjects would occur with reading later in the 1920s. He did annotate a copy of C. G. Jung's *Collected Papers on Analytical Psychology* (1916; *YL* 1050), however.

[9] The term is cognate with "*Anima Mundi*" or "Great Memory" in *PASL* (see *Myth* 345–46).

entire strangers, and preserved in a kind of impersonal mirror, often simply called the "record," which takes much the same place in his system [as] the lower strata of the astral light does among the disciples of Elephas Levi. This does not exhaust the contents of dreams for we have to account also for certain sentences, for certain ideas which are not concrete images and yet do not arise from our personal memory, but at the moment I have merely to account for certain images that affect passion or affection. Robartes writes to Aherne in a letter dated May 15th, 1917: "No lover, no husband has ever met in dreams the true image of wife or mistress. She who has perhaps filled his whole life with joy or disquiet cannot enter there. Her image can fill every moment of his waking life but only its counterfeit comes to him in sleep; and he who classifies these counterfeits will find that just in so far as they become concrete, sensuous, they are distinct individuals; never types but individuals. They are the forms of those whom he has loved in some past earthly life, chosen from *Spiritus Mundi* by the subconscious will, and through them, for they are not always hollow shades, the dead at whiles outface a living rival." They are the forms of Over Shadowers as they are called.[10] All violent passion has to be expiated or atoned, by one in life, by one in the state between life and life, because, as the Judwalis believe, there is always deceit or cruelty; but it is only in sleep that we can see these forms of those who as spirits may influence all our waking thought. Souls that are once linked by emotion never cease till the last drop of that emotion is exhausted—call it desire, hate or what you will—to affect one another remaining always as it were in contact. Those whose past passions are unatoned seldom love living man or woman but only those loved long ago, of whom the living man or woman is but a brief symbol forgotten when some phase of some atonement is finished; but because in general the form does not pass into the memory, it is the moral being of the dead that is symbolised. Under certain circumstances, which are precisely described, the form indirectly, and not necessarily from dreams, enters the living memory; the subconscious will, as in Kusta-ben-Luki in the story, selects among pictures, or other ideal representations, some form that resembles what was once the physical body of the Over Shadower, and this ideal form becomes to the living man an obsession, continually perplexing and frustrating natural instinct. It is therefore only after full atonement or expiation, perhaps after many lives, that a natural deep satisfying love becomes possible, and this love, in all subjective natures, must precede the Beatific Vision.

When I wrote ["]An Image from a Past Life["], I had merely begun my study of the various papers upon the subject, but I do not think I misstated Robartes' thought in permitting the woman and not the man to see the Over Shadower or Ideal Form, whichever it was. No mind's contents are necessarily shut off from another, and in moments of excitement images pass from one mind to another with extraordinary ease, perhaps most easily from that portion of the mind which for the time being is outside consciousness. I use the word "pass" because it is familiar, not because I believe any movement in space to be necessary. The second mind sees what the first has already seen, that is all.

---

[10] See note 5, above.

THE SECOND COMING[1]

Turning and turning in the widening gyre
The falcon cannot hear the falconer;
Things fall apart; the centre cannot hold;
Mere anarchy is loosed upon the world,
The blood-dimmed tide is loosed, and everywhere
The ceremony of innocence is drowned;
The best lack all conviction, while the worst
Are full of passionate intensity.

Surely some revelation is at hand;
Surely the Second Coming is at hand.
The Second Coming! Hardly are those words out
When a vast image out of Spiritus Mundi[2]
Troubles my sight: a waste of desert sand;
A shape with lion body and the head of a man,
A gaze blank and pitiless as the sun,
Is moving its slow thighs, while all about it
Wind shadows of the indignant desert birds.
The darkness drops again but now I know
That twenty centuries of stony sleep
Were vexed to nightmare by a rocking cradle,
And what rough beast, its hour come round at last,
Slouches towards Bethlehem to be born?

---

[1] The poem was written in Jan. 1919, according to George Yeats (see *YPM* 237); it first appeared in *The Dial*, Nov. 1920, and in *The Nation* (London), 6 Nov. 1920. Anne Butler Yeats was born on 26 Feb. 1919. "The Second Coming" and "A Prayer for my Daughter" are frequently anthologized together, following the precedent established in the Cuala collection of 1921. On 6 June 1918, Yeats told Pound that he was "thinking out" a prose work on "the Egyptian Sphinx which becomes jealous of Christ & thinks of being born" (*CL InteLex* 3447). "The Second Coming" was not used in *AVA* or *AVB* as was "Leda and the Swan," which dramatizes the rise and fall of the profane era of Hellenic civilization just as "The Second Coming" anticipates the demise of the Christian era that followed, with the return of Christ to judge mankind, as predicted in Matt. 24 and in St. John's description of the beast of Apocalypse in Revelations. A fragment of "The Second Coming" (ll. 1–6), with most of "Toward Break of Day," may be found in the Occult Papers of W. B. Yeats (NLI 36,263/29, not cited in Parkinson's Cornell edition), as well as "<Where Kusta ben Luki got his philosophy> ~~Michael Robartes and the Judwali Doctor,~~" eventually adapted for use as interjected commentary by Owen Aherne in *AVA*, Book IV, "The Gates of Pluto," section XIII, "Communications with Spirits and the Nature of Sleep." "Leda and the Swan" famously succeeds the figure of "The Historical Cones" in *AVA*, Book III, "Dove or Swan" (retained in Book V of *AVB*). So it is possible that Yeats contemplated the use of "The Second Coming" as an extract to illustrate either the "Expanding and Contracting Gyres" or the modern moment at the end of the Christian cycle.

[2] Again, here and in Yeats's Note on the poem, below, the term "Spititus Mundi" is cognate with "*Anima Mundi*" or "Great Memory" in *PASL* (see *Myth* 345–46).

YEATS'S NOTE ON "THE SECOND COMING"[3]

Robartes copied out and gave to Aherne several mathematical diagrams from the *Speculum*, squares and spheres, cones made up of revolving gyres intersecting each other at various angles, figures sometimes of great complexity. His explanation of these, obtained invariably from the followers of Kusta-ben-Luki, is founded upon a single fundamental thought. The mind, whether expressed in history or in the individual life, has a precise movement, which can be quickened or slackened but cannot be fundamentally altered, and this movement can be expressed by a mathematical form. A plant or an animal has an order of development peculiar to it, a bamboo will not develop evenly like a willow, nor a willow from joint to joint, and both have branches, that lessen and grow more light as they rise, and no characteristic of the soil can alter these things. A poor soil may indeed check or stop the movement and a rich prolong and quicken it. Mendel has shown that his sweet-peas bred long and short, white and pink varieties in certain mathematical proportions, suggesting a mathematical law governing the transmission of parental characteristics. To the Judwalis, as interpreted by Michael Robartes, all living mind has likewise a fundamental mathematical movement, however adapted in plant, or animal, or man to particular circumstance; and when you have found this movement and calculated its relations, you can foretell the entire future of that mind. A supreme religious act of their faith is to fix the attention on the mathematical form of this movement until the whole past and future of humanity, or of an individual man, shall be present to the intellect as if it were accomplished in a single moment. The intensity of the Beatific Vision when it comes depends upon the intensity of this realisation. It is possible in this way, seeing that death is itself marked upon the mathematical figure, which passes beyond it, to follow the soul into the highest heaven and the deepest hell. This doctrine is, they contend, not fatalistic because the mathematical figure is an expression of the mind's desire, and the more rapid the development of the figure the greater the freedom of the soul. The figure while the soul is in the body, or suffering from the consequences of that life, is frequently drawn as a double cone, the narrow end of each cone being in the centre of the broad end of the other.

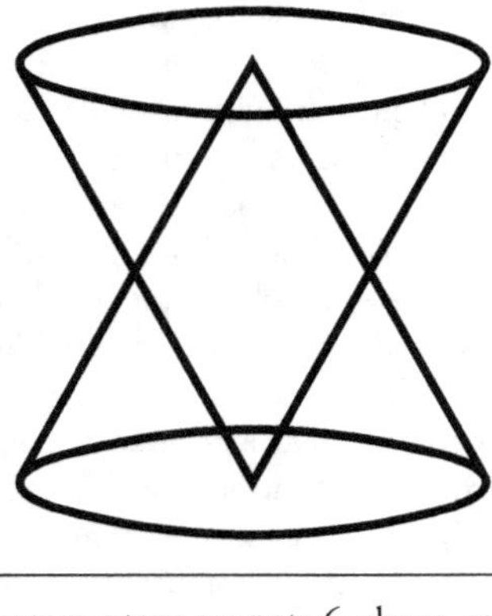

[3] On the writing of Yeats's commentary, see note 6, above, on "An Image from a Past Life."

It has its origin in a straight line which represents, now time, now emotion, now subjective life, and a plane at right angles to this line which represents, now space, now intellect, now objective life; while it is marked out by two gyres which represent the conflict, as it were, of plane and line, by two movements, which circle about a centre because a movement outward on the plane is checked by and in turn checks a movement onward upon the line; & the circling is always narrowing or spreading, because one movement or other is always stronger.[4] In other words, the human soul is always moving outward into the objective world or inward into itself; & this movement is double because the human soul would not be conscious were it not suspended between contraries, the greater the contrast the more intense the consciousness. The man, in whom the movement inward is stronger than the movement outward, the man who sees all reflected within himself, the subjective man, reaches the narrow end of a gyre at death, for death is always, they contend, even when it seems the result of accident, preceded by an intensification of the subjective life; and has a moment of revelation immediately after death, a revelation which they describe as his being carried into the presence of all his dead kindred, a moment whose objectivity is exactly equal to the subjectivity of death. The objective man on the other hand, whose gyre moves outward, receives at this moment the revelation, not of himself seen from within, for that is impossible to objective man, but of himself as if he were somebody else. This figure is true also of history, for the end of an age, which always receives the revelation of the character of the next age, is represented by the coming of one gyre to its place of greatest expansion and of the other to that of its greatest contraction.[5] At the present moment the life gyre is sweeping outward, unlike that before the birth of

---

[4] The figure on the facing page is explained in *AVA* (*CW13* 104–08) in terms of *Anima Hominis* and *Anima Mundi* (as we understand the concepts from *PASL*). So much more of Yeats's note on "The Second Coming" involves the human soul than we might have expected. Also, considerably more of Blake's influence is apparent in *AVA* than in revised *AVB*, especially regarding Blake's enigmatic poem "The Mental Traveller," quoted selectively in Book II, "What the Caliph Refused to Learn," section III, "Blake's Use of the Gyres." This follows the introduction to the system in "The Wheel and the Phases of the Moon," the prolusion to Book I, and "Desert Geometry or the Gift of Harun al-Raschid," the gateway to Book II. In Blake's poem, the countervailing gyres are a woman and a man "growing at one another's expense, but with Blake it is not enough to say that one is beauty and one is wisdom, for he conceives this conflict as that in all love…which compels each to be slave and tyrant by turn" (108). See Chapman, "'Metaphors for Poetry,'" *YVEC* 217–51, especially 237–39. Also, in the same collection, see Neil Mann, "'Everywhere that antinomy of the One and the Many': The Foundation of *A Vision*," 1–21.

[5] Curiously, Yeats offers comparatively little, beyond this point, on the historical play of the "life gyre" in connection with Christ, less than the title and second stanza of the poem would suggest. As in his commentary for "An Image for a Past Life," the *Speculum* of Giraldus and the mysteries of the Judwalis seem useful to Robartes mainly to explain moments of revelation in individual psychology. If not altogether clear beyond that, Yeats allows that "Robartes had little help from the Judwalis…because they cannot grasp events outside their experience, or because certain studies seem to them unlucky."

Christ which was narrowing, and has almost reached its greatest expansion. The revelation which approaches will however take its character from the contrary movement of the interior gyre. All our scientific, democratic, fact-accumulating, heterogeneous civilization belongs to the outward gyre and prepares not the continuance of itself but the revelation as in a lightning flash, though in a flash that will not strike only in one place, and will for a time be constantly repeated, of the civilization that must slowly take its place. This is too simple a statement, for much detail is possible. There are certain points of stress on outer and inner gyre, a division of each, now into ten, now into twenty-eight, stages or phases. However in the exposition of this detail so far as it affects the future, Robartes had little help from the Judwalis either because they cannot grasp events outside their experience, or because certain studies seem to them unlucky. "'For a time the power' they have said to me," (writes Robartes) "'will be with us, who are as like one another as the grains of sand, but when the revelation comes it will not come to the poor but to the great and learned and establish again for two thousand years prince & vizier. Why should we resist? Have not our wise men marked it upon the sand, and it is because of these marks, made generation after generation by the old for the young, that we are named Judwalis.'"

Their name means makers of measures, or as we would say, of diagrams.[6]

[6] Yeats to Lady Gregory (4 Jan. 1918): "I am writing it all out in a series of dialogues about a supposed medieval book, the *Speculum Angelorum et Hominum* by Giraldus, and a sect of Arabs called the Judwalis (diagrammatists). Ross has helped me with the Arabic" (*L* 644). Yeats to Edmund Dulac (10 Jan. 1918): The neglect of Giraldus is "only comparable to that which has covered with the moss of oblivion the even more profound work of Kusta iben Luka of Bagdad, whose honour remains alone in the obscure sect of the Jadwalis [*sic*]" (*CL InteLex* 3388).

NOTE ON "THE ONLY JEALOUSLY OF EMER"[1]

While writing these plays, intended for some fifty people in a drawing-room or a studio, I have so rejoiced in my freedom from the stupidity of an ordinary audience that I have filled "The Only Jealousy of Emer" with those little known convictions about the nature and history of a woman's beauty, which Robartes found in the *Speculum* of Gyraldus and in Arabia Deserta among the Judwalis. The soul through each cycle of its development is held to incarnate through twenty-eight typical incarnations, corresponding to the phases of the moon, the light part of the moon's disc symbolizing the subjective and the dark part the objective nature, the wholly dark moon (called Phase 1) and the wholly light (called Phase 15) symbolizing complete objectivity and complete subjectivity respectively. In a poem called "The Phases of the Moon" in *The Wild Swans at Coole* I have described certain aspects of this symbolism which, however, may take 100 pages or more of my edition of the Robartes papers, for, as expounded by him, it purports to be a complete classification and analysis of every possible type of human intellect, Phase 1 and Phase 15 symbolizing, however, two incarnations not visible to human eyes nor having human characteristics. The invisible fifteenth incarnation is that of the greatest possible bodily beauty, and the fourteenth and sixteenth those of the greatest beauty visible to human eyes. Much that Robartes has written might be a commentary on Castiglione's saying[2] that the physical beauty of woman is the spoil or monument of the victory of the soul, for physical beauty, only possible to subjective natures, is described as the result of emotional toil in past lives. Objective natures are declared to be always ugly, hence the disagreeable appearance of politicians, reformers, philanthropists, and men of science. A saint or sage before his final deliverance has one incarnation as a woman of supreme beauty.

---

[1] Yeats reported to Lady Gregory that he had finished the play on 14 Jan. 1918; it was then published in *Poetry* (Chicago) in Jan. 1919 and, with *The Dreaming of the Bones* (without notes), in *Two Plays for Dancers* (Dundrum: Cuala, Jan. 1919). The note, written around the summer of 1920, was appended to *Four Plays for Dancers* (London: Macmillan, 1921) when the play was reprinted with *At the Hawk's Well*, *The Dreaming of the Bones*, and *Calvary*. Of the four plays, only *At the Hawk's Well* was entirely written before Yeats's marriage and thus before the automatic scripts and dialogues were conceived; hence the first note simply accommodated text, about the play's historic performance in 1916, taken from the preface to the play in *Harper's Bazaar* (Mar. 1917) and *Theatre Arts Magazine* (Jan. 1919). Notes on the other three plays are original work for and may be read as a piece in *Four Plays for Dancers*. Like the preface and notes for *Michael Robartes and the Dancer* (1921), the occasion provided an opportunity to elucidate strange new matter apart from that of the Japanese and Irish traditions about which he had written in an introduction to *Certain Noble Plays of Japan*, ed. Ernest Fenollosa and Ezra Pound (Dundrum: Cuala, 1916), reprinted as an essay in *The Cutting of an Agate* (1919; *E&I* 221–37). However, the source of his new material—that of the supposed discoveries of Michael Robartes "in the *Speculum* of Gyraldus and in Arabia Deserta among the Judwalis"—could not be revealed. Ergo, Yeats drew once more on the story-frame of the Robartes-Aherne dialogues and their esoteric content to entertain or instruct a very exclusive audience, beginning with the general concept of the Great Wheel, 28 Embodiments, and "supreme beauty" located at the heart of it all as Robartes had recited in "The Phases of the Moon."

[2] Baldassare Castiglione (1478–1529), *The Book of the Courtier*, trans. Thomas Hoby (*YL* 351).

In writing these little plays I knew that I was creating something which could only fully succeed in a civilization very unlike ours. I think they should be written for some country where all classes share in a half-mythological, half-philosophical folk-belief which the writer and his small audience lift into a new subtlety. All my life I have longed for such a country, and always found it quite impossible to write without having as much belief in its real existence as a child has in that of the wooden birds, beasts, and persons of his toy Noah's Ark. I have now found all the mythology and philosophy I need in the papers of my old friend and rival, Robartes.

Note on "The Dreaming of the Bones"[1]

Dervorgilla's few lines can be given, if need be, to Dermot,[2] and Dervorgilla's part taken by a dancer who has the training of a dancer alone; nor need that masked dancer be a woman.

The conception of the play is derived from the world-wide belief that the dead dream back,[3] for a certain time, through the more personal thoughts and deeds of life. The wicked, according to Cornelius Agrippa,[4] dream themselves to be consumed by flames and persecuted by demons; and there is precisely the same thought in a Japanese "Noh" play, where a spirit, advised by a Buddhist priest she has met upon the road, seeks to escape from the flames by ceasing to believe in the dream. The lovers in my play have lost themselves in a different but still self-created winding of the labyrinth of conscience. The Judwalis distinguish between the Shade which dreams back through events in the order of their intensity, becoming happier as the more painful and, therefore, more intense wear themselves away, and the Spiritual Being, which lives back through events in the order of their occurrence, this living back being an exploration of their moral and intellectual origin.

All solar natures, to use the Arabian terms, during life move towards a more objective form of experience, the lunar towards a more subjective. After death a lunar man, reversing the intellectual order, grows always closer to objective experience, which in the spiritual world is wisdom, while a solar man mounts gradually to the most extreme subjective experience possible to him. In the spiritual world subjectivity is innocence, and innocence, in life an accident of nature, is now the highest achievement of the intellect. I have already put the thought in verse.[5]

---

[1] *The Dreaming of the Bones* was written between 15 May and 11 June 1917 and rewritten in the summer of 1918. See Wayne K. Chapman, ed., *"The Dreaming of the Bones" and "Calvary": Manuscript Materials* (Ithaca, NY: Cornell University Press, 2003), xxxii; transcription of Yeats's note of 1920 is given on pp. 235–41. First published in Jan. 1919 in *Two Plays for Dancers* and *The Little Review* (Jan. 1919), the play was reprinted in *Four Plays for Dancers*, notes included.

[2] Young Man, a 1916 rebel, meets these cursed spirits who betrayed Ireland 700 years ago.

[3] The doctrine of "dreaming back" as enunciated by Theodor Fechner, *On Life after Death* (1914; *YL* 665), which Yeats began reading in Feb. 1918.

[4] Cf. *Myth* 354, where Yeats quotes the passage he paraphrases here, from *Opera* (*YL* 24).

[5] The following lines are from "Shepherd and Goatherd," finished 19 Mar. 1918 (*YPM* 236).

He grows younger every second
That were all his birthdays reckoned
Much too solemn seemed;
Because of what he had dreamed,
Or the ambitions that he served,
Much too solemn and reserved.
Jaunting, journeying
To his own dayspring,
He unpacks the loaded pern
Of all 'twas pain or joy to learn,
Of all that he had made.
The outrageous war shall fade;
At some old winding whitethorn root
He'll practise on the shepherd's flute,
Or on the close-cropped grass
Court his shepherd lass,
Or run where lads reform our daytime
Till that is their long shouting playtime;
Knowledge he shall unwind
Through victories of the mind,
Till, clambering at the cradle side,
He dreams himself his mother's pride,
All knowledge lost in trance
Of sweeter ignorance. [*VP* 342–43, ll. 89–112]

The Shade is said to fade out at last, but the Spiritual Being does not fade, passing on to other states of existence after it has attained a spiritual state, of which the surroundings and aptitudes of early life are a correspondence. When, as in my poem, I speak of events while describing the ascent of the Spiritual Being, I but use them as correspondence or symbol. Robartes writes to John Aherne,[6] under the date of May 1917, a curious letter on this subject: "There is an analogy between the dreaming back of the Body of Passion" (I have used instead of this term the more usual term Shade), "and our ordinary dreams—and between the life of Spirit and Celestial Body taken together" (I have substituted for both terms the less technical, though, I fear, vague term Spiritual Being), "and those coherent thoughts of dreamless sleep, which, as I know on my personal knowledge, coincide with dreams. These dreams are at one time their symbols, and at another live with an independent life. I have several times been present while my friend, an Arab doctor[7] in Bagdad, carried on long conversations with a sleeping man. I do not say a hypnotized man, or even a somnambulist, for the sleep seemed natural

[6] As in the notes Yeats prepared for "An Image from a Past Life" and "The Second Coming," bearing extracts from fictitious Robartes-John Aherne letters of May 1917, both this and the following note draw upon the procedure of the "Version B," c. June 1920 shift from dialogue to extracts.

[7] Relates to "Michael Robartes and the Judwali Doctor" in NLI 36,263/29 and short extracts interjected by Owen Aherne in *AVA* 245–47; this line of invention continues in the *Calvary* note.

sleep produced by fatigue, though sometimes with a curious suddenness. The sleeper would discuss the most profound truths and yet while doing so make, now and again, some movement that suggested dreaming, although the part that spoke remained entirely unconscious of the dream. On waking he would often describe a long dream, sometimes a symbolic reflection of the conversation, but more often produced by some external stimulus—a fall in temperature in the rooms, or some condition of body perhaps. Now and again these dreams would interrupt the conversation, as when he dreamed he had feathers in his mouth and began to blow. Seeing, therefore, that I have observed a separation between two parts of the nature during life, I find no difficulty in believing in a more complete separation, affirmed by my teachers, and supported by so much tradition, when the body is no longer there to hold the two parts together."

I wrote my play before the Robartes papers came into my hands, and in making the penance of Dermot and Dervorgilla last so many centuries I have done something for which I had no warrant in these papers, but warrant there certainly is in the folklore of all countries. At certain moments the Spiritual Being, or rather that part of it which Robartes calls "the Spirit," is said to enter into the Shade, and during those moments it can converse with living men, though but within the narrow limits of its dream.

Note on "Calvary"[1]

I have written the little songs of the chorus to please myself, confident that singer and composer, when the time came for performance, would certainly make it impossible for the audience to know what the words were. I used to think that singers should sing a recipe for a good dish, or a list of local trains, or something else they want to get by heart, but I have changed my mind and now I prefer to give him some mystery or secret. A reader can always solve the mystery and learn the secret by turning to a note, which need not be as long as those Dante put to several of the odes in the *Convito*.[2] I use birds as symbols of subjective life, and my reason for this, and for certain other things, cannot be explained fully till I have published some part at any rate of those papers of Michael Robartes, over which I have now spent several years. The following passage in a letter written by Robartes to Aherne in the spring of 1917 must suffice.[3] "At present I rather pride myself on believing all the superstitions of the Judwalis, or rather in believing that there is

---

[1] Influenced by readings in Fechner of Feb./June 1918, Yeats's writing of this play extended through 1919 to the date stamp (7 Oct. 1920) on the galley proof of the note for *Four Plays for Dancers*. See Chapman, *"The Dreaming of the Bones" and "Calvary": Manuscript Materials* xxxv–xlii and (for the note) 247–59. George Harper sees the automatic script made on 26 Oct. 1918 as especially important and pivotal in Yeats's thinking about *Calvary* in its writing: "A play planned as a 'Judas play' became a Christ play" after that (*MYV2* 153).

[2] Same analogy, almost verbatim, as in the preface to *Michael Robartes and the Dancer* (1921).

[3] See note 6, above, on Yeats's *Dreaming of the Bones* commentary in relation to the procedure of extracts from Robartes papers and paraphrased conversations.

not one amongst them that may not be true, but at first my West European mind rebelled. Once in the early morning, when I was living in a horse-hair tent among other similar tents, a young Arab woke me and told me to come with him if I would see a great wonder. He brought me to a level place in the sand, just outside the tent of a certain Arab, who had arrived the night before and had, as I knew, a reputation as a wonder-worker, and showed me certain marks on the sand. I said they were the marks of a jackal, but he would not have this. When he had passed by a little after sunrise there was not a mark, and a few minutes later the marks were there. No beast could have come and gone unseen. When I asked his explanation he said they were made by the wonder-worker's 'Daimon' or 'Angel.' 'What,' I said, 'has it a beast's form?' 'He goes much about the world,' he said; 'he has been in Persia and in Afghanistan, and as far west as Tripoli. He is interested in things, in places, he likes to be with many people, and that is why his Daimon has the form of a beast, but your Daimon would have a bird's shape because you are a solitary man.' Later on, when I mastered their philosophy, I came to learn that the boy had but classified the wonder-worker and myself according to their division of all mankind into those who are dominated by objects and those who are dominated by the self or *Zat*,[4] or, as we would say, into objective and subjective natures. Certain birds, especially as I see things, such lonely birds as the heron, hawk, eagle, and swan, are the natural symbols of subjectivity, especially when floating upon the wind alone or alighting upon some pool or river, while the beasts run upon the ground, especially those that run in packs, are the natural symbols of objective man. Objective men, however personally alone, are never alone in their thought, which is always developed in agreement or in conflict with the thought of others and always seeks the welfare of some cause or institution, while subjective men are the more lonely the more they are true to type, seeking always that which is unique or personal."

I have used my bird-symbolism in these songs[5] to increase the objective loneliness of Christ by contrasting it with a loneliness, opposite in kind, that unlike His can be, whether joyous or sorrowful, sufficient in itself. I have surrounded Him with the images of those He cannot save, not only with the birds, who have served neither God nor Caeser, and await for none or for a different saviour, but with Lazarus and Judas and the Roman soldiers for whom He has died in vain. "Christ," writes Robartes, "only pitied those whose suffering is rooted in death, in poverty, or in sickness, or in sin, in some shape of the common lot, and he came especially to the poor who are most subject to exterior vicissitude." I have therefore represented in Lazarus and Judas types of that intellectual despair that lay beyond His sympathy, while in the Roman soldiers I suggest a form of objectivity that lay beyond His help. Robartes said in one of the conversations recorded by

---

[4] "Zat" is the term for the self of God in mystical Sufi Islam.

[5] I.e., songs in *Calvary*. Yeats's bird-symbolism derives from an annotated copy of Swedenborg's *Arcana Coelestia* and the veritable bestiary, or aviary, he obtained from the automatic script and its attendant card file, rather than an Arabian source; see Chapman, *"The Dreaming of the Bones" and "Calvary": Manuscript Materials* xxxvii.

Aherne: "I heard much of *Three Songs of Joy*,[6] written by a certain old Arab, which owing to the circumstances of their origin were considered as proofs of great sanctity. He held the faith of Kusta ben Luki, but did not live with any of the two or three wandering companies of Judwalis. He lived in the town of Hâyel[7] as servant to a rich Arab merchant. He himself had been a rich merchant of Aneyza[8] and had been several times to India. On his return from one of these journeys he had found his house in possession of an enemy and was himself driven from Aneyza by the Wahâbies[9] on some charge, I think of impiety, and it was then he made his first song of joy. A few years later his wife and child were murdered by robbers in the desert, and after certain weeks, during which it was thought that he must die of grief, his face cleared and his step grew firm and he made his second song. He gave away all his goods and became a servant in Hâyel, and a year or two later, believing that his death was near, he made his third song of joy. He lived, however, for several months, and when I met him had the use of all his faculties. I asked him about the 'Three Songs,' for I knew that even on his deathbed, as became the votary of a small contentious sect, he would delight in exposition. I said, (though I knew from his songs themselves, that this was not his thought, but I wanted his explanation in his own words): 'You have rejoiced that the Will of God should be done even though you and yours must suffer.' He answered with some emotion: 'Oh, no, Kusta ben Luki has taught us to divide all things into Chance and Choice;[10] one can think about the world and about man, or anything else until all has vanished but these two things, for they are indeed the first cause of the animate and inanimate world. They exist in God, for if they did not He would not have freedom, He would be bound by His own Choice. In God alone, indeed, can they be united, yet each be perfect and without limit or hindrance. If I should throw from the dice-box there would be but six possible sides on each of the dice, but when God throws He uses dice that have all numbers and sides. Some worship His Choice; that is easy; to know that He has willed for some unknown purpose all that happens is pleasant; but I have spent my life in worshipping His Chance, and that moment when I understand the immensity of His Chance is the moment when I am nearest Him. Because it is very difficult and because I have put my understanding into three songs I am famous among my people.'"

---

[6] Untraced.

[7] Ha'il, Ha'yel, or Hayil—a city in northwestern Saudi Arabia.

[8] Another city in Saudi Arabia cited for hostilities with the Wahhabis in Charles M. Doughty's *Wanderings in Arabia*, an abridgement of the two-volume *Travels in Arabia Deserta*, ed. Edward Garnett (1908; *YL* 539), one of Yeats's main sources, here, besides *Arabian Nights*.

[9] Adherents of religious sect, or radical branch of Islam. Most Sunni and Shia Muslims today disapprove of Wahhabism, nowadays associated with global terrorism.

[10] As early as Dec. 1917, the Robartes-Aherne dialogues began to explore the idea of "Chance & Choice" in an exchange so labeled (NLI 36,263/7[5]): "I once paid a visit to Damascus to speak with a student of 'The Way of the Soul' who had set up there as a doctor, & had some knowledge of European Methods of thought & owe it largely to him that I have been able to find meaning in certain obscure passages.... It is something one, as it were, alludes to in the midst of pre-occupation with something else—an object introduced by Chance" (ff. 1–2).

THE GIFT OF HARUN-AL-RASHID[1]

Kusta-ben-Luka is my name,[2] I write
To Abd-al-Rabban[3]; fellow roisterer once
Now the good Caliph's learned Treasurer,
And for no ear but his.
Carry this letter
Through the great gallery of the Treasure House
Where banners of the Caliphs' hang, night-coloured[4]
But brilliant as the night's embroidery,
And wait war's music; pass the little gallery;
Pass books of learning from Byzantium
Written in gold upon a purple stain,
And pause at last, I was about to say,
At the great book of Sappho's song[5]; but no
For should you leave my letter there, a boy's
Love-lorn, indifferent hands might come upon it
And let it fall unnoticed to the floor.
Pause at the Treatise of Parmenides[6]
And hide it there, for Caliphs' to world's end
Must keep that perfect, as they keep her song
So great its fame.

---

[1] The poem was written in 1923 as Yeats became frustrated with a long, fifth Noh adaptation set at Ballylee, honoring his wife by analogy to Mary Hynes, the Helen of local legend cited in "The Tower" III, stanzas 3–5. The first page of manuscript for "The Gift of Harun Al-Rashid" (in latest spelling) is misfiled with a version of the unfinished play, eventually published in *YA* 17 (2007) and reprinted in *YPM* 97–127, 246–89, and 313–19. Harun al-Rashid, frequently figuring in the tales of *Arabian Nights*, was the fifth Abbasid Caliph, who ruled from Bagdad during the Golden Age of Islam, between 786 and his death in 809, too early to have had actual dealings with Yeats's Kusta.

[2] W. B. Yeats in the guise of Qusta ibn Luqa (820–912), also Costa ben Luca, Constabulus, from Heliopolis, Lebanon, a Byzantine Greek Christian, traveler, and translator of Greek texts into Arabic.

[3] Al-Rabban ("the rabbi") is the eponymous Harun Al-Rashid's treasurer, introducing to Yeats's apocryphal contribution to the tales of *Arabian Nights* a "dialogue of three religions (Islam, Christianity, and Judaism)," according to Mazen Naous in "The Turn of the Gyres: Alterity in 'The Gift of Harun Al-Rashid' and *A Thousand and One Nights*," *The Ashgate Research Companion to Nineteenth-Century Spiritualism and the Occult*, ed. Tatiana Kontou and Sarah Willburn (London: Ashgate, 2012), 204.

[4] A short note on p. 41 of *The Cat and the Moon and Certain Poems* reads: "The banners of the Abbasid Caliphs were black as an act of mourning for those who had fallen in battle at the establishment of the Dynasty."

[5] Attic Greek poet (c. 630–570 BC) from Lesbos, Sappho's songs on the theme of love are almost entirely lost, surviving in fragments. See Yeats's note below.

[6] Parmenides, pre-Socratic Greek philosopher who lived just prior to 500 BC. Yeats refers, evidently, to *On Nature*, extant today only in fragments.

When fitting time has passed
The parchment will disclose to some learned man
A mystery that else had found no chronicler
But the wild Bedouin. Though I approve
Those wanderers that welcomed in their tents
What great Harun-al-Rashid, occupied
With Persian wars or Greek ambassadors,
Or those who need his bounty or his law,
Must needs neglect; I cannot hide the truth
That wandering in a desert, featureless
As air under a wing, can give birds' wit.
In after time they will speak much of me
And speak but phantasy. Recall the year
When our beloved Caliph put to death
His Vizir Jaffer[7] for an unknown reason;
'If but the shirt upon my body knew it
I'd tear it off and throw it in the fire.'
That speech was all that the town knew, but he
Seemed for a while to have grown young again;
Seemed so on purpose, muttered Jaffer's friends,
That none might know that he was conscience struck—
But that's a traitor's thought. Enough for me
That in the early summer of the year
The mightiest of the princes of the world
Came to the least considered of his courtiers;
Sat down upon the fountain's marble edge
One hand amid the goldfish in the pool;
And thereupon a colloquy took place
That I commend to all the chroniclers
To show how violent great hearts can lose
Their bitterness and find the honeycomb.

'I have brought a slender bride into the house;
You know the saying "Change the bride with Spring,"
And she and I, being sunk in happiness,
Cannot endure to think you tread these paths,
When evening stirs the jasmine, and yet
Are brideless.'

---

[7] Ja'far ibn Yahya (767–803), the vizier of Caliph Harun al-Rashid and member of the Barmakid family. He was executed for having an affair with the Caliph's sister and figures in several *Arabian Nights* tales.

'I am falling into years'
'But such as you and I do not seem old
Like men who live by habit. Every day
I ride with falcon to the river's edge
Or carry the ringed mail upon my back,
Or court a woman; neither enemy,
Game-bird, nor woman does the same thing twice;
And so a hunter carries in the eye
A mimicry of youth. Can poet's thought
That springs from body and in body falls
Like this pure jet, now last amid blue sky
Now bathing lily leaf and fishes' scale,
Be mimicry?'
'What matter if our souls
Are nearer to the surface of the body
Than souls that start no game and turn no rhyme!
The soul's own youth and not the body's youth
Shows through our lineaments. My candle's bright
My lantern is too loyal not to show
That it was made in your great father's reign.'

'And yet the jasmine season warms our blood'

'Great prince forgive the freedom of my speech;
You think that love has seasons, and you think
That if the spring bear off what the spring gave
The heart need suffer no defeat; but I
Who have accepted the Byzantine faith,[8]
That seems unnatural to Arabian minds,
Think when I choose a bride I choose for ever;
And if her eye should not grow bright for mine
Or brighten only for some younger eye,
My heart could never turn from daily ruin,
Nor find a remedy.'
'But what if I
Have lit upon a woman,[9] who so shares
Your thirst for those old crabbed mysteries,
So strains to look beyond our life, an eye
That never knew that strain would scarce seem bright,
And yet herself can seem youth's very fountain,
Being all brimmed with life.'

[8] As a Melkite Christian of Greek origin.
[9] I.e., Bertha Georgie ("George") Hyde Lees Yeats.

'Were it but true
I would have found the best that life can give,
Companionship in those mysterious things
That make a man's soul or a woman's soul
Itself and not some other soul.'
'That love
Must needs be in this life and in what follows
Unchanging and at peace, and it is right
Every philosopher should praise that love.
But I being none can praise its opposite.
It makes my passions stronger but to think
Like passion stirs the peacock and his mate,
The wild stag and the doe; that mouth to mouth
Is a man's mockery of the changeless soul.'
And thereupon his bounty gave what now
Can shake more blossom from autumnal chill
Than all my bursting springtime knew. A girl[10]
Perched in some window of her mother's house
Had watched my daily passage to and fro;
Had heard impossible history of my past;
Imagined some impossible history
Lived at my side; thought Time's disfiguring touch
Gave but more reason for a woman's care.
Yet was it love of me, or was it love
Of the stark mystery that has dazed my sight
Perplexed her phantasy and planned her care?
Or did the torchlight of that mystery
Pick out my features in such light and shade
Two contemplating passions chose one theme
Through sheer bewilderment? She had not paced
The garden paths, nor counted up the rooms,
Before she had spread a book upon her knees
And asked about the pictures or the text;
And often those first days I saw her stare
On old dry writing in a learned tongue,
On old dry faggots that could never please
The extravagance of spring; or move a hand
As if that writing or the figured page
Were some dear cheek.

---

[10] George Yeats in her mother's house in London, one of various residences of Edith Ellen Woodmass Tucker and husbands William Gilbert Hyde Lees and Harry T. ("Uncle Bunk") Tucker familiar to Yeats.

Upon a moonless night
I sat where I could watch her sleeping form,
And wrote by candle-light; but her form moved,
And fearing that my light disturbed her sleep
I rose that I might screen it with a cloth.
I heard her voice 'Turn that I may expound
What's bowed your shoulder and made pale your cheek';
And saw her sitting upright on the bed;
Or was it she that spoke or some great Djinn?
I say that a Djinn spoke. A live-long hour
She seemed the learned man and I the child;
Truths without father came,[11] truths that no book
Of all the uncounted books that I have read,
Nor thought out of her mind or mine begot,
Self-born, high-born, and solitary truths,
Those terrible implacable straight lines
Drawn through the wandering vegetative dream,
Even those truths that when my bones are dust
Must drive the Arabian host.

The voice grew still,
And she lay down upon her bed and slept,
But woke at the first gleam of day, rose up
And swept the house and sang about her work
In childish ignorance of all that passed.

A dozen nights of natural sleep, and then
When the full moon swam to its greatest height
She rose, and with her eyes shut fast in sleep
Walked through the house. Unnoticed and unfelt
I wrapped her in a heavy hooded cloak, and she,
Half running, dropped at the first ridge of the desert
And there marked out those emblems on the sand[12]
That day by day I study and marvel at,
With her white finger. I led her home asleep
And once again she rose and swept the house
In childish ignorance of all that passed.

---

[11] On George Yeats's self-birth ("Self-born, high-born, and solitary truths," l. 141), see Neil Mann, "George Yeats and Athanasius Kircher," *YA* 16 (2005): 178.

[12] See Yeats's notes, above, to *The Dreaming of the Bones* (on "a sleeping man") and *Calvary* (on "a certain Arab…a wonder-worker" and "certain marks on the sand"). Also, see Owen Aherne's "Introduction" to *AVA*, below at ll. 120–25 (on Judwali children learning doctrine "by the aid of diagrams drawn by old religious men upon the sands"). George Yeats's activities observed while sleeping are famously described in *A Packet for Ezra Pound* III and XI (*AVB* 9–10, 20–22).

Even today, after some seven years
When maybe thrice in every moon her mouth
Murmured the wisdom of the desert Djinns,
She keeps that ignorance, nor has she now
That first unnatural interest in my books.
It seems enough that I am there; and yet
Old fellow student, whose most patient ear
Heard all the anxiety of my passionate youth,
It seems I must buy knowledge with my peace.
What if she lose her ignorance and so
Dream that I love her only for the voice,
That every gift and every word of praise
Is but a payment for that midnight voice
That is to age what milk is to a child!
Were she to lose her love, because she had lost
Her confidence in mine, or even lose
Its first simplicity, love voice and all,
All my fine feathers would be plucked away
And I left shivering. The voice has drawn
A quality of wisdom from her love's
Particular quality. The signs and shapes;
All those abstractions that you fancied were
From the great treatise of Parmenides;
All, all those gyres and cubes and midnight things[13]
Are but a new expression of her body
Drunk with the bitter sweetness of her youth.
And now my utmost mystery is out.
A woman's beauty is a storm-tossed banner;
Under it wisdom stands, and I alone—
Of all Arabia's lovers I alone—
Nor dazzled by the embroidery, nor lost
In the confusion of its night-dark folds,
Can hear the armed man speak.

1923.

[13] A second short note from p. 41 of *The Cat and the Moon and Certain Poems* reads as follows: "'All those gyres and cubes and midnight things' refers to the geometrical forms which Robartes describes the Judwali Arabs as making upon the sand for the instruction of their young people, & which, according to tradition, were drawn or described in sleep by the wife of Kusta-ben-Luka." The note is referred to the wrong page and line in the text, reflecting changes in the typesetting that affected the page run.

Yeats's Note on "The Gift of Harun-Al-Rashid"[1]

This poem is founded on the following passage in a letter of Owen Ahern's,[2] which I am publishing in 'A Vision'.

'After the murder for an unknown reason of Jaffer, head of the family of the Barmecides, Harun-al-Rashid seemed as though a great weight had fallen from him, and in the rejoicing of the moment, a rejoicing that seemed to Jaffar's friends a disguise for his remorse, he brought a new bride into the house. Wishing to confer an equal happiness upon his friend, he chose a young bride for Kusta-ben-Luka. According to one tradition of the desert, she had, to the great surprise of her friends, fallen in love with the elderly philosopher, but according to another Harun bought her from a passing merchant. Kusta, a christian like the Caliph's own physician, had planned, one version of the story says, to end his days in a Monastery at Nisibis,[3] while another story has it that he was deep in a violent love affair that he had arranged for himself. The only thing upon which there is general agreement is that he was warned by a dream to accept the gift of the Caliph, and that his wife a few days after the marriage began to talk in her sleep, and that she told him all those things which he had searched for vainly all his life in the great library of the Caliph and in the conversation of wise men. One curious detail has come down to us in Bedouin tradition. When awake she was a merry girl with no more interest in matters of the kind than other girls her age, and Kusta, the apple of whose eye she had grown to be, fearing that it would make her think his love but in self-interest, never told her that she talked to him in her sleep. Michael Robartes frequently heard Bedouins quoting this as proof of Kusta-ben-Luka's extraordinary wisdom . . . . even in the other world Kusta's bride is supposed to remain in ignorance of her share in founding the religion of the Judwalis, and for this reason young girls, who think themselves wise, are ordered by their fathers and mothers to wear little amulets on which her name has been written. All these contradictory stories seem to be a confused recollection of the contents of a little old book, lost many years ago with Kusta-ben-Luka's larger book,[4] in the desert battle which I have already described. This little book was discovered according to tradition, by some Judwali scholar or saint, between the pages of a greek book which had once been in the Caliph's library. The story of the discovery may however be the invention of a much later age to justify some doctrine, or development of old doctrine, that it may have contained.'

---

[1] What follows is part VI of *The Cat and the Moon* (1924) "Notes." Yeats grants himself considerable license to exaggerate in his note: "I have amused myself by imagining incidents and metaphors that are related to certain beliefs of mine as are the patterns upon a Persian carpet to some ancient faith or philosophy" (*VPl* 805). The footnotes below do not identify figures already addressed in my notes to the poem (WKC).

[2] The poem, not the letter by Owen Aherne, is published in *AVA*.

[3] School of Nisibis, place of a monastic revival in the late 5th century in East Syria.

[4] "called TARĪQAT UN-NUFUS BAYN AL-QUMUR WA'L-SHUMUS, the Way of souls between the Moons & the Suns" in the "'Discoveries' Manuscript" (*YVP4* 70).

In my poem I have greatly elaborated this bare narrative, but I do not think it too great a poetical licence to describe Kusta as hesitating between the poems of Sappho and the treatise of Parmenides[5] as hiding places. Gibbon[6] says the poems of Sappho were still extant in the twelfth century, and it does not seem impossible that a great philosophical work, of which we possess only fragments, may have found its way into an Arab library of the eighth century. Certainly there are passages of Parmenides, that for instance numbered one hundred and thirty by Burkitt,[7] and still more in his immediate predecessors, which Kusta would have recognised as his own thought. This from Herakleitus for instance 'Mortals are Immortals and Immortals are Mortals, the one living the other's death and dying the other's life.'[8]

---

[5] On the lost Sappho songs and Parmenides treatise, see footnotes 5 and 6, above, on Yeats's poem.

[6] Edward Gibbon (1737–1794), author of *The History of the Decline and Fall of the Roman Empire*, 7 vols. (1909–1914; *YL* 746).

[7] F. C. Burkitt, as in *AVA* 132 (spelled "Birkett"), is a mistake for John Burnet, *Early Greek Philosophy* (London and Edinburgh: Adam and Charles Black, 1892; *YL* 308).

[8] One of Yeats's favorite expressions, translated by Burnet, p. 138; also quoted or paraphrased in *AVA* and elsewhere. See Chapman, "Metaphors for Poetry," in *YVEC* 238 and *YPM* 180.

THE LOVER SPEAKS

A strange thing surely that my Heart when love had come unsought
Upon the northern upland or in that poplar shade,
Should find no burden but itself and yet should be worn out,
It could not bear that burden and therefore it went mad.

The south wind brought it longing, and the east brought in despair,
The west wind made it pitiful, and the north wind afraid.
It feared to give its love a hurt with all the tempest there;
It feared the hurt that she could give and therefore it went mad.

I can exchange opinion with any neighbouring mind,
I have as healthy flesh and blood as any rhymer's had,
But oh my Heart could bear no more when the upland caught the wind;
I ran, I ran from my love's side because my Heart went mad.

THE HEART REPLIES

The Heart behind its rib laughed out, 'You have called me mad' it said.
'Because I made you turn away and run from that young child;
How could she mate with fifty years that was so wildly bred?
Let the cage bird and the cage bird mate and the wild bird mate in the wild.'

'You but imagine lies all day, O murderer', I replied.
'And all those lies have but one end poor wretches to betray;
I did not find in any cage the woman at my side.
O but her heart would break to learn my thoughts are far away.'

'Speak all your mind' my Heart sang out, 'speak all your mind; who cares,
Now that your tongue cannot persuade the child till she mistake
Her childish gratitude for love and match your fifty years.
O let her choose a young man now and all for his wild sake.'

After appearing as separate poems in *The Dial* (June 1924) and *The Cat and the Moon* (1924), "The Lover Speaks" and "The Heart Replies" were united as one two-part poem, entitled "Owen Aherne and his Dancers," in *The Tower* (1928) and thereafter. The poems were written, respectively, on 24 and 29 Oct. 1917, as observed by Mrs. Yeats (*YPM* 239). Yeats's note in *The Tower* is confusing as it glosses only "The Gift of Harun Al-Rashid" and fails to mention Owen: "Part of an unfinished set of poems, dialogues and stories about John Ahern and Michael Robartes, Kusta ben Luka, a philosopher of Bagdad, and his Bedouin followers" (*VP* 830).

INVENTIONS AND EXTRACTS FOR *A VISION: AN EXPLANATION OF LIFE FOUNDED UPON THE WRITINGS OF GIRALDUS AND UPON CERTAIN DOCTRINES ATTRIBUTED TO KUSTA BEN LUKA* (1925)

On 15 July 1918, Yeats reported to Ezra Pound on progress "now at the 30th page of my prose dialogue expounding this symbol [of the Great Wheel] & there will be 3 dialogues of some 40 pages each, full of my sort of violence and passion" (*CL InteLex* 3461). Enclosed for placement in a journal (though none followed) was the completed poem "The Phases of the Moon," which, after appearing first in *The Wild Swans at Coole* (1919, 1920), assumed a signal position in *A Vision* (1925) as "1. The Wheel and The Phases of the Moon," between Owen Aherne's "Introduction" and, in Book I: "What the Caliph Partly Learned," Owen Aherne's second submission to Yeats's treatise, "2. The Dance of the Four Royal Persons." By then, the dialogue, or "conversations," between Robartes and Aherne had become a manuscript of nearly 60 pages (Draft 4, ready for typing on 3 October 1918) and then a typescript under 40 pages (Draft 5, by late 1918), finally abandoned to a body of heavily illustrated "fragments, partly extracts from letters written by Robartes... ~~partly redactions~~ to John Aherne" (*YVP4* 141) as well as ostensible "conversations" and drawings from the spring of 1919, when Robartes is supposed to have returned from the Middle East. The invention of circumstance by Yeats in a headnote signed "WBY. June. 1920" created a source of some 116 pages of loosely organized material, with a 10-page appendix (counting versos), called "Version B" in light of its derivation from "The Discoveries of Michael Robartes." This repository of new tales and compounded extracts from preceding drafts in dialogue amounted to a source from which Yeats drew when composing notes and commentary, as we've seen, for a number of poems and plays published between 1919 and 1924. In another letter to Pound, when Yeats considered the prospects of publishing direct extracts from recent Robartes-Aherne writings, he could only hope for the future:

> The only other prose work I have in my head is a bundle of stories & dialogues concerning Michael Robartes.... I intend these tales & dialogues to be simply works of art. I will use certain philosophical ideas to give subjective hardness as Dante used Aquinas—It was lack of an Aquinas that denied to Milton & I think also to Shelley a refuge from Rhetoric. Subjective hardness is what we['re] all trying to get in different ways. In poetry it is the escape from imagination, the only vast pattern. All the rest is haycocks in the flood. (June 6 1918, dictated; *CL InteLex* 3447)

On 13 February 1922, Yeats wrote to Allan Wade, who must have seen the notes and prefaces that had begun to appear in recent Cuala Press and Macmillan titles, to enlighten him on the resurrection of Michael Robartes and on the appearance of John Aherne. See, for example, Yeats's prefaces to *The Wild Swans at Coole* and *Michael Robartes and the Dancer*, and especially the long notes appended to *Four Plays for Dancers* (1921) that cited "the Robartes papers," "my old friend and rival, Robartes." Acknowledging his bibliographer's mystification in a query of 25 November 1921 (*Four Plays* was published on 28 October), Yeats was somewhat coy although Wade may have known the reason behind the elaborate ruse, as were the Pounds, the Dulacs, Iseult Gonne, Sir Edward Ross, Lady Gregory, and other close friends:

> I have brought [Robartes] back to life. My new story is that he is very indignant because I used his real name in describing a number of fictitious adventures, and that because I called my fictitious hero by his name, many people have supposed him to be dead. He lived for years in Mesopotamia, but when the war came there returned to England for a short time. In England he got into communication with a certain John Aherne, and through him got into correspondence with me, and finally conveyed to me, without quite forgiving me, the task of editing and publishing the philosophy which he has discovered among certain Arabian tribes. That philosophy now fills a very large tin box upon which my eyes at this moment are fixed[;] I am giving it to the world in fragments, poems, notes, and a Cuala volume. (*CL InteLex* 4068)

We can easily imagine Yeats's "very large tin box," replete with "Version B," "Discoveries" drafts, and associated automatic scripts. If he was already thinking of the time when his "stories" might be presented and read apart from the philosophy, it would take him another eight years to get around to doing just that. However, he would soon deliver to the world by way of the Cuala Press another long poem and related set of notes in *The Cat and the Moon and Certain Poems* (1924). The poem was the dramatic monologue "The Gift of Harun Al-Rashid," which initiated Book II: "What the Caliph Refused to Learn" in *AVA* as "1. Desert Geometry or The Gift of Harun Al-Raschid."

But the process of redacting extracts from a mixed body of fiction and esoteric philosophy was not as simple and merely mechanical as it may sound. It was in fact painfully hard work, as Yeats acknowledged to Dulac in the following year: "I am toiling at a last higher tec[h]nical chapter of my philosophy & that done will enjoy life writing Robartes['s] little romantic interpolations" (23 October [1923], *CL IntLex* 4384). For sake of measurement, the pain may be deduced between the dates "March 13 [1923]," when Yeats reported only slow progress to T. Werner Laurie, and "October 23 [1925]," when final proofs were returned to Laurie, according to the record of their correspondence in the W. B. Yeats Collection (Manuscript Collection No. 600, Box 2, folders 21–44) at the Stuart A. Rose Manuscript, Archives, and Rare Book Library, Emory University. By mid-August

1924, Yeats expressed dissatisfaction with *A Vision*, with delays of various sorts following. No later than its publication on 15 January 1926, he was already at work on the subtantial rewriting that produced the revised edition of 1937 (*AVB*). Among other changes of consequence, "The Gift of Harun Al-Rashid" was removed from the book, as were all of the Robartes extracts and Aherne interpolations, save "The Phases of the Moon." When "The Gift" was collected in *The Tower* and delivered, in 1927, to Macmillan for printing, it bore the following, almost dismissive note: "Part of an unfinished set of poems, dialogues and stories about John Ahern and Michael Robartes, Kusta ben Luka, a philosopher of Bagdad, and his Bedouin followers" (*VP* 830). Even so, the poem's climactic position in *The Tower* was more satisfactory, preceding "All Souls' Night," which was the tail-piece there as in both editions of *A Vision*, than was its relegation to the "Narrative and Dramatic" section of *The Collected Poems* (1933), where its anomalous relation to the Celtic pieces is striking.

Maintaining the conceit that Robartes was the principal source and inspiration for the volume's philosophical discourse, rather than Mrs. Yeats and the spirit guides, was now critical to publishing fully the occult discoveries of several years of marital collaboration. Fiction provided a narrative frame for organizing and conveying fantastic truths, "philosophical ideas to give subjective hardness" to tales regarded as "simply works of art," as Yeats had told Pound. Psychologically, the strategy appealed to his own experience from laboring with poet, author, painter Edwin J. Ellis on *The Works of William Blake* for four years, during which time Ellis had entertained him by mixing "philosophical discussion varied with improvised stories, at first folk-tales which he professed to have picked up in Scotland, and, though I had read and collected many folk-tales, I did not see through the deceit" (*Au* 162). Extracts compiled from imaginary papers on Kusta ben Luka in Yeats's notes for *Calvary* and "The Gift of Harun Al-Rashid" are largely original tales as if taken from *The Arabian Nights*, as is Owen Aherne's rendition of "The Dance of the Four Royal Persons" (see below), only more so. A life-long fan of the exotic Arabian tales, Yeats would have been encouraged to witness in his own illustrated copy of the popular *New Arabian Nights* by Robert Louis Stevenson (Scribner, 1913; *YA* 4: 288) two clusters of contemporary stories, "The Suicide Club" and "The Rajah's Diamond" (mostly set in London), attributed to "my Arabian author" with framing links, in italics, between each of the seven stories of those clusters. The unifying device is cousin to Yeats's organization of material and to the titles he cast in Books I and II of *AVA* and, thereafter, in the interjection of materials signed or abbreviated "Owen Aherne," "O. Aherne," or simply "O.A."

Eventually, in developing structures for the changing logic of the book between 1925 and 1937, Yeats traded out old for new sequences of invention in fiction and poetry. Having initially struggled to write a long dialogue or as many as four dialogues between Owen Aherne and Michael Robartes, Yeats had abandoned this plan to the *AVA* scheme, where these two characters are given to quarrel with Yeats and each other in a counterfeit introduction supposedly by the imaginary Aherne. The scene shifts as conflict continues in the prologue of Book I, "The Phases of the Moon," where the speakers rehearse the book's philosophy, and Aherne presents a short narrative entitled "The Dance of the Four Royal Persons," which is actually lifted from "Version B," or "the Robartes MSS," vowing to "discuss all these matters at length in [his] own book upon the philosophy and its sources" (*AVA* 11). Both the 1925 and 1937 editions of *A Vision* conclude with an elegiac tribute to three of Yeats's *actual* friends from his early life as a creative mystic, "All Souls' Night: An Epilogue"—a tribute to William Horton, Florence Farr, and MacGregor Mathers, the latter being one of the models for Robartes. "The Gift of Harun Al-Rashid" was extravagant and charming. Yet worry was always there that the poet's excitement over the book's philosophy might not be matched by his poetry-reading public. One precaution taken was the limited first edition. Another was to issue a caveat in *AVA*'s "Dedication: To Vestigia" (i.e., to Moina Mathers, MacGregor's wife), acknowledging that he had doubts that certain parts of the book would elicit enthusiasm from such readers:

> I have moments of exaltation like that in which I wrote "All Souls' Night," but I have other moments when remembering my ignorance of philosophy I doubt if I can make another share my excitement. As I most fear to disappoint those that come to this book through some interest in my poetry and in that alone, I warn them from that part of the book called "The Great Wheel" and from the whole of Book II, and beg them to dip here and there in the verse and into my comments upon life and history. (*AVA* xii)

The reconfiguration of the narrative frame itself, in light of such concerns, is matter for Part Four of this study, on the making of "Stories of Michael Robartes and his Friends: An Extract Made by his Pupils" in 1929–1931.

All excerpts/exhibits given on the following pages of this section are from the first edition of *A Vision: An Explanation of Life founded upon the Writings of Giraldus and upon certain Doctrines Attributed to Kusta ben Luka* (T. Werner Laurie, 1925). Textual commentary not otherwise presented in the apparatus as footnotes and collations will be presented in the Notes on pages 158–64, according to the arrangement of these units in that edition. Exceptions include

- from Book I: "What the Caliph Partly Learned," "1. The Wheel and the Phases of the Moon" (as the poem appears on pages 106–110, above); and
- from Book II: "What the Caliph Refused to Learn," "1. Desert Geometry or the Gift of Harun al-Raschid" (which appears on pages 133–38, preceding Yeats's note on 139–40).

Introduction

By Owen Aherne

In the spring of 1917 I met in the National Gallery a man whom I had known in the late Eighties and early Nineties, and had never thought to see again. Michael Robartes and I had been intimate friends and fellow-students for a time, and later, after matters of theological difference arose between us, I lost sight of him, but heard a vague rumour that he was wandering or settled somewhere in the Near East. At first I was not certain if this were indeed he, and passed him in hesitation several times, but his athletic body, and his skin that had seemed, even when I first met him, sundried and sun-darkened, his hawk-like profile, could belong to no other man. I wish the thirty years had changed me as little, for I saw no change in that erect body except that the hair that had been some kind of red, was grey, and in places, fading into white. I had known him as an uncompromising Pre-Raphaelite, and there he stood before the story of Griselda pictured in a number of episodes, the sort of thing he had admired thirty years ago. Even when I had made him understand who I was I drew him from the picture with difficulty, because his indignation that the authorities of the gallery had not thought it was worth saving from the German bombs had heightened his admiration for all pictures of that type and his need for its expression. "The old painters," he said, "painted women with whom they would if they could have spent the night or a life, battles they would if they could have fought in, and all manner of desirable houses and places, but now all is changed, and God knows why anybody paints anything. But why should we complain, things move by mathematical necessity, all changes can be dated by gyre and cone, and pricked beforehand upon the Calendar." I brought him to a seat in the middle of the room, and I had begun to speak of the changed world we met in when he said: "Where is Yeats? I want his address. I am lost in this town and I don't know where to find anybody or anything." I felt a slight chill, for we had both quarreled with Mr Yeats on what I considered good grounds. Mr Yeats had given the name of Michael Robartes and that of Owen Aherne to fictitious characters, and made those characters live through events that were a travesty of real events. "Remember," I said, "that he not only described your death but represented it as taking place amid associations which must, I should have thought, have been highly disagreeable to an honourable man." "I was fool enough to mind once," he said, "but I soon found that he had done me a service. His story started a rumour of my death that became more and more circumstantial as it grew. One by one my correspondents ceased to write. My name had become known to a large number of fellow-students, and but for that rumour I could not have lived in peace even in the desert. If I had left no address I could never have got it out of my head that there was a vast heap of their letters lying somewhere, or even crossing the desert upon camel back." I did not know where Mr Yeats lived, but said that we could find out from Mr Watkins the book-seller in Cecil's Court: and having so found out, he said we must call upon Mr Yeats, and we started, keeping as much as possible from the main streets that we might have silence for our talk. "What have you to say to Yeats?" I said, and instead of answering he began to describe his own life since our last meeting. "You will remember the village riot which Yeats exaggerated in 'Rosa Alchemica.' A couple of old friends died of their injuries, and that, and certain evil results of another kind, turned me for a long time from my favourite studies. I had all through my early life periods of pleasure, or at least of excitement, that alternated with periods of asceticism. I went from Paris to Rome, and from Rome to Vienna, in pursuit of a ballet dancer, and in Vienna we quarreled. I tried to forget my sorrow in wine, but in a few weeks I had tired of that, and then, with some faint stirring of the old interest I went to Cracow, partly because of its fame as a centre of printing, but more I think because Dr. Dee and his friend Edward Kelly had in Cracow practiced alchemy and scrying. There I took up with a fiery handsome girl of the poorer classes, and hired a couple of rooms in an old tumble-down house. One night I was thrown out of bed and when I lit my tallow candle found that the bed, which had fallen at one end, had been propped up by a joint stool and an old book bound in calf. In the morning I found that the book was called 'Speculum Angelorum et Hominorum,' had been written by Giraldus and printed at Cracow in 1594, a good many years before the celebrated Cracow publications, and was of a very much earlier style both as to woodcut and type. It was very dilapidated and all the middle pages had been torn out; but at the end of the book were a number of curious allegorical pictures; a woman with a stone in one hand and an arrow in the other; a man whipping his shadow; a man being torn in two by an eagle and some kind of wild beast; and so on to the number of eight and twenty; a portrait of Giraldus and a unicorn; and many diagrams where gyres and circles grew out of one another like strange vegetables; and there was a large diagram at the beginning where lunar phases and zodiacal signs were mixed with various unintelligible symbols—an apple, an acorn, a cup. My beggar maid had found it, she told me, on the top shelf in a wall cupboard where it had been left by the last tenant, an unfrocked priest who had joined a troup of gypsies and disappeared, and she had torn out the middle pages to light our fire. What little remained of the text was in Latin, and I was piecing the passages together and getting a little light on two or three of the diagrams when a quarrel with my beggar maid plunged me into wine and gloom once more. Then turning violently from all sensual pleasure I decided to say my prayers at the Holy Sepulchre, and from there I went to Damascus that I might learn Arabic for I had decided to continue my prayers at Mecca, and hoped to get there in disguise. I had gone the greater portion of the way when I saw certain markings upon the sands which corresponded almost exactly to a diagram in the 'Speculum.' Nobody could explain them or say who made them, but when I discovered that an unknown tribe of Arabs had camped near by a couple of nights before and that they had moved in a northerly direction, I took the first opportunity of plunging into the desert in pursuit. I went from tribe to tribe for several months, learnt nothing and found myself at last in a remote town where, thanks to a small medicine chest which I always carry, I became first doctor, and then a kind of steward to an Arab chief or petty king. I constantly spoke about those markings upon the sand but learnt nothing till our town or village was visited by a tribe of Judwalis. There are several tribes of this strange sect, who are known among the Arabs for the violent contrasts of character amongst them, for their licentiousness and their sanctity. Fanatical in matters of doctrine, they seem tolerant of human frailty beyond any believing people I have met. One of them, an old man well known for his piety, asked me to prescribe for some complaint of his. When he came into my house, the book lay open upon a table, the frontispiece spread out: he turned towards it because it was European, and everything European filled him with curiosity, and then, pointing to the lunar phases and the mythological emblems, declared that he saw the doctrines of his tribe. The Judwali had once possessed a learned book called "The Way of the Soul between the Sun and the Moon" and attributed to a certain Kusta ben Luka, Christian Philosopher at the Court of Harun Al-Raschid, and though this, and a smaller book describing the personal life of the philosopher, had been lost or destroyed in desert fighting some generations before his time, its doctrines were remembered, for they had always constituted the beliefs of the Judwalis who look upon Kusta ben Luka as their founder. As my attempt to understand the diagrams of Giraldus, in the absence of other intellectual interests, had come to fill all my thoughts, I persuaded him to accept me into his tribe and for some years wandered with the Judwalis, though not always with the same tribe. I found that though their Sacred Book had been lost they had a vast doctrine which was constantly explained to their growing boys and girls by the aid of diagrams drawn by old religious men upon the sands, and that these diagrams were in many cases identical with those in the "Speculum Angelorum et Hominorum." I am convinced, however, that this doctrine did not originate with Kusta ben Luka, for certain terms and forms of expression suggest some remote Syriac origin. I once told an old Judwali of my conviction upon this point but he merely said that Kusta ben Luka had doubtless been taught by the desert djinns who lived to a great age and remembered ancient languages."

We had come by this to the little Bloomsbury court where Mr Yeats had his lodging; but when I told him so, he said, "No, it will be better to write and make an appointment. He is almost certain to be out." The evening had begun to darken and I pointed to a gleam of light through a slit in the curtain of the room on the second floor, but he said "No, no, I will write," and then "I have great gifts in my hands and I stand between two enemies; Yeats that I quarrelled with and have not forgiven; you that quarrelled with me and have not forgiven me." He began to walk away and I followed, and presently we fell into talk about indifferent things. I dined with him at the hotel and after dinner he brought out diagrams and notes, and began explaining their general drift. The sheets of paper which were often soiled and torn were rolled up in a bit of old camel skin and tied in bundles with bits of cord and bits of an old shoe-lace. This bundle, he explained, described the mathematical law of history, that bundle the adventure of the soul after death, that other the interaction between the living and the dead and so on. He saw that I was interested and asked if I would arrange them for publication. Such things fascinate me and I consented and from then on for months we were travelling companions, and he explained notes and diagrams in words almost as obscure. Certainly no man had ever less gift of expression. He came with me to France and later on to Ireland because of his wish to see once more places that he had known. In Dublin we stayed for a time in my Dominick Street house, described so extravagantly in "The Tables of the Law," which keeps its eighteenth century state, though slum children play upon its steps and the windows of the next house are patched with brown paper. On a walking tour in Connaught we passed Thoor Ballylee where Mr Yeats had settled for the summer, and words were spoken between us slightly resembling those in "The Phases of the Moon," and I noticed that as his friendship with me grew closer, his animosity against Mr Yeats revived.

Suddenly, however, our friendship was shattered by a violent scene like those of our youth. We had returned to London and I had there written eighty or ninety pages of exposition. He complained in exaggerated language that I interpreted the system as a form of Christianity, that only those aspects of character that were an expression of Christianity interested me—*primary* character to use the terms of philosophy—and that I was neither informed nor interested when I came to the opposite type. I contended that there could be nothing incompatible between his system and Christianity. St. Clement of Alexandria had taught the re-birth of the Soul and had remained a saint, and in our own time the Capuchin Archbishop Passivalli has taught it and keeps his mitre. Through lack of it, I said, the mediaeval Church got into a labyrinth of absurdity about Limbo and unbaptized children, but a certain number of modern Catholics have come to think that God may very well command a soul that has left its work unfinished to leave Purgatory and return to the world. Nothing, however, would persuade him, and he declared that he would give all his material to Mr Yeats and let him do what he like with it. Now it was my turn to get angry, for I had spent much toil upon his often confused and rambling notes. "You will give them to a man," I said, "who has thought more of the love of woman than of the love of God." "Yes," he replied, "I want a lyric poet, and if he cares for nothing but expression, so much the better, my desert geometry will take care of the truth." I replied—I think it better to set my words down without disguise—"Mr Yeats has intellectual belief but he is entirely without moral faith, without that sense, which should come to a man with terror and joy, of a Divine Presence, and though he may seek, and may have always sought it, I am certain that he will not find it in this life." This increased Robartes' anger, for I had almost repeated words of his own, and he accused Christianity of destroying Greco-Roman art and science, because it thought nothing mattered but faith. I denied this but said that even barbarism had not been too great a price to pay for pity and a conscience, and I reminded him that the system itself made the realisation of God one half of life. He then used ungenerous words, revived a quarrel of thirty years before, said that I was always the same, that I was but a free man for the moment, and even asked if I had consulted my confessor.* He called next day with some kind of apology but said I must come to see Mr Yeats and that he had made an appointment for us both. At Mr Yeats's Bloomsbury lodging he talked of his travels and his discovery, and as during the night I had thought the matter over and thought myself well out of a troublesome and thankless work, I helped his exposition. He had brought the Giraldus diagrams, and they seemed to interest Mr Yeats at first sight as much as they had Robartes himself. Mr Yeats consented to write the exposition on the condition that I wrote the introduction and any notes I pleased, and would have persuaded me to accept a portion of the profits but this I refused as later on I may publish my own commentary.

Two days later Robartes returned to Mesopotamia, for the armistice had made some spot, where he planned to spend his declining years, habitable once more, and from that day to this I have heard neither of him nor from him. This silence that has closed round him has made it natural to write, as I knew he wished that I should, as if his conversation and his foibles were already a part of history. In all probability he will never read what Mr Yeats or I have written, and he has lived so long out of Europe that he has no friends to find offence in a too candid record.

Mr Yeats's completed manuscript now lies before me. The system itself has grown clearer for his concrete expression of it, but I notice that if I made too little of the *antithetical* phases he has done no better by the *primary*. I think too that Mr Yeats himself must feel that the abstract

*I think Mr Aherne has remembered his own part in this conversation more accurately than that of his opponent.—W. B. Y.

foundation needs some such exploration as I myself had attempted. The twelve rotations associated with the lunar and solar months of the Great Year first arose, as Mr Yeats understands, from the meeting and separation of certain spheres. I consider that the form should be called elliptoid, and that rotation as we know it is not the movement that corresponds most closely to reality. At any rate I can remember Robartes saying in one of his paradoxical figurative moods that he pictured reality as a number of great eggs laid by the Phoenix and that these eggs turn inside out perpetually without breaking the shell.

O. A.

London, *May*, 1925

191–201 Allan Wade was first to notice that a rejected version of this passage existed in a draft of Owen Aherne's "Introduction" of December 1922. So our attention focuses on a range of manuscripts in NLI 36,264/7–14 (Introduction for *AVA* xv-xxiii). George Harper and Walter Hood attribute the date "Dec 1922" to "much more than Book I," including Yeats's revision and expansion of text for an installment to send Werner Laurie early in 1923 (*CVA* xxxvi, xxxviii–xxxix). The first version of the "Introduction" is cited in *CW13* xxxvii and 214, n. 26, in addition to the later revision borne in a typescript dated 26 July 1923. Both versions are discussed by Diana Poteat Hobby in "William Butler Yeats and Edward Dulac: A Correspondence, 1916–1938," PhD diss., Rice University, 1981. The "Dec 1922" Wade version of lines 191–201 is paraphrased in *CW13* xxxviii. The full text is as follows:

> "He [Robartes] called upon me the next day, made some kind of an apology, and said that I must come to see Mr. Yeats and that he had made an appointment for us. At Woburn Buildings he told of his Arabian discoveries and spread out upon the table his diagrams, his notes, my written commentary without even explaining that it was mine; and after a couple of hours' exposition, and answering many questions, asked Mr. Yeats to undertake the editorship.
>
> "Mr. Yeats opened a large gilded Moorish wedding chest, took out a number of copy-books full of notes and diagrams; showed that our diagrams and his were almost exactly the same; that our notes only differed from his because our examples were Arabian whereas his were drawn from European history and literature.
>
> "'You can only have found that all out,' said Robartes, who was pale and excited, 'through the inspiration of God.'
>
> "'Is not that a rather obsolete term?' said Mr. Yeats. 'It came in the first instance quite suddenly. I was looking at my canary, which was darting about the cage in rather brilliant light, when I found myself in a strangely still and silent state and in that state saw with the mind's eye symbols streaming before me. That still and silent state always recurs in some degree when I fix my mind upon the canary.'" (*L* 700)

Barbara L. Croft points out that the process Yeats describes with the canary is "scrying…, a kind of out-of-body travel, induced by self-hypnosis" practised by Dr. Dee in Cracow, a reason why Robartes had been attracted to the city (*"Stylistic Arrangements": A Study of William Butler Yeats's* A Vision [Lewisburg, PA: Bucknell University Press, 1987], 109–10).

214–22 Much later in *AVA* (p. 175), in a section entitled "The Cones—Higher Dimensions," Yeats makes use of the paradox of the Phoenix eggs, nonchalantly referring to Aherne as his authority. Five years later (in *SMR*, p. 1), the narrator John Duddon testifies that "Michael Robartes called the universe a great egg that turns inside out perpetually without breaking its shell," adding (mischievously for Yeats's part), "and a thing like that always sets Owen off." The 1925 text reads as follows:

> "One of the notes upon which I have based this book says that all existence within a cone has a larger number of dimensions than are known to us, and another identifies *Creative Mind, Will* and *Mask* with our three dimensions, but *Body of Fate* with the unknown fourth, time externally perceived. When I saw this I tried to understand a little of modern research into this matter but found that I lacked the necessary training. I have therefore ignored it hitherto in writing this book. The difference between a higher and a lower dimension explains, however, the continual breaking up of cones and wheels into smaller cones and wheels without changing the main movement better than Swedenborg's vortex, his gyre made up of many gyres. Every dimension is at right angles to all dimensions below it in the scale. If the Great Wheel, say, be a rotating plane, and the movement of any constituent cone a rotation at right angles to that plane the second movement cannot affect the first in any way. In the same way the rotation of the sphere will be a movement at right angles to a circumference which includes all movements known to us. We can only imagine a perpetual turning in and out of that sphere, hence the sentence quoted by Aherne about the great eggs which turn inside out without breaking the shell." (*AVA*, p. 175)

2. THE DANCE OF THE FOUR ROYAL PERSONS

By Owen Aherne

MICHAEL ROBARTES gives the following account of the diagram called "The Great Wheel" in Giraldus. A Caliph who reigned after the death of Harun Al-Raschid discovered one of his companions climbing the wall that encircled the garden of his favourite slave, and because he had believed this companion entirely devoted to his interests, gave himself up to astonishment. After much consideration he offered a large sum of money to any man who could explain human nature so completely that he should never be astonished again. Kusta ben Luka, now a very old man, went to the palace with his book of geometrical figures, but the Caliph, after he had explained them for an hour, banished him from the palace, and declared that all unintelligible visitors were to be put to death. A few days later four black but splendidly dressed persons stood at the city gate and announced that they had come from a most distant country to explain human nature, but that the Caliph must meet them on the edge of the desert. He came attended by his Vizir, and asked their country. "We are," said the eldest of the four, "the King, the Queen, the Prince and the Princess of the Country of Wisdom. It has reached our ears that a certain man has pretended that wisdom is difficult, but it is our intention to reveal all in a dance." After they had danced for several

---

1–7 When Haroun El Rashid died El-Muktedir became Calif (this celebrate[d] man lived much earlier. The story is plainly folk lore. O. A.) He discovered one of his companions climbing the wall that encircled the garden of his favorite slave and because...interests gave himself up to astonishment. *NLI 36,265/7 and 36,265/8/A*

10–15 Kusta Ben Luki now a very old man went to the palace and showed Calif El-Muktedir a book full of geometrical figures but after he had explained them for an hour banished him from the palace and declared that all unintelligible men who came there were to be put to death. *NLI 36,265/7 and 36,265/8/A*

16 persons cam[e] to the city gate [and] *NLI 36,265/7 and 36,265/8/A*

18 nature but that Calif El-Muktedir *NLI 36,265/7 and 36,265/8/A*

20–24 Visier and..."The King, the Prince and the Princess...difficult but *NLI 36,265/7 and 36,265/8/A*

minutes the Caliph said: "Their dance is dull, and they dance without accompaniment, and I consider that nobody has ever been more unintelligible." The Vizir gave the order for their execution, and while waiting the tightening of the bow-strings, each dancer said to the executioner: "In the Name of Allah, smooth out the mark of my footfall on the sand." And the executioner replied, "If the Caliph permit." When the Caliph heard what the dancers had said, he thought, "There is certainly some great secret in the marks of their feet." He went at once to the dancing place, and, having stood for a long time looking at the marks, he said: "Send us Kusta ben Luka, and tell him that he shall not die." Kusta ben Luka was sent for, and from sunrise to sunset of the day after, and for many days, he explained the markings of the sand. At last the Caliph said: "I now understand human nature; I can never be surprised again: I will put the amount of the reward into a tomb for the four dancers." Kusta ben Luka answered: "No, Sire, for the reward belongs to me." "How can that be?" said the other, "for you have but explained the marks upon the sand, and those marks were not made by your feet." "They were made by the feet of my pupils," said ben Luka. "When you banished me from the Palace they gathered in my house to console me, and the wisest amongst them said, 'He that dies is the chief person in the story,' and he and three others offered to dance what I chose." "The reward is yours," said the Caliph, "and henceforth let the figure marked by their feet be called the Dance of the Four Royal Persons, for it is right that your pupils be rewarded for dying."

26–28 minutes Calif El-Muktedir said "Their dance is dull and they dance without accompaniment and I consider that <nobody has ever been more> ~~They are so~~ unintelligible" ~~as Xx any man has ever been or ever can be to the end of the world"~~ The Visier *NLI 36,265/7 and 36,265/8/A*

31–34 executioner, "In the name of Allah, smooth out ~~my~~ the mark…sand", and…permit." Then El-Muktedir…thought "There *NLI 36,265/7 and 36,265/8/A*

36–41 place and…said "Send us Kusta Ben Luki…die" Kusta Ben Luki…days he…marking of the sand. At last El-Muktedir said, *NLI 36,265/7 and 36,265/8/A*

43–45 again;…dancers." But Ben Luki answered, "No, sire, for *NLI 36,265/7 and 36,265/8/A*

49–52 pupils" said Ben Luki, "When…palace…said "He…story. And *NLI 36,265/7 and 36,265/8/A*

53–55 aid El-Muktedir,…the dance *NLI 36,265/7 and 36,265/8/A*

56a Owen Ahearne [centered] *NLI 36,265/7 and 36,265/8/A*

According to the Robartes MSS. the Dance of the Four Royal Persons is one of the names for the first figure drawn by the Judwali elders for the instruction of youth and is identical with the "Great Wheel" of Giraldus.

I am inclined to see in the story of its origin a later embodiment of a story that it was the first diagram drawn upon the sand by the wife of Kusta ben Luka, and that its connection with the lunar phases, the movements and the nature of the *Four Faculties* and their general application to the facts of human life, were fully explained before its geometrical composition was touched upon. The Judwali doctor of Bagdad, who is mentioned elsewhere in this book, said that the whole philosophy was so expounded in a series of fragments which only displayed their meaning, like one of those child's pictures which are made up out of separate cubes, when all were put together. The object of this was, it seems, to prevent the intellect from forming its own conclusions, and so thwarting the Djinn who could only speak to curiosity and passivity. I cannot, however, let this pass without saying that I doubt the authenticity of this story, which Mr Yeats has expanded into the poem "Desert Geometry or The Gift of Harun Al-Raschid,"at least in its present form, and that an almost similar adventure is attributed in one of the Robartes documents to a Mahometan grammarian of a much later date. I will, however, discuss all these matters at length in my own book upon the philosophy and its sources.

O. A.

May, 1925

57–60 Note. According . . . MSS the. . . Judwaylie. . . youth. It is, it seems, identical with The Great Wheel of Gyraldus. *NLI 36,265/7 and 36,265/8/A*

61–84 *lacking in NLI 36,265/7 and 36,265/8/A*

Initials and date: *date lacking in NLI 36,265/7 and 36,265/8/A*

Interjections by Owen Aherne in "The Gates of Pluto"

In IX, Beatitude (*AVA* 235–36)—

(Mr Yeats, indulgent to Christian or primary prejudice, permits me to say that in the Robartes Papers I find this passage—"The *Celestial Body* is the Divine Cloak lent to all; at the Consummation the Cloak falls for the Christ is revealed." A passage that reminds me of Bardesan's "Hymn of the Soul" where a king's son asleep in Egypt is sent a cloak which is also an image of the body of him to whom it is sent—the *Celestial Body* acting through the *Mask*—and the king's son sets out to his father's kingdom clad in the cloak. I find also that the *Ghostly Self* is so named, not as it might seem because it is shadowy but because the *Beatitude* and the two states that follow correspond to the 13th, 14th and 15th Cycles which correspond in their turn to Holy Ghost, Son and Father.—Owen Aherne.)

In X, The States Before Birth, called The Going Forth and the Foreknowing (*AVA* 237–38)—

(Robartes told me that while in Arabia his work was constantly interfered with by illness, his own or somebody else's, and that he came to know the presence of *Frustrators* by animal odours like that of the excrement of some beast, or by the smell of a guttering candle. He said that these odours were objective, for anybody who came into the tent smelt them. He blamed the *Frustrators* for the inadequacy and confusion of all his own notes which deal with the life between death and birth, and insisted that the original revelation to Kusta Ben Luka had been, so far as this subject is concerned, left unfinished for the same reason. A curious point of his was that souls immediately before birth frequently thought of themselves as becoming small, and that this called up an imagination of small beasts, birds and flies. He had known, he said, two Arab women who found, one a mouse in her shoe, the other in her bed, the night before their first children were born. He thought that mice, constrained by the imagination of the unborn, were perhaps really there.—Owen Aherne.)

In XIII, Communications with Spirits and the Nature of Sleep (*AVA* 245–46)—

(Robartes told me that at Bagdad he came across an old Judwali doctor who had taken a medical degree in France, and made under his direction certain experiments upon an Arab boy. This boy was a patient of the doctor's for some physical ailment which had no connection with the fact that he talked in his sleep and would answer questions. Sometimes Robartes carried on conversations upon the most profound problems of the soul with an automatic personality which seemed sometimes the boy's own spirit and sometimes an extraneous being. He discovered that the boy's *Passionate Body* continued to dream during these conversations, but he only became aware of this dream when some physical action arising out of it interfered with articulation. Once the sleeper lapped like a cat under the influence of some chance word spoken in his hearing before he fell asleep; upon another occasion he dreamt that his mouth was full of feathers; and so on. If afterwards Robartes asked the boy what he had dreamt it was the dream of the *Passionate Body* and that alone he remembered. Upon one occasion when the boy was lapping Robartes imitated the barking of a dog as he might for a child. The boy's terror was great, the beating of his heart violent and yet Robartes had scarcely made any attempt at mimicry. Some part of the boy's mind must have accepted the suggestion deliberately; the dream must have been a self-created terror. Robartes told me that the dream of the *Passionate Body* after death was so created and that the *Spirit* while it shared the dream could be sufficiently apart from it to see men, scenes, other spirits, though it could not act or speak outside the dream.—O. Aherne.)

AND A SECOND INTERJECTION IN XIII (*AVA* 246–47)—

(During the sleep of the boy I described in a previous note, Robartes once arranged a code with the automatic personality. When the boy, who knew nothing of all this was wide awake, perhaps eating or at some work, the dream created being would comment upon Robartes' conversation or action by tapping with the boy's foot or with his fork or in some similar way. Sometimes he would speak through the boy's lips and at such moments the boy heard nothing, though the voice was loud and clear, and though he heard everything that Robartes said and every sound in the room and everything that he himself said except those words. Gradually as the automatic personality increased in power it made visible or other signs outside the body of the boy, a sudden light, a sudden heat or cold or some strong fragrance, that of a flower frequently, and this fragrance was generally perceptible to anybody who came into the room. Once Robartes listened to the sleeping boy talking to a number of spirits, and pausing for their answers. The boy spoke to them as though he knew who they were, their capacities, and when they lived. There was something they wanted to tell him that he might know what to do in a certain difficult matter, and that they might be able to impress it on his mind they were evidently insisting that he should go away by himself at a certain hour the next day. He reluctantly consented, being a very sociable person. Next morning he knew nothing of his dream, but when the hour came round said he wanted to be alone and strayed away into the fields. On his return, he said that he had made up his mind what to do in that difficult matter. Robartes' comment was that he had obeyed an order received in sleep without knowing that he did so and received a thought without knowing that it was not his own, and that this showed how strong is the control of the *Daimons* over human life.—Owen Aherne.)

Notes on *AVA* Extracts (glossed by line or numeral)

Introduction by Owen Aherne

Lines 1–19: Save for the date ("spring of 1917"), the content parallels that of the "Discoveries" Typescript (Draft 5 of dialogue), first two speeches, setting the scene for Aherne's and Robartes's chance reunion in the National Gallery, London, before the painting of Griselda, indignant that authorities "had not hidden it from the German bombs" (*YVP4* 13).

Lines 25–40: The subject of Yeats as *Secret Rose* author is raised as well as the offense taken by the two old men for having been depicted as fictitious characters in the 1890s; this follows precedent in the "Discoveries" Typescript as well as earlier drafts of the dialogue. However, the language is closer to that of the "Discoveries" Manuscript (Draft 4) when Robartes explains how the false impression that he had died was of service to him, providing him with peace to pursue wisdom in the Arabian desert. See *YVP4* 63.

Lines 43–48: Having obtained Yeats's address (18 Woburn Buildings, Euston Road, London, on the edge of Bloomsbury) from John M. Watkins, book-seller at No. 21 Cecil Court, London, Aherne acknowledges familiarity with Watkins Books, famous Mecca for pilgrim readers of the hermetic, esoteric, and Theosophical arts. At this point, Aherne suggests that he and Robartes look up Yeats, keeping to the main streets to "have silence for [their] talk." This passage is a reworking of the "Discoveries" Typescript, p. 1 (*YVP4* 13), but also "Discoveries" Manuscript, p. 2 (*YVP4* 63) yet not earlier drafts, where the two men eventually happen by Yeats's lodgings without turning in. See, for example, *YVP4* 122.

Lines 48–53: Reference to the riot at the end of "Rosa Alchemica" is introduced without ever mentioning the discussion of *Per Amica Silentia Lunae* in the typescript or manuscript drafts. This is because Yeats has shifted the date of the occasion from January 1918, when *PASL* was published, to spring 1917.

Lines 54–83: "I went from Paris to Rome, and from Rome to Vienna in pursuit of a ballet dancer…"; thus begins the central story of Robartes's discovery of the *Speculum* of Giraldus as one finds the account building by accretion since the first draft of the Robartes-Aherne dialogue. Up to this point, the most detailed depiction of the woodcuts in the *Speculum* is that of the "Discoveries" Typescript (*YVP4* 16); however, once that becomes part of Aherne's "Introduction" in *AVA*, this rendition is so close to the wording used in *SMR* (1931) as to suggest later copying directly from *AVA*.

Lines 83–107: "the Holy Sepulchre, and from there I went to Damascus… Mecca" (cf. p. 5 of "Discoveries" Typescript, *YVP4* 16–17), also close to the language of Robartes on how he came to serve the Judwalis as a "doctor, and then

[as] a kind of steward" (but not on "certain markings upon the sands which corresponded exactly to a diagram in the 'Speculum'"). This is from the first extract of "Version B," p. 4 (*YVP4* 142). For the significance of sand-marks, see Aherne's next piece based on "the Robartes MSS.," "The Dance of the Four Royal Persons."

Lines 107–22: "'The Way of the Soul between the Sun and the Moon'... attributed to Christian Philosopher at the Court of Harun Al-Raschid"; see "Discoveries" Typescript, "Discoveries" Manuscript, and "Version B" (*YVP4* 17, 70, and 143), as well as *CW13* 226, n. 51, on the fictitious title that coalesced rudiments from poetry collections by W. T. Horton, Cecil French, and Lord Tennyson, with a transliteration from English to Arabic by Sir Edward Denison Ross in 1918. It has been noted earlier that a fragment of dialogue from 1917, labeled "Chance & Choice" and citing "a certain obscure passage" to "The Way of the Soul," may be the earliest instance of the title in manuscript. Regarding the authority of Kusta ben Luka, see also notes by Yeats and by this editor on *Calvary* and "The Gift of Harun Al-Rashid."

Lines 123–27: Robartes's doubts about the origin of the doctrine of the Judwalis that attributes Kusta ben Luka as its source compares with Aherne's doubts (in "The Dance of the Four Royal Persons," ll. 76–84 as presented below) about the credibility of Mr. Yeats in the story he "expanded" in "The Gift of Harun Al-Rashid."

Lines 128–36: The scene at Yeats's door in Bloomsbury and Robartes's decision to walk away are rehearsed in the Robartes-Aherne dialogue of Draft 2 (NLI 36,263/7/2, folio 7^r) onward to Draft 5, where Aherne discerns Yeats's presence from the light in the window (*YVP4* 17). However, when Aherne points this out here, Robartes declines to stop for a different reason: his preference "to write and make an appointment," instead, because of the complicated circumstance of finding himself literally flanked by two associates with whom he disagrees, perhaps with exaggeration—"I stand between two enemies; Yeats that I quarreled with and have not forgiven; [and] you that quarreled with me and have not forgiven me."

Lines 136–44: The "Introduction" now departs from all versions of the dialogue. Content telescopes as the geometry and philosophical doctrine have become the body of *A Vision* to be interpreted by Yeats for the most part. Robartes and Aherne retire from the scene, dine, and then discuss the same in "general drift" over two groups of papers that Robartes has made the centerpiece of his studies: one "the mathematical law of history, that bundle the adventure of the soul after death, [and] that other the interaction between the living and the dead and so on." Because of Aherne's interest in these subjects and his fascination with the papers themselves, he is invited to "arrange them for publication," which seems rather more the task of an editor than that of an author or publisher. Agreeing to the request, Aherne establishes himself as an uncomfortable rival to Yeats, who, later in the "Introduction," is assigned the task of "exposition" over Aherne.

Lines 144–56: With their old friendship restored on this extraordinary day in the "spring of 1917," Aherne and Robartes become "travelling companions," venturing first to France, then to Ireland—where they "stayed for a time in my Dominick Street house" in Dublin ("described so extravagantly in 'The Tables of the Law'"; cf. *Myth* 302–04)—and to Connaught, where, in passing Yeats's summer home, Thoor Ballylee, they have a conversation "slightly resembling" the one reported in "The Phases of the Moon," the poem interposed between Aherne's "Introduction" and "The Dance of the Four Royal Persons." The relationship between the two friends is the mathematical inverse of their relationship to Yeats, growing closer as their animosity builds toward Yeats.

Lines 157–73: However, they reach a dramatic turning-point in their relationship with each other and with respect to Yeats and the so-called Robartes papers over the bias of Aherne's adherence to Catholic (i.e., orthodox Christian) doctrine on the interpretation of Robartes's system. The two men return to London, and their differences come to a head after Aherne writes "eighty to ninety pages of exposition" (a little less than Yeats's "Version B") and Robartes complains that the system had been characterized "as a form of Christianity." In self-defense, Aherne's logic is riddled with inaccuracies, possibly not deliberate ones by Yeats. Titus Flavius Clemens (d. 215 AD), Greek theologian and head of the catechetical school of Alexandria, is confused with St. Clement I of Rome. Capuchin Luigi Puecher-Passivalli, who delivered the opening sermon for the Vatican Council in 1869, is worthy of a note on the mitre as a Roman Catholic headdress for bishops and on Yeats's confusing his popes (see *CW13* 228, n. 59) in connection with the "labyrinth of absurdity" of Limbo and Purgatory in the "mediaeval Church" (see also *CW13* 228, n. 60).

Lines 173–91: Robartes's angry declaration that he would give his papers to Yeats raises the ire of Aherne, who needs little provocation to assail the poet for loving women better than loving God, an insult as memorable as the one he had hurled to Yeats's face in "Anglo Ireland: a conversation": "You protestants have no quibbles but I do not see much Platonics about you" (NLI 30,103, f. 4). Tempers flare until Robartes employs "ungenerous words," reviving a quarrel from youth, that Aherne was only free to think with his confessor's approval. (Yeats's comic footnote feigns impartiality while suggesting that Robartes may have had objections to Aherne beyond the ones recalled in the "Introduction"; see *L* 700, n.1).

Lines 191–201: Robartes goes to Woburn Buildings to convey his manuscripts (including diagrams from the *Speculum*) and to discuss his travels and various discoveries, leaving Aherne to conclude that he had been freed from "troublesome and thankless work." Consequently, Aherne becomes an aid to Yeats's project, agreeing to contribute "the introduction and any notes" that Aherne pleases but declining royalties in order to publish a commentary of his own. The agreement with Yeats occurs on or about 9 November 1918, as we deduce from lines 202–05.

Lines 202–09: "Two days later," Robartes returns to Mesopotamia, never to be seen or heard from again (until *SMR*, that is), the war's having ended with the Armistice of Compiègne, the agreement between the Allies and Germany that stopped the fighting in Europe on 11 November 1918. (Robartes's romantic side as a character is later enhanced by the invention of a service record for him beside "young Colonel Lawrence" of Arabia prior to Robartes's demobilization in 1917—see *SMR* 10).

Lines 210–17: Aherne expresses a general reservation about *AVA* ("Mr Yeats himself must feel that the abstract foundation needs some such exploration as I myself attempted"). The adverb "now" is defined by a series of roughly co-extant dates laid beside various placenames in the book, for example: "LONDON, May, 1925" and "May, 1925" beneath the initials "O. A." at the end of the "Introduction" and "The Dance of the Four Royal Persons"; in addition to the inscriptions "CAPRI, February, 1925" (beneath the initials "W. B. Y." at the end of the "Dedication") and "Finished at Capri, February, 1925" and "Finished at Syracuse, January, 1925" at the end of Books III and IV, respectively. Significantly, Book I of *AVA* is inscribed at the end, too: "Finished at Thoor, [*sic*] Ballylee, 1922, | in a time of Civil War."

Lines 217–222: A version of the Robartesian paradox of "eggs [that] turn inside out perpetually without breaking the shell" also concludes a paraphrasing by Yeats in Book II.2.xxiii ("The Cones—Higher Dimensions"), p. 174, and gives a punch-line to the opening paragraph of *SMR*, p. [1], where Daniel O'Leary introduces himself, having just left the study as Robartes makes analogy to the universe ("a thing like that always sets Owen off"). See endnotes attached to the full text of the "Introduction," above.

THE DANCE OF THE FOUR ROYAL PERSONS BY OWEN AHERNE

From Book I: "What the Caliph Partly Learned," I have omitted "1. The Wheel and the Phases of the Moon" here because the verse-dialogue is reprinted above in the chronological arrangement of selections from *The Wild Swans at Coole* (1919). Moreover, Dulac's figure of "The Great Wheel," placed in *AVA* on p. [xiv], is reproduced below, with the text of *SMR* (1931). For the next two pages, commentary on "2. The Dance of the Four Royal Persons by Owen Aherne" follows the same procedure as applied to the "Introduction by Owen Aherne."

Lines 1–2: Cf. the opening paragraphs of "Appendix by Michael Robartes" on "The Great Diagram from the Speculum Angelorum…which is the frontispiece" (NLI 36,263/7/3, ff. 1^r and 2^r). After these first lines, the story shifts away from Giraldus in the sixteenth century to Kusta ben Luka in the ninth, following the death of Caliph Harun Al-Rashid in 809 AD, during the reign of a successor, given by Yeats in a variant to be El-Muktedir (for Al-Muqtadir), caliph in Bagdad from 908 to 932. The problem is that the historic Qusta ibn Luqa al-Ba'albakki was born in 820 and died in 912 and, though he would have been "a very old man" (l. 11) under this later caliph, he would not have been living at the time of the fabled Harun Al-Rashid of *Arabian Nights* fame. Yeats's exercise of poetic license in "Desert Geometry or The Gift of Harun Al-Raschid" is humorously rebutted at the end of the present story. Hence "The Dance of the Four Royal Persons" is offered by Aherne as a corrective to the exaggerated poetic invention that Yeats presents at the head of Book II.

Lines 3–15: Nearly a hundred years after the death of Harun Al-Rashid, then, Bagdad's later caliph wagers a "large sum of money" to anyone capable of explaining human nature to him so that he might avoid astonishment. Nevertheless, he does expect to be entertained as well as enlightened, for, when the venerable Kusta ben Luka bears his "book of geometrical figures, called 'The Way of the Soul between the Sun and the Moon'" in Aherne's "Introduction," the caliph banishes him from the palace after an hour's instruction and decrees that "all unintelligible visitors" "were to be put to death."

Lines 15–22: The story's four Royal Persons arrive. The expression "Royal Persons" refers to alchemical symbols, according to the editors of *CW13*, but also to the quarters of Giraldus's Great Wheel, and "are reminiscent of the Yeatsian quarternaries" (232, n. 19). The editors do not say that the story was initially composed as extract "V" in "Version B" to explain "Why Kusta ben Luki was banished from court & ~~what~~ under what circumstance he returned" (*YVP4* 151–53); signed "Owen Aherne," it is followed by extract "VI," called "~~The Four Faculties.~~ | The Dance of the Four Royal Persons," which is, in fact, an exposition of the preceding story in terms of the Yeatsian Faculties of "Self," "Intellect," "Body of Fate," and "Image," or, in *AVA*, the "*Four Faculties* which constitute the *Tinctures*—the *Will*, the *Creative Mind*, the *Body of Fate*, and the *Mask*" (14). Much of "Version B" after that (153–237) appears to be a first-draft version of *AVA* Book I (from Part I.3.ii: "The Four Faculties") through Part I.4: "The Twenty-Eight Embodiments," minus the intervening tables—in other words, the unit of work said to have been completed in 1922 at Thoor Ballylee, dramatically "in a time of Civil War." The remaining "Appendix" to "Version B" relates to Yeats's Flaubertian exploration of "La Spirale" as the geometry takes over in the early pages of Book II: What the Caliph Refused to Learn, immediately after "1. Desert Geometry or The Gift of Harun Al-Raschid." In line 20, the "Vizir" is obviously not Ja'far ibn Yahya, vizier of Al-Rashid, for Ja'far was put to death for consorting with the caliph's sister. An allusion to Kusta ben Luka is made when the eldest of the dancers says that "a certain man has pretended that wisdom is difficult" (ll. 23–24).

Lines 25–29: Stupidly, after observing only "several minutes" of dancing without accompaniment, the Caliph is bored by the Royal Persons (king, queen, prince, and princess from the Country of Wisdom); so he pronounces them most unintelligible of all and sentences them to be executed on the spot.

Lines 29–38: Apparently in unison, the four Persons beg the executioner to "smooth out" the marks their feet have left in the sand, whereupon the Caliph stops the proceedings and calls for Kusta ben Luka to be brought back to interpret the meaning of the marks, suspecting that a "great secret" might be discovered.

Lines 39–56: Kusta ben Luka successfuly interprets the writing in the sand and, over "many days," brings the Caliph to understand human nature. One would expect to find a source for this phenomenon in either the abridged 1908 or complete, two-volume, 1923 edition of Charles M. Doughty's *Travels in Arabia Deserta* (*YL* 538 and 537), or perhaps in *Aspects of Religious Belief and Practice in Babylonia and Assyria* (1911, *YA* 4: 284), a work of omen and divination literature by Morris Jastrow, Jr. But it seems likely that the source is a combination of ritual aspects of the Hermetic Students of the Golden Dawn, the four Tarot suits, and Dervish dance (see *CW13* 232–33, nn. 19 and 23). Because the dancers are Kusta's own pupils, he claims priority—the right of authorship, as it were—and is granted the treasure promised to them by the Caliph; they had only danced as he had taught them during his banishment. Hence the dancers are executed, and the dance, as well as the figure produced in its performance, is proclaimed to be "the Dance of the Four Royal Persons, for it is right that [Kusta's] pupils be rewarded for dying."

Lines 57–60: Aherne vouches that this story stands on the authority of "the Robartes MSS," that it gives its name to "the first figure drawn by the Judwali elders for the instruction of youth" and is equivalent to the "'Great Wheel' of Giraldus."

Lines 61–84: The remainder of Aherne's story digs at Yeats for comic effect and is absent from NLI 36,265/7 and 36,265/8/A. The story is original if Yeats's poem "The Gift of Harun Al-Rashid" is apocryphal because it claims "the first diagram drawn upon the sand [to be] by the wife of Kusta ben Luka." For the "Judwali doctor of Bagdad, who is mentioned elsewhere in this book" (*AVA* 11), see "The Gates of Pluto" XIII (first and second interjections by "O. A." below, re: "Michael Robartes and the Judwali Doctor"). See also Yeats's poem and notes from *The Cat and the Moon* (above). Yeats's objective in such work, according to Aherne, is obfuscation, "thwarting the Djinn," genie or Daimon, "who could only speak to curiosity and passivity." Moreover, in lines 76–84, Aherne deftly accuses Yeats of misrepresenting authority and possibly plagiarizing, alleging that Kusta ben Luka should not be the speaker of the poem, "at least in its present form," as the story resembles "an almost similar adventure…attributed in one of the Robartes documents to a Mahometan grammarian of a much later date." Absurdly, Aherne promises to discuss the whole quandary: "at length in my own book upon the philosophy and its sources."

"The Cones—Higher Dimensions"

"Desert Geometry or the Gift of Harun al-Raschid," the prelude to *AVA* Book II, "What the Caliph Refused to Learn," has been omitted here because the dramatic monologue is reprinted in its chronological position as a selection from *The Cat and the Moon and Certain Poems.* Most of *AVA* II.2.xxiii, "The Cones—Higher Dimensions," is reprinted and discussed in the endnotes to Owen Aherne's "Introduction," where it is placed as a convenience to facilitate comparison.

Interjections by Owen Aherne from Book IV: "The Gates of Pluto"

"IX. Beatitude": Again acknowledging "Christian or primary prejudice," Aherne is allowed a short parenthetical rebuttal added later "to a much revised page of typescript" (*CW13* 329, n. 53).

"X. The States before Birth…": Harper and Paul note that Owen Aherne's parenthetical interjection was inserted "after the typescript," suggesting that it was introduced as a precaution to disguise the fact that Yeats was himself "well acquainted with 'the two girls'" that Aherne attributes to two Arab women of Robartes's acquaintance. On that point and on the Frustrators of the automatic script, see *CW13* 330, nn. 58 and 59.

"XIII. Communications with Spirits and the Nature of Sleep": Both of Aherne's interjections into this movement were once part of a longer, four-page, typed version entitled "Michael Robartes and the Judwali Doctor" (NLI 36,263/24/1–2), prepared for the first section of Book IV (see *CW13* 334–35, nn. 84 and 86). A fragment also exists in NLI 36,263/29 with poem "The Second Coming" and "Towards Break of Day." Aherne's second interjection continues from the first one to constitute a single tale, which had taken root as a seedling in dialogue form in the "Discoveries" Typescript (*YVP4* 17) after an initial sowing in the discarded fragment "Chance & Choice" (NLI 36,263/7[5]), with glimmerings in "Untitled Manuscript" (*YVP4* 122) and "Version B" ("I met in Bagdad an Arab doctor, whose parents had been of this [Judwali] sect"; *YVP4* 143). Harper and Paul observe that the textual environment into which Aherne has interjected his Robartesian content is "very close to…the note published in 1921 to 'An Image from a Past Life'…[a]lthough contain[ing] deliberately misleading dates" so as to direct attention away from the automatic script (334, n. 83). Similar evidence of Yeats's recycling invented matter on his wife's dreaming and sleep-talking is to be found in the notes of *Four Plays for Dancers* (also in 1921), on *The Dreaming of the Bones* ("I have several times been present while my friend, an Arab doctor in Bagdad carried on long conversations with a sleeping man") and on *Calvary* (wherein the nocturnal marvels of an Arab "wonder-worker's 'Daimon' or 'Angel'" are related). Those texts are reproduced above. See also *CW14* 8–14, for Yeats on the automatic writing of his wife and sleep exposition.

Part Four: 1929–1931

The Making of "Stories of Michael Robartes and His Friends"

for *Stories of Michael Robartes and His Friends: An Extract from a Record Made by His Pupils: and a Play in Prose* (Cuala Press, 1931)

later revised and reprinted in *A Vision* (Macmillan, 1937)

The Making of *Stories of Michael Robartes and His Friends*, 1929–1931

In the third chapter of *"Stylistic Arrangements,"* Barbara L. Croft's comparative study of *AVA* and *AVB*,[1] a case is made for the greater artistic merit of "Stories of Michael Robartes and His Friends: An Extract from a Record Made by His Pupils" based on the work's organic integration into *AVB* as a whole. This thesis has been challenged in a review by George Mills Harper (*YAACTS* 6 [1988]: 291–94), who states that,

> outside of Yeats's brilliant and carefully written introduction [*AVB* 8–25, or most of the 1929 Cuala Press text of *A Packet for Ezra Pound*], I consider much of the remaining cover material more or less extraneous. To Croft, in contrast, the "Stories of Michael Robartes" are "autobiographical and represent both Yeats's intentions to acknowledge, under the veil of fiction, his emotional debts and to assert his convictions regarding determinism and instinct" (127). That, I suggest, is a heavy burden for these "absurdist" stories.... Indeed, the very condition of the "manuscript" of *A Vision* when it was submitted to Macmillan in December 1934 suggests its inorganic character. (*YAACTS* 6: 293)

Harper's view is sustained by the evidence considered in most parts of the present study, too, especially in this section and ones to follow, which deal with the organic integrity of "Stories" in its own right while acknowledging that it was eventually attached to *A Vision* to assuage fear that the latter might not stand alone.[2]

Perhaps as early as October 1923, it had occurred to him that to enjoy life "writing Robartes little romantic interpolations" as in *AVA* might not be secured apart from the toil of writing "technical chapters" for his philosophy (*CL InteLex* 4384). Hence the writing of "Stories of Michael Robartes" came after that of *A Packet*, the designated introduction to *A Vision,* which Yeats had hoped to have ready, before long, in revised form. Even so, the rewriting of his play *The Resurrection*, from the early version of 1927 to the version accompanying "Stories" in *SMR* (1931), introduced organic contingencies more to the point of the stories well before the front half of *SMR* (prologue through page 26) was ever submitted to Macmillan as partial copy text for *AVB*. He speaks nowhere of this circumstance in *A Packet* (and therefore in *AVB*). Yet he associates the disclosure that he was not the "sole author" of *AVA* (his wife being "unwilling that her share should be known") with the need to "amend" and publish "an unnatural story of an Arabian traveller" (Robartes, Kusta ben Luka, Giraldus) because he had been "fool enough to write half a dozen poems that are unintelligible without it" (*AVB* 19). He does not in that section of *A Packet*, dated "November 23rd. 1928" (*Wade* 163), say that "Stories" would "find a place" one day in the cover material of *AVB*. He *was* able to say, on 13 September 1929, that an essay in *A Packet* would introduce "a new edition of 'The Vision' under the name of 'The Great Wheel,'" work that he planned to take with him to Rapallo with the expectation of sending it to the press in spring 1930; also, among other projects planned at that time:

> I shall begin…the new version of the Robartes stories. Having proved, by undescribed process, the im[m]ortality of the soul to a little group of typical followers, he will discuss the deductions with an energy & a dogmatism & a cruelty I am not capable of in my own person. I have a very amusing setting thought out. (WBY to Olivia Shakespear, *CL InteLex* 5285)

Serious illness got in the way of an ambitious time-table. *A Packet for Ezra Pound* had just been published in August 1929. If "Feb 1930," chosen for the date of John Aherne's epistle, has any bearing on the progress of the writing (see NLI 13,577, folio 25^r), then the stories were moving ahead faster than were revisions of the philosophy. Still, it would be another six months before Yeats would be able to write to an also frail Lady Gregory, promising that "[w]hen I have finished my present task[,] 'Stories of Michael Robartes & his friends[,]' it will be advertised with 'Coole'" (23 August 1930, *CL InteLex* 5373).[3] By 13 September 1930, the poet reported to his wife from Coole Park: "Have been writing notes in diary & correcting Robartes. Robartes is finished—they [will] get me a registered envelope in Gort today. I will send it on Monday" (*CL InteLex* 5381). Two days later, he wrote to her again to say: "I send script of Robartes—I couldn't get a registered envelope when [I] asked for their largest[,] the Gort post office sent one for letters. Had no other I suppose" (*CL InteLex* 5383). By "script," Yeats presumably meant a manuscript copy, the typing of which she was to arrange. It could hardly have been the complete holograph draft of NLI 13,577, presented below in 83 pages, because that copy was much too rough for any typist to manage unsupervised and was too large for a letter envelope, as the manuscript notebook was mounted inside a heavy, ornately embossed, leather attaché cover with enlaced edges (26 cm x 34 cm), like the Rapallo notebooks and the White Vellum Notebook, prize possessions in which revisions were drafted and kept for *The Resurrection* and the new edition of *A Vision*, and in which numerous poems were written, including several, in July 1931, related to and including "Huddon, Duddon and Daniel O'Leary," the prologue for *SMR* that originally had been intended as an epigraph for *The Resurrection*.[4]

Yeats worked on this play for more than nine years, from January 1925 to the first performance at the Abbey Theatre in July 1934. First printed in *The Adelphi* (in June 1927), the play's rewriting commenced in January 1930 and ended in September 1931, with second publication to follow in *SMR* in March 1932 and a reprinting after that in *Wheels and Butterflies* (1934), when an introduction was added to it. Rewriting partly occurred in the White Vellum Notebook and in

Rapallo Notebook E (NLI 13,582) between late November 1930 to 8 July 1931, roughly coincidental to, but somewhat after, the extant holograph version of "Stories of Michael Robartes." The typescript of the play was prepared in March 1931 for the *SMR* typesetting. Yeats's temporary secretary at that time was Alan Duncan, who undertook its typing on 10 February 1931 and finished it on 14 March.[5] With the writing of stories for Robartes's students and the amalgamation of stories for the title character himself (from the Robartes-Aherne dialogues, "Version B," and *AVA* extracts), Yeats saw an opportunity to integrate elements of both projects and seized it in an extraordinary way, particularly with regard to rejected material from the old *Adelphi* version of the play that would become integral to the last adventure of Michael Robartes and Owen Aherne.

In order to instill dramatic tension in the play where discursive dialogue prevailed in the early version, Yeats deleted The Hebrew's account of a Spartan temple that the latter had visited, as a tourist might, "to see the sights" (*VPl* 916), giving emphasis to the central conceit of the crucified Christ's still-beating heart.[6] The excised passage extends what we already knew about Yeats's sources for his famous sonnet "Leda and the Swan," from a few years before. The following exchange, then, inspired the talismanic centerpiece of the 1931 "Stories":

> *The Hebrew:* You think that if we can but keep our faith in a phantom, in an appearance, in an illusion, in some kind of trick, we can overcome the Greeks?
>
> *The Egyptian:* Did He not say that faith moved mountains?
>
> *The Hebrew:* I have not told you all that I saw in that temple. The guide—there is always a guide—showed me a piece of an old oar that had been used by Oddysseus [*sic*], and there above the altar a great egg hung from the roof by a long gold chain, an unhatched egg of Leda's.
>
> *The Egyptian:* An egg of Leda, did you say? And unhatched? What frustrated destiny!
>
> *The Hebrew:* From another of her eggs came Helen. Helen and Odysseus will give the Greeks mastery of the human race for ever, for even I, at sight of that old piece of an oar and that egg, could hardly keep from prostrating myself before the altar. What phantom can prevail against the treasure of Sparta! Paris found a beating heart in Helen's breast.
>
> *The Egyptian:* Odysseus and Helen died; Christ only seemed to die. (*VPl* 918)

In *SMR*, Leda's unhatched egg is delivered in a dramatic paragraph narrated by Robartes (as recorded by Duddon) but interrupted by Aherne to show that invention, or poetic license, is at work as the old men, with Mary Bell as bearer of the egg, prepare to make a long desert trek to witness the miraculous birth of an avatar, "the terror that is to come" (19):

> Mary Bell then opened the ivory box and took from it an egg the size of a swan's egg, and standing between us and the dark window curtains, lifted it up that we might all see its colour. 'Hyacinthine blue, according to the Greek lyric poet', said Robartes 'I bought it from an old man in a green turban at Teheran; it had come down from eldest son to eldest son for many generations'. 'No', said Aherne 'you never were in Teheran.' 'Perhaps Aherne is right' said Robartes. 'Sometimes my dreams discover facts, and sometimes lose them, but it does not matter. I bought this egg from an old man in a green turban in Arabia, or Persia, or India. He told me its history, partly handed down by word of mouth, partly as he had discovered it in ancient manuscripts. It was for a time in the treasury of Harun Al-Rashid and had come there from Byzantium, as ransom for a prince of the imperial house. Its history before that is unimportant for some centuries. During the reign of the Antonines tourists saw it hanging by a golden chain from the roof of a Spartan Temple. Those of you who are learned in the classics will have recognised the lost egg of Leda, its miraculous life still unquenched. I return to the desert in a few days with Owen Aherne and this lady chosen by wisdom for its guardian and bearer. When I have found the appointed place, Owen Aherne and I will dig a shallow hole where she must lay it and leave it to be hatched by the sun's heat.' He then spoke of the two eggs already hatched, how Castor and Clytaemnestra broke the one shell, Helen and Pollux the other, of the tragedy that followed, wondered what would break the third shell. Then came a long discourse founded upon the philosophy of the Judwalis and of Giraldus, sometimes eloquent, often obscure. I set down a few passages without attempting to recall their context or to arrange them in consecutive order. (19–20; cf. 50–52).

Some of Robartes's "ancient manuscripts" are manifest in this passage. One source is Pausanias, *Description of Greece*, translated by W. H. S. Jones: "In Sparta is a lounge called Painted, and by it hero-shrines.... Near is a sanctuary of Hilaeira and of Phoebe....Here there has been hung from the roof an egg tied to ribands, and they say that it is the famous egg that legend says Leda brought forth."[7] These shrines and this particular sanctuary is associated with Tyndareus, king of Sparta, husband to Leda, and father of the Dioscuri, heroes Castor and Pollux. We hear more of them in Yeats's second source though one notices a conflation of "ribands" (not *ribbons*) into a single "long gold chain," "a golden chain" suspending the egg from the roof of the "Spartan Temple" in *The Resurrection* and in Robartes's account. We have a virtual genealogy in Apollodorus, *The Library*, James George Frazer's 1921 translation, where variants according to hearsay or legend are acknowledged, making paternity a complicated affair and allowing the possibility that two eggs were hatched and up to two consorts were involved liaising with Zeus:

> Tyndareus and Leda had daughters, to wit, Timandra, whom Echemus married, and Clytaemnestra, whom Agamemnon married; also another daughter Phylonoe, whom Artemis made immortal. But Zeus in the form of a swan consorted with Leda, and on the same night Tyndareus cohabited with her; and she bore Pollux and Helen to Zeus, and Castor and Clytaemnestra to Tyndareus. But some say that Helen was a daughter of Nemesis and Zeus; for that [Nemesis], flying from the arms of Zeus, changed herself into a goose, but Zeus in his turn took the likeness of a swan and so enjoyed her; and as the fruit of their loves she laid an egg, and a certain shepherd found it in the groves and brought and gave it to Leda; and she put it in a chest and kept it; and when Helen was hatched in due time, Leda brought her up as her own daughter.[8]

Leda's *finding* the egg is also the story-line followed by Sappho, "the Greek lyric poet" Robartes cites as his authority for the "Hyacinthine blue" color of the swan's egg: "Leda they say once found an egg hidden under hyacinth-blossoms" (*YL* 1835).[9] She does not say the shell was blue. In a footnote to Apollodorus, Frazer deviates from the foundling-egg story to return to the question of the number of eggs laid by Leda and to the children sired by Zeus:

> According to one account…Castor, Pollux, and Helen all emerged from a single egg; according to another account [also that of First Vatican Mythographer], Leda laid two eggs, one of which produced Castor and Pollux, and the other Clytaemnestra and Helen. In heaven the twins Castor and Pollux had each, if we may believe Lucian, half an egg on or above his head in token of the way in which he had been hatched. (24)

From such sources, Yeats would have been encouraged to invent a third, "lost egg of Leda, its miraculous life still unquenched" (*SMR* 20). Therefore, why shouldn't he participate in the mythologizing of Zeus and Leda after the fact of the momentous cuckolding of Tyndareus at the influx of the heroic age? If one tradition held that one egg gave issue to offspring and another tradition posited two eggs, with more than one sire, then why not three eggs? Helen's relation to the Dioscuri as delivered from a second egg, the issue of Zeus (Swan) and Nemesis (Goose), might have inspired the invention of a mysterious third egg entirely fitting with the cuckoo associated with John Bond and Mary Bell. In other words, the ancient mysteries gave license for Yeats's modern one.[10]

The modern mystery is cousin to Blake's "Mundane Egg" (*Milton* 1: 15), Jacob Bryant's Orphic world-egg, and Robartes's "great egg" of the universe "that turns inside out perpetually without breaking its shell" (*SMR* 1).[11] Leda's eggs compare with Robartes's picture of reality, "as a number of great eggs laid by the Phoenix," at the end of Aherne's "Introduction" to *AVA*: they "turn inside out perpetually without breaking the shell" (xxiii; see also 175). Yeats's mythographic use of Leda is ingenious. For the third egg establishes the end of a continuum of symbolic annunciations—between the influx of Olympian and polytheistic dispensations in "Leda and the Swan" (c. 2100 BCE) and, in "The Mother of God" and "The Second Coming," that of the present Christian and monotheistic dispensations (starting at c. 1 CE) and the next dispensation, to come in the comparatively near future (at c. 2100 CE)—each one a parody of the one before.[12] Beyond Leda is Hera (or Juno) whose peacock screams as civilization ends. Brian Arkins is recommended for his treatment of classical myth, religion, and history in *The Resurrection*.[13] Other connections go to the heart of the story. Not surprisingly, these are about light/illumination, burning out, darkness, and Robartes's particular quandary on the paradox of love.

Both the rewritten version of *The Resurrection* and the Robartes story of 1931 are true because in their construction they impart a sense of verity, as fables do, from their articulated themes and personae. The untitled prologue, ["Huddon, Duddon and Daniel O'Leary"], speaks to both works that follow it, perhaps most audaciously to the play. The "three persons" who "despair and keep the pace | And love wench-wisdom's cruel face" are unmistakably Peter Huddon, John Duddon, and Daniel O'Leary in the story (acolytes whose names are adapted from an Irish folktale in *FFTIP*)[14] but are also, on the love of women, John Bond, Mr. Bell, and, most of all, Robartes himself. In *The Resurrection*, we have The Hebrew, The Greek, and The Syrian, after Yeats cut The Egyptian from the 1927 version; and the risen Christ appears, masked, at the end, having taken the place of the dead god Dionysus at the climax of the bacchanal. As is the custom in Yeats's plays for dancers, there are three musicians to preside over the play and to perform the choral opening and closing ceremonies. The women in the story are the amoral Denise, who has formed a *ménage* with Huddon and Duddon (the relationship is clearer after her story is added in *AVB*), and Mary Bell, adulteress and therefore suitable guardian of Leda's egg. Mary's cuckolding of her husband, with Bond, leads to the birth of an illegitimate heir. Robartes says, "We will call them John Bond and Mary Bell from the characters in a doggrel of Blake's."[15] The triangles compare with Robartes's involvement with a ballet-dancer and, on the rebound, with "an ignorant girl of the people" (7). The women in the play are Mary the mother of Jesus, Mary the mother of James, and "other women" accompanying—"the Galilean women"—as well as the pagan worshippers of Dionysus (including transgender boys and men) who participate in a frenzied orgy and "sing the death of the god and pray for his resurrection" (35).

In the prologue, Yeats recalls three outrageous characters in a folktale that astonished him as a child—"hard-living men" who "burn their bodies up" and "mock us burning out" (13–15). Love and fate for Robartes, like love and faith in Christ for the disciples, are iterated themes understood in terms of a solar-lunar binary. "Stories of Michael Robartes" opens late at night around the fire when

Huddon, Duddon, and Denise are first introduced to O'Leary, whose "great interest is the speaking of verse" (1). His comic demonstration of that interest is counterpointed by Yeats's instructions in the headnote of the play, which is followed directly by the ceremonial reference to "the fierce virgin and her Star | Out of the fabulous darkness" (27–28). We have, on the one hand, the fire that has been fed by the pages of the *Speculum* of Giraldus (8) and, on the other, a Messiah who exhausts suffering "as though it were all together in the spot of burning glass" (33). "Shakespeare's bright particular star" (22), denoting sexual love in *All's Well That Ends Well* 1.1.86–91, is juxtaposed to both "Babylonian starlight" and "man's darkening thought…fabulous formless darkness" (45). To be sure, the play's curtain lines are sad ones: "Whatever flames upon the night | Man's own resinous heart has fed" (46). For all of Robartes's quenchless desire, love "has been no ever-burning lamp" (9); "civilizations come to an end when they have given all their light like burned out wicks," he says, and "ours is at its end" (19).

Both "Stories of Michael Robartes" and *The Resurrection* are about living proof to the immortality of the soul, the objective that Robartes's teaching proves with personal testimony and with the preposterous tale of Mary Bell's counterfeit production of a cuckoo's nest so that her elderly scientist-husband might die a happy man. Man's heart ambiguously feeds the flame of his undoing, and, as Yeats asserts in *AVA* on the annunciation of Leda, "all things are from antithesis" (181), or, as Robartes explains in the story, from Kantian antinomies. This principle is an important addition to Robartes's own story (not anticipated in Aherne's introduction of 1925) and especially evident in a difficult part of the manuscript. Following the narratives of O'Leary and Duddon (counted also for that of Huddon) and, in *AVB*, before Denise's burlesque supplement, Robartes's personal testament bears the weight of an exemplar's concession. Central to them all, his story required special attention in the art of storytelling to become noticed as a dramatic turning-point. The necessity posed some difficulty for Yeats on folio 9^{r} of NLI 13,577, where, beneath scribbled-out lines 16–21, we may discern an abandoned first attempt (simplified here for sense): "I have pursued women…but have always known that love should be changeless.…[M]y loves burned themselves out like a candle"; also, picking up on suffering according to the "first antinomy of [I]mmanuel Kant" (at the foot of the page), we read that love "has burned into us [as if] it were flame & fuel" (lines 30–31). We are referred in three places to the verso ("See back"), where, on 9^{v}, lines 18–23, we see clearly the result of drafting worked out in a fragmentary scrap that only seems to have survived on microfilm, as SB 0400771, in the Department of Special Collections, State University of New York, Stony Brook:

> I had nothing now to distract my thoughts that ran through my past loves, neither numerous <nor> ~~now~~ happy[,] back to that platonic love of boy hood[,] the most <impassioned> ~~impassioned~~ of all. ~~&~~ I was plunged into hopeless misery. I have always known that love should be changeless

> & yet mine <soon drank their oil> ~~confer consumed their fuel~~ & died – there has been <no> ~~however~~ ever burning lamp.

Before continuing further in this vein, Yeats composed a short theme, just as he might in jotting down a prose subject for one of his poems, but at the far end of his notebook, at 43^v (the verso of the last folio). He even gave it a title, "Concerning love," stylistically rehearsing Robartes's critical self-revelation from the point where he had left off:

> We cry "it is for ever", & [as] we cry that out it passes & yet if we did not cry that out, it would not be love – but desire which does not pass away. Love dies.... The anguish of its birth & death meet in that cry.[16]

At the top of folio 10^r (page number "12" of the manuscript), Yeats introduces the antinomial elements of the argument and carries on from there with the gist of 43^v:

> Thesis there is no beginning. Antithesis there is a beginning, or as I prefer to put it[,] There is...no end & yet there is an end.... I cry out "My love will never end["]...and exhausted by that cry [it] passes away[;] without that cry it were not love but desire, desire does not pass.... The anguish of birth & death cry out in the same instant.

So this is the crux of Robartes's personal story concerning love, as we have it in *SMR*, page 9:

> 'Love contains all Kant's antinomies but it is the first that poisons our lives. Thesis, there is no beginning; antithesis, there is a beginning; or, as I prefer; thesis, there is no end. I cry out "My love will never end." Exhausted by that cry it ends; without that cry it were not love but desire, desire does not end. The anguish of birth and death cry out in the same instant....'

In *AVB*, Yeats is still polishing his phrasings and balancing the periods of these sentences, but the conclusion of the argument is fundamentally the same: "Life is no series of emanations from divine reason such as the Cabbalists imagine, but an irrational bitterness, no orderly descent from level to level, no waterfall but a whirlpool, a gyre" (40). The exhaustion of love, like "Everything that man esteems," is fleeting; hence "Love's pleasure drives [man's] love away" in *The Resurrection* (*SMR* 45). Of greater consequence to Robartes, as an old man (in manuscript, at line 17 of folio 9^r, with "desire almost dead in me"), is Kant's third antinomy: "thesis: freedom; antithesis: necessity" (21). This is restated as follows: "Every action of man declares the soul's ultimate, particular freedom,...the soul's disappearance in God; declares that reality is a congeries of beings and a single being...life itself which turns, now here, now there, a whirling and a bitterness." At the end of the play, the words of Heraclitus ring out: "God and man die each other's life, live each other's death" (45). Questions raised by the Syrian—"What if the irrational return? What if the circle begin again?" (42)—may seem only rhetorical compared with Robartes's blunt, final imperative: "Love war because of its horror, that belief may be changed, civilization renewed. We desire belief and lack it. Belief comes from shock and is not desired.... Belief is renewed continually in the ordeal of death" (22). To this, Owen Aherne objects, one of the few times he does so outside his brother's letter: "why should war be necessary?... You are not sane when you talk like that" (22).

Fortunately, we remember the reason behind Robartes's role in the "Extract" and "Record" made by his students, including Yeats as a character in the story's anti-climax, three pages from the end in *SMR*, where "a resemblance between [his] face and that of Giraldus in the *Speculum*" is noted (24). Facing that observation is the tipped-in woodcut by Dulac that had served as the frontispiece of *AVA*. The manuscript even concludes (at folio 27^{v}) with a cancelled postscript by John Aherne: "PS. I enclose some photographs Duddon took ~~from~~ of Wood Cuts in Speculum. He says that Gyraldus is a portrait so like you that he may [have] been one of your incarnations. I cannot myself see the resemblance." The humor in the remark recalls the candor of Yeats's admission to Olivia Shakespear that Robartes was to take up "deductions with an energy & a dogmatism & a cruelty I am not capable of in my own person" (*CL InteLex* 5285).

Hereafter, this commentary is intended to guide one through the many textual exhibits that follow. The guide addresses selected features of the manuscript that highlight its progress as a composition, in some cases reflecting a relative ease in the writing, in others the difficulty that certain aspects of invention posed to Yeats until he found solutions by working his way through or around them.

Folios 1–16 are loose, having been removed from the notebook but reinstated in correct sequence. From folio 17 onward, the leaves of the notebook are still bound in place, except for folios 26 and 27, which were torn out and are loose at that point, followed by 16 bound leaves. The latter are entirely blank except for the verso of the last one (folio 43^{v}), bearing the single paragraph entitled "Concerning love." Rectos are assigned page numbers; and most versos, according to Yeats's habit, were used to revise or extend content from the right-hand pages. All pages are fairly large ones (22 cm x 30 cm), compared with those of the inexpensive exercise booklets he tended to use for prose works. The white paper of the notebook is unlined and without watermarks. The cover (aside from the tooled leather case used to keep everything together) consists of paper boards decorated with blue blossoms stamped in a pattern of white ovals in a gold setting.

The four sections of the story are next to consider because of confusion Yeats created for himself and the typist and typesetter for the *SMR* printing at the Cuala Press. There is no section "IV" as such in *SMR*, only "I", "II," "III," and "V." When correction was made for *AVB* at Macmillan, the final episode began in a different place in the text. See NLI 13,577, folios 19^{r}, 20^{r}, 20^{v}, and 21^{r} to see how the mistake was made. As a consequence, the following table compares divisions between the 1931 and 1937 printings of *SMR* and *AVB*.

PARTS I–III are coordinate in both versions, but Denise's story has been inserted near the beginning of III in *AVB*.

PART IV is lacking in *SMR*, perhaps intended for the space left between the two paragraphs of page 16 (line 403 in the text).

PART IV in *AVB* begins between the second and third paragraphs of page 18 in *SMR*.

PART V (lacking in *AVB*) occurs on page 19 of *SMR*, which is where Mary Bell opens the box to reveal the unhatched egg of Leda.

NLI 13,577, FOLIOS 1^{R}, 2^{R}, 2^{V}, 3^{R}, 4^{R}, 4^{V}, 5^{R}, 5^{V}, AND 6^{R} (LINES 1–8)

Initially, the framing of Yeats's central narrative is unsettled, which is reason enough for him to occasionally confuse who is speaking. But the problem is compounded by the embedding of speakers and quotes within quotes. Besides confusing the brothers Owen and John Aherne, the original conception was to have presented "Stories" in the form of a letter "from Daniel O'Leary to John Ahern" as "edited by WB Yeats." The subtitle was soon amended to "an extract from a manuscript book" (since Yeats was composing in one) maintained by Robartes's "pupils" up to "May 1924." The date is not actual but invented to suggest an attributed source of fictional "extracts" like those contributed to *AVA* by Owen Aherne. This source would follow the supposed "diary kept by…Owen during [his] tramp in Ireland in 1922 and 1923" with Robartes, as John writes to Yeats (*SMR* 23) in the letter dated "Feb 1930" in manuscript (line 15 of folio 25^{r}). The setting is understood to be contemporary after O'Leary's "letter" is replaced by Duddon's "report." Following the substitution of Duddon's name for O'Leary's at line 21 of folio 1 (an error in view of the final text), the writing came to Yeats fairly easily for most of the story that would eventually tell how O'Leary came to live with Robartes and his disciples in a house in Albert Road, Regents Park, London. There is a jump between the last line of folio 2^{r} and the first line of 3^{r}, bridged by a "P.T.O." ("Please Turn Over") at 2^{r}, line 28 and a continuation, onto 2^{v}, with matter revised from the half-page cancellation that occurs on 3^{r}, lines 1–14. Similarly, a vexed issue at 4^{r}, lines 6–9 is resolved by referring to the folio verso—"(see back) X"—where a corresponding "X", on 4^{v}, marks the substituted passage. Aside from those slight detours, there are few mysteries here except to wonder why Yeats had given Duddon O'Leary's interest in "the speaking of verse" and O'Leary Duddon's romantic co-dependency on Denise and Huddon when the rhymed names from Irish folktale would dictate otherwise. After the change was made and "Stories" completed, however, O'Leary was given the role of mediating his master's prophecies in "Michael Robartes Foretells" (see Part Five: 1932–1937, pages 312–39, below).

Another mystery—probably an unsolvable one—concerns two pages (up to two leaves) missing from the manuscript notebook. Torn out and discarded, these pages may have contained content that Yeats copied out (and abridged as he did so) onto the extant first folio, assigning to it the compound number "1–2. & 3 | ~~3~~." Therefore, extant folios 2–27 are accordingly numbered 4–29.

Writing with rapidity, Yeats compounded the error of folio 1 by allowing O'Leary (at 4^{r}, line 20) to introduce himself, Denise, and "<Peter> ~~Michael~~ Huddon" as a group. O'Leary is thus the artist who produces paintings that Huddon compulsively purchases. Character names are still shown to be in flux. For instance, O'Leary says: "~~for some time Michael Dudden & myself have been as two twins~~" (lines 22–23), forgetting that the character John Duddon had been introduced already by his right name but in wrong person. Name toggling continues at the top of 5^{r}, but misattributed identities hardly impede the progress of Yeats's storytelling. He refers to the back of the page, at line 13, only to develop Owen Aherne's unfortunate misadventure as the unlucky gentleman clubbed "outside the Ritz" (later the Café Royal), in place of Huddon, and taken to a chemist's for treatment. As a result, fairly clean copy is produced on 5^{v} for substitution in place of 5^{r}, lines 14–23. Apart from momentary spelling lapses and word-choice impediments in that vicinity, the narrative cruises to the end of part I at folio 6^{r}, line 8. At this point, two of the stories have been told, albeit with transposed narrators.

Folios 6^{R} (lines 9–29), 7^{R}, 7^{V}, 8^{R}, and 8^{V}

Part II begins with the entrance of Robartes and Aherne, who introduce themselves to Huddon, Duddon, O'Leary, and Denise. Thumbnail descriptions of the elders, mixed with the repartee of introductions, make the writing seem fitful as the demands of narrative required details not provided in the dialogues of 1917–1920 nor in subsequent notes, prefaces, and poems. Robartes is "lank, brown, muscular, & clean shaven," reminiscent of the Ancient Mariner, whereas Aherne is "stout & sedentary & bearded & dull of eye," the "alert ironical eye" with which he surveys the young guests. The repartee acknowledges differences in age and profession. Figurative word-play on "Love" and "War" emboldens Denise, whose profession is "Love" and who is only shy of *old* men, to request of Robartes that he tell her the story of his life. So Aherne fetches "a very old book…an old battered book" from a bookcase, and Robartes proceeds to tell the assembled company about this book, how he found it, "what followed from the finding of it & what is still to follow" (7^{r}, line 19).

Robartes begins to tell his story, basically a retelling of accounts by now familiar to us from the early dialogues, especially the more developed narrative within the "Discoveries" Typescript (*YVP4* 16) and the extract quoted by Aherne in his introduction to *AVA* (xvii).[17] The very familiarity of such antecedents introduced a complication to the manuscript of "Stories," however, in that a kind of lateral expansion occurred that required greater use of facing versos in the interpolation of material. For example, a passage on Robartes's frustration with cabalistic philosophy at 8^{r}, lines 6–19, leads in two directions: first, to a full-page redaction on 7^{v} as Yeats directs one to "See back of | previous page" and, second, to a rejected revision on 8^{v}, where he worked on his depiction of the "fiery handsome girl of the poorer classes" with whom Robartes lived when he discovered the *Speculum* of Giraldus. These locutions, backward and then forward, are hard to follow; moreover, a deep tear along the upper-left side of folio 8^{r} has left a lacuna in the manuscript and corresponding transcription. Even so, all goes well for the remainder of the folio, from line 20 onward, because the text follows closely *AVA* xvii, except for the cancelled observation that the title of Giraldus's book was "in the ungrammatical dog latin of the time" (in line 25), recalling the rebuke of F. P. Sturm, in 1926, that "[h]owever dog the Latin you can't keep '*hominorum*' because it isn't latin."[18] Robartes's attraction to Cracow, "because Dr Dee and his friend Edward Kelly had…practiced alchemy and scrying" there (*AVA* xvii), had also prompted Sturm to volunteer highlights from Dee's Latin treatise *Monas Hierglyphica* (1564), including the book's first diagram called the Eagle's Egg. Although we see Yeats pulling away from Dee and alchemy with cancellations in folios 8^{r} and 7^{v}, the Eagle's Egg interested Yeats as it would seem a close relative of Robartes's universal egg that turns inside out without breaking its shell: "The Latin text is crabbed & cob-webby, like the mind of Dee.… He says that the great work of dissolving the Eagle's Egg is accomplished when the white disappears in the yolk, and is enveloped in it *as if by many revolving spirals*" (Sturm 96; see Yeats's response on 98–99).

FOLIOS 9^{R}, 9^{V}, 10^{R} AND 11^{R}

In the concluding part of Robartes's life story, we have not only the crux on love, in his estimation, as discussed at length above, but we also have development on the significance of Robartes's find and how the desire to interpret it as a palimpsest leads to more travel, namely to Jerusalem and the sands of Arabia. Again, the nearest textual antecedent to folio 9^{r}, lines 1–12, is in Aherne's introduction to *A Vision*, with the dialogues providing parallels only more distantly related. We can actually follow Yeats through the first 16 lines of 9^{r} and the first 13 lines of 9^{v} as he uses this text as a crib:

> …at the end of the book were a number of curious allegorical pictures; a woman with a stone in one hand and an arrow in the other; a man whipping his shadow; a man being torn in two by an eagle and some kind of

> wild beast; and so on to the number of eight and twenty; a portrait of Giraldus and a unicorn; and many diagrams where gyres and circles grew out of one another like strange vegetables; and there was a large diagram at the beginning where lunar phases and zodiacal signs were mixed with various unintelligible symbols—an apple, an acorn, a cup. My beggar maid had found it, she told me, on the top shelf in a wall cupboard where it had been left by the last tenant, an unfrocked priest who had joined a troup of gypsies and disappeared, and she had torn out the middle pages to light our fire. What little remained of the text was in Latin, and I was piecing the passages together and getting a little light on two or three of the diagrams when a quarrel with my beggar maid plunged me into wine and gloom once more. (*AVA* xvii-xviii)

Based on this text, Yeats obtained more and better details for *SMR* than he might have from other versions available to him. (Among them, only the "Discoveries" Manuscript lacks description of the woodcut figures, for some reason.) The others vary from each other by degree (see note 17) although the "Discoveries" Typescript is representative:

> It was indeed full of curious allegorical woodcuts, astronomical diagrams, where drawings of Noah's Ark and the Tables of the Law were mixed up with Zodiacal signs and phases of the moon and geometrical diagrams where cones containing gyres sprang out of each other like strange vegetables. (*YVP4* 16)

This earlier description, from late 1918, shows that by 1925 Yeats had visualized the effaced *Speculum* in a way that conveys to his reader a veritable picture of a mutilated Renaissance-era allegorical treatise from which most of its Latin content has been removed, leaving behind certain cryptic figures to speak for themselves. And more so than the geometrical diagrams of *AVA*, Book II, the "strange vegetables" that give the impression of propagating gyres actually resemble the jumble of figures in the Appendix of "Version B" (*YVP4* 238–46). That is one element of the tableau that Yeats kept. Giraldus's portrait, the printer's device of the unicorn, and The Great Wheel from *A Vision* are clearly recognizable in the tableau because these figures were recycled for use at strategic points in *SMR*. But what of the "allegorical pictures" themselves, "all…the unintelligible diagrams"—"a man torn in two by an eagle and some sort of wild beast, a man whipping his shadow, a man between a hunchback and a fool in cap and bells" (*SMR* 8)?

Kathleen Raine's much-illustrated monograph *Yeats, the Tarot and the Golden Dawn* is a good place for one to start looking for sources in context. However, there is an allegorical book with which Yeats was familiar and which his description seems to parody, a peculiarly illustrated text that he spent hours studying as a young man.

This paid work involved copying the *Hypnerotomachia Poliphili*, written in the fifteenth century by Fra Francesco Colonna in Latin, Greek, and Italian, but translated by "R.D." (probably Sir Robert Dallington) as *Hypnerotomachia: The Strife of Love in a Dream* (London: Simon Waterson, 1592) in a partial printing of woodcuts. Yeats's copy-work contributed text for *The Strife of Love in a Dream, being the Elizabethan Version of the First Book of the Hypnerotomachia of Francesco Colonna*, a new edition by Andrew Lang, M.A. (London: David Nutt, 1890). As he told Katharine Tynan, he had spent a week at Oxford in the Bodleian Library, "six & a half hours each day... and should be contented enough here but for the miserable al[le]gory I copy out for Nutt" (*CL1* 177–72). Though he projected finishing by 16 August 1889, he reported on the 8th that he was there "by evil fortune...copying out for Nutt the publisher...a dull old al[le]gory about love written by an Italian, who deserved to be forgotten long ago, & translated into fairly good English & published in a book full of misprints by an Elizabethan who wrote well enough to have known better" (180). On the 14th, in sight of finishing, he was able to joke about "a long S" that had gotten into his letter "out of the book I am copying." The 1592 edition he copied from, incomplete and as badly produced as he let on, was remedied in the Nutt edition by drawing woodcuts directly from the original Italian edition. Reproductions were available in *The Dream of Poliphilus: Facsimiles of One Hundred and Sixty-Eight Woodcuts in "Poliphili Hypnerotomachia," Venice, 1499,* edited by J. W. Appell (London: Reproduced for the Department of Science and Art in Photo-Lithography by W. Griggs, 1888)—almost exclusively woodcuts.[19] Yeats may have known about this aspect of the project to which he contributed a year later. But by 1921 much of the experience was beginning to fade from memory when he recalled "a few days at Oxford copying out a seventeenth-century translation of Poggio's *Liber Facetiarum* or the *Hypnerotomachia* of Poliphilo for a publisher—I forget which, for I copied both" (*Au* 154).[20] By far, of all Yeats's critics to date, Giorgio Melchiori remains the leading expert on Colonna's possible influence on Yeats, much of this because of three extraordinary woodcuts on the annunciation of Leda (her "Triumph") and the vaginal delivery of two eggs and their presentation to the Temple of Apollo (in side decorations to Leda's triumphal car).[21] Calling Colonna "the Beardsley of his time" (113), Melchiori notes the proximity of dates between *The Strife of Love in a Dream* (1592) and the *Speculum* of Giraldus (1594), and then ventures to suggest even more: "It is interesting to see, by the description Yeats gives of the imaginary book by Giraldus, with its quaint symbolic engravings, that he was visualizing a book of much the same kind" (228n).

As to the manuscript's contribution to speculation about Giraldus's basis in fact, Robartes did have his own theory, which proved to be wrong; he "had made a fruitless attempt...to prove or disprove...that Giraldus was Giraldus of Bologne" (9^v, lines 14–15), or Bologna in *SMR* (8). Robartes's failure does not rule out Gerard of Cremona (Gerardus Sablonetanus), as Sturm reasonably suggested to Yeats in 1924, due to the latter Gerard's (or Gerald's) twelfth-century translations of "everything from Aristotle to Kusta ben Luki" (Sturm 86). Richard Taylor asserts (in Sturm 46) that Yeats *blundered* in substituting Gerardo di Bologna for the more plausible historical figure, missing Yeats's point, which might be a joke rather than an error in deduction or judgment. He did not want his fable pinned to some one "medieval persona," not even to the Celtic Giraldus Cambrensis. For the point of the story is Robartes's failure: his spiritual crisis as well as his transient love.

Relieved to find his beggar mistress gone and himself "in mere disgust of… gloom and preoccupation" (folio 9^{v}, lines 16–17), Robartes comes to terms with himself in a dark-night logic presented in the manner of Kant, after which he mourns "for love itself" and feels the need to pray "at the Holy Sepu[l]cre" (10^{r}, lines 13–16). He tells his listeners that he had grown calmer in the realization that "Christ did not belong to me,…that [H]e did not understand my despair, that [H]e belongs to order & reason!" (lines 17–21). Then, as if bidden, an old Arab walks into his room, the next day, to interpret the markings on the *Speculum*'s Great Wheel according to "the doctrines of his tribe," the Judwalis, or "diagram[m]atists" (11^{r}, line 5). He seems derived from earlier narratives, such as the "Discoveries" Typescript and its predecessors. But Robartes concludes by holding back details from those sources. In short, we learn that Robartes joined the tribe, accepted their dress and morality, their politics, rose to authority, even fought in their wars beside the famous English colonel T. E. Lawrence ("Lawrence of Arabia"), who "never suspected the nationality" (i.e., Irish) of the "old ~~warlike~~ fighting Arab ~~who fought~~ at his side" (11^{r}, lines 8–14). Although the better part of his life has been withheld in the telling, Robartes concludes part II of "Stories" epigrammatically, conscious of his role as instructor and of the audience he has assembled: "I have completed my life," he says, "balanced every pleasure with a danger lest my bones might soften" (lines 15–16).

FOLIOS 12^{R}, 13^{R}, 13^{V}, 14^{R}, 15^{R}, 15^{V}, AND 16^{R}

The passion of Robartes is uncommon, self-effacing, dignified, ironic, like that of his friend in "The Tables of the Law," where Aherne comes to much the same conclusion about himself but from a different perspective: "I am not among those for whom Christ died.… I have seen the whole, and how can I come again to believe that a part is the whole? I have lost my soul because I have looked out of the eyes of the angels" (*Myth* 305–06). This passion is beyond the experience of the neophytes that have been taken in at Albert Road to be schooled "without interruption" by Robartes (*SMR* 10), or "disturbed in certain studies & researches" (folio 12^{r}, line 4). The speaker is now John Duddon (a correction from O'Leary in part I), so part III begins as we have it in *SMR* and *AVB*, save for the spelling of Denise's Christian name: "Some six weeks later Huddon, Denys, O'Leary & I sat <in silence> around the same fire" (12^{r}, lines 1–2). Denise is eager to tell the indecent story behind her decision to abandon her family name in favor of the *nom d'amour* "de L'Isle Adam" after Conte Villiers de l'Isle-Adam, the author of *Axel*. But she is prevented from doing so, at line 8, due to the entrace of Aherne, Robartes, and newcomers also bearing assumed names: Mary Bell and John Bond (see note 15). Denise's story will be inserted at this point in 1936, but here the only complication concerns the momentary introduction of a third "new friend," "a young man in a black shirt" whom Robartes ignores before Yeats cuts him altogether from the company (in lines 10 and 15). At first, Denise—then Aherne, and finally Robartes (at lines 4–5)—is given the responsibility of carrying "in a little chest of carved ivory,…~~a painted casket box~~…a ~~small painted cask~~ chest of carved [wood?] some eighteen inches long by some nine inches in ~~bredth~~ width & in depth" (lines 5 and 11–13)—a treasure chest worthy of Sinbad or Aladdin. Suggestion of a rivalry to come, between the two women (at least from the competitive Denise's point of view), is introduced when Robartes announces that Mary "is the only suitable guardian & bearer for [what] I carry in this box" (lines 26–27). At that point in the text, a long drawn-line carries the narrative directly to folio 13^{r}, where John Bond begins to tell their story.

The tale John tells of illicit love that cannot be arrested at first sight and held at bay in a Platonic condition was easily generated by Yeats, for the most part. He had only a little difficulty explaining why Mary was sent to the Riviera, unescorted by her much older husband after five years of childless marriage (at 13^{r}, lines 5–12, cancelled). With few, very local setbacks from folio 13^{r} through 15^{r} (save for the revision, on 13^{v}, of lines 5–12 of the former), only Church of Ireland doctrine (on folio 14^{r}, lines 1–9) was enough of an issue to justify the deletion of substantial text. Fortunately, too, Mary Bell's husband and John Bond, her lover, are both ornithologists, an improbable coincidence that allowed Yeats to cut corners as he raced the plot of this romance to its tragi-comic, more or less inevitable conclusion, when the three characters meet. The technicalities and specifics of bird-lore and natural science make folio 15^{r} a little congested, but Yeats found that he could easily push the narrative ahead on the enviable environment of Mr. Bell's Anglo-Irish estate by directing the typist to "P.T.O" (or "Please Turn Over" to the verso, 15^{v}), when he continued the scene at another sitting, apparently after completing much of part III, at least as far as (or up to) folio 18^{r}. The Irish Big House of Mary's great-uncle-in-law, Peter Bell, "the famous Chancery Judge ~~&~~ the friend of Goldsmith & Burke"[22] (16^{r}, lines 16–17), is surely based on Yeats's first-hand knowledge of the great house of Sir William Gregory and his wife, Lady Gregory, at Coole Park; the demesne and residence of the Gore-Booth family at Lissadell; as well as similarly admired country estates in England.

FOLIOS 17^{R}, 18^{R}, 19^{R}, AND 20^{R}

John Bond is impressed by the material culture in evidence on "~~walls packed hung with oil paintings, engravings, duelling swords & portraits~~, framed letters from Chatham…& ~~Walpole~~ Horace Walpole <duelling…swords & pistols> ~~engravings mez[z]otints, family portraits~~ one a Peter Lely…arranged upon the walls by generations" (17^{r}, lines 1–4).[23] Attention given to the "duelling swords & pistols" (in manuscript and in *SMR* 15) is apt as Bond is led to the bedroom where old Bell is dying amid "copies" (not originals) "of paintings by Muril[l]o & his contemporaries" as well as, hanging "[o]ver the Murillo piece," a portrait of Bell's wife, Mary, "painted by Sargent <in her early twenties>" (lines 14–20).[24] If Bond feels the suspense as he climbs the stair to meet so distinguished a cuckold—and is in a heightened state of anxiety to face the man he betrayed, to face a possibly vengeful spouse who says he "wants to see [him] alone,"[25] wondering what the man will have to say to him—we find that Yeats struggled with the description for five lines (17–20), essentially got stuck, before abandoning the face to the weak voice of Mr. Bell, as "[h]e smiled & tried to rise from the pillow" (20–21), ironically, within the canopy of his "great four poster" (12) bed. Again, memorable lines from "Coole Park and Ballylee, 1931" are not far off, as well as a passage from the play *Purgatory*.[26]

Oddly, the Cuala Press typesetter interpreted an episodic shift at this point in the narrative and introduced (at *SMR* 16) an unnecessary vertical space. Thereafter, Yeats seems sure of the story he had worked out in his head, improving the expression of old Bell's puzzled happiness when he decides, "after the birth of a son[,] that it was not wrong to give nothing in return" and to apply himself to the good work of teaching "dumb brutes" the art of proper nesting; for "the passions of Adam…mirroured in nature became the birds & beasts of Eden," and as "partakers in original sin they can be partakers in salvation" (folio 18^{r}, lines 8–9 and 17–19). As a saintly fool, the old man delivers a punch-line worthy of the comic stage in both timing and delivery: "I knew that <the> longest life could do but little, & wishing especially to benefit those that…lacked what I possessed…I decided to devote my life to the cucko[o]s" (lines 20–22). Of course, those lines were kept. Yet, with difficulty mirrored in the manuscript, the old man's breathless attempt to convey his frustration and suffering in trying to persuade "obstinate," "unteachable" caged birds to build nests for themselves is almost enough to take his last breath away. Moreover, at this point, Yeats was himself in earnest to discover the end of the episode.

Mary's too perfectly timed presentation of the completed cuckoo's nest, one that she has made with her own hands, was an even easier chore to carry out on folio 19^{r}. "Now may thy servant depart in peace," the old man murmurs, giving his last words in benediction for a life's work that is finished (and has failed in reality)—though Bond has been asked to continue it and will raise the son he has produced with Mary as if the boy were the legitimate heir to the great estate. Mary lays the nest on the pillow. Then Yeats inscribed the numeral "IV" in the center of the page to signify the end of the scene. The old man turns over and closes his eyes.

However, less than two lines into the next day's breakfast scene, in which Mr. Bell's death is announced, Yeats changed his mind, scribbled out the numeral, those two lines, and returned to the previous scene to give Mary a comic but evidently true curtain-line (spoken to Bond, in his arms): "we have given him great happiness" (line 28). On folio 20^{r}, therefore, Yeats inscribed the numeral "IV" again and proceeded to write Bond's account of the next morning's announcement, his covenant with Mary to raise their son in accordance with Bell family tradition, and their strange meeting with "Mr Owen Aherne" at the funeral. They learn from him that certain intimate scenes in their lives had "risen before Mr Robartes['s] eyes on several successive mornings as he awaited his early tea" (20^{r}, lines 17–18). So startled are they that they "set out for London that very evening" (line 23), at which point Yeats inscribed the numeral "IV" a third time, only to strike it out once more and to continue the narrative from the foot of the page to the top of the verso, folio 20^{v}, via his customary direction "P.T.O" ("Please Turn Over"). He had decided to begin the fourth part of "Stories" with the mysterious task that Mary Bell and Michael Robartes are to undertake together at the end of the story.

FOLIOS 20^{V}, 21^{R}, 22^{R}, AND 22^{V}

Folio 20^{v} is the fullest if not the busiest page to transcribe. One reason for this is that Yeats had nowhere to work out revisions at the opening in the notebook, having already written the next page (folio 21^{r}) and having designated that to be the beginning of part "IV," wherein Robartes opens the large box to reveal Leda's unhatched egg. It was a good start, but he realized that he must first transition the scene from Ireland to London. So he did this by having Robartes ask Duddon (who is recording) and the three other pupils if he has proven "by practical demonstration…that the soul survives the body" (20^{v}, lines 8–10). Circumscribed at the top of the page, a reference is made to Swift's "essay upon the dissensions of the Greeks & [R]omans" (lines 13 and 14, in order of composition),[27] and, as the circumscription partly intersects the numeral "IV," Yeats became confused, at a later sitting, and struck out the numeral on 21^{r} (thus: "~~IV~~") and replaced it with the numeral "V." When the manuscript was typed, the numeral "IV" was missed on 20^{v}. Thus, no part IV is evident in *SMR* though remedied in *AVB* to follow the 20^{v} instance.

Folios 21^{r}, 22^{r}, and 22^{v} are about Leda's lost third egg, how Robartes came to purchase it, and what he proposes to do with it—all of which have been discussed at length, above. As the one chosen to become the guardian of the egg, Mary's connection with Robartes's view of reality as "a congeries of beings & a single being" (22^{r}, line 25; see *Ex* 305) is somewhat hard to follow in the manuscript, but is elucidated by what I have already said, both on Leda and on Robartes's Kantian projections of "a whirling & a bitterness" in a future not far off.[28]

FOLIOS 23^{R}, 24^{R}, AND 25^{R} (LINES 1–14)

Continuing a succession of short passages from Robartes's discourse "without… context or…consecutive order," as Yeats imagined Duddon might recall them, gives the impression one might have after listening to a philosophical treatise "sometimes eloquent, often obscure" (*SMR* 20). Eloquence was the hard part to work out in the spaces Yeats allotted between rows of "X"s, the first appearing at the bottom of folio 22^r, with the others appearing on 23^r and 24^r–much laboring for five paragraphs, most amounting to pithy sayings, only one of which relates to old Mr. Bell in his four-poster bed: "The marriage bed is the symbol of the solved antinomy, and were more than symbol could a man lose and keep his identity, but he falls asleep. That sleep is the same as the sleep of death" (*SMR* 21; folio 23^r, lines 17–21). Another saying turns on an Old Testament verse about the Witch of Endor (1 Samuel 28) after Kant has fallen out of the picture and is stricken from the frame (see lines 4–16). Another quotes Shakespeare (*All's Well* 1.1.86) but cites Milton, and then (most fraught of all) goes on to commend war: "Test art, morality, custom, thought, by Thermopylae" (*SMR* 22; cf. *CW14* 337, n. 50). And so it is just that Aherne should interrupt to object (at folio 24^r, lines 18, 26–29, and folio 25^r, lines 1–4). The pupils are silent at that, except Denise, who whispers, because Duddon's eye has fallen on Mary: "She <has done> ~~did it~~ very well, ~~but I~~ but Robartes should have asked me to hold it [the egg] for I am taller, & my training as a model would have helped" (25^r, lines 7–9). This silly remark, erotically toned, with just the suggestion of Metaphysical *double-entendre,* also undercuts the dramatic moment of Robartes's departure. His beckoning "~~to the man in the black shirt~~" (Aherne, presumably, at line 13) seems almost a gesture to the political young men of the shirts in "Michael Robartes Foretells," written in the next couple of years. Finally, Duddon signs his name.

Folios 24^V, 25^R (lines 15–34), 26^R, 26^V, 27^R, and 27^V

Yet there is more: dated "Feb 1930" and labeled in manuscript "Appendix" and "~~Introductory letters~~" (in folio 25^r, line 15), the polyphonic narrative of mixed voices gives place to an imaginary epistle addressed to, and edited by, Yeats himself. John Aherne writes to acknowledge a trove of related papers in his possession beyond "John Duddon's long narrative" (*SMR* 23), just concluded. We have two drafts of the "Appendix": the first one beginning at line 15 of 25^r, including an editor's note keyed by an asterisk to line 17, and ending on folio 24^v; and the second draft starting over and proceeding more clearly from folio 26^r to the end of the composition on 27^v. The other papers in John Aherne's possession include his brother's diary from 1922–1923, kept during his "tramp" in Ireland with Robartes lecturing on the philosophy of the Judwalis and their founder Kusta ben Luka, matter largely withheld from Duddon's extracts of parts I-[IV] and V in *SMR.* Also understood to be available as an unpublished supplement is the record made by Robartes's other pupils in London, including "his diagrams & their explanation" (26^r, lines 15–16), which compare favorably with accounts made by Yeats in his poems "The Phases of the Moon," "The Double Vision of Michael Robartes," and "The Gift of Harun Al-Rashid." The record of these pupils John Aherne finds to be in accord with the new version of *A Vision* that Yeats had sent him ("corrected, clarified, & completed after five years almost continuous labour"), making an endorsement of the method by which Yeats had "found what was lost in the *Speculum*," the palimpsest of Giraldus, because "I recall what Plato said of memory & suggest…that your automatic script…may well have been but a process of remembering" (26^{v}, lines 5–6, 8–10, and 16–18). The resemblance between Yeats and the woodcut image of Giraldus is uncanny when the evidence is presented, enough so that the cancelled postscript on 27^{v} cleverly suggests that Yeats is Giraldus reincarnated.

Self-reflexive, but not self-regarding, Yeats renders his portrayal of John as a good *brother*, remembering his own, the painter Jack Yeats, in the course of writing John's letter (at 26^{r}, lines 11–13 and *SMR* 23). The tone is amicable, one might say filial, as John recalls the grief caused Owen by Yeats's exaggeration of "slight incident" in the triptych, especially "Rosa Alchemica," more than thirty years before, transmuting "some kind of ritual" in "an old shed on Howth pier" into "an orgy in honor of the pagan gods" and a window broken by "herring or mackerel sorters & some girls" into the apparent "murder of Robartes & his friends" (27^{r}, lines 5–6, 9, 11, and 13–16). For the first time, Michael Robartes and more orthodox Owen Aherne are said to be co-founders of "a society…for the study of Kaballa Denudata & similar books" (lines 7–8), mirroring Yeats's acquaintance with S. L. MacGregor Mathers and with Christian Knorr von Rosenroth's *Kabbala Denudata seu Doctrina Hebræorum transcendentalis et metaphysica atque Theologica* (Sulzbach, 1677–1678), partly translated by Mathers as *The Kabbalah Unveiled* (London: George Redway, 1887; see *YL* 1292). Robartes's objection to the elaborate style of those stories is a ribbing Yeats had been giving himself ever since he resurrected the two characters in 1917.

Notes

1. *"Stylistic Arrangements": A Study of William Butler Yeats's* A Vision (Lewisburg, PA: Bucknell University Press, 1987). Chapter 3 is entitled "A Comparison of the Fiction in the Two Versions of *A Vision*."
2. WBY to Hansard Watt, 14 Dec. 1930; *CL InteLex* 5419. Much of this letter is quoted below in "'Michael Robartes Foretells': A Rejected Ending."
3. Lady Gregory's memoir *Coole,* with Yeats's poem "Coole Park" (later "Coole Park, 1929") as its preface, was finished at the Cuala Press on 30 Apr. 1931, thereafter published in July.
4. WBY to George Yeats, [?28 July 1931], *CL InteLex* 5493. The other poems were "Tom the Lunatic," "Old Tom at Cruachan," and "Old Tom Again." See "Related Matter in the White Vellum Notebook," pages 272–78 below, on the making of the *SMR* prologue, its proposed placement relative to *The Resurrection*, and a rejected note for *SMR* that defines the play in terms of equivalents to "some of the themes described…by Robartes."
5. For these dates, I am indebted to Jared Curtis and Selina Guinness in W. B. Yeats, *The Resurrection: Manuscript Materials,* ed. Jared Curtis and Selina Guinness (Ithaca, NY: Cornell University Press, 2011), xix and xxxv, n. 85.
6. See Curtis Bradford, *Yeats at Work* (Carbondale and Edwardsville: Southern Illinois University Press,1965), 245–50; as well as Curtis and Guinness (eds.), *The Resurrection: Manuscript Materials* xxix, 160–65, 202–03, 258–61.

7. Pausanias, *Description of Greece*, trans. W. H. S. Jones and H. A. Ormerod (Cambridge, MA: Harvard University Press; London: W. Heinemann, 1966), vol. 2 (Laconia, xv.8–11, and xvi), 95 and 97. Yeats owned the Jones translation from the 1918 Loeb Classical Library (*YL* 1545).
8. Apollodorus, *The Library*, trans. James George Frazer (London: W. Heinemann; New York: G. P. Putnam's Sons, 1921), vol. 2: 23 and 25.
9. Sappho, *Memoir*, trans. Henry Thornton Wharton, 3rd ed. (London: John Lane, 1895). Billed as "a literal translation," the fragment is preferable to the amateurish poem "Leda," made in dithyrambs by John Myers O'Hara in Sappho, *The Poems* (Chicago, 1907), autographed by O'Hara (*YL* 1836). As a literalist, Wharton disputes what the Greeks meant by "hyacinth": "it probably had nothing in common with our hyacinth, and it seems to have comprised several flowers, especially the iris, gladiolus, and larkspur" (106). Recent translations follow Wharton but alter the syntax slightly. Only Eva-Maria Voigt, in her compendium *Sappho at Alcaeus: Fragmenta* (Amsterdam: Athenaeum, 1971), 146, specifies color: "that once upon a time Leda found hidden an egg of hyacinthine blue." See P. Th. M. G. Liebregts, *Centaurs in the Twilight: W. B. Yeats's Use of the Classical Tradition* (Amsterdam and Atlanta: Rodopi, 1993), 280.
10. For a whole treatise on this line of invention, see Giorgio Melchiori, *The Whole Mystery of Art: Pattern into Poetry in the Work of W. B. Yeats* (London: Routledge & Kegan Paul, 1960).
11. See Kathleen Raine, *From Blake to "A Vision"* (Dublin: The Dolmen Press, 1979), 13–31, 34–37, and plates 7, 10, 24, and 25. Inscribed into a copy of Bryant's *A New System, or, An Analysis of Ancient Mythology* (1774, British Library copy C.144.e.6), Yeats noted that "the influence of Bryant is strong in [Blake's] later Prophetic Books[,] 'Jerusalem['] particularly. I compared them with other writings by Bryant[—]what I forget. This ~~was the~~ book was however the great influence[,] I think."
12. See diagram of the historical gyres of religion and civilization (with junctures of annunciation) in *YVEC*. Cf. Liebregts 279. Yeats's famous delineation of the ages is given in both editions of *A Vision*, in books entitled "Dove or Swan" (III and V, respectively). Right after a diagram of "The Historical Cones" and his sonnet of 1923, alternatively called "Leda," as well as a short movement of "Stray Thoughts," he begins to discuss the period "2000 B.C. to A.D. 1," thus: "I imagine the annunciation that founded Greece as made to Leda, remembering that they showed in a Spartan temple, strung up to the roof a holy relic, an unhatched egg of hers; and that from one of her eggs came Love and from the other War" (*AVA* 181, *AVB* 268). Notably, his source, Pausanias, does not say that the temple relic was an "unhatched" egg.
13. Brian Arkins, *Builders of My Soul: Greek and Roman Themes in Yeats* (Savage, MD: Barnes and Noble, 1990), 101–16. See also Liebregts 291–97.
14. Yeats calls the tale "Donald and His Neighbours" and credits it to *Hibernian Tales*, "[a] chapbook mentioned by Thackery in his *Irish Sketch Book*"; see *YPM* 318, n. 45, as well as "Related Entries in the White Vellum Notebook" (below), *passim*. A cursory search on the internet will reveal dozens of folktale variants.
15. Actually the names are adapted from two poems by Blake: "William Bond" and "Long John Brown & Little Mary Bell" in *WWB3* 79–80 and 81.
16. This possible "subject" for poetry and its relation to "Stories of Michael Robartes" in *SMR* and *AVB*, to the last stanza of "Two Songs from a Play," and to other lyrics from the same period, was first examined in my treatment of themes in chapter 1 of *YPM*, pp. 3–5 and 290, nn. 1–2.
17. Robartes's departure from Ireland for Paris, Rome, Vienna, and Cracow is described in the following texts of *YVP4*: "Untitled Manuscript" (120), "Discoveries" Manuscript (68–69), "Discoveries" Typescript (16), and "Version B" (142). Among those texts, "Discoveries" Typescript compares more closely with *AVA* xvii than do the others.
18. Frank Pearce Sturm, *His Life, Letters, and Collected Work*, ed. Richard Taylor (Urbana: University of Illinois Press, 1969), 94.

19. See *The Dream of Poliphilo*, related and interpreted by Linda Fierz-David, translated by Mary Hottinger, with a foreword by C. G. Jung (New York: Pantheon, 1950). A photo-facsimile edition of the Dallington text is available in Francesco Colonna, *Hypnerotomachia: The Strife of Love in a Dreame (1592)*, translated by R.D., a facsimile reproduction with an introduction by Lucy Gent (Delmar, NY: Scholars' Facsimiles and Reprints, 1973). For an unexpurgated edition of this classic of typography and graphic art, see Francesco Colonna, *Hypnerotomachia Poliphili: The Strife of Love in a Dream*, trans. and intro. by Joscelyn Godwin, with the original woodcut illustrations (New York: Thames & Hudson, 1999).
20. William O'Donnell and Douglas Archibald note, in *CW3* 449, n. 78, that Yeats copied out in the Bodleian Library "part of Caxton's edition of Aesop's *Fables*, with those of Avion, Alfonso, and Poggio," for David Nutt, in August 1888. Poggio Bracciolani's Latin *Liber Facetarium* (1478) was represented, in English translation, by a few selections. Yeats transcription (subject to the editor's review) are in vol. 2 of *The Fables of Aesop, as First Printed by William Caxton in 1484, with Those of Avian, Alfonso and Poggio*, ed. Joseph Jacobs (London: David Nutt, 1889), 2 vols.
21. See Melchiori 133–37 and 191–94.
22. Yeats's invention of an Irish pedigree for Mary Bell's husband, who, with a Scottish family name, requires considerable license. The great-uncle in question, first "Matthew" and then "Peter" Bell, is given the forename of an Apostle and a profession, as an "~~Irish lord Chancery Judge~~," simplified (in 16^r, line 16) to "the famous Chancery Judge" before no name, at all, was set in type, with demotion to "famous Chancery lawyer." In fact, as Yeats knew, Peter Bell was the eponymous subject of a long narrative poem by Wordsworth, published in 1819 and satirized in doggeral verse by Shelley, in "Peter Bell the Third," under the pen-name "Miching Mellecho." If Judge Bell served the Irish Court of Chancery (1858–1877), he might have known Edmund Burke (1729–1797), Irish statesman and political theorist, as well as Oliver Goldsmith (1728–1774), Irish novelist, playwright, and poet. He might have had his portrait done by the dominant portrait-painter of the third quarter of the eighteenth century, Thomas Gainsborough (1727–1788). His patrilineal nephew might have owned some of the 274 portrait engravings and autotypes made for political members of London's Grillion Club, beginning in 1812, without being a member. So Mary Bell's husband might have his brief history in the British Foreign Office. In the balance between realism and farce, Yeats chose to be vague and sympathetic enough to be plausible.
23. "Chatham" is William Pitt (the Elder, also known as The Great Commoner), 1st Earl of Chatham (1708–1778), English statesman of the Whig party. The others are Horace Walpole (1717–1797), Whig politician, man of letters, and art historian; and Peter Lely (1618–1680), English painter of Dutch origin and chief portrait-painter during the reign of Charles II.
24. Bartolomé Esteban Murillo (1617–1682), Spanish Baroque painter best known for religious works, paintings of women, children, and everyday scenes; and John Singer Sargent (1856–1925), an American painter, the most famous of his generation for portraits evoking Edwardian luxury. Since Mary is a woman of thirty-five in "Stories," Bond is viewing the likeness made of her around 1918, just after the war and at the time of her marriage and "Grand Tour" of the continent.
25. Yeats wrote "Bell" when he meant "Bond" and did not make the correction until at least his second pass through the Cuala page proofs (NLI 30,019 at p. 15).
26. See *VP* 491, lines 35–37; and *VPl* 1043, lines 61–68.
27. The reference is to Jonathan Swift, *Discourse of the Contests and Dissensions between the Nobles and Commons in Athens and Rome* (London: John Nutt, 1701).
28. Robartes's serious parody of the Kantian method is informed by a marked passage, entitled "The Cosmological Idea," and succeeding demonstrations in Immanuel Kant, *Kant's Critical Philosophy for English Readers*, 3rd ed., vol. 2: *The Prolegomena*, trans. J. P. Mahaffy and J. H. Bernard (London: Macmillan, 1915), 103; *YL* 1052.

NLI 13,577 [1r]

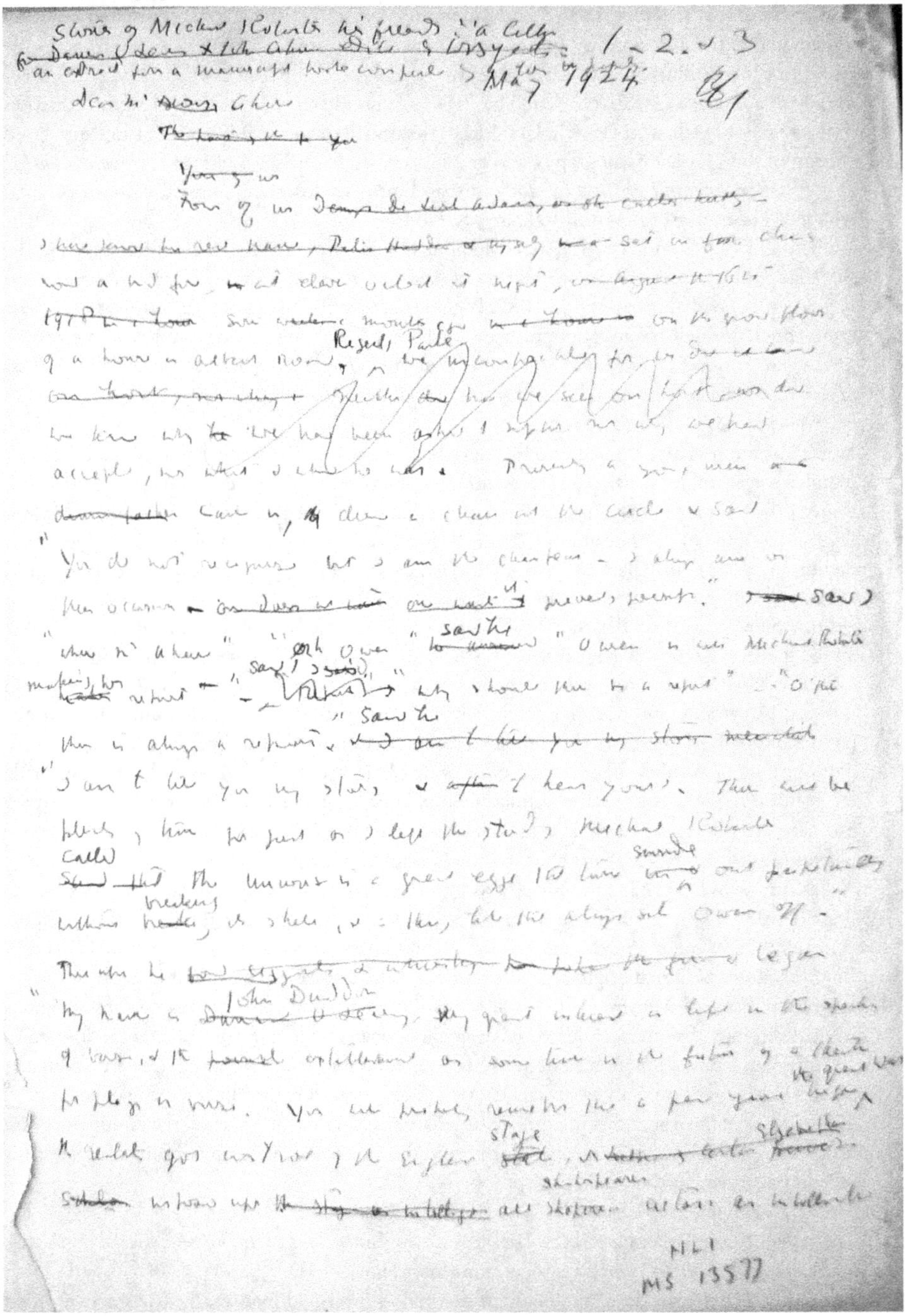

Originally, at least one folio preceded this one, as suggested by the fragment seen in the lower left-hand corner of this photograph. Evidently, to allow for discarded material, folio 1r (or page "3") was re-numbered "1–2. & 3" at upper right.

[1r]

Stories of Michael Robartes his friends: "a letter
~~from Daniel O Leary to John Ahern edited by WB Yeats~~ 1–2. &3
an extract from a manuscript book [?compiled] by his ~~[?]~~ pupils
May 1924
Dear Mr ~~Owen~~ Ahern ~~3~~
1 ~~The part of the for you~~
~~Your of us~~
2 Four of us ~~Denys De Lisle Adam, as she calls herself~~
3 ~~I have know her real name, Peter Hudden & myself in a~~ sat in four chairs
4 round a [?bon] fire, ~~in~~ at eleven o clock at night, ~~on August the 16th~~
5 ~~1918 in a house~~ some ~~weeks~~ a month ago ~~in a house in~~ on the ground floor
Regents Park
6 of a house in Albert Road,^ we [were] uncomfortable for we did not know
7 ~~our host, nor why &~~ neither ~~did~~ had we seen our host, nor did
8 we know why ~~he~~ we had been asked to supper nor why we had
9 accepted, nor what & who he was. Presently a young man ~~in a~~
10 ~~dinner jacket~~ came in, ~~&~~ drew a chair into the circle & said
11 "You do not recognise [me] but I am the chaufeur — I always am on
it
12 these occasions ~~— one does not want one wants to~~ prevents gossip." ~~I said~~ Said I
said he
13 "Where[s] Mr Ahern" "~~Oh~~ Owen" ~~he answered~~ "Owen is with Michael Robartes
making his said I ~~I said~~
14 ~~making~~ report" " ^ ~~"Report"~~, "Why should there be a report" — "O that
" said he
15 there is always a report, ~~& I am to tell you my story meanwhile~~
16 "I am to tell you my story & ~~after~~ to hear yours. There will be
17 plenty of time for just as I left the study Michael Robartes
called sinside [=inside]
18 ~~said that~~ the universe is a great egg that turns ~~in &~~ out perpetually
breaking
19 without ~~breaking~~ its shell, & a thing like that always sets Owen off."
20 There upon he ~~found ciggarettes & whiskey be taken the fire~~ & began
John Duddon
21 "My name is ~~Daniel O Leary~~, my great interest in life is the speaking
22 of verse, & ~~possible~~ establishment in some time in the future of a theatre
the Great War
23 for plays in verse. You will probably remember that a few years before^
stage Elizabethan
24 the realists got control of the English ~~state~~, & ~~helped by certain perverse~~
Shakespearean
25 ~~scholars~~ imposed upon ~~the stage as intelligent~~ all ~~Shaperean~~ actors an intollerable

---

6–11 coalesce as follows: "of a home in Albert Road, Regents Park. Presently a young man" (close to *SMR*).

NLI 13,577 [2r]

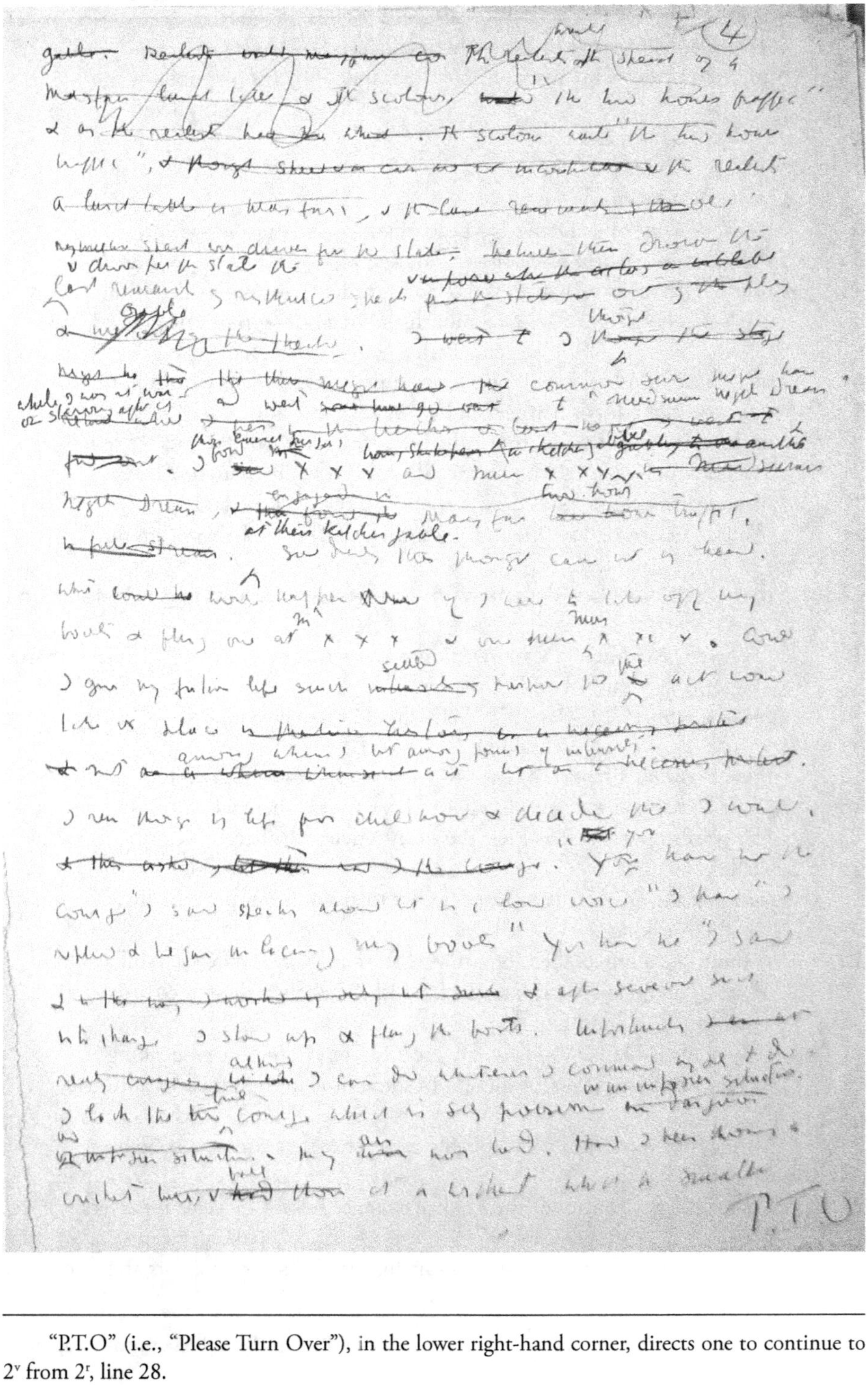

"P.T.O" (i.e., "Please Turn Over"), in the lower right-hand corner, directs one to continue to 2v from 2r, line 28.

[2r]

would 4
~~gable~~ [=gabble]. ~~Realists wanted mayfair even~~ The realists often speak of a
Mayfair [?lunch] later & the scholars ~~wanted~~ "the two hours traffic"
& as ~~the realists had the wheel~~. ~~The scholars wanted "the two~~ hours
traffic", ~~& thought speed & a car are not incompatible &~~ the realists
~~a lunch table in Mayfair~~, & the ~~last remnants of the~~ old
~~rhythmical speech were driven from the state~~, ~~between~~ then drove the
& drove from the state the &~~impose upon the actors an intolerable~~
^last remnants of rhythmical speech ~~from the state & out of the~~ play
~~gable~~ thought
~~& me out of the theatre~~. ~~I went to~~ I ~~thought the stage~~
^
~~might be There~~ ~~That there might have the~~ common sense might have
while I was at war and went some time ago ~~out~~
or starving after it to "Midsummer Nights Dream"
~~returned while~~ ~~I was in the trenches & last night I went to~~
those Eminent persons gabble
found ~~turning Shakespeare in kitchen gabling to the audience~~
find out. I ~~saw Mr~~ XXX and Miss XXXXX ~~in Mid Summers~~
~~engaged in~~ ~~two hour~~
~~Nights Dream~~, ~~& then found~~ the Mayfair ~~two hour~~ traffic.
At their kitchen gable.
~~in full stream~~.^Suddenly this thought came into my head.
What ~~could be~~ would happen ~~if one~~ if I were to take off my
Mr Miss
boots & fling one at XXX & one [at] ^ XXXX. Could
settled the
I give my future life such ~~intensity of~~ purpose that ~~h~~ act could
take its place ~~in theatre history as a necessary protest.~~
among whims but among forms of intensity
~~&~~ not ~~as a whim whimsical~~ act ~~but as a necessary protest.~~
I ran through my life from childhood & decided that I could.
~~But~~ You
~~& then asked if but then had I the courage.~~ "~~You~~^ have not the
courage" I said speaking aloud but in a lower voice "I have" I
replied & began unlacing my boots "You have not" I said
& ~~in this way I worked my self into such~~ & after several such
interchanges I stood up & flung the boots. Unfortunately ~~I am not~~
although
~~really courageous~~, ~~but when~~ I can do whatever I command myself to do
true in an unforeseen situation.
I lack the ~~true~~ courage which is self possession ~~in dangerous~~
an aim
~~or unforseen situations~~. My ~~arm~~ was bad. Had I been throwing a
ball
cricket ~~ball, & had thrown~~ at a wicket which [is] a smaller
P.T.O.

NLI 13,577 [2v]

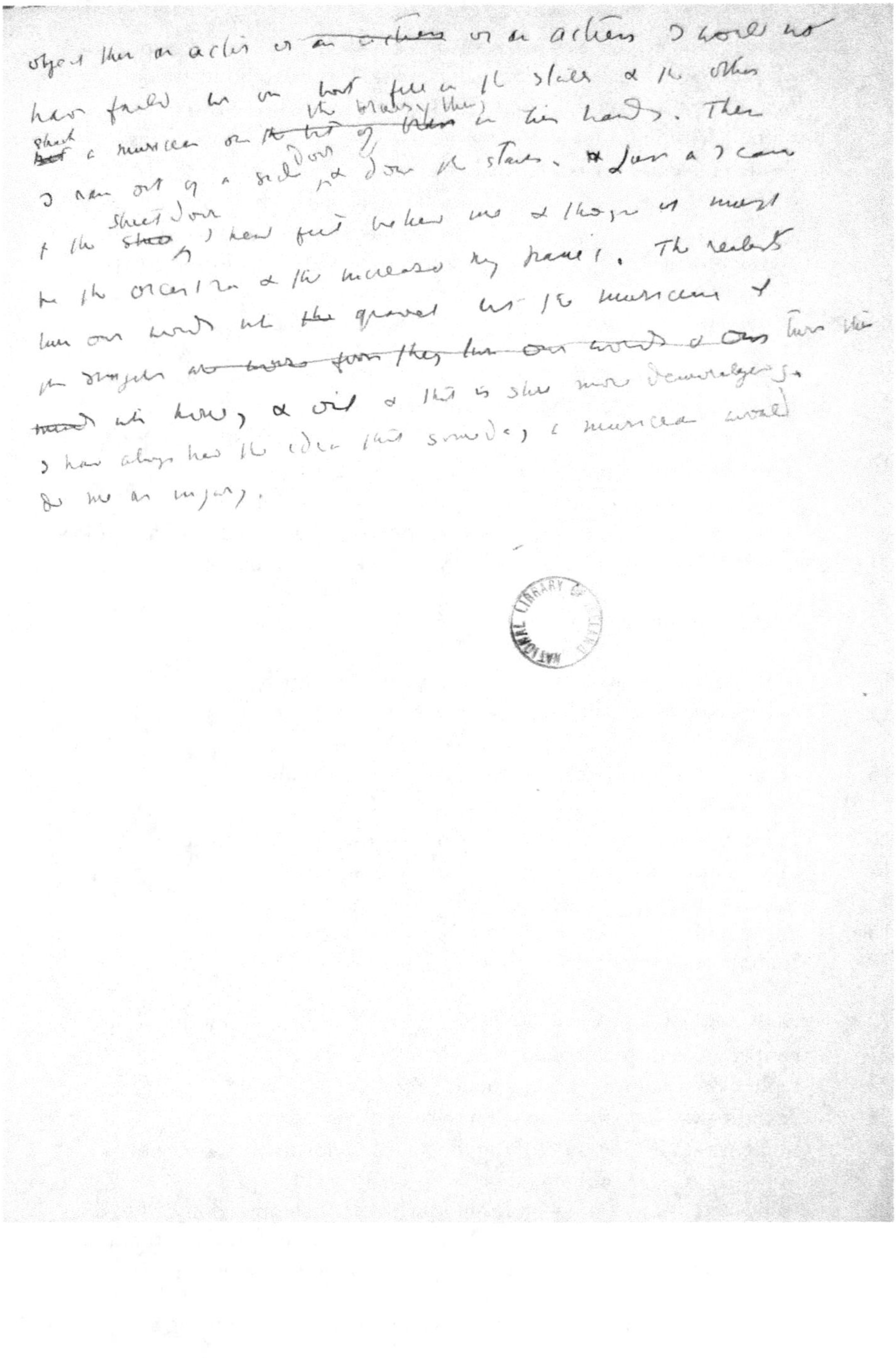
object than an actor or ~~an orchestra~~ or an actress I would not
have failed to one but fell in the stalls & the others
~~but~~ shook a musician on ~~the top of~~ ~~[illegible]~~ the braces they in their hands. Then
I ran out of a side door of & down the stairs. ~~x~~ Just as I came
to the ~~stage~~ street door I heard feet behind me & thought it must
be the orchestra & the increased my panic. The residents
have our words with the gravest but the musicians &
the strangers ~~are~~ ~~[illegible]~~ ~~from they have our words & ours~~ turn their
~~[illegible]~~ with horror, & oil & that is still more demoralizing to
I have always had the idea that some day a musician would
do me an injury.

2v follows directly from 2r.

[2v]

1 object than an actor or ~~an actress~~ or an actress I would not
2 have failed for one boot fell in the stalls & the other
struck the brassy thing
3 ~~hit~~ a musician on ~~the bit of brass~~ in his hands. Then
door
4 I ran out of a side ^ & down the stairs. "Just a[s] I came
street door
5 to the ~~street~~ ^ I heard feet behind me & thought it must
6 be the orchestra & that increased my panic. The realists
7 turn our words into ~~the~~ gravel but the musicians &
8 the singers ~~are worse from they turn out words & our~~ turn them
9 ~~minds~~ into honey & oil & that is still more demoralizing.
10 I have always had the idea that someday a musician would
11 do me an injury.

1–11 These lines, facing folio 3r, revise the first thirteen and a half lines of page "5," continuing from 2r, line 28.

8 Read "for" for "from" for sense.

NLI 13,577 [3r]

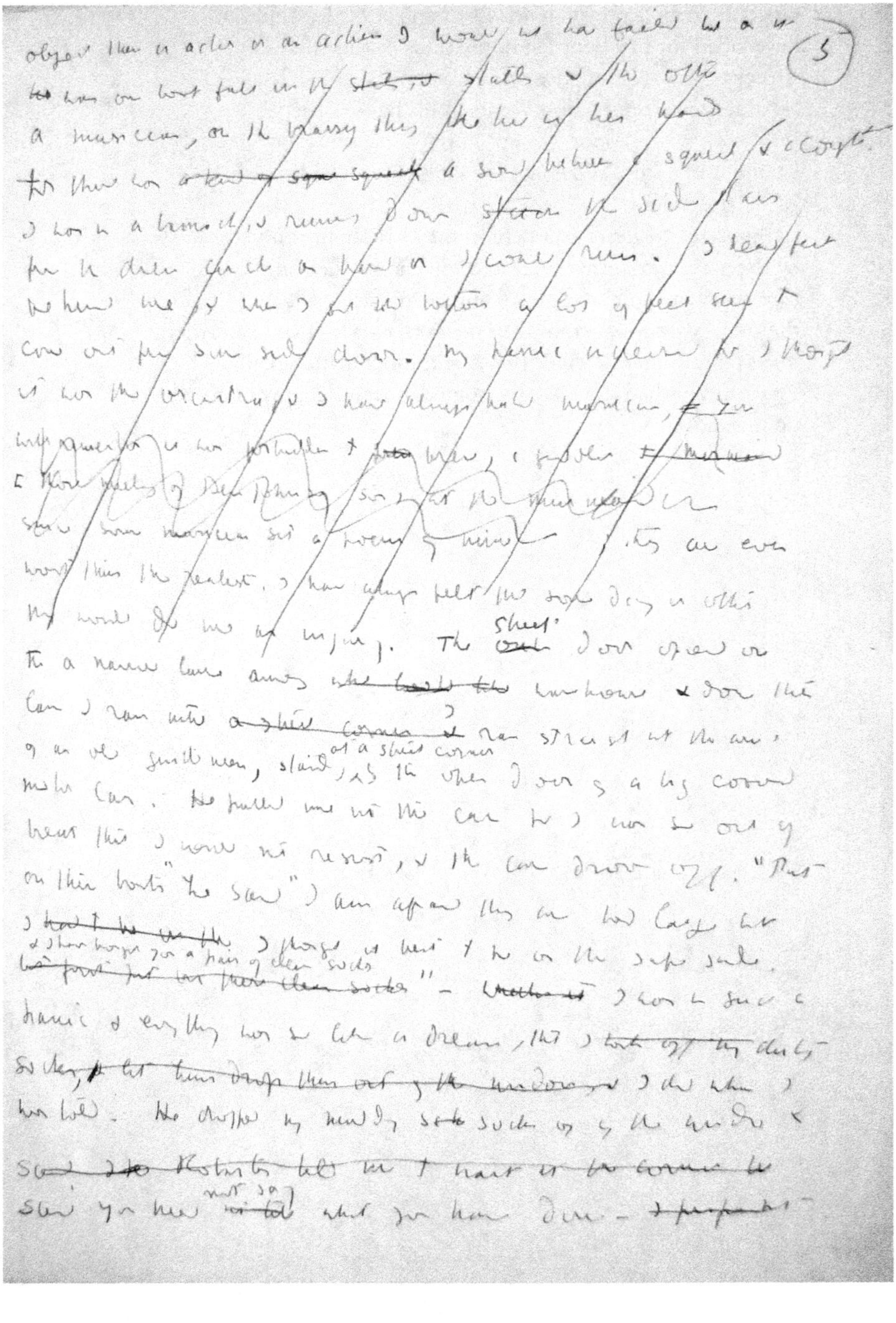
object than an actor or an action I would we had failed but a
~~[illegible]~~ was our worst fall in the ~~[illegible]~~ stalls & the other
a musician, or the greasy thing the hue of her hand
~~for there was a kind of some squeak~~ a sort between a squeal & a cough.
I was in a hammock, & running down ~~stairs~~ the side stairs
for the door could not have been I could run. I heard feet
behind me & when I got to the bottom a lot of feet seemed to
come out from some side door. My panic increased for I thought
it was the orchestra & I have always hated musicians, ~~for~~ you
[illegible] & [illegible] wine, & fiddles ~~[illegible]~~
& those [illegible]
[illegible] of [illegible] even
worst than the [illegible], I have always felt [illegible] some day or other
they would do me an injury. The street door opened on
to a narrow lane among ~~[illegible]~~ warehouses & down this
lane I ran into ~~a street corner &~~ I ran straight into the arms
of an old smith man, standing at a street corner by the other door of a big covered
motor car. He pulled me into the car for I was so out of
breath that I could not resist, & the car drove off. "Put
on these boots" he said" I am afraid they are too large but
~~[illegible]~~ I thought it best to be on the safe side. & I have brought you a pair of clean socks
~~[illegible]~~" — ~~[illegible]~~ I was in such a
panic & everything was so like a dream, that I ~~took off my dirty~~
socks, ~~& let him drop them out of the window~~ & did what I
was told. He dropped my new dry socks out of the window &
~~said [illegible] Robartes told me to wait at the corner to~~
said you need not say ~~or tell~~ what you have done — ~~[illegible]~~

[3r]

object than an actor or an actress I would not have failed but as it
~~ha~~ was one boot fell in the ~~stats, &~~ stalls & the other (5)
a musician, on the brassy thing that he [had] in his hands
~~for~~ there was ~~a kind of sque squeek~~ a sound between a squeel & a cough.
I was in a [?panic], & running down ~~stairs~~ the side stairs
from the dress circle as hard as I could run. I heard feet
behind me, & when I got toward bottom a lot of feet seem[ed] to
come out from some side door. My panic increased for I thought
it was the orchestra, & I had always held musicians, ~~you~~
~~will remember it was forbidden to prair~~ bring a fiddle, ~~to Mermaid~~
~~to those meetings of Ben johnson sons at the Mer maid~~
~~since some musician set a poem of mine~~ they are even
worse than the realists. I have always felt that someday or other
street
they would do me an injury. The ~~out~~ door opened on
to a narrow lane among ~~which [?toward] the~~ warehouse & down this
lane I ran into ~~a street corner &~~ I ran straight into the arms
at a street corner
of an old gentleman standing ^ by the open door of a big covered
motor car. He pulled me into the car for I was so out of
breath that I could not resist, & the car drove off. "Put
on these boots" he said "I am afraid they are too large but
I ~~had to be sure the~~ I thought it best to be on the safe side
& I have brought you a pair of clean socks
~~but first put on these clean socks~~"— ~~Whether it~~ I was in such a
panic & everything was so like a dream, that ~~I took off my dirty~~
~~socks & let him drop them out of the window, &~~ I did what I
was told. He dropped my muddy ~~sch~~ socks out of the window &
~~said I to Robartes told me to wait at the corner he~~
not say
said you need ~~not tell~~ what you have done~~—I prefer not~~

Cancelled lines 1–14, before "The street door opened on," are revised on 2v.

NLI 13,577 [4r]

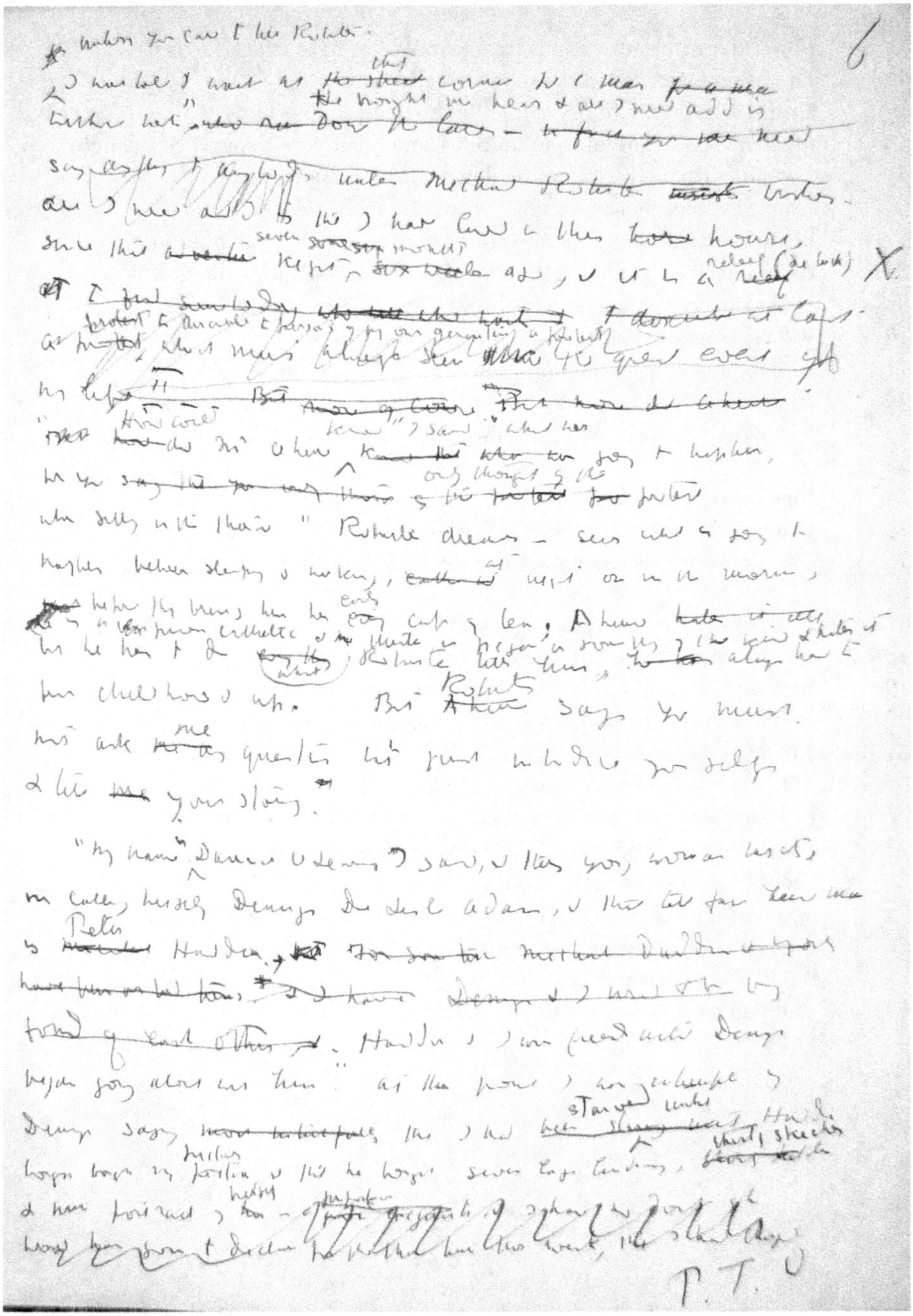

The "X" in the extreme right margin at line 6, beside the parenthetical direction to "see back," refers one to 4v, lines 6–14.

"P.T.O" (i.e., "Please Turn Over") at the foot of 4r refers both to the continuation and resolution of cancelled lines 28–29 (after "herself") and to revision for lines 6–9.

[4r]

1 ~~for~~ unless you care to tell Robartes. 6

that

2 ^I was told to wait at ~~the street~~ corner for a man ~~for a man~~

He brought me here & all I need add is

3 without boots." ~~who runs down the lane in fact you nee need~~

4 ~~say any thing to any body unless Michael Robartes insists wishes~~.

5 All I need add to this I have lived in this ~~hose~~ house,

seven ~~some six~~ months relief (see back) X

6 since that ~~adventure~~ night ^~~six weeks~~ ago, & it is a ~~relif~~

7 ~~[?to] to find somebody who will who wants to to describe at last~~

~~protest~~ to describe to persons of my generation a protest

8 a ~~protest~~ which must always seem ~~[?to me]~~ the great event yet

9 My life — ~~— But more of course~~. ~~But more did Aherne~~

How could know" I said "What was

10 "~~But how did~~ Mr Aherne^ ~~know that what was~~ going to happen,

only thought of

11 for you ~~say that you only thought of that protest~~ ~~pro~~ protest

12 when sitting in the theatre "Robartes dreams—sees what is going to

at

13 happen between sleeping & waking, ~~either at~~ night or in the morning

early

14 ~~[?just]~~ before they bring him his ~~early~~ cup of tea; Aherne ~~hates it all~~

15 he is a ~~true~~ pious Catholic & ~~he~~ thinks it Pagan or something of the kind & hates it

16 for he has to do everything Robartes tells him, ~~he has~~ always had to

what Robartes

17 from childhood up. But ~~Ahern~~ says you must

me

18 not ask ~~me any~~ questions but just introduce your self

19 & tell ~~me~~ your story."

20 "My name ^is Daniel O Leary I said, & this young woman insists

21 on calling herself Dennys De Lisle Adam, & that tall fair haired man

Peter

22 is ~~Michael~~ Hudden, ~~but for some time Michael Dudden & myself~~

~~&~~

23 ~~have been on bad terms, & I have Dennys & I used to be~~ very

24 ~~fond of each other~~. Huddon & I were friends until Denys

25 began going about with him." At this point I was interrupted by

starved until

26 Denys saying ~~most unfitfully~~ that I had ~~been starving until~~ Huddon

pictures thirty sketches

27 bought bought my ~~picton~~ & that he bought seven large landscapes, ~~twenty sketches~~

herself ~~proportion~~

28 & nine portraits of ~~her~~ – a ~~grave exageration, & I have no doubt she~~

29 ~~would have gone to declare for [?] there have this week, that I had charged.~~

P. T. O.

NLI 13,577 [4v]

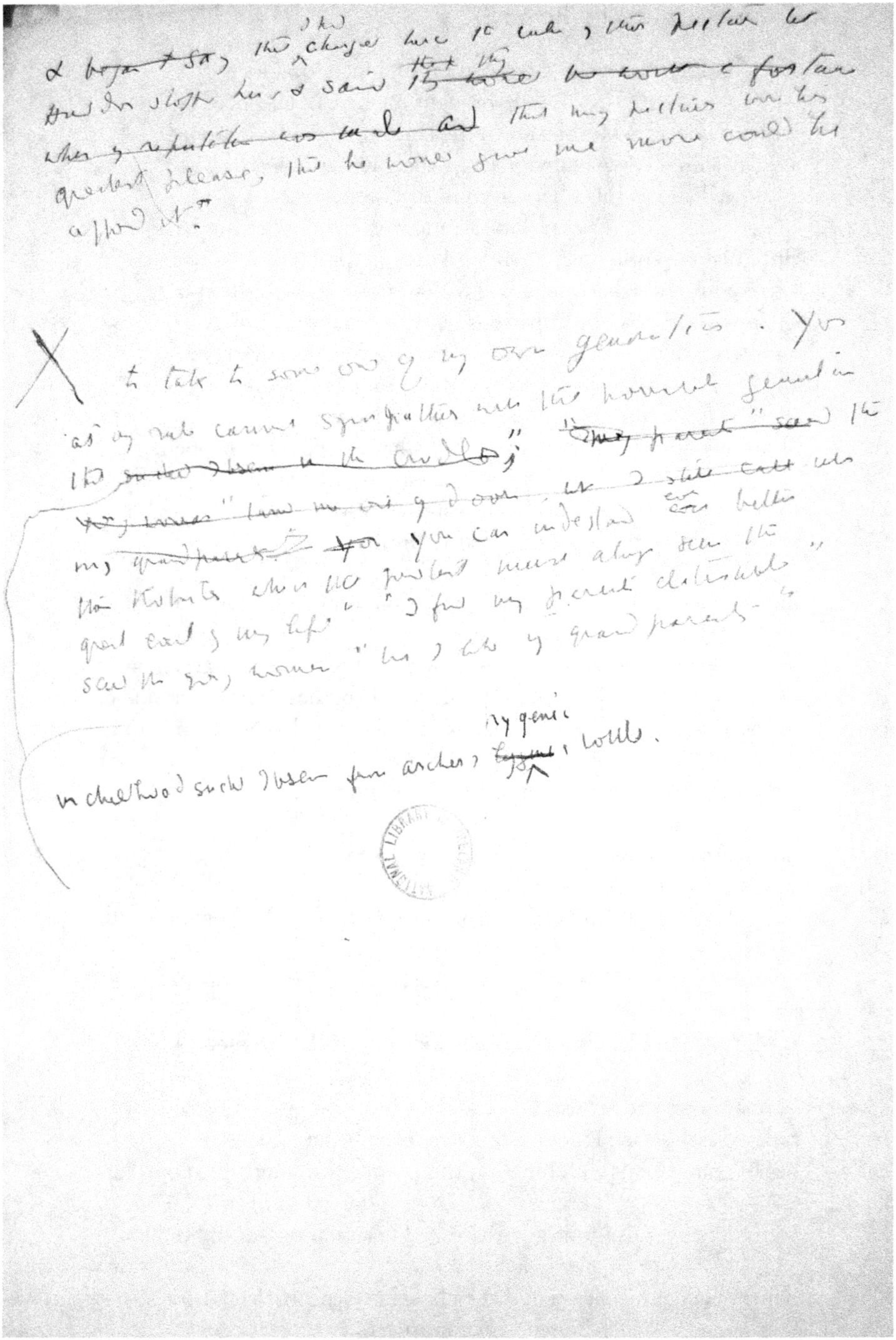

[4ᵛ]

I had

1 & ~~began to say~~ that^charged twice the value of these pictures but

~~the p~~ they

2 Huddon stopped her, & said ~~they would be worth a fortune~~

3 ~~when my reputation was made and~~ that my pictures were his

4 greatest please [=pleasure], that he would give me more could he

5 afford it."

6 X to talk to some one of my own generation. You

7 at any rate cannot sympathise with that horrible generation

8 that ~~sucked Ibsen in the cradle~~"; "~~My parents" said the~~

10 ~~young woman "turned me out of doors, but I still call upon~~

even

11 ~~my grandparents. You~~ You can understand ~~even~~ better

12 than Robartes which [=why] that protest must always seem the

13 great event of my life" "I find my parents detestable"

14 said the young woman "but I like my grand parents"

hygenic

9 in childhood sucked Ibsen from Archers ~~hyginee~~ bottle.

^

The following page "7" (folio 5ʳ) actually continues from the end of page "6" (4ʳ), the "P.T.O" at the bottom of which allows incorporation of lines 1–5 above. The vexed issue at 4ʳ, lines 6–9, is resolved with "(see back) X," which is keyed to lines 6–14 above, marked for insertion on the recto.

NLI 13,577 [5r]

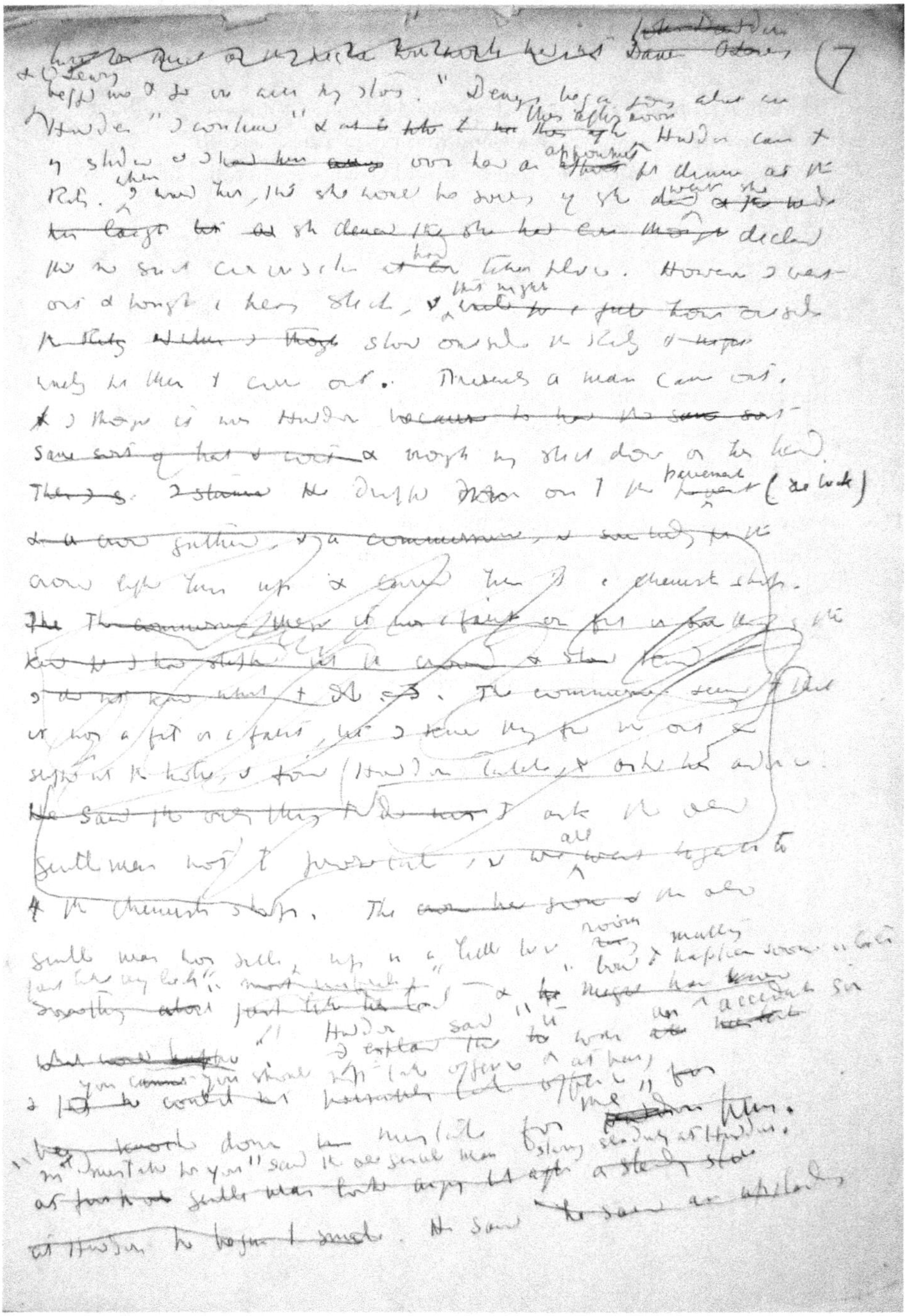

Page "7" continues the story of Huddon, Duddon, and Denise as compares, roughly, with *SMR*, p. 4, at a point near the bottom of the page. The circumscribed and cancelled lines 13–23, as indicated at line 13 (right), are amended on 5v (i.e., "See back").

[5r]

~~John Duddon~~
~~twice as much as the pictures were worth had not Dane O Leary~~ \7
& O Leary
^begged me to go on with my story. “Denys began going about with
this after noon
Hudden” I continued “& ~~[?not to]~~ ~~take~~ ~~to see this after~~^Huddon came to
appointment
my studio and I ~~heard him calling~~ over heard on ~~appoint~~ for dinner at the
When went she
Ritz. ^ I warned her, that she would be sorry if she ~~did~~^ ~~& that made~~
~~her laugh~~ ~~but~~ ~~And~~ She ~~denied that she had ever thought~~ declared
had
that no such conversation ~~had ever~~ taken place. However I went
that night
out & bought a heavy stick, &^ ~~waited for a full hour~~ outside
~~the Ritz and when I thought~~ stood outside the Ritz ~~at night~~
waiting for them to come out. Presently a man came out
& I thought it was Huddon ~~because he had the same sort~~
~~same sort of hat & coat~~ & brought my stick down on his head.
pavement
~~Then I s- I shivere[d]~~ He dropped ~~down~~ on to the ~~pavemt~~ (See back)
~~& a crowd gathered & a commissioner & some body from~~^ ~~the~~
crowd lifted him up & carried him to a chemists shop.
~~The The commissioner thought it was a faint or fit or some thing of the~~
~~kind for I had stepped into the crowd & stood stood~~
~~I did not know what to do. I~~ The commissioner seemed to think
it was a fit or a faint, but I knew my friend was out so
slipped into the hotel, & found Huddon['s] table, & asked his advice.
~~He said the only thing to do was~~ to ask the old
all
gentleman not to prosecute, & we^ went to~~gether to~~
~~to the chemists sho~~p. The ~~crowd had gone & the~~ old
room
gentle man was sitting up in a little back ~~room~~ muttering
“Just like my luck” ~~“most unfeeling”~~ “bound to happen sooner or later
~~something about~~ ~~Just like his luck—~~& ~~he might have known~~
^ Huddon said “it an accident Sir
~~what would happen I explained that~~ ~~he~~^was ~~was mistaken~~
You ~~cannot~~ You should not take offence at being
& t~~hat he could not possibly take offence~~ ~~for~~
me”
~~being knocked~~ down ~~m~~ mistake[n] for ~~Huddon him~~.
“In mistake for you said the old gentle man staring steadily at Huddon.
~~as for the old gentle man looked angry but after a steady stare~~
~~at Huddon he began to smile.~~ He said ~~he said an upstanding~~

NLI 13,577 [5v]

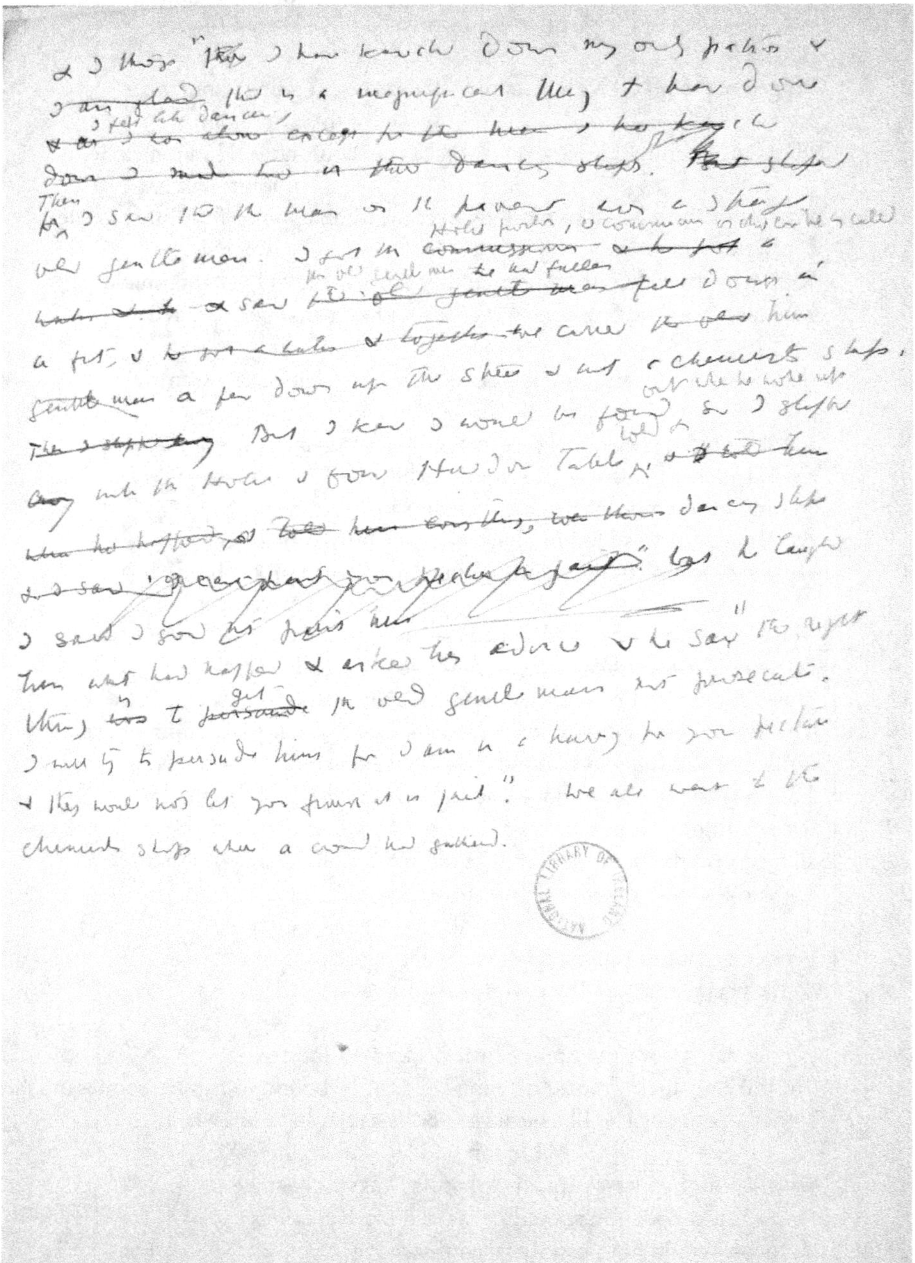

[5^{v}]

& I thought "~~There~~ I have knocked down my only patron &
~~I am glad~~ that is a magnificent thing to have done
I felt like dancing
~~& as I was alone except for the man I had knocked~~
~~down I made two or three dancing steps. But stop[p]ed~~
Then
~~for~~$_{\wedge}$I saw that the man on the pavement was a strange
Hotel porter, or commicier or what ever he is called
old gentle man. I got an ~~commissioner & he got~~ a
the old gentle man ~~he~~ had fallen
~~waiter & he~~ & said ~~the old gentle man fell~~ down in
a fit, & ~~he got a waiter & together~~ we carried ~~the old~~ him
~~gentle man~~ a few doors up the street & into a chemists shop.
out when he woke up
~~Then I slipped away~~ But I knew I would be found$_{\wedge}$so I slipped
told
~~away~~ into the Hotel & found Huddon['s] table$_{\wedge}$, ~~& I told him~~
~~what had happened, & told him everything, even thou[gh]~~ dancing steps
~~& I said "I cant paint your pictures in jail" but~~ he laughed
~~I said~~ I good not paint [?them]
him what had happened & asked his advice & he said "The right
is get
thing ~~was~~ to ~~persuade~~ the old gentle man not [to] prosecute.
I will try to persuade him for I am in a hurry for your picture
& they would not let you finish it in jail." We all went to the
chemists shop where a crowd had gathered.

As directed at line 13 of 5^{r}, "(see back)", 5^{v} renders text for insertion. Hence, after 5^{v}, lines 1–19, the narrative continues on 5^{r}, lines 23–31, completing the first episode on 6^{r} (page "8"), lines 1–8.

6 "~~commissioner~~…<Hotel porter, or commicier or what ever he is called>": the word Yeats may be searching for is *concierge*, or perhaps *consigliere.*

14 "good" is a scribal error for "could."

NLI 13,577 [6r]

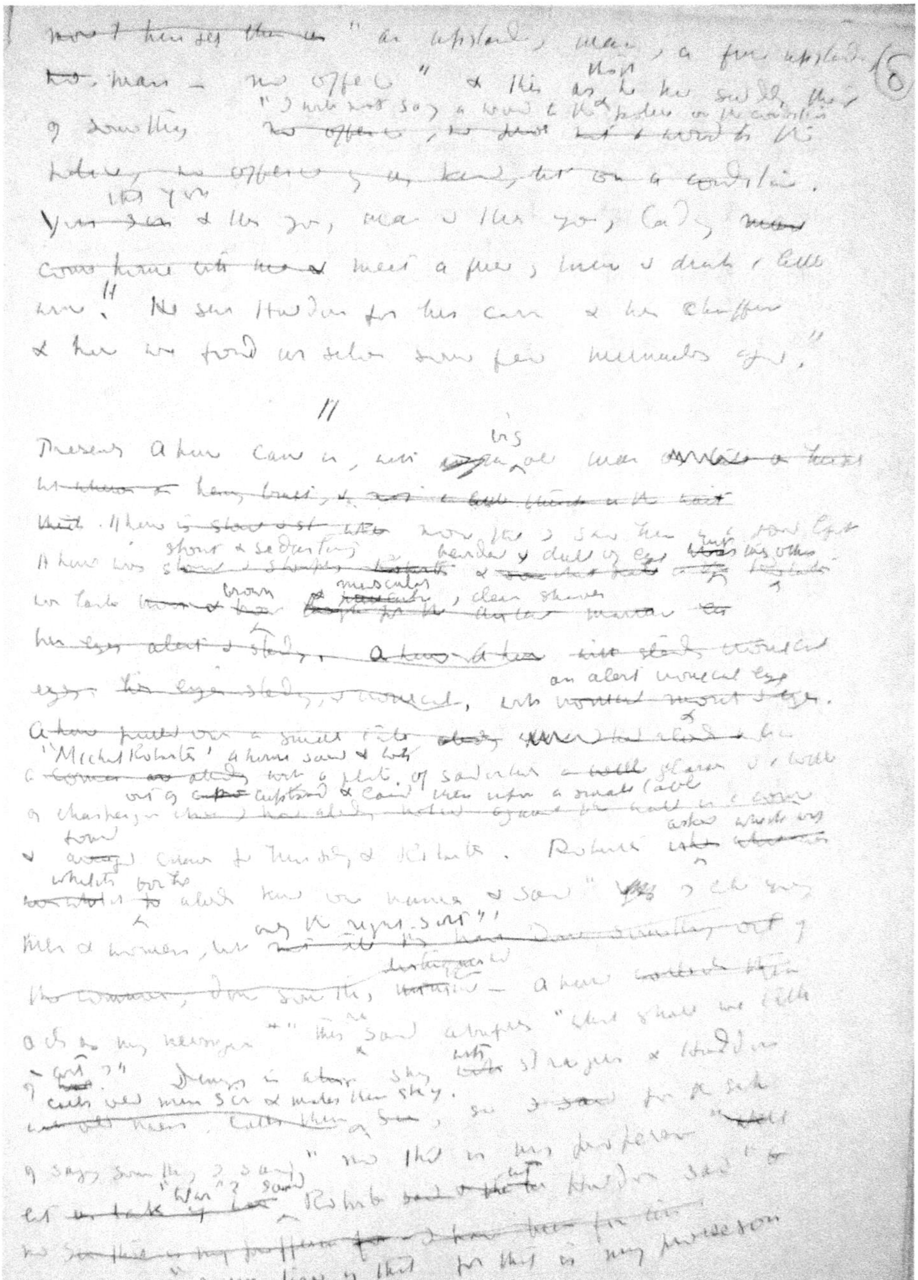

The composition on this folio follows directly from the bottom of 5r (page "7").

[6r]

1 ~~more to himself than us~~ "An upstanding man, a fine upstanding (8)
though
2 ~~ma~~ man— no offense" & this as^he had suddenly thought
"I will not say a word to the police on the condition
3 of something ~~no offence, no prob~~ ~~not a word to~~ the
4 ~~police, no offence of any kind, but on a condition.~~
that you
5 ~~You sir~~ & this young man & this young lady ~~must~~
6 ~~come home with me &~~ meet a friend of mine & drink a little
7 wine." He sent Huddon for his car & his chauffeur
8 & here we found our selves some few minutes ago."

II

big
9 Presently Aherne came in, with ~~another~~^old man ~~as tall as himself~~
10 ~~but [?where] as heavily built, & not a little thick in the waist~~
11 ~~thick~~ Aherne ~~is stout & sl[?] when~~ now that I saw him in good light
but
stout & sedentary bearded & dull of eye ~~whereas~~ the other
12 Aherne was ~~stout & stooping~~ ~~Robartes~~ & ~~some what pale~~ ~~and the~~ ~~Robartes~~
muscular ^
brown ~~musculr~~ & clean shaven
13 was lank ~~brown & brow~~ ~~enough for the ancient mariner~~ ~~ey~~
^
14 ~~his eyes alert & steady. Aherne Aherne~~ ~~with steady ironical~~
an alert ironical eye
15 ~~eyes his eyes steady, & ironical.~~ With ~~ironical mouth & eyes~~
^
16 ~~Aherne pulled over a small ta[b]le~~, ~~already when I heard a loud &~~ [?]
"Michael Robartes" Aherne said & took
17 & ~~comes are already with~~ a plate of sandwiches ~~a bottle~~ glasses & a bottle
out of a cupboard & laid them upon a small table
18 of champagne ~~which I had already noticed against the wall in a corner~~
found asked which was
19 & ~~arranged~~ chairs for himself & Robartes. Robartes ~~askes~~ ~~which ever~~
whitch for he ^
20 ~~was whitch~~^~~for~~ already knew our names & said "~~Yes~~ I like young
only the right sort
21 men & women, but ~~not till they have done something out of~~
~~distinguished~~
22 ~~the common, done something~~ ~~[?unusual]~~ —Aherne ~~collects them~~
he
23 acts as my messenger" "This^said abruptly "What shall we talk
—art with
24 of war?" Denys is ~~always~~ shy ~~with~~ strangers & Huddon
calls old men Sir & makes them shy.
25 ~~with old men, calls them~~^~~Sir~~, so ~~I said~~ for the sake
26 of saying something I said "No that is my profession" ~~which~~
"War"? said but
27 led ~~us back to war~~ Robartes ~~said & then [?he]~~ Huddon said "~~[?O]~~
28 no ~~Sir that is my profession for I have been for tire~~
29 "I am tired of that for this is my pro[f]ession

NLI 13,577 [7r]

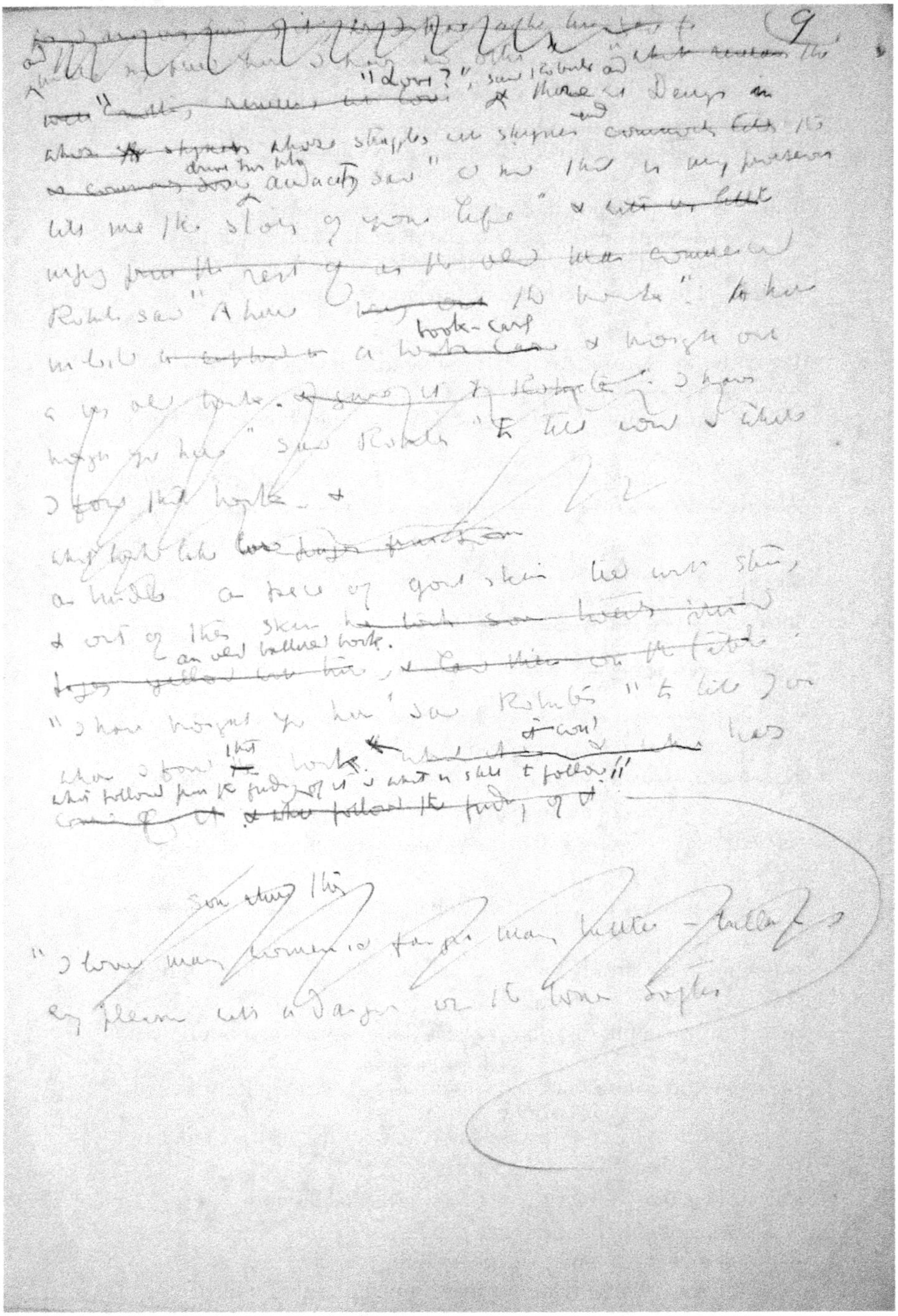

[7r]

~~for I am very tired of it, for I that after her gave f~~ 9
and
^aside [from] my friends here I have no other" "~~What remains~~ then
"Love?", said Robartes and
well "~~nothing remain but love.~~^& thereat Denys in
end
~~whose sh shyness~~ whose struggles with shyness ~~commonly takes~~ the
drive her into
~~is commonly some~~^audacity said "O no that is my profession
tell me the story of your life" & ~~with very little~~
urging ~~from the rest of us the old man commenced~~
Robartes said "Aherne ~~bring out~~ the book." Aherne
book-case
unlocked ~~a cupboard in~~ a ~~book case~~ & brought out
a very old book. ~~& gave it to Robartes~~. "I have
brought you here" said Robartes "to tell how & where
I found that book, &
What looked like ~~loose~~ pages from some
~~a bundle~~ a piece of goat skin tied with string
& out of the skin ~~he took some twenty printed~~
an old battered book.
~~pages yellow with time~~, ~~& laid them on the table~~.
"I have brought you here" said Robartes "to tell you
that ~~it~~ could
where I found ~~the~~ book." ~~what it is & where~~ has
what followed from the finding of it & what is still to follow"
~~come of it & what followed the finding of it"~~

~~some where this~~
"I loved many women & fought many battles—ballance
every pleasure with a danger or the bones soften

20 The drawn curving line indicates where the text carries over to page "10" (8r), lines 1–5.

NLI 13,577 [7v]

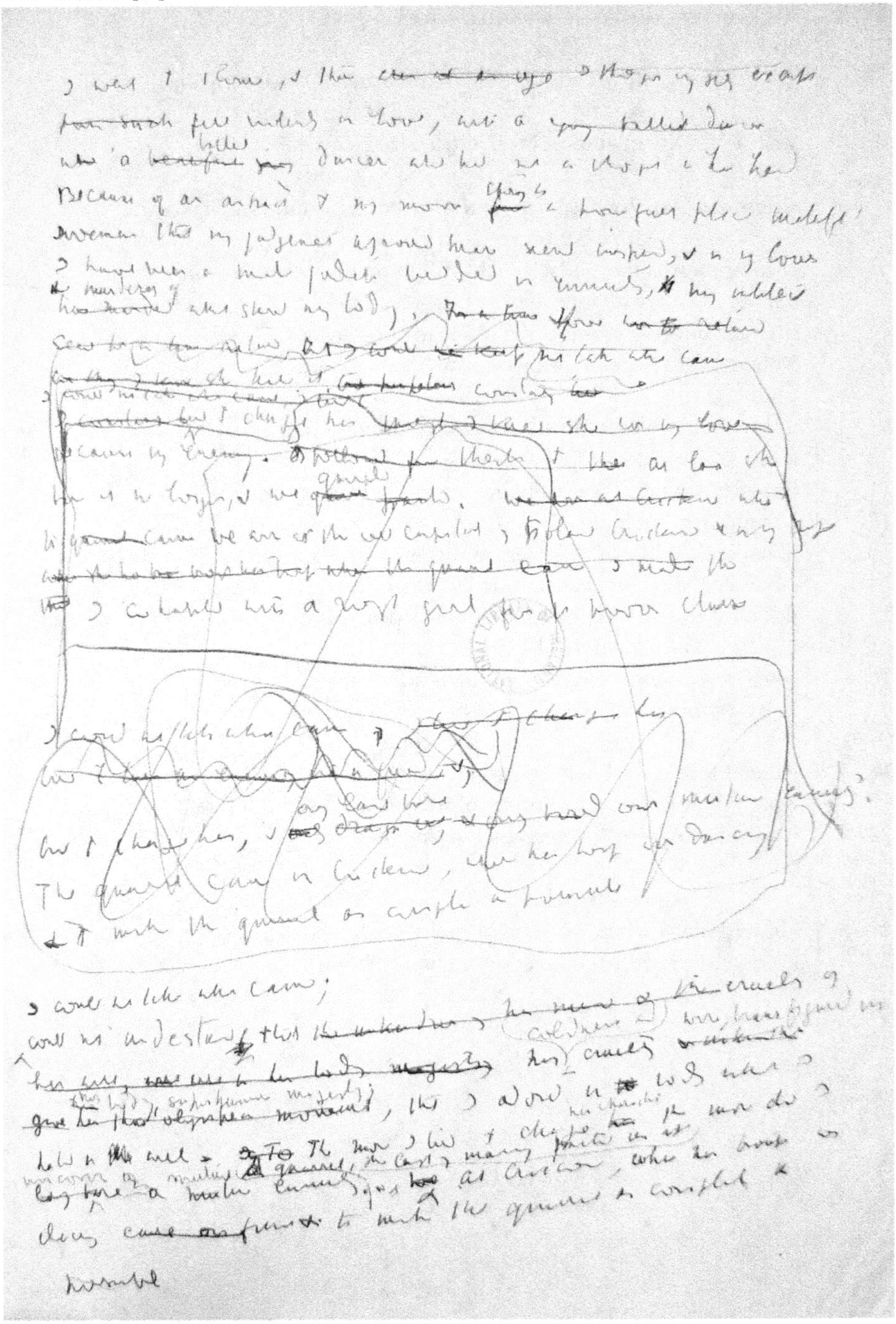

7v, lines 1–28 (in spite of the muddle of lines 8–21) were presented as an insert for 8r (page "10"), lines 6–19, where one is directed to "See back of | previous page."

[7v]

1 I went to Rome, & there ~~when at an age I thought my self exempt~~
2 ~~from such~~ fell violently in love, with a ~~young ballet dancer~~
ballet
3 who a ~~beautiful young~~ dancer who had not a thought in her head
though
4 Because of an aspect to my moon ~~from~~ a powerfull place [?malefic]
5 women that my judgement ap[p]roved more seemed insipid, & in my loves
6 I have been a male Judith bedded in enmity, & my intel[l]ect
the murderer of
7 ~~has murdered~~ what stirred my body. ~~For a time~~ L~~o~~ve ~~was to returned~~
8 ~~seemed for a time returned, but I could not keep not take what came~~
9 ~~even though I knew she hated it tried perpetually~~ constantly ~~tried~~
10 ~~I could not take what came, I tried~~
11 I constantly tried to change her though I knew she was my love—
12 because my enemy. I followed from theatre to thea[tre] at [?last] she
quarreled
13 bore it now longer, & we ~~quarel~~ ~~parted~~ ~~We were at Crakow~~ When
14 the ~~quarrel[ing]~~ came we were at the old capitol of Poland Crakow in my rage
15 ~~where she had bro brought her troup when the quarrel[ing] came I made~~ then
16 ~~that~~ I cohabited with a rough girl from the poorer classes

17 I could not take what came, ~~I tried to change~~ her
18 ~~tried to turn an enemy into a friend,~~ &,
only laid bare
19 tried to change her, & ~~only~~ ~~drag[g]ed out,~~ & only bared our mutual enmity?
20 The quarrel came in Crackow, where her troop was dancing
21 ~~&~~ I made the quarrel as complete as possible

22 I could not take what came;
23 ^could not understand ~~[?]~~ that ~~the unkindness of her mind & the~~ cruelty of
coldness and were, transfigured in
24 ~~her will was all in her body majesty~~ her cruelty ~~& unkindness~~
her
~~her~~ body, superhuman majesty
25 ~~gave her that olympean movement~~ that I adored in ~~h~~ body what I
her character
26 hated in ~~the~~ will. ~~A To~~ The more I tried to change ~~her~~ the more did I
uncover ~~a~~ mutual A quarrel, the last of many parted us
27 ~~lay bare~~ a ~~mutu~~ enmity. ~~here~~ at Crackow, where her troop was
^ ^
28 dancing ~~came on~~ fierce & to make the quarrel as complete as
possible.

NLI 13,577 [8r]

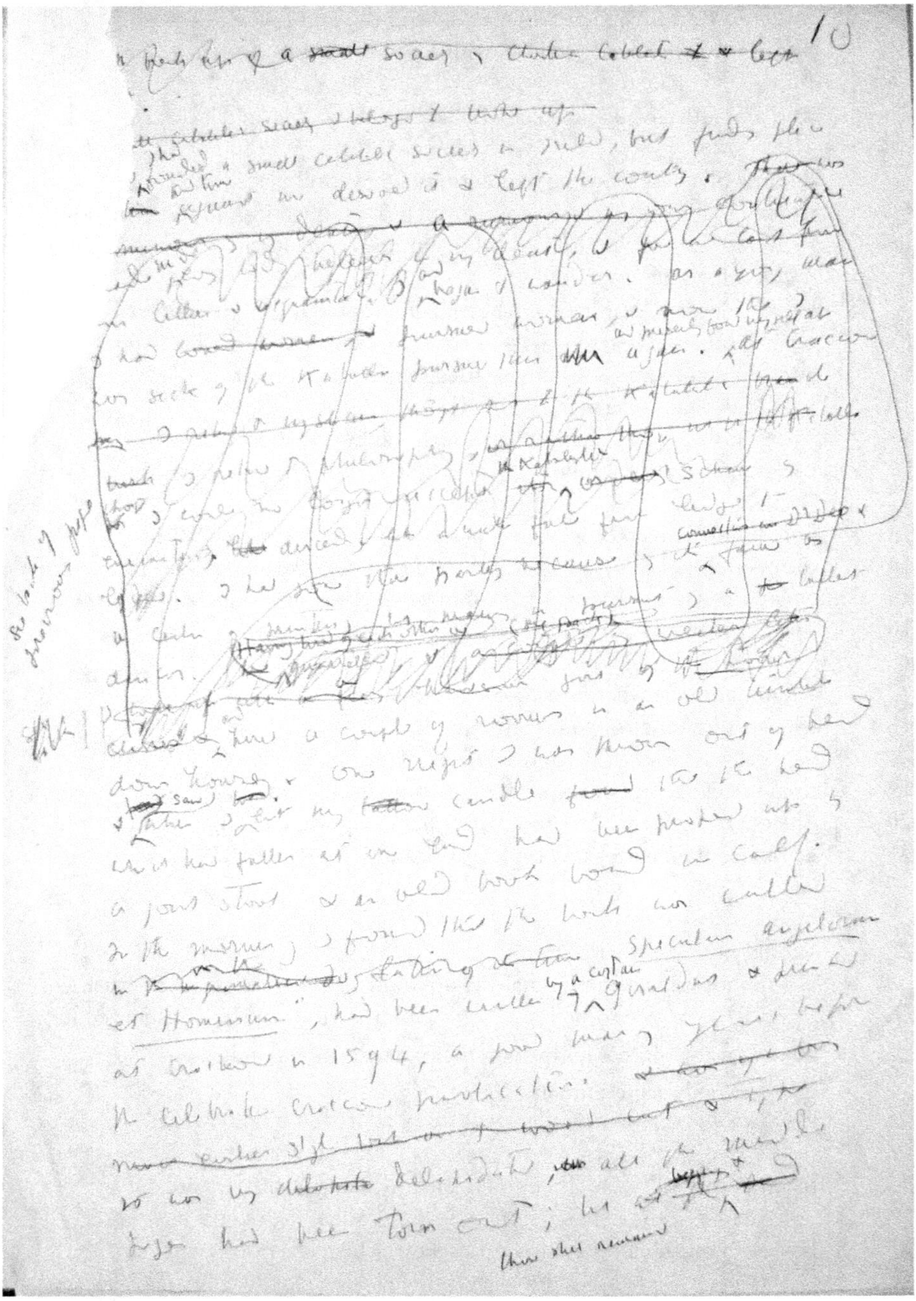

A small piece of the page (upper left) is missing from the time the leaf was torn out of the notebook, the facing page of which (7v) is referred to as revised text for the circumscribed and heavily cancelled lines 6–19. At lines 17–19, cancelled notes to "See back" refer to the 9 stricken lines on 8v.

[8r]

10
[?] break up of a ~~small~~ society of Christian Cabalists ~~[?]~~ & left
[…]
~~[…] [sma]ll Cabalistic society I belonged to broke up~~
I had
[…] ‸founded a small Cabalistic society in Ireland, but finding place
and time
[…]~~time~~‸against me dissolved it & left the country. ~~There was~~
[…] ~~rumour of my death & a rumour of my own [?conversion]~~
~~made~~
~~[??]ade‸every body believe in my death, and free at last from~~
and
[…] ~~letters & acquaintances, I~~‸began to wander. As a young man
I had ~~loved women, &~~ pursued women, & now that I
and presently found myself at
was sick of the Kaballa pursued them ~~[?over]~~ again. ‸At Cracow
~~my I returned to mysticism, though not to the Kabalistic branch~~
~~branch~~ I returned to philosophy, ~~or rather not in the Kaballa~~
though the Kabalistic
~~for~~ I could no longer accept ~~its~~‸~~orderly~~ scheme of
emanation, ~~like~~ descending like a water fall from ledge to
~~connection with Dr Dee~~ &
ledge. I had gone there partly because of its‸fame as
a center of printing but mainly in pursuit of a ~~d~~ ballet
(~~Having tired of each other we~~) (~~see Back~~)
dancer. We‸quarreled, & ~~a couple of weeks later~~
I took up with a fiery handsome girl of the poorer
and
classes &‸hired a couple of rooms in an old tumble
down house. One night I was thrown out of bed
~~found~~ saw ~~had~~
& when I lit my ~~tallow~~ candle ~~found~~ that the bed
which had fallen at one end had been prop[p]ed up by
a joint stool & an old book bound in calf.
In the morning I found that the book was called
in that
in ~~the ungramatical dog latin of the time~~ Speculum Angelorum
by a certain
et Hominum," had been written ~~by~~‸Giraldus & printed
at Crakow in 1594, a good many years before
the celebrated Cracow publications ~~& was of a very~~
~~much earlier style [?work] as to woodcut & type~~
It was very ~~delapila~~ delapidated, ~~[?for]~~ all the middle
~~beginning &~~
pages had been torn out; but ~~at the~~‸~~end~~
there still remained

See back of previous page

~~See back~~

NLI 13,577 [8ᵛ]

[8^{v}]

1 ~~Just~~
2 ~~I discussed her~~ &
3 after a quarrel the last of many we parted—Because of a
malefic the have found
4 powefully supported ~~planet~~ in ^ Seventh House ~~and~~ I ~~find~~
5 all women that my judgement approved insipid;—~~so~~ seemed a
for intellect
~~their innocense~~ has murdered
6 male Judith bedded in enmity; ~~I must murder~~
~~st~~ all this stirred my body.
~~what in body desire~~ ^
7 ~~what stirs my flesh~~. To make the quarrel ~~as~~ complete
at once
8 I ~~took up with a rough girl of~~ I ^ cohabited with a
9 rough girl from the poorest classes

1–9 (cancelled) are abandoned lines to amend 8^{r}, lines 17–19. See 7^{v}, lines 1–28, which supersedes this.

NLI 13,577 [9r]

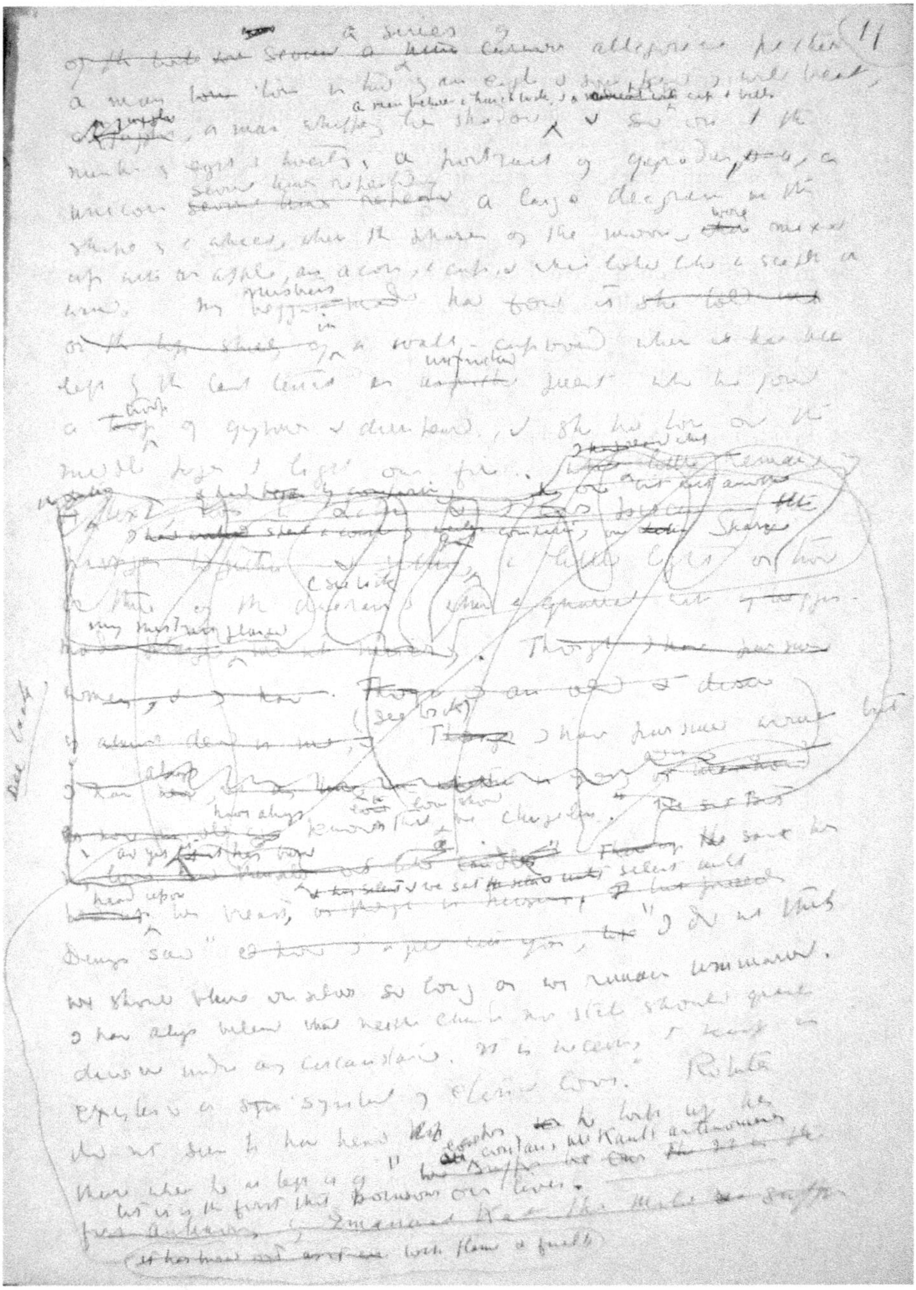

Three directions are given, in left margin and parenthetically over lines 15 and 18, to "See back"—that is, to an insertion on 9v to amend the circumscribed and thoroughly cancelled lines 12–21.

[9r]

~~[?was]~~ a series of 11
~~of the book were several a utter[?ly] curious allegorical pictures~~
a man ~~torn~~ torn in two by an eagle & some kind of wild beast, fool in
~~a juggler~~ a man between a hunchback, & a ~~medieval with~~^ cap & bells
~~a juggler~~, a man whipping his shadow, & so on to the
member of eight & twenty, a portrait of Grya[l]dus, ~~& a~~ a
several times repeated
unicorn ~~several times repeated~~ a large diagram in the
were
shape of a wheel, where the phases of the moon, ~~where~~ mixed
up with an apple, an acorn, a cup, & what looked like a scepter or
mistress
wand. My ~~beggar maid~~ had found it ~~she told me~~
in
~~on the top shelf of~~^ a wall cupboard where it had been
unfrocked
left by the last tenant an ~~unfrocked~~ priest who had joined
troop
a ~~troop~~^ of gypsies & disappeared & she had torn out the
I had read what
middle pages to light on fire. ~~What little re~~mained of
~~The Latin~~ & had begun by comparing
~~the text was in Latin & I was piecing the~~
I ~~had worked~~ spent a couple of weeks comparing one ~~Latin~~ [?S] passage
~~got~~
passage together & getting^ a little light on two
(See back)
or three of the diagrams, when a quarrel with ~~my beggar~~
my mistress plunged
~~made plunged me into misery~~. ~~Though I have pursued~~
~~women, & I have~~. ~~Though I am old & desire~~
(See back)
~~is almost dead in me, & though~~ I have pursued women but
~~always~~ or in
~~I have never, in my time, in whether m youth or manhood~~
have always ~~love~~ that love should
~~as now in old age~~ known that^ be changeless" He said But
"~~And ye~~t ~~about~~ it has burned a
~~my loves burned themselves out like~~^ ~~candle~~" ~~There upon~~ He sank his
head upon ^ ~~& was silent &~~ we sat ~~in silence until~~ silent until
~~head up~~^ his breast ~~as though in misery [?] but presently~~
Denys said "~~and how & I agree with you, let~~" I do not think
we should blame ourselves so long as we remain unmarried.
I have always believed that neither church nor state should grant
divorce under any circumstance. It is necessary to keep in
existence a ~~sym~~ symbol of eternal love." Robartes
did not seem to have heard ~~her,~~ for he took up his
~~All~~ love contains all Kant's antinomies
theme where he had left it off" ~~We suffer be~~ ~~Our~~ ~~The It is the~~
but it is the first that Poisons our lives.
~~first antinomy of Emanuel Kant that makes us suffer~~
~~it has burned into us it were~~ with flame & fuel")

See back

NLI 13,577 [9v]

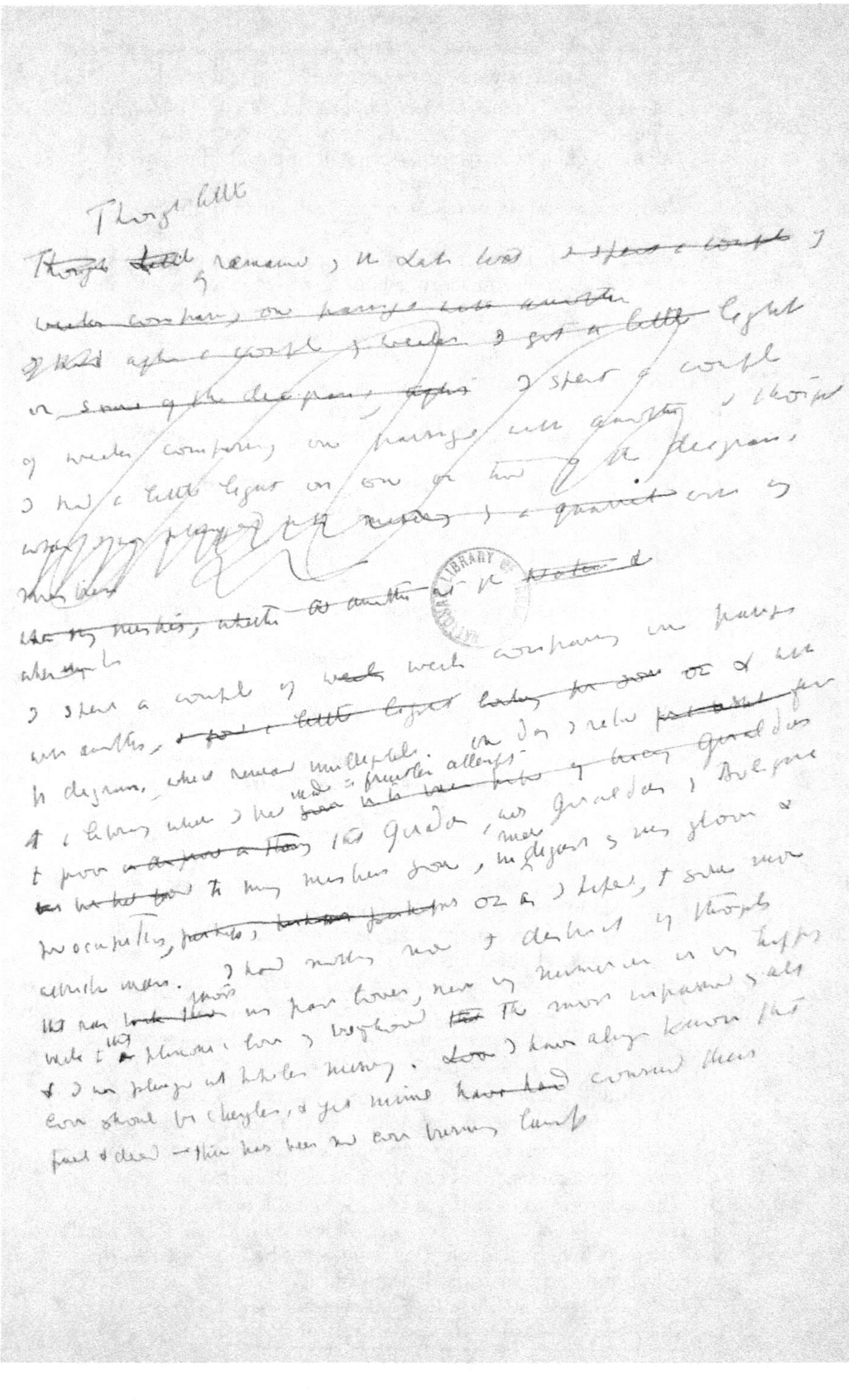

[9^{v}]

Though little
~~Though Little~~∧remained of the Latin text ~~I spent a couple~~ of
~~weeks comparing one passage with another~~
~~I had after a couple of weeks I got a little~~ light
~~on some of the diagrams, after~~ I spent a couple
of weeks comparing one passage with another & thought
I had a little light on one or two of the diagrams
~~when I was plunged into misery by a quarrel~~ with my
mistress
~~when my mistress, whether and another~~ at the ~~Nature [?]~~
~~when my [?]~~

I spent a couple of ~~weeks~~ weeks comparing one passage
with another, ~~& found a little light looking for some one~~ & with
the diagrams, which remained unintelligible. One day I returned ~~as usual~~ from
made a fruitless attempt
~~t~~ a library where I had ~~given into one hope of tracing Giraldus~~
to prove ~~or disprove a theory~~ that Giraldus, was Giraldus of Bologne
mere
~~but but had found~~ that my mistress gone, in∧disgust of my gloom &
preoccupation, ~~perhaps perhaps perhaps~~ or as I hoped, to some more
attractive man. I had nothing more to distract my thoughts
through
that ran ~~back through~~ my past loves, never very numerous or very happy
that
back to ~~a~~ pla[t]onic love of boyhood ~~that~~ The most impassioned of all
& I was plunged into hopeless misery. ~~Love~~ I have always known that
love should be changeless, & yet mine ~~have had~~ consumed their
fuel and died—there has been no ever burning lamp

All of this to be inserted in place of the cancelled block in the middle of page "11" (9^{r}, lines 12–21).

NLI 13,577 [10r]

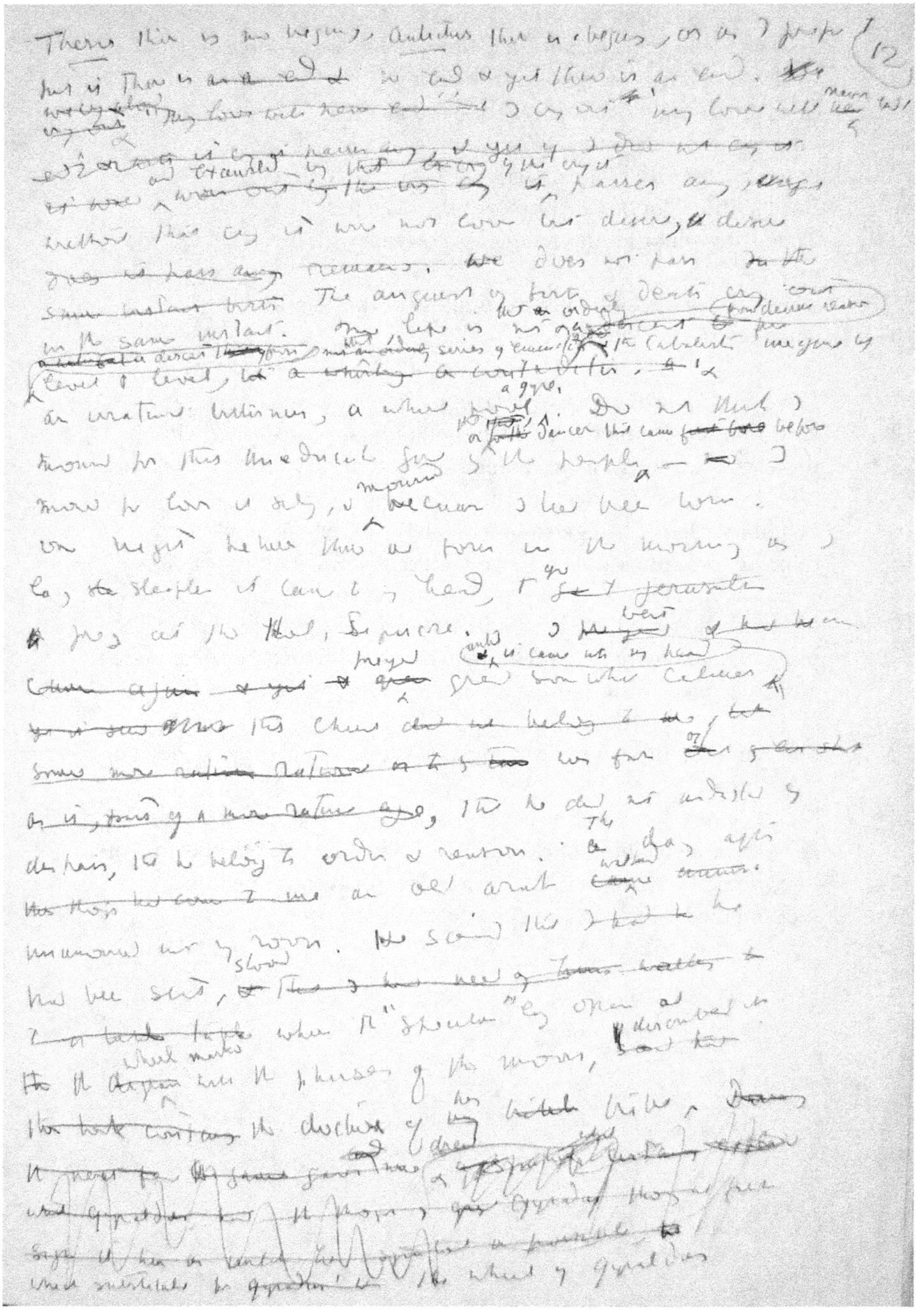

The significance of this page is that it works out the impassioned confession of Robartes that Yeats anticipated at the far end of his notebook (on folio 43v) in a rehearsal called "Concerning love." The antinomial logic of Kant was worked and reworked in the proof copies of *SMR* (p.9) and *AVB*, as shown in Part Three, section 2, below.

[10r]

(12

<u>Thesis</u> there is no beginning, <u>Antithesis</u> there is a beginning, or as I prefer to
put it There is ~~an an end &~~ no end & yet there is an end. ~~We~~
~~we cry aloud~~ never
~~cry out~~^ "~~My love will never end~~" I cry out "My love will ~~n~~^end
~~end & with [?that] cry it passes away, & yet if I did not cry it~~
and exhausted by ~~that cr cry~~ by that cry it
~~it would~~^ ~~worn out by the very cry~~ it^passes away and yet
without that cry it were not love but desire, ~~&~~ desire
~~does not pass away~~ ~~remains~~ ~~we~~ does not pass ~~In the~~
~~same instant birth~~ The anguish of birth & death cry out
that ~~an~~ orderly (from devine reason)
in the same instant. No life is not^an descent ~~[?]~~ from
(~~a waterfall~~ descent ~~[?]~~ from) ~~not~~^~~that orderly~~ series of emanations^the Cabalists imagine it
^level to level but ~~a whirling a contradiction a~~ &
a gyre
an irrational bitterness, a whirl pool,^. Do not think I
or for the dancer that came ~~first fore~~ before
mourned for this uneducated girl of^the people^~~—no~~ I
mourned
mourned for love it self, & because I had been born.
One night between three and four in the morning as I
go
lay ~~sle~~ sleepless it came to my head, ~~to~~ ~~go to Jerusalem~~
went
~~[?to]~~ prey at the Holy Sepu[l]cre. I ~~preyed~~ & ~~had become~~
preyed (~~&~~ it came into my head)
~~come again & yet &~~ ~~grew~~ grew somewhat calmer^
^
~~yet it seemed to me~~ that Christ ~~did not belong to me, like~~
off
~~some more ration rational or to my [?time]~~ was far ~~out of earshot~~
~~as it [=if?] part of a more rational age~~, that he did not understand my
The
despair, that he belongs to order & reason. ~~A~~ day after
walked
~~this thought had come to me~~ an old arab ~~came~~ ~~unann~~
unannounced into my room. He said that ~~I had be~~ he
stood
had been sent ~~&~~ ~~that I had need of him~~ ~~walked to~~
~~to a table table~~ where the "Speculum" lay open at
wheel marked described it
~~the~~ the ~~diagram~~ with the phases of the moon, ~~said that~~
his
~~this book containing~~ the doctrines of ~~my~~ ~~trible~~ tribe. During
~~and~~ drew which
~~the next few~~ ~~He gave gave was~~^~~a symbol certainly explains~~
~~what Gyraldus had~~ ~~the thought of gry Gyra[l]dus though first~~
~~sight it was as unlike his symbol as possible, but~~
which substituted for ~~Gyra[l]dus' w~~ the wheel of Gyraldus

NLI 13,577 [11r]

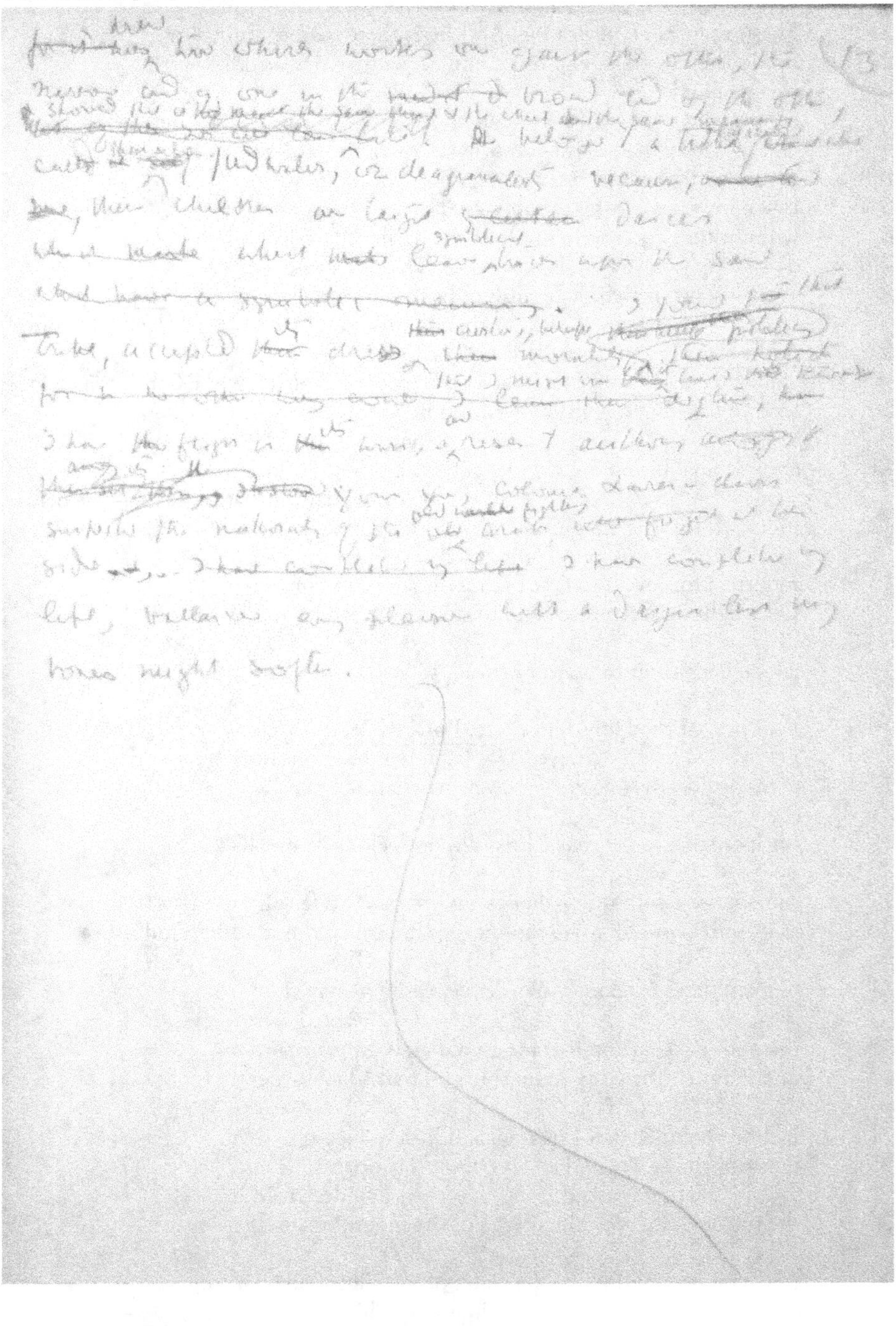

[11r]

drew
1 ~~for it was~~ ^ two whorls working one against the other, the (13
2 narrow end of one in the ~~midst d~~ broad end of the other
3 showed that it ~~had meant the same thing~~ & the wheel had the same ~~meaning~~
(of arabs)
4 ~~but of this you will learn later~~. He belonged to a tribe ~~which~~ who
themselves
5 called ~~it self~~ Judwalis, or diagramatists because, ~~as he told~~
^
6 ~~me~~, their children are taught ~~by certain~~ dances
symbolical
7 ~~which mark~~ which ~~make~~ leave ^ traces upon the sand
8 ~~which have a symbolic meaning~~. I joined ~~the~~ that
its ~~their~~ customs, beliefs (~~their beliefs their~~ politics)
9 tribe, accepted ~~their~~ dress ^ their morality, ^ ~~their politics~~
that I might win ~~their~~ its trust & ~~their~~ its knowledge
10 ~~for in no other way could I learn their doctrine~~, ~~ha~~
its and
11 I have ~~tho~~ fought in ~~their~~ wars, & risen to authority ~~amongst~~
~~among~~ its
12 ~~themselves then, & I stood~~ Your young Colonel Lawrence never
old ~~warlike~~ fighting
13 suspected the nationality of the ~~old~~ ^ Arab ~~who fought~~ at his
14 side— —, ~~I had completed my life~~ I have completed my
15 life, ballanced every pleasure with a danger lest
16 my bones might soften.

The drawn line at line 16, leading to lower right, evidently signifies that 11r, lines 1–16 complete the episode, for part "III" follows immediately on the next page.

1–3 seem to be describing the double cones or possibly the sign of Cancer. See "Concerning love," on 43v, where cardinal signs of the zodiac, especially Cancer and Capricorn, beside fire and water symbols, are drawn below the entry. The signs also appear on "The Great Wheel" (see Part Four, section 2, below). The figure is tipped in between pages 8 and 9 in *SMR*.

NLI 13,577 [12r]

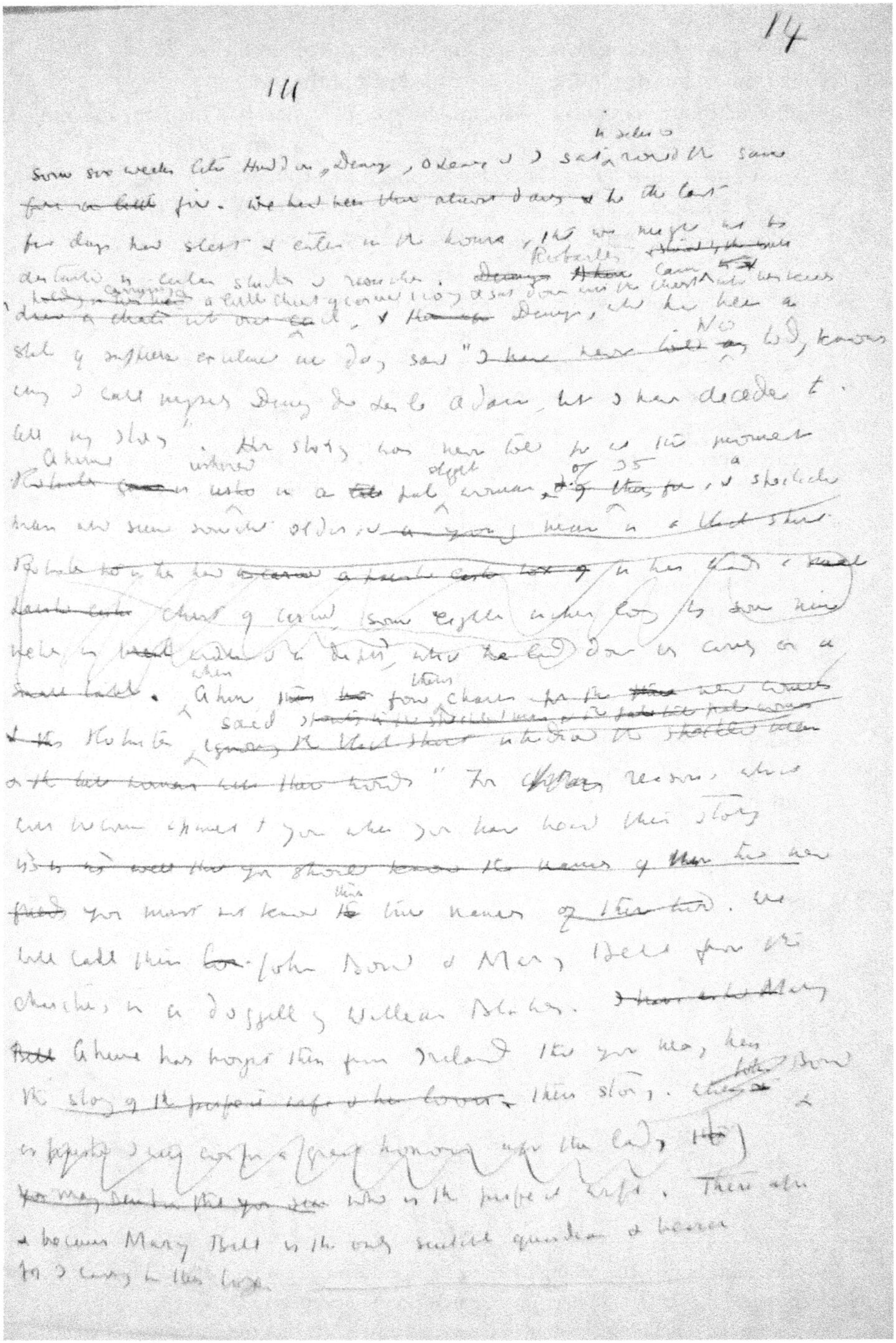

[12r]

14

III in silence

Some six weeks later Huddon, Denys, O'Leary & I sat‸round the same
~~fire a little~~ fire. ~~We had been there almost daily &~~ for the last
few days had slept & eaten in the house, that we might not be
Robartes ~~& stood by the wall~~
disturbed in certain studies & researches. ~~Denys Aherne~~ came ~~in w~~
carrying
in ~~holding in his hands~~ a little chest of carved ivory & sat down with the chest upon his knees
~~drew a chest into our circle~~, & ~~there upon~~ Denys, who had been [in] a
^ No
state of suppressed excitement all day said "~~I have never told any~~ body knows
why I call myself Denys de Lisle Adam, but I have decided to ^
tell my story". Her story was never told for at that moment
Aherne ushered slight of 35 a
~~Robartes came in~~ ~~ushed~~ in a ~~tale~~ pale woman, ~~& I~~ ~~therefore~~, & spectacled
^ ^ ^
man who seemed somewhat older, ~~& a young man in a black shirt~~
Robartes had in his hand ~~a carved~~ ~~a painted casket box of~~ in his hands a ~~small~~
~~painted cask~~ chest of carved [wood?] some eighteen inches long by some nine
inches in ~~bredth~~ width & in depth, which he laid down very carefully on a
When them
small table.‸Aherne ~~then bro~~ found‸chairs for the ~~three~~ new comers
said ~~speaking to the spectacled man & the pale tall pale woman~~
~~& then~~ Robartes ^ ~~ignoring the black shirt~~ introduced the ~~spectacled man~~
& ~~the tall woman with these words~~ "For ~~[certain]~~ reasons which
will become apparent to you when you have heard their story
~~it is not well that you should know the names of these two new~~
their
~~friends~~ you must not know ~~the~~ true names ~~of these two~~. We
will call them ~~bon~~ John Bond & Mary Bell from the
characters in a doggrell of William Blakes. ~~I have asked Mary~~
~~Bell~~ Aherne has brought them from Ireland that you may hear
~~John~~ Bond
~~the story of the perfect wife & her lover~~ their story. When ~~it~~ ^
is finished I will confer a great honour upon this lady ~~that~~
~~you may mention that you [had] seen~~ who is the perfect wife. There upon
& because Mary Bell is the only suitable guardian & bearer
for [what] I carry in this box. ————————————

27 A drawn line to the right indicates that the paragraph is to carry on with 13r (page "15"), line 1 without a break.

NLI 13,577 [13^{r}]

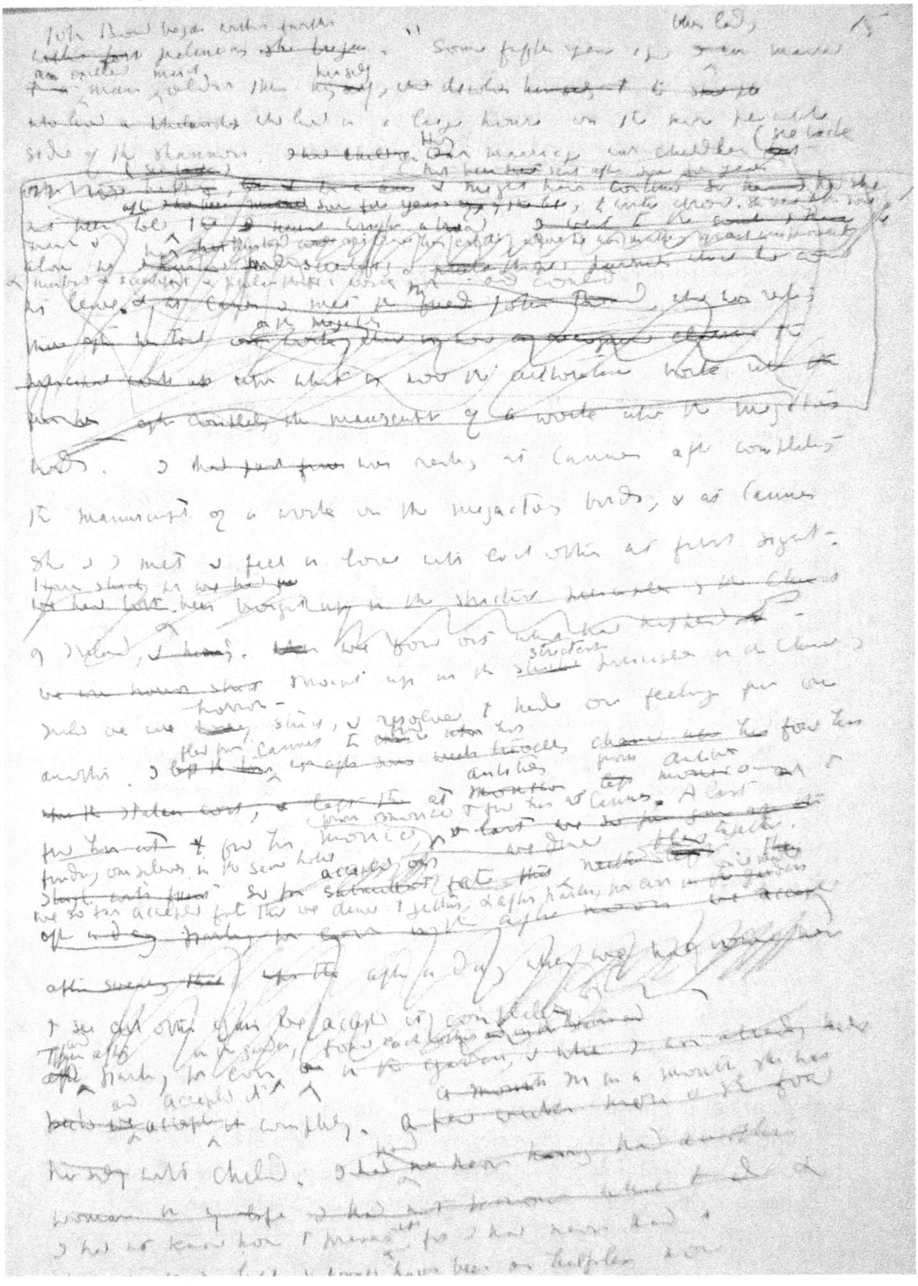

At the end of line 4 and, just over the vigorously cancelled, circumscribed passage inclusive of lines 5–13, one is referred to "see back." That ensnarled passage is amended by the four lines on 13^{v}.

[13r]

John Bond began without further   this lady   15
~~Without furt~~ preliminaries ~~she began~~. "Some fifteen years ago ~~I [?]~~ married
an excellent much   herself
~~to the~~ ^ man ^ older than ~~myself~~, ~~who devoted himself to the stud[y] [?]~~
~~who lived a philanthrop~~ who lived in a large house on the more peaceable
His
side of the Shannon. ~~I had children~~ ~~Our~~ marriage was childless ~~but~~   (see back
~~(see back)~~   not been ~~sent~~ sent after some five years
~~other wise happy~~, ~~till~~ ~~& for a time~~ & might have continued so ~~had I~~ had she
after ~~I had been married~~ some ~~five years [?] of this life~~, to winter abroad. She went to the south of
not been told ^ ~~that I must winter abroad~~. ~~I went to the south of France~~
France & her ~~her~~ husband could not leave his estate, where he was making ~~great~~ improvmt
^ alone for ~~I husband his scientific &~~ ^ ~~philothropic pursuits which he~~ could
husband & scientific & philanthropic work and could
not leave. ~~& at Cannes I met this~~ my ~~friend John Bond, who was resting~~
on the migration
~~there after his toil on work that is now a recognized classic~~ the
~~principal work up~~ upon what is now the authoritative work upon The
~~from him after completing the manuscript of a work upon the migratory~~
~~birds~~. ~~I had just finis~~ was resting at Cannes after completing
the manuscript of a work on the migratory birds, & at Cannes
she & I met & fell in love with each other at first sight.
~~Horror struck for we had been~~
~~We had both~~ ^ been ~~brought up in the strictest principles of the Church~~
of Ireland, ~~& horror~~. ~~When we found out what had happened [?]~~
strictest
~~we were horror struck~~ & brought up in the ~~strict~~ principles of the Church of
horror
Ireland we were ~~horry~~ struck, & resolved to hide our feelings from one
fled from Cannes to <find> ~~chance upon~~ her
another. I ~~left the town~~ ^ ~~but after some weeks travelling~~ ~~chanced upon her~~ found her
Antibes   from Antibes
~~upon the Italian coast, & left then~~ at ~~Monaco~~, ~~left~~ ~~Monaco~~ only to
from Monaco to find her at Cannes. A[t] last
~~find her at~~ & found her at Monaco, ^ ~~at last we~~ ~~so we gave up sta~~
finding ourselves in the same hotel
accepted our   we dined   ~~fled~~ together
~~I [?high] with faint~~ so far ~~submitted to~~ fate that ^ ~~neither left~~ ~~There~~   once more
we so far accepted fate that we dined together, & after parting for ever ~~in the garden~~
~~after a day parting for ever in the after noon we accepted~~
~~after swearing that~~ ~~upon the~~ after a day when we had vowed never
to see each other again we accepted it completely
And
~~Then~~ after   in the garden found each other ~~and~~ on the stairs and
~~after~~ ^ parting for ever ^ we ^ ~~in the garden, & when I was already [?having]~~
and accepted it   ~~A month~~ In in a month she was
~~packed we~~ ^ ~~accepted it~~ completely. ~~A few weeks more & she found~~
had
~~herself~~ with child. I ~~had not never having had another~~
~~woman in my life I had not known what to do~~ &
it
I had not known how to prevent ^, for I had never had a
woman in my life, & would have been as helpless now

NLI 13,577 [13v]

her happy & might have continued so had she not in the ninth ~~seventh~~
~~ninth~~ year of her marriage been told to winter abroad. She
went alone to the South of France for her husband
his scientific & philanthropic work that he could not leave

[13v]

ninth

but happy & might have continued so had she not in the ~~seventh month~~ ~~ann~~ year of her marriage been told to winter abroad. She went alone to the south of France for her husband had scientific & philanthropic work that he could not leave

1–4 amend 13r (page 15), lines 5–13.

NLI 13,577 [14r]

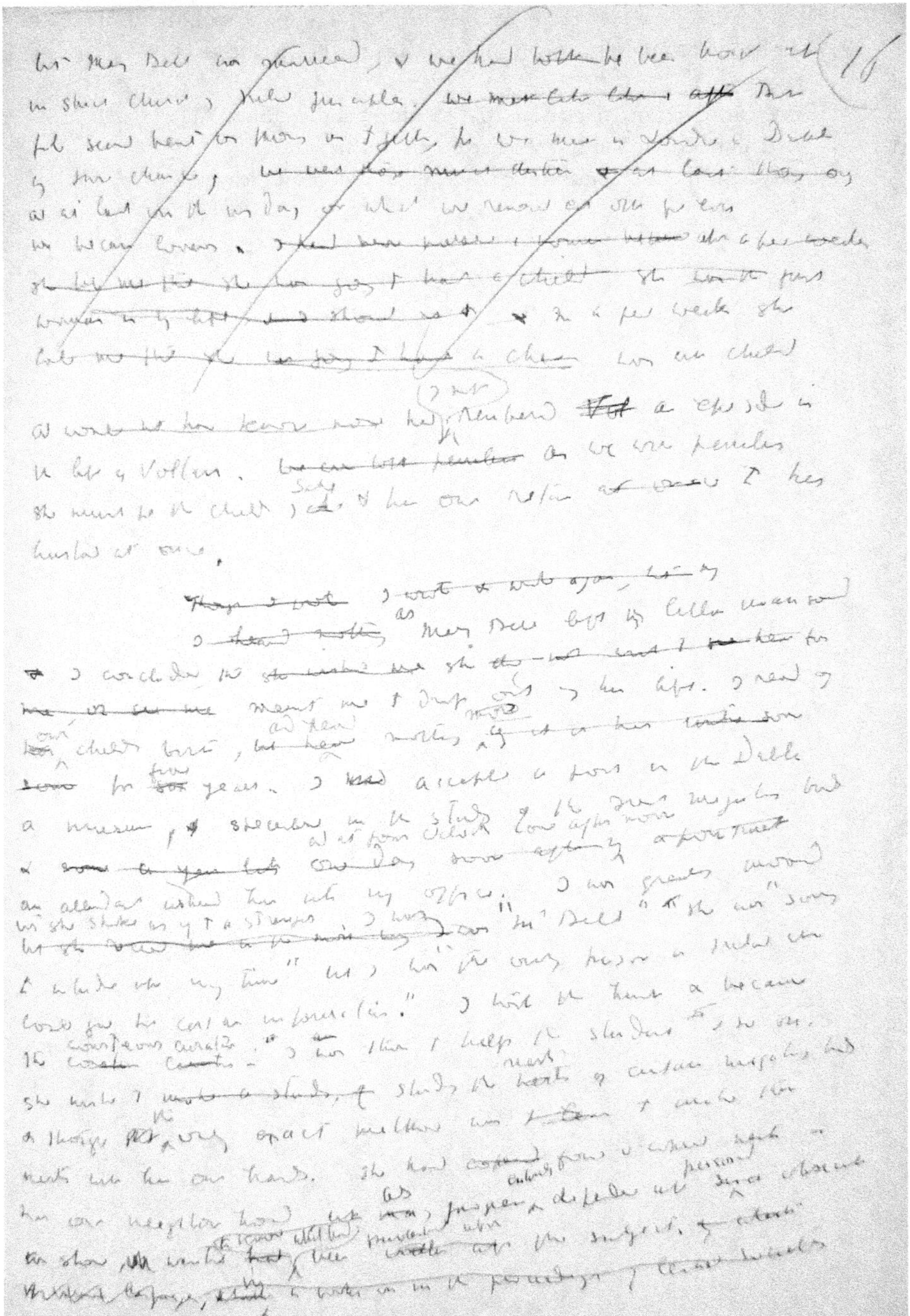

[14ʳ]

1 but Mary Bell was married, & we had ~~both be~~ been brought up 16
2 in strict Church of Ireland principles. ~~We met later later after~~ But
3 fate seemed bent on moving us together, for we met in London & Dublin
4 by some chance, ~~we were there much destined & at last though only~~
5 and at last on the very day on which we renounced each other for ever
6 we became lovers. ~~I had never possessed a woman before~~ after a few weeks
7 ~~she told me that she was going to have a child. She was the first~~
8 ~~woman in my life, & I showed no [?]~~ & In a few weeks she
9 ~~told me that she was going to have a child~~ was with child

I not
10 and ~~would not have known now~~ had ^ remembered ~~Vol~~ an episode in
11 in the life of Voltaire. ~~We were both penniless~~ As we were penniless

sake
12 she must for the childs ~~sake~~ & her own return ~~at once~~ to her
13 husband at once.
14 ~~Though I wrote I wrote & wrote again, but my~~
15 ~~I heard nothing~~ as Mary Bell left my letters unanswered
16 ~~&~~ I concluded that ~~she wished me~~ she ~~did not wish to see hear from~~
17 ~~me, or see me~~ meant me to drop out of her life. I read of

our and heard ~~more~~
18 ~~her~~ ^ childs birth, ~~but never~~ nothing ~~of it or her until some~~

five ^ ^
19 ~~some~~ for ~~six~~ years. I ~~had~~ accepted a post in the Dublin
20 a museum, ~~&~~ specialised in the study of the Irish migratory birds

and at four o clock one after noon
21 & ~~some~~ ~~a year later~~ ~~one day~~ ~~soon after~~ my ^ appointment
22 an attendant ushered her into my office. I was greatly moved

but she spoke as if to a stranger I was
23 ~~but she received me in the [?usual] way I~~ was "Mr. Bell" "she was "sorry
24 to intrude on my time" but I was "the only person in Ireland who
25 could give her certain information." I took the hint & became

courteous curator ~~am~~
26 the ~~courte~~ ~~careter~~. "I was there to help the student" & so on.

nests
27 She wished to ~~make a study of~~ study the ~~nests~~ of certain migratory birds

that
28 & thought ~~that~~ ^ only exact method was ~~to leave~~ to make their
29 nests with her own hands. She had ~~copied~~ found & copied nests in

as entirely personal
30 her own neighbor hood, but ~~may~~ progress ^ depended upon ~~such~~ observation

to know what had published upon ^
31 was slow, ~~&~~ wanted ~~had~~ ^ been ~~written up~~ the subject. ~~of which~~

in
32 ~~in various languages, whether in books or in the proceedings of learned societies.~~

^

NLI 13,577 [15^{r}]

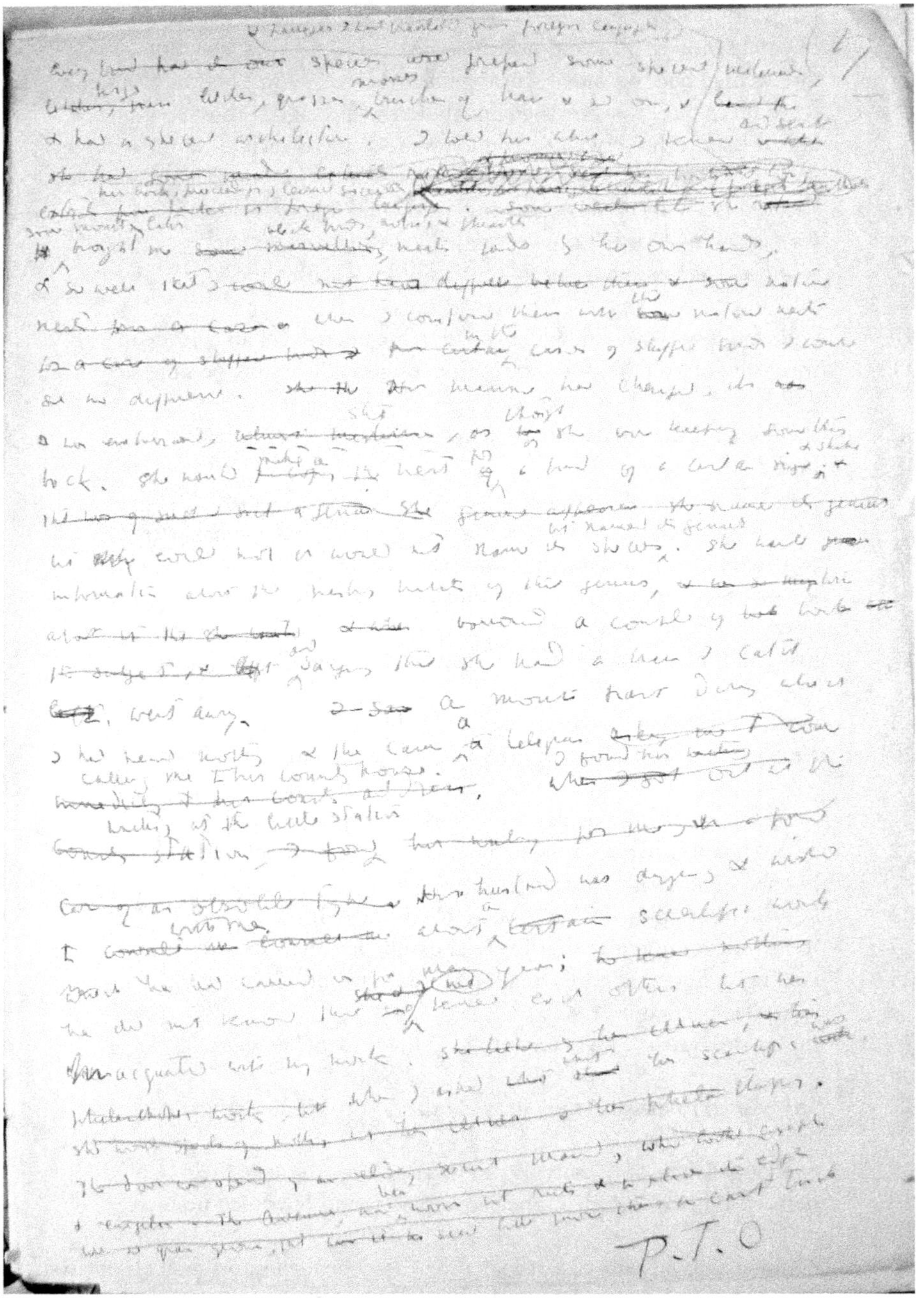

[15r]

(& passages I had translated from foreign languages) (17
Every ~~bird had is own~~ species ~~used~~ prepared some special materials,
twigs mosses
~~litchens, grass~~ litchens, grasses,^ bunches of hair & so on, & ~~learned the~~
& had a special architecture. I told her what I knew ~~& when~~
~~& promised her~~
~~she had gone made extracts & [?returning] home sent her books & long~~
her books, proceedings of learned societies ~~translations and passages translated from foreign authors~~
~~extracts from books in foreign languages. Some weeks later she returned~~
some months later black birds, robins & throstles
~~for~~^ ~~brought me some marvellous~~^ nests made by her own hands
& so well that ~~I could not have difference between them & some~~ natural
the
~~nests from a case or~~ When I compared them with ~~some~~ natural nests
in the
~~from a case of stuffed birds I from certain~~^ cases of stuffed birds I could
see no difference. ~~She the~~ her manner had changed. She ~~was~~
stet though
~~[?]~~ was embarrassed, ~~almost misterious~~, as ~~[?if]~~ she were keeping some thing
make a for ^ & shape
back. She wanted ~~to copy the~~ nest ~~of~~ a bird of a certain size^ ~~of~~
~~that was of such & such a genus She general appearance she named its genus~~
but named its genus
but ~~only~~ could not or would not name its species^. She wanted ~~facts~~
information about the nesting habits of the genus, ~~& was so mysteri[ous]~~
~~about it that she wanted & when~~ borrowed a couple of ~~bok~~ books ~~on~~
and
~~the subject, & but~~^ saying that she had a train to catch
~~left~~ went away. ~~I saw~~ A month past during which
a
I had heard nothing & then came^ ~~a~~ telegram ~~asking me to come~~
calling me to her country house. I found her ~~waiting~~
~~immediately to her country address. When I got out at the~~
waiting at the little station
~~country station~~, ~~I found~~^ her waiting for me, in a good
car of an obsolete type. Her husband was dying, & wished
with me a
to ~~consult me consult me~~ about^ ~~certain~~ scientific work
which he had carried on for many years; ~~he knew nothing~~
~~she & I~~ (we)
he did not know that ~~we~~^ knew each other but was
~~[?]~~ acquainted with my work. ~~She talked of his illness, & his~~
what was
~~philanthropic work, but~~ when I asked ~~what about~~ his scientific ~~work~~,
~~she would speak of nothing but his illness & his philanthropy.~~
~~The door was opened by an elderly servant maid, who looked capable~~
been
~~& energetic. The Avenue had~~^ ~~worn into ruts & in places its edges~~
~~were so grass grown, that now it was seemed little more than a cart track~~
P. T. O

---

11 "almost misterious" (marked "stet") has been restored.

31 (lower right) "P.T.O" directs that, from lines 27, the narrative continues on 15v.

NLI 13,577 [15v]

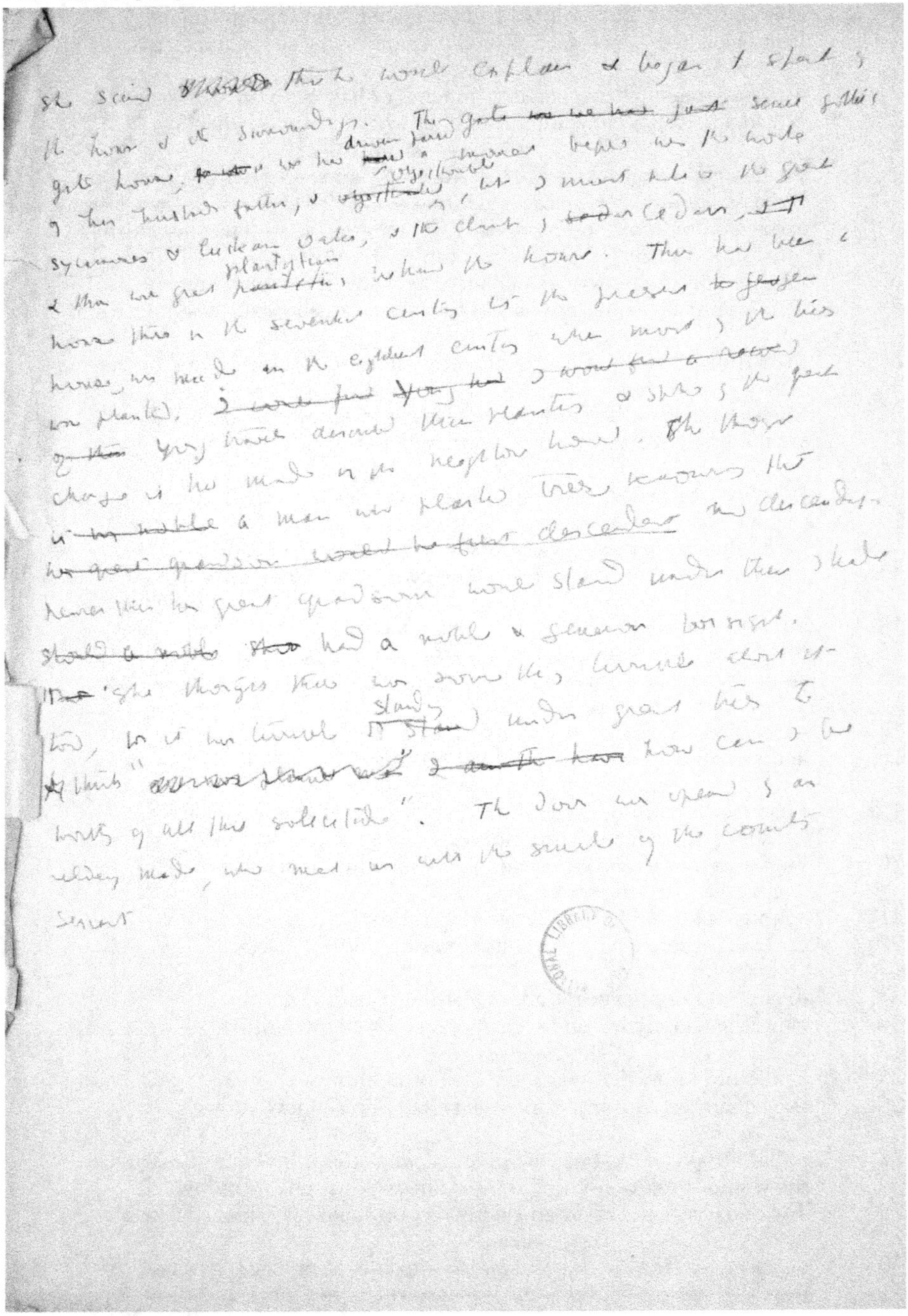

[15^{v}]

She said ~~I would~~ that he would explain & began to speak of
the house & its surroundings. The ~~Gate we we had just~~ semi gothic
driven passed
gate house, ~~from which~~ we had ~~passed~~ a moment before was the work
objectionable
of her husbands father, & ~~objectionded~~$_{\wedge}$, but I must notice the great
sycamores & luckam oaks, & the clump of ~~cedars~~ cedars, ~~& th~~
plantations
& there were great ~~plantations~~ behind the house. There had been a
house there in the seventeenth century but the present ~~the Georgian~~
house, was made in the eighteenth century when most of the trees
were planted. ~~I would find Young had I would find a record~~
~~of this~~ Young travels described their planting & spoke of the great
change it had made in the neighbor hood. She thought
~~it very noble~~ a man who planted trees, knowing that
~~his great grandson would be first descendent~~ no descendent
nearer than his great grandson would stand under their shade
~~should a noble should~~ had a noble & generous fore sight.
~~But~~ She that there was some thing terrible about it
standing
too, for it was terrible ~~to stand~~ under great trees to
~~[?say]~~ think "~~All was planned [?once]" I am the have~~ how can I be
worthy of all this solicitude". The door was opened by an
elderly made, who met us with the smile of the country
servant

5 "luckam" eventually spelled "lucombe" in *SMR* and *AVB*.
20 "made" for "maid."

NLI 13,577 [16r]

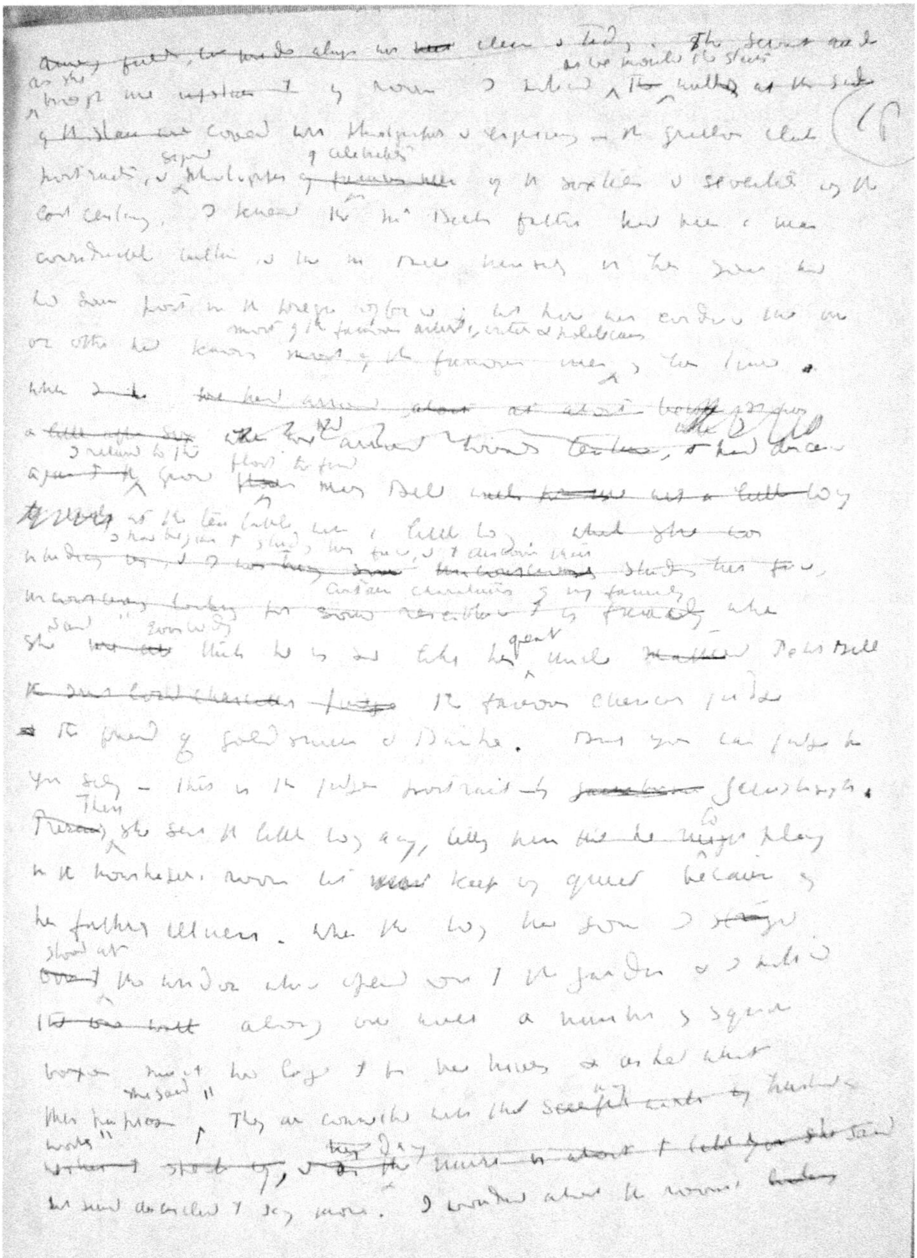

[16ʳ]

1 ~~Among fields, was made always was neat clean & tidy. The servant~~
As she as we mounted the stairs
2 ‸brought me ~~upstairs~~ to my room I noticed‸~~the~~‸walls ~~I~~ ~~at the side~~
3 ~~of the stairs~~ were covered with photographs & engravings—the Grillion Club (18)
signed of celebrities
4 portraits, &‸photographs ~~of famous men~~ of the sixties & seventies of the
5 last century. I knew that Mr Bells father had been a man [of]
6 considerable culture, & the Mr Bell himself in his youth had
7 had some post in the foreign office; but here was evidence that one
most of the famous artists, writers & politicians
8 or other had known ~~most of the famous men~~‸of his time.
9 When ~~I h~~ ~~we had arrived about~~ ~~at about before it was~~
had
10 ~~a little after six~~ ~~when we arrived toward towards tea time & had descended~~
I returned to the floor to find
11 ~~again to the~~‸ground ~~flour~~ Mary Bell ~~waiting for us with a little boy~~
12 ~~to lunch~~ at the tea table with a little boy. ~~While she was~~
I had begun to study his face, & to discover there
13 ~~introducing us, & I was being serv[ed]~~ ~~unconsciously studying his face~~
certain characteristics of my family
14 ~~unconsciously looking for some resemblance to my family~~ when
said everybody great
15 she ~~we all~~ thinks he is so like his‸uncle ~~Matthew~~ Peter Bell
16 ~~the Irish lord Chancer[y]~~ ~~Judge~~ the famous Chancery Judge
17 ~~&~~ the friend of Goldsmith & Burke. But you can judge for
18 your self—that is the judges portrait by ~~gainsbrou~~ Gainsborough.
Then to
19 ~~Presently~~‸she sent the little boy away, telling him ~~that he might~~ play
20 in the housekeepers room but ~~must~~ keep very quiet because of
21 his fathers illness—When the boy had gone I ~~strayed~~
stood at
22 ~~over to~~‸the window which opened out to the garden & I noticed
23 ~~that one wall~~ along one wall a number of square
24 boxes much too large to be bee hives & asked what
She said my
25 their purpose‸"They are connected with that ~~scientific work my~~ husbands
work" ~~his~~ day
26 ~~wishes to~~ ~~speak of~~, ~~& as the~~ ~~nurse is about to tell you she said~~
‸
27 but seemed disinclined to say more. I wandered about the room, ~~looking~~

NLI 13,577 [17r]

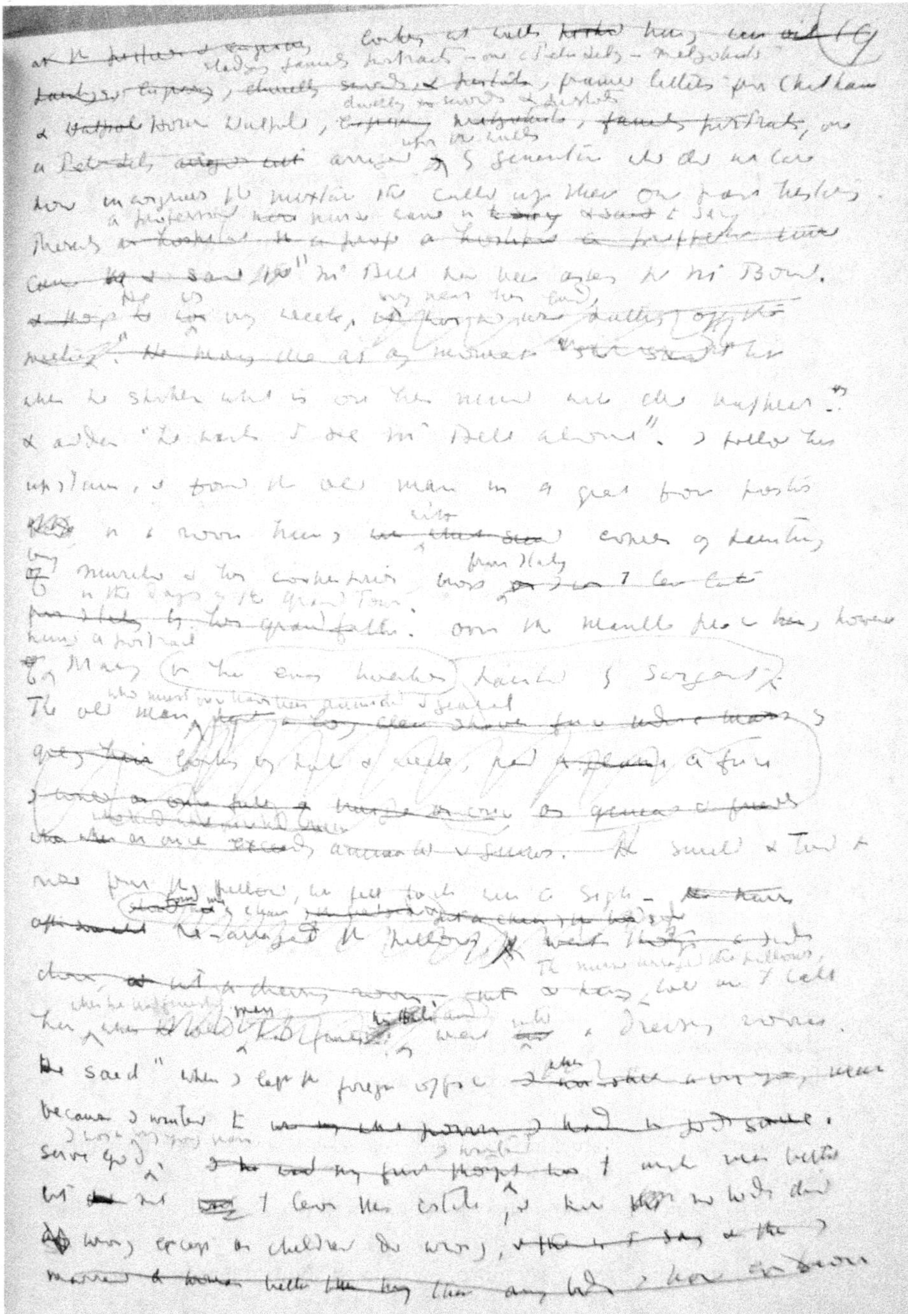

[17r]

~~at the pictures & engravings~~ ~~looking at walls packed hung with oil~~ 19
studying family portraits—one a Peter Lely—metzotints
~~paintings, engravings,~~ ~~duelling swords & portraits~~, framed letters from Chatham
duelling ~~w~~ swords & pistols
& ~~Walpole~~ Horace Walpole, ~~engravings~~ ~~metzotints~~, ~~family portraits,~~ one
upon the walls
a Peter Lely ~~arranged out~~ arranged ^ by generations who did not care
how incongruous the mixture that called up their own past history
a professional ~~nerse~~ nurse came in ~~to say~~ ~~& said~~ to say
Presently ~~an hospital [?nurse]~~ ~~a prof~~ ~~a hospital~~ ~~a profession~~ ~~nurse~~
~~came in & said~~ ~~that~~ "Mr Bell has been asking for Mr Bond.
He is very near his end,
~~& though he~~ ~~was~~ very weak, ~~it was no use putting off that~~
^
~~matter." He may die at any moment" she said~~ "but
when he [has] spoken what is on his mind will die happier."
& added "he wants to see Mr Bell alone". I followed her
up stairs, & found the old man in a great four poster
with
~~bed~~, in a room hung ~~with what seemed~~ copies of paintings
by from Italy
~~of~~ Muril[l]o & his contemporaries, brought ^ ~~as I was to learn later~~
in the days of the Grand Tour.
~~from Italy by his grand father~~. Over the Murillo piece ~~hung~~ however
hung a portrait
of ^ Mary (in her early twenties) painted by Sargent ^
who must once have been animated & ~~geneal~~
The old man ^ ~~had a long clean shaven face under a mass of~~
~~grey hair~~ looking very pale & weak, had ~~a plane~~ a face
~~I could at once face an image at once~~ ~~as genial & friendly~~
who had what once had been
~~[?which] when as once exceeding[ly] animated & genial.~~ He smiled & tried to
rise from the pillow, but fell back with a sigh ~~— the nurse~~
found me
(~~showed me~~ a chair ~~by the bed side &~~)
~~after some while~~ re-arranged the pillows ^ & ~~went~~ ~~through a side~~
The nurse arranged the pillows,
~~door, & into a dressing room. that was nearby~~ ^ told me to call
when he had finished man his tale and into
her ^ ~~when the old~~ ^ ~~had finished~~ ^ went ~~out~~ a dressing room.
when
He said "When I left the foreign office ~~I was still a very young man~~
because I wanted to ~~use my what powers I had in gods service.~~
I was a very young man I wanted
serve God ^ . ~~I had want~~ ~~my first thought was~~ to make men better
but ~~did~~ not ~~want~~ to leave this estate, & here ~~they~~ no body did
~~any~~ wrong except as children do wrong, ~~& that is to say~~ ~~& then I~~
~~married a woman better than any than any body & [?became] anxious~~

NLI 13,577 [18r]

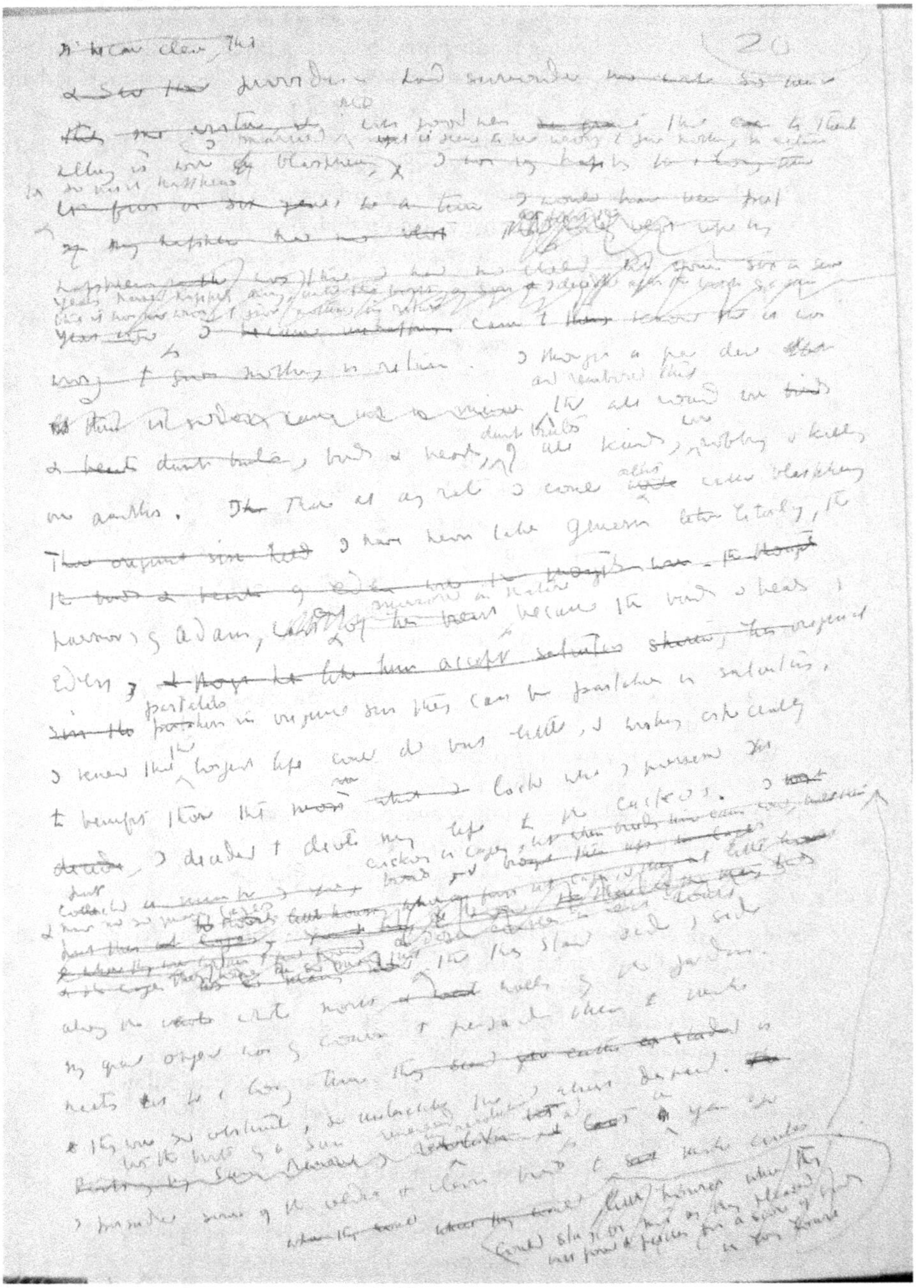

[18r]

~~It became clear that~~ 20
~~& said that~~ providence had surrounded ~~me with so much~~
me
~~this me virtue, it~~ ^ with goodness ~~so great~~ that ~~even~~ to think
I married ~~yet~~ it seemed to me wrong to give nothing in return
altering it were ~~a~~ blasphemy ^ ~~I was very happy~~ ~~for a long time~~
for so much happiness
^ ~~for five or six years~~ ~~for a time~~ ~~I would have been~~
~~At first the~~
~~If my happiness had no blot~~ ~~the only blot upon my~~
~~happiness in the was that I had no child but some six or seven~~
years passed happily away until ~~the birth [of] a son &~~ I decided after the birth of a son
that it was not wrong to give nothing in return
~~years ago~~ ^ I ~~became unhappy~~ came to ~~think~~ know that it was
I thought a great deal ~~about~~
~~wrong to give nothing in return~~ and remembered that
~~but then it sud[d]enly came into my mind~~ ^ that all round one ~~birds~~
dumb brutes were
~~& beasts~~ ~~dumb brutes~~, birds & beasts, ^ of all kinds, ^ robbing & killing
alter
one another. ~~I ha~~ There at any rate I could ~~work~~ without blasphemy
^
~~There original sin held~~ I have never taken Genesis ~~liter~~ literal[l]y, the
~~birds & beasts of Eden were the thoughts born the thoughts~~
~~out~~ mirroured in nature
passions of Adam, ~~cast~~ ^ ~~off his breast~~ ^ became the birds & beasts of
Eden, ~~& though he like him accept salvation~~ ~~sharing his original~~
partakers
~~sin the~~ ~~pertakers~~ in original sin they can be partakers in salvation.
the
I knew that ^ longest life could do but little, & wishing especially
~~w~~
to benefit those that ~~most~~ ~~what I~~ lacked what I possessed ~~I~~
~~decided~~ I decided to devote my life to the cucko[o]s. I ~~bought~~
put cuckos in cages, ~~but when breeding time came round, built them~~
~~collected a number of young birds,~~ & ~~brought them up in cages~~
& have now so many cages
~~the roosts~~ ~~little houses which at first were cages, & then but little houses~~
~~put them into cages, you d say & now there~~ there were so many birds
~~in which they were contained to find food a dozen couples in each house~~
~~These houses are so many that~~
~~& the cages~~ ~~are so many now~~ ^ that they stand side by side
along the ~~whole~~ whole north ~~& west~~ walls of the garden.
My great object was of course to persuade them to make
nests but for a long time ~~they seemed given either [?] studied or~~
~~[?]~~ they were so obstinate, so unteachable that I almost despaired. ~~The~~
but the birth of a son renewed my resolution ~~but~~ and a
~~Birth of my son~~ ~~renewed my resolution, &~~ ~~last~~ ~~[?a]~~ year ago
^ ^ ^
I persuaded some of the oldest & cleverest birds to ~~build~~ make circles
~~where they would~~
~~where they could~~
~~little houses where they could stay or nest as they pleased with food & perches for a score of birds in every house~~

24

NLI 13,577 [19r]

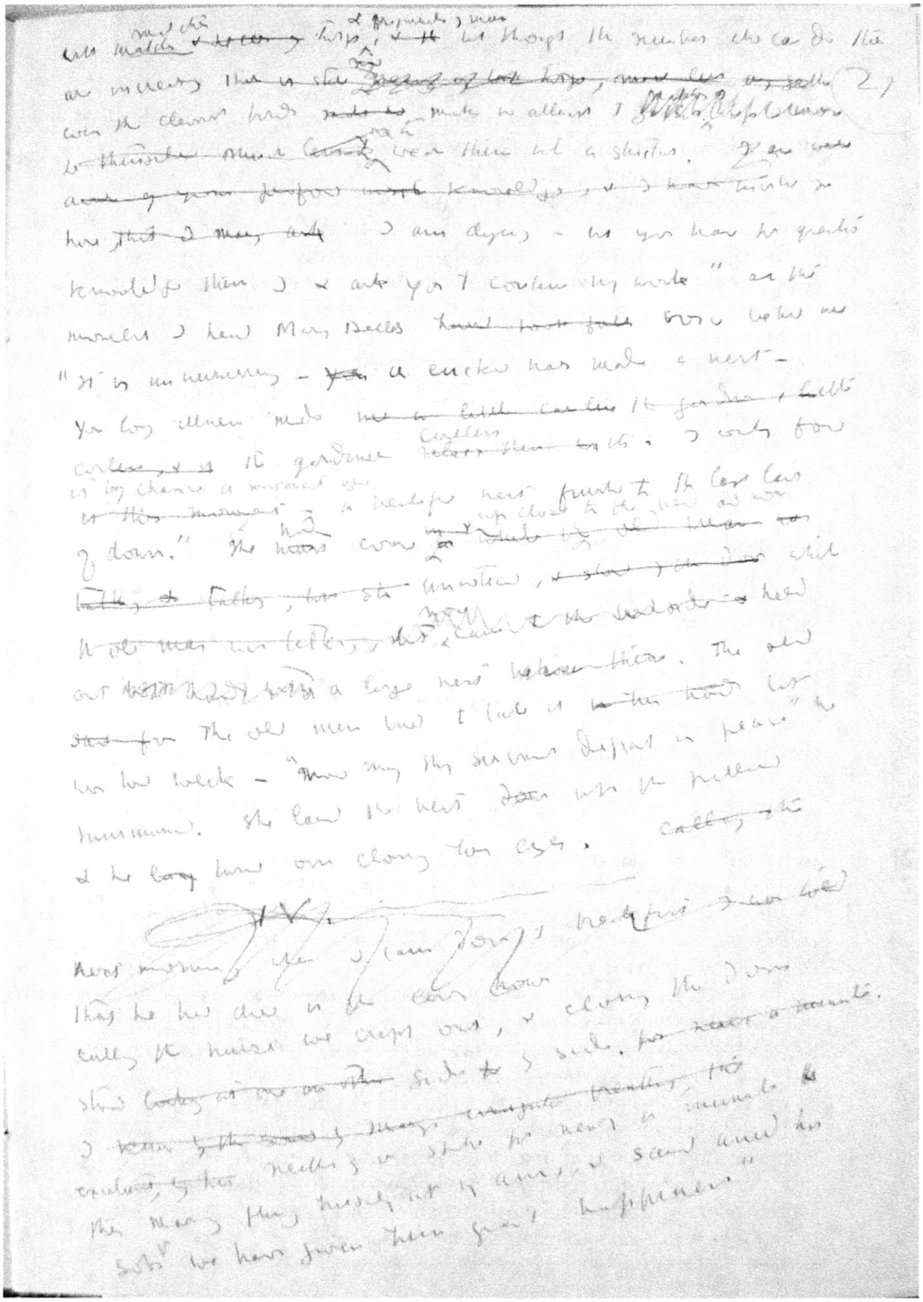

[19^r]

matches & fragments of moss
with ~~matches & pieces of~~ twigs^, ~~& the~~ but though the number who can do this
no
are increasingly ~~that us still~~^ ~~weaving of tree twigs, much less any gather~~ (21
[?matches] ~~of~~
even the cleverest of birds ~~make no~~ make no attempt to ~~gather~~^ ~~twigs & more~~
~~[?return]~~
~~for themselves~~ ~~much~~ ~~less to~~^ weave them into a structure. ~~I am well~~
~~aware of your profound insite knowledge, & I have invited you~~
here ~~that I may ask~~ I am dying—but you have far greater
knowledge than I & ask you to continue my work" at that
moment I heard Mary Bells ~~hand book fall~~ voice behind me
"It is unnecessary—~~you~~ a cucko[o] has made a nest—
Your long illness made ~~me a little care less~~ ~~the gardeners a little~~
careless
~~careless, & [?]~~ the gardeners ~~relax their watch~~. I only found
it by chance a moment ago
~~it this moment~~—a beautiful nest finished to the last lay[er]
had ~~in &~~ up close to the bed and was
of down." She ~~must~~ come^ ~~in while the old man was~~
~~talking & talking, and sto~~ unnoticed, ~~& stood by the door~~ while
now
~~the old man was talking, but~~^ ~~came to the bed side &~~ held
out ~~both hands with~~ a large nest ~~between them~~. The old
~~said from~~ The old man tried to take it ~~from her hands~~ but
but was too weak—"Now may thy servant depart in peace" he
murmered. She laid the nest ~~down~~ upon the pillow
& he ~~lay~~ turned over closing his eyes. ~~Calling the~~

~~IV~~

Next morning when I came down to breakfast I was told
that he had died in the early hours
calling the nurse we crept out, & closing the door
stood ~~looking at one another~~ side ~~to~~ by side ~~for nearly a minute~~
I ~~knew by the sound of Marys irregular breathing, the~~
~~excitement, of her~~ Neither of us spoke for nearly a minute ~~th~~
Then Mary flung herself into my arms, & said amid her
sobs "we have given him great happiness"

The cancellation of "IV" at line 21, as well as on page 22, at lines 1 and 24, might have contributed to the unusual omission of the numeral in *SMR*. See Part Four, section 2 below.

NLI 13,577 [20r]

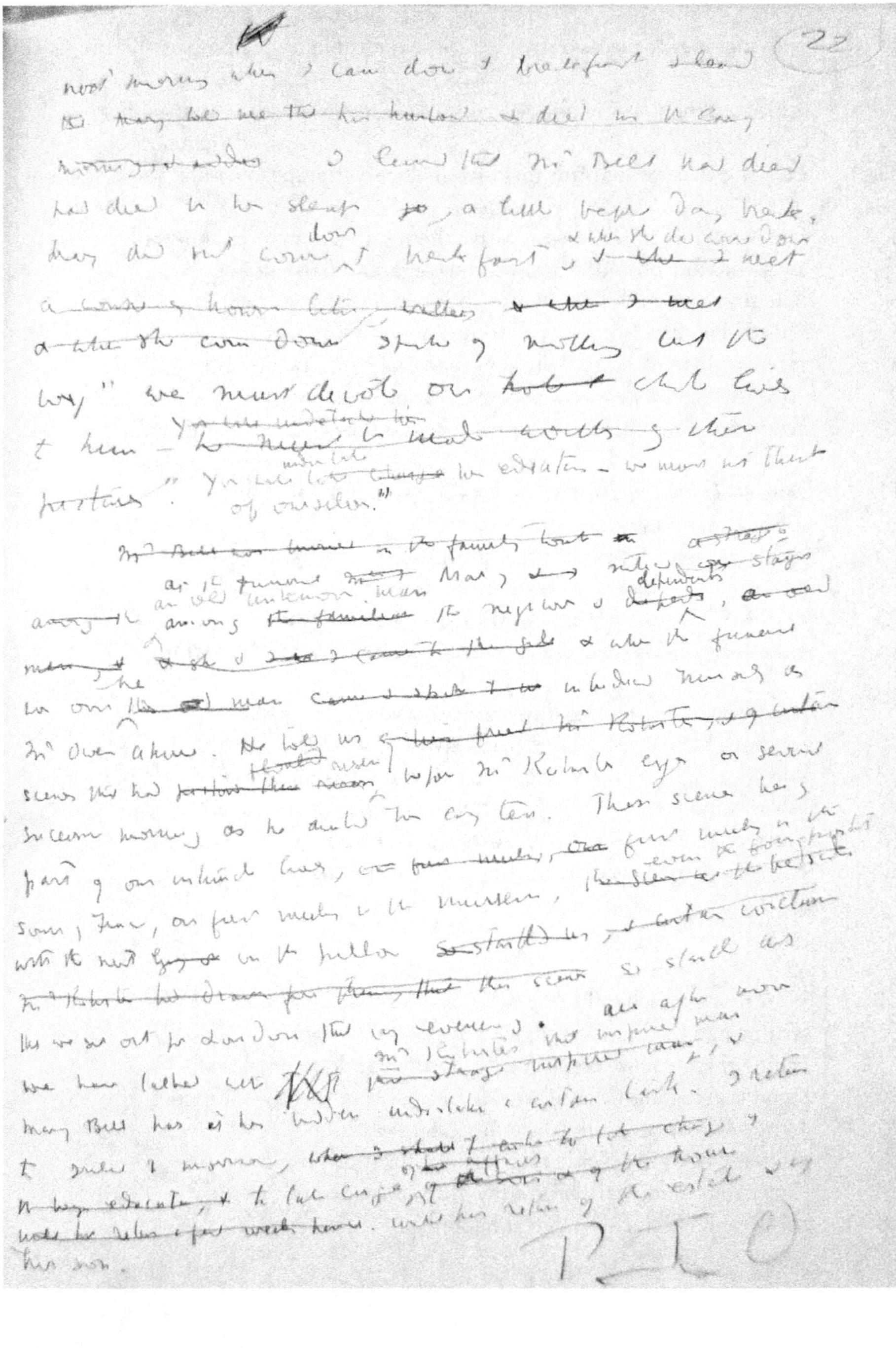

22

next morning when I came down to breakfast I learned [illegible] I learned that Mrs Bell had died had died in her sleep a little before day break. Mary did not come down to breakfast & when she came down I met [illegible] speaking of nothing but the way" we must devote our [illegible] child lives to him – [illegible] parties" You will undertake his education – we must not think of ourselves."

At the funeral Mary & [illegible] stayed among the neighbours & dependents [illegible] & when the funeral [illegible] he [illegible] as Mr Owen Aherne. He told us [illegible] scenes that had risen before Mr Robartes eyes on several successive mornings as he awoke from his long trance. These scenes being part of our inherited lives, [illegible] even the [illegible] seen, then, on [illegible] in the mansion, [illegible] with the [illegible] in the hollow [illegible] so startled us [illegible] the scene [illegible] all after noon that we set out for London that very evening. [illegible] Mr Robartes [illegible] & we have talked [illegible] Mary Bell has [illegible] undertaken a certain task. I return to [illegible] tomorrow, [illegible] & to take charge of [illegible] the house [illegible] until her return of the [illegible] with her son.

P. T. O.

[20^{r}]

~~IV~~ (22)

Next morning when I came down to breakfast ~~I learned~~
~~that Mary told me that her husband had died in the early~~
~~morning, & added~~ I learned that Mr Bell had died
had died in his sleep ~~in~~, a little before day break.
down & when she did come down
Mary did not come$_{\wedge}$to breakfast, ~~& when I me~~t
~~a couple of hours later, nothing & when I met~~
~~& when she came down~~ spoke of nothing but the
boy "We must devote our ~~hole l~~ whole lives
You will undertake his
to him~~—he must be made worthy of~~ these
undertake
~~pictures.~~~~"~~ You will ~~take charge~~ of his education—we must not think
of ourselves."
~~Mr Bell was buried in the family tomb in~~ ~~a stranger~~
At the funeral ~~M^{rs} B~~ Mary ~~& I~~ noticed ~~one stranger~~
an old unknown man dependants
~~among the~~$_{\wedge}$among ~~the familiar~~ the neighbors & ~~depends~~, ~~an old~~
$\wedge$
~~man, & & she & I we I came to the gate~~ & when the funeral
he
was over$_{\wedge}$ ~~this old man came & spoke to us~~ introduced himself as
Mr Owen Aherne. He told us ~~of his friend Mr Robartes, & of certain~~
~~floated~~ risen
of scenes that had ~~pictured there risen~~$_{\wedge}$before Mr Robartes eyes on several
successive mornings as he awaited his early tea. These scenes being
part of our intimate lives, ~~our first meeting, our~~ first meeting in the
even the four-poster
south of France, our first meeting in the Museum, ~~the scene at the bedside~~
with the nest ~~lying on~~ on the pillow ~~so startled us, & certain conclusions~~
~~Mr Robartes had drawn from them, that these scenes~~ so startled us
that we set out for London that very evening. All after noon
Mr Robartes that inspired man
we have talked with ~~IV~~ ~~that strange inspired man~~$_{\wedge}$, &
Mary Bell has at his bidding undertaken a certain task. I return
to Ireland to morrow, ~~where I shall to enter to take charge~~ of
~~of her affairs~~
~~the boys education, &~~ to take charge$_{\wedge}$~~of the son & of the house~~
~~until her return a few weeks hence.~~ until her return of the estate & of
her son. P. T. O

28 The direction "P.T.O" refers one to the verso of this folio (20^{v}), a long single page of work to constitute episode "IV," the beginning of which had false starts on pages 21 and 22.

NLI 13,577 [20v]

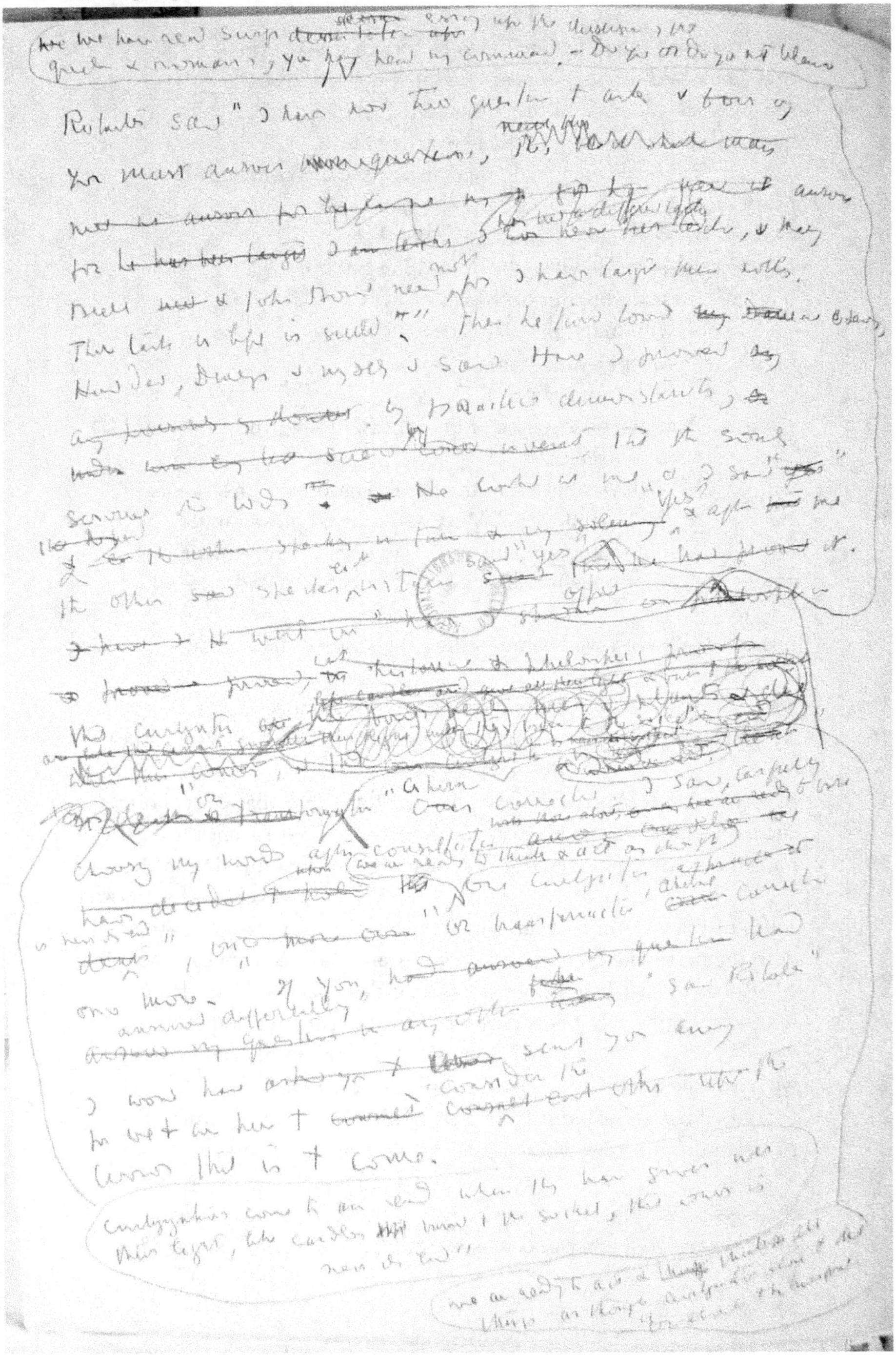

[20[v]]

~~essay~~ essay upon the dissensions of the
13 ~~We~~ We have need Swifts ~~dissertation upon~~
14 Greeks & romans, you have heard my comments—Do you or do you not believe
IV
1 Robartes said "I have now two questions to ask & four of
~~need this~~
2 you must answer ~~those questions~~ ~~This black shirt man~~
3 ~~need not answer for he is not my [?s] for he need not~~ answer
~~have had a different teacher~~
4 for ~~he has been taught~~ ~~I am teacher~~ ~~I was never his teacher,~~ & Mary
not
5 Bell ~~need~~ & John Bond need^for I have taught them nothing.
6 Their task in life is settled.~~"~~ " Then he turned toward ~~my~~ ~~Daneal~~ O Leary,
7 Huddon, Denys & myself & said Have I proved by
8 ~~any possibility of doubt~~ by practical demonstrations, ~~or~~
~~by~~
9 ~~under~~ ~~with every test science could invent,~~ that the soul
10 survives the body.~~"~~ we He looked at me & I said "~~yes~~"
~~then repeated~~ "Yes"
11 & ~~to the others speaking in turn & very solemnly~~^&after" ~~that~~ me
^ each said "Yes"^
12 the others ~~said~~ speaking^in turn ~~said~~ ~~that~~ ~~he had proved~~ it
offered ^
15 ~~I have I He went on "have I shown a philosophic~~
with
16 ~~& proved—proved,~~ ~~in~~ ~~historical and philosophical proofs~~
~~like candles and give all their light & burn to the socket~~
17 that civilizations ~~are~~ ~~like birds beasts men & plants & die~~
~~are like that cannot give all their light until they burn to the socket & end~~
18 ~~When this comes,~~ ~~& that our civilization has reached its end~~ ~~death~~
~~is near its end~~

NLI 13,577 [20v]

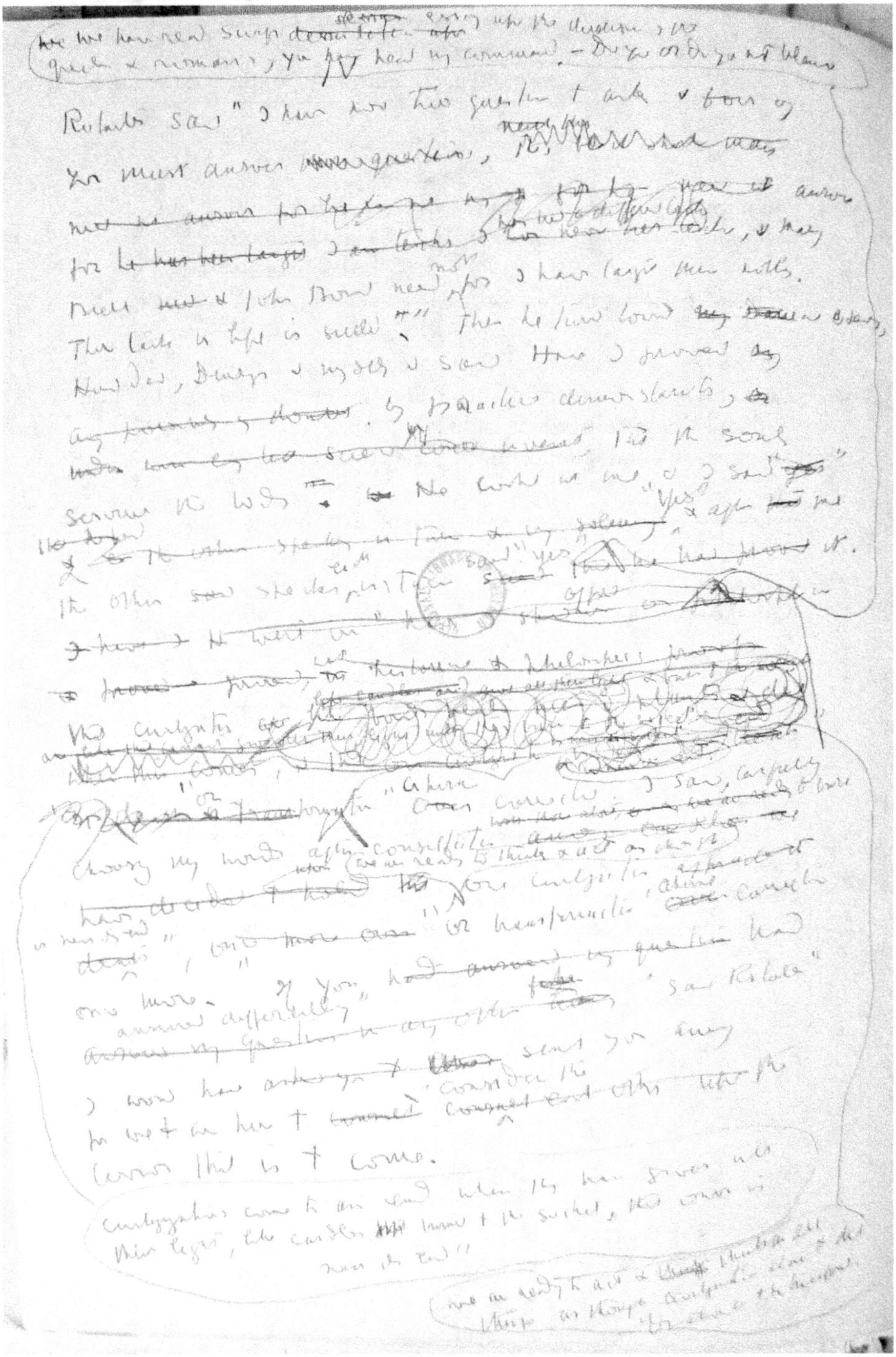

[20ᵛ continued]

“or Aherne

19 “~~Its~~ ~~death & transformation~~” ~~Owen~~ corrected. I said, carefully

~~with those about & as we are ready~~ to bare

26 choosing my words after consultation ~~among ourselves~~ ~~we~~

~~upon~~ We are ready to think & act as though,

27 ~~have decided to hold~~ ~~that~~ our civilization ~~approaches its~~

is near its end Aherne

28 ~~death~~”, ~~once more our~~ “Or transformation” ~~Owen~~ corrected

29 once more. If you ~~had answered my question~~ had

answered differently ~~fashion~~

30 ~~answered my question in any other way.~~” said Robartes “

31 I would have ~~asked you to leave~~ sent you away

consider the

32 for we ~~[?]~~ are here to ~~comment~~ ~~consult each other upon~~ the

^

33 terror that is to come.

20 Civilizations come to an end when they have given all

21 their light, like candles ~~that~~ burned to the socket, that ours is

22 near its end”

23 We are ready to act & ~~think~~ think in all

24 things as though civilization about to die

25 or about to be transformed

The transcription of this busiest of all pages of the manuscript is here complete.

NLI 13,577 [21r]

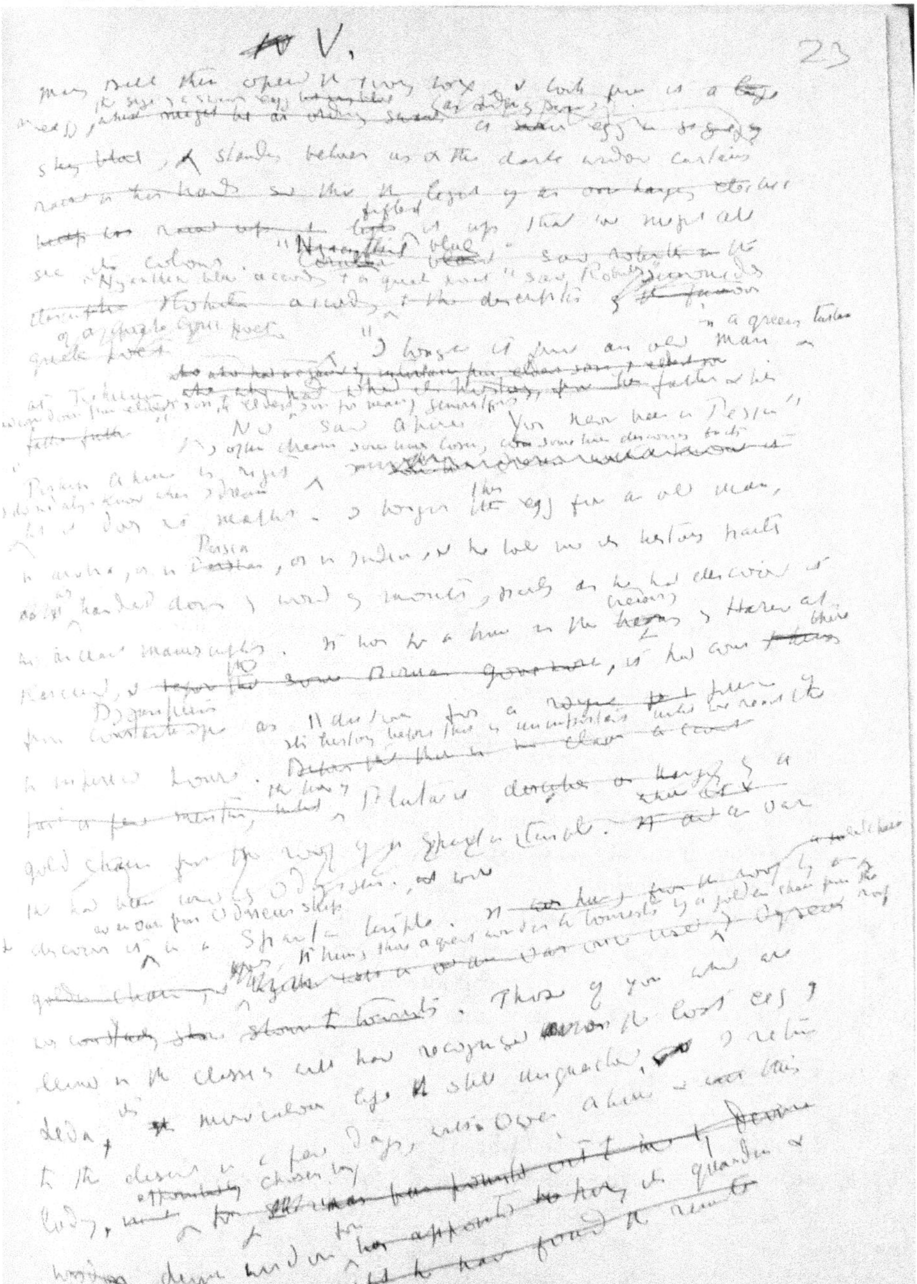

[21r]

~~IV~~ V. 23

Mary Bell then opened the ivory box, & took from it ~~a large~~
the size of a swans egg ~~but very blue~~ (an ordinary swans egg)
an egg, ~~which might be an ordinary swans~~ ~~a swans egg in size and~~^ ~~but~~
~~sky blue~~, & standing between us & the dark window curtains
~~raised in her hands so that the light of an over hanging electric~~
lifted
~~lamp was~~ ~~raised up to~~ ~~light~~^ it up that we might all
"Hyacythine blue"
see its colour "~~Cerulean bleu~~" ~~said Robartes in~~ the
"Hya[ci]nthine blue according to a Greek poet" said Robartes, ~~according [to]~~
~~descriptions~~ ~~Robartes according~~^ ~~to the descriptions~~ ~~of the famous~~
of a Greek lyric poet
~~Greek poet~~ in a green turbon
^ "I brought it from an old man^
~~who~~ ~~who had acquired it by inheritance from eldest son to eldest son~~
at Teheran ~~who~~ ~~who had what its history from his father & his~~
It had come down from eldest son for many generations"
~~fathers father~~" ^ "No" said Aherne "You never been in Persia"
I often dream some times losing [?but] some times discovering facts
"Perhaps Aherne is right^ ~~I some times dream without know[ing] it~~
I do not always know when I dream this
^but it does not matter. I bought ~~the~~ egg from an old man,
Persia
in Arabia, or in ~~Persha~~, or in India, & he told me its history partly
as
~~as it~~^ handed down by word of mouth, partly as he had discovered it
treasury
in ancient manuscripts. It was for a time in the ~~treasury~~ of Harun al
that there
Raschid, & ~~before that some Roman governor~~, & had come ~~to him~~
Byzantium
from ~~Constantinople~~ as ransom for a ~~royal~~ ~~prin~~ prince of
Its history before that is unimportant until we read that
the imperial house. ~~Before that there is no clear account~~
that line of
~~just a few mentions, which~~^ Plutarch ~~describes as hanging~~ by a
~~where it &~~
gold chain from the roof of a Spartan Temple. ~~It and~~ an oar
that had been owned by Odysseus, ~~was~~ were
and an oar from Odysseus ship ~~a golden chain~~
He discovered it^ in a Spartan temple. ~~It was hung from the roof by a~~^
~~hung~~ it hung there a great wonder to tourists by a golden chain from the
~~golden chain, &~~^ ~~together with old an oar once used by Odysseus~~ roof
was ~~constantly~~ ~~shown~~ ~~shown to tourists~~. Those of you who are
learned in the classics will have recognized ~~it as~~ the lost egg of
its
Leda, ~~its~~ miraculous life ~~st~~ still unquenched, ~~& I~~ I return
to the desert in a few days, with Owen Aherne & ~~with~~ this
~~appointed by~~ chosen by
lady, ~~chosen~~^ for^ ~~she has been pointed out to me by devine~~
for
~~wisdom~~ devine wisdom^ ~~has appointed M Mary~~ its guardian &
bearer. ~~Which we have found the remote~~

NLI 13,577 [22r]

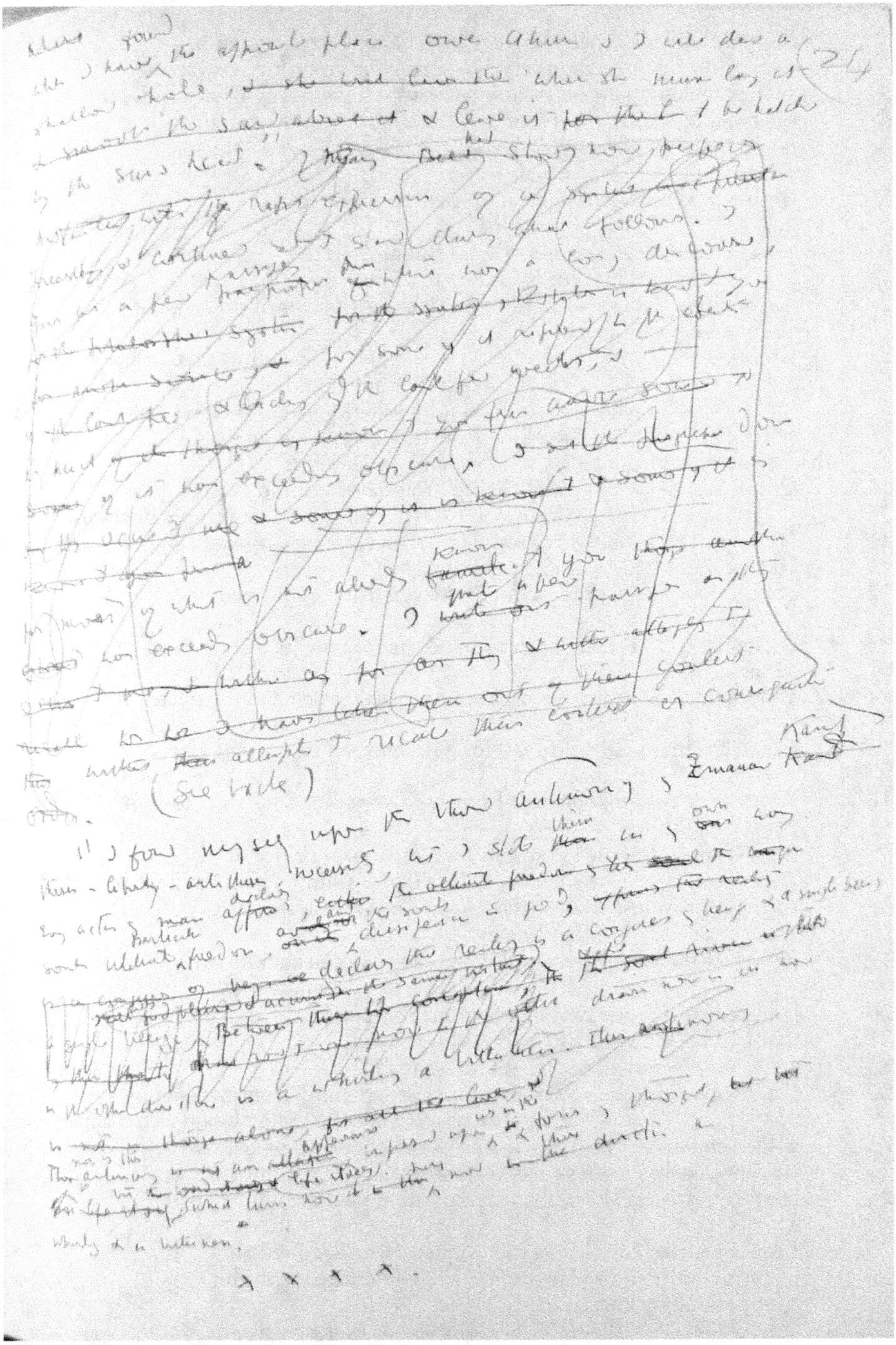

The thoroughly cancelled, circumscribed passage in the upper half of this page is revised on the verso (22v), as directed at line 20: "(See back)".

[22r]

~~Aherne~~ found
When I have ^ the appointed place Owen Aherne & I will dig a (24
shallow hole, ~~& she will leave the~~ where she must lay it
~~& smooth the sand about it~~ & leave it ~~for the h~~ to be hatched
had
by the suns heat." ~~Mary Bell stood now perfectly~~
distracted with the rapt expression of a ~~Sybil or a priestess~~
priestess & continued so to stand during what followed. I
passages from
gave out a few ~~paragraphs~~ ~~of~~ what was a long discourse,
~~from the philosophical system~~ ~~from the system of Robartes is known to you~~
~~from another source, &~~ for some of it referred to the events
of ~~the last few~~ & teachings of the last few weeks, &—
for much ~~of the thought is known to you from another source~~ &
~~some~~ of it was exceedingly obscure, ~~I set the paragraphs~~ down
~~as they occur to me~~ ~~& some of it is known to [you?] & some of it~~ is
~~known to you from a~~ known
for most of what is not already ~~familiar~~ to you ~~through another~~
quote a few
~~extract~~ was exceedingly obscure. I ~~write out~~ passages as they
~~occur to me, & without any~~ ~~for as they~~ ~~& without attempting to~~
~~recall~~ ~~for [?that] I have taken them out of their context~~
~~thus~~ ~~without their attempting to recall their context or consequitive~~
~~order.~~ (See back)
I Kant
"I found myself upon the third antinomy of {I/E} manua[l] ~~Kand~~
them own
thesis—liberty—antithesis—necessity, but I state ~~them~~ in my ~~own~~ way
declares
Every action of man ~~affirms~~, ~~either~~ ~~the ultimate freedom of his soul~~ ~~the unique~~
and
particular ~~and its or~~
souls ultimate ^ freedom, ~~on its~~ ^ dissappearance in god, ~~affirms that reality~~
~~is a congeries of beings or~~ declares that reality is a congeries of beings & a single being
(~~I call god blessed & accurst~~) ~~In the same instant~~ ^ ~~Life~~
a single being ^ between these two conceptions, in ~~the soul riven in [?two]~~
~~by these theses to draw now to one now to the other~~ ~~drawn now in one now~~
in the other direction in a whirling bitterness. This antinomy
~~is not in thought alone, for all that lives~~ &
nor is this appearance us in the
~~This~~ ^ antinomy ~~is not~~ an ~~illusion~~ imposed upon ^ ~~a~~ ^ form of thought, ~~but~~ ~~but~~
but ~~to ward itself &~~ (life itself) here there
~~upon life itself~~, which turns now ~~to~~ ~~in this~~ ^ now ~~in that direction~~ a
whirling & a bitterness"

XXXX

NLI 13,577 [22v]

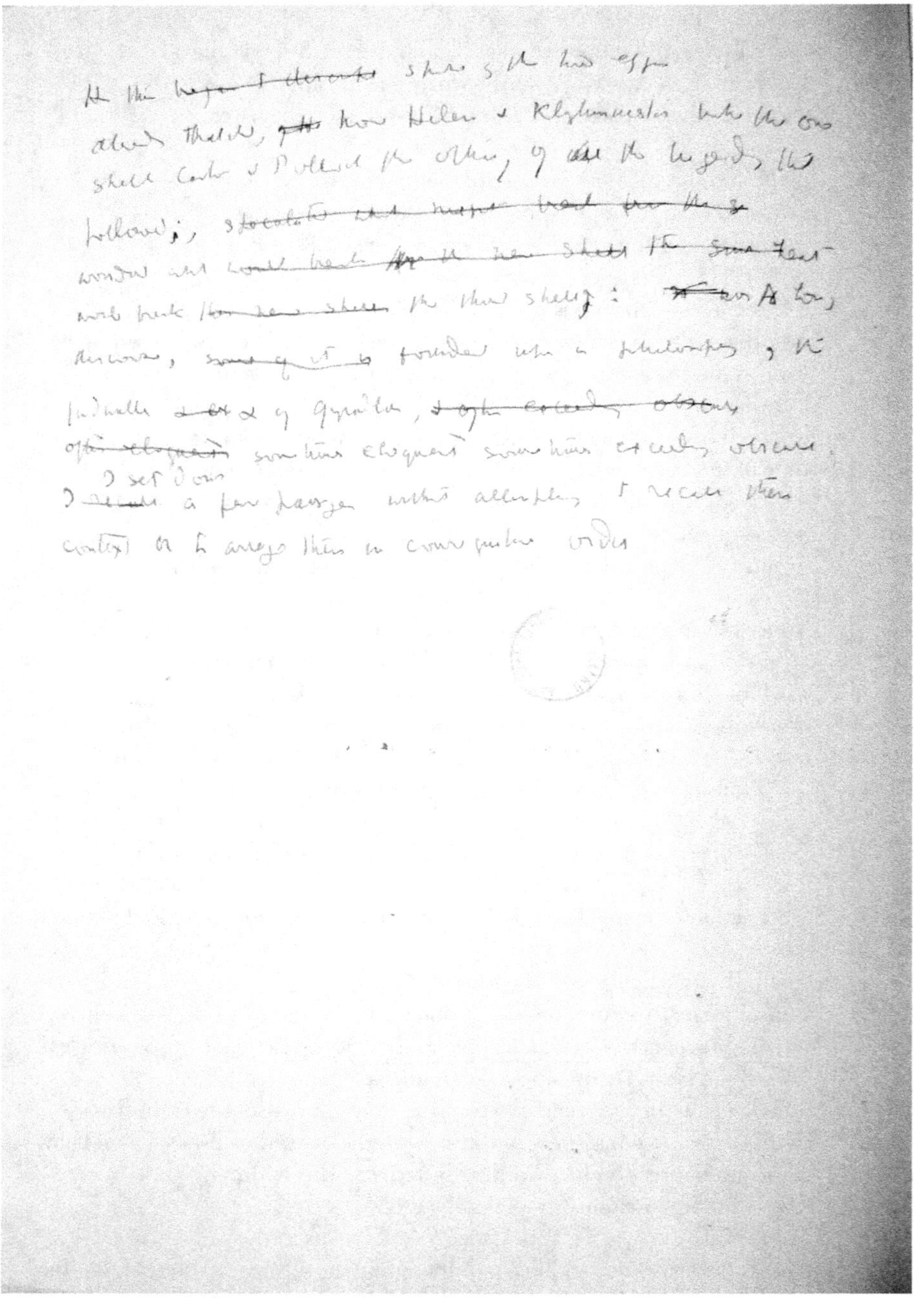
At this [illegible] shows the two eggs
already hatched, how Helen & Klytemnestra broke the one
shell Castor & Pollux the other, of all the legends, the
following; [illegible]
wonder [illegible]
[illegible] the third shelf: [illegible]
discourse, [illegible] is founded upon a philosophy, the
[illegible] of Gyraldus, [illegible]
[illegible] sometimes eloquent sometimes exceedingly obscure.
I set down a few passages without attempting to recall their
context or to arrange them in convenient order

[22v]

He then ~~began to describe~~ spoke of the two eggs
already hatched, ~~of He~~ how Helen & Klytemnestra broke the one
shell Castor & Polluck the other, of ~~all~~ the tragedy that
followed;, ~~speculated what might break from the sh~~
wondered what ~~would break from the new shell~~ ~~The suns heat~~
word break ~~this new shell~~ the third shell) : ~~It was~~ {A / a} long
discourse, ~~some of it was~~ founded upon the philosophy of the
Judwallis ~~& ex~~ & of Gyraldus, ~~& often exceeding[ly] obscure~~
~~often eloquent~~ sometimes eloquent some times exceeding[ly] obscure
I set down
I ~~recall~~ a few passages without attempting to recall their
context or to arrange them in consequetive order

Lines 1–10 amend 22r, lines 4–20 as directed there.
11 "consequetive" for "consecutive"?

NLI 13,577 [23r]

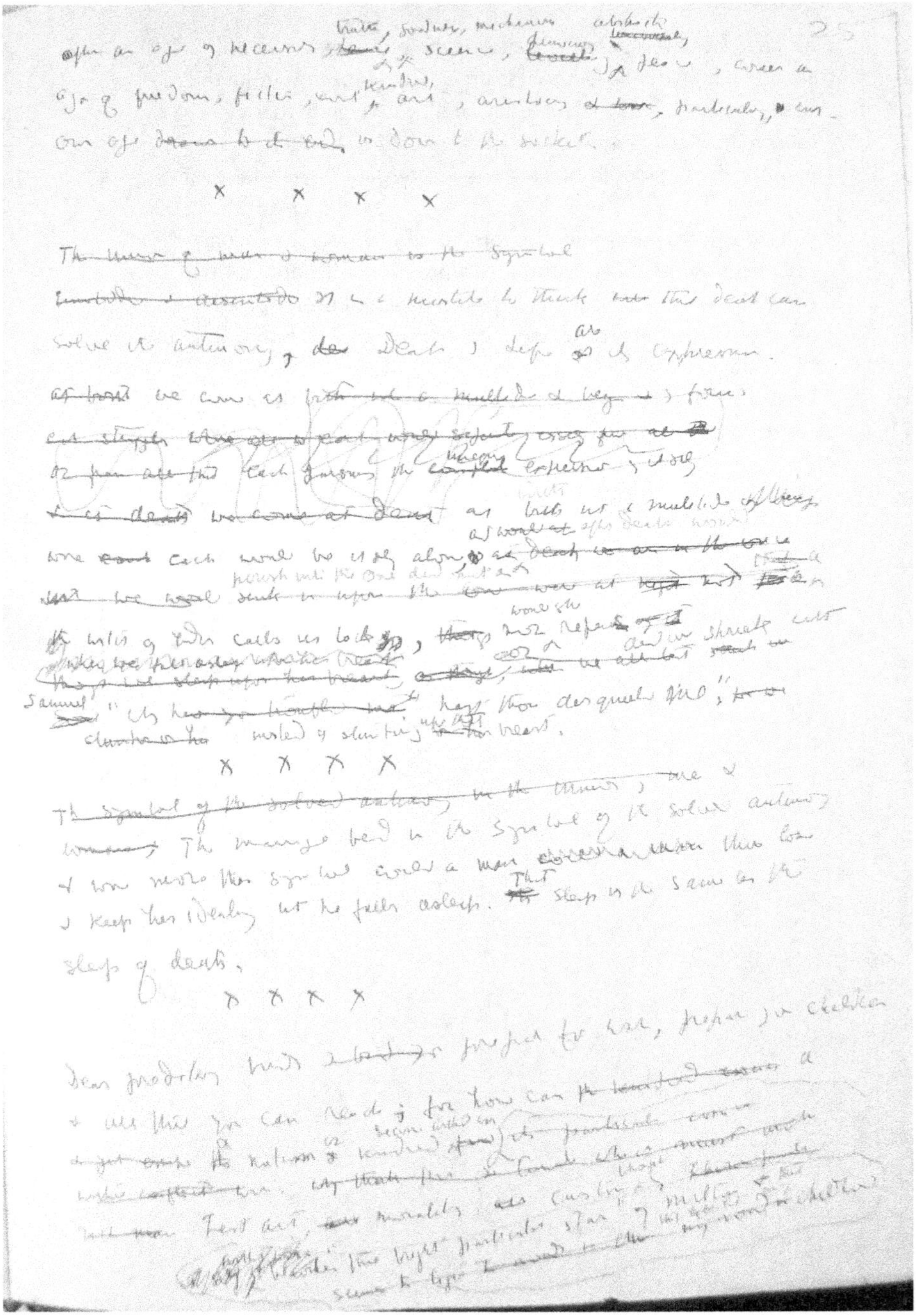

Page "25" continues from page "24," line 32.

[23r]

goodness, mechanism abstraction
truth, democracy ~~universality~~ 25
1 After an age of necessity, ~~peace~~^,^science, ~~levelling~~^peace, comes an
kindred
2 age of freedom, fiction, evil,^art, aristocracy ~~& war~~, particularity, ~~&~~ war.
3 Our age ~~draws to its end~~ is down to the socket.

X X X X

4 ~~The union of man & woman is the symbol~~
5 ~~Embodi[ments] & descents do~~ It is a mistake to think ~~with~~ that death can
are
6 solve the antinomy of ~~dea~~ Death & Life ~~[?or]~~ its expression.
7 ~~At birth~~ We come at birth ~~into a multitude & begin & by focusing~~
8 ~~our struggle~~ ~~Where all [?and] each could separate itself from all that~~
unique
9 ~~or from all that~~ each pursues the ~~complete~~ expression of itself
birth
10 ~~& at death~~ ~~we come at death~~ at ~~birth~~ into a multitude ~~of beings~~
and ~~would at~~ after death would
11 one ~~comes~~ each would be itself alone, and ~~at~~^ ~~death we are in the once~~
perish into the One did not a ~~that~~ a
12 ~~[?] we would~~ ~~sink in upon the One were at night not that the~~^
would she
13 ~~the~~ Witch of Endor calls us back ~~[?]~~, ~~though~~ nor^repent ~~of it~~
~~& when we fall asleep upon her breast~~ or did we shriek with
14 ~~though we sleep upon her breast~~, ~~or though~~, ~~[?when] we all but~~ ~~shriek with~~
Samuel
15 ~~Saul~~ "Why ~~have you troubled me~~" hast thou disquieted me," ~~for we~~
upon that
16 ~~slumber on her~~ instead of slumbering ~~on her~~ breast.

X X X X

17 ~~The symbol of the solved antinomy in the minds of the me[n]~~ &
18 ~~women~~; The marriage bed is the symbol of the solved antinomy
19 & were more than symbol could a man ~~could a man~~ there lose
That
20 & keep his identity but he falls asleep. ~~Its~~ sleep is the same as the
21 sleep of death.

X X X X

22 Dear predatory birds ~~I bid you~~ prepare for war, prepare your children
23 & all that you can reach; for how can ~~the kindred essence~~ a
a or become without war
24 & yet escape ~~the~~ nation ~~&~~ kindred^ ~~find~~^ ~~its particular essence~~
27 ~~without conflict war~~. ~~Why think that the tenets which must make~~
thought
28 ~~rich man~~ Test art, ~~all~~ morality, ~~all~~ custom,^by ~~Thermopolae~~
~~without war~~
25 ~~itself~~^ ~~to~~ become "that bright particular star" of Milton ~~&~~ that
that ~~light~~ lit my
26 ~~seems to light the roads in child~~ ~~my road in~~ childhood

NLI 13,577 [24r]

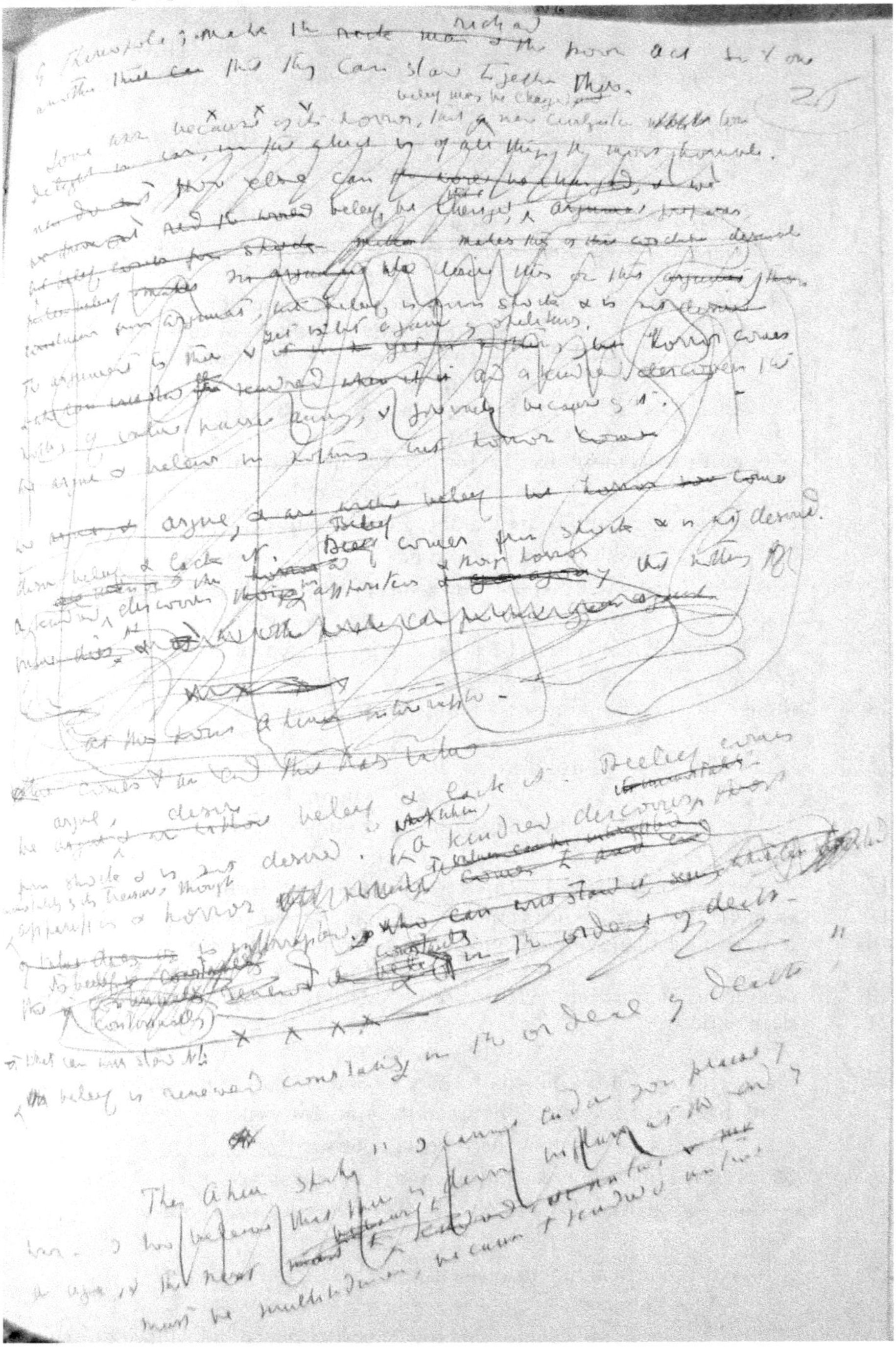

Continues directly from page "25" (23r, line 28).

[24r]

rich and
by Thermopole; make the ~~rich man & the~~ poor act so to one
another ~~that can~~ that they can stand together there. (26)
X X X belief may be changed ~~and~~
Love war because of its horror, that ~~a~~ new civilization ~~may be~~ born
^
~~delight in war, in that which is of all things the most horrible~~.
~~man did not~~ How else can ~~the world be changed, & we~~
~~that a~~
~~we drive out~~ ~~rid the world~~ belief be changed,^ ~~argument~~ prepares
~~but belief comes from shock~~ ~~makes~~ ~~makes this or that conclusion [?discernible]~~
{W/w}
~~makes belief~~ ~~makes~~ ~~In argument~~ {W/w}e desire this or that ~~argument~~ ~~through~~
conclusion from argument, but belief is from shock & is not ~~desired~~
yet is but a game of speculation
The argument is there & ~~it is not~~ ~~yet is nothing~~, ~~but~~ horror comes
~~& who can withstand the kindred when it is~~ And a kindred discovers that
nothing of value passes away, & prevails because of it.
we argue & believe in nothing but horror comes

We ~~argue, &~~ argue, ~~& are without belief but horror some times~~
Belief
desire belief & lack it. ~~Bealf~~ comes from shock & is not desired
the ~~horror of~~
~~a man or~~ an & through horror
a kindred^ discovers ~~through~~^ apparition ~~& agon agony~~ that nothing of
~~value dies," & not no other people can prevail over a question~~
~~X X X X~~
At this point Aherne interrupted.
~~Value comes to an end that has value~~
argue, desire
We ~~argue & are without~~ belief & lack it. Bealief comes
~~which~~ (When) ~~its immortality~~
from shock & is not desired. ^A kindred discovers^ ~~through~~
the immortality of its treasure, through ~~its value can be interrupted~~
^apparition & horror ~~that nothing~~ ~~comes to~~ an ~~end~~
~~of value dies or~~ is interrupted., ~~who can with stand it, seeing~~ ~~what can with stand~~
~~that belief has constantly~~ ~~constantly~~
that & ~~continually~~ renewed it ~~belief~~ in the ordeal of death
^ continually
~~X X X X~~
~~it~~ what can with stand
^~~that~~ belief is renewed continually in the ordeal of death."
~~X~~
Then Aherne spoke "I cannot endure your praise of
war. I too believe that there is divine influx at the end of
~~because t~~
an age, & the next ~~must t[he] kindred, or nation, or man~~
must be multitudiness, because the kindred & nations

NLI 13,577 [24v]

[24v]

upon heresay
I have compared those poems in "A Vision" which is founded ~~on what~~ you ^
~~have learned from Daniel O Leary~~
~~I~~ with certain written records
& 'The Vision of Michael Robartes'
^ 'The Phases of the Moon,^ allowing for the condensations & hightening
of verse ~~records~~ ~~corresponds~~ is in the same as the record
~~of his own & Robartes from conversations made by Aherne in "the~~
Vision of Michael Robartes" or sufficiently like his own record
in Ahernes Diary ~~of his~~ {R / ~~M~~} ~~obartes & Robartes Irish journey~~

Though cancelled, 24v, lines 1–8 were drafted to amend the circumscribed, heavily cancelled lines 25–28 on page "27" (25r), as indicated by the two short drawn lines leading to the right edge of this still-bound page in the notebook.

NLI 13,577 [25[r]]

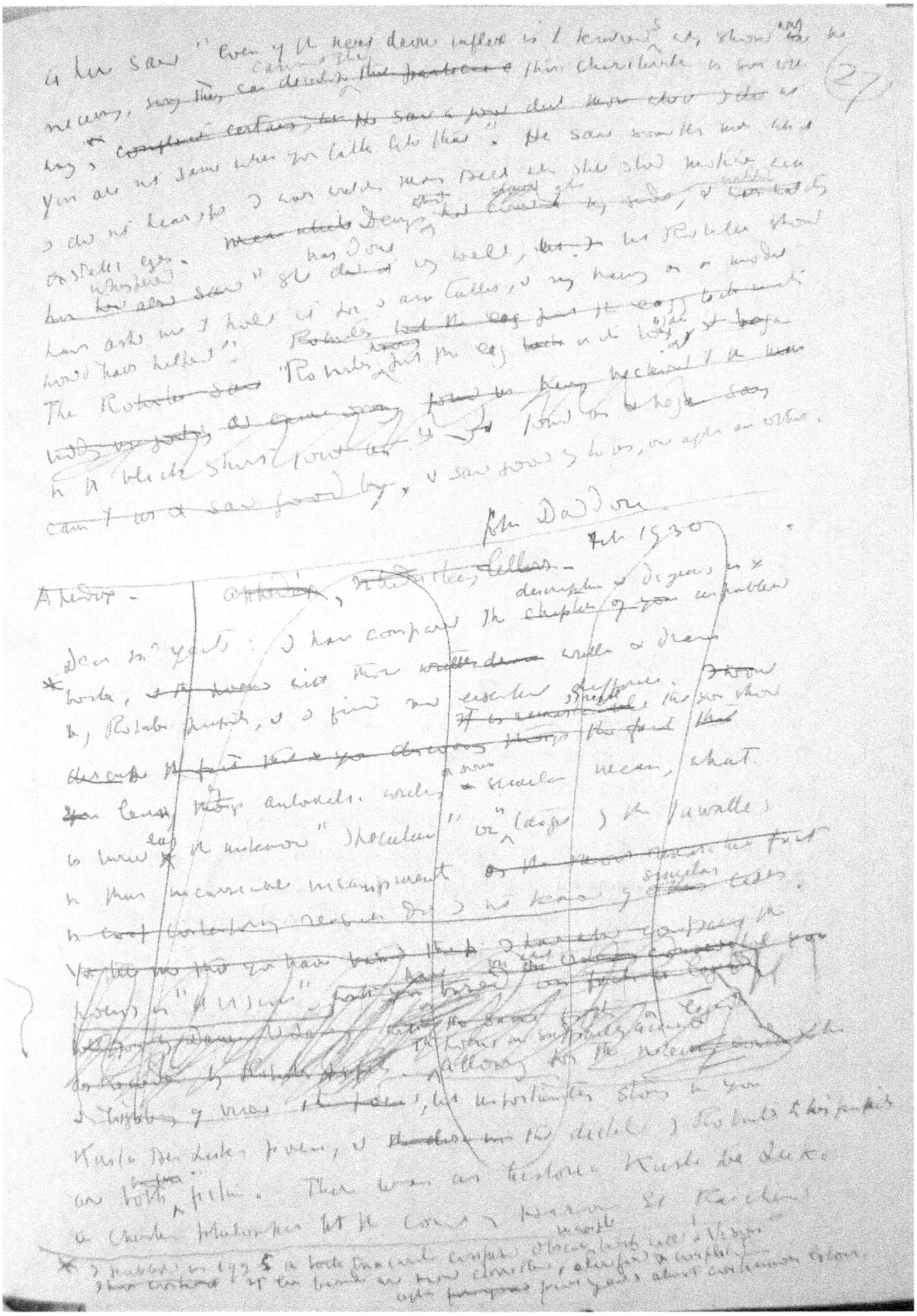

Cancelled lines 25–28 were to have been amended by 24[v] until Yeats's revision there was also cancelled. The whole "Appendix" begins again on 26[r].

[25r]

s war
1 Aherne said "Even if the next devine influx is to kindred^ ~~why~~ should ~~war~~ be
cannot they
2 necessary, ~~surely they can develop~~^ ~~their particular &~~ their characteristics some other
3 way.** ~~Conflict certainly, but~~ ~~He said a good deal more which I did not~~
4 You are not sane when you talk like that". He said something more which (27
5 I did not hear, for I was watching Mary Bell who still stood motionless with
~~who~~ ~~should~~ also ~~watched~~
6 ecstatic eyes. ~~Mean while~~ Denys^ ~~had come to my side, &~~ ~~was watching~~
whispered has done
7 ~~her too also said~~ "She ~~did it~~ very well, ~~but I~~ but Robartes should
8 have asked me to hold it for I am taller, & my training as a model
9 would have helped." ~~Robartes took the egg put the egg back in its~~
10 ~~having~~ again
11 Then ~~Robartes said~~ Robartes^ put the egg ~~back~~ in its box^, ~~& began~~
12 ~~bidding us good by~~ ~~and came among~~, ~~joined us having beckoned to the man~~
13 in the black shirt ~~joined us~~ ~~[?]~~, & joined us & began saying
14 ~~came to us & said good by~~. & said good by to us, one after an other.
John Duddon.

---

15 Appendix. ~~Appendix~~, ~~Introductory letters.~~ Feb 1930
description & diagrams in your
16 Dear Mr Yeats: I have compared the ~~chapter of your~~ unpublished
17 * book, ~~& the poems~~ with those ~~written drawn~~ written & drawn
18 by Robartes pupils, & I find no essential difference. ~~I would~~
It is remarkable <strange>that you should
19 ~~This case~~ ~~the fact that that [?] your~~ ~~discovery through the fact that~~
by or some
20 ~~You~~ learn ~~through~~ automatic writing ~~&~~ similar means, what
lost
21 is buried^ in the unknown "Speculum" or "taught by the Ju[d]wallis
22 in their inaccessible encampments ~~as the most remarkable fact~~
similar
23 ~~in cont contemporary research did I not know of other cases~~
24 ~~You tell me that you have based the p~~ I ~~have also~~ comparing the
what
have ~~on [?] O Leary converse told you~~
25 poems in "A Vision", note^ you based on facts and legends
26 ~~told you by Daniel O Leary with the same facts or legends~~
The poems are sufficiently accurate
27 ~~as recorded by Robartes pupils.~~ ^ allowing for the poems ~~condensations~~
28 ~~& heightening of verse, the poems~~, but unfortunately story in your
29 Kusta Ben Luka poem, & ~~the description~~ that dictated by Robartes to his pupils
~~a fine~~
30 are both^ fiction. There was an historic Kusta be[n] Luka
31 a Christian philosopher in the court of Harun El Raschid

---

incomplete
32 *I published in 1925 a ~~book~~ inaccurate confused obscure^ book called "a Vision"
33 ~~I have corrected it~~ It lies beside me now corrected, clarified & completed—
34 after ~~five years~~ five years almost continuous labour.

NLI 13,577 [26r]

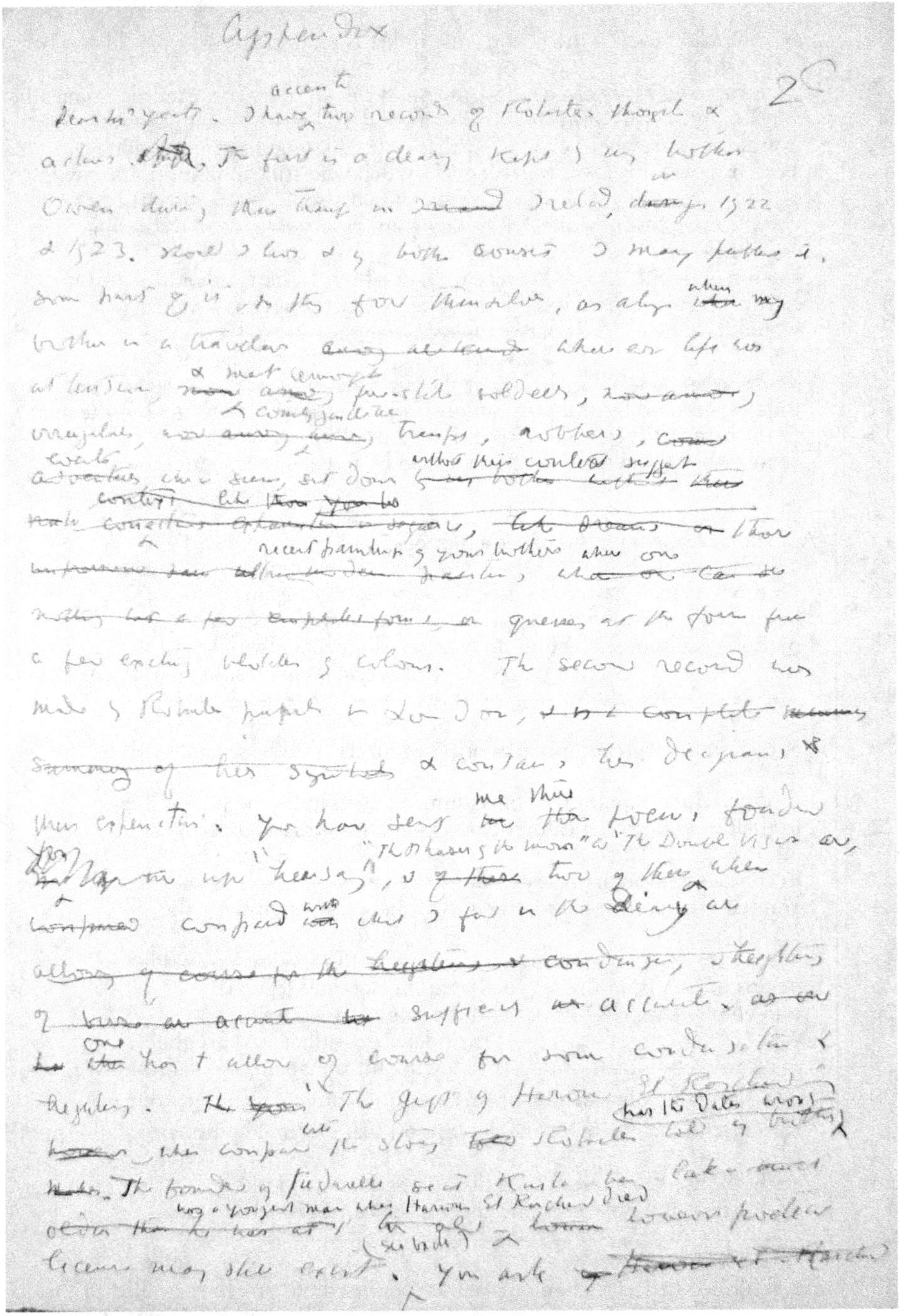

Supersedes 25r, lines 15–34.

[26r]

Appendix

access to
1 Dear Mr Yeats. I have^two records of Robartes thought & 28
2 actions ~~& firstly,~~ The first is a diary kept by my brother
in
3 Owen during their tramp in ~~Ireland~~ Ireland, ~~during~~ 1922
4 & 1923. Should I live & my brother consent I may publish it.
when
5 Some part of it, for they found themselves, as always ~~when~~ my
6 brother is a traveler ~~among all kinds~~ where every life was
& met enough
7 at tension, ~~now~~^~~among~~ free-state soldiers, ~~now among~~
country gentlemen
8 irregulars, ~~now among~~^~~among~~ tramps, robbers, ~~com~~
events without their context suggest
9 ~~adventures~~ which seem, set down ~~by my brother without there~~
~~context like those you had~~
10 ~~natu connections explanations or sequence, like dreams or~~ those
^ recent paintings of your brother where one
11 ~~impressions pain~~^~~ultra modern painting~~ ~~where one can see~~
12 ~~nothing but a few~~ ~~emphatic forms~~, one guesses at the forms from
13 a few exciting blotches of colour. The second record was
14 made by Robartes pupils in London, ~~& is a complete summary~~
15 ~~summary of his symbols~~ & contains his diagrams &
me three
16 their explanations. You have sent ~~me three~~ poems founded
~~You~~ "The Phases of the Moon" and "The Double Vision["] are
17 ~~have~~ ~~[?] me~~ upon "hearsay," & ~~of these~~ two of these^when
with
18 ~~compared~~ compared ~~with~~ what I find in the diary are
19 ~~allowing of course for the heightening & condensing & heightening~~
20 ~~of verse are accurate~~ ~~[?but]~~ sufficiently ~~as~~ accurate, ~~as one~~
One
21 ~~has~~ ~~when~~ has to allow of course for some condensation &
22 heightening. ~~The~~ ~~Your~~ "The Gift of Harun El Raschid"
with (has the dates wrong)
23 ~~however~~, when compared the story ~~told~~ Robartes told my brother^
24 ~~makes~~. The founder of Judwallis sect Kusta-ben-luka ~~much~~
was a youngish man when Harun El Raschid died
25 ~~older than he was at t was old~~^~~however~~ however poetical
(See back)
26 licence may still exist. ^ You ask ~~of Harun El Raschid~~

26 "(See back)" directs one to 26v, where the narrative continues unabated.

NLI 13,577 [26v]

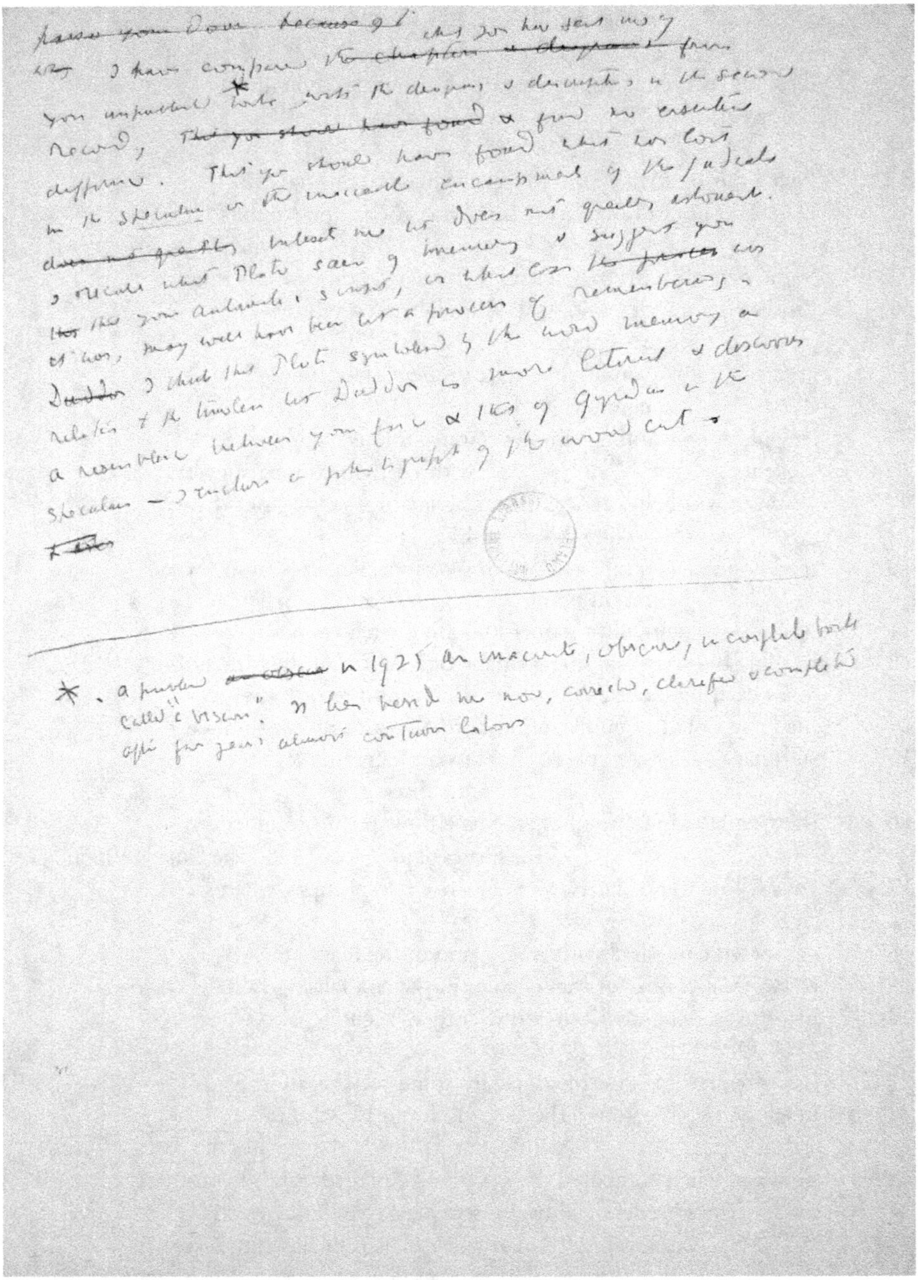

[26v]

~~passed your door because of t~~
what you have sent me of
~~why~~ I have compared ~~the chapters & diagrams from~~
your unpublished *book, with the diagrams & descriptions in the second
record, ~~that you should have found~~ & found no essential
difference. That you should have found what was lost
in the Speculum or the inaccessible encampments of the Judwali
~~does not greatly~~ interests me but does not greatly astonish.
I recall what Plato said of memory & suggest you
~~the~~ that your automatic script, or what ever ~~the process~~ was
it was, may well have been but a process of remembering.
~~Duddon~~ I think that Plato symbolised by the word memory a
relation to the timeless but Duddon is more literal & discovers
a resemblance between your face & that of Gyraldus in the
Speculum—I enclose a photograph of the wood cut.
~~& ask~~

---

*A published ~~an obscure~~ in 1925 an inaccurate, obscure, incomplete book
called "a Vision." It lies beside me now, corrected, clarified & completed
after five years almost continuous labour

These lines are interjected into the narrative from the bottom of 26r, before the words "You ask ~~of Harun El Raschid~~," which are picked up at the top of 27r (page "29").

NLI 13,577 [27r]

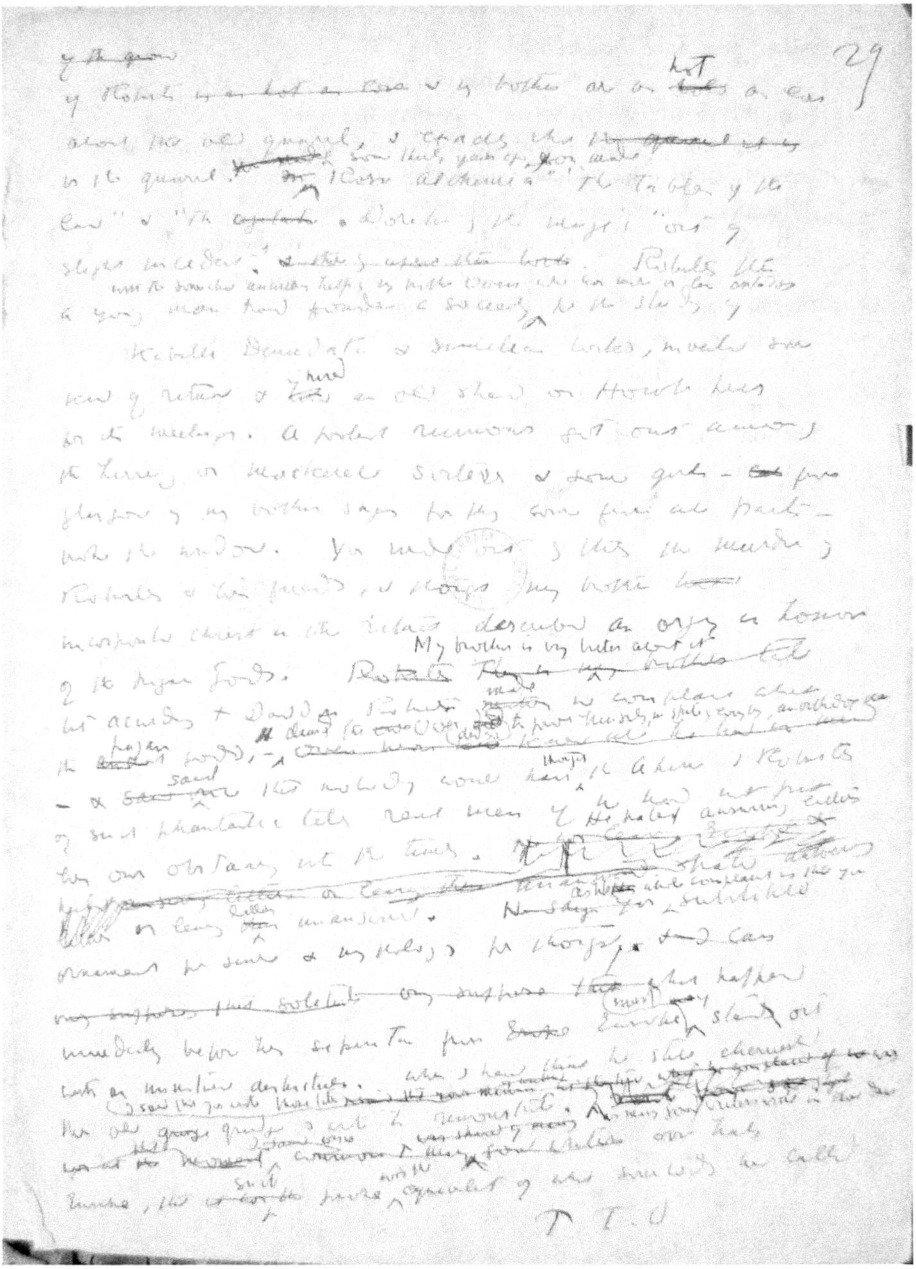

Page "29" carries the narrative forward, from the bottom of 26r, on the cue: "You ask. . . ." Subsequently, below line 30 on page "29," the notation "P.T.O" directs one to 27v, where the draft is completed.

[27r]

~~if the quarrel~~ hot 29
if Robartes ~~is as hot as ever~~ & my brother are as ~~cold~~ as ever
about that old quarrel, & exactly what ~~the quarrel it is~~
~~You made~~ Some thirty years ago, you made
is the quarrel. ~~In~~ ‸ "Rosa Alechmica" "The Tables of the
law" & "The ~~Agitation~~ Adoration of the Magi", "out of
slight incident." ~~& there by upset them both~~. Robartes then
with the somewhat unwilling help of my brother Owen who was more or less orthodox
a young man had founded a society ‸ for the study of
Kaballa Denudata & similar books, invented some
hired
kind of ritual & ~~hired~~ an old shed on Howth pier
for its meetings. A foolish rumour got out among
the herring or mackerel sorters & some girls—~~lads~~ from
Glasgow as my brother says for they came from all parts—
broke the window. You made out of this the murder of
Robartes & his friends, & though my brother ~~had~~
incorporated Christ in the ritual described an orgy in honor
My brother is very bitter about it
of the pagan gods. ~~Robartes~~ ~~Then in my brothers tale~~
made
but according to Duddon, Robartes ~~makes~~ no complaint about
~~but~~ dreamed that ~~Owe~~ Owen ~~did~~ to prove himself in spite of everything,
pagan (did so) [an orthodox man
the ~~ancient~~ gods,— ‸ ~~Owen never kno knew all he had in mind~~
said thought
—& ~~said once~~ that nobody would have ‸ the Aherne & Robartes
‸
of such phantastic tales real men if he had not put
He hated answering letters
his own obituary into the Times. ~~He was leaving Europe &~~
~~hated answering letters or leaving them unanswered hated answering~~
letters As his ~~His~~ whole complaint is that you
~~letters~~ or leaving ~~them~~ unanswered. He ~~says you~~ ‸ substituted
ornament for sense & mythology for thought. ~~& I can~~
~~only suppose that soletude only suppose that~~ what happened
(must) ~~may~~
immediately before his separation from ~~Erope~~ Europe ‸ standout
with an unnatural distinctnes[s]. When I heard that he still cherished
~~of writing~~
I said that you wrote those tales ~~I said that your manner at the time which he complained of~~ was
this old ~~gruge~~ grudge I wrote to remonstrate. ‸ I ~~wrote you about style~~
~~that~~ ~~I said once~~ ~~who shared by many~~ as many good writers wrote in those days
~~was at the moment~~ ‸ ~~common to many~~ ‸ ~~good writers~~ over half
such was the
Europe, that ~~it was the~~ prose ‸ equivalent of what somebody had called
P. T. O

NLI 13,577 [27v]

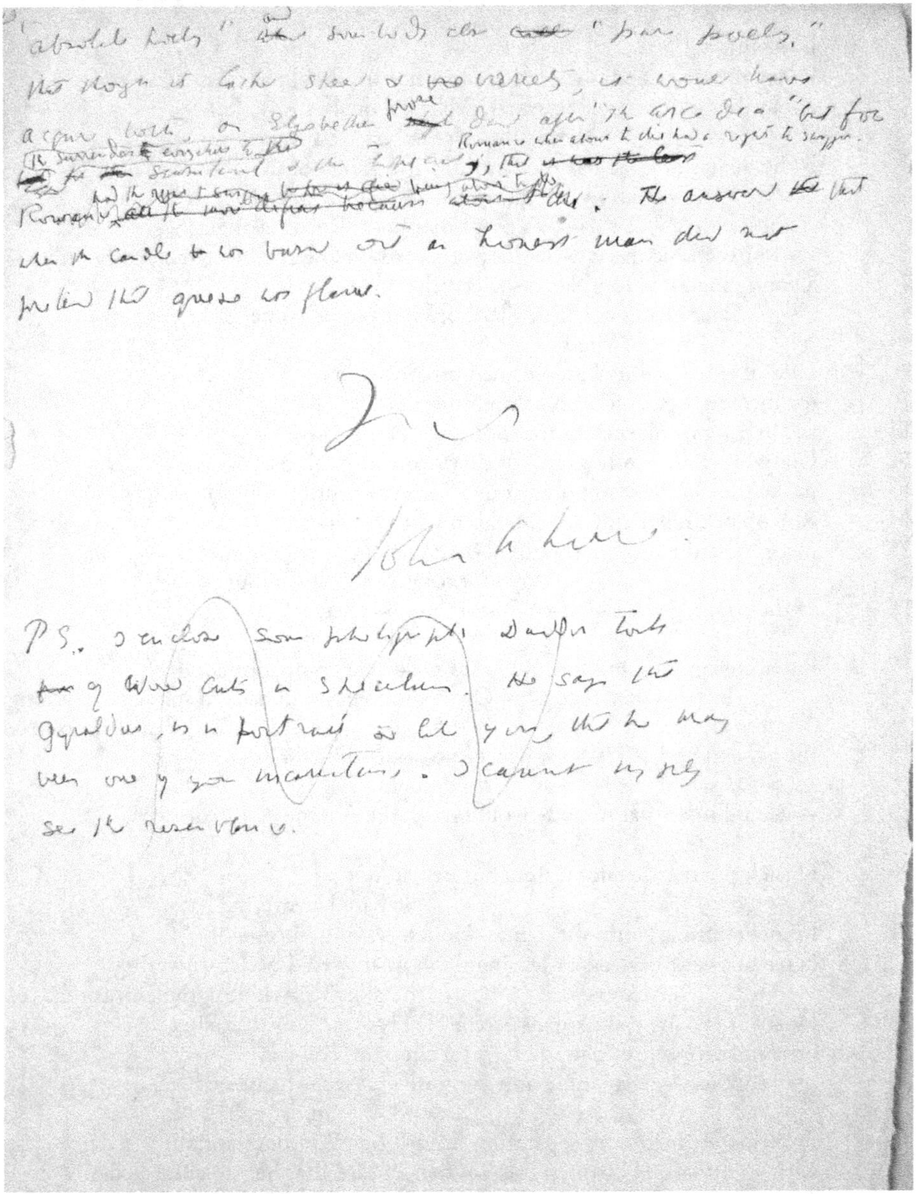

when the candle [?] burn out an honest man did not pretend that grease was flame.

Yrs

John Aherne.

P.S. I enclose some photographs

[27ᵛ]

and
"absolute poetry" ~~which~~ some body else ~~called~~ "pure poetry."
that though it lacked speed & ~~vre~~ variety, it would have
prose
acquired both, as Elizabethan ~~style~~ did after "The Arcadia" but for
(to surrender ~~to~~ everywhere to the) Romance when about to die had a right to swagger.
~~but~~)^ ~~for the~~ sensational & the topical, that it was the last
~~had the right to swagger before it died being about to die~~
~~Romance~~^ ~~all the more defiant because about to die~~. He answered ~~the~~ that
when the candle ~~has~~ was burnt out an honest man did not
pretend that grease was flame.

Y[ours] s[incerely]

John Aherne

PS. I enclose some photographs Duddon took
~~from~~ of Wood Cuts in Speculum. He says that
Gyraldus, is a portrait so like you, that he may [have]
been one of your incarnations. I cannot myself
see the resemblance.

3–9 Evidently prepared as a taped-over insert to correct the ending of a typescript (now lost), the typed fragment NLI 30,465 presents an almost final version of these lines, unfavorably comparing, as prose stylists, Yeats to poet and courtly romance writer Sir Philip Sidney. The fragment completes John Aherne's observation from mid-sentence and gives Robartes the rhetorically loaded, final word: "both as Elizabethan prose did after the Arcadia, but for the surrender everywhere to the sensational and the topical; that romance driven to its last ditch had a right to swagger. He answered that when the candle was burnt out an honest man did not pretend that grease was flame. | John Aherne". Which writer's prose is "flame" and which "grease" is implied, a joke Yeats played on himself, like the mischievous postscript that followed in lines 10–14 of the holograph.

10–14 As indicated, the postscript suppressed the revelation that Edmund Dulac's portrait of Giraldus was actually a portrait of Yeats in disguise. The joke is precious but reveals more than necessary to be appreciated by most readers.

NLI 13,577 [43v]

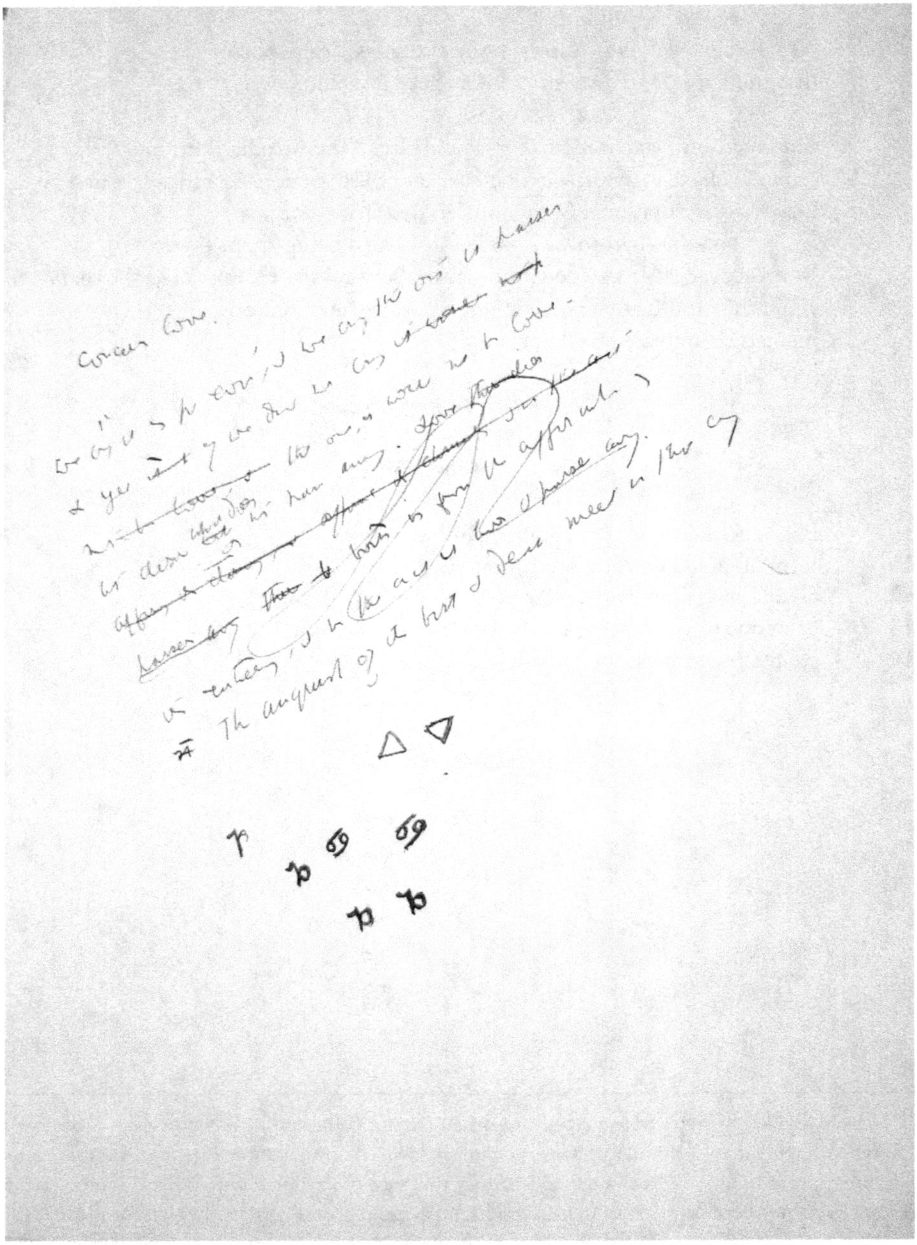

[43v]

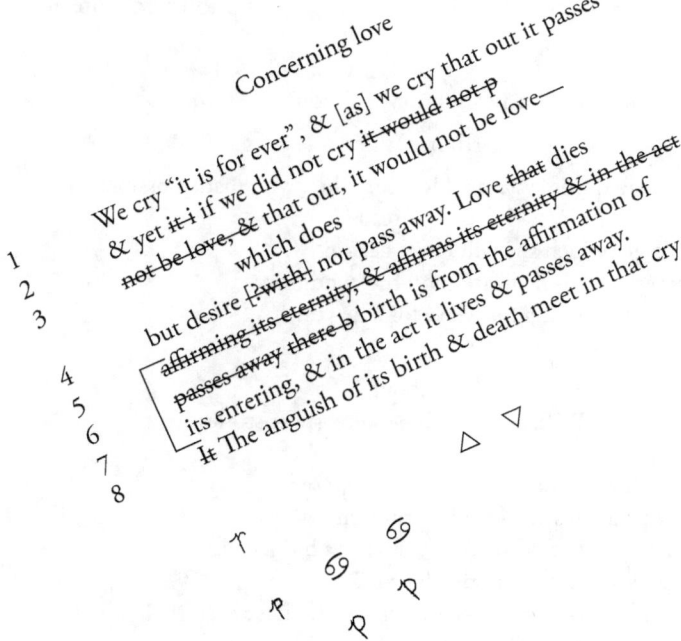

Concerning love

We cry "it is for ever", & [as] we cry that out it passes
& yet ~~it i~~ if we did not cry ~~it would~~ ~~not p~~
~~not be love, &~~ that out, it would not be love—
which does
but desire ~~[?with]~~ not pass away. Love ~~that~~ dies
~~affirming its eternity, & affirms its eternity & in the act~~
~~passes away~~ ~~there b~~ birth is from the affirmation of
its entering, & in the act it lives & passes away.
~~It~~ The anguish of its birth & death meet in that cry

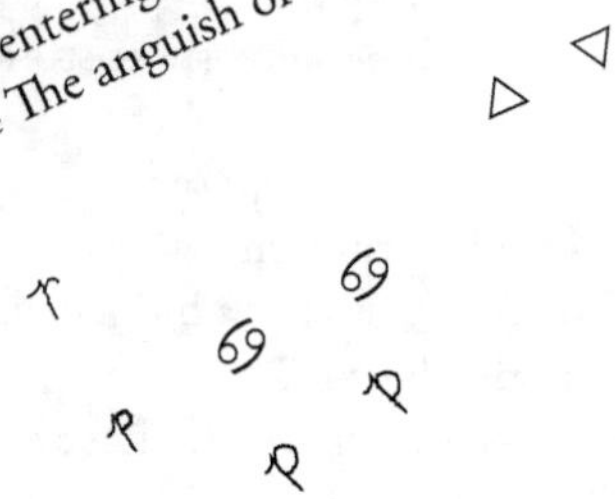

Well removed from the rest of the manuscript, on the verso of the last folio in the notebook, this entry reads like the prose subject of a poem. It rehearses Robartes's important self-revelation worked out on folio 10r (page "12"), lines 1–9. See above as well as Yeats's attention to the passage in corrected proof copies of *SMR* and, later, in *AVB* (see Part Four, section 3, page 290, below).

The drawn figures beneath line 8 represent Fire and Water, as well as Cancer and variant forms for the symbol Capricorn. In *AVA*, Cancer is placed in the 4th quarter of The Great Wheel, with Fire and Capricorn in the 2nd quarter with Water. In *SMR*, Capricorn and Water appear in the 4th quarter, with Cancer and Fire in the 2nd. See page 289, below. In *AVB*, Capricorn and Fire are placed in the 4th quarter whereas Cancer and Water occur in the 2nd.

Related Matter in the White Vellum Notebook[1]

Folio 89^{v} (or p. [178] as numbered by Curtis Bradford prior to SUNY Stony Brook filming), an unused dedication for *A Vision*, and an unpublished note for 1931 *SMR*, rejected:

Dedication for "a Vision"

To my Wife

Who created this system which bores her, who made possible
read
these pages which she will never ~~head~~ & who
has accepted this dedication on the condition
that I write nothing but verse for a ~~Ye~~ year.

about
Thirty years ago M^{r} W B Yeats wrote ~~three~~ ~~some short stories~~
and
~~about~~ a certain Michael Robartes, ~~who~~ his supposed
death in a riot. In the present story he brings him
back from the Arabian desert, where he has been hidden all
these years, & shows him surrounded by ~~a group of~~
deciples, ~~who have each his own his own story~~ who have each their
own adventures to describe. "The Resurrection" is a
play in prose, which takes up again some of the themes
described ~~by Robartes & his Deciples~~.
by Robartes.

[The last sentence makes clear that themes in "SMR" rehearse or anticipate the new edition of *The Resurrection* that joined "SMR" in 1931, but less clearly those of *AVB*. Use of third-person voice in reference to "Mr W B Yeats" echoes John Aherne at the end of "SMR" (lines 631–55). Notebook entries run from 23 November 1930 through 1933.

On p. {161}, Yeats inscribed what Bradford calls the "Final version" of "Huddon, Duddon and Daniel O'Leary" as it appeared in *SMR* (1931). This is according to Bradford's inventory of the notebook (item 35), where the poem falls between the final version of "Tom the Lunatic" (p. {159}), dated July 27, and a late version of "The Seven Sages" (pp. {161} and {163}) dated January 30. But see p. {173}, where a rough draft of "Tom the Lunatic" occurs just two pages before

[1] Location of the White Vellum Notebook (also called MBY 545 or "*WVNb*") is presently unknown. I have worked from images on microfilm, Reel V, in the W. B. Yeats Papers, 1908–1934 (F47–1), Houghton Library, Harvard University. The pages are unnumbered in this earliest and most legible of three copies made for study.

the introductory note, transcribed above, and four pages before the rough draft of "Huddon, Duddon and Daniel O'Leary" occurs on pp. {180}, {181} and {183}. The date of composition therefore would seem to be c. July 1931. David R. Clark argues, conservatively, for its completion as sometime after January 1931 because of the position of the fair-hand version in apposition to "The Seven Sages." The Cuala Press printing of *SMR* occurred officially on 31 October 1931; see following transcriptions.]

Folio 90^{v} (p. [180]):

Huddon, Duddon & D/aniel O Leary
Delighted me as a chil/d
But once that roaring/ranting crew
\ \ [?] \ raced \ \
Danced, ~~drank~~, ~~[?] loved fought~~ thought Danced, laughed, loved, fought through
There brief lives I never knew though put
I ~~have set~~ my
~~Some~~ ~~I set there~~ scholours in their place
Huddon, Duddon & Daniel O Leary ~~Scholours have taken name & place~~
Delighted me as a child keep
I dare not mock the dead & yet That despair & help the pace
On some that neither race nor bet And love wench wisdoms cruel face
Those great forgotten name[s] I set
Scholours there Now
~~There schools take their name & place~~ ~~My~~ scholours take their name & place
~~my~~ ~~their~~
~~And lone~~ Scholours ~~have~~ taken name & place
~~That dour~~ There that despair and
~~Despair, exult~~ laugh ~~Despair, exult~~ & keep the pace
~~Exult~~ exult ~~&~~ ~~loved~~ love wench
Despair, ~~laughing & loving~~ [?] [?] And love ~~that~~ wisdoms cruel face
the
And ~~w~~ wench wisdoms cruel face Three reckless s

Huddon, Duddon and Daniel O Leary
Delighted me as a child
Hard living men & men of thought
I send their substance upon nought
And please ~~it~~ the most when burning out
Burn their bodies up for ~~naught~~ nought
~~And please the most when burning out~~
But how they mock us
~~And scorn our substance~~ burning out

Folio 91[r] (p. [181]):

Huddon, Duddon & Daniel O Leary
Those names delighted me as a child
~~What sort of~~ god forsaken god forsaken crew
Where that ~~hell & leather crew~~ Where that [?~~reward~~] for
~~Broke their necks on~~ Drank & loved & ranted th
~~Cracked their heads/~~ ~~Cursed & loved & ranted~~/through Their brief lives I never knew
Health & wealth ~~I never knew~~

Huddon & Duddon & Daniel O Leary
Those names delighted me as a child
And seem as fit for men of thought They mocked & the men of [thought
Both spend their substance upon nought Spend their substance on [nought
~~cheer~~ the burning
please[2] | And ~~Light light~~ it most when ~~bury~~ out And light as most when burning out

Huddon & Dud

~~Sages, jockeys racing men~~
And have not mocked the dead & yet
~~Those~~
~~Or other men, those names I set~~
~~That neither rode~~
~~Those famous ancient names I set~~
~~On the~~
~~Those great~~
Their great forgotten names I set
~~On [?] where no men ride or~~
~~Where no[ne] has raced~~
Where none race, or dice or bet.

---

[2] "please…burning out" etc.—that is, "please the most when burning out"—see the last sentence of *SMR* 1931 (ll. 670–72): "He answered that when the candle was burnt out an honest man did not pretend that grease was flame." Lines 13–15 in the poem become "Hard-living men and men of thought | Burn their bodies up for nought | But how they mock us burning out" (and in *AVB*: "…I mock at all so burning out"), anticipating the last lines of *The Resurrection* as they appeared first in *SMR* and subsequently in "Two Songs from a Play," II (15–16) in *CP*, *Wheels and Butterflies*, and *CPl*: "Whatever flames upon the night | Man's own resinous heart has fed."

Folio 92[r] (p. [183]; folio 92[v] [p. 182] being blank):

"The
to go before ^Resurrection"

Huddon, Duddon and Daniel O Leary
Delighted me as a child;
But wheres that roaring ranting crew
\ \ \
Danced, laughed, loved, fought through
Their brief lives I never knew.

Huddon, Duddon and Daniel O Leary
Delighted me as a child.
three persons
I put ~~my scholours~~ in their place
That despair & keep the pace
And love wench wisdoms cruel face.

Huddon, Duddon & Daniel O Leary
Delighted me as a child,
Hard living men & men of thought
bodies
Burn their ~~substance~~ up for naught
But how they mock us, burning out.

~~Note~~
~~as I[=a] child~~ as though
As I[=a] child I pronounced the word to rhyme with "dairy."
^

Correction of ~~li~~ certain lines in "The Tower"

Odour of blood when Christ was slain
Attic
Made all ~~all Attic~~ tolerance & vain
Vain all Doric dicipline.

[Cf. lines 6–8 of "Two Songs from a Play," II (i.e., "…Made Plato's tolerance in vain | And vain the Doric discipline"), where pt. I was the opening song in *The Resurrection* and pt. II was the first of two stanzas of the closing song.]

March 4. 1933. This correction is later in
date than another which is somewhere in this book

[*CP* was published in November 1933; the correction was made then.]

Folio 81r (p. 161):

introductory lines for Stories of Robartes

Huddon, Duddon & Daniel O Leary
Delighted me as a child;
But where that roaring, ranting crew
Danced, laughed, loved, fought through
Their brief lives I never knew

Huddon, Duddon & Daniel O Leary
Delighted me as a child.
I put three persons in their place
That despair & keep the pace
And love wench wisdoms cruel face.

Huddon, Duddon & Daniel O Leary
Delighted me as a child.
or
Hard living men & of thought
They
Burn their bodies up for naught
But How they mock us burning out.

[This fair-hand copy, based on the draft from folio 92r (p. [183]), is not identical with the first published version in punctuation, spelling, and the exact wording of stanza 3. The most significant difference between the two pages, however, is in Yeats's decision to use the poem to introduce "SMR" rather than *The Resurrection*, as indicated by directions laid at the the top of each page. The Curtis/Guinness edition of the manuscripts of the play[3] does not hint at what point Yeats may have changed his mind while revising the play from its original published state of 1927 to the Cuala version of 1931.

The draft lyric on 81r is followed immediately by lines from "The Seven Sages," as Clark observed, whereas the antecedent draft was followed, on 93r, by scratch notes on Judas and, on 93v–94r, by the opening lines of the play. Still, "Huddon, Duddon and Daniel O'Leary" must have been all but finished by the time Yeats wrote to his wife from Coole Park that he had "written two good poems & hope to do a third. They are about "'old Tom the lunatic that sleeps under the canopy,'" conjecturally dated "[July 1931]" on microfilm but not collected in *CL InteLex* by John Kelly. Imposed over stanza 2 of "Tom the Lunatic,"

[3] W. B. Yeats, *The Resurrection: Manuscript Materials*, ed. Jared Curtis and Selina Guinness (Ithaca and London: Cornell University Press, 2011).

the letter occurs on folio 87^{r} (p. [173]): "Huddon, Duddon, [and] Daniel O'Leary | Holy Joe the beggarman," etc.[4]

Huddon and Duddon (only spelled -en rather than -on) are rival farmers in "Donald and his Neighbors," a tale reprinted by Yeats in *FFTIP*, giving the source as a "chap-book" entitled "Hibernian Tales" as "mentioned by Thackeray in his *Irish Sketch Book*" (1842 and later), where the story is quoted in full. Other versions are known, as one finds today on the internet. The Thackeray-Yeats version was reprinted in a 10-volume compendium, *Irish Literature*, ed. Justin McCarthy, Lady Gregory, Douglas Hyde, et al. (New York: Bigelow, Smith, 1904), to which Yeats contributed as an editor and author. However, he seems to have known another version of the tale, entitled "Huddon, Duddon and Donald O'Neary" and credited to Alfred Nutt, appearing in *Celtic Fairy Tales*, ed. Joseph Jacobs (1892 and later; see Edward O'Shea, "The 1920s Catalogue of W. B. Yeats's Library," *YA* 4 [1986]: 284). In the epigraph to "SMR" in *SMR* (1931) and *AVB* (1937), the names Huddon, Duddon, and Daniel O'Leary are made to conform with those given to characters in the story—Peter Huddon, John Duddon, and Daniel O'Leary—without other notable correspondences. The apocryphal Yeats poem is wry but also perplexing in suggesting that the eponymous charcters from the folktale have been applied to his fictional characters the same way a subtext applies to a text: "I put three persons in their place | That despair and keep the pace | And love wench Wisdom's cruel face" (8–10).

Perhaps more challenging than perplexing is the possibility of linking themes and characters with the play that followed them both in 1931, as suggested by the introductory note on folio 89^{v}. The challenge comes from thinking of *SMR* as *AVB* preliminary matter, which was not Yeats's objective until later. The fact that he ever considered placing the introductory rhymes before *The Resurrection* shows that making the play and the Robartes stories fit together as a pair would have taken priority over other options. Rewriting the play fully from its 1927 version while writing its lively fictional companion were matters requiring at least some rough alignments of theme and motif, as was discussed earler at some length. Otherwise, in *AVB*, the epigraph would seem to initiate the narrative as a transition from Pound's lyric "The Return," quoted at the end of "To Ezra Pound": "See, they return; ah, see the tentative | Movements, and the slow feet, | The trouble in the pace and the uncertain | Wavering." Yeats's epigraph is apocryphal because it was subsequently deleted from the canon entirely, with only a trace resemblance of it left to be observed in "Tom the Lunatic," first published in *Words for Music Perhaps* (1932) and *The Winding Stair* (1933). The characters Peter Huddon, John Duddon, and Daniel O'Leary take up (with others) the themes of their supposed

---

[4] Yeats only attributed the date of this possibly unsent letter to "Wednesday (I think) no Thursday"; but cf. WBY to GY, "Tuesday" [? July 28 1931]: "Have written two poems—queer & I think good" (*CL InteLex* 5493). The other two poems were "Old Tom at Cruachan" and "Old Tom Again."

spiritual master, Robartes, who has returned from the deserts of Arabia to hear their stories. In its several versions, the folktale is always about the fleecing of gullible yokels. Thus, by an association that Yeats made with the epigraph, "Stories of Michael Robartes and his Friends" can be read as a tongue-in-cheek counterpoint to the serious point of Yeats's open letter to Pound on the authority of *A Vision*. In support of this assertion, we also have Yeats's word to Olivia Shakespear (of 13 September [1929]) that in the exposition of these stories his own "deductions" might be projected "with an energy & a dogmatism & a cruelty I am not capable of in my own person" (*CL InteLex* 5285). By "deductions," he alludes to "the System" but also to human costs extracted from any bearer of revelation.

> Everything that man esteems
> Endures a moment or a day.
> Love's pleasure drives his love away,
> The painter's brush consumes his dreams;
> The herald's cry, the soldier's tread
> Exhaust his glory and his might:
> Whatever flames upon the night
> Man's own resinous heart has fed.
> ("Two Songs from a Play," II; *VP* 438, 9–16)

This stanza was first added to the closing rhymes of *The Resurrection* in 1931.]

STORIES OF MICHAEL ROBARTES AND HIS FRIENDS: AN EXTRACT FROM A RECORD MADE BY HIS PUPILS: AND A PLAY IN PROSE BY W. B. YEATS.

THE CUALA PRESS
DUBLIN, IRELAND
MCMXXXI

The full text of Yeats's "Stories of Michael Robartes and His Friends: An Extract from a Record Made by His Pupils" follows from the Cuala Press printing of 31 Octobert 1931. Collated against this base text are the substantive later variants of *A Vision* (Macmillan, 1937) and the earlier, corrected Cuala proofs (NLI 30,019), of which there were six partial sets to make up the whole, excluding, of course, those of the accompanying "Play in Prose," *The Resurrection*. Chronologically, the constituent units are abbreviated SMR_1, SMR_2, SMR_3, SMR_4, SMR_5, and SMR_6. These are somewhat shuffled out of order in the NLI file. They are defined here as follows: SMR_1 encompasses text and corrections for pages 1–8; SMR_2 (marked "Revise") covers pages 9–16; SMR_3 (marked "Press") also covers pages 9–16; SMR_4 (marked "Revise") extends from page 17 through 26; SMR_5 (marked "Press") covers pages 17–24; and SMR_6 (marked "Press") covers pages 25–32, the last two pages of the story and the first six pages of the play.

Variants introduced with *A Vision* (1937) are referred to as *AVB*. Macmillan's substitution of double for single quotation marks, transposition of commas and periods to fall within end quotes, commas after attribution phrases in dialogue, and use of single quotation marks for embedded dialogue are pervasive in *AVB* and generally not reported in this collation, except in the long interpolation of Denise's story at lines 265–77.

Also included in the collation are two short fragments, SB 0400771 (a Story Brook holograph, Vol. 3 #231–239) and NLI 30,465 (a typed slip prepared as an insert to a manuscript, evidently lost). Respectively, these fragments rehearse text appearing on pages 8–9 and at the very end of the Cuala proofs and published edition.

Huddon, Duddon and Daniel O'Leary*
Delighted me as a child ;
But where that roaring, ranting crew
Danced, laughed, loved, fought through
Their brief lives I never knew.

Huddon, Duddon and Daniel O'Leary
Delighted me as a child.
I put three persons in their place
That despair and keep the pace
And love wench-wisdom's cruel face.

Huddon, Duddon and Daniel O'Leary
Delighted me as a child.
Hard-living men and men of thought
Burn their bodies up for nought
But how they mock us burning out.

W. B. Y.

**As a child I pronounced the word as though it rhymed to 'dairy.'*

---

14 nought] nought, *AVB*

15 But how they mock us...] I mock at all so... *AVB*

16 Note follows a superscript number "1" in *AVB* and is not italicized.

1, 6, 11 These refrain lines are echoed in line 7 of the contemporary lyric "Tom the Lunatic," dated "July 27 [1931]" by Yeats and the editor David R. Clark in *Words for Music Perhaps and Other Poems: Manuscript Materials* (Cornell University Press, 1999), 611. A fair-hand version of "Huddon, Duddon, and Daniel O'Leary" (as "Introductory lines for Stories of Robartes") was inscribed on leaf 42^r of Yeats's White Vellum Notebook (MBY 545, or NLI 30,545 although the item was never deposited in the National Library of Ireland). Clark infers from the poem's position in the Notebook, in relation to other dated work, that the poem "was probably composed after January 1931, the date given for 'The Seven Sages,' which begins at the bottom of the same page" (612). Jared Curtis and Selina Guinness, in *The Resurrection: Manuscript Materials* (Cornell University Press, 2011), 271, report further that "Huddon, Duddon and Daniel O'Leary" was accompanied by Yeats's note, "To go before 'The Resurrection,'" i.e. "To precede the play in *Stories of Michael Robartes and His Friends,*" although he subsequently decided to move it into its present location as "introductory lines," or epigraph, in relation to "Stories" if not the whole volume (see MBY 545, folio 81^r, above). The Cuala proofs of NLI 30,019 lack the poem and begin with the "b" signature, provided on the following page.

16 Yeats might have added to this note that he has in mind a particular tale, "Donald and His Neighbors," reprinted in *FFTIP*, giving as the source a "chap-book" entitled "Hibernian Tales." There were others, as noted in the commentary.

STORIES OF MICHAEL ROBARTES AND HIS FRIENDS; AN EXTRACT FROM A RECORD MADE BY HIS PUPILS.

I

Three of us, two young men and a young woman, sat round a fire at eleven o'clock at night on the ground floor of a house in Albert Road, Regent's Park. Presently a third young man came in, drew a chair into the circle and said: 'You do not recognise me, but I am the chauffeur : I always am on these occasions, it prevents gossip.' Said I 'where is Mr Owen Aherne?' 'Owen' said he, 'is with Michael Robartes making his report.' Said I 'why should there be a report?' said he 'O, there is always a report. Meanwhile I am to tell you my story and to hear yours. There will be plenty of time, for as I left the study Michael Robartes called the universe a great egg that turns inside out perpetually without breaking its shell, and a thing like that always sets Owen off.

'My name is Daniel O'Leary, my great interest is the speaking of verse, and the establishment some day or other of a small theatre for plays in verse. You will remember that a few years before the great war the realists drove the last remnants of rhythmical speech out of the theatre. I thought common sense

[1]

---

3 Road, *rev from* Road SMR_1
6 chauffeur: *rev from* chaffeur– SMR_1
7 Said I 'where *rev from* Said I, "Where SMR_1
10 said he 'O,] Said he, "Oh, *AVB*
16 off. *rev from* off.' SMR_1
17 'My *rev from* –My SMR_1
20 great war] Great War *AVB*

Above the title, in top margin of SMR_1, Yeats circumscribes a note that he entirely cancels afterward: "I shall want yet another 'revise' | but it will do when you send me the | proof with diagrams ~~in them~~ Etc." In the lower right-hand corner, someone has inscribed in pencil: "17 September | Coole."

might have returned while I was at war or in the starvation afterwards, and went to Romeo and Juliet to find out. I caught those well-known persons Mr . . . . and Miss . . . . at their kitchen gabble. Suddenly this thought came into my head, what would happen if I were to take off my boots and fling one at Mr. . . . . . . and one at Miss . . . . . ? Could I give my future life such settled purpose that the act would take its place not among whims but among forms of intensity? I ran through my life from childhood and decided that I could. "You have not the courage," said I, speaking aloud but in a low voice, "I have," said I, and began unlacing my boots. "You have not," said I, and after several such interchanges I stood up and flung the boots. Unfortunately, although I can do whatever I command myself to do, I lack the true courage, which is self-possession in an unforeseen situation. My aim was bad. Had I been throwing a cricket ball at a wicket, which is a smaller object than an actor or an actress, I would not have failed, but as it was, one boot fell in the stalls and the other struck a musician or the brassy thing in his hand. Then I ran out of a side door and down the stairs. Just as I came to the street door I heard feet behind and thought it must be the orchestra and that increased my panic. The realists turn our words into gravel but the musicians and the

2

24–25 Romeo and Juliet] *Romeo and Juliet AVB*

27–28 head, what] head: What *AVB*

29 Miss. . . . . ? *rev from* Miss . . . . . SMR_1

32 intensity? *rev from* intensity. SMR_1

37–38 Unfortunately,] ¶ Unfotunately *AVB*

41 cricket ball] cricket-ball *AVB*

43 failed,] failed; *AVB*

48 orchestra] orchestra, *AVB*

49 but] but, *AVB*

singers turn them into honey and oil. I have always had the idea that some day a musician would do me an injury. The street door opened on to a narrow lane, and down this lane I ran until I ran straight into the arms of an old gentleman standing at a street corner by the open door of a big covered motor car. He pulled me into the car, for I was so out of breath that I could not resist, and the car drove off. 'Put on these boots' he said, 'I am afraid they are too large but I thought it best to be on the safe side, and I have brought you a pair of clean socks.' I was in such a panic, and everything so like a dream, that I did what I was told. He dropped my muddy socks out of the window and said "You need not say what you have done, unless you care to tell Robartes. I was told to wait at the corner for a man without boots." He brought me here; all I need add is that I have lived in this house since that night some six or seven months ago, and that it is a great relief to talk to people of my own generation. You at any rate cannot sympathise with that horrible generation that in childhood sucked Ibsen from Archer's hygienic bottle. You can understand even better than Robartes why that protest must always seem the great event of my life.'

'I find my parents detestable,' said the young woman, 'but I like my grandparents.' 'How could

3

50 oil. *rev from* oil, SMR_1

55 motor car] motor-car *AVB*

58 large] large, *AVB*

64 Robartes. *rev from* Robartes, SMR_1

66 here; all] here. All *AVB*

70 that horrible] a horrible *AVB*

Mr. Aherne know' said I, 'what was going to happen? You only thought of the protest when sitting in the theatre.' 'Robartes' said O'Leary 'sees what is going to happen, between sleeping and waking at night, or in the morning before they bring him his early cup of tea. Aherne is a pious Catholic, thinks it Pagan or something of the kind and hates it, but he has to do what Robartes tells him, always had to from childhood up. But Robartes says, you must not ask me questions, but introduce yourselves and tell your story.'

'My name is John Duddon,' said I, 'and this young woman insists on calling herself Denise de L'Isle Adam, and that tall fair young man is Peter Huddon. He gets everything he wants and I hate him. We were friends until Denise began going about with him.' At this point I was interrupted by Denise saying that I had starved until Huddon bought my pictures, that he had bought seven large landscapes, thirty sketches from life, nine portraits of herself, and that I had charged twice their value. Huddon stopped her, said that he would give more could he afford it, for my pictures were his greatest pleasure, and O'Leary begged me to continue my story. 'This afternoon' I said Huddon came to my studio and I overheard an appointment for dinner at the Café Royal. When I warned her that she would be sorry

4

85 says,] says *AVB*

99 afford it, *rev from* afford it SMR_1

101 said Huddon] said, "Huddon *AVB*

102 Café *rev from* Cafe SMR_1

if she went, she declared that no such conversation had taken place. However I bought a heavy stick & tonight stood outside the Café Royal waiting till they came out. Presently a man came out. I thought it was Huddon and brought my stick down on his head. He dropped on the pavement and I thought "I have knocked down my only patron, and that is a magnificent thing to have done", and I felt like dancing. Then I saw that the man on the pavement was a strange old gentleman, I found the café porter, said the old gentleman had fallen down in a fit, and we carried him a few doors up the street and into a chemist's shop. But I knew the truth would come out when he woke up, so I slipped into the hotel, found Huddon's table and told him what happened and asked his advice. He said "The right thing is to get the old gentleman not to prosecute". So we went to the chemist's shop where a small crowd had gathered. The old gentleman was sitting up in a little back room muttering "Just like my luck....bound to happen sooner or later". Huddon said "It was an accident, Sir, you cannot take offence at being knocked down in mistake for me". "In mistake for you?" said the old gentleman staring steadily at Huddon. "An upstanding man, a fine upstanding man—no offence." And then as though he had suddenly thought of something "I will not

5

---

105 However...&] However,...and *AVB*
106 outside the Café *rev from* onside the Cafe SMR_1 ; tonight] to-night *AVB*
111 done", *rev from* done" SMR_1
113 café *rev from* cafe SMR_1
116 chemist's *rev from* chemists SMR_1
117 hotel] café *AVB*
118 table and told] table, told *AVB*
121 chemist's *rev from* chemist SMR_1
123 muttering] muttering. *AVB*
125 Sir,] sir; *AVB*
127 gentleman] gentleman, *AVB*
130 something "I *rev from* something" I SMR_1

In the bottom margin (right), an indecipherable, one-word inscription is scribbled out.

say a word to the police on the condition that you and this young man and this young woman meet a friend of mine and drink a little wine."'

II

Presently Aherne came in with a big old man. Aherne, now that I saw him in a good light, was stout and sedentary-looking, bearded and dull of eye, but this other was lank, brown, muscular, clean-shaven, with an alert, ironical eye. 'This is Michael Robartes' said Aherne, and took a plate of sandwiches, glasses and a bottle of Champagne out of a cupboard and laid them upon a small table, and found chairs for himself and Robartes. Robartes asked which was which for he already knew our names and said 'I want the right sort of young men and women for pupils. Aherne acts as my messenger. What shall we talk about? Art?' Denise is shy with old men, and Huddon calls old men 'Sir' and makes them shy, so for the sake of saying something, I said 'No. That is my profession' 'War?' said Robartes, and Huddon said 'That is my profession, Sir, and I am tired of it'. 'Love?' said Robartes, and Denise whose struggles with shyness always drive her into audacity, said 'O, no. That is my profession. Tell me the story of your life.' 'Aherne, the book' said Robartes. Aherne unlocked a bookcase and

6

---

131 you *rev from* you, *SMR*$_1$
133 wine.'" *rev from* wine." *SMR*$_1$
136 eye, *rev from* eye' *SMR*$_1$
140 Champagne] champagne *AVB*
141 a cupboard *rev from* a a cupboard *SMR*$_1$
143 which for] which, for *AVB*
144 names] names, *AVB*
147 old men *rev from* oldmen *SMR*$_1$; 'Sir'] "sir" *AVB*
149 No. That *rev from* No, that *SMR*$_1$
150 Sir,] sir, *AVB*
152 Denise] Denise, *AVB*
153 'O,] "Oh, *AVB*
154 the story *rev from* thestory *SMR*$_1$

brought out a bit of goatskin and out of this an old battered book. 'I have brought you here' said Robartes, 'to tell you where I found that book, what followed from the finding of it, what is still to follow. I had founded a small cabalistic society in Ireland; but, finding time & place were against me, dissolved it and left the country. I went to Rome and there fell violently in love with a ballet-dancer who had not an idea in her head. All might have been well had I not been content to take what came; had I understood that her coldness and cruelty were in the transfiguration of the body an inhuman majesty; that I adored in body what I hated in will; that judgment is a Judith and drives the steel into what has stirred its flesh; that those my judgment approves seem to me, owing to an infliction of my moon, insipid. The more I tried to change her character the more did I uncover mutual enmity. A quarrel, the last of many, parted us at Vienna where her troup was dancing, and to make the quarrel as complete as possible I cohabited with an ignorant girl of the people and hired rooms ostentatious in their sordidness. One night I was thrown out of bed and saw when I lit my candle that the bed, which had fallen at one end, had been propped up by a broken chair and an old book with a pig-skin cover. In the morning I found that the book was called 'Speculum Angelorum et

7

---

160 Ireland; *rev from* Ireland SMR_1 ; cabalistic] Cabalistic *AVB*

161 &] and *AVB*

166 were] became *AVB*

174 troup] troupe *AVB*

182 'Speculum Angelorum et] *Speculum Angelorum et AVB*

177–78 A stroke in right margin accompanied by an erasure, which seems correspondent with an erased stroke through the word "bed" in l. 178.

Hominum', had been written by a certain Giraldus and been printed at Cracow in 1594, a good many years before the celebrated Cracow publications. It was very dilapidated, all the middle pages had been torn out ; but there still remained a series of allegorical pictures, a man torn in two by an eagle and some sort of wild beast, a man whipping his shadow, a man between a hunchback and a fool in cap and bells, and so on to the number of eight and twenty, a portrait of Giraldus, a unicorn several times repeated, a large diagram in the shape of a wheel where the phases of the moon were mixed up with an apple, an acorn, a cup, and what looked like a sceptre or wand. My mistress had found it in a wall cupboard where it had been left by the last tenant, an unfrocked priest who had joined a troup of gypsies and disappeared, & she had torn out the middle pages to light our fire. Though little remained of the Latin text I spent a couple of weeks comparing one passage with another and all with the unintelligible diagrams. One day I returned from a library, where I had made a fruitless attempt to identify my Giraldus with Giraldus of Bologna, and found my mistress gone, whether in mere disgust at my preoccupation or, as I hope, to some more attentive man. I had nothing now to distract my thoughts that ran through my past loves, neither numerous, nor happy, back to

8

---

183 Hominum',...Giraldus] *Hominum*,...Giraldus, *AVB*

184 and] had *AVB*

198 gypsies *rev from* gipsies *SMR*$_1$

199 fire. *rev from* fire, *SMR*$_1$; &] and *AVB*

200 text] text, *AVB*

201 passage *rev from* passsage *SMR*$_1$

205 and found *rev from* to find *SMR*$_1$

207–14 I had nothing now to distract my thoughts, that ran | through my past loves, neither numerous nor happy, | back to that platonic love of boyhood the most impassioned | of all. & I was plunged into hopeless misery. I have | always known that love should be changeless & yet mine | ~~confer consumes their food~~ <soon drank their oil> & died—there has been [?] <no> ever | burning lamp. SB 0400771

The tipped in figure of "The Great Wheel," located between pages 8 and 9 in the 1931 printing was lacking in the proofs. See Yeats's marginal note on p. 1, above, where "The Great Wheel" and, near the end, the figure of Giraldus are referred to as "diagrams." Both of these were relocated to different points in *AVB*.

The Great Wheel

the platonic love of boyhood, the most impassioned of all, and was plunged into hopeless misery. I have always known that love should be changeless and yet my loves drank their oil and died—there has been no ever-burning lamp.' He sank his head upon his breast and we sat in silence, until Denise said 'I do not think we should blame ourselves as long as we remain unmarried. I have always believed that neither Church nor State should grant divorce under any circumstances. It is necessary to keep in existence the symbol of eternal love.' Robartes did not seem to have heard, for he took up his theme where he had left it. 'Love contains all Kant's antinomies but it is the first that poisons our lives. Thesis, there is no beginning; antithesis, there is a beginning; or, as I prefer; thesis, there is no end. I cry out "My love will never end". Exhausted by that cry it ends; without that cry it were not love but desire, desire does not end. The anguish of birth and death cry out in the same instant. Life is no series of emanations from divine reason such as the cabalists imagine, but an irrational bitterness, no orderly descent from level to level, no waterfall but a whirlpool, a gyre. One night between three and four in the morning as I lay sleepless, it came into my head to go pray at the Holy Sepulchre. I went, prayed, grew somewhat calmer, until I said to myself "Jesus Christ

9

---

210 the platonic love of boyhood *rev from* platonic love of my boyhood SMR_2

220 symbol *rev from* sybol SMR_2

221 heard, *rev from* heard SMR_2

224 antithesis,...beginning; or, *rev from* anthi-thesis,...beginning; or SMR_2

225 as I prefer; thesis, there is no end. I cry out "My *rev from* as I prefer, I cry out "My SMR_3 *rev from* as I prefer, there is no end. I cry out "My SMR_2 ; prefer; thesis, there is no end.] prefer: thesis, there is an end; antithesis, there is no end. *AVB*

226 end." Exhausted...ends; *rev from* end, exhausted...ends, SMR_2 ; Exhausted by that cry it ends;] Exhausted by the cry that it can never end, my love ends; *AVB*

228 and death] and that of death *AVB*

230 cabalists] Cabalists *AVB*

233 One night] ¶ "One night, *AVB*

234 morning] morning, *AVB*

236 "Jesus *rev from* 'Jesus SMR_2

Top margin (right, in Yeats's handwriting): "Revise" in SMR_2; "Press" in SMR_3

Top margin (centered, in another hand): "L.C. Pursers suggestions". SMR_3

Top margin (circumscribed and in Yeats's hand): "I accept all Pursers | suggestions that I have not crossed out" SMR_3

does not understand my despair, He belongs to order and reason." The day after, an old Arab walked unannounced into my room. He said that he had been sent, stood where the *Speculum* lay open at the wheel marked with the phases of the moon, described it as the doctrine of his tribe, drew two whorls working one against the other, the narrow end of one in the broad end of the other, showed that my single wheel and his two whorls had the same meaning. He belonged to a tribe of Arabs who called themselves Judwalis or Diagrammatists because their children are taught dances which leave symbolical traces upon the sand. I joined that tribe, accepted its dress, customs, morality, politics, that I might win its trust and its knowledge. I have fought in its wars and risen to authority. Your young Colonel Lawrence never suspected the nationality of the old Arab fighting at his side. I have completed my life, balanced every pleasure with a danger lest my bones might soften.'

III

Some six weeks later, Huddon, Denise, O'Leary and I sat in silence round the same fire. For the last few days we had slept and eaten in the house that Robartes might teach us without interruption. Robartes came in with a little chest of carved ivory and sat

10

---

238 reason." The...Arab *rev from* reason. The...arab SMR_2

243 whorls *rev from* whirls SMR_2

243–44 narrow end *rev from* narrowend SMR_2

246 Arabs *rev from* arabs SMR_2

247 Diagrammatists *rev from* Di-agrammatists SMR_2

249 symbolical traces upon the sand.] upon the sand traces full of symbolical meaning. *AVB*

257 Some six weeks] Three months *AVB*

261 with] carrying *AVB*

down, the chest upon his knees. Denise, who had been in a state of suppressed excitement all day, said: 'Nobody knows why I call myself Denise de L'Isle Adam, but I have decided to tell my story.' Her story was never told; for at that moment Aherne ushered in a pale slight woman of thirty five and a spectacled man who seemed somewhat older. When Aherne had found them chairs Robartes said : 'We will call them John Bond and Mary Bell from the characters in a doggerel of Blake's. For reasons which will become apparent when you have heard their story you must not know their true names. Aherne brought them from Ireland that you may hear it and because Mary Bell's a suitable guardian and bearer for what I carry in this box.' John Bond began without further preliminary; 'Some fifteen

[11, in part]

---

265 my story.'] my story". *AVB*
266 told; for *rev from* told for SMR_2
271 doggerel *rev from* doggerell SMR_2

265–77 Her story…further preliminary; *lacking in AVB*. At this point, almost certainly as a lengthy insertion introduced into the proof of *A Vision* in late 1936 and submitted to Macmillan in 1937 (see Part Five, below, on the interpretation of Denise's story and its making), "Stories of Michael Robartes and His Friends" was amplified as follows:

> "You told that story," said Huddon, "half a dozen times at the Café Royal and should be satisfied."
>
> At that moment, to my great relief, Aherne ushered in a pale slight woman of thirty-five and a spectacled man who seemed somewhat older. When Aherne had found them chairs, Robartes said: "This is John Bond and this is Mary Bell. Aherne has brought John Bond from Ireland that you may hear what he has to say, and Mary Bell because I think her a suitable guardian for what I carry in this box. Before John Bond tells his story, I must insist upon Denise telling hers; from what I know of her, I feel certain that it will be a full and admirable introduction."
>
> Denise began: "I was reading *Axel* in bed. It was between twelve and one on the 2nd June last year. A date that I will never forget, because on that night I met the one man I shall always love. I was turning the pages of the Act where the lovers are in the vault under the castle. Axel and Sarah decide to die rather than possess one another. He talks of her hair as full of the odour of dead rose leaves—a pretty phrase—a phrase I would like somebody to say to me; and then comes the famous sentence: 'As for living, our servants

[Cuala p. 11 continued]

---

will do that for us'. I was wondering what made them do anything so absurd, when the candle went out. I said, 'Duddon, I heard you open the window, creep over the floor on your toes, but I never guessed that you would blow the candle out'. 'Denise,' he said, 'I am a great coward. I am afraid of unfamiliar women in pyjamas.' I said: 'No, my dear, you are not a coward, you were just shy, but why should you call me unfamiliar? I thought I had put everything right when I told you that I slept on the ground floor, that there was nobody else on that floor, and that I left the window open.' Five minutes later I said: 'Duddon, you are impotent, stop trembling; go over there and sit by the fire. I will give you some wine.' When he had drunk half a tumbler of claret, he said: 'No, I am not really impotent, I am a coward, that is all. When Huddon tires of a girl, I make love to her, and there is no difficulty at all. He has always talked about her, but if he had not, it would not make much difference. He is my greatest friend, and when she and he have been in the same bed, it is as though she belonged to the house. Twice I have found somebody on my own account, and been a failure, just as I have to-night. I had not indeed much hope when I climbed through the window but I had a little, because you had made it plain that I would be welcome.' I said: 'Oh, my dear, how delightful; now I know all about Axel. He was just shy. If he had not killed the Commander in the Second Act—and it would have been much more dramatic at the end of the play—he could have sent for him and all would have come right. The Commander was not a friend, of course; Axel hated him; but he was a relation, and afterwards Axel could have thought of Sarah as a member of the family. I love you because you would not be shy if you had not so great respect for me. You feel about me what I feel about a Bishop in a surplice. I would not give you up now for anything.' Duddon said, wringing his hands: 'Oh, what am I to do'. I said: 'Fetch the Commander'. He said, getting cheerful at once: 'I am to bring Huddon?'

"A fortnight later Duddon and I were in Florence. We had plenty of money, for Huddon had just bought a large picture, and were delighted with each other. I said: 'I am going to send Huddon this little cigarette-case'. It was one of those pretty malachite things they sell in Florence. I had had it engraved with the words: 'In memory of the 2nd June'. He said: 'Why put into it only one cigarette?' I said: 'Oh, he will understand'.

"And now you know," said Denise, "why I have named myself after the author of *Axel*." I said: "You wish always to remember that upon that night I introduced you to Huddon". She said: "What a fool you are. It is you that I love, and shall always love." I said: "But you are Huddon's mistress?" She said: "When a man gives me a cigarette, and I like the brand, I want a hundred, but the box is almost empty".

"Now", said Robartes, "the time has come for John Bond." John Bond, after fixing a bewildered eye, first upon Denise and then upon me, began. He had evidently prepared his words beforehand. "Some fifteen (*AVB* 42–44)

[N.B.: with the addition of Denise's story in *AVB*, Yeats has omitted Robartes's remark that John Bond and Mary Bell are pseudonyms based on "the characters in a doggerel of Blake's" (lines 270–71, above). Actually, the names derive from two poems from the Pickering Manuscript: "John Brown & Little Mary Bell" and "William Bond." See *WWB3* 82 and 79, respectively.

[Cuala p.11 continued]

years ago this lady married an excellent man, much older than herself, who lived in a large house on the more peaceable side of the Shannon. Her marriage was childless but happy and might have continued so had she not in its ninth year been told to winter abroad. She went alone to the south of France, for her husband had scientific and philanthropic work that he could not leave. I was resting at Cannes after completing the manuscript work on the migratory birds, and at Cannes we met and fell in love at first sight. Brought up in the strictest principles of

11

280 Shannon. Her *rev from* Shannon, her *SMR_2*

283 France, *rev from* France *SMR_3*

284 philanthropic *rev from* philathrophic *SMR_2*

287 birds, *rev from* birds *SMR_2*

the Church of Ireland we were horror-struck and hid our feelings from one another. I fled from Cannes to find her at Monaco, from Monaco to find her at Antibes, from Antibes to find her at Cannes, until chancing upon the same hotel we so far accepted fate that we dined at the same table, and after parting for ever in the garden accepted fate completely. In a little while she was with child. She was the first woman that had come into my life, and had I not remembered an episode in the life of Voltaire I had been helpless. We were penniless; for the child's sake and her own she must return to her husband at once.

'As Mary Bell left my letters unanswered I concluded that she meant me to drop out of her life. I read of our child's birth, and heard nothing for five years. I accepted a post in the Dublin Museum, specialised in the subject of Irish migratory birds, and at four o'clock one afternoon an attendant brought her into my office. I was greatly moved, but she spoke as if to a stranger. I was "Mr. Bond," she was "sorry to intrude upon my time" but I was "the only person in Ireland who could give her certain information". I took the hint and became the courteous Curator, I was there "to help the student". She wished to study the nests of certain migratory birds and thought the only exact method

12

---

289 Church *rev from* church SMR_2 ; Ireland] Ireland, *AVB*
298 Voltaire *rev from* Voltaire. SMR_2
301 once. *rev from* once.' SMR_2
304 birth, and heard nothing] birth, heard nothing more *AVB*
307 birds, *rev from* birds SMR_2
311 "the *rev from* 'the SMR_2
312 information". *rev from* information'. SMR_2
313 "to help *rev from* 'to help SMR_2
313–14 stu- dent". *rev from* student'. SMR_2
315 birds and thought] birds, thought *AVB*

was to make their nests with her own hands. She had found and copied nests in her own neighbourhood, but as progress, entirely dependent on personal observation, was slow, wanted to know what had been published on the subject. Every species preferred some special materials, twigs, lichens, grasses, mosses, bunches of hair and so on, and had a special architecture. I told her what I knew and sent her books, proceedings of learned societies, and passages translated from foreign tongues. Some months later she brought me swift's, swallow's, corncrake's, and red-warbler's nests made by her own hands and so well that when I compared them with the natural nests in the cases of stuffed birds I could see no difference. Her manner had changed, it was embarrassed, almost mysterious, as though she were keeping something back. She wanted to make a nest for a bird of a certain size and shape. She could not or would not name its species but named its genus. She wanted information about the nesting habits of that genus, borrowed a couple of books, and saying that she had a train to catch went away. A month later a telegram called me to her country house. I found her waiting at the little station. Her husband was dying, and wished to consult with me about a scientific work he had carried on for many years; he did not know that we knew each other but was acquainted with my work. When I asked what his

13

---

316 her own *rev from* their own *SMR*$_2$
323 knew and sent] knew, sent *AVB*
324 passages *rev from* passages, *SMR*$_2$
326 swift's, swallow's, corncrake's, *rev from* swifts, swallows, corncrakes *SMR*$_2$
326–27 and red-warbler's *rev from* red-warblers *SMR*$_2$
328 that] that, *AVB*
329 birds *rev from* birds, *SMR*$_2$; birds, *AVB*
330 changed,] changed; *AVB*
330–31 embarras- sed *rev from* embar- assed *SMR*$_2$
337 catch] catch, *AVB*

326–7 The list of birds with the incorrect placement of apostrophes might have been corrected in *SMR*$_3$ but was not. Correctly marked in *SMR*$_2$ (in red pencil) the typesetter transposed each terminal "s" with the intended apostrophes. The errors remained in *AVB* and stand uncorrected in subsequent editions of *A Vision*.

scientific work was, she said that he would explain, and began to speak of the house and its surroundings. The deplorable semi-gothic gateway we had passed a moment before was the work of her husband's father, but I must notice the great sycamores and lucombe oaks and the clump of cedars, & there were great plantations behind the house. There had been a house there in the seventeenth century, but the present house was made in the eighteenth century, when most of the trees were planted. Arthur Young had described their planting and spoken of the great change it would make in the neighbourhood. She thought a man who planted trees, knowing that no descendent nearer than his great-grandson could stand under their shade, had a noble and generous confidence. She thought there was something terrible about it, for it was terrible standing under the great trees to say "Am I worthy of that confidence?" The doors were opened by an elderly maid who met us with the smile of the country servant. As she brought me to my room and as I mounted the stairs I noticed walls covered with photographs and engravings, the Grillion Club portraits, photographs signed by celebrities of the sixties and seventies of the last century. I knew that Mr. Bell's father had been a man of considerable culture, that Mr. Bell himself had been in the Foreign Office as a young man, but here was the evidence that one or

14

---

345 and its *rev from* andits SMR_2
346 gateway *rev from* gateway, SMR_2
347 before *rev from* before, SMR_2
349 &] and *AVB*
361 "Am *rev from* 'Am SMR_2
361–62 con- fidence?' *rev from* con- fidence.' SMR_2
362 The doors] ¶ "The doors *AVB*
368–69 fa- ther *rev from* Father SMR_2
371 man, *rev from* man SMR_2

---

349 "lucombe" is underscored in red pencil and marked for deletion in SMR_2, but the edit is stricken in black ink.

other had known most of the famous writers, artists, and politicians of his time. I returned to the ground floor to find Mary Bell at the tea table with a little boy. I had begun to discover in his face characteristics of my family when she said "Everybody thinks he is so like his great-uncle, the famous Chancery lawyer, the friend of Goldsmith and of Burke, but you can judge for yourself, that is his portrait by Gainsborough." Then she sent the little boy away but told him not to make a noise because of his father's illness. I stood at a window which opened on to the garden, noticed a number of square boxes much too large to be beehives, and asked their purpose. She said, "they are connected with Mr. Bell's work", but seemed disinclined to say more. I wandered about the room studying family portraits; one a Peter Lely; mezzotints, framed letters from Chatham and Horace Walpole, dueling swords & pistols arranged upon the walls by generations who did not care how incongruous the mixture that called up their own past history. Presently an hospital nurse came to say "Mr. Bell has been asking for Mr. Bond. He is very weak; very near his end; but when he has spoken what is on his mind will die happier. He wants to see Mr. Bond alone." I followed her upstairs and found the old man in a great fourposter, in a room hung with

15

---

373 politicians *rev from* pol- iticians *SMR*$_3$; time. I returned *rev from* time. Returned *SMR*$_2$

374 tea table] tea-table *AVB*

376–77 "Every- body *rev from* Everybody *SMR*$_2$

380 Gainsborough." *rev from* Gainsborough.' *SMR*$_2$

385 purpose. She said, "They *rev from* purpose, she said, 'they *SMR*$_2$

386 work", *rev from* work', *SMR*$_2$

388 portraits; one a Peter Lely; *rev from* portraits—one a Peter Lely— *SMR*$_2$; portraits; a Peter Lely; *AVB*

390 & pistols. *rev from* and pistol *SMR*$_2$; &] and *AVB*

393 "Mr. Bell *rev from* 'Mr. Bell *SMR*$_2$

397 Bond alone." *rev from* Bell alone." *SMR*$_3$ rev from Bell alone.' *SMR*$_2$

398 fourposter] four-poster *AVB*

---

373 The notation "poli/ticians" at the top of the page in *SMR*$_3$ attempts to correct the hyphenation in *SMR*$_2$. Earlier revisions made on the letterpress, in justifying lines of type, made hyphenation unnecessary.

390 Similarly, the resetting of type made necessary the substitution of "&" for "and" in this line. This occurred after *SMR*$_3$ was marked for "Press."

copies of paintings by Murillo and his contemporaries brought from Italy in the days of the Grand Tour, and one modern picture, a portrait of Mary painted by Sargent in her early twenties.

The old man who must have been animated and genial once, smiled and tried to rise from his pillow but fell back with a sigh. The nurse arranged the pillows, told me to call her when he had finished, and went into a dressingroom. He said: "When I left the Foreign Office because I wanted to serve God I was a very young man. I wanted to make men better but not to leave this estate, and here nobody did wrong except as children do. Providence had surrounded me with such goodness that to think of altering it seemed blasphemy. I married, & it seemed wrong to give nothing in return for so much happiness. I thought a great deal and remembered that birds and beasts, dumb brutes of all kinds, were robbing and killing one another. There at any rate I could alter without blasphemy. I have never taken Genesis literally. The passions of Adam, torn out of his breast, became the birds and beasts of Eden; partakers in original sin, they can be partakers in salvation. I knew that the longest life could do but little, and wishing especially to benefit those who lacked what I possessed, I decided to devote

16

---

402 painted by Sargent in her early twenties.] in her early twenties, painted by Sargent *AVB*

403 The old man who *rev from* The old man 'who *SMR_3* *rev from* 'The old man, who *SMR_2*; "The old man who *AVB*

404 genial once, *rev from* genial once' *SMR_3* *rev from* genial once *SMR_2*

407 "When *rev from* 'When *SMR_2* ; dressingroom] dressing-room *AVB*

413 seemed *rev from* seem *SMR_3* ; &] and *AVB*

421 Eden; partakers] Eden. Partakers *AVB*

---

403 The extra space before this line is an accident, not intended as an episodic shift in narrative. In *SMR_3*, the space was occupied by "ties" from the hyphenation of "twenties." Thus, a resetting of type that subsequently occurred caused line 402 to contract. *AVB* perpetuates the miscue while tabbing for the new paragraph at line 403.

my life to the cuckoos. I put cuckoos in cages, and have now so many cages that they stand side by side along the whole southern wall of the garden. My great object was of course to persuade them to make nests; but for a long time they were so obstinate, so unteachable, that I almost despaired. But the birth of a son renewed my resolution and a year ago I persuaded some of the oldest and cleverest birds to make circles with matches, twigs, and fragments of moss, but though the numbers who can do this are increasing, even the cleverest birds make no attempt to weave them into a structure. I am dying, but you have far greater knowledge than I and I ask you to continue my work." At that moment I heard Mary Bell's voice behind me "it is unnecessary, a cuckoo has made a nest. Your long illness made the gardeners careless. I only found it by chance a moment ago, a beautiful nest, finished to the last layer of down." She had crept unnoticed into the room and stood at my elbow holding out a large nest. The old man tried to take it but was too weak. "Now let Thy servant depart in peace" he murmured. She laid the nest upon the pillow and he turned over, closing his eyes. Calling the nurse we crept out, and shutting the door stood side by side. Neither of us spoke for almost a minute, then Mary flung herself into my arms and said amid her sobs "We have given him great happiness."

17

---

438 work." *rev from* work.' *SMR*$_4$
439 "it *rev from* 'it *SMR*$_4$; me "it] me. 'It *AVB*
443 down." *rev from* down.' *SMR*$_4$
445 "Now let *rev from* 'Now may *SMR*$_4$
446 peace" *rev from* peace' *SMR*$_4$
447 over, *rev from* over *SMR*$_4$
451 "We *rev from* 'We *SMR*$_4$
452 happiness." *rev from* happiness.'*SMR*$_4$

Inscribed in upper right-hand margin: "Revise".

Next morning when I came down to breakfast I learnt that Mr. Bell had died in his sleep a little before daybreak. Mary did not come down, and when I saw her some hours later she spoke of nothing but the boy. "We must devote our whole lives to him. You must undertake his education. We must not think of ourselves."

'At the funeral Mary noticed an old, unknown man among the neighbours and dependants, and when the funeral was over he introduced himself as Mr. Owen Aherne. He told us of scenes that had risen before Mr. Robartes' eyes on several successive mornings as he awaited his early tea. These scenes being part of our intimate lives, our first meeting in the South of France, our first meeting in the museum, even the four-poster with the nest on the pillow, so startled us that we set out for London that very evening. All afternoon we have talked with Mr. Robartes, that inspired man, and Mary Bell has at his bidding undertaken a certain task. I return to Ireland tomorrow to take charge until her return of the estate and of her son'.

Said Robartes 'I have now two questions to ask, and four of you must answer. Mary Bell and John Bond need not, for I have taught them nothing. Their task in life is settled'. Then he turned towards O'Leary, Denise, Huddon and myself, and said: 'Have I proved by practical demonstration that the

18

---

453 Next *rev from* 'Next *SMR*$_4$; "Next *AVB*

456 later she *rev from* later. She *SMR*$_4$

457 "We *rev from* 'We *SMR*$_4$

458 undertake] think *AVB*

459 ourselves." *rev from* ourselves.' *SMR*$_4$

460 'At *rev from* At *SMR*$_4$

473 tomorrow] to-morrow *AVB*

475 ¶ IV ¶ Said *AVB*

476 answer. *rev from* answer, *SMR*$_5$

In *SMR*$_5$ editor's space markings are laid in at lines 466 and 473 to indicate that words are set too tightly.

475 This is still the first line of a new paragraph. But it has finally been noticed, in correcting text for *A Vision*, that the fourth episode has lacked the designation of a numeral "IV" (inserted between lines 474 and 475 in *AVB*).

soul survives the body?' He looked at me and I said 'Yes' ; and after me the others, speaking in turn, said 'Yes'. He went on 'We have read Swift's essay upon the dissensions of the Greeks and Romans; you have heard my comments, corrections, amplifications. Have I proved that civilisations come to an end when they have given all their light like burned out wicks, that ours is near its end?' 'Or transformation' Aherne corrected. I said, speaking in the name of all, 'you have proved that civilisations burn out and that ours is near its end'. 'Or transformation' Aherne corrected once more. 'If you had answered differently', said Robartes 'I would have sent you away, for we are here to consider the terror that is to come.'

V

Mary Bell then opened the ivory box and took from it an egg the size of a swan's egg, and standing between us and the dark window curtains, lifted it up that we might all see its colour. 'Hyacinthine blue, according to the Greek lyric poet', said Robartes 'I bought it from an old man in a green turban at Teheran; it had come down from eldest son to eldest son for many generations'. 'No', said Aherne 'you never were in Teheran.' 'Perhaps Aherne is right' said Robartes. 'Sometimes my dreams discover facts, and sometimes lose them, but it does not matter. I

19

481 body?...said *rev from* body'?...said *SMR_5 rev from* body'?...said, *SMR_4*

487–88 burned out] burned-out *AVB*

495–96 V *lacking in AVB*

498 Window curtains] window-curtains *AVB*

488 end?' *rev from* end.' *SMR_4*

500 lyric poet', said *rev from* Lyric poets', said *SMR_5 rev from* Lyric poets', 'said *SMR_4* ; Robartes] Robarts. *AVB*

503 'you *rev from* 'You *SMR_4*

505 Robartes. *rev from* Robartes *SMR_4*

495–96 With the addition of the missing numeral "IV" at only the beginning of the preceding paragraph, the fourth part of the narrative now continues without interruption until the introduction of John Aherne's epistle, at line 587. Division and numeral V lacking in *AVB*.

bought this egg from an old man in a green turban in Arabia, or Persia, or India. He told me its history, partly handed down by word of mouth, partly as he had discovered it in ancient manuscripts. It was for a time in the treasury of Harun Al-Rashid and had come there from Byzantium, as ransom for a prince of the imperial house. Its history before that is unimportant for some centuries. During the reign of the Antonines tourists saw it hanging by a golden chain from the roof of a Spartan Temple. Those of you who are learned in the classics will have recognized the lost egg of Leda, its miraculous life still unquenched. I return to the desert in a few days with Owen Aherne and this lady chosen by divine wisdom for its guardian bearer. When I have found the appointed place, Owen Aherne and I will dig a shallow hole where she must lay it and leave it to be hatched by the sun's heat.' He then spoke of the two eggs already hatched, how Castor and Clytaemnestra broke the one shell, Helen and Pollux the other, of the tragedy that followed, wondered what would break the third shell. Then came a long discourse founded upon the philosophy of the Judwalis and of Giraldus, sometimes eloquent, often obscure. I set down a few passages without attempting to recall their context or to arrange them in consecutive order.

20

---

511 treasury *rev from* Treasury SMR_5

514–15 During the reign of the Antonines *rev from* During the reign of Antonines SMR_5 *rev from* In the time of Augustus SMR_4

516 Temple.] temple. *AVB*

525 Castor *rev from* Helen SMR_4

526 Clytaemnestra *rev from* Clytemnestra SMR_4

526 Helen *rev from* Castor SMR_4

---

515 Prior to the change from Augustus to Antonines, Yeats begins a correction in the left margin as follows: "Marcus | Au" (which he cancels and then makes the revision noted above for lines 514–15, entered in the top margin of SMR_4 and directed into the text with a drawn line. A similar procedure was followed in the bottom margin for the transposition of names in lines 525–26. All in black ink.

'I found myself upon the third antinomy of Immanuel Kant, thesis: freedom; antithesis: necessity; but I restate it. Every action of man declares the soul's ultimate, particular freedom, and the soul's disappearance in God; declares that reality is a congeries of beings and a single being; nor is this antinomy an appearance imposed upon us by the form of thought but life itself which turns, now here, now there, a whirling and a bitterness.

'After an age of necessity, truth, goodness, mechanism, science, democracy, abstraction, peace, comes an age of freedom, fiction, evil, kindred, art, aristocracy, particularity, war. Has our age burned to the socket?

'Death cannot solve the antinomy: death and life are its expression. We come at birth into a multitude and after death would perish into the One did not a witch of Endor call us back, nor would she repent did we shriek with Samuel : "Why has thou disquieted me?" instead of slumbering upon that breast.

'The marriage bed is the symbol of the solved antinomy, and were more than symbol could a man there lose and keep his identity, but he falls asleep. That sleep is the same as the sleep of death.

'Dear predatory birds, prepare for war, prepare your

21

534–35 Imman- uel Kant, thesis: freedom; antithesis: *rev from* Emanuel Kant, thesis—freedom; antithesis— SMR_4

542 bitterness.] bitterness." AVB

547 socket?] socket?" AVB

548 'Death *rev from* "Death SMR_4

552 Samuel: *rev from* Samuel:" SMR_4

554 breast.] breast." AVB

555 'The *rev from* The SMR_4

558 death.] death." AVB

559 'Dear *rev from* Dear SMR_4

children and all that you can reach, for how can a nation or a kindred without war become "that bright particular star" of Shakespeare, that lit the roads in boyhood? Test art, morality, custom, thought, by Thermopylae; make rich and poor act so to one another that they can stand together there. 'Love war because of its horror, that belief may be changed, civilization renewed. We desire belief and lack it. Belief comes from shock and is not desired. When a kindred discovers through apparition and horror that the perfect cannot perish nor even the imperfect long be interrupted, who can withstand that kindred? Belief is renewed continually in the ordeal of death'.

Aherne said:

'Even if the next divine influx be to kindreds why should war be necessary? Cannot they develop their characteristics in some other way? You are not sane when you talk like that.' He said something more which I did not hear, for I was watching Mary Bell standing motionless with ecstatic eyes. Denise whispered 'She has done very well, but Robartes should have asked me to hold it, for I am taller, and my training as a model would have helped.'

Robartes put the egg in its box again, and said good-bye to us one after the other.

John Duddon

22

561 without war become *rev from* become without war, SMR_5 *rev from* become without war SMR_4

562 Shakespeare, *rev from* Milton SMR_4

563 boyhood? *rev from* boyhood. SMR_4

564 Thermopylae; *rev from* Thermophylae SMR_4

566 'Love] Love *AVB*

571 nor even the *rev from* nor the SMR_5

576 necessary? *rev from* necessary'? SMR_4

577–78 You are not sane when you talk like that. *lacking in AVB*

579 hear, *rev from* hear SMR_4

583 helped.' *rev from* helped. SMR_4

Dear Mr. Yeats

I have access to two records of Robartes' thought and action. The first is a diary kept by my brother Owen during their tramp in Ireland in 1922 and 1923. Should I live, and my brother consent, I may publish some part of it, for they found themselves, as always, where life is at tension, and met, amidst Free State soldiers, Irregulars, country gentlemen, tramps and robbers, events that suggest, set down as they are without context or explanation, recent paintings by Mr. Jack Yeats where one guesses at the forms from a few exciting blotches of colour. The second record was made by Robartes' pupils in London and contains his diagrams and their explanations, and John Duddon's long narrative. You have sent me three poems founded upon 'hearsay' as you put it, *The Phases of the Moon, The Double Vision*, and *The Gift of Harun Al-Rashid*. The first two compared with what I find in the diary are sufficiently accurate. One has to allow of course for some condensation and heightening. *The Gift of Harun Al-Rashid* seems to have got the dates wrong, for according to the story Robartes told my brother, the Founder of the Judwali Sect, Kusta ben Luka, was a young or youngish man when Harun Al-Rashid died. However poetic license may still exist.

23

---

589 The first is a diary] There are diaries *AVB*

590 in 1922] in 1919, 1922 *AVB*

592 it,] these, *AVB*

593 always, where…met, amidst *rev from* always where…met amidst SMR_4

594 Irregulars,] irregulars, *AVB*

595 suggest, *rev from* suggest: SMR_5 *rev from* suggest— SMR_4

596 explanation, *rev from* explanation: of SMR_5 *rev from* explanation those of SMR_4

599 The second record was] There is a record *AVB*

605 diary] diaries *AVB*

609 wrong, *rev from* wrong SMR_4

612 Harun Al-Rashid *rev from* Harun-Al Rashid SMR_4

603–04, 607–08 The titles of Yeats's poems are removed from italics and presented within quotation marks in *AVB*.

I have compared what you have sent of your unpublished book* with the diagrams and explanations in the second record, and find no essential difference. That you should have found what was lost in the *Speculum* or the inaccessible encampments of the Judwalis, interests me but does not astonish. I recall what Plato said of memory, and suggest that your automatic script, or whatever it was, may well have been but a process of remembering. I think that Plato symbolised by the word 'memory' a relation to the timeless, but Duddon is more literal and discovers a resemblance between your face and that of Giraldus in the *Speculum*. I enclose a photograph of the woodcut.

You ask if Robartes and my brother are as hot as ever about that old quarrel and exactly what is the quarrel. This is what I found after questioning various people. Some thirty years ago you made *Rosa Alchemica, The Tables of the Law* and *The Adoration of the Magi*, out of 'a slight incident'. Robartes, then a young man, had founded a society, with the unwilling help of my brother Owen, for the study of the *Kabbala Denudata* and similar books, invented

**I published in 1925 an inaccurate, obscure, incomplete book called 'A Vision.' It lies beside me now, corrected, clarified and completed after five years' work and thought.*

24

615 * *lacking in AVB*

615–16 in the second record,] recorded by his pupils, *AVB*

618 or the] or survives in the *AVB*

634 society, *rev from* society SMR_4

639 years' *rev from* year's SMR_5 *rev from* years SMR_4

637–40 *lacking in AVB*

626 Yeats marks an "X" beside "Giraldus" and underscores the terminal "s" to indicate a light impression in print.

631–33 The titles of Yeats's short stories are removed from italics and presented within quotation marks in *AVB*.

The figure of Giraldus that follows this page in the 1931 edition is lacking in SMR_4 and SMR_5. It was moved forward in *AVB* to approximately the point which had been occupied by the figure of "The Great Wheel" in the 1931 edition of *SMR*. (See p. 8 note.) As noted in the top margin of SMR_1, the woodcut designs by Edmund Duloc were yet coming with a final press setting.

some kind of ritual and hired an old shed on Howth Pier for its meetings. A foolish rumour got out among the herring or mackerel sorters, and some girls (from Glasgow, my brother says, for they come from all parts) broke the window. You hatched out of this the murder of Robartes and his friends, and though my brother incorporated Christ in the ritual, described a sort of orgy in honour of the pagan gods. My brother is very bitter about the pagan gods but is so, according to Robartes, to prove himself an orthodox man. Robartes makes no complaint about your description of his death and says nobody would have thought the Aherne and Robartes of such fantastic stories real men but for Owen's outcry. He is however (and this I confirm from my own knowledge) bitter about your style in those stories and says that you substituted sound for sense and ornament for thought. What happened immediately before his separation from Europe must stand out with an unnatural distinction. I wrote once to remonstrate. I said that you wrote in those tales, as many good writers wrote at the time over half Europe, that such prose was the equivalent of what somebody had called 'absolute poetry' and somebody else 'pure poetry'; that though it lacked speed and variety, it would have acquired both, as Elizabethan prose did after the *Arcadia*, but for the surrender everywhere to the sensational & the topical;

25

---

643 mackerel *rev from* mackrel SMR_4

644 girls (from *rev from* girls: from SMR_6; *rev from* girls: SMR_4 (a revision from "girls—")

645 parts) *rev from* parts: SMR_6 also SMR_4 (a revision from "parts—")

647–48 in the ritual *rev from* in ritual SMR_6; also "the" deleted before "described" and "honour"

650 gods] gods, *AVB*

655 however (and *rev from* however: and SMR_6; rev from however: SMR_4 (a revision from "however—"); is] is, *AVB*

656 knowledge) *rev from* knowledge: SMR_6 also SMR_4 (a revision from "knowledge—"); knowledge)] knowledge), *AVB*

661 tales,] tales *AVB* 668 &] and *AVB*

Top margin inscription in SMR_4: "Revise".

644–45 and 655–56 corrections listed here lack the intervening, or final, correction of the colons to parentheses (open or closed) as would have been marked on the final press copy.

that romance driven to its last ditch had a right to swagger. He answered that when the candle was burnt out an honest man did not pretend that grease was flame.

John Aherne

[26]

The SMR_4 proof copy bears no corrections, and SMR_5 lacks pages 25 and 26. The typed fragment NLI 30,465 agrees with lines 669–73 in every respect, having been used at some late stage in producing setting copy at the Cuala Press.

The Resurrection follows directly on page [27].

Part Five: 1932–1937

Afterword: Unpublished and Published Additions

Prepared for *A Vision* (Macmillan, 1937)

"Michael Robartes Foretells": A Rejected Ending

On 14 March 1926, nearly a year after Yeats wrote in his notebook that he had "finished" the first edition of *A Vision*, he recorded that the last part of it, Book IV, especially section 2.xii ("The Spirits at Fifteen and at One"), was the "slightest & worst," rather than "the most important in the book" (NLI 13,576, folio 7^{v}). *A Vision* (1925) had only been available to subscribers since 15 January 1926. He wondered if the problem might be ameliorated on the subject of a man and a woman interacting "like East & West. Love must become an image of civilization." Possibly, he might "write it [as] a letter from Robartes to two young Arab lovers. That would make it more credible—the Rose of the Arab poets to help. Look up Hafiz."[1] In that vicinity (*AVA* Book IV.2.ix-x and xiii), he had placed parenthetical extracts from the fictitious "Robartes papers" as if inserted by Owen Aherne. The imaginary letter was never written although the precedent for a solution such as that must have seemed promising.

Similarly, a thought to introduce Robartes at the end of the rewritten edition of 1937 came to nought sometime before Yeats submitted his manuscript to Macmillan in December 1934. "Michael Robartes Foretells," as the new movement was called, was an extension of the body of fiction he had composed in 1930, seen completed in proof at the Cuala Press on All Hallows' Eve (31 October) 1931, and celebrated, in March 1932, with publication of *Stories of Michael Robartes and His Friends: an Extract from a Record Made by His Pupils: and a Play in Prose*. When a complimentary copy was sent to George Russell ("AE"), one of Yeats's models for Robartes (and a sympathetic fellow mystic, senator, editor, and Irish man of letters), Russell responded with advice that might have inspired "Michael Robartes Foretells" as a means of making "credible" some changes in style that he noted in the booklet:

> I had already a copy of the Robartes Stories but I am pleased indeed to have a copy from yourself. They are a great change in style from the earlier tales and I think the intellectual atmosphere so strange that to make it credible you must write two or three stories in the same style. It is curious how an atmosphere becomes credible if it is breathed not once but two or three times. Any one of Dunsany[']s Pegana tales[2] would be without weight, but a volume of them convinces the reader that the fantasy is natural to him and is therefore humanly credible & we surrender to the fantasy. I imagine the subsidence of Ireland from the heroic mood of O'Grady & his contemporaries to the mood of abject piety before the coming of the Eucharist Congress has crystalized your moods into intellectual sharpness and where before you had a dream mood you now exercise yourself with an intellectual dagger. Ireland today forces us to a heretical revolt, and if your mood and mine and O[']Connor[']s and others are symbolical we may be

> forerunners of an Irish Voltaire.... The verses which conclude the play are very fine. I found the book intellectually exciting. But think over what I said about the tale not being able to stand by itself. It requires three of the same mood to create an atmosphere which is believable, just as one man by himself may be a human peak but three believing the same things may become a movement. (G. Russell to Yeats, 6 March 1932, *LTWBY2* 531).

Russell's judicious reviews of *AVA* and *A Packet for Ezra Pound* in *The Irish Statesman* of 13 February 1926 (714–16) and 7 September 1929 (11–12), respectively, were valued for their honesty. In the latter, Russell had noticed a "dream world" atmosphere in connection with the revelation of the true source of *A Vision*. Michael Robartes's blistering attack on Yeats's *fin de siècle* style in *SMR* (24–26) really amounts to a comic self-indictment by the poet—a critique that focuses attention squarely on style as a topic. If Russell was not simply alluding to the three early stories of 1896–97, the shift to "intellectual sharpness...where before you had a dream mood" might recall his impression of the brilliant narrative destined to accompany "the Robartes Stories" as a preliminary movement of *AVB*.

To come at the problem the other way around, Yeats was also aware that *AVB* should probably not stand alone. He made the point emphatically in a letter to Hansard Watt, on 14 December 1930, when proposing a "seventh volume for the ordinary collected edition of my work" to contain

> 1. The two little volumes of "Diaries" published at Cuala [i.e., *Estrangement* {1926} and *The Death of Synge* {1928}, both subtitled "Extracts from a Diary Kept in 1909"]
>
> 2. A collection of philosophic stories about to be published at Cuala [i.e., *SMR*]
>
> 3. "A Packet for Ezra Pound" published at Cuala two years ago [actually 1929]
>
> 4. "A Vision" published privately by Werner Laurie in, I think, 1922 or 1923 [actually finished in 1925 and published in 1926]
>
> These four sections support each other. "A Vision" is not the crude book published by Laurie; I have worked years on it since then. The philosophic stories, which were written this summer and are amongst the best things I have written, expound its fundamental ideas. "A Packet for Ezra Pound" is the introduction to "A Vision" and the "Diaries" which are probably my best critical writings have sufficient relation to it not to seem out of harmony. I don't want to publish "A Vision" by itself for various reasons. (*CL InteLex* 5419)

By the time *AVB* was finally published by Macmillan, lacking the autobiographical "Diaries," the order of items 2 and 3 had been transposed. The new ending portending prophecies for "A Vision" had been withheld. If "Michael Robartes Foretells" was to have held such a prominent place in the treatise, for reasons of stylistic *credibility* as Russell suggested or to conclude the book's argument about history by completing the fictional frame of the stories, bending like an arc over the treatise, when did Yeats begin to write it? When did he decide to cast it away with a long diagonal stroke drawn across its first page? And *why*?

Before this, the story has been presented twice before, first by Hazard Adams in 1955 (with almost no commentary), and next by Walter Kelly Hood in 1975 (with little more). (See the footnote to NLI 36,272/33, folio 1, below.) In neither case was the text presented diplomatically, although the silently emended Hood version is annotated and occasionally acknowledges revisions but is usually content to cite parallel ideas or features elsewhere in *AVB*. Neither Adams nor Hood were aware that the typist's trove of manuscript material existed beyond Yeats's own copy and included two carbon copies in the H. Lytton Wilson Collection of the Morris Library, Southern Illinois University-Carbondale. (Again, see footnote to folio 1.) In the context of the mass of materials related to *AVB* in the Wilson Collection, it seems probable that Mrs. Wilson typed "Michael Robartes Foretells"[3] and the other parts of the book in her possession in the 1932–1933 time-frame. Walter Hood exceeds his usual care about dates by asserting that the text "can be dated with some accuracy" (*YO* 215), suggesting that it was the story that Yeats wrote to amuse Dorothy Wellesley in the summer of 1936. (However, see the final chapter in this study and the holograph presented there.) More likely, "Michael Robartes Foretells" was indeed one of the seven attempts that Yeats made by July 1933 to rewrite the section of Book V, "Dove or Swan," that deals with the future.[4] We also know from the reference on folio 1 to "Coole House" and its "now empty rooms" that composition necessarily post-dated the furniture auction of 8–9 August 1932 and a cooling-off period for Yeats to whom the empty house was deeply upsetting.[5]

Other circumstantial evidence in the text points generally to 1932. On the third page, Daniel O'Leary speaks from his notes about the next Cycle, "That...its Schools and Universities...would combine some Asiatic philosophy...with the latest results of that psychical research founded by William Crookes,...preparing all to face death without flinching, perhaps even with joy" (NLI 36,272/33, folio 3, ll. 39–43). In Yeats's introduction to *Fighting the Waves,* typed by Mrs. Wilson[6] and published in *The Dublin Magazine* (April-June 1932), he hedged an extraordinary prophecy:

> Yet it may be that our science, our modern philosophy, keep a subconscious knowledge that their raft, roped together at the end of the seventeenth century, must...part and abandon us to the storm, or it may be, as Professor Richet[7] suggests at the end of his long survey of psychical research from the first experiments of Sir William Crookes to the present moment, that all it can do is...to prove the poverty of human intellect, that we are lost amid alien intellects...more incomprehensible than the most distant stars.

> We may…plunge as Rome did in the fourth century according to some philosopher of that day into "a fabulous, formless darkness." (*VPl* 571)

Published in advance of the play, this part of the introduction (with two others) was deleted in *Wheels and Butterflies* (1934).[8] The prediction compares, too, with the long note at the end of "Michael Robartes Foretells," where O'Leary's summary shifts to Yeats's own voice on the collapse of Roman civilization along the lines of present and future developments:

> We must consider the Roman cycle as two or three centuries later than that of Greece. I accept Sc[h]neider's identification[9] of Virgil, Ovid, Nero, Epictetus with certain logical developments of Roman thought and I name those developments Phases 24, 25, 26, and 27. (NLI 36,272/33, folio 9).

"Michael Robartes Foretells" consists of two parts, numbered accordingly "1" and "2," a conversational scene involving Robartes's followers from *SMR* (lacking Mary Bell, John Bond, and of course Robartes and Aherne) and a recitation by O'Leary culminating in the prophecy Robartes left on his departure to the deserts of Arabia (now at least his third such departure in the character's history) and in the note just cited. The first part is light enough and reminiscent of *SMR* in style and content. The second part might easily be mistaken for the philosophical matter that Yeats articulates in *A Vision* beyond the two Cuala booklets appended to it. To reject the second part would leave the first without point. To foretell or not to foretell? That is the question Yeats must have asked himself in the summer of 1933 without much mystery, for prophecy was denied, at last, if it had not been suppressed by doubt. Instead, he wrote:

> nothing comes—though this moment was to reward me for all my toil. Perhaps I am too old. Surely something would have come when I meditated under the direction of the Cabalists. What discords will drive Europe to that artificial unity—only dry and drying sticks can be tied into a bundle—which is the decadence of every civilisation? (*AVB* 301–02)

No matter how clever or entertaining the device of the fictional frame in part 1 of the new story, it was little more than a third of the whole piece and could not withstand the decision to suspend part 2. Adams says that if "the system gave Yeats the ability to predict pseudoscientifically and dogmatically, the final edition finally wiped away all such suggestions" (*The Contrary Vision* 247). To put it bluntly: "Yeats finally rejected prediction" (248). Walter Hood comes to much the same conclusion. In noting parallels with *AVB*, he points to "Foretells," folio 4, lines 71–77, and detects in the cancelled first sentence ("~~It is only to prophesy in abstract; every term has <innumerable> a hundred possible, particular expressions~~") an echo of Yeats's later disclaimer, in *AVB* 302: "Then I understand. I have already said all that can be said. The particulars are the work of the *Thirteenth Cone* or cycle which is in every man and called by every man his freedom."[10]

But it is possible that a mitigating circumstance might justify rejection of "Michael Robartes Foretells" without allowing, necessarily, that Yeats had recanted the particulars of part 2—that is, the "particular expressions" of the absent Robartes and his own presence in the concluding footnote of folio 9. His presence is in fact ironic because Robartes's revelations are presented at Thoor Ballylee when Yeats is away, having sent O'Leary "the key" so that he might sit at a window and contemplate the nearby mansion and demesne much as Yeats imagined himself doing in "Coole Park and Ballylee, 1931." In the story, that is the place "where fine work has been planned or accomplished, where a great Irish social order climaxed and passed away" (folio 1, ll. 11–13). In the poem, first published in November 1932, the "spot whereon the founders lived and died" becomes an absence of presence whereas "We shift about—all that great glory spent— | Like some poor Arab tribesman and his tent" (*VP* 491: 33, 39–40). Yeats's absence from Ballylee and pining for Coole Park coincides with an uptake in his appearances at Garsington and London among the Morrells and Bloomsbury's literary elite.

Time is vaguely defined as contemporary in *SMR*, so the setting in "Foretells" is "seven years since Michael Robartes disappeared into Arabia" (folio 1, 11. 17–18), or roughly 1938, which Yeats must have projected for *AVB*. Duddon remarks that "[i]n London there are young men fresh from the Universities who perplex us.... One night I brought in some London Journalist...[and] said that the Proletariat was an abstraction and must disappear before the German and Italian conception of the State," to which, we are told, "the Journalist derided the ~~Absolute~~ State, ~~and~~ argued that nothing mattered but internationalism, democracy and disarmament" (folio 2, ll. 22, 24–29). The inner circle of Bloomsbury's political elders, Maynard Keynes and Leonard Woolf, was deeply committed to those things and, as editors, exercised considerable influence on the contributors to and audience of *The New Statesman*, *The Nation & The Athenaeum*, and *Political Quarterly*, the latter of which Woolf helped to launch in 1930. (Hitler became chancellor of Germany in 1933.) Probably not the "London Journalist" in "Michael Robartes Foretells," Leonard Woolf wrote and edited books in those days—for instance, *Imperialism and Civilization* (1928), *The Intelligent Man's Way to Prevent War* (1933), and *Quack, Quack!* (1935)—that provided talking-points at gatherings hosted by Lady Ottoline Morrell, a mutual friend of the Yeatses and the Woolfs.[11] Leonard Woolf respected Yeats's authority on government but would have regarded his mystical ideas as "honest quackery," as opposed to the *dishonest* kind. The two men had a common interest in Oswald Spengler's *The Decline of the West*, discussed by Yeats in *AVB* and reviewed by Woolf in "The World of Books" column during his literary editorship of *The Nation & The Athenaeum* in the 1920s.[12]

However, the Journalist was probably a young man, closer to Duddon in age but also university educated. Like O'Leary, the Journalist had heard Robartes speak of "the next Cycle...and of the influx at the second, third and fourth Phases" and of "some Asiatic Nation" (perhaps Japan) that "would base its whole civilization upon War" (folio 2, ll. 31–35), Notably, Robartes had insisted upon the paradox "that the old age of our civilization begins with young men marching in step, with the shirts and songs that give our politics an air of sport" (folio 6, 118–21).[13] Nevertheless, the civil war in Spain (1936–39), which found volunteers among young activists associated with the Woolfs of the Hogarth Press ("Living Poets" such as W. H. Auden, Julian Bell, and Stephen Spender),[14] was outside the storyline, an unforeseen event of the future.

One of these fellows, Auden, collaborated with the proletarian Group Theatre, which almost persuaded Yeats, in 1934, to commit *A Full Moon in March, The Player Queen*, and *The Resurrection* to productions alternating with a double-bill of Auden's *The Dance of Death* and Eliot's *Sweeney Agonistes,* plays of "rival schools."[15] The Woolfs' favorite nephew, Julian Bell, went to China in 1932 but returned to London impatient to join the Loyalists' cause in Spain, where he was killed driving an ambulance—more activist than listener. On the other hand, Stephen Spender has testified to Yeats's taking on a bit of the Robartes persona when speaking of occult matters at one of Lady Ottoline's parties. To entertain Bloomsbury's radically progressive mindset is also a matter treated in the next chapter.

In this instance, Yeats was in London to discuss with Rupert Doone, director of the Group Theatre, the proposition cited above, which seems to have gone well despite lingering doubts on Yeats's part. In her diary, Virginia Woolf, who greatly admired Yeats's poetry, noted the subjects he discussed once she had rescued the young poet-essayist Spender from an awkward moment:

> Yesterday at Ottoline's [25 October 1934]. Old Yeats.
>
> What he said was, he had been writing about me. The Waves....
>
> The Occult [after a list of half a dozen items in paragraphs]. That he believes in firmly. All his writing depends on it. Was walking with Robinson Ellis. The words came to him "The world is the excrement of God": 2 minutes afterwards R. E. said them. This convinced Yeats of the existence of another mind. A woman accused him of being the father of her child. He went to Lady Jowett. She wrote a message in Greek—Oh sweet singer—showed it to Waley at Brit. Mus[eum]: said it was written by an Englishman[?] 200 years ago. Anyhow this proves absolutely the existence of another mind. Neither religion nor science explains the world. The occult does explain it. All in Plotinus. Has seen things. His coat hanger advanced across the room one night. Then a coat on it, illuminated: then a hand in it....
>
> [*Later*]...Somebody had cast his horoscope & given him a character, the very opposite of his own conception; but as he now saw, this was his real character. He believes entirely in horoscopes. Will never do business with anyone without having their horoscope. Is trying to get a play acted

in London, at the Gate. But no actor can produce a play. Actors only know their own parts. They cant see that theres a piebald horse outside the window.[16]

Yeats had rehearsed his winning compliment to Virginia Woolf in part III of his 1932 introduction to *Fighting the Waves*, where he considers "change in European thought" from Stendahl to the present. Succinctly and beautifully, he made his case there for an influx of new literature:

Certain typical books—*Ulysses*, Mrs. Virginia Woolf's *Waves*, Mr. Ezra Pound's *Draft of XXX Cantos*—suggest a philosophy like that of the *Samkara* school of ancient India, mental and physical objects alike material, a deluge of experience breaking over us and within us, melting limits whether of line or tint; man no hard bright mirror dawdling by the dry sticks of a hedge, but a swimmer, or rather the waves themselves. (*VPl* 568–69)

Spender recalls in his autobiography, *World Within World,* having conversed with Yeats earlier and having produced a dilemma for himself and his hostess:

he looked at me fixedly and said: "What, young man, do you think of the Sayers?" This took me aback and I murmured that I had not read any. "The Sayers," he repeated, "the Sayers." Lady Ottoline then explained that he was speaking of a certain troupe of speakers [Rupert Doone's players] who recited poetry in chorus. I knew even less of these than of detective fiction and had to admit so. Lady Ottoline…saw that I was a failure. She left the room and telephoned to Virginia Woolf to get in a taxi and come round from Tavistock Square at once. Virginia, highly amused, arrived a few minutes later.[17]

For more than a page, Spender supplements the content of Yeats's performance as noted in Woolf's diary for the hour she sat with Yeats on the sofa and Spender listened in, "relieved not to have to take part in the conversation." Then, after Woolf had taken leave at the introduction of another poet, John Pudney, Spender gives more of what Yeats had to say on the occasion, this time on the future:

Then he spoke about the political views in the writings of my friends and myself, contrasting it with his own interest in spiritualism. "We are entering," he said, "the political era, dominated by considerations of political necessity which belong to *your* people. That will be bad enough, but there will be worse to come. For after that there will be an age dominated by the psychologists, which will be based on the complete understanding by everyone of all his own motives at every stage of his life. After that, there will be the worst age of all: the age of *our* people, the spiritualists. That

> will be a time when the separation of the living from the dead...will be completely broken down, and the world of the living will be in full communication with that of the dead."
>
> Yeats expressed these ideas in a half-prophetic, half-humorous vein, and I may have distorted them in recording them....It is difficult to understand how seriously to take such a prophecy. What is clear[,] though, is that he saw spiritualism as a revolutionary social force as important in its power to influence the world, as [is] politics, psychology, or science. (*World Within World* 165)

A few days later, Virginia Woolf wrote to Spender and made a light-hearted pronouncement of the bits that she had heard:

> I liked talking to Yeats, but Lord!—what a grind those [Ottoline] parties are! And after an hour's hard work, the occult appeared—an illuminated coat hanger, a child's hand, and a message about an unborn baby in Greek—at which I gasped, like a dying alligator, and Ottoline supplied a Mr Pudney[,] a poet."[18]

Thereafter, Spender follows Woolf's example, admiring Yeats the great writer, but less so the apparently foolish man for expressing bizarre ideas and outrageous opinions concerning the anti-democratic "moral and spiritual Nationalism" that he had predicted for the future, organizing the disgust of minorities to "create a turbulence, like that we see about us to-day," an outcome of "knowledge enforced upon Primary Minds of antithetical civilization" and *vice versa* ("Michael Robartes Foretells," folio 9, ll. 175–79). If seen as honest quackery from the Woolf perspective, *A Vision* in its final state seemed interesting enough for Spender to make a reasonable assessment of it in *The Criterion* (April 1938: 536–37). But he was mortified by the questionable judgment Yeats exhibited (especially on the omission of the war poets) in the *Oxford Book of Modern Verse*, and said so in a hostile review, "Modern Verse—Minus the Best of It" in the *Daily Worker* (16 December 1936: 7). Yeats and Spender were on less than friendly terms after that.

In sum, there is no definite *model* for the Journalist in "Michael Robartes Foresees"—only a collective zone of identity on the political left of the literary milieu in early 1930s London. But, as Yeats said, "Auden, Spender, all that seem the new movement *look* for strength in Marxian socialism, or in Major Douglas; they want marching feet" (*LDW* 7). So they will do for example.

If Yeats had determined by mid-1933 or 1934 not to use the new Robartes story for an off-hand ending of *A Vision,* in spite of its rhetorical suitability for a meeting with O'Duffy, the Fascist organizer (*L* 812), perhaps it was because he found the piece *played out* and at a dead end. Social occasions among friends were opportunities to rehearse and test the reception of ideas. It was, after all, common practice for

Yeats to test plays on an audience before publishing. For, even if he hadn't changed his mind about making predictions, discretion *is* said to be the better part of valor. As prophesying and storytelling call for equal measures of art, one can imagine that discarding "Michael Robartes Foretells" might have happened because it does not measure up to the "Stories of Michael Robarties and His Friends." Thus closure in *AVB* as a volume was left to the elegiac poem "All Souls' Night," as in *AVA*, but newly subtitled "AN EPILOGUE." Indeed, a more charming face can hardly be imagined than the one Yeats gave "The End of the Cycle" in the 1937 edition.

Notes

1. Shirâzi Hâfiz, *Selections from the Rubaiyat & Odes of Hafiz*, trans. by a member of the Persian Society of London, with an account of Sufi Mysticism (London: John M. Watkins, 1920); *YL* 826.
2. Lord Dunsany [Edward John Moreton] (1878–1957), Irish playwright and author of short stories that greatly influenced J. R. R. Tolkien and others in the fantasy genre. The short fiction to which Russell refers includes Dunsany's collections *The Gods of Pegana* (1905), *Time and the Gods* (1906), and *The Sword of Welleran* (1908). A copy of the second of these Yeats owned in the 1920s (*YA4* 282), along with a copy of *Plays of Gods and Men*, containing Dunsany's two-act romance *The Tents of the Arabs*, which was produced at the Abbey Theatre on 24 May 1920 and undoubtedly encouraged Yeats's inventions concerning the Judwali tribe. A Dunsany book that Yeats acquired, possibly around the time of Russell's critique, is *The Travel Tales of Mr. Joseph Jorkens* (1931); *YL* 591. Yeats also retained his copy of *The Sword of Welleran* (*YL* 590).
3. Recently, Adams suggests that George Yeats may have been the typist, obviously still unaware of the Yeats Papers in the Wilson Collection. See Hazard Adams, *Academic Child: A Memoir* (Jefferson, NC: McFarland, 2008), 100.
4. Yeats to Olivia Shakespear, 23 July 1933: "I have just re-written for the seventh time the part of *A Vision* that deals with the future" (*L* 812). Connie Hood, in "The Remaking of *A Vision*, *YAACTS* 1 (1983), 52, counts the last of the seven to be "The End of the Cycle" (*AVB* 301–02) and regards "Michael Robartes Foretells" to be the sixth. Walter Hood acknowledges the letter but draws no such conclusion. See *CW14* 462, n. 134, which observes that this section of the book was "reworked many times," citing texts ranging in date from 16 Oct. 1931 to Sept. 1932.
5. My thanks to Neil Mann for the inference based on the auction dates. Personal correspondence 13 Mar. 2017. Lady Gregory died on 22 May 1932.
6. See Box 1, Folder 10 in the William Butler Yeats Papers from the H. Lytton Wilson Collection, Southern Illinois University at Carbondale.
7. Charles Richet, *Thirty Years of Psychical Research: A Treatise on Metaphysics,* trans. Stanley De Brath (London: W. Collins, 1923); *YL* 1743.
8. Steven Winnett's transcriptions in Appendix III ("Yeats's Introductions to *Fighting the Waves* [1932–1934]) may be instructive, in W. B. Yeats, "*The Only Jealousy of Emer" and "Fighting the Waves": Manuscript Materials*, ed. Steven Winnett (Ithaca, NY: Cornell University Press, 2004), 375–86. Curiously, another reference to Sir William Crookes in the 1932 introduction (*VPl* 569) was also eliminated in *Wheel and Butterflies*; however, there, at the end of Yeats's Introduction to *The Resurrection*, a reading of Crooke's *Studies in Psychical Research* (from "years ago") is recalled as the source of the central incident of the play (*VPl* 935).
9. Hermann Schneider, *The History of World Civilization: From Prehistoric Times to the Middle Ages*, trans. Margaret M. Green, 2 vols. (New York: Harcourt, Brace, 1931); *YL* 1853 annotated but not, unfortunately, inscribed with a date of acquisition. The marginal comments in both volumes

are about the Egyptians. For its authority on the "marriage of Europe and Asia" and "the symbolic wheel [as] timeless and spaceless," Schneider's book is cited in *AVB* 205, 206, and 206, n. 1.

10. Hood makes this point in *YO* 221, n. 38. Several other notes, on pp. 221–23, observe co-incidental parallels between part 2 of the rejected ending and *AVB* elsewhere. Presented here in pairs, they are as follows: folio 5, ll. 82–83 / *AVB* 93; folio 5, l. 95 / *AVB* 67 (on Heraclitus); folio 5, ll. 98–100 and marginalia / *AVB* 166 (23rd Phase); folio 6, ll. 104–08 / *AVB* 111–12; folio 6, ll. 111–12 / *AVB* 84, 166; folio 7, ll. 140–45 / *AVB* 206 (on Achilles and Aeneas); and folio 8, ll. 157–62 / *AVB* 107, 135–36.
11. Recalling one amusing occasion, Woolf demonstrates empathy with Yeats, who "sat in the place of honour, but was grumpy and silent, and Virginia was commandeered, much too obviously, by Ottoline to go over and sit next to him and talk him, if possible, into a better mood"; *Downhill All the Way: An Autobiography of the Years 1919–1939* (London: The Hogarth Press, 1970), 106.
12. See Wayne K. Chapman, "Spengler's *The Decline of the West* and Intellectual Quackery: Checking the Climate with Leonard Woolf and W. B. Yeats," *Virginia Woolf and the Natural World*, ed. Kristin Czarnecki and Carrie Rohman (Clemson, SC: Clemson University Press, 2011), 220–27; see also Chapman's "Synthesizing Civilizations: Leonard Woolf, the League of Nations, and the Inverse of Imperialism, 1928–1933," *Virginia Woolf and the Common(wealth) Reader*, ed. Helen Wussow and Mary Ann Gillies (Clemson, SC: Clemson University Press, 2014), 18–26.
13. The League of Youth, or Blueshirts (*Na Léinte Gorma*), was an Irish, far-right, paramilitary organization led by General O'Duffy, who commissioned Yeats to write lyrics for marching songs in the 1930s. Yeats's letter to Olivia Shakespear of 23 July 1933 (*L* 812) is mostly about what he soon called the "political comedy" of O'Duffy and his "body of young men" (815). Eventually, some of them fought for the Nationalists in Spain. Also on the right were the Brownshirts, or Stormtroopers, in Germany and Mussolini's Blackshirts in Italy. On the left, again in Germany, were the Red Front Fighters of the Communist Party.
14. All selected by Yeats for his controversial edition of the *Oxford Book of Modern Verse* (Oxford: At the Clarendon Press, 1936), xxxv–xxxviii and 427–33.
15. See Appendix B: "The Poets' Theatre" in Michael Sidnell's *The Dance of Death: The Group Theatre of London in the Thirties* (London: Faber and Faber, 1984), 266–69.
16. Virginia Woolf, *The Diary of Virginia Woolf*, vol. 4: *1931–1935*, ed. Anne Olivier Bell, assisted by Andrew McNeillie (New York: Harcourt Brace Jovanovich, 1983), 255–57. For more on the Virginia Woolf/W. B. Yeats relationship, with Ottoline Morrell acting as mediator, see Wayne K. Chapman, "Woolf, Yeats, and the Writing of 'Spilt Milk,'" *Contradictory Woolf*, ed. Derek Ryan and Stella Bolaki (Clemson, SC: Clemson University Press, 2012), 265–70.
17. Stephen Spender, *World Within World* (New York: St Martin's Press, 1994), 163–64.
18. Virginia Woolf, *The Letters of Virginia Woolf*, vol. 5: *1932–1935*, ed. Nigel Nicolson and Joanne Troutmann (New York: Harcourt Brace Jovanovich, 1979), 341.

APPENDIX

(SEE THE NEXT EIGHTEEN PAGES)

Facsimiles of the Amended Typescript (ribbon copy) and Transcriptions of "Michael Robartes Foretells" (NLI 36,272/33). Two clean, identical carbon copies survive in Box 1, Folder 9 of the H. Lytton Wilson Collection (see footnote on the next page). P. 1 of the carbon sets lack paragraph tabs, so p. 1 of the ribbon copy had been re-typed.

NLI 36,272/33, folio 1

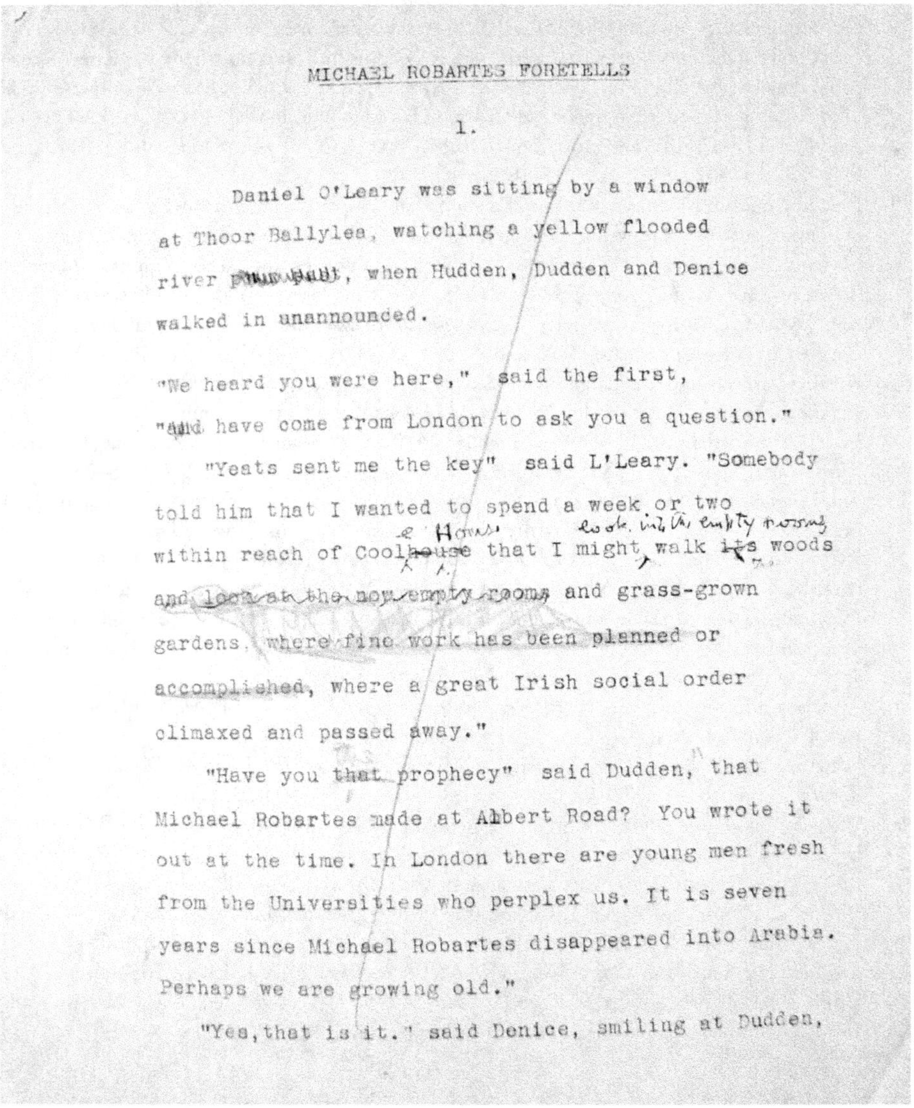

MICHAEL ROBARTES FORETELLS

1.

Daniel O'Leary was sitting by a window at Thoor Ballylee, watching a yellow flooded river ~~pour past~~, when Hudden, Dudden and Denice walked in unannounced.

"We heard you were here," said the first, "~~and~~ have come from London to ask you a question."

"Yeats sent me the key" said L'Leary. "Somebody told him that I wanted to spend a week or two within reach of Cool~~house~~ e House that I might look into the empty rooms walk ~~its~~ the woods and ~~look at the now empty rooms~~ and grass-grown gardens, ~~where fine work has been planned or accomplished~~, where a great Irish social order climaxed and passed away."

"Have you ~~that~~ prophecy" said Dudden, that Michael Robartes made at Albert Road? You wrote it out at the time. In London there are young men fresh from the Universities who perplex us. It is seven years since Michael Robartes disappeared into Arabia. Perhaps we are growing old."

"Yes, that is it." said Denice, smiling at Dudden,

Edited transcripts of "Michael Robartes Foretells" have been introduced by Hazard Adams, in *Blake and Yeats: The Contrary Vision* (Ithaca, NY: Cornell University Press, 1955) 301–305, and Walter Kelly Hood, in "Michael Robartes: Two Occult Manuscripts," *Yeats and the Occult,* ed. George Mills Harper (London: Macmillan Press, 1975) 219–24. Two uncorrected carbon copies of the typescript are located in Box 1, Folder 9 of the William Butler Yeats Papers from the H. Lytton Wilson Collection, Special Collections, Southern Illinois University, Carbondale, Illinois. Mrs. Wilson was Yeats's typist. The conspectus to the collection reports only that the "carbon typescripts vary in minor details from [the Hazard Adams] version."

MICHAEL ROBARTES FORETELLS

1.

Daniel O'Leary was sitting by a window at Thoor Ballylea, watching a yellow flooded river ~~pour past~~, when Hudden, Dudden, and Denice walked in unannounced.

"We heard you were here," said the first, "~~and~~ have come from London to ask you a question."

"Yeats sent me the key" said L'Leary. "Somebody told him that I wanted to spend a week or two within reach of Cool{e}**~~house~~** {House} **that I might** {look into the empty rooms,} **, walk ~~its~~** {the} **woods ~~and look at the now empty rooms~~ and grass-grown gardens, ~~where fine work has been planned or accomplished,~~ where a great Irish social order climaxed and passed away."**

"Have you ~~that~~ {the} **prophecy" said Dudden, "that Michael Robartes made at Albert Road? You wrote it out at the time. In London there are young men fresh from the Universities who perplex us. It is seven years since Michael Robartes disappeared into Arabia. Perhaps we are growing old."**

Yes, that is it." said Denice, smiling at Dudden,

The intention of the long diagonal stroke through the text of folio 1 is unclear. Although it appears to cancel the first three paragraphs of the story, it may actually indicate Yeats's decision to reject the whole work. This premise is supported by the fact that neither Hazard Adams nor Walter Kelly Hood mention the conspicuous mark in their commentaries, ignoring it, in effect.

NLI 36,272/33, folio 2

[and at last completely intelligible]

2.

"Even I am faithful to the past."

"One night I brought in some London Journalist," Dudden went on, "You began a Communistic arguement; I said that the Proletariat was an abstraction and must disappear before the German and Italian conception of the State ~~as shaped~~ [moulded] by History[, yet transparent to reason]; then the Journalist ~~denounced~~ [derided] the Absolute State ~~and~~ argued that nothing mattered but internationalism, democracy and disarmament."

"Oh, yes, I remember." said O'Leary. "Robartes talked of the next Cycle, forgetting that the Journalist was ignorant of our terms, of the influx at the second, third and fourth Phases, said that some Asiatic Nation would base its whole civilisation upon War, that its governing class would take care of the common people as our governing class ~~cannot~~ [could not] or ~~will~~ [would] not, that they might obey in War and be loyal in defeat."

and at last completely intelligible

2.

"Even I am faithful to the past."

"One night I brought in some London Journalist,"
Dudden went on, "You began a Communistic arguement;
I said that the Proletariat was an abstraction and
must disappear before the German and Italian con-
moulded yet transparent to reason
ception of the State ~~as shaped~~ by History/; then the
derided ^ ^
Journalist ~~denounced~~ the ~~Absolute~~ State, ~~and~~ argued
^
that nothing mattered but internationalism, democracy
and disarmament."

"Oh, yes, I remember." said O'Leary.
"Robartes talked of the next Cycle, forgetting that
the Journalist was ignorant of our terms, of the
influx at the second, third and fourth Phases, said
that some Asiatic Nation would base its whole
civilization upon War, that its governing class
would take care of the common people as our govern-
could not would
ing class ~~cannot~~ or ~~will~~ not, that they might
^ ^
obey in War and be loyal in defeat.~~"~~

---

38 end quotation mark is stricken as Yeats indicates with a drawn line that the paragraph continues in O'Leary's voice on the next page

NLI 36,272/33, folio 3

3.

"That ~~it would incorporate in the teachings of~~ its Schools and Universities [would combine some] ~~an~~ Asiatic philosophy [with] ~~and~~ the latest results of that psychical research founded by William Crookes, [preparing all to] ~~that men may~~ face death without flinching, perhaps even with joy. As according to [their philosophy] ~~that teaching,~~ the dead will not pass to a remote Heaven, but return to the Earth, it will seem as though the soldier's dead body manured [the] fields, ~~that~~ he himself would till. Furthermore, that they would subordinate class to class, that certain virtues created in leisure might descend to all; [whatever music, dancing,] ~~music~~, painting, literature ~~and~~ ~~the dance would express~~ [best served] the perpetuation or perfection of the [race] ~~race~~ or man's ultimate deliverance ~~abroad~~. Yet the State would be but little in men's [minds] ~~thoughts~~, for the State, [as an idea] whatever definition we make of it, is but [a] ~~one~~ degree less abstract than [that of] the Proletariat. Men's [minds] ~~thoughts~~ will dwell upon some company of governing men whom, though they seem every man's, even every base man's [my] ~~inner~~ self, it is natural to call noble."

"You are speaking from memory, I thought [you] had notes," said Hudden.

"No, not of those words. When you had shown the Journalist out and gone to your beds, I asked Robartes if I might

3.

~~"~~That ~~it would incorporate in the teachings of~~ its
would combine some with
Schools and Universities ~~an~~ Asiatic philosophy ~~and~~ with/
^
the latest results of that psychical research founded
preparing all to
by William Crookes, ~~that men may~~ face death without
^ their philosophy
flinching, perhaps even with joy. As according to ~~that~~
^
~~teaching~~, the dead will not pass to a remote Heaven,
but return to the Earth, it will seem as though the
the
soldier's dead body manured fields~~, that~~ he himself
^
would till. Furthermore, that they would subordinate
class to class, that certain virtues created in leisure
~~and~~ whatever music, dancing
might descend to all {;/.} ~~Music~~, painting, literature ~~and~~
best served ^
~~the dance would express~~ the perpetuation or perfection
Race
of the ~~Rave~~ or man's ultimate deliverance, ~~depend~~. Yet
^ minds
the State would be but little in men's ~~thoughts~~, for ~~minds~~/
as an idea / **the State,/ whatever definition we make of it, is but**
a that of
~~one~~ degree less abstract than the Proletariat. Men's
^ ^
minds| **~~thoughts~~ will dwell upon some company of governing men**
whom, though they seem every man's, even every base man's
very
~~inner~~ self, it is natural to call noble."
^ you
"You are speaking from memory, I thought had notes," said
^
Hudden.

"No, not of those words. When you had shown the Journal-
ist out and gone to your beds, I asked Robartes if I might

---

39 quotation mark stricken; see folio 2, line 38.
53 an erased inscription occurs over the words "State, whatever."

NLI 36,272/33, folio 4

4.

put them down. He said, no, that he made them up while talking and didn't know whether they were true or not; that he knew nothing of the next cycle except that it would be the reverse of ours. I begged him to say what we who took the gyres and cones as the framework of our thought might safely prophesy, and on that night and the two following, we sat late. I made notes and thisxitx a few days later I wrote what I could remember. Here it is."

II.

"~~It is only possible to prophesy in abstract; every term has a hundred possible, particular expressions.~~

"We know that our own life, or the year, or the civilisation must pass through certain changes, that we, or it, approach the prime, or have passed it, that this or that character must increase or decrease, but we cannot know the particulars. When we speak of the past, we can say that the Divina Comedia, or the Russian Revolution, expressed such and such a phase, but we are mixixed misled the moment we imagine some future work of art or historical event.

4.

put them down. He said, no, ~~that~~ he made them up while talking and didn't know whether they were true or not; ~~that~~ he knew nothing of the next cycle except that it would be the reverse of ours. I begged him to say what we who took the gyres and cones as the framework of our thought might safely prophesy, and on that night and the two following, we sat late. I made notes and ~~this is~~ a few days later I wrote what I could remember. Here it is."

II.

~~"It is only possible to prophesy in abstract; every term has a hundred possible, particular expressions.~~
innumerable

" **We know that our own life, or the year, or the civilisation must pass through certain changes, that we, or it, approach the prime, or have passed it, that this or that character must increase or decrease, but we cannot know the particulars. When we speak of the past, we can say that ~~the~~** La **Divin{a/e} Comedi{a/e}, or the Russian Revolution, expressed such and such a phase, but ~~we~~ are ~~mislead~~ misled the moment we ~~try to~~** try to **imagine some future work of art or historical event.**

---

73 quotation mark added at the onset of the line following the cancellation of lines 71 and 72.
75 the first two commas are stroked in by Yeats.

NLI 36,272/33, folio 5

wins its victory & returns. All our morality is heroic & this falling, or falling asleep brings its gains with it those conventions, formulas, mechanism. I reject Hegel's all containing, all sustaining, all satisfying final [illegible]. I reject

5.

I will re-examine the Wheel. Every triad of phases is a separate Wheel. Whatever existence we think of, a Civilisation's or an individual's, it arises from ~~the~~ the general mass ~~returns to the general mass. All our morality is heroic, this or defeat its falling back brings its gains with it. We cannot therefore accept Hegel's conception where civilisation ends in the self-sufficing all-containing State nor~~ Marxian Socialism, in so far as it is derived from him.

NP The general mass, call it Nature, God, the Matrix, the Unconscious, what you will, becomes a unity when interlocked with some separating or subsiding existence; nor is it ~~[illegible]~~ greater than that existence, the Will and Creative Mind of the one, the Mask and Body of Fate of the other, Each ~~dies~~ dying the others life, ~~lives~~ living the others death.

~~We are agreed that~~ The 22nd. phase of our civilisation has just passed, ~~and it seems clear that~~ the Russian violence and ~~much of~~ the art and thought of our time, [illegible] represent the 23rd. phase, the first phase of the first Primary Triad; ~~that~~ the Dictatorships in various parts of the world, including the Russian, are the approach of the 24th. Phase. So much we deduce from our general knowledge and from our Cones and Symbols. ~~[illegible]~~

where our logic has compelled the evolution & expression of a single element

wins its victory & returns. All our morality is heroic ~~[?]~~ ;
back though
this falling ^ or falling asleep brings its gains with it ~~but~~ conventionalised,
formalised, mechanised. I reject Hegel's all containing, all
sustaining, all sadisfying final wakefulness. I reject
~~thought~~

5.

And derelict

" I will re-examine the Wheel. Every triad of phases

is a separate Wheel. Whatever existence we think of,

'*s* '*s* the general mass

a Civilisation or an individual, it arises from and ^

~~returns to the general mass. All our morality is heroic,~~

this or defeat we die, wise, wealthy & ~~derelict.~~

~~its falling back / brings its gains with it. We cannot~~

We reject ripe old age

~~therefore accept Hegel's conception where civilisation~~

his all satisfying we reject

~~ends in the self-suffering all-containing State, nor~~

Marxian Socialism, in so far as it is derived from him.

NP

" The general mass, call it Nature, God, the Matrix, the

Unconscious, what you will, becomes a unity when inter-

locked with some separating or subsiding existence {;,} nor

~~[?ever]~~ greater

is it ~~greater~~ than that existence {;,} the Will and Creative

^ ^

Mind of the one, the Mask and Body of Fate of the other.

dying living

Each ~~dies~~ the others life, ~~lives~~ the others death.

~~Wherever I~~
Where ever logic
has compelled the
isolation & exageration
of a single element

^ "The ^

"~~We were agreed that the~~ 22nd. phase of our civilis-

ation has just passed, ~~and it seems clear that~~ the

Russian violence and ~~much of~~ the art and thought of our

~~Wherever it se[?perates] & exagerates some single~~

~~time~~, represent the 23rd. phase, the first phase of the

^

first Primary Triad {;,} ~~that~~ the Dictatorships in various

parts of the world, including the Russian, are the approach

of the 24th. Phase. So much we deduce from our general

knowledge and from our Cones and Symbols. ~~But look~~

NLI 36,272/33, folio 6

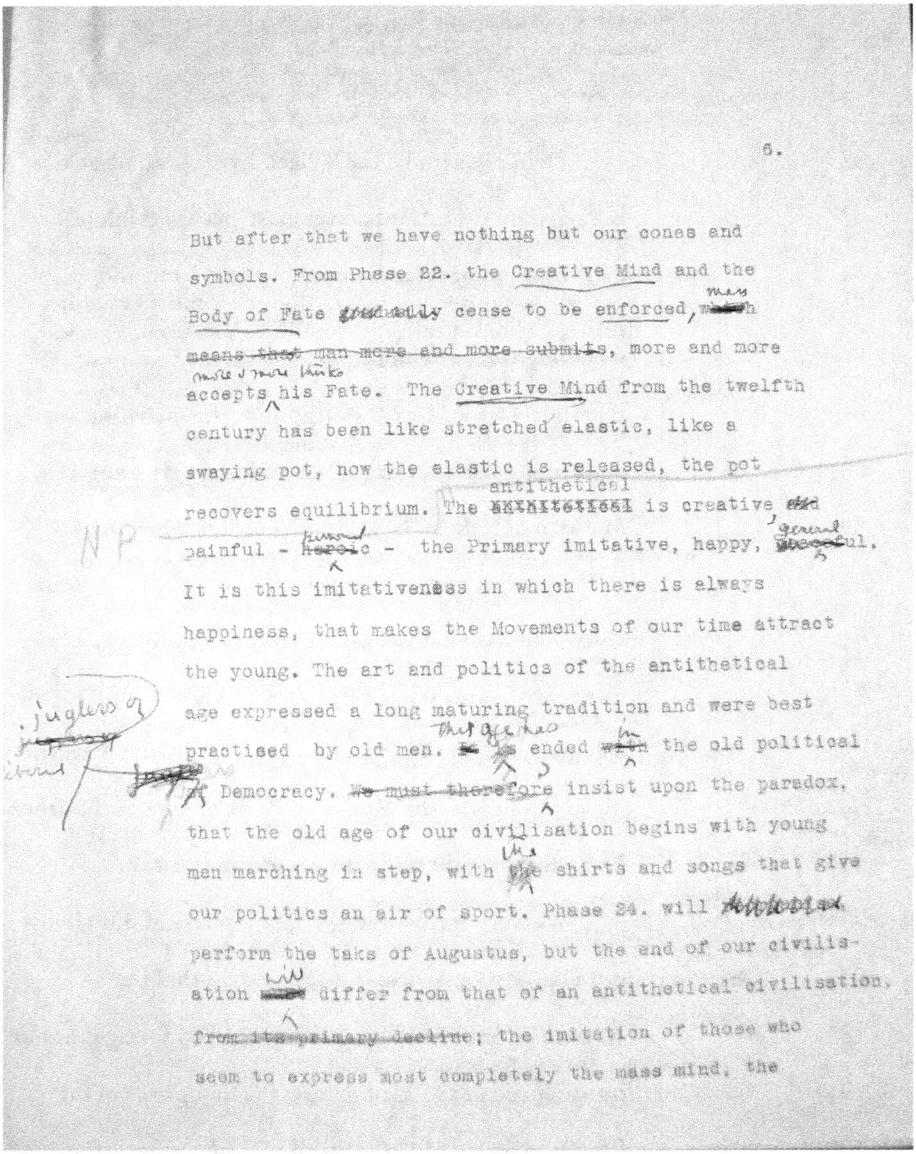

6.

But after that we have nothing but our cones and symbols. From Phase 22. the Creative Mind and the Body of Fate ~~gradually~~ cease to be enforced, ~~which means that man more and more submits~~, more and more accepts his Fate. The Creative Mind from the twelfth century has been like stretched elastic, like a swaying pot, now the elastic is released, the pot recovers equilibrium. The antithetical is creative ~~and~~ painful - ~~heroic~~ - the Primary imitative, happy, ~~peaceful~~. It is this imitativeness in which there is always happiness, that makes the Movements of our time attract the young. The art and politics of the antithetical age expressed a long maturing tradition and were best practised by old men. ~~It is~~ ended ~~with~~ the old political ~~of~~ Democracy. ~~We must therefore~~ insist upon the paradox, that the old age of our civilisation begins with young men marching in step, with ~~the~~ shirts and songs that give our politics an air of sport. Phase 24. will ~~[illegible]~~ perform the taks of Augustus, but the end of our civilisation ~~[illegible]~~ differ from that of an antithetical civilisation, ~~from its primary decline~~; the imitation of those who seem to express most completely the mass mind, the

6.

But after that we have nothing but our cones and
symbols. From Phase 22. the <u>Creative Mind</u> and the
man
<u>Body of Fate</u> ~~gradually~~ cease to be <u>enforced</u>, ~~which~~
~~means that man more and more submits~~, more and more
more & more thinks
accepts his Fate. The <u>Creative Mind</u> from the twelfth
^
century has been like stretched elastic, like a
swaying pot, now the elastic is released, the pot
antithetical
recovers equilibrium. "The ~~anthitetical~~ is creative, ~~and~~
NP personal **general**
painful – ~~heroic~~ – the Primary imitative, happy, ~~peaceful~~.
^ ^
It is this imitativeness in which there is always
happiness, that makes the Movements of our time attract
the young. The art and politics of the antithetical
age expressed a long maturing tradition and were best
juglers of That age has in
~~jugglers of~~
practised by old men. ~~It is~~ ended ~~with~~ the old political
liberal/ ~~Juglers~~ ^ I ^
/~~of~~ Democracy. ~~We must therefore~~ insist upon the paradox,
^
that the old age of our civilisation begins with young
the
men marching in step, with ~~the~~ shirts and songs that give
^
our politics an air of sport. Phase 24. will ~~reorganise,~~
perform the taks[=task] of Augustus, but the end of our civilis-
will
ation ~~must~~ differ from that of an antithetical civilisation,
^
~~from its primary decline~~; the imitation of those who
seem to express most completely the mass mind, the

---

111 new paragraph indicated by "NP" and drawn lines.
122 "taks" is a typographical error for "task."

NLI 36,272/33, folio 7

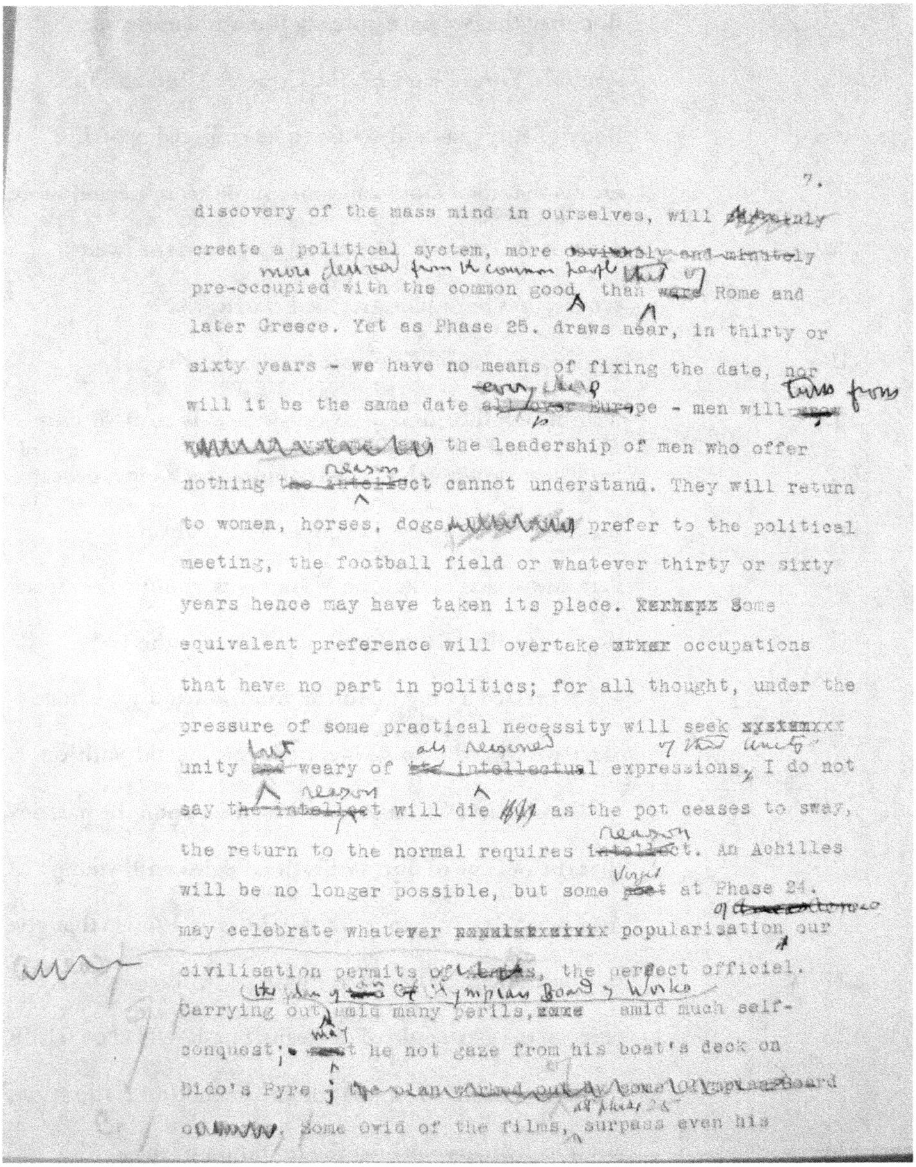

7.

discovery of the mass mind in ourselves, will certainly create a political system, more derived from the common people than that of Rome and later Greece. Yet as Phase 25. draws near, in thirty or sixty years - we have no means of fixing the date, nor will it be the same date everywhere - men will turn from the leadership of men who offer nothing the reason cannot understand. They will return to women, horses, dogs, prefer to the political meeting, the football field or whatever thirty or sixty years hence may have taken its place. Some equivalent preference will overtake occupations that have no part in politics; for all thought, under the pressure of some practical necessity will seek unity but weary of all reasoned expressions of that unity. I do not say the reason will die as the pot ceases to sway, the return to the normal requires reason. An Achilles will be no longer possible, but some Virgil at Phase 24. may celebrate whatever popularisation of our civilisation permits, the perfect official. Carrying out the plans of the Olympian Board of Works amid many perils, amid much self-conquest; may he not gaze from his boat's deck on Dido's Pyre; Some Ovid of the films, surpass even his

7.

discovery of the mass mind of ourselves, will ~~certainly~~
create a political system, more ~~obviously and minutely~~
more derived from the common people that of
pre-occupied with the common good, than ~~were~~ Rome and
^ ^
later Greece. Yet as Phase 25. draws near, in thirty or
sixty years – we have no means of fixing the date, nor
everywhere turn from
will it be the same date ~~all over Europe~~ – men will ~~grow~~
^ ^
~~weary of systems, and~~ the leadership of men who offer
reason
nothing ~~the intellect~~ cannot understand. They will return
^
to women, horses, dogs. ~~They will~~ prefer to the political
meeting, the football field or whatever thirty or sixty
years hence may have taken its place. ~~Perhaps~~ Some
equivalent preference will overtake ~~other~~ occupations
that have no part in politics; for all thought, under the
pressure of some practical necessity will seek ~~system~~
but all reasoned of that unity
unity ~~and~~ weary of ~~its intellectual~~ expressions. I do not
^ reason ^ ^
say ~~the intellect~~ will die ~~out~~ as the pot ceases to sway,
^ reason
the return to the normal requires ~~intellect~~. An Achilles
Vergil
will be no longer possible, but some ~~poet~~ at Phase 24.
of ~~Aneanes Aeneas~~
may celebrate whatever ~~populist civi~~ popularisation our
~~Aeneas~~/ /as Δ
civilisation permits ~~of Aenias~~, the perfect official.

an
(the plan of [?some] ~~Ol~~ Olympian Board of Works[)]
¶/ **Carrying out ^ amid many perils, ~~come~~ amid much self-**
may
conquest; ~~must~~ he not gaze from his boat's deck on
^
Dido's Pyre; ~~the plan worked out by some Olympian Board~~
at Phase 25
lc/ **~~of Works.~~, Some Ovid of the films,^ surpass even his**

NLI 36,272/33, folio 8

8.

popularity by celebrating ~~of~~ our common
casual pleasures. ~~Man will accept his fate, will~~ his
~~fate, think his fate, he will struggle - Will and Mask~~
~~have to be enforced - but~~ every event will compel ~~his~~
acceptance of the external mask, objective man, life
lived in common. Fate is multiple ~~and~~ particular,
has as it were personality, but the Mask is always one."

Merely personal distinction, as past times
used the word, will be out of date, will no longer exist
~~exist~~ archaic studious circles, or as ~~imitation and~~
~~formula~~ pretentions of the vulgar; the ugly will sting
man to life because it rids him of the desire and hope
he can no longer employ. I cannot say these things
NP without hatred, I am an antithetical man ~~of an~~ antithetical age, yet the men of that day, lacking our in-
equality, lacerations, artificialities, judged by any
accepted standard will be happier than we are.

Phases 24. and 25. must see the completion of
a public ideal, its assimilation in the common civilisation,
where all, whatever degree of rank and station remain,
will live and think in much the same way. But at Phase 26.

8.

popularity by celebrating ~~at Phase 25~~. our common
casual pleasures. ~~Man will accept his fate, will~~ his
~~fate, think his fate, he will struggle. Will and Mask~~
E ~~mens &~~ man's free
~~have to be enforced – but~~ {e} very even will compel ~~his~~
^ ^
acceptance of the external mask, objective man, life
lived in common. Fate is multiple, ~~and~~ particular,
has as it were personality, but the Mask is always one.~~"~~

" **Merely personal distinction, as past times**
used the word, will be out of date, will no longer exist
except in a
~~exist~~ archaic studious circles, or as ~~imitation and~~
~~formula~~ pretentions/ of the vulgar; the ugly will sting
man to life because it rids him of the desire and hope
he can no longer employ. "**I cannot say these things**
NP born in a still
without hatred, ~~"~~**I am antithetical man~~, of an~~ anti-**
~~NP~~ ^
thetical age, yet the men of that day, lacking our in-
equality, lacerations, artificialities, judged by any
accepted standard will be happier than we are.

"**Phases 24. and 25. must see the completion of**
a public ideal, its assimilation in the common civilsation,
where all, whatever degree of rank and station remain,
will live and think in much the same way. But at Phase 26.

---

156 end quotation mark inserted, then stricken.
157 quotation mark inserted.
162 quotation mark inserted as new paragraph is indicated by "NP" and drawn lines.
163 quotation mark inserted but stricken as Yeats changes his mind about starting a new paragraph ("NP") here, with drawn lines partially erased.
167 quotation mark inserted.

NLI 36,272/33, folio 9

9.

will come, enforced by some intellectual necessity or change of circumstances impossible to foreknow, the knowledge of a form of existence, of a private aim opposite to any that our civilisation has pursued. This knowledge affecting minorities, and organising their disgust, will create a turbulence, like that we see about us to-day, but moral and spiritual; the knowledge of antithetical civilisation enforced upon Primary Minds.[1]

Note: In finding concrete events for the dates given me by my instructors, I considered that the historical chart must be that of the Christian Era and what led to it. I have considered this Era as a distinct cycle, different from those of Greece and Rome, but have the authority of my instructors for making it coincide at certain points with that of Greece. We must consider the Roman cycle as two or three centuries later than that of Greece. I accept Sneider's identification of Virgil, Ovid, Nero, Epictetus with certain phases of Roman thought and I name those phases, Phases. 24. 25. 26. 27. The personal exaggeration of Nero and his Court may be described as an antithetical vision of a Primary Ideal. In Epictetus that ideal is clearly seen, a Universal Being present in every particular person. A Primary Vision of an antithetical ideal might at Phase 26. be a moral and spiritual Nationalism, antinomeen differences, personal in its final form, seen as differing ways of life.

developement

9.

will come, enforced by some intellectual necessity
or change of circumstances impossible to foreknow,
a private aim
the knowledge of a form of existence, of ~~an [?aim]~~
any ^ ^
opposite to ~~all that~~ our civilisation has ~~known~~ pursued,
^
This knowledge ~~at first~~ affecting minorities, and
organising their disgust, will create a turbulence,
like that we see about us to-day, but moral and
spiritual; the knowledge of antithetical civilisation
enforced upon Primary Minds. [i]

Note: In finding concrete events for the dates given me by my instructors, I ~~have~~ considered that the historical chart ~~must be~~ was **that of the Christian Era and what led to it. I ~~have~~ considered this Era as a distinct cycle, different from those of Greece and Rome, but have the authority of my instructors for making it** arise **~~coincide at/ certain points with that of Greece. I accept Sceneider's identification~~** from that of Greece **We must consider the Roman cycle as two or three centuries later than that of Greece. I accept Scneider's identification of Virgil, Ovid, Nero, Epictetus with certain /~~phases~~** logical developements **of Roman thought and I name those ~~phases~~, Phases 24. 25. 26. ~~and~~ 27. The personal exaggeration of Nero and his Court may be described as an antithetical vision of a Primary Ideal. In Epictetus that ideal is clearly seen, a Universal Being present in every particular person. A Primary Vision of an antithetical ideal might at Phase 26. be a moral and spiritual Nationalism, ~~antinomean~~ antinomean differences, ~~each~~ personal in ~~its~~** their **final form, seen as differing ways of life.**

~~with the~~
with or contain[?ing] the Athenian
and Byzantine cycles

developments

but first

Note lines 7 and 8: "Scneider" is a misspelling for one of Yeats's sources, Hermann Schneider, *The History of World Civilization: From Prehistoric Times to the Middle Ages,* trans. Margaret M. Green, 2 vols. (New York: Hancourt, Brace, 1931); see *AVB,* pp. 205, 206.

Denise's Story: W. B. Yeats, Dorothy Wellesley, and the Re-making of "Stories of Michael Robartes and His Friends: An Extract from a Record Made by His Pupils"

Forty years after publishing the triptych of Robartes and Aherne stories from *The Secret Rose* (1896) and *The Tables of the Law & The Adoration of the Magi* (1897), Yeats made his final addition to a body of writings that had grown substantially since 1917, usually in connection with philosophical and creative work inspired by the remarkable collaboration with his wife. In the way of last chapters, therefore, the following narrative begins with a recapitulation of relevant facts.

In 1923, Yeats committed to publisher T. Werner Laurie the manuscript of *A Vision: An Explanation of Life founded upon Certain Doctrines Attributed to Kusta Ben Luka* (1925), first issued to subscribers on 15 January 1926. But already, in a long entry of 14 March 1926, he had begun to plan in his diary (NLI 13,576) major revisions for the substantially rewritten version of *A Vision* that materialized on 7 October 1937, when the standard edition was published by Macmillan, without subtitle. Referred to as *AVA* and *AVB*, these two renditions of the same book posed very different assumptions about the author in relation to his sources, both fictional and actual. Although Yeats registers no qualms in the diary about how close *AVA* adhered to the research source of his wife's automatic writing, Richard Ellmann has stated that she opposed an elucidated second edition that would acknowledge the spirit guides who informed the work's mystic philosophy:

> Mrs. Yeats was absolutely opposed to this, and they had then, as she told me, the first and only serious quarrel of their marriage. Yeats prevailed, but included his mythical variations as well as his realistic account. The second edition of 1937 made room for many second thoughts and also many doubts. When Allan Wade asked him if he believed in *A Vision*, he said evasively—though accurately, "Oh, I draw from it images for my poetry." The book hovered between philosophy and fiction, bread and cake.[1]

To put some perspective on the quarrel, it should be noted that Yeats's private revelations to friends put an end to George Yeats's "philosophical sleeps" on 27 November 1923.[2] Yeats subsequently disclosed their *modus operandi* in *A Packet for Ezra Pound* (Cuala Press, 1929), revealing that they were the same "Two contemplating passions [who had] chose[n] one theme | Through sheer bewilderment" in "Desert Geometry or The Gift of Harun Al-Raschid" (*AVA* 125, ll. 32–33). The disclosure motivated a number of maneuvers implemented, eventually, in *AVB*. The chief maneuver required that one of Yeats's masks, that of Kusta ben Luka, be omitted, along with the poem just cited and preliminary matter by the fictitious character Owen Aherne, so that Giraldus (the likeness of Yeats, bearded and turbaned, by Edmund

Dulac) might yet preside though moved from the frontispiece to the interior of a whole new body of fiction called "Stories of Michael Robartes and His Friends: An Extract from a Record Made by His Pupils" (privately published by the Cuala Press in 1931 in company with the play *The Resurrection*). Gambits involving the fabled Judwalis and the education of the Caliph had given place to the contemporary scene of bohemian artists and mystics retrieved from the pages of *The Secret Rose* (1897), especially from the story "Rosa Alchemica" augmented by "The Tables of the Law" and "The Adoration of the Magi." The objective of setting straight "Dear Mr. Yeats" by means of transcripts signed by John Aherne, Owen's brother, and by John Duddon, another new character based on an old Irish tale about the fleecing of gullible yokels, offers a tongue-in-cheek counterpoint to the serious point of Yeats's open letter to Pound on the authority of *A Vision*.[3] As Ellmann suggested, the former inventions might be regarded as cake to the bread of the latter philosophy and that of the partitioned main body of *AVB* proper, Books I-V.

In time, difficulties within the marriage led Yeats to cultivate interests in other women. Almost as a premonition of the philandering "wild old wicked man" of the 1930s, Yeats also wonders (in the diary entry of March 14, 1926) that *AVA* revised might require, on the nature of love, a final section in the form of a letter by Michael Robartes to "two young eastern lovers" to illustrate the juxtaposition of Mask and Creative Mind compared with changes of civilization. The problem was to "help the *Phantasmagoria*" without the method of writing intruding too obviously with "generalization" to compose a letter to make "more credible" the historical gyres and civilization as abstractions. Eventually, a short narrative called "Michael Robartes Foretells" was written but withheld from *AVB*, leaving the poem "All Souls' Night," as before, to serve the entire book as an epilogue.[4] However, on the nature of love, subject to a man's and a woman's interaction in life "like East and West," the epitome of love as an experience is precisely rendered in *AVB* in Robartes's personal account of himself as a lover:

> Love contains all Kant's antinomies, but it is the first that poisons our lives. Thesis, there is no beginning; antithesis, there is a beginning; or, as I prefer: thesis, there is an end; antithesis, there is no end. Exhausted by the cry that it can never end, my love ends; without that cry it were not love but desire, desire does not end. The anguish of birth and that of death cry out in the same instant. Life is no series of emanations from divine reason such as the Cabalists imagine, but an irrational bitterness, no orderly descent from level to level, no waterfall but a whirlpool, a gyre. (*AVB* 40)[5]

For the most part, the writing of the 1931 *Stories of Michael Robartes and His Friends* was taken down first in a large notebook, bound handsomely in embossed leather with enlaced edges (NLI 13,577), and completed in a series of Cuala proofs (NLI 30,019) and a typed fragment for the ending (NLI 30,465)—all of which is examined in Part Four of this study. The focus here, on the other hand, is on a single textual gene that Yeats had suppressed until he was well into the correction of proof copy for *AVB* and motivated by a desire to entertain and perhaps shock Lady Dorothy Wellesley, who became an intimate friend from June 1935 to January 1939, when she stood vigil with her partner, Hilda Matheson, at Yeats's deathbed in the south of France.

Like MacGregor Mathers, the host of Yeats's "Paris friends" in the 1890s, Robartes plays host to an assortment of wayward characters in the bundle of stories joined in the eponymous 1931 version. One such character is a capricious young woman who calls herself Denise de L'Isle Adam (*sic*), inspired by *Axel,* the play by Count Villiers de l'Isle-Adam that Yeats reviewed in 1894 and, in 1924, remembered in a preface to H. P. R. Finberg's translation.[6] Denise is understood to be an emancipated *habitué* of Parisian (or, here, London) café society in the 1920s. Her sexual promiscuity is suggested but undeclared until she is permitted by Robartes, in *AVB,* to tell her story over the objection of the men with whom she is engaged in a *ménage à trois.* She had been interrupted in the earlier version by Aherne's ushering in of the adulterous lovers John Bond and Mary Bell, who, besides Robartes's fantastic story about recovering much of the lost *Speculum Angelorum et Hominum* by Giraldus while being thrown out of bed by an "ignorant girl" with whom he had been cohabiting, are the evening's featured attraction as cuckoo and bearer, respectively, of the lost egg of Leda. In "a state of suppressed excitement," Denise prevails to tell her story over Huddon's protest that she had done so "a dozen times at the Café Royal and should be satisfied" (*AVB* 42), but only because Robartes has broken in before Bond can speak and insists that Denise be given her turn, observing that, "from what I know of her, I feel certain that it will be a full and admirable introduction" (42). An error in judgment, as it turns out.

The body of her story was composed on three folios (1^r, 2^r, and 3^r), constituting a holograph fragment (NLI 30,390) housed in the National Library of Ireland. The fragment is given in facsimile and transcribed in the Appendix (below). The published equivalent is paragraph 3 of part III, as follows:

> Denise began: "I was reading *Axel* in bed. It was between twelve and one on the 2nd of June last year. A date that I will never forget, because on that night I met the one man I shall always love. I was turning the pages of the Act where the lovers are in the vault under the castle. Axel and Sarah decide to die rather than possess one another. He talks of her hair as full of the odour of dead rose leaves—a pretty phrase—a phrase I would like somebody to say to me; and then comes the famous sentence: 'As for living, our servants will do that for us.' I was wondering what made them do anything so absurd, when the candle went out. I said, 'Duddon, I heard you open the window, creep over the floor on your toes, but I never guessed that you would blow the candle out.' 'Denise,' he said, 'I am a

> great coward. I am afraid of unfamiliar women in pyjamas.' I said: 'No, my dear, you are not a coward, you were just shy, but why should you call me unfamiliar? I thought I had put everything right when I told you that I slept on the ground floor, that there was nobody else on the floor, and that I left the window open.' Five minutes later I said: 'Duddon, you are impotent, stop trembling; go over there and sit by the fire. I will give you some wine.' When he had drunk half a tumbler of claret, he said: 'No, I am not really impotent, I am a coward, that is all. When Huddon tires of a girl, I make love to her, and there is no difficulty at all. He has always talked about her, but if he had not, it would not make much difference. He is my greatest friend, and when she and he have been in the same bed, it is as though she belonged to the house. Twice I have found somebody on my own account, and been a failure, just as I have to-night. I had not indeed much hope when I climbed through the window but I had a little, because you had made it plain that I would be welcome.' I said: 'Oh, my dear, how delightful; now I know all about Axel. He was just shy. If he had not killed the Commander in the Second Act—and it would have been much more dramatic at the end of the play—he could have sent for him and all would have come right. The Commander was not a friend, of course; Axel hated him; but he was a relation, and afterwards Axel could have thought of Sarah as a member of the family. I love you because you would not be shy if you had not so great respect for me. You feel about me what I feel about a Bishop in a surplice. I would not give you up now for anything.' Duddon said, wringing his hands: 'Oh, what am I to do.' I said: 'Fetch the Commander.' He said, getting cheerful at once: 'I am to bring Huddon?' [. . ."] (*AVB* 42–43)

"Full," but hardly "admirable" for the occasion, Denise's story is a joke at the expense of youthful enthusiasm—hers and formerly Yeats's own. As Marilyn Gaddis Rose writes in her "Translator's Foreword" to *Axel,* Denise "nonchalantly distorts the characterizations, even attributes a key speech to the wrong character" (ix). Presumably, Rose alludes to Sara's lines in Act IV, Scene 4: "Let me veil you in my hair so you may inhale the attar of roses of all time" (155) and "[*smiling, inhaling* AXEL'S *hair*] You smell like bright autumn leaves, O my huntsman!" (157). It is still some pages in the Rose translation before Axel issues his famous line: "As for living? Our servants will do that for us" (170). Rather than acknowledging the chaste but erotically yearning protagonists' dilemma in choosing life-in-death instead of several forms of death-in-life (including the satiation of carnal passion), Denise distorts the characters and the play to a bottom-line of sexual impotence. The play's eroticism is apparent, and evidently all she sees: "What quiverings rise at the sight of you! My love? My desires?... They crush you, penetrate you, O beloved! They swell and die in you..." (156–57); but the suppression of desire is a perversity, as Axel says just before bitterly declaiming the famous sentence about the servants: "Realize this, Sara: in our strange hearts we have destroyed the love of life" (169). To have created naughty Denise de L'Isle Adam, Yeats's estimation of *Axel* had to have changed to allow him to exploit for comic effect one of the sacred books of his youth. The change is almost one with our dating of the story.

In May 1935, while reading and selecting poems for his notorious *Oxford Book of Modern Verse* (1936), Yeats encountered at the home of his friend Lady Ottoline Morrell the poem "Horses" by Dorothy Wellesley, later the Duchess of Wellington.[7] Excited by what he read, he began corresponding at once and, in a few days, visited her at her romantic estate, Penns in the Rocks, on the Sussex-Kent border. They became fast friends, though not without a serious spat on liberties he began taking with her poetry writing. Subsequently, he promoted her writing in the *OMBV* and, also in 1936, pronounced her genius in an introduction for *Selections from the Poems of Dorothy Wellesley*.[8] They collaborated as editors on the second series of *Broadsides* (Cuala Press, 1937), to which they contributed poems with eroticized content written, essentially, in competition with one another. His correspondence to her, *Letters on Poetry from W. B. Yeats to Dorothy Wellesley*, first published in 1940, after his death, with a second edition in 1964. Extraordinary for Yeats's view of modern verse and the making of poems, the book is also endowed with an abundance of material on their complex relationship.[9]

In Yeats's letters to Wellesley from 26 July 1936 up to 4 May 1937, his progress on *A Vision* is regularly cited. In the first of these, he promises to send "Lapis Lazuli" as soon as he can have it typed and refers, significantly, to the drafting of Denise's story: "To-morrow I write a story to be added to the Michael Robartes series (a prelude to *A Vision* which I am now revising in proof). It is almost an exact transcript from fact. I have for years been creating a group of strange disorderly people on whom Michael Robartes confers the wisdom of the east" (*LDW* 83). If Yeats kept to this schedule, the story was written on 27 July 1936. But what is meant by "almost an exact transcript of fact"? With only one minor difference in punctuation, the text of the letter in *LDW* agrees with that given in Allan Wade's selected edition of Yeats's *Letters* (London: Macmillan, 1955), 859. In 1985, though, Richard Ellmann was to explain what Yeats meant, supplying most of a passage omitted by Wellesley and Wade as a precaution to protect the living, no doubt. Ellmann's revelation was published in *The New York Review of Books* 32.8 (9 May 1985): 10–18 as "Yeats's Second Puberty" and reprinted elsewhere.[10] Because Yeats associated sexual virility with the ability to create passionate poetry, according to the biographer, impotence was of great interest to the poet from his Steinach operation in 1934 onward. Today, more than thirty years after the Ellmann essay and fifteen years after the issuance of the first electronic edition of *The Collected Letters of W. B. Yeats*, a complete *literatim* text of the letter bridges the misleading gulf that Wellesley and Wade left in their versions of the letter without so much as an ellipsis to indicate editorial intervention.

Hence, we can now restore the omitted passage that has been standing invisibly after the words "transcript from fact," between the second and third sentences quoted above. As follows, the omission certainly strikes one as a choice secret that one might only share with a very close friend in confidence. The scene is roughly 1920, when the Yeatses resided in Oxford but toured America:

> We let our house in the Broad, Oxford to some American girl students. In the middle of the night Alan Porter (late editor or sub editor of the Spectator) climbed through the window & got into bed with one of the girls. He was welcomed but found to be impotent. He explained that he had a great friend & when that friend had tired of a girl had always taken her for himself. If he found a girl for himself he was impotent. The student said fetch your friend. He did. And after that all went well. Alan Porter had the student 14 times in 10 days. I have worked it up into a charming fantasy on the nature of shyness. If the girl lay with the friend he felt she belonged to the family, once was enough.[11]

Salacious gossip? To be sure. In the course of their relationship with Ottoline Morrell, Yeats and his wife often amused one another with stories obtained from their visits to Garsington. Probably he knew that Wellesley, whose social circle intersected with that of the Morrells and their Bloomsbury friends (and now his own), would appreciate the tale and his sharing as an invitation to further intimacy. The counting of coups, or scoring of Porter's successful "times" with the student, seems kindred to adolescent locker-room talk and in that way affirms Ellmann's claim that Yeats was in his "second puberty." Yeats seems to be initiating with such talk the least prurient aspect of his late wickedness with women, too—particularly the "rich women" of whom Auden disapproved, being homosexual, like Dorothy Wellesley: "You were silly like us: your gift survived it all; / The parish of rich women, physical decay, / Yourself" ("In Memory of W. B. Yeats," ll. 32–34).[12] Moreover, Yeats seems to have delighted in his own naughtiness, judging from at least one of his contributions to *Broadsides: A Collection of New Irish and English Songs* (Dublin: Cuala Press, 1937) soon after gathered and expanded to a whole sequence in *New Poems* (Dublin: Cuala Press, 1938). Inspired by Wellesley's poem "The Lady, The Squire, and the Serving-maid" and its illicit triangle involving a courtly lady, her chambermaid, and their male lover, Yeats's "The Three Bushes" is attributed to a fictitious source given in its subtitle: "the 'Historia mei Temporis' of the Abbé Michel de Bourdeille."[13] The ruse is reminiscent of the function of texts by Villiers and Giraldus cited in *AVB,* and the common "incident" in the two poems recalls an inference that Ellmann draws from Yeats's story: that "Denise loves one man with her soul and accepts the other with her body," twisting conventional morality and theology in a comic circumstance worthy of Chaucer; thus, "the soul may keep its distance while the body embraces, and vice versa."[14]

Yeats had already launched a sort of competition in verse before writing Denise's story. On July 2nd, he returned to Wellesley her poem, revised and declared a "masterpiece," his having only "put in the rhymes" to make a ballad of it (*LDW* 70). On July 10th, he sent another version of stanzas II and III due to an "inadmissible rhyme," to which she responded, curtly, enclosing her amended poem and noting that she "regard[ed] it as written" at this point, and she asked him to send his ballad, at last (*LDW* 71–72). He did as she requested but not without sending another full version of her poem, apparently failing to appreciate the offense she had taken at liberties he was taking with her as a poet and the degree of his intervention as her co-editor.[15] In his next three letters, he defends his poem, point by point, against her "slanging" criticism (*LDW* 80), but finally conceded that he had been overzealously engaged with her work: "Ah my dear how it added to my excitement when I re-made that poem of yours to know it was your poem. I re-made you and myself into a single being. We triumphed over each other and I thought of [Shakespeare's] *The Turtle and the Phoenix*" (*LDW* 82).[16] So then, in his next letter, crossing in the mail with one of her own that observed "a dark unhappy day reading Virginia Woolf and Edith Sitwell," Yeats humored her with his "transcript from fact" on the new story for the Michael Robartes series.

One doubts that the account of Alan Porter's escapades in Mr. and Mrs. Yeats's leased premises in Broad Street, Oxford, shocked the author of "The Lady, The Squire, and the Serving-maid," though its alleged authenticity was eyebrow-raising. Denise's story, told from the perspective of the American "girl" with whom Porter overcomes his sexual shyness in the company of his "great friend," is a counterpoint to "The Three Bushes," even though her presentation of it is embedded, within quotes, in an "Extract from a Record" signed by John Duddon, artist and writer, the lover she prefers while serving as the mistress of Peter Huddon, who supports them both. The story is amusing but, as a *vignette*, still wants to be married to Duddon's entire account of Robartes's pupils and assorted friends. The way Yeats cut back to his 1931 copy text[17] is literally an extraordinary case so far as textual biography goes. For, now separated, the new story and a new poem to appease and please Wellesley were originally laid out contiguously in the same manuscript notebook. When he started to write Denise's story, it was 27 July 1936. When he finished the poem—"To D. W." in *LDW*, "To a Friend" in *The London Mercury* and *New Poems*, and "To Dorothy Wellesley" in *Last Poems and Plays*—it was August 1st, and on the 2nd and 5th he made and dispatched corrections for individual verses. In a few days, the work was done in both instances, although he could not report that *A Vision* proofs were "off [his] hands" (*LDW*), finally, until a year later.

As seen in the Appendix below, the folio on which Yeats completed the story by transitioning back to Robartes's introduction of Mary Bell and John Bond has been withdrawn and filed with materials generally associated with *New Poems* and

Last Poems (NLI 13,593), folder 16 ("To Dorothy Wellesley"). In the shuffle, the capital letter "B" was inscribed on the upper-left corner of the recto side of the sheet to distinguish it from the verso, labeled "A," bearing a 13-line rough draft of the 16-line poem. With the "B" side on top, a note ("P. 'B' Prose | Huddon & Duddon | stories") has been clipped to the lot.[18] To achieve a visual reconstruction of Yeats's notebook, then, one finds that the assembly sequence for the story is NLI 30,390 (1^r), (2^r), (3^r), (3^v), and NLI 13,593 (16), p. "B." Due to spatial limitations, the only verso in this sequence, page (3^v), has been moved to the end of the Appendix, with Yeats's drawn lines simulated by graphics in the transcriptions of "B" and 3^v to make apparent, when viewed in apposition, exactly how the latter came into play in Robartes's speech, which would thereafter carry on essentially as it had done in the Cuala text of 1931.

The visual impression one has in viewing the beginning of the sequence (at 1^r) and the revision at the end (at 3^v) is that splicing presented a little more work than most other parts of the composition. One imagines a typist preparing slips directly from this draft for insertion into the copy text or into Macmillan proof copy (see note 17), and one surmises that the sentence marked for inclusion on 3^v was not used because it repeated text introduced on 1^r. Consequently, page "B" came to agree in most respects with the following passage (starting at the bottom of 3^r but continuing in a single paragraph):

> "A fortnight later Duddon and I were in Florence. We had plenty of money, for Huddon had just bought a large picture, and were delighted with each other. I said: 'I am going to send Huddon this little cigarette-case.' It was one of those pretty malachite things they sell in Florence. I had had it engraved with the words: 'In memory of the 2nd June.' He said: 'Why put into it only one cigarette.' I said: 'Oh, he will understand.'["] "And now you know," said Denise, "why I have named myself after the author of Axel." I said: "You wish always to remember that upon that night I introduced you to Huddon." She said: "What a fool you are. It is you that I love, and shall always love." I said: "But you are Huddon's mistress?" She said: "When a man gives me a cigarette, and I like the brand, I want a hundred, but the box is almost empty."
>
> "Now," said Robartes, "the time has come for John Bond." John Bond, after fixing a bewildered eye, first upon Denise and then me, began. He had evidently prepared his words beforehand. . . . (*AVB* 43–44)[19]

Interestingly, Yeats was still making metaphors of cigarettes on 1 August 1936, when he wrote Ethel Mannin: "It is a curious experience to have an infirm body & an intellect more alive than it has ever been. One poem leads to another as if I were smoking cigarettes & lit them from each other! Nothing now interrupts the chain" (*CL InteLex* 6627). On the same day, he wrote to Olivia Shakespear and boasted his vigorous output of poetry though invalided to a wheelchair, happy as the man in an old play who gives away his last possession, his wooden leg, to declare, "now I am ready to enjoy life" (*CL InteLex* 6626). In Denise's story, the device of a last cigarette borne in a valuable, almost empty case seems a similar trope. Given the story's content, we are invited to read as Freudian Denise's punch-line, or declaration, of love as a preference ("always") for one of two men. But can Duddon believe her? As their master teaches, only desire does not end. Conversely, containing all of Kant's antinomies, love ends in the declaration that it is without end. Like Hic and Ille (This and That), the characters Huddon and Duddon function as antinomies just as they do in their comic source,[20] to which Yeats had alluded in the epigraph. They are "Hard-living men," "men of thought" who "Burn their bodies up for nought," and their "burning out" the poet mocks (*AVB* 32). Just so, burning light (a "torch on high") is the important figure on which Yeats constructs his compliment in "To Dorothy Wellesley." The conflict in the poem, as he explained to her, originated deep in subconsciousness: "I dream of clear water…(the moon of the poem), then come erotic dreams. Then…I write with sex for theme. Then comes the reversal—[as] it came when I was young with some dream or some vision between waking and sleep with a flame in it. Then for weeks I get a symbolism like that in my Byzantium poem or in 'To D. W.'" (*LDW* 86–87).

It seems unlikely from this that Dorothy Wellesley had ever been shocked when she read the new version of "Stories of Michael Robartes and His Friends"—indeed, assuming that she eventually read *A Vision*—and then remembered the "transcript from fact," the theme of a new Michael Robartes story, which Yeats had given to amuse her in a letter, perhaps as a peace offering. According to Deborah Ferrelli, whose otherwise exhaustive treatment of the influence the two poets had on each other makes no reference to this gesture, Yeats's follow-up tribute to Wellesley understandably draws attention away from "strange disorderly people" (*LDW* 83), directing attention to the poets themselves. Accordingly, Ferrelli writes, "'To Dorothy Wellesley' allowed Wellesley to be internalized by Yeats at the same time as she was internalized in the ballads" (258). Their relationship was never quite the same after that.[21]

This final addition to the Robartes-Aherne canon brings to a spirited conclusion the first genetically conceived, chronologically arranged edition of that extraordinay body of work, considered in both published and unpublished states. Whether illuminating philosophical verses or longer pieces as framing vignettes, or enjoyed for their own sake as "simply works of art," such compositions gave Yeats much pleasure to write and frequently rise to the level of his most inventive writing.

Notes

1. Richard Ellmann, "At the Yeatses'," in *along the riverrun* (New York: Alfred A. Knopf, 1989), 247.
2. Ann Saddlemyer, *Becoming George: The Life of Mrs. W. B. Yeats* (Oxford: Oxford University Press, 2002), 306. See *YPM* 122 and 318, n. 51.
3. See Chapman, "Metaphors for Poetry," *YVEC* 236. John Duddon and his counterpart, Peter Huddon, derive from the rival farmers in the tale "Donald and His Neighbours," which, more than forty years earlier, Yeats had reprinted in his anthology *Fairy and Folk Tales of the Irish Peasantry* (1888), his source being a "chap-book" entitled "Hibernian Tales," credited by Thackeray in his *Irish Sketch Book* (1842 and later), where the story is quoted in full. In *AVB*, most of *A Packet for Ezra Pound* (1929) preceded matter from *Stories of Michael Robartes and His Friends* (1931), the two Cuala texts serving together as preludes.
4. See preceding chapter. "Michael Robartes Foretells" continues Yeats's narrative method from "Stories of Michael Robartes" in *AVB* by gathering at Thoor Ballylee the friends Huddon, Duddon, Daniel O'Leary, and Denise for the reading of Robartes' prophecy on the next Cycle before he disappeared into Arabia.
5. For an additional account of the emergence of Robartes's opinion of love as given in his own story (part II), see *YPM* 3–5, regarding Yeats's rehearsal of these lines from a manuscript theme entitled "Concerning love."
6. Yeats's preface, dated "September 20th, 1924," is reprinted in Villiers de l'Isle-Adam, *Axel*, trans. Marilyn Gaddis Rose (Dublin: The Dolmen Press, 1970), xiii-xv; the quote is from p. xiii. For the preface, Yeats adapted three sections of his review of the play from the *Bookman* of April 1894. Entitled "A Symbolical Drama in Paris," the review is available in *The Collected Works of W. B. Yeats*, vol. 9: *Early Articles and Reviews*, eds. John P. Frayne and Madeline Marchaterre (New York: Scribner, 2004), 234–37.
7. W. B. Yeats, ed., *The Oxford Book of Modern Verse 1892–1935* (Oxford: At the Clarendon Press, 1936); hereafter cited as *OBMV*. See pages xxxii–xxxiii and 309–24. Wellesley's poems were "Fire," "Horses," "Asian Desert," "Fishing," "From 'Lenin,'" "From 'Matrix,'" "The Buried Child," and "The Morning after"—one more poem and two more pages than Yeats allotted to T. S. Eliot, and five more poems and nine more pages than he gave to his "poetic son" Ezra Pound. Yeats and his wife were fond of Lady Ottoline, who, within a few days, drove him to Wellesley's home and introduced them. Wellesley, like Morrell, was a link to Bloomsbury as she served as an editor for the Hogarth Press Living Poets series despite Leonard Woolf's antipathy. An admiring Virginia Woolf was introduced to Yeats by Morrell, and he wrote a poem about it in 1930; see Chapman, "Woolf, Yeats, and the Making of 'Spilt Milk,'" 265–70.
8. Yeats's introduction is best found today in *The Collected Works of W. B. Yeats*, vol. 6: *Prefaces and Introductions*, ed. William H. O'Donnell (New York: Macmillan, 1989), 182–85.
9. The study employs the later edition: W. B. Yeats, *Letters on Poetry from W. B. Yeats to Dorothy Wellesley*, intro. by Kathleen Raine (London: Oxford University Press, 1964); hereafter cited as *LDW*. Besides this book, the best treatment of the personal and professional relationship between Yeats and Wellesley is Deborah Ferrelli's "W. B. Yeats and Dorothy Wellesley," in *Influence and Confluence; Yeats Annual No. 17: A Special Number*, ed. Warwick Gould (London: Palgrave Macmillan, 2007), 227–305. Also see Tim Armstrong, "Giving Birth to Oneself: Yeats's Late Sexuality," *Yeats Annual* 8 (1991): 39–58; and Joseph M. Hassett, *W. B. Yeats and the Muses* (Oxford: Oxford University Press, 2010), 185–97.
10. The other printings are a booklet entitled *W. B. Yeats's Second Puberty: A lecture delivered at the Library of Congress on April 2, 1984* (Washington, DC: Library of Congress, 1985) and a chapter in Ellmann's posthumous essay collection *Four Dubliners: Wilde, Yeats, Joyce, and Beckett* (New York: George Braziller, 1987), 38–63; both are identically illustrated.

11. *CL InteLex* 6622. To "belong to the family" meant, according to Denise, to belong to the "house" (see NLI 30, 390, 3ʳ, line 2).
12. The lines are too famous not to recall them from *The Norton Anthology of English Literature*, vol. 2, eds. M. H. Abrams et al. (New York: Norton, 1962), 1626–28. Yeats's awareness of her sexual preference is signaled in a passage cut from *LDW* (109) about the "charge" against Casement, as well as on the homosexuality of Charles Ricketts and T. E. Lawrence (of Arabia); Yeats to Dorothy Wellesley, 2 Dec. [1936], *CL Intelex* 6737.
13. *VP* 569–75. In W. B. Yeats, *The Collected Poems of W. B. Yeats: A New Edition*, ed. Richard J. Finneran (New York: Macmillan, 1989), 296–301, the poems are "The Three Bushes," "The Lady's First Song," "The Lady's Second Song," "The Lady's Third Song," "The Lover's Song," "The Chambermaid's First Song" and "The Chambermaid's Second Song." Finneran's note on the supposed sixteenth- or seventeenth-century source is useful although speculative, translating "Historia mei Temporis" as "History of my Times" and deriving a possible pun from the name Bourdeille in the conflation of "*bourde* ('a fib or humbug') and *bordel* ('a brothel')" (506).
14. Ellmann, *W. B. Yeats's Second Puberty* 15.
15. The dispute was settled between them, as Wellesley noted in her edition of their letters, with a correct text in "D.W.'s own words…published in the Cuala Broadsides" and with "three final verses" restored "on an erratum slip" (*LDW* 69). See the editors' Appendix III: "Yeats and Dorothy Wellesley Collaboration" in W. B. Yeats, *New Poems: Manuscript Materials*, eds. J. C. C. Mays and Stephen Parrish (Ithaca, NY: Cornell University Press, 2000), 379–91.
16. The sexual double-entendres and transgender implications suggested in the passage are relevant here and sustain much of Ferrelli's account of the Yeats/Wellesley relationship. In a number of instances, Yeats says he is attracted to her masculine beauty. His "wildness" as an old man recalls Crazy Jane as well as Eliot's Tiresias: "My dear, my dear—when you crossed the room with that boyish movement, it was no man who looked at you, it was the woman in me. It seems that I can make a woman express herself as never before. I have looked out of her eyes. I have shared her desire" (*LDW* 108; cf. Ferrelli, 255). In his letter of July 21, Yeats means *The Phoenix and the Turtle*, Wellesley's favorite poem, according to Ferrelli (269, n. 72), a copy of which Yeats gave to her on Christmas 1937.
17. At this writing, it is certain that Yeats prepared, at that time, either an insert to send with a corrected copy of the Cuala booklet or, more likely, an insert directly into proof copy. But if the "Stories of Michael Robartes" were already before him in *AVB* proof copy when he added the latest tale, that stage of the production has been entirely lost. We know that a setting copy of the 1931 edition of *Stories of Michael Robartes and His Friends*…was prepared and still exists in the private collection of the late Michael B. Yeats, "used as copy for the corresponding section of the 1937 edition of *A Vision*," as Connie K. Hood reports in "The Remaking of *A Vision*," *Yeats: An Annual of Critical and Textual Studies*, 1 (Ithaca, NY: Cornell University Press, 1983), 47. The book has been thoroughly marked with compositor's galley numbers and house style changes. But "only one substantive change is marked (*hotel* to *café* at 5.14)" in that copy, leading to the conclusion that "all the substantive changes that appear in the 1937 edition must have been made by Yeats on various stages of galleys" (47), the most substantive alteration being the "interpolation of Denise's story (*SMR* 11; AV-B* 42.8–44.20)." See the collation of variants in Part Four (above) for such changes introduced in galley both in 1930–31 and 1936–37.
18. All but the "B" page of this file is available in facsimile and transcription (with much of page "A" in conjectural state) in Mays and Parrish, eds., *New Poems: Manuscript Materials* 106–11.
19. The dialogue exchanges between Denise and Duddon may be confusing to the reader who fails to note that, in the second paragraph here, the narrative voice shifts from her to him (i.e., "I " refers to Duddon whereas the pronoun formerly referred to Denise). A bracketed

close-quotation mark has been added to indicate that the embedded narrative frame has concluded.

20. See note 3.
21. A *coda* to this whole episode might be constructed from the evidence assembled in Appendix IV ("Ballads Left Unpublished by Yeats") of *New Poems: Manuscript Materials*, where the editors wisely refuse to attribute much authority to Yeats in the "deliberately bizarre" case of "Poem of Launcelot Switchback" (and the related "Billy Boy"), written in collaboration with doggerel poet Oliver St. John Gogarty "…PRIMARILY TO SHOCK DOROTHY WELLESLEY, WHICH IT DID, SAYS MRS. YEATS." Such a *coda* might resemble Conrad Balliet's essay "W. B. Yeats: Literary Masochism and Poetic Stimulation in the Previously Unpublished 'Poem of Lancelot Switchback,'" *Yeats: An Annual of Critical and Textual Studies* 9 (1991), 3–10. Balliet's case, however, has been so devastatingly repudiated by A. Norman Jeffares, in "Know Your Gogarty," *Yeats Annual* 14 (2001), 298–305, that it seems prudent not to go there. Yet, to have it both ways, Mays and Parrish note, in the introduction to Appendix III ("Yeats and Dorothy Wellesley in Collaboration"), that Wellesley withheld "The Lady, The Squire, and the Serving-Maid" from *Early Light* (1955), a collection of verse including "all [she] wish[ed] to preserve," and that she cut her copy of Yeats's *New Poems* (1938) *short* of the signature bearing "To a Friend" (i.e., "To Dorothy Wellesley"), suggesting that unpleasantness for her was better left out of sight. Mays and Parrish, eds., *New Poems: Manuscript Materials* 381.

Appendix

(see the next eight pages)

Manuscript Facsimiles and Transcriptions for Denise's Story, composed in July/August 1936 and introduced into "Stories of Michael Robartes and His Friends: An Extract from a Record Made by His Pupils" (1931) as preliminary matter for *A Vision* (London: Macmillan, 1937).

Inserted as Yeats corrected a proof copy of the latter, the final version of the story was printed in *AVB* 42–44. See note 17 (above). Since publication of the book on 7 October 1937, the setting copy has been lost, bearing text to editors at Macmillan Ltd. (London) for interpolation by printers at R. & R. Clark, Ltd. (Edinburgh). Macmillan's outgoing letterbooks acknowledge receipt of "corrected slip proofs from Yeats" on 24 February 1937, intermittent delays, and finally "proofs of pp. 1–192 of *A Vision* passed for press" by Yeats on May 24th (British Library Add 55791, f. 284 through Add 55794, f. 487), with occasional references to inserted materials.

The following exhibits correspond with Yeats's original draft, not later marked proof and inserted copy, presumably typed.

NLI 30,390 (1[r])

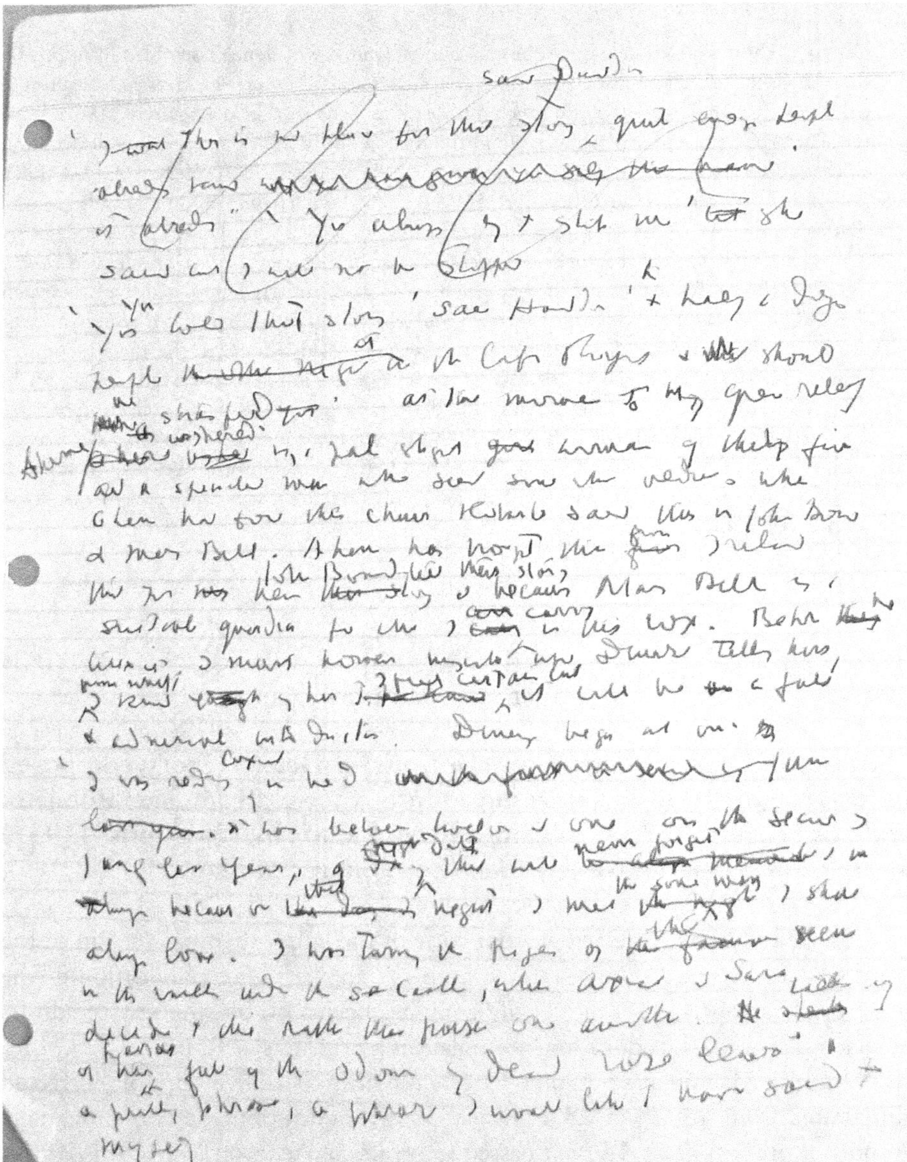

NLI 30,390 (1r):

Said Duddon
'~~I will~~ This is no place for that story ^ quite enough people
already know ~~why you have given yourself than name~~'
it already" 'You always try to stop me' ~~let~~ she
said but I will not be stopped

you to
'You told that story' said Huddon '[?] half a dozen
at
people ~~the other night in~~ the Café Royal & ~~that~~ should
be
~~have~~ satisfied ~~you~~' at the moment to my great relief
[?~~then~~] ushered
Aherne/~~aherne~~ ~~ushed~~ in a pale slight ~~girl~~ woman of thirty five
and a spectacled man who seemed some what older. When
Aherne had found them chairs Robartes said this is John Bond
from
& Mary Bell. Aherne has brought them ~~from~~ Ireland
John Bond tell their story
that you ~~may~~ hear ~~their story~~ & because Mary Bell is a
~~arr~~ carry he
suitable guardian for what I ~~cary~~ ^ in this box. Before ~~they~~
tells it, I must however insist upon Denise telling hers,
from what I feel certain that
^I know ~~enough~~ of her ~~I~~ ~~kn~~ ~~know~~ it^will be a full
& admirable introduction. Denise began at once ~~I~~
Axel
'I was reading^in bed ~~on the first or second of June~~
~~last year~~. It was between twelve and one on the second of
~~night~~ date never forget
June last year, a ~~day~~^that will ~~be always memorable~~ to me
that the same man
~~always~~ because on ~~that day I~~ night I met ~~the nigh~~^I shall
that
always love. I was turning the pages of ~~the famous~~ scene
in the vault under the castle, when Axel & Sara
talks of
decide to die rather than possess one another. He ~~speaks~~
hair as
~~of har~~ ^^ full of the odour of dead rose leaves',
a pretty phrase, a phrase I would like to have said to
myself

NLI 30,390 (2r)

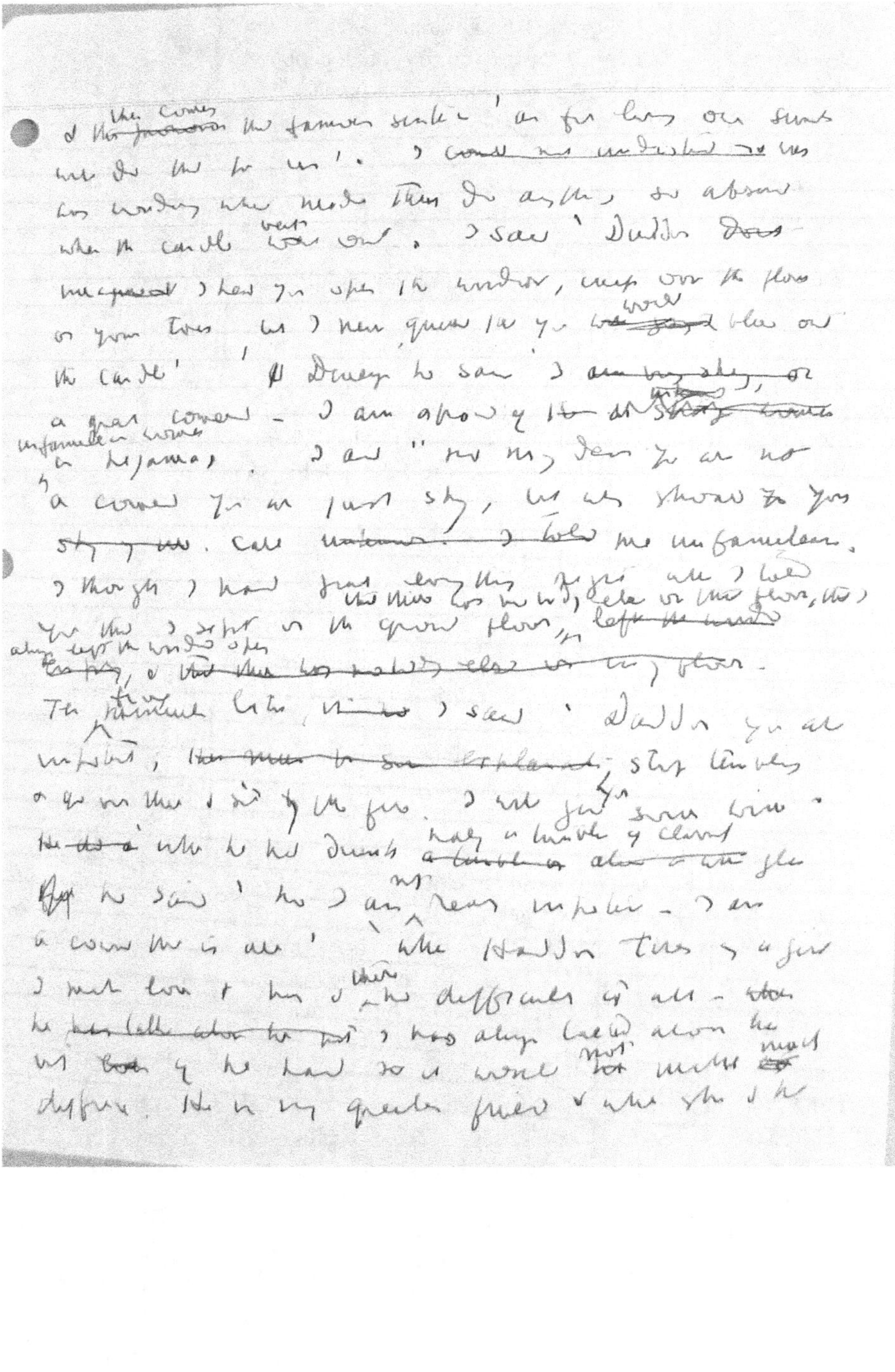

NLI 30,390 (2^{r})

then comes
& ~~then pronounces~~ that famous sentence 'as for living our servants
will do that for us'. I ~~could not understand it~~ was
was wondering who made them do anything so absurd
went
when the candle ~~wen~~ out. I said "Duddon ~~don't~~
~~imagine &~~ I heard you open the window, creep over the floor
would
on your toes but I never guessed that you ~~were going to~~ blow out
the candle' 'O Denys['] he said 'I ~~am very shy, or~~
~~unknown~~
a great coward – I am afraid of ~~the~~ ~~all strange women~~
unfamiliar women
^ in pajamas.['] I an[swered] "No my dear you are not
a coward you are just shy, but why should ~~yo~~ you [be]
~~shy of me~~. call ~~unknown I told~~ me unfamiliar.
I thought I had put every thing right after I told
that there was nobody else on that floor, that I
you that I s[l]ept on the ground floor, ^ ~~left the window~~
always left the window open
~~empty~~, & ~~that there was nobody else on my floor.~~
five
Then ^ minutes later, ~~[?] no~~ I said 'Duddon you are
impotent; ~~there must be some explanation~~; stop trembling
you
& go over there & sit by the fire. I will give some wine'
Half a tumbler of claret
~~He did as~~ When he had drunk ~~a tumbler or~~ ~~above & with~~ glee
not
~~he~~ he said 'no I am ^ really impotent – I am
a coward that is all' 'When Huddon tires of a girl
theres
I make love to her &^no difficulty at all – ~~when~~
he ~~had talked about her [?wit]~~ I had always talked about her
not much
wit ~~even~~ if he had not it would ~~bu~~t make ~~m~~
difference. He is my greatest friend & when she & he

NLI 30,390 (3[r])

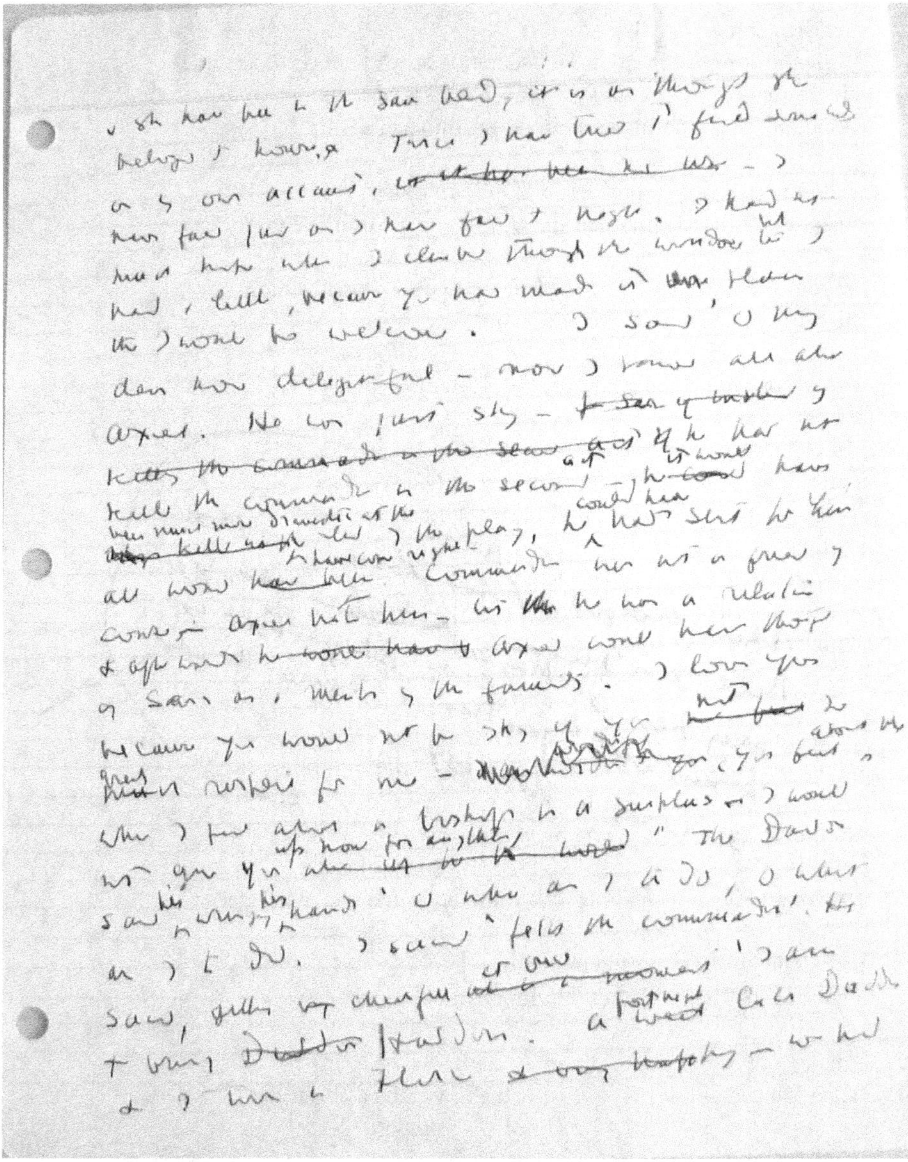

NLI 30,390 (3^{r})

& she have been in the same bed, it is as though she
belonged to [the] house. Twice I have tried to find some body
on my own account, ~~but it has been no use~~ – I
have fail[ed] just as I have failed to night. I had not
but
much hope when I climbed through the window ~~but~~ I
had a little, because you had made it [?] plain
that I would be welcome. I said 'O my
dear how delightful – now I know all about
Axel. He was just shy – ~~for Sara~~ ~~if instead~~ of
~~killing the commander in the second act~~ If he had not
act it would
killed the commander in the second – ~~he could~~ have
been much more dramatic at the could have
~~always killed at the~~ ^ end of the play, he ^ had sent for him
have come right–
all would ~~have been~~ Commander was not a friend of
course – Axel hated him – but [?] he was a relation
& after wards ~~he would have to~~ Axel could have thought
of Sara as a member of the family. I love you
not
because you would not be shy if you ~~have feelings~~ so
great wonderful about me
~~much~~ respect for me – ~~I am neither to you~~ & you feel ^
where I feel about a bishop in a surplus – I would
up now for anything
not give you ~~[?now] up for the world~~" Then Duddon
no his
said ^ wringing ^ hands 'O what am I to do, o what
am I to do.['] I said 'fetch the commander'. He
at once
said, getting ~~very~~ cheerful ~~all in a moment~~ 'I am
fortnight
to bring ~~Duddon~~ Huddon. A ~~week~~ later Duddon
& I were in Florence ~~& very happy~~ – we had

NLI 13,593 (16), page "B"

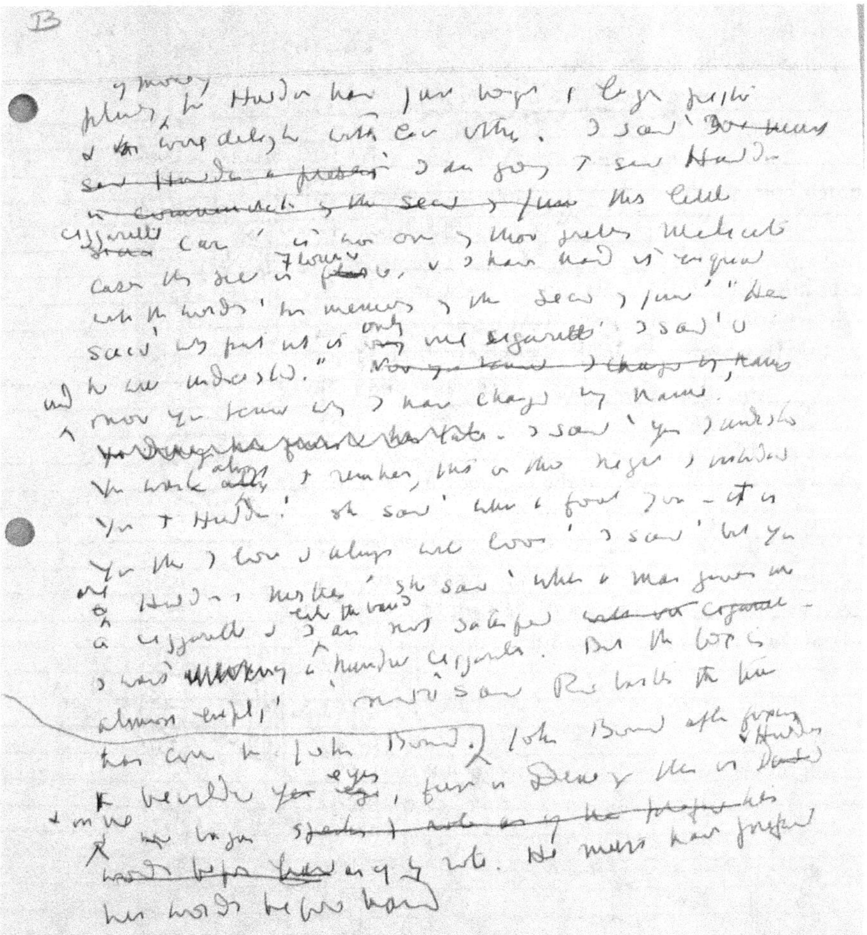

NLI 30,390 (3[v])

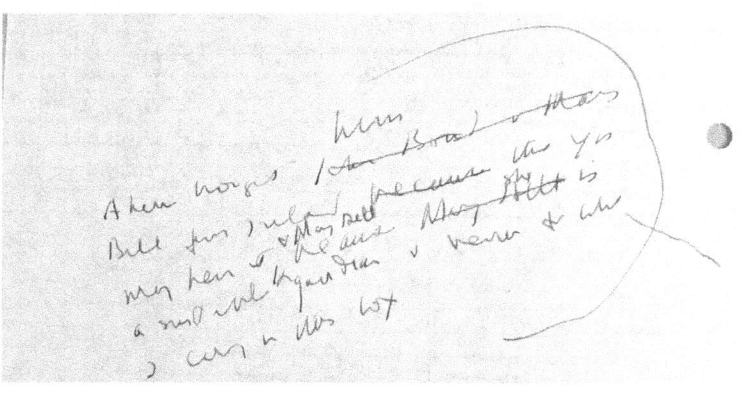

NLI 13,593 (16), page "B"

of money
plenty ^ for Huddon had just bought a large picture
I
& we were delighted with each other. I said '~~We must~~
~~send Huddon a present~~' 'I am going to send Huddon
~~in commemoration of the second of June~~ this little
ciggarette
[?silver] case' it was one of those pretty malachite
Florence
cases they sell in ~~florence~~, & I have had it engraved
with the words 'In memory of the second of June' He
only
said 'Why put into it ~~only~~ one cigarette' I said 'O
he will understand." ~~Now you know I changed my name~~
and now you know why I have changed my name.'
^ ~~Your Denys has finished & has late~~ – I said 'Yes I understand
always
You want ~~always~~ to remember, that on that night I introduced
You to Huddon.' She said 'What a fool you [are] – it is
You that I love & always will love' I said 'but you
are
[?] ^ Huddons mistress' She said 'when a man gives me
like the brand
a cigarette & I ^ am not satisfied ~~with one cigarette~~
I want ~~a lot of~~ a hundred cigarettes. But the box is
almost empty' Now said Robartes the time
has come for John Bond. ^ John Bond after fixing *[insert at caret NLI 30,390 (3^{v})]*
eyes & Huddon
his bewildered ~~yes eye~~, first on Denys then on ~~Duddon~~
& on me
^ ~~& me~~ began ~~speaking by rote as if he prepared his~~
~~words before hand~~ as if by rote. He must have prepared-
his words before hand

NLI 30,390 (3^{v})

him
Aherne brought ~~John Bond & Mary~~
Bell from Ireland ~~because~~ that you
& Mary Bell she
may hear it because ~~Mary Bell~~ is
a suitable guardian & bearer for what
I carry in this box

[to insert in NLI 13,593 (16), page "B" as indicated by the drawn lines]

Manuscript Materials Cited

British Library Add. 54902–54904, Macmillan Archive, Correspondence with A. P. Watt and Sons, 14 Mar. 1933–17 Apr. 1939.

British Library Add. 55750–55833, Macmillan Archive, Outgoing Letterbooks, 16 Mar. 1934–3 Jan. 1940.

"MBY 545" (from Harvard microfilm), manuscript drafts of "Huddon, Duddon and Daniel O'Leary" and related entries in the privately owned White Vellumn Notebook (location unknown).

"Michael Robartes Foretells," two uncorrected carbon typescripts (Box 1, Folder 9), H. Lytton Wilson Collection, Morris Library, Southern Illinois University, Carbondale. Box 1, Folder 9.

SB 0400771: a short fragment of "Stories of Michael Robartes," 1 p. holograph (1 page), William Butler Yeats Microfilmed Manuscripts Collection 294, Special Collections, Melville Library, State University of New York, Stony Brook.

SPEC COL/PR5906.A553 1929: the setting copy of *A Packet for Ezra Pound* (1929) prepared for *A Vision* (1937), in the Stuart A. Rose Manuscript, Archives, and Rare Book Library, Emory University, Atlanta.

W. B. Yeats to T. Werner Laurie, correspondence and papers, Box 2, folders 21–44, Manuscript Collection No. 600, in the Stuart A. Rose Manuscript, Archives, and Rare Book Library, Emory University, Atlanta.

National Library of Ireland (listed by accession number):

NLI 8774(14), *The Only Jealousy of Emer.*

NLI 13,576, a manuscript diary/notebook begun April 7, 1921, at 4 Broad Street, Oxford.

NLI 13,577, notebook bearing drafts of "Stories of Michael Robartes and His Friends."

NLI 13,582, Rapallo Notebook E, containing MS of *The Resurrection*, *A Vision*, and other works.

NLI 13,587(21), "The Phases of the Moon" (with a fragment of "The Living Beauty").

NLI 13,593(16), "To Dorothy Wellesley" (page "B" gives remainder of NLI 30,390 fragment).

NLI 30,019, page proofs of *Stories of Michael Robartes and His Friends* (1931).

NLI 30,030, page proofs of *Mythologies* from the "Coole Edition" (1931); corrections by Yeats used for 1939 Macmillan edition.

NLI 30,103, "Anglo Ireland. a conversation" (MS prose dialogue between Yeats and Owen Aherne).

NLI 30,358, 64^v and 67^r, "Ego Dominus Tuus," in brown leather MS book.

NLI 30,361, maroon notebook containing *Calvary*, *The Player Queen*, and "A People's Theatre."

NLI 30,390, manuscript fragment of "Stories of Michael Robartes and His Friends" (Denise's story).

NLI 30,465, typed fragment of the concluding lines of "Stories of Michael Robartes and His Friends."

NLI 30,525, manuscript of Robartes-Aherne dialogue (June 1920).

NLI 36,263/3, "The Discoveries of Michael Robartes." Typescript with MS alterations. Draft 5.

NLI 36,263/4, "The Discoveries of Michael Robartes." Manuscript. Draft 4.

NLI 36,263/7/1–2, two exercise books, "Aherne & Robartes Dialogue Etc. – imperfect." Drafts 1 and 2.

NLI 36,263/7/3, "Appendix by Michael Robartes" (in the hand of George Yeats).

NLI 36,263/7/4, untitled sequence of Robartes-Aherne dialogue, 26 loose, perforated sheets.

NLI 36,263/7/5, untitled sequence of Robartes-Aherne dialogue, 6 loose sheets.

NLI 36,263/9, "Untitled Manuscript" (precedes NLI 36,263/4 as a Robartes-Aherne dialogue). Draft 3.

NLI 36,263/10/1–2, "Version B" (a short dialogue and Robartes "extracts"). Follows NLI 36,263/3 in order of composition.

NLI 36,263/24/1–2, draft note to "The Gift of Harun Al-Raschid," condensed story in *A Vision* (1925), etc.

NLI 36,263/29, early draft of the basic system, including "Michael Robartes and the Judwali Doctor," a fragment of "The Second Coming," "Towards Break of Day," etc.

NLI 36,265(2), includes a fragment of an older version of "The Phases of the Moon."

NLI 36,265/7, "The Dance of the Four Royal Persons," carbon typescript with MS correction.

NLI 36,265/8/A, "The Dance of the Four Royal Persons," carbon typescript with MS correction.

NLI 36,272/33, amended typescript of "Michael Robartes Foretells," rejected epilogue for *A Vision* (1937).

Index

www.ingramcontent.com/pod-product-compliance
Lightning Source LLC
Chambersburg PA
CBHW071140100726
47908CB00002B/196
* 9 7 8 1 3 5 0 2 1 0 7 4 5 *